THE PARADOX OF

SOUTHERN PROGRESSIVISM,

1880–1930

✦

THE FRED W. MORRISON SERIES

IN SOUTHERN STUDIES

THE UNIVERSITY OF NORTH CAROLINA PRESS

CHAPEL HILL & LONDON

THE
PARADOX OF
SOUTHERN
PROGRESSIVISM,
1880–1930

WILLIAM A. LINK

Library of Congress
Cataloging-in-Publication Data
Link, William A.
  The paradox of Southern progressivism,
1880–1930 / William A. Link.
      p.   cm. — (The Fred W. Morrison series
in Southern studies)
    Includes bibliographical references (p.   ) and
index.
  ISBN 0-8078-2040-7 (cloth: alk. paper)
    1. Southern States—Politics and
government—1865–1950.   2. Southern
States—Social conditions.   3. Progressivism
(United States politics) I. Title.   II. Series.
F215.L56   1992
306.2'0975—dc20   92-1328
                                    CIP

Portions of chapter 1 appeared in a different
form in "The Social Context of Southern
Progressivism, 1880–1930," in *The Wilson Era:
Essays in Honor of Arthur S. Link*, edited by
John Milton Cooper, Jr., and Charles Neu,
copyright © 1991 by Harlan Davidson, Inc.
Reprinted by permission of the publisher.

Portions of chapter 5 appeared in a different
form in " 'The Harvest Is Ripe, but the Laborers
Are Few': The Hookworm Crusade in North
Carolina, 1909–1915," in *North Carolina
Historical Review* 67 (January 1990): 1–27.
Reprinted by permission.

Portions of chapter 7 appeared in a different
form in "Privies, Progressivism, and Public
Schools: Health Reform and Education in the
Rural South, 1909–1920," in *Journal of
Southern History* 54 (November 1988): 623–42.
Copyright © 1988 by the Southern Historical
Association. Reprinted by permission of the
managing editor.

FOR MY PARENTS

CONTENTS

◆

ILLUSTRATIONS

———— ◆ ————

PREFACE

At the beginning of the twentieth century, a thoroughgoing restructuring transformed social and political institutions and instrumentalities in the United States, with the result that, between about 1900 and 1930, bureaucratic intervention in education, public health, child welfare, and public morality replaced traditional governance, which had relied on voluntarism and community control. The new bureaucratic presence reflected the influence of reformers who attempted to impose new forms of government in which administrative expertise and efficiency became the primary standards, and what is loosely called "progressivism" swept over all regions of the United States in the early 1900s.

In no region was there a sharper conflict between traditional and modernizing governance, or between republican libertarianism and the trend toward a more powerful state, than in the South. Scholars of southern reform have reached a consensus, as have historians of American progressivism, on progressivism's general features. They agree that reformers created new structures for twentieth-century political, cultural, and social institutions; that they and their followers came mostly from the urban middle classes; and that they sought to transform the relationship between individuals and government. But here agreement ends and controversy begins.[1]

This study argues that southern progressivism should be understood as a clash between radically divergent views of the social contract. On the one hand, southern traditionalists, located in farms, villages, and small towns, understood "community" in local, neighborhood terms; accordingly, they viewed social problems passively and often indifferently. Like Populists and other rural southerners of the nineteenth century, traditionalists articulated a powerful version of southern political culture that exalted the values of participatory democracy and discourse; these values reinforced localism and opposition to outside interference. Like the Populists, they opposed strong centralized power and resisted the intrusion of large, impersonal forces into matters heretofore under community control. Like generations of Americans before them, they sought equity and justice, yet on this point the traditionalists of the Progressive Era diverged significantly. For Populists, equity meant the regulation of large economic enterprise and freedom from the tentacles of the market economy. For traditionalists of the early twentieth century, in contrast, equity was defined in antigovernment terms and meant freedom from the intrusions of government. Populists and early twentieth-century social reformers, in sum, were dealing with different spheres of activity. Populists concerned themselves mainly, although not exclusively, with equity and the political economy. Favoring a new national monetary policy and what could be called the beginnings of regulation, Populists were antimonopoly and antirailroad. In contrast, rural opponents of reform were antigovernment. Insular in thinking, traditionalists were suspicious of outsiders and strongly resisted any threats to their autonomy.

Progressive Era reformers, on the other hand, saw "community" differently. Originating in a middle-class white urban environment, they were impelled by a new degree of Protestant humanitarianism that was reshaping public life across the nation. What traditionalists took for granted reformers often viewed as appalling; familiar social conditions became problems in need of solution. Reformers located the source of these problems in the structure of governance; they saw solutions through the expansion of coercive state intervention.

In this dialectic, two fundamental values clashed: the paternalism of reformers and the localism and community power of traditionalists. Paternalism explains the often erratic behavior of reformers: how they embraced uplift and progress, yet believed in a hierarchy of race and culture; how they were fervent advocates of democracy, yet also endorsed measures of coercion and control. Functioning with an assumption of the superiority of their new, modern culture over rural culture—or over the culture of southern blacks—reformers offered uplift and improvement but wanted to limit local participation and control. They eventually discovered that their success depended on the cooperation of communities that more often than not were reluctant to sacrifice neighborhood control. In a small-scale war between centralizers and localists, reformers were forced to confront the integrity of the communities that they sought to change.

This book is not a comprehensive history of southern progressivism. Rather, by concentrating on the struggle between paternalist reformers and localist communities, this study represents an extended essay on a central paradox of early twentieth-century reform. I have deliberately said little about political reform, or, for that matter, about the politics of social reform. It is clear that the social policy changes of the early twentieth century could not have occurred without the transformation of the political structure. The political reforms that the rest of the United States experienced in the early decades of the twentieth century also swept through the South and made possible a new administrative state that, in turn, laid the basis for a new social policy. Political reform is best considered in a separate context; it has been more fully explored elsewhere and need not be repeated. Nonetheless, scholars await a fuller treatment of the nature and creation of the new administrative state.[2]

It is almost a cliché among historians to plead for further scholarship, but my hope is that this book will kindle further interest in Progressive Era reform. That scholarship is most particularly needed at the state and community levels, where much of the paternalist-localist struggle was acted out. I have attempted to include local material, but I have incorporated it into a southern regional typology; my purpose has been to sketch out some general tendencies rather than to include all the voluminous evidence about a vast topic. Readers should be warned that I have adopted a rather catholic definition of "the South." I have dealt with Alabama, Arkansas, the Carolinas, Florida, Georgia, Kentucky, Louisiana, Mississippi, Tennessee, Texas, and Virginia, yet I make no claim that this work tells the full story of reform in those states. Rather, I have attempted to explain, with the social context surrounding it, the nature of the interplay between reformers and the local communities that they sought to transform.

This book could not have been written without the advice, support, encouragement, and help of a number of people. Financial support for travel to the sources and for time off from teaching was particularly critical. Grants from the American Association of State and Local History, the Rockefeller Archive Center, the Southern Regional Education Board, and the University of North Carolina at Greensboro (UNCG) Research Council financed travel to manuscript repositories and archives. A semester's leave from UNCG made much of this travel possible, while timely support for summer writing also came from the UNCG Excellence Fund and the National Endowment for the Humanities (Grant # FT-33913-90).

Like all scholars, I am indebted to a legion of archivists and librarians, most of whom too often remain unthanked for their essential labors. I am grateful to the staffs of those private manuscript collections and state archives that I visited. At these institutions, I encountered degrees of courtesy, helpfulness, and high standards that scholars have come to expect from the professionals staffing them. I must particularly thank David Moltke-Hansen, Richard Shrader, and John White of the Southern Historical Collection, University of North Carolina at Chapel Hill Library; Wayne Moore of the Tennessee State Library and Archives; Nadine Doty-Tessel of the Florida State Archives; Beth Howse of the Special Collections Department, Fisk University Library; Mimi Jones of the Alabama Department of Archives and History; Virginia Shadron of the Georgia Department of Archives and History; Michael Plunkett of the Manuscripts Department, University of Virginia Library; Conley Edwards III and Minor Weisiger of the Virginia State Library and Archives; William Bynum and Diana Sanderson of the Presbyterian Church (U.S.A.), Department of History, Montreat, North Carolina; and John R. Woodard of the North Carolina Baptist Collection, Wake Forest University Library. For help with photographs, I must also thank William Bynum, Jerry Cotten, Beth Howse, Gail Miller, Emilie W. Mills, Ellen Nemhauser, Elaine Owens, Carolyn Parsons, Thomas Rosenbaum, and Diana Sanderson. I appreciate the willingness of President Bruce Dodd of the Rabun Gap-Nacoochee School in Atlanta to permit me to examine his institution's records. The staff members of the Presbyterian Church (U.S.A.), Department of History, Montreat, North Carolina, formerly known as the Historical Foundation, extended me many courtesies; they not only made available several of their fine collections but also provided a wonderful work environment during writing and revision. The rich collections of the Rockefeller Archive Center were especially useful. Director Darwin H. Stapleton and his staff were friendly, helpful, and thoroughly professional during my visits to the center, and my stay was inestimably aided by the knowledge of Thomas Rosenbaum.

In the course of travel, I frequently imposed on friends and family. I enjoyed the hospitality of Margaret and John Hebron Moore of Florida State University and Tallahassee, and I appreciate the many kindnesses that they extended to me while I was there. Arthur C. Jones III, then of Ringwood, New Jersey, generously put me up on two occasions and loaned me an automobile for commuting. Other friends and family members who housed me during research trips include Jim and Lou Douglas, William and Wayne Harbaugh, Chuck Harmon and Elizabeth Miles, John T. Kneebone and Suzanne Freeman, Peggy M. Link, John and Veronica Oldfield, and Bruce A. Ragsdale. While on a trip to Richmond, I profited from the stimulating collegiality of the Publications Division of the Virginia State Library and Archives and its staff, Edward D. C. Campbell, John Kneebone, Jon Kukla, Brent Tarter, and Sandra Gioa Treadway.

The History Department at UNCG has provided an atmosphere of mutual support and cooperation and an exceptional environment for scholarship. I appreciate the help, logistical and otherwise, of both Bobbie Carter and Shirley Roll. The professional staff of UNCG's Jackson Library contributed indispensable help and patience in ordering reels of microfilm. At the university, Chancellor William E. Moran, Provost Donald V. DeRosa, Dean Joanne V. Creighton and then Walter Beale of the College of Arts and Sciences, Stephen R. Mosier and Beverly R. Maddox of the Office of Research

Services, and the staff of the UNCG Academic Computer Center have all unfailingly supported my research and writing.

This study, like most other works of history, involved the help and active collaboration of numerous scholars. At an early stage, the UNCG History Club sponsored the presentation of some undigested ideas in this book. Subsequently, presentations at the American Association for the History of Medicine, the North Carolina Medical History Group, the Organization of American Historians, and the Southern Historical Association helped me to focus and refine these ideas. I was the beneficiary of the generosity of a number of people who were willing to share their own research. Robert M. Calhoon shared portions of his important research on southern evangelicals. James H. Locke, Jr., generously provided me with sources on child labor reform, and Robert C. McMath, Jr., introduced me to important materials while I visited Atlanta. At various stages in the conceptualization of this book, Lewis Bateman, Orville Vernon Burton, Robert M. Calhoon, Kenneth Caneva, Ronald C. Cassell, Stanley Coben, John M. Cooper, Jr., John Duffy, Elizabeth Etheridge, John Ettling, Missy Foy, Dewey W. Grantham, William H. Harbaugh, Bruce A. Ragsdale, and Todd L. Savitt all contributed much-needed suggestions. Edward L. Ayers, Robert M. Calhoon, John Kneebone, Allen W. Trelease, and Marjorie Spruill Wheeler read the entire manuscript, as did, for the University of North Carolina Press, Jack Temple Kirby and an anonymous reader, and I have profited from their thorough critiques. I have not always followed the advice of these scholars, but the final product is certainly improved by their suggestions.

I have also benefited from the professionalism and guidance of the staff of the University of North Carolina Press. I must thank Matthew Hodgson for his interest in my work and steady support for it. Managing editor Sandra Eisdorfer and copyeditor Stevie Champion guided the manuscript toward publication. Lewis Bateman has monitored this project since its inception and throughout has provided advice, support, and criticism. I deeply appreciate his abilities as an editor and his friendship, as I do the abilities and contributions of many others at the Press.

Like most authors, I have imposed most of all on the time of my family. My best friend and wisest adviser, Susannah J. Link, has personal and professional standards that continue to amaze me; she has always provided confidence and love. Our three daughters, Percy, Maggie, and Josie, still trying to decide what it is exactly that their father does for a living, have very generously resisted impulses to play on the computer, and I thank them for their consideration. My parents, to whom this book is dedicated, have inspired it with their example of personal and professional integrity. Many people—friends, acquaintances, and sometimes even adversaries—will testify to their literary standards and their uncompromising dedication to free inquiry, genuine interest in people, good humor, and personal warmth. They have also always been among my best critics, and in this case as in others I have relied on their advice. Over the years, their patience, constant support, and high expectations created a debt that I will never fully repay.

ABBREVIATIONS

AFL
American Federation of Labor

ASL
Anti-Saloon League

CES
Conference for Education in the South

CF
Commonwealth Fund

CIC
Commission on Interracial Cooperation

CU
Congressional Union

ERA
Equal Rights Association Club, New Orleans

GEB
General Education Board

IHB
International Health Board, Rockefeller Foundation

IHC
International Health Commission, Rockefeller Foundation

ISHB
Interdepartmental Social Hygiene Board

JRF
Julius Rosenwald Fund

LSRM
Laura Spellman Rockefeller Memorial

NAWSA
National American Woman Suffrage Association

NCLC
National Child Labor Committee

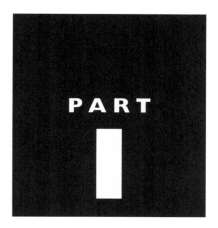

PART

I

LOCALISM IN TRANSITION

◆

THE CONTOURS OF

SOCIAL POLICY

◆

Post-Reconstruction southerners shared a common tradition of governance. Imbued with rural republican traditions, they despised concentrated power, most of all the governmental coercion and intervention that they believed anticipated military dictatorship and a negation of personal liberty. Like their parents and grandparents, they tolerated the functioning of local, state, and federal governments only under strict constraints. This tradition of governance placed near-absolute control in the hands of local instrumentalities, which, in turn, functioned more or less independently of any outside control. The operation of local government was rarely democratic; power, especially in rural communities, was lodged in few hands. Yet what most often mattered to the people involved was that, in this hierarchical system, the local community enjoyed primacy in the management of public affairs.

♦ ♦ ♦

CATEGORIES OF SOCIAL POLICY

In the nineteenth century the cultural setting for social policy—broadly defined as any exercise of governance designed to shape individual and community behavior—was distinctive. Aside from postmasters and an occasional tax collector, the federal government rarely touched the lives of southerners in the isolated rural communities and villages that the great majority of them inhabited. The role of state and local governments was no greater. In such areas as public education, public health, the regulation of moral behavior, and public welfare, state and local officials scrupulously respected home rule and the sanctity of local autonomy. Public welfare—community responsibility for the care of the poor, infirm, mentally ill, and dependents—offers one example of nineteenth-century social policy in operation. By sponsoring poorhouses and apprenticing the poor, county and parish governments extended relief by establishing a sort of social safety net that provided for the destitute and prevented outright starvation. Yet this welfare policy was rooted in a traditional view of charity that sought to discourage dependency, assumed that poverty was the product of individual character flaws rather than social environment, and stigmatized relief recipients.[1]

Public education was another important example of social policy in operation. While New England and the Midwest established publicly financed, tuition-free common schools between 1820 and 1860, the South created a more elitist structure. Antebellum southern schools, of course, excluded blacks, both free and slave; but even whites had only limited access to common schools. Underfunded by states and localities, they operated in erratic fashion, barely surviving the shabby poverty and popular hostility that hobbled them. Their designation as charity schools or *free schools*— a term that survived for much of the nineteenth century—set them apart from northern common schools. The fate of southern free schools also exposed cultural attitudes that were strongly hostile toward public education, beneath which lay a fundamentally different conception of education and social policy. Rather than being the symbols of a common culture of literacy, antebellum southern schools were seen as a poor man's alternative to private and denominational education. Like the poorhouse, free schools— in a culture that stressed independence and feared white "slavery"—became stigmatized as charity institutions.

During and after Reconstruction, the common school model slowly superseded the free school model. Mississippian Belle Kearney remembered that during the immediate postwar years, it was considered "scarcely respectable" to patronize public schools; those who taught in them were "brave indeed." In what she called a "revolution" that reflected a "blossoming" of public opinion, schools became permanent fixtures of the southern social landscape. Political and constitutional factors spurred on attitudinal changes. By the 1880s, as a result of Reconstruction state constitutions, every southern state required universal education, including black education. The connections between Reconstruction and education were close, for northern and southern Republicans believed that grafting New England–style common schools on the South would subvert the aristocratic social order. Other features of the New England model of common schooling figured prominently in late nineteenth-century schools. Tuition-free and financed by state and local property taxes, the new southern common schools were administered by a skeletal state bureaucracy headed by a state superintendent who was located in the state capitol; they were operated at the local level by county superintendents and local trustees. Yet, rather than the transplantation of northern cultural institutions to the South, what occurred was a process of assimilation of northern educational values and institutions into southern culture. Although the New England township system supplied the popular model for Reconstruction school administration, there was significant variation. Some states had county-run systems, others had schools operated by townships, and still others granted total autonomy to neighborhoods. In some states, school officials were elected; in others, they were appointed.[2]

Although important differences persisted among whites and blacks, both races embraced education during the post-Reconstruction era. The approval by blacks was immediate, enthusiastic, and millennial; in their communities, schools symbolically but decisively repudiated the intellectual and psychological underpinnings of slavery. Many whites clung to antebellum attitudes; their acceptance of Reconstruction-style schools came slowly. Although the social stigma of charity schools persisted into the 1880s, disappearing only gradually, southern whites steadily incorporated public schools into the fabric of community life. As southerners adapted to schools, schools adapted to southerners. Facing an often-hostile public opinion, school officials discovered that survival required a recognition of the limits of social policy. Although school superintendents emerged as figures of some stature, few of them had any illusions about their powers. Their main purpose was to secure community approval and support for education. Real control lay with communities, on whose good favor and participation the effective functioning of schools depended, and power over educational policy resided in the dispersed neighborhoods of the rural South.

Public health similarly functioned under a community-controlled admin-

Keithville School, Caddo Parish, Louisiana, ca. 1920.
(Courtesy of the Special Collections Department, Fisk University Library)

istrative system. Although a few states possessed an antebellum public health apparatus, like the educational system, it underwent redefinition during Reconstruction. Even so, only as a temporary response to the emergency of epidemics did states begin to establish public health systems. The creation of the National Board of Health in 1878—in response to a devastating epidemic in the Mississippi Valley in that year—marked a brief and largely unsuccessful experiment in a coordinated national public health policy. New state and local health boards came into existence during the 1870s and 1880s. In states such as Alabama, Louisiana, and Florida, which contained ports of entry for tropical diseases, state health bureaucracies were granted strong emergency powers.[3] In Alabama, the legislature in 1875 revitalized the antebellum State Board of Health by making the state medical association the state board of health and investing it with new powers. It also empowered the state board to convert county medical associations into county boards of health, whose primary duties were to collect and record vital statistics. In Florida, a state health system was created after the devastating impact of a yellow fever epidemic in 1888. In response, the assembly enacted legislation creating both a State Board of Health and a system of maritime quarantine.[4]

The regulation of the manufacture, distribution, and consumption of alcohol is another example of the limited scope of prebureaucratic governance.

Rather than regulating or directly attempting to limit alcohol consumption, the state awarded franchises or officially sanctioned permits. As with schools and public health, public power was abdicated to private, nongovernmental groups. At the local level, this meant that the execution of policy fell mostly to local power blocs. Beginning in the colonial period, most southern states, in part to control consumption and in part to obtain revenue, adopted a system that provided for fees and licensing and the nominal regulation of taverns and saloons. During the Civil War the federal government also imposed an excise tax on whiskey manufacturers, which the U.S. Internal Revenue Service enforced.[5]

Yet the implementation of alcohol policy also operated under limitations that public opinion and local custom imposed. A tradition of drinking balanced restrictions on alcohol. Visitors often noted alcohol-induced southern hospitality; if anything, the prevalence of drink had increased by the end of the nineteenth century. Because of these strong traditions of alcohol consumption, nineteenth-century state and local governments made few efforts at regulation. Although local option spread across the rural South in the post-Reconstruction period, there is ample evidence that it was violated almost routinely. Despite local option laws, federal internal revenue agents regularly collected taxes in dry counties. Blind tigers (illegal saloons) were a common phenomenon in the post-Reconstruction South; in the absence of legislation to prevent the importation of alcohol from wet into dry counties, bootleggers worked out cunning and effective systems of distribution.[6]

Whether in education, health, or public poor relief, southern state and local governments exercised social policy in a manner that most late twentieth-century Americans would consider strange, even alien. Rather than providing continuous, regular, and bureaucratic government, states and localities were concerned primarily with factors such as political party, class, locality, kinship, and denomination. Few features of social policy were compulsory or coercive; except for grave emergencies, the sanctity of the individual and of personal liberty remained sacrosanct. This was a system of government in which bureaucracy played no role at all.[7]

◆ ◆ ◆
PUBLIC OPINION AND SOCIAL POLICY

Social policy and governance in the post-Reconstruction South were shaped by and responsive to public opinion. For nineteenth-century southerners, as for most Americans, public opinion most commonly mirrored political culture, which combined an ideology of republicanism and resistance to power with a structure strongly shaped by partisanship.[8] Southerners shared this political culture, and its accompanying political attitudes, with other Americans. Yet other distinctive conditions also made social policy and its relationship with public opinion unique in the rural South. The lack of good overland transportation facilities made the already-imposing barriers of a large number of often-impassable streams and mountains formidable. The impact of the South's rural landscape was striking to northern visitors, many of whom noticed that crossing the Potomac from Washington, D.C., into Virginia brought stark changes. When a northern-born traveler, Olive Dame Campbell, visited the South in 1908, she was struck by its exotic qualities. She noted changes in the landscape once her train crossed into Virginia. The rural qualities of the South immediately struck her; she noted the absence of large cities and the monotony of "stretches and stretches of woodlands and corn fields."[9]

Even starker changes awaited the more adventurous travelers willing to depart the railroads. Harvard historian Albert Bushnell Hart visited the South and in 1910 published his observations in a sociological guidebook for northern visitors, *The Southern South*. Hart urged students of southern life to probe beneath the surface. He wrote that visitors who went only to boom towns, textile centers, mining and lumbering centers, and forges and foundries accepted stereotypes about widespread progress. Yet the prevalence of change did not always mean progress, for once observers entered the hinterlands, as did Hart, they discovered a very different environment, one composed of "straggling" cities, "small and often decaying towns," and "remote and isolated" rural communities.[10]

This social environment was distinctive. The fact that an undiluted "Anglo-Saxon" race populated the South fascinated Hart, as it did many other early twentieth-century observers. But while he praised white southerners for their racial purity, their backwardness baffled him: southern Anglo-Saxons, he wrote, were as "lazy, unprogressive and densely ignorant" as the blacks with whom they lived in close proximity, while they were also, he believed, indisputably "brutal, licentious, monicidal, and cruel." But the white masses were dominated to an extraordinary extent by class constraints. Although he acknowledged that "a comparatively small number of persons" made the "great decisions" in all societies, Hart asserted that southerners lived under a rigid hierarchy of elite domination; in no other region did a small aristocracy exercise such prestige and influence. For Hart, elite control meant leadership by the "best" people. With some admiration, he mused that—to the amazement of northerners—in the South the well-to-do, the cultured, the educated, and the well connected absolutely controlled society, while public opinion showed unusual unity. In most categories of public behavior and social policy, there existed a "recognized standard." Any deviations from that standard were regarded with great suspicion.[11]

Yet public opinion also cut across class lines. Despite the rigid social hierarchy that Hart suggested, community solidarity against outside threats was a significant factor. Southerners rallied against northern intervention; North Carolinians and Mississippians expressed equally enthusiastic state patriotism, and the basic loyalty was to the community, most often to the rural neighborhood. Encircled by their kin and churches, southerners recognized a fundamental individual and group identity, and, at this community level, they forged their strongest allegiances. The settlement pattern of the colonial period had much to do with determining these attitudes: rather than settling in compact villages typical of Europe and New England, most southerners followed a pattern of dispersed settlement. The result was a rural isolation that became, over the centuries, a culturally determinative characteristic. Most people, Hart observed, lived in sparsely settled and dispersed communities that had retained frontier characteristics. Villages with pretentious-sounding names were nothing more than hamlets of several houses, where churches, schools, and "mournful little cemeteries" often lay at a crossroads. White Carolinians, wrote rural sociologist Eugene Cunningham Branson, lived in isolated farms; compactly settled rural communities, "conscious of common necessities and organized to secure common advantages," were rare. A concept of community meant one thing in the Middle West and the Northeast; in the South, it meant quite another. Geographic isolation also affected rural blacks, according to a contemporary who noticed stronger, mutually binding relationships in the black community. Especially in majority-white counties, blacks lived in closer proximity to one another. In rural Rutherford County, Tennessee, a white observer wrote that blacks lived in colonies of scattered homes; like rural whites, the dispersed population maintained a nucleus around which they formed.[12]

Geographic isolation contributed to social isolation, which for most southerners made the locality into the important gemeinschaft. Remoteness bred adherence to kin, denomination, neighborhood—and aloofness toward outsiders. What Branson observed in 1916 about North Carolina was true for the rest of the region. "Far removed from socialism in any sense, good or bad," southerners were "but a hair's breadth away from individualism, raw, raucous and unorganizable." Nor was isolation, and a sense of community that excluded the outside world, confined to any of the subregions of the South. Rural isolation affected mountaineers, he wrote, no more than Tidewater people.[13]

Like most Americans, nineteenth-century southerners were infused with a rural republican ideology that emphasized independence and self-reliance and provided a rhetoric for resisting outside interference. Again Branson aptly described the social environment. Living in an isolated world of "language, manners, and customs of a past long dead elsewhere," rural Carolinians could often be "suspicious, secretive, apathetic, and unapproachable." The result was a society of sharp contrasts: within the sound of college bells, a rural North Carolina family lived in a state of suspended animation, isolated from the shifting and dynamic currents of the outside world, "ghettoed in the midst of present day civilization." Although condescending toward rural culture, Branson's description expresses an essential truth about this social environment: isolation strengthened traditional hostility toward coercive government. As passionate defenders of self-government, southerners valued the "spirit of revolt against centralized power"; again and again, they symbolically wrested "from tyranny its crown and scepter." Rural communities, standing vigilant against any threats to their independence, embraced "personal liberty," that is, freedom from the scrutiny and coercion of outsiders.[14]

The conditions described above were present in varying degrees throughout the South, but nowhere in more amplified form than in the mountain region. According to a sympathetic observer of its culture, extreme individualism prevented the exercise of strong governance. Although democratic, this was a sort of democracy that resented and rejected aggressive local leadership of any kind. Public opinion coalesced only in response to outside threats; the community worked in concert most frequently when it opposed influences that it regarded as foreign.[15]

In order to achieve a minimum of effectiveness, nineteenth-century public officials adapted themselves to the peculiarities of public opinion and achieved a kind of equilibrium in governance. Depending on an extraordinary level of community support and participation, government successfully harnessed the potentially divisive force of localism, and, in the process, underwent a small-scale expansion. But social policy—and indeed government generally—was *au fond* passive. Rather than being concentrated in the hands of state or local officials, power tended to devolve into isolated pockets, without a core. In sum, governance was centrifugal rather than central.

◆ ◆ ◆

THE ROLE OF THE STATE

In 1911 Charles Lee Coon, a reform-minded eastern North Carolina school official, described this loose and vaguely defined system of social policy by way of a parable. He told of an indigent schoolmaster in need of a new pair of trousers who, thinking himself too poor to have them tailored, accepted a small patch as a start toward a new garment. He added more patches gradually, until enough material was available to piece the trousers together. But when the teacher appeared in school, the odd trousers caused so much ridicule that he was forced to discard them and begin all over again in search of new ones. Coon went on to point up the meaning of the story. Instead of a coherent, systematic, and state-directed social policy, North Carolina possessed a system of governance composed of "multi-colored patches," pieced together in a "variegated handiwork." [16]

The half century after the Civil War was marked by the steady growth of social policy in the South, particularly in the two fields of education and public health. As for schools, this growth can best be measured by the numbers of enrollments, schools, and teachers—all of which increased across the South. In health policy, a similar expansion occurred, as state boards of health enjoyed some success in limiting the impact of epidemics. Deep South states from Florida to Texas developed state boards of health that imposed quarantines and other controls to restrain the spread of epidemics of yellow fever, smallpox, and dengue fever. [17]

Yet practitioners of southern social policy in education and public health shared a common bond of powerlessness. In both fields, a state system existed with a governing board, an executive officer, and local representatives of the state system. Aside from the collection of mostly inaccurate statistics, the writing of annual reports, and periodic tours to the hinterlands, however, state education superintendents and state health officers remained isolated from developments in the heartland, and they exercised little effective control over local communities. This administrative power vacuum became apparent to one observer, John C. Campbell, when he visited the southern Appalachian region in 1908 and 1909. As the best evidence of a flawed administrative system, he cited the absence of accurate data. In search of statistics for a study of the mountain region, Campbell could find no authority willing to help him. He first wrote to state educational and health authorities. Once it became evident that they possessed little reliable data, he tried the county authorities. Unsuccessful with them, Campbell began to gather his own data. [18]

Campbell's experience was not exceptional. The typical school superintendent performed even the most fundamental responsibility—the gathering of statistics—carelessly. Data were incomplete and unreliable, because superintendents sometimes considered it "a perquisite of their offices" not to reply to requests for statistical information. A similar carelessness typified county health officials. North Carolina state health officials greeted a report of a low death rate in one county skeptically. One of two things was evident: either there was "a mistake somewhere in collecting these statistics" or that county was "the healthiest spot upon the earth."[19]

This was only part of a larger pattern of powerlessness, which most state officials readily admitted. Post-Reconstruction state officials often lamented the absence of both funding and coercive power. In the late 1870s a sanitarian complained that, although the Tennessee State Board of Health had been legally empowered to control epidemics, it was effectively "without authority, and without pay, and therefore without respectability." His grandchildren might live "to see reform in these matters, but we need not dream of it." A similar mood of pessimism afflicted the North Carolina state health officer almost three decades later. When asked by one community for help in testing milk, he responded sarcastically. A budget of only $2,000 per annum for the entire state health bureaucracy, he explained, prevented him from being able to indulge in "luxuries" like sanitation and preventive public health.[20]

Most health bureaucrats had only a scant understanding of the etiology of disease and knew even less about how to prevent it. An observer was not far from the truth during the 1930s when he claimed that a schoolboy then knew more about yellow fever than the entire Mississippi State Board of Health when it was created in 1877. Few of these officials, and fewer physicians, knew how to contain an epidemic disease. In the case of yellow fever, physicians in Mississippi, in order to repel airborne infections, often skinned a calf and hung the meat. Others fired cannons, burned pitch, and prescribed limewater, garlic, and onions as ways to ward off the yellow-fever-bearing miasmas. Treatment after infection was no more effective.[21]

With weak and often ill-defined powers, state officials exercised what authority they had with great caution. Carefully avoiding conflicts over the issue of local control, they protected themselves by insisting that they served only in an advisory capacity. "I can only advise—it is up to you and your county authorities to act," the North Carolina state health officer informed a local official in 1912. In most instances, state health officials refused to intervene in local matters, the Florida state health officer explained, "where the police powers of the Municipality are sufficient if only exercised." What this meant, as he wrote when sending an agent on an inspection tour, was that state officials acted only in "an advisory capacity." A little "persuasion and coaxing" in this instance and others became the preferred method; in place of coercion, he urged "advising, and cautioning, and counselling." He then pointedly added that the agent should "incur no expense."[22]

School administrators were similarly hamstrung. Like health officials, they possessed neither money nor compulsory powers, both of which would give them leverage over local communities. For the South as a whole, even the weak compulsory attendance laws, typical of the rest of the country at the end of the nineteenth century, were the exception rather than the rule.[23] Sensible officials acted cautiously to avoid unpopular decisions. The records of the early twentieth-century North Carolina educational bureaucracy are filled with examples of its refusal to intervene in local matters. Especially in controversial issues, the state superintendent had severely limited powers. When the Yancey County School Board appealed to the state superintendent to resolve a school location dispute in 1912, the state superintendent pronounced it a local matter under the "entire control" of the county board, whose decision was "final and not reviewable by me or any body else." His relationship to local authorities, he stressed in language familiar to health bureaucrats, was "simply advisory."[24]

Consequently, health and school officials limped along from year to year in the "multi-colored" and "variegated handiwork" described by Coon. They necessarily delegated responsibility to those officials who served as their representatives—county superintendents and the boards of health and education that had elected them to office. County officials performed most of the important functions of state administration. In every southern state except Arkansas—where the office was optional until World War I—county school superintendents served a dual function: as representatives of state authority and as the executive officers of county school boards.[25] In consultation with school boards, southern superintendents exerted final authority over decisions such as locating schools, selecting teachers, appropriating funds, paying teachers, and reporting to the state superintendent. For their efforts they received a salary, but rarely was it enough to make the position full-time. School superintendents were usually nonprofessionals. In North Carolina, according to one account, some were preachers, some farmers, and "all but some half a dozen" received salaries that could not possibly support them. They were chosen less for their ability than because they were "the only men to be had at the price fixed by law."[26]

County health officials were elected by county health boards—when and if they were organized. In Alabama, which created a theoretically vigorous local public health system, county health officers were burdened with time-consuming responsibilities. State officials, who considered them direct representatives of the state system, expected local officials to perform duties such as compiling vital statistics, maintaining a complete directory of physicians and midwives, and visiting and inspecting the entire county. As the state health officer said, the county health officer should perform all these duties directly: he should "see with his own eyes and hear with his own ears where the fault

A rural school in North Carolina, ca. 1900.
(Courtesy of University Archives, University of North Carolina at Greensboro Library)

may be; should give information and advice with his own lips; and should put his own hands and brains to work for the correction of any evils he may find to exist."[27]

But state power rarely achieved effective execution. Florida's system placed little confidence in local officials. After a brief experiment with local health boards, the legislature abolished them in 1889 and instead provided for the appointment of district agents who, according to one contemporary, inspected local sanitary conditions "from time to time." But their powers assumed a familiarly limited form; their appointments were "commissions of honor and trust," their main influence "moral." In normal circumstances, explained a Mississippi county health officer in 1890, he did "nothing more than advise"; too often, that advice was "simply thrown away." As a result, southern health officers performed the minimum, taking their position seriously only after the outbreak of an epidemic. These minimum duties included regular inspections and fumigation of the courthouse and jail.[28]

County school officers were also weakly tied to state authority. Possessing little conception of professional, bureaucratic administration, superintendents communicated with state officials only infrequently; when they did communicate, they were granted wide latitude. An Alabama school superintendent assured the state superintendent about the progress of his county's schools by noting parenthetically that he had worked hard "to have it all OK." "Indeed I have," he added, "and have done the very best in my power under the circumstances." Semiautonomous local officials, as this person suggested, had little to fear from state authorities, and there were ample opportunities for abuse. An Etowah County, Alabama, woman wrote of a superintendent who paid teachers only sixty dollars per three-month session and claimed a commission of five dollars. Another western North Carolina superintendent held both the superintendency and a school principalship, despite the protests of the state superintendent against plural office holding. Partisanship also influenced school administration. In a Middle Tennessee county in the 1920s, the county superintendent—who, like many others in Tennessee, was a woman—exerted little real authority aside from moral suasion. The real power lay with the county school board, whose chairman was a professional politician. He controlled finances and hiring and was not above ensuring that contracts for painting school buildings were awarded to his company.[29]

The absence of effective administration pervaded most aspects of social policy. Nowhere in the South did any state government succeed in establishing effective local school and health bureaucracies. Most state officials acknowledged failure. At the turn of the twentieth century, Eugene Clyde Brooks was the superintendent of a North Carolina Piedmont town school system; he later became state superintendent and president of North Carolina State College. In January 1902 he published an indictment of decentralized school governance in the *Raleigh News and Observer*. Referring to a fictional, but also typical, Clarendon County, he described a system without responsibility or power. The county superintendent, underpaid at two hundred dollars a year and knowing "nothing about teaching, nothing about supervision," took little interest in facilities, teaching, or curriculum. His work was "worthless"; he served as a "mere clerk," whose main function was to gather statistics in an annual report. Local school boards did little better, and they avoided vigorous administration. What bothered Brooks and other reformers most about the schools were two fundamental conditions of late nineteenth-century social policy: weakly exerted state power and low professional standards. County school boards appointed "almost any one" to the office of county superintendent, complained Coon in 1911. The result was that preachers, lawyers, doctors, newspaper editors, and others filled the ranks. Yet this sometimes occasioned a "social tragedy" because many of these superintendents were incapable of supervising or training teachers. Southern sanitarians voiced similar complaints. For example, one health official was described as doing good work "in a way" without knowing "what he does do."[30]

Local officials had plenty of problems. Low salaries was one. In one Alabama county, the health officer received no salary at all, and he felt that it was an injustice to himself and his family to work for nothing. His visits on behalf of public health were not "very extensive." Understandably, most physicians considered the job unattractive. As one explained, there was "not a small amount of work connected with its duties," and most physicians were too poor to donate time without pay. Health officers were also practicing physicians, and low salaries necessitated that the position be only part-time. The pay was so low, explained one county health officer, that the amount would not justify a man in "leaving his work and going to other parts of the Co. and working up these things personally." If the job "payed [sic] better a man could afford to ride around and see his assistants," explained another, but "the Law does not require this of him and he cannot spare or give away this time that belongs to patients who do pay him."[31]

The powerlessness of local representatives of state power reflected popular attitudes about the proper role of government in everyday life. Southerners preferred minimal government and were almost instinctively suspicious of it when it crossed accepted boundaries; in nineteenth-century governance, they got what they wanted. This was so because many of the functions of government required community participation. Beyond that, the proper functioning of prebureaucratic governance relied almost exclusively on community support.

◆ ◆ ◆

SOCIAL POLICY AND COMMUNITY CONTROL

County officials especially depended on local officials, whose participation linked the state system with the local community. Realizing that little was possible without community consensus, state educational and health officials usually appointed village or district boards to represent the local power structure and satisfy local opinion. Their duties and responsibilities varied. In the case of schools, local trustees did most of the real work: they located the schools, hired the teachers, and attempted to settle community squabbles—although, nominally, these were the responsibilities of the county superintendents. Although their duties were far less extensive and time-consuming, local health officers were expected to fulfill the essentially similar obligations of assessing public opinion and carrying out policy.

Local officials were, almost always, more accountable to the community than they were to state officials. In Florida, school boards, which were elected, regarded neighborhood interests as paramount. Trustees carefully studied popular sentiment, commented a visitor, and "dexterously" accommodated themselves to it. Although in most states local officers were appointed, unpopular trustees served shortened terms, as school patrons soon voiced their dissatisfaction. In one typical example, a group of North Carolina parents, who charged that local school officials were "not giving satisfaction," circulated a petition in the neighborhood calling for their ouster. In most localities, the community exerted particular influence over the day-to-day administration of schools. As today, parents expected that home standards of youth socialization would, more or less automatically, transfer to schools. Rural parents, for this reason, commonly complained less about excessive than insufficient corporal discipline. Insufficient discipline meant a disorderly school and bad teaching, according to popular wisdom. Unruly students revealed, to one northern Piedmont North Carolina community, the teacher's lack of control; to patrons, corporal discipline was the only evidence that the school was properly disciplined.[32]

New schools came into existence only at local initiative. As a contingent of Cullman County, Alabama, patrons reported in 1889 to the state superintendent, a majority had settled on the location of a school, while the others agreed to give land and build "a good house." Long after the school's establishment, parents continued to take an active part in crucial decisions. In fictional Clarendon County, North Carolina, Eugene Brooks described the extraordinary degree of parental participation in key decisions such as teacher selection. Meeting in early October to hire the teacher, members of the local school committee sent out a call for applicants; during the next few days, they visited the different members of the school board and went into the community to obtain endorsements. Based on these informal interviews and on the comments they evoked, the board made its decision.[33]

Community control over teacher selection and other important decisions was common throughout the rural South. As in Clarendon, other communities offered opinions about teachers that they expected authorities to respect. In some neighborhoods, parents acted in concert through a traditional means of community expression—petitioning. In 1873 a Louisiana neighborhood endorsed Dennis Clark, a teacher described in a petition as "getting along teaching very well," adding, in a character reference, that he was "no whisky drinker, neither gets drunk." Parents commonly expressed themselves through a vote. When asked at the turn of the twentieth century how teachers were selected, the school superintendent of Habersham County, Georgia, wrote that the choice was made by popular vote or from a list drawn up by school patrons.[34]

Local school officials remained well attuned to community opinion. In

Alabama, beat (or district) school superintendents were expected to hold regular consultations with parents about teacher hiring and school location, as one official stressed, "with a view to subserve their wishes[,] interest[,] and convenience." To serve parental "convenience," local officials scheduled school openings with careful regard for local economic needs. When public schools were first organized in a Louisiana community in 1871, the school board specified that the opening of the schools would occur only after "the farmers had pretty well finished working their little crops." Similar sentiments prevailed in Catoosa County, Georgia, where the school superintendent wrote that schools usually began whenever parents could "spare their children . . . out of their farms best." Thus, school opening tended to occur during lulls in the agricultural economy.[35]

Irregular attendance patterns also reflected a child labor economy. In the absence of compulsory attendance laws, the alternatives of school or work changed weekly or even daily for rural children because of what one Georgia superintendent in 1902 described as a "want of appreciation of [the] value of education" and a "spirit of Commercialism" among parents, which compelled them to keep children "to work on [the] Farm when not absolutely necessary." An Arkansas rural community, where schools were described in 1923 as "regulated to suit the crops" and where children were imported to cotton, berry, and truck-farming fields in caravans, was not atypical.[36]

During the last third of the nineteenth century, a striking phenomenon occurred: while tax support and school terms either remained the same or actually declined, the number of schools, along with enrollment, underwent a dramatic expansion.[37] This expansion was linked to a locally centered enthusiasm for schools. Numerous accounts confirm a pattern of growth within a locally driven system. In every North Carolina community, explained Charles Lee Coon, the "cry of a school house at every man's door" prevailed. But school diffusion was a product of social environment and geography, and it reflected a distinctive environment. Olive Dame Campbell described the roles and expectations surrounding mountain schools. Although the schools were small and isolated, she pointed out that these characteristics embodied community conditions. Mountaineers wanted schools nearby because of a "lack of community spirit," a state of mind that arose out of intense isolation and, more specifically, in response to the risks of sending children across often treacherous terrain. The result, Campbell concluded, was a "multiplicity" of schools that divided funds, shortened school terms, and clustered resources in mountain valleys.[38]

Because the hiring of teachers had long been a local prerogative, the primary criterion of their employment was the satisfaction of community standards. Local, "home" candidates always received preference, but often controversy erupted when candidates from neighboring localities were considered. Family connections were important, and the line dividing nepotism and fair hiring often grew indistinct. North Carolina trustees were usually half asleep when considering the most important decisions, according to one critic of school governance. The only instances of "warm feeling" occurred when a relative applied for the position, and the feeling "was over the relative and not over the school." Local autonomy in one Tennessee community was so unchallenged in the 1920s that trustees routinely employed underage relatives as teachers. In numerous cases, when faced with local appeals for help, state officials rarely if ever intervened, even in instances of flagrant nepotism.[39]

Local autonomy inevitably affected the status of teachers, even after they were hired. Although the case was not necessarily typical, a trustee in Tennessee reportedly drove teachers out of the county because they would not submit to his "immoral demands." When a teacher contracted to teach in a school in the North Carolina mountains, he soon discovered that isolation and high illiteracy made it impossible for him to conduct the school "as it should be." The teacher then sought the district board's permission to quit, and it agreed if he could find a substitute. Although he secured one, the board subsequently refused to pay him, and when he asked the state superintendent for relief, the official refused to intervene. This episode was not an isolated example; teachers working under local control were often paid erratically.[40]

◆ ◆ ◆

COMMUNITY POWER AS PARALYSIS:
PUBLIC HEALTH IN ALABAMA

Nineteenth-century sanitarians realized that public health depended on community approval and participation. County and state officials encouraged the formation of town boards of health that exercised emergency epidemic and sanitary powers, while everywhere county health officers depended on substantial support, especially from local physicians. But local autonomy in southern public health had predictable consequences. Most North Carolina rural and village communities were "c[a]reless" and "indifferent" about their responsibilities, according to one observer; possessing complete autonomy, they "could if desired, do nothing, and allow contagious diseases originating within [their] borders to spread beyond and into other towns and counties."[41]

Perhaps the best example of the tenuousness of this community-state partnership occurred Alabama, where beat, or district, health officers aided in the enforcement of an ambitious state and county vital statistics program that had begun during the 1870s. Consistent with prevailing conceptions of local officials and social policy, nonsalaried beat health officers were appointed to represent the local community. Their major responsibility, in theory, was to ensure the enforcement of the reporting of births and deaths by physicians and midwives. But in practice beat health officers served as barometers of the shifting winds of public opinion and divided their loyalties between the state and the local community—with the greater share going to the locality. As a health official in Alabama put it, because community participation was essential to the success of public health, he needed to exercise governmental power "cautiously & with a great [d]eal of leniency."[42]

Alabama, despite its pretensions of state power, lacked effective administrative control. State health officer Jerome Cochran, who spent nearly two frustrating decades attempting to enforce the state's vital statistics law, encountered virtually insuperable obstacles of geography, isolation, and race. In the 1880s and 1890s local communities permitted only erratic compliance. County health officers, even with the assistance of beat officers, faced widespread indifference. Health officials, all of whom were white, found stonewalling and resistance especially common in black communities. Reacting almost instinctively by avoiding white authority, most rural Alabama blacks were born without physicians attending; as one official wrote, they died in a similar manner. Unless some white official heard of births and deaths in the black community and personally confirmed them, no report resulted. Other observers soon concluded that widespread noncompliance, resulting from ignorance of the law or resistance to white authority, was the rule in the black community.[43]

Faced with obstacles at the local level, Cochran fell back on berating local health officers, but they frequently confessed their inability to enforce the law. Even in performing innocuous functions such as inspecting public buildings, county health officers encountered hindrances. When the Bibb County health officer visited the jail and poorhouse, he recommended a general cleanup. Although the poorhouse subsequently improved, the jail, he discovered on later visits, remained "very filthy." His recommendations, he complained, went unnoticed by local government. Why was it necessary for him even to visit the jail, he asked, when the sheriff told him that he had not cleaned it at all?[44]

Behind the frustration of Alabama health officials lay powerful local obstructions. One county health officer was described as having made himself "so obnoxious" that several physicians "*swore* they would report no more nor assist him at all." When it became clear that he would get no help, he quit. Midwives and physicians—because they were expected to provide accurate birth and death data—frequently resisted state authority. Yet prosecution of delinquents was not easy. A county health officer expressed reluctance to coerce a delinquent midwife in Bibb County for fear that "she at once would get up the cry that the 'Drs' were envying her in her work and wanted to persecute her." Still another county health official, after experiencing local stonewalling, concluded that "any man's work here, is all in vain." Even if he worked full-time at public health, he would not accomplish anything.[45]

Although local officials often requested intervention, even minimal interference by state officials could provoke a backlash. Cochran's "dictatorial manner" had alienated local doctors; his successor, W. H. Sanders, was advised to adopt different tactics. Cochran's needling of careless officials or delinquent physicians provoked other strong reactions. Acknowledging problems with his statistical report, one county health officer exploded. It was needless to remind him of the inaccuracy of his reports, but, he asked, was it his fault? Was he expected to "go over the county to get up the reports?" Instead, he suggested that an effective vital statistics law depended on the beat officers who had to collect accurate data.[46]

The nub of the problem, explained one county health officer, was in the lack of accountability. He was criticized without cause, he wrote to Cochran: "I do not know what to do, or who[m] to report to." Echoing these attitudes, a Chambers County health official passed the buck. He had tried "hard enough to get certain parties to look well to their duty," but the real problem was "a culpable carelessness" among physicians. Yet the problem of public health lay more with an ineffective administrative system. Despite the good intentions of one county health officer, his list of physicians and midwives—against which he checked his beat officers' reports—was "a fright." One thing was certain— that the health officers had to report the delinquents to him or he could not report them to Cochran. Accurate reporting ultimately was impossible, however, because it depended on unreliable physicians and midwives, and their statistics were equally unreliable. Was he to report all those not on his report as delinquent—even if they claimed no deaths or births? Without any law to compel them, threats of prosecution were to "no avail, at least in my Beat." Other officials were blunter. Anticipating a reprimand from Cochran, a county health officer admitted that his report, which included no deaths and "nothing like the full number of births," was "verry [sic] defective." Still, he washed his hands of the matter: "I have cleared my own skirts and I hope that you will not fly on to me because the doctors and midwives of the county have failed to discharge their duty." From Choctaw County came other excuses. Apologizing for his monthly report, the health officer there offered three causes for "it coming up badly": negligence on the part of beat officers, "contrariness" among physicians, and ignorance on the part of some of the midwives and heads of households.[47]

Local medical societies, as well as individual practitioners, were supposed to cooperate with county health officials. Yet from all across Alabama came complaints about the profession's indifference, hostility to sanitarian efforts, and squabbling and factionalism. "Ignorance, ignorance, oh there is so much ignorance among doctors!" lamented a health official in Dallas County about his medical society. Another observer said that a conception of professional obligation was only rarely evident; he preferred "the Task of Converting Old Jackson [County] to Prohibition than to gather into the fold of the Med Society the Out Standing Drs." Neighborhood rivalries aggravated mutual suspicion and animosity among physicians; localism, sanitarians complained, worked against professionalism. "We are not a band of brethren," said a Chambers County doctor; "such feelings as *envy, Jealousy, back bitings &c*" plagued the medical society.[48]

Self-improvement, or voluntary cooperation, was not typical of rural physicians. In Blount County, the health officer complained that doctors avoided public health responsibilities and refused to enforce a law that was "for their benefit, & their children, and & childrens['] children to a thousand generations." Even the president of the county's medical society admitted that physicians were indifferent. In the same county thirteen years later, the health officer, noting that his reports were "far from complete," asserted that he had tried to get the doctors to report to him. He wrote to them regularly and posted notices in the newspaper warning of penalties for noncompliance. But it was "all in vain," for rural physicians openly flouted the law. They had become so accustomed to nonreporting that "they thought they could not be made [to] do so."[49]

Nonreporting physicians usually enjoyed the protection of the community, which seldom tolerated outside, state interference and could always withdraw what little funding it provided for enforcement. Local opposition toward public health, or the potential for it, affected the attitude of government decisively. In Butler County, the county health officer glumly reported that the county commissioners refused to pay him anything, "as there is much prejudice and opposition," while the county's political leadership pressed for repeal of the state's vital statistics law. In a candid moment, Cochran admitted that one of the "greatest obstacles" to enforcement of the law was the "attitude of indifference, and even of passive antagonism, sometimes assumed by courts of county commissioners."[50]

Openly delinquent physicians usually escaped prosecution. Greeted with a menacing letter from the state health officer, one such doctor responded in an almost carefree tone. "Forgetfulness," he wrote, had only partly caused his failure to report. The real reason was that he resented state intrusion and considered the gathering of vital statistics to be "foolishness" and unnecessarily demanding of his "time & pocket." It was "ridiculous folly" to expect a rural physician "to drop his business & appropriate time that his patients or family needs." The result, he said, was that most physicians executed the law carelessly, and consequently the reports are not "verry reliable." He warned Cochran to send no more threatening letters: "I am human & dislike perhaps as much as you the idea of being driven." [51]

The inability of the Alabama health bureaucracy to perform its obligations revealed the general characteristics of southern social policy. Lacking coercive powers, aspiring bureaucrats of the New South faced seemingly endless frustrations. As a county health official pointed out to the Alabama state health officer in 1897, the powerlessness of social policy, specifically vital statistics, was rooted in the voluntary, noncompulsory nature of the system. The value and completeness of county officials' reports depended on local physicians and midwives; the state health officer's report hinged on county statistics. Where did true responsibility lie? "I am not going to pass any such criticism upon your report," he wrote, "notwithstanding it could be as truthfully done as yours were upon mine." But as long as the reports' accuracy depended on the "ignorant masses" of physicians and midwives, the system was a failure. [52]

◆ ◆ ◆
COMMUNITY CONTROL: THE POLICY CONSEQUENCES

Health and educational officials frequently found conditions in the rural hinterlands to be so overwhelming as to discourage any hope for improvement. What was true in Alabama was true throughout the South: powerless state health officials made few attempts at preventive health and instead awaited periodic sweeps of epidemic disease. As a western North Carolina health official explained to the state health officer, Watson S. Rankin, local sensitivities necessitated that he "proceed slowly"; excessive zeal would "rub the hair" of local physicians the wrong way. But when he suggested that the official write a letter praising his sanitary efforts, Rankin could stomach it no more. How, he asked, could he congratulate him "upon the observance of law which you say is not observed?" [53]

Other accounts confirm that, for the mass of southerners, illness went both untreated and unprevented. Most southern women, especially black women, experienced the hazards of pregnancy and childbirth aided only by midwives, most of whom were unlicensed and uneducated in modern sanitation.

While black women in northern Alabama made no preparation for their confinement, according to one physician, they accepted the services of any old woman who chanced to be available. Most physicians and health officials, like this one, barely tolerated midwives, who existed completely outside of the medical profession and the public health structure. As late as 1913, North Carolina midwives were virtually unregulated; "they do as they please," wrote the state health officer, "in so far as their patients will allow them." Yet midwives functioned close to the community. A rare defender from the ranks of public health workers explained the importance of this symbiosis. Midwives were often accused of being "dirty, ignorant and superstitious," but they were faithful and would answer a call when no one else would.[54]

Health officials did virtually nothing to prevent disease and acted only after the appearance of serious epidemics. In Mississippi, a county health officer complained in 1880 that public health work was "an up-hill business" in which local people followed "the old beaten track" of a blind confidence in Providence. Once an epidemic imminently threatened, he wrote, they placed trust in "their powers of locomotion." Elsewhere, community resistance was more openly displayed. The health officer of another Mississippi county told of a "manifest disposition" among some to "ignore the Rules and Orders of the State Board as well as the Health Officer," especially those relating to quarantine. After an eastern North Carolina health official imposed a quarantine on a black family following an outbreak of smallpox, the family escaped by fleeing to a neighbor's house off the main road. Aided by an unlicensed black folk doctor, the family openly violated the quarantine, confident that the solitary county health officer was "the whole show in this quarantine business." Warning that this open defiance could render the law "very ineffective in the future," the health officer appealed for an official reprimand of the lawbreakers. Rankin refused, however, with the observation that this was "too much in the nature of a bluff," which would reduce the "influence of this office with the people generally in the enforcement of health laws." The county health officer responded by resigning.[55]

Lacking preventive powers, state health officials were often powerless to improve health conditions. With the incorporation of the South into the world transportation network during the last decades of the nineteenth century, the incidence of smallpox, yellow fever, diphtheria, and measles increased. Health officials, particularly in the lower South, made significant progress in eliminating yellow fever by containing access from Latin America and in reducing smallpox through quarantine. Even so, epidemics persisted, primarily because of the weakness of state authorities. The Mississippi state health officer in the early 1880s warned of the spread of yellow fever from Latin America through the state's Gulf Coast counties, which, he explained, were "almost constantly infected." Accordingly, state authorities sought greater powers to control quarantines in local communities, which were "necessarily wanting" in their "concert of action and reach of authority." A Texas health official lamented that, without central control, counties adopted what regulations suited "their peculiar ideas or prejudices," and that "no power" could "undo them." Understandably, when epidemics appeared, the rank and file had little confidence in public health measures. When a yellow fever epidemic afflicted Montgomery, Alabama, the citizenry quickly became "panic stricken." Those who could fled the city, while public health officials attempted to combat the outbreak by burning pine chips.[56]

A more common occurrence was a smallpox outbreak, which occasioned public panic, not so much because of high mortality as because of the disfiguring results of the disease. In trying to control smallpox, health officials discovered that traditional, localistic governance was ineffective. Because the market economy stimulated interregional community contacts and mass population migration, disease pools mingled with greater ease. The real cause of the spread of smallpox, complained one Alabama mayor, was from tramps and hoboes traveling by way of freight trains and from epidemic refugees leaving the trains. In 1885 a Mississippi observer explained that the expansion of transportation facilities had fostered a "frequent and easy intercourse of our citizens with each other as well as with outside communities" that brought frequent smallpox epidemics. The disease could be eradicated only through compulsory vaccination, but that was possible, given "the present state of public opinion and among a heterogenous population like ours," only in the face of immediate danger. Yet locally oriented epidemic control policies usually failed. A health official near Mobile, Alabama, complained that nearby Escambia County took "little or no cognizance of Smallpox," even though its cooperation was "*absolutely* necessary, otherwise like the poor, it will always be with us." Was cooperation, he asked, impossible? Morale in his county was "excellent," but residents wondered why Escambia failed to observe proper quarantine. Similarly, in Texas, the state health officer wrote in 1892 that, although smallpox had "gained a foothold" in forty-two of that state's counties, "great contrariety of opinions" existed among local officials about how to deal with the problem.[57]

Behind the health bureaucracy's largely futile struggle to control disease lay at least two factors. The first was the powerful popular reflex against coercive governance. Rural southerners had long resisted vaccination for smallpox because of the risk; they regarded other public health measures such as quarantine suspiciously. In one Union County, North Carolina, community, despite a severe outbreak of smallpox, local health officers who attempted to enforce compulsory vaccination encountered "all sorts of obstacles & resistances." One teacher refused to allow vaccinations; as the county health officer said, "he almost ordered us off the place." Although public health officials insisted on universal inoculation, explained one North Carolinian, this could not be done except by military force, with results probably worse than smallpox. This observer, whose son had had a bad reaction from a smallpox vaccination, was dubious about its value.[58]

A second factor hamstrung the efforts of health officials: the discouraging environment of ill health that it could do little to change. When a Florida health agent came upon a village of about two hundred persons built along the railroad, he described it as "very slovenly and unkept [in] appearance." Yards were filled with trash, and pigs ran wild through the streets. The village's most unsanitary feature, however, was its sewage system: outhouses were closely situated to dwellings, few of them employing disinfectants, and the flies that seemed "especially numerous in this section" enjoyed easy access to both toilets and kitchens. Despite these unsanitary conditions, the health official admitted that, because he lacked a "sanitary nuisance" to justify his intervention, he was powerless to act.[59]

Close observers perceived other sources of ill health. A subtle but prevalent affliction was mosquito-borne malaria, which prevailed in a wide belt from Maryland to Texas and was concentrated in river valleys and coastal alluvial plains. When Rockefeller Foundation officials surveyed the Mississippi Delta region of eastern Arkansas in 1917, they were shocked to discover that 90 percent of the population of two townships had a history of malaria. Rather than killing its sufferers, malaria more commonly enervated them and became part of the social landscape. "I right you in reguard to the health of the people in this settlement," appealed a North Carolinian to the state health officer. "Nearly every family" experienced "chills or malaria," and he wondered whether they could "make a living be sides." Malaria was no less common in one Alabama community, where "on the river & creek bottoms every year we have more or less intermittent fever."[60]

Typically, the careless disposal of animal and human waste imperiled health. Town and village residents kept livestock with little or no regard for waste disposal. In a Florida town, an ill-kept hog pen became "a great breeding place for flies, and filth of every kind," while in a western North Carolina town the residents kept cows in poorly constructed, poorly maintained stalls. Many cows had no stalls at all but were lodged underneath residences, in houses constructed on hillsides with long pillars. An even more serious threat to community health in rural areas was soil and water pollution resulting from the unsanitary disposal of human waste. Rural communities had no privies, as a rule, noted one observer; "in the woods without privies," according to another, was the prevalent style. In small towns and villages, open-surface privies bred disease and filth and were, according to one health official, "a menace to the health of any community." With an assortment of intestinal parasites associated with a polluted water supply and soil came other filth-borne diseases, the most serious of which was typhoid. Disease and its consequences, debilitation or death, were thus part and parcel of rural society. The burden, as it does in any society with untreated disease and high mortality, fell disproportionately upon children. Few families were spared the tragedy of infant death; in one instance, a twenty-eight-year-old mother wrote and explained how all four of her children had died, one of meningitis, two of digestive tract complications, and a fourth of heart failure.[61]

Decentralized governance had another result: the shabby and ill-equipped school facilities that were so common throughout the rural South. Almost without exception, visitors were appalled. A teacher in western North Carolina reported backwoods districts with "unpainted Houses, with abominable seats, Black Boards &c. &c., and unkept and improperly clad children." Insufficient facilities were typical. One visitor to South Carolina schools described dilapidated building and grounds, unreliable supplies of water and fuel, and insufficient blackboards, maps, and books. An observer of Arkansas schools found the teacher and pupils during wintertime "huddled about the stove trying vainly to keep warm, while snow blew into the room thru the places where glass should have been." A visitor to Texas rural schools found a "very unattractive, base, ugly" school interior, which had a "poor arrangement of windows, and rusty stoves." To her apparent surprise, an old plowshare held by wire from an oak tree served as the gong that called the pupils. While the facilities of white schools in his county were bad, concluded a Georgia superintendent in 1902, those of black schools were worse.[62]

Many reformers, who exposed these conditions to rally public opinion behind reform, discovered that the deficiencies of schools were rooted in their social environment. The deficiencies of rural schools reflected not only rural poverty but also apathy. In western North Carolina, a county superintendent characterized schools as "sadly neglected"; very few of them were not abused. In Macon County, Alabama, a supervisor for the General Education Board described white schools as scattered and poor, but the chief cause of their poverty was community indifference, measured not just in shabby facilities but also in low attendance. This was, concluded the visitor, "the remnants of a white civilization which has moved away."[63]

Local democracy did not always bring harmony and bliss. Frequently, dif-

Privies, Austin, Texas, ca. 1920.
(Courtesy of Emory University Library)

ferent schools and the communities they represented competed for scarce resources. Location was crucial, since too many congested schools would deplete attendance and, because state support was based on attendance, threaten the flow of funds. Thus, the question of school location, reached by school authorities in a kind of annual ritual, brought intercommunity rivalries to the surface.[64]

In Alabama, interneighborhood conflict over school location and finance was complicated by the state's system of finance. The state's first constitution of 1819 established a school fund in which the proceeds of the rental of public lands (the sixteenth section) were allocated to school districts. Yet community schools frequently complained that the distribution of these funds was unfair. In northern Alabama, the Tennessee River divided a school district in Jackson County into two squabbling neighborhoods that competed for the scarce sixteenth-section funds. On the southern end of the river, school patrons complained that "the north side of the Township" was undervaluing the rental of the land and that "their whole interest has ever been to ruin the school interest of the whole township." Other Alabama communities clashed for scarce resources. In Randolph County, two schools located at the southeastern and northeastern corners of the school district enjoyed exclusive access to the sixteenth-section funds. Over time, however, as other community schools sprang into existence, they pressed their claim for public financial support. The older schools became unhappy because funds were "cut short . . . as there has been more schools located." They vented their wrath by pressing for the removal of the county superintendent.[65]

Intracommunity conflict also often erupted over the vital decisions affecting the community school, most particularly over the annual choice of a teacher. When school trustees hired an Alabama teacher without consulting with patrons, the patrons complained to the state superintendent that they had not "seen any Law" giving him the right to make decisions "contrary to the wishes of the majority of the patrons." In most communities, black or white school patrons exerted an effective veto power over teacher selection. In Georgia, the common practice was for superintendents to submit the issue of teacher selection to a neighborhood vote. Elsewhere, parents often reminded trustees and superintendents of their lack of power. The warning by a group of South Carolina parents that a teacher was "objectionable" was enough to doom her candidacy. Patrons in a North Carolina community made a clearer point when they objected to a teacher and predicted that the school would "go down" in the face of a local boycott. Similarly, an Alabama teacher lost pupils and attendance fell below the minimum. Although the teacher was "eminently qualified and satisfactory to all who send," a disaffected half of the community boycotted the school because their favorite did not teach.[66]

Intracommunity conflicts over teachers were sometimes papered over by appeals to character and moral leadership. In his county, explained a Georgia superintendent, teachers not only had to be "native" and secure the consent of a clear majority of parents, they also had to possess "irreproachable character." Communities would tolerate no hint of dalliance between teachers and pupils, as one young teacher discovered in Davidson County, North Carolina. After reports of a love affair with a student, the community "stood it as long as they could, and asked him to close the school." In other instances, charges of immoral behavior simply masked intracommunity conflict. In eastern Tennessee, a feud between a teacher and another man led the latter to instigate a campaign charging the teacher with immorality. "His company during the nights and on Saturdays & Sundays," charged a petition, was "with a class of people that is, not of good repute and his conduct in general is such that [it] is degrading rather [than] elevating." School officials, despite contradictory evidence, fired the teacher.[67]

Although most southerners lived in a world with little bureaucracy, they were hardly insulated from new social forces that were transforming their region. As Robert H. Wiebe pointed out a quarter century ago, the creation of a national and world transportation system was the beginning of the end of the "island communities" of rural and small-town America.[68] The late decades of the nineteenth century brought, among other changes, railroads, industrialization, and urbanization, and these forces had remade the landscape by the turn of the twentieth century. Even in rural areas, southerners experienced a transformation of agriculture, landholding, and social organization.

Yet the onset of this wider social process did not mean that most southerners were prepared to abandon traditional attitudes toward society and government. If anything, those attitudes became, perhaps paradoxically, more entrenched in the face of change, while the same forces that transformed their environment also spawned groups that embraced new approaches toward social problems and the ability to relate them to local, regional, and national conditions. Even as personal liberty and community autonomy continued to be the watchwords for most people, especially in rural communities, others regarded the prebureaucratic system of community organization as deficient. Whereas rural southerners took for granted a close relationship between community and government, and the democracy that accompanied it, others saw in that system only ineffectiveness and impotence in dealing with a new agenda of social problems. As early as the 1870s social reformers began to define a reform agenda, and they became leading critics of the process of governance that prevailed throughout the South.

GOVERNANCE AND THE

MORAL CRISIS

◆

Although social reformers were active in the post-Reconstruction South in
efforts as diverse as good-government and convict-lease reform, before the
late 1890s they were generally frustrated and isolated.[1] At least part of the reformers' failure lay in their isolation from social and political realities, their
fragmentation, and their lack of a shared, common vision of reform. Despite
agreement that nineteenth-century governance was an obsolete barrier to necessary change, few common threads held reformers together, while rhetoric
and political language fundamentally divided them. Health and educational
professionals, who had an obvious stake in reform, spoke the language of the
technician; good-government reformers were primarily political; and humanitarians were guided by ostensibly selfless motives. Not until what Daniel T.
Rodgers has called a single "language of discontent" emerged to supply an
"ideational glue" for these differing approaches did a coherent reform movement arrive in the South.[2] In that region, this "ideational glue" came in the
last two decades of the nineteenth century from reformers concerned about
the moral and social consequences of alcoholism and excessive drinking. Un-

like the agenda of other social critics, their program enjoyed a significant degree of popular support. That it did so reflected their language and imagery, which were deeply rooted in evangelical notions of human behavior, sin, and the social order.

◆ ◆ ◆

TEMPERANCE AND THE INNER MORAL CRISIS

Writing in the early 1880s, a Virginia Baptist confirmed that a fundamental attitudinal change toward drinking had occurred during the previous generation. Typically, a minister used to take "his julep to prepare himself for the duties of the pulpit, or his toddy to brace up his wearied powers after his services were over." At the homes of ministers and members alike, decanters, tumblers, pitchers of water, and sugar sat on sideboards, "free to every visitor." A new culture of temperance had "surely wrought a great change in all these customs."[3]

Another observer noted the same change in Florida. Fifty years earlier, he reported, deacons, members, and clergy kept strong drink in their homes. On social occasions, they brought "forth the decanter and the glass from the cupboard" and invited "all to pour out and partake." Ministers, like those in Virginia, often drank a "stimulating draught" immediately before church service; on leaving it, they drank "for refreshment from their weariness." Like his counterpart in Virginia, however, the Floridian noted a dramatic change in these attitudes. By the 1880s no churchman who kept intoxicating beverages or served them to visitors could be regarded as "an orderly and consistent disciple of a self-denying Christianity."[4]

This attitudinal transformation was the result of an ambitious and widespread attempt, lasting for most of the nineteenth century, to modify the voracious drinking habits of Americans. Between the 1820s and the passage of the Volstead Act in 1919, many Americans participated in a campaign to restrict and, eventually, to eliminate excessive drinking. The temperance and prohibition movement was perhaps the most misunderstood attempt to modify human behavior in human history. It significantly altered the role of alcohol in American society.[5]

Although the South has long enjoyed a reputation for teetotaling, not until after the Civil War did prohibitionist sentiment emerge in the region. Before then, and until about the mid-1880s, southerners of an evangelical persuasion seldom crossed the line dividing the secular from the religious. Rather, through churches and temperance societies, southerners rejected alcohol by creating an alternative, nonalcoholic culture. While radical in its message of abstinence and abnegation, the new culture of temperance emphasized an individual, inner world of temperance and self-restraint that blended into Victorian culture.

In the mid-nineteenth century, an inner-directed, sentimental worldview of southern evangelicalism clashed with the culture of alcohol. With growing frequency, evangelical churches felt free to discipline drinking members. Temperance became entrenched in the three largest Protestant denominations—Presbyterians, Baptists, and Methodists—by the 1850s. The Methodist Discipline, or book of order, classified intemperance as immoral as early as 1832. Among both Baptists and Presbyterians, internal church discipline was the rule. Public drunkenness, as one churchman explained in 1868, was incompatible with Christianity.[6]

Among evangelicals, the conviction that Christianity and the "monster" of alcoholic culture were incompatible was commonplace. Wherever saloons flourished, concluded a Mississippian, churches withered and died, Sunday schools were abandoned, and virtue declined. Contributions to the saloon replaced weekly contributions to the church; the saloon, the center of alcoholic culture, was devoid of any "religious thought and pious emotion." To combat this invasive and threatening influence, churches sought to insulate themselves from external contamination and to purge themselves of internal corruption. As the chief bulwark of order, stability, and structure, wrote an Alabama Methodist, Christians should keep the church pure, for its impact on public sentiment would ensure that drunkenness and whiskey would be banished.[7]

To expunge the "monster," southern evangelicals sought to create an insulated world. Church leaders urged congregations to expel drinking members and create an alcohol-free community. Church members, a Florida Baptist admonished, should forgo Christmas eggnog and "eat the eggs and do not have the whisky." Churches offered "the best temperance organization," explained a group of Methodists. Intemperance was "the most formidable of all the enemies of the cause of Christ," a "hell-born evil" that undermined evangelical religion and openly defied its precepts. Temperance, for evangelicals, meant acceptance of the church prohibition against drinking; violating these rules exposed members to expulsion.[8]

Such vigilance was necessary because evangelicals faced an internal danger. In Tennessee, liquor-selling church members worked for the "devil all the week" and on Sunday participated in the Holy Communion. Although they claimed "to know God," by their actions they denied Him, making clear that they knew "nothing about the love of God" and cared "nothing for the present or future interest of their fellow-man." Temperance advocates extended this condemnation to drinkers as well as liquor sellers. Too many churchmen drank more than was "conducive to either their piety or their usefulness." With "bloated faces, red noses, trembling lips," these men made liquor "a constant and welcome guest in their households"; even while they preached a life of purity, they spoke in tones "thick and husky with drink." The verdict of one North Carolinian was typical. The sooner churches rid themselves of "habitual dram drinkers," he declared, "the better for the cause of Christ." Drunkenness was a "foul blot on the character of any church member." The communal piety and purity that was so central to the southern evangelical experience also required a ministry free of drink. A North Carolinian complained in 1871 about Methodist ministers who had hindered "the progress of reform" by becoming "stumbling blocks to many tempted ones, among their flocks." He urged other Protestants to force the clergy to flush out supporters and opponents. If ministers opposed temperance, then "we ought to know it and know their objections, so as to be able to combat them." As members of the culture of temperance, ministers were expected not only to support temperance but also to become practicing teetotalers.[9]

Throughout the last three decades of the nineteenth century, southern evangelicals rooted out drinkers from the ranks of the clergy. Southern Methodists in their church discipline explicitly barred "drunkenness or drinking of spirituous liquors" among either members or ministers. But abuses persisted, as a national meeting of southern Methodists acknowledged in 1871. Intemperance, they declared, had "invaded our very pulpits," and "fallen" clergy brought reproach upon the ministry and the church. Public drunkenness was a common affliction among Protestants. A Tennessee Baptist complained that a preacher held services even while under the influence. He held on to the pulpit to avoid falling, and his delivery was incoherent. But when brought up on charges before the congregation, he claimed that he was sober because he had not fallen down and was not drunk as long as he could stand up and preach. In his defense, he claimed that a few drams made "a man more spiritual."[10]

While the temperance movement strenuously opposed alcoholic culture, it imposed limitations on individual behavior consistent with nineteenth-century conceptions of personal liberty and community responsibility. Temperance advocates accepted and often strongly endorsed the popular tradition against intrusive governance. As late as 1890 the Tennessee Baptist State Convention expressed a combination of intense hostility toward alcohol and determined reluctance to embrace solutions through public policy. While condemning the liquor trade, it refrained from accepting state-enforced prohibition. The solution, it said, instead lay in the Christian community working "in the constant, persistent, and never ceasing business of preaching repentance toward God and faith toward our Lord Jesus Christ."[11]

Temperance fraternities across the South reinforced this inner-directed approach to individual behavior and community responsibility. These fraternities constituted a secular equivalent of the evangelical culture of temperance. Although rivalry among the churches and the lodges occasionally erupted, most temperance reformers endorsed a working alliance. Within the "moral vineyard," explained a member of the North Carolina Sons of Temperance in 1871, the fraternal orders served only as an "auxiliary" and "legitimate off-spring" of churches. Temperance lodges were independent of church organization, though "permeated and sanctified by the spirit of the master." The earliest formally organized temperance societies appeared in the South, as they did nationally, in the 1820s. Yet southerners were noteworthy for their rejection of those temperance groups that endorsed publicly oriented activities and their acceptance of those that embraced an inner-directed view of temperance. In the antebellum period, nowhere in the South did the American Temperance Society or other reform-oriented associations make much headway. It was also significant that, whenever temperance legislation was considered, it encountered strong political opposition from southerners denouncing a dangerous constraint on personal liberty.[12]

Most popular were fraternities such as the Washingtonians and the Sons of Temperance, both appearing in the 1840s, which offered an alternative to the world of alcohol and the saloon but eschewed any political involvement. The insistence of southern temperance workers on the rejection of state intervention often clashed with a determination on the part of northerners to embrace it, and the result was internal fracture. In North Carolina, for example, Washingtonians, a primarily working-class movement that attracted as many as 12,000 members statewide, foundered when it embraced prohibition legislation in the 1850s. The Sons of Temperance enjoyed similar popularity during the 1840s and 1850s, survived the Civil War, but then suffered desertions over the question of black membership. The societies that replaced it, such as the Independent Order of Good Templars, the Friends of Temperance, and the Templars of Temperance, succeeded only by avoiding public involvement.[13]

Temperance societies, with the rituals of secret societies—secret grips, signs, and symbols—created an alternative, nonalcoholic world. In a mirror image of the masculine world of the tavern or saloon, the temperance lodge was infused with the traditions of nineteenth-century male culture. For example, when the Bennettsville, South Carolina, chapter of the Sons of Temperance debated the question "Is woman man's equal," it decided, not surprisingly, in the negative. In a ritual that paralleled the all-male act of voting, the taking of the pledge signified public commitment to a new temperance ethos. Often the signing of the pledge constituted a sort of male coming of age. This ritual lay at the very center of the building of an insulated, male-bonded community. Much of the appeal of alcohol lay rooted in all-male culture, the "social feeling" that young men experienced when they imbibed together. Drinking men came "honestly to the pledge," with "high resolve" and a male sense of honor. Drinkers were at least partly attracted to alcohol because of companionship, and a major conflict in pledging abstinence was their ability to relinquish their companions, defy their ridicule, and "resist all their temptations." The ritualized signing of the pledge rendered resistance easier: in violating it, any honor-bound male violated a "solemn obligation." Temperance societies replaced one male code of behavior and sense of community with another. "I became a member of the Sons of Temperance soon after I came hear [sic]," wrote a young Alabama planter in 1849. He claimed that he had honored the pledge and was part of "quite a flourishing Institution."[14]

Temperance societies sought to attract moderate drinkers, rather than outright drunkards, to their ranks. These were men who drank occasionally or habitually, without apparent injury to themselves. Although they never staggered, lay sprawled in the street, or drank to excess at home, they were part of an alcoholic culture. It was these moderate drinkers who unwittingly were under an "evil influence," and they soon developed a habitual use of alcohol. There was another danger, reformers believed, in moderate drinking. By providing a middle ground between total abstinence and drinking, it threatened the integrity and separateness of temperance culture. The moderate drinker frustrated reform; he acted, sometimes unknowingly, "in partnership with the rum seller and the devil in the manufacture of drunkards." Moderate drinkers influenced others by continuing a "course of self-indulgence, regardless of the injury" to others. Men were social creatures, and intemperance was a social vice. Drinking in moderation constituted a kind of "selfishness" that denied "this individual responsibility" and was "as criminal and deadly in the 'moderate drinker' as the dramseller."[15]

Temperance advocates pitched their appeal particularly to young males, those most tempted by the culture of alcohol. Warnings about the temptations and disastrous results of drinking were commonplace. As a Florida Baptist described it in 1885, alcoholic culture devoured manhood. Young men, usually unaware of the implications of their actions, handed their money to other young men who parted "their hair in the middle"; in return, they received "that fiery spirit called rum-fiend," eventually grew to love it, and, in the end, threw their lives away. Young males were particularly susceptible to peer pressure. Even the young man who took the pledge had to be constantly vigilant, for the social influence of his companions and their "mockery at his weakness" could undermine his convictions and lead him toward ruin.[16]

Temperance societies, like churches, readily disciplined their own. When a member of the Bennettsville lodge violated his pledge, lodge members, after a formal hearing, expelled him. Complaints about backsliders were frequent elsewhere. In North Carolina, it was charged that men too often joined temperance societies because of a "prudential policy" instead of "a high and honorable sense of duty." Many lodge members were not "heart and soul" part of the temperance community; when pressed, they crept back "to the bar-room and to freedom from the restraints (?) of the Order." Yet the discipline of their members also suggests that the cohesion and survival of these temperance societies were often problematic. Few members, complained one North Carolinian, willingly accepted the logical consequences of membership. Temperance would triumph only if workers were "true to themselves and their principles." But this required disassociation from those who drank and sold liquor—a position that few temperance men were willing to accept.[17]

◆ ◆ ◆

TEMPERANCE, THE INDIVIDUAL, AND COMMUNITY RESPONSIBILITY

Mid-nineteenth-century southern moral reformers articulated a value structure that was consistent with the prevailing Victorian ethos. Temperance reformers, a North Carolinian observed, rejected the assumption that they could "make men virtuous by statute, or to regulate their appetites by law." Drunkenness was a matter of individual choice and responsibility, and its effects were societal only insofar as they distorted the individual capacity for reason and self-restraint. The temperance press repeated a common message: drinking's impact on the community came primarily through its progressive destruction of individual character. An immediately recognizable term to most nineteenth-century Americans was that of the *moral sense*, which, under the influence of alcohol, became perverted. In 1881 the members of the Council of the United Friends of Temperance of Black Hawk, Mississippi, were told that drink destroyed reason, blunted the moral sense, and broke "the force of the will." Damaged by demon drink, men lost the capacity to distinguish between right and wrong. Alcohol made men dishonest and deceitful; they sought "a private place, the backroom, or the cellar, or the cover of darkness to indulge the habit."[18]

Reformers subscribed to a notion of community that was defined exclusively and included only those who, by shunning the world of alcohol, held membership in the temperate community. In North Carolina, a temperance man described a "thriving little town" that embodied the ideal of an exclusive community. Walking up the main street, he was proud to observe that temperance men dominated the town's business life; among the young, respect and "honorable employment" prevailed as long as they traversed "the sunny path of temperance." Despite the threat of "heavy fire" from the forces of intemperance and the "sad havoc" it brought within temperance ranks, this was a community that was "prospering finely."[19]

Temperance advocates adopted a new litmus test of community—drinking cold water in an almost ritualistic way. Cold water, rather than destroying health, "mental gearing," and "our soul-powers," epitomized total abstinence from alcohol. In Mississippi, temperance workers composed a ditty in which the image of cold water as a beverage sharpened the distinction between drinker and teetotaler: "Men may sing if they will, with a drunken leer / Of the virtues of whiskey and cider and beer; I pray from the curse of them to be free. / Cold Water, pure water for me / Cold Water, pure water for me."[20]

A negative reference—the monstrous evil that alcohol represented—united the temperance community. Demon Rum and the alcoholic culture that surrounded it resorted "to every possible scheme" to fight temperance to the bitter end, declared a South Carolina Baptist; it was "linked with the world of darkness and has for its champion the prince of evil." Temperance was a struggle between the forces of civilization and barbarism, according to a Mississippian. In this worldview, a battle raged "between order and disorder, between intemperance and sobriety, between peace and violence, between quietness and disturbance, between happiness and misery, and between the church and the saloon."[21]

Temperance advocates differentiated their community by appealing to conspiratorial images and symbols that resonated with central symbols in American Protestantism. A North Carolina temperance advocate likened alcoholic culture to a "serpent that biteth like an adder, whose sting is venomous," through whose evil effects scores were dispatched "to a premature grave." The liquor traffic was not only monstrous, it was also the work of the devil. A North Carolina newspaper described a "co-partnership" between the saloon keeper and the devil. Bring him the "industrious, the sober, the respectable," the devil promised, and he would return drunkards and paupers. Alcohol also promoted social discord, family disintegration, and vice—all satanic objectives. The rum seller occupied a central place in this scenario of evil. Temperance leaders warned their friends not to be deluded by his superficial success and status. Those sympathetic to temperance might be impressed enough to conclude that it was "better to sell liquor and become rich and ride in a fine carriage, than to belong to the Friends of Temperance, and be hard pressed for money." But these riches were "all stained with blood, and besprinkled with tears." An avenging God would, in due time, "*dash* his ruined soul into that pit of eternal despair."[22]

While communitarian, reformers were also highly individualistic; they stressed a message of individual responsibility and piety that precluded any form of governmental interference. Most temperance advocates foresaw a day in which, through a voluntary process, drinkers would join the culture of temperance; societal redemption was possible only through personal redemption. Changing individual behavior, most temperance advocates assumed before the 1880s, could not be legislated. They argued that the Maine Law of 1851, the model for state-level prohibition legislation, had failed because it lacked community and individual assent. Temperance reform could produce a new society only when its values had triumphed in a sort of temperance millennium. A North Carolina Methodist eagerly foresaw a time when "the grogshops shall be closed for the want of customers." Yet this would become possible only through the "rapid spread of the *Gospel* of Jesus Christ," once a "mighty phalanx" had worked in lockstep against intemperance.[23]

In the last two decades of the nineteenth century, this approach to temperance reform underwent a significant transformation: temperance increasingly embraced more public solutions. Reform focused less on individual redemption than on the restriction and even eradication of the liquor "traffic," the trade that made the culture of alcohol possible. Behind this transformation were several factors, the most important of which was the rapid change that had begun to alter traditional conceptions of family, gender roles, work, and leisure. By the 1880s, when the spread of the market economy began to transform both southern agriculture and industry, excessive use of alcohol became a metaphor for anxiety about the larger disintegration of community and moral values. This message was less a testimony about the decline and destruction of moral sense and individual character than it was one of societal breakdown.[24]

This shift in focus from individual to community had important implications. Rather than being a problem that affected only men, alcoholic culture endangered the entire family structure. In 1896 the *Alabama Christian Advocate* urged the nurturing of children and their protection from the harsh realities of the world. The years of childhood were lost too quickly to the "cares and struggles of maturity." While they could, children should participate in "the fresh innocent joys of childhood." "Let them grow gradually and there will be more sturdiness about their maturity. . . . Don't rob your children of childhood." Child nurture necessitated protection and regulation and an ideology of nurture meshed with an ethos of temperance.[25]

New conceptions of childhood and adolescence were juxtaposed against anxieties about the changing nature of family hierarchy. Within the family, alcohol became a focal point for fears about the assertion of independence and autonomy within a constrained, patriarchal family. Assertiveness, especially on the part of the young, was often portrayed as evidence of the breakdown of the traditional, cohesive family hierarchy. Dram shops were filled with "beardless youth," boys who asserted a right of individual self-government. In these "dens of infamy," parents had "yielded their sceptre to strangers' hands"; the "family circle" had become so broken that domestic tranquility was shattered. Although drinking had been banished from churches, observed a Virginian, it remained the "direst curse in our homes." Most families, "however high—and the higher, the greater the peril," had sons who faced the prospect of filling a drunkard's grave. Many other young men followed a similar course, according to a North Carolinian, in which "early training" gave way to "evil associations" that "led to ruin." Ignoring their filial duty, they plunged headlong into a "vortex of dissipation."[26]

Alcohol also undermined the traditional position of women within the family. Vivid, even lurid, imagery aroused Victorian sensibilities. One pamphlet told the story of a fictional Philip Raymond, a drunkard, who preferred drinking with male companions to nurturing his family and whose "love for strong drink overcame his love for home and family." Was there not a Philip Raymond among us all, asked the pamphlet, and were its readers not afraid they would become one? The point was not subtle: drinking men were also husbands and fathers, and alcohol impoverished and destroyed their families.[27]

By brutalizing women and making a "kind father into an unfeeling tyrant,"[28] alcohol undermined the traditional sanctity of marriage and family. If women entered into the bonds of matrimony in good faith, wondered one temperance advocate, could they be expected to honor their vows in the face of a drunken and abusive husband? As innocent victims of the alcohol traffic, women bore "the burden of shame" and wore "the rags of poverty," declared a woman reformer in 1884; pale cheeked, their eyes grew "dim" with the dissipation of the patriarch. This sort of critique was not uncommon. A Florida woman, adding her testimony, told how she had married a drinker without understanding what life with a drunkard truly meant. There was not a "young girl in this building," she told an audience of temperance workers, that truly understood it. "Girls, believe me when I tell you that to marry a drunkard, to love a drunkard, is the crown of all misery." Alcohol abuse to other observers was also a chief cause of the increasing trend of family breakup. To reformers, liquor poisoned marriage and the family and became an independent agent of social breakdown. Drunkards should never be husbands, advised a Tennessee Baptist, because they possessed the power to inflict misery, which they were sure to use to the utmost. Drunken men were capable of such abuses that to compare them to "the brutes of the stall or the beasts of the jungle" would libel the animals. Drink eroded the ability to sustain mutual relationships; selfishness consumed "the very heart" of the husband-father, who otherwise should be the object of "reverence and love." [29]

By invading the sanctum of the home, alcohol had consequences wider than early temperance reformers had admitted, and by the 1880s reformers were associating a welter of social problems with drink. Writing in the *North Carolina Prohibitionist*, one observer described its ill effects: "homes that were once beautiful and pleasant converted into places of wretchedness and woe," dissipated sons, and husbands who had begun marriage with "a courageous heart to breast the storms of life" but who were "brought low by excessive drinking." These were all innocents in a larger pattern: a "traffic" that was "of expense to every person," whose effects were "here and there all over the land." [30]

What caused most social problems, asked another reformer. Whiskey, and the liquor traffic, was at its root, but the key point, as this observer put it, was a system that tolerated and even encouraged alcohol abuse. "Do our people know these facts?" he asked. Certainly they did, but the reason they tolerated it was because of the money that the system produced. The problem was less individual sin than it was a widely extended system. It was best exemplified in saloons or in the more generalized "Liquor Traffic" that dominated the entire community and encouraged social decay and degeneration. Its objective was to "tear down, never to build up," wrote one prohibitionist in 1894, and although some were enriched by it, the community was "surely impoverished." [31]

This kind of discourse increasingly rendered old assumptions about temperance irrelevant, as did other factors. Ted Ownby's recent study of southern evangelicals has found that, among evangelical churches, moral discipline, especially over drinking-related transgressions, eroded during the last decades of the nineteenth century. [32] Meanwhile, most of the all-male temperance lodges entered a state of suspended animation during the 1880s; those that survived began to stress prohibition. [33] In Mississippi, for example, the Verona chapter of the Order of Good Templars resolved in 1883 to condemn the liquor traffic and to endorse "all honorable efforts to suppress the sale, manufacture and use of alcoholic bever[a]ges." In this way, reformers were constructing a wider appeal to what another southerner described as a "deep and deep[e]ning feeling" against the "waste and ruin caused by the liquor traffic." This "feeling," he hoped, would blossom into "a great movement" to abolish the liquor traffic and to restore "hope, peace and plenty to many desolate homes."[34]

◆ ◆ ◆

THE MOBILIZATION OF MORAL REFORM

In September 1880, in a scene repeated countless times across the South, the citizens of Meridianville, Alabama, assembled and sent a petition to the governor. The petition's signers, like those of many other communities in the 1880s, announced their support for local option prohibition. Asserting a right of community control and self-regulation, they predicted that such a law "would promote the peace, good order, and the prosperity of the public and would relieve said community, and the churches and schools in said village, from much disorder and disturbance." What occurred in Meridianville was just one instance of a widespread, grassroots movement. There was an obvious change in the reformers' rhetoric and imagery, which began to be apocalyptic. A petition from a group of Florida Baptists was typical: the Bible condemned both drunkenness and the use of alcohol; alcohol had sent "its thousands yearly in disgrace to their grave[s]; and their souls to a burning hell." It was the duty of all Christians to combat anything "in opposition to Christianity" and to deny any "encouragement of or aiding of the accursed traffic, either manufacturing or selling intoxicating drinks." This kind of language became commonplace. A Georgia minister in 1885 described saloons and the liquor traffic as "traders in inequity," "vampires," and "ulcers" eating "deeper into our flesh." Individuals faced a stark choice between good and evil. "We are either for God or the Devil," declared a North Carolina Baptist. How could any man say that he belonged to God when he willingly chose the liquor traffic? Those on God's side should unite to destroy the common enemy.[35]

Mobilized Christians like these eagerly endorsed an aggressive campaign against the liquor traffic. Regulation of liquor was impossible, wrote a Tennessean; such a policy was simply "legalized lawlessness." The only solution was to be "out with it." "After all these years of prayer & effort & waiting & hoping," declared a Woman's Christian Temperance Union activist from Augusta, Georgia, in 1892, God had revealed Himself in a way in which there could be no mistaking. The time, she believed, had never been more propitious for reform: out among the people there was "great enthusiasm &

encouragement." A "marvelous religious awakening in all the churches" had brought "a mighty upheaval on the liquor question, thank God!"[36]

Prohibitionists framed their appeal in terms that many Americans would readily understand. By raising the specter of corruption, conspiracy, and decline, they appealed directly to republican values. Moral reformers equated the liquor traffic with other vast, impersonal forces threatening the Republic. Along with "Romanism" and the "Money Power," according to one reformer, the "Liquor Power" constituted a "great evil" that operated against the best interests of the people. The threat of this sprawling conspiracy gave prohibition added urgency during the 1880s and 1890s. The problem of alcohol promised "greater perils to all the interests of our people than any which we have had to face since the dark days of reconstruction and negro domination," declared a South Carolinian. As part of "true manhood and loyal citizenship," defenders of the Republic should "meet the emergency with a determined purpose."[37]

Prohibitionists further maintained that the corruption of the liquor traffic had poisoned the political system. They portrayed traditional politics as being under the domination of whiskey dealers or indifferent to community interests. There was no reason to hope for much in the way of prohibition from either of the old political parties, complained a Tennessee reformer in 1888, because they were both afraid of the question. The "whiskey power" was too great for them, and it held the balance of political power. The alternatives under the traditional political system seemed grim. Supporting an independent prohibitionist party violated strong taboos and aroused fears of black political power. Yet reformers were determined to have a political impact. Prohibitionists should "elect no man to any office, from the highest to lowest," declared an Alabamian, "who drinks." To further the cause of reform, he wrote, "Let Christian men make it a *sine qua non* for their votes that a candidate shall 'touch not, taste not, handle not the unclean thing.'"[38]

Two groups—women and Protestant activists—spearheaded the prohibition mobilization. Whereas the temperance movement had been primarily male, in the 1880s prohibition involved greater numbers of women and was part of a larger infusion of women into public affairs during the last quarter of the nineteenth century. Yet this infusion occurred with considerable ambivalence about its precise shape and extent. Women addressed the issue of their involvement gingerly at first, then with greater aggressiveness. In the early 1870s a North Carolina woman complained to a state temperance newspaper that women were shut out of moral reform. Women should properly work "to save erring man from the drunkard's grave" through "kind words and loving smiles from the tempter's snare." But women were also directly affected by male drinkers as "the grief stricken mother [or] wife . . . of the erring one." With the aid of women, the temperance movement would "uproot the evil from our land." More than a decade later, a Mississippi prohibitionist took a more assertive tone. She urged women to make drinking "unfashionable and disgraceful" among their suitors, since no young man could safely be trusted with the happiness of any woman. Women, she believed, played a special role in mobilizing public opinion by making it regard alcohol with "scorn, contempt and ridicule." Women, through public activism, could ensure that decanters decorating the tables of households would become consigned to the "cob-webs of the cellar," and that the "whiskey rings" would fall, "never to be resurrected." Another reformer in the 1880s urged women to exert their moral influence. Women should purge "the matchless evil" from society by refusing "to smile upon the men who sell or drink the firey [sic] fluid"; they would be declared "unfit for the society of a *true woman*" and reform would fol-low, "bringing peace upon its wings." While disputing the notion that women should be confined exclusively to the home, a Mississippi woman added that activism against saloons would "abate not one jot . . . of home influence." [39]

Others promoted a more directly political role. Responding to a Texas anti-prohibitionist who scolded women for sacrificing the home for the public sphere, an Alabama editorialist affirmed the duty of women to shape public opinion in their "high and holy mission to become a factor in all moral re-forms." The woman, as custodian of the family, suffered most from alcohol's devastation; if "any being on earth" deserved to loathe it, she did: drink had "robbed her a thousand times of all the comforts that made home happy" and stolen away the love of her husband, transforming him into a "brute" and a "broke[n] and dishonored wreck." [40]

Still others took political involvement to a radical, if logical, conclusion. Votes for women, according to some prohibitionists, translated into votes for the restriction of drink. To one Alabama woman prohibitionist, the system was flawed when less intelligent men possessed the franchise, while capable women had no political power. Was it just, she asked, when women stood aside "with folded hands and mute lips" while ignorant men, some of them black and foreign, decided questions that so materially affected the sanctity of their homes and hearts? Was it just that women had no voice over legislation governing their children and demanding their obedience, while an ignorant man possessed "the legal right to assist in forming laws by his free vote"? And was it just that women should have no influence over the existence of saloons that tempted "the innocent feet of the most precious ones down the slippery ways to spiritual, mental and physical ruin"? [41]

The most important vehicle for women's activism in prohibition was the Woman's Christian Temperance Union, founded in Ohio in the mid-1870s and first organized in the South in the early 1880s. Recent studies of the WCTU have emphasized how it provided an important arena for women's activism and autonomy in the public sphere. Yet the organization also typified and embodied the contradictory impulses behind the involvement of women in prohibition. Whereas the northern WCTU became directly involved in politics, even to the extent of supporting both an independent prohibitionist party and endorsing a broad plank of social reforms, including woman suffrage, southern WCTU members were more cautious and stressed temperance education and coalitions with other prohibitionists.[42]

Although strongly committed to and involved in prohibition, southern WCTUs respected well-delineated limits. The records of the Richmond, Virginia, chapter of the WCTU are illustrative. In 1882 the chapter was established after the visit of a South Carolina organizer who stressed that women should avoid closing saloons themselves, "but, by their influence and labors, try to obtain Prohibition, or, at least, Local Option." Then and later, the chapter remained torn between its existence as a staid women's club or its advocacy of a more public role. As a single-sex organization, as the chapter's minutes expressed it in 1883, the women were "indeed united & work as sisters should." They asserted a moral right to work "to banish from our beloved city the fiend that is destroying both the bodies and souls of our young men." But, at the same time, the organization worked in coalition with other groups to lobby for local option prohibition.[43]

Another important ingredient in the popular mobilization behind prohibition was the changed attitude of Protestant evangelicals. As early as 1879 North Carolina Methodists denounced the liquor traffic as "the greatest source of evil and crime" and endorsed prohibition, and within a year the state's Baptists had concurred in this view. In Alabama, Methodists and Baptists both spearheaded prohibition. In 1881 the state's Baptist convention condemned the liquor trade and two years later began a full-scale campaign to enact local option; in 1882 the state Methodist conference endorsed prohibition.[44]

Although interdenominational rivalries remained strong, in some instances prohibitionists overcame them and forged working alliances. In Mississippi, for example, Pontotoc County evangelicals formed an interdenominational Prohibition Association to shape "public sentiment on questions of public interest." More specifically, the association pledged to employ "all honorable means" to press the prohibition cause. Although the group announced that it would avoid "any political issue whatever," it sought, as a new single-interest organization, the accomplishment of "prohibition and the enforcement of the law against the liquor traffic."[45]

The mobilization of churches behind local option and other forms of restriction began to yield results during the last two decades of the nineteenth century in the form of statewide local option legislation. The Virginia General Assembly enacted fairly typical legislation in 1886. It provided that local administrative units—either incorporated towns or unincorporated magisterial districts—could hold popular elections to ban the licensing of saloons and liquor establishments. Sixteen years of local option legislation resulted in widespread rural prohibition. By 1902 local option prevailed in twenty-three of the commonwealth's one hundred counties. Even more significant, about three-quarters of its unincorporated magisterial districts were dry in that year.[46]

In states where general local option legislation met opposition, prohibitionists succeeded in enacting other restrictive legislation. In some states, they settled for general dispensary legislation, which, sometimes in conjunction with local option, permitted the establishment of state-run dispensaries by referenda. In South Carolina, local option occurred only by special legislative enactment, and the state adopted a dispensary system in 1892 in part to forestall statewide prohibition. In Tennessee, the legislature refused to pass strong general local option laws in 1873, 1875, and 1879; instead, in 1877 it enacted the famous Four Mile Law. By banning the sale of intoxicating liquor within four miles of any school, it became—because schools were widely dispersed throughout the state—one of the most effective examples of temperance legislation in the late nineteenth-century South. Alabama passed a general local option bill in 1883, and over the next twenty-four years twenty-one counties took advantage of it. But just as effective were a variety of laws passed across the South that extended prohibition by banning drinking in areas surrounding churches, schools, factories, voting precincts, coal mines, and railroad stations.[47]

The emergence of prohibition sentiment at the grassroots level during and after the 1880s constituted a fundamental alteration of southern public opinion. The power and appeal of the temperance movement during the 1850s, 1860s, and 1870s lay in its promise of cultural isolation; mid-nineteenth-century temperance advocates stressed individual redemption, usually of male drinkers. In the last two decades of the nineteenth century, a new critique emerged that endorsed coercive prohibition. Rather than stressing the breakdown of character, prohibitionists emphasized the social threat of alcoholic culture. The Reverend O. P. Fitzgerald, a southern Methodist, told the National Reform Association in 1890 that, under the influence of alcohol, cultural, racial, or political conflict quickly escalated into a social crisis. Whether in a strike in the North, vigilante justice in the West, or an instance of "race trouble" in the South, alcohol usually inflamed passions and aggravated the crisis. The closing of saloons and the abolition of drunkenness, he declared, would mean that southern racial violence would become as "scarce as prayer-meetings among the anarchists in Chicago." The stability of the Republic depended on political virtue and intelligence, commented a southern prohibitionist in 1883. The liquor traffic corrupted the vote, debauched legislatures, and sought "to dictate its policy of corruption and death to the nation." The saloon power had descended upon state capitals and demanded its legitimization as a "controlling power." The liquor traffic had "proclaimed its purpose to rule, govern and dominate the politics of the country," declared another prohibitionist, and had pledged itself to the defeat of all opposing politicians. It was high time for southerners "to raise the black banner of Prohibition and stand shoulder to shoulder under it as one man."[48]

Stressing social over individual sin, prohibitionists emphasized the wider, systemic consequences. From saloons and the cancerous network of liquor manufacture, sale, and distribution sprang crime and disorder. When Mississippi prohibitionists organized a statewide Prohibition Union in 1883, they proclaimed themselves composed of people who were "tired of the reign and ruin of rum" and of "murder, the direct result of drunken brawls." In Georgia, according to one observer, the local option campaigns of the early 1880s arose most frequently in counties where social disorder and crime prevailed. Spalding County, where crime and drinking were "universal," joined the prohibition column, as did Clayton County, long a "resort of desperation." To this observer, local option had become an effective tool for the reestablishment of law and order.[49]

The changing social landscape of the late nineteenth century made old assumptions about alcohol obsolete. A central assumption of mid-century temperance—that the battle against alcohol could be won through "moral suasion"—came under increasing criticism. Moral suasion was ineffective in the war against evil, declared the *Clinton Argus* in 1883. Only legal compulsion could eradicate vice and immorality. Moral suasion taught reverence; legal compulsion placed "its sentries to guard each church door from intrusion or disturbance." Moral suasion and legal compulsion were mutually dependent; the two were "joined" and together did "their best work." Other prohibitionists argued that moral suasion meant an ineffective and failed compromise with evil. In 1887 an Alabamian described it as a "complete failure." Proselytizing could save people, but "good, wholesome prohibition laws" provided the most effective method for this "gracious work." The "giant evil" of alcohol rendered old assumptions obsolete, declared the Minister's Union of Montgomery, Alabama, in 1899. Those who championed "social order, good government and good morals" could no longer rely exclusively on moral suasion. Some mistakenly believed that there could be temperance without prohibition, warned a reformer, but such reasoning implied that moral suasion might succeed with thieves, burglars, murderers, and perjurers—and do away with jails and gallows. Because moral suasion worked neither with these criminals nor with the liquor traffic, state-required prohibition remained the only "wholesome restraint."[50]

To combat the "Liquor Power," prohibitionists articulated a sophisticated understanding of the problem of alcohol. They saw alcohol abuse as part of a systemic corruption typified by local saloons but tied into a highly profitable alcohol trade. Its tentacles were national and affected every community in the country; drink cursed not only the community that manufactured it, but the whole nation as well. The entire system was a "fountain head of corruption, woe and misery" whose "poisoned waters" flowed everywhere, "polluting the very atmosphere as they go." Its "demoralizing and destructive influence" could be felt "not only in the country, in the mountains, and in the valleys, but in our villages, towns, and cities."[51]

Stressing manufacture and distribution rather than abuse, prohibitionists conceived of the social problem of alcohol differently. Although prohibitionists and mid-century reformers shared the assumption that drinking reflected moral decline and corruption, prohibitionists saw its fundamental causes as social rather than individual sin. Prohibition sought less to control drinking than it did to smash the all-pervasive system. Instead of making "bad men good" or "dishonest men honest," prohibition would punish the makers and sellers of this "deadly poison." Retailing alcohol was an evil, wholesaling "a greater evil." Responsibility for this corruption "increased in proportion to the amount made and sold."[52]

◆ ◆ ◆

THE ROLE OF GOVERNMENT

The logic of the prohibitionists' argument led them to a broader reconsideration of the role of government in southern society. Abandoning moral suasion meant accepting governmental compulsion, yet this could not be accomplished without another step—locating corruption in government itself. Because the high license system, which regulated the alcohol trade by imposing a tax on retailing, provided substantial revenues, government became, reformers contended, an active partner in the liquor trade.

Under the license system, they argued, government protected saloons and the alcohol trade. Under "the cover and protection of law," wrote a Nashville prohibitionist in 1900, organized vice encouraged lawlessness and social disorder. The licensing system legalized the liquor traffic, which sought legitimization and was willing to sacrifice profits for official recognition and sanction. A "bastard in the great family of civilized exchange," the liquor trade yearned for the legitimacy that licensing provided. In exchange for a licensing fee, the saloon received public recognition and participation in its trade, contended the *North Carolina Baptist*. Licensing officially tolerated the liquor traffic, permitting it for "a consideration." By licensing saloons, government had lost its neutral standing.[53]

The dispensary system was another matter. Moderate and conservative reformers saw state-run dispensaries as a way of uprooting corruption by exerting state control over distribution. Probably most prohibitionists, however, saw dispensaries as yet another copartnership with evil. When South Carolina established a statewide dispensary system in 1892, a prohibitionist described the law establishing it as "the State of South Carolina saying that the liquor traffic is such a *bad* thing, such a *very bad* thing that her citizens ought not and shall not engage in it, but—the *State herself will.*" The liquor business was under the control of "the devil and his angels," a condition that legislative enactment left unchanged. Government fostered the liquor traffic under its protection, a meeting of South Carolina prohibitionists resolved in May 1892. A leading prohibitionist in that state, Lysander Childs, described licensing as an association between the community and evil. Taxing liquor was equivalent to protecting it; licensing meant becoming a "party to the business with all its consequences." The government had no right to engage in a partnership that injured its citizens, both by participating in evil and by then sacrificing "the victim to that evil."[54]

The only solution to the moral quagmire of government's relationship with the liquor trade, most reformers had concluded by the early twentieth century, was unqualified prohibition—and a reconsideration of the role of the state. Although the *Nashville Christian Advocate* opposed "an officious paternal government" and was convinced that the state should remain out of the private affairs of its citizens, the issue of prohibition offered exceptional circumstances. The temperance cause required the sacrifice of individual autonomy and necessitated a "*strong* government, one that acts, when it acts at all, with resistless force." Government was legally protecting and promoting the liquor traffic, wrote a North Carolina prohibitionist; it should henceforth use the same powers to destroy it. Personal liberty did not mean "the right to tempt men to drunkenness." The old adage that it was impossible to "legislate morality into men" was untrue, editorialized South Carolina's *Baptist Courier.* Governmental coercion could never perfect men, but it was a "great educative force" whose restraining power contributed to public and private morality. Although the law was not the only vehicle of civilization and morals, nothing along these lines could be done without it.[55]

In this transformation to advocacy of active governance, prohibitionists attacked some long-standing notions. One was the distinction between church and state. Moral government, argued reformers, did not mean theocratic government. Church and state both exercised moral and temporal functions, argued a Tennessee Baptist: the state possessed the right to punish "licentiousness, in the name of a church," while churches could protest against immoral government. Evangelicals committed to prohibition could properly offer their moral support, as well as their protest, against those laws fostering the liquor traffic in favor of those sponsoring its legal prohibition.[56]

Another, even more central political conception that prohibitionists attacked was that of "personal liberty." When an aged Jefferson Davis in 1887 opposed a prohibition amendment to the Texas constitution on the ground that the world was "governed too much," a prohibitionist, John H. Reagan, former postmaster general in Davis's cabinet, responded that limiting individualism was sometimes necessary for the good of society and the protection of its members. All laws, he maintained, required limitations over individual freedom; the greatest of them, the Ten Commandments, did the same thing. Such limitations were part of human civilization. They protected the persons, the reputations, the lives, and the property of the people. "Personal liberty" enjoyed no constitutional protection, and if the liquor traffic was evil and produced drunkenness and crime, caused poverty and individual ruin, deprived families of their homes, and inspired men to abuse and murder, then surely personal liberty was an irrelevant concept. Unlimited individual rights belonged "only to the savage," maintained a South Carolinian, and orderly society was based on consensual agreement to the limitation of individual freedom for the common good. One man, for example, might claim a right to utter profanity, but this right "to his tongue" was restricted by his "neighbor's right to that neighbor's ears." Similarly, the right to drink was limited by the greater public good of temperance. Civilized society was based on the mutual surrender of personal rights, an Alabama Methodist editorialized in 1887. To protect the liquor traffic in the name of "personal liberty" was equivalent to defending the rights of Satan to travel "through Paradise and to crush out the life of every fair flower that blooms there."[57]

By the late 1890s, then, prohibitionists had concluded that individual temperance efforts were not sufficiently compulsive; that the problem of alcohol was complex, and responsibility for it pervaded the social and political system; and that the solution lay in restricting individual freedom through governmental coercion. Thus did moral reformers, in the closing decades of the nineteenth century, change the terms of debate from individual to social redemption.

◆ ◆ ◆

MORAL REFORM AND THE BOURGEOIS INTERIOR

The coalescence of a prohibitionist critique during the 1880s and thereafter had wider implications. Other reformers by then took its message of social and moral decline and the need for the reassertion of traditional order and applied it to a broader analysis of southern society. Like moral reformers elsewhere, they believed that rapid social change in the post-Reconstruction South had eroded the traditional family structure and the moral system that it upheld. Few could question the need "for a decided change in the present order of things," declared a North Carolinian in 1891. Vice had "seized our young men and even boys of very tender age," while "obscenity, vulgarity, and blasphemy" prevailed among them. A clear decline was under way in the standards of parental control. The lack of parental control was a familiar theme in the southern denominational press of the 1890s and thereafter. In South Carolina, a commentator noted the "growing lack of respect for constituted authority" among the young, which he traced to a softer family. Although the "firmness" of the traditional family had seemed "in many instances harsh and unwise," it yielded "manly men and womanly women" and was far better than "the weak yielding of parent to the control of insistent juveniles." "Pampered and indulged and cajoled" children were the products of families "indoctrinated" with a "false theory" of child nurture.[58]

Husbands and wives similarly disregarded the sanctity of marriage; divorce was on the rise. With virtual unanimity, reformers condemned the tendency toward the liberalization of divorce laws. Divorce imperiled the family, the fundamental ingredient of human civilization, observed an Atlanta minister; it destroyed home, church, and state and encouraged social chaos. Those favoring or even tolerating divorce were confederates with evil and recruiters for "the myrmidons of hell." The growth of divorce, wrote a Baptist, suggested that marriage was regarded as temporary rather than permanent, existing only as long as it might suit personal convenience. Instead, marriage was the "foundation of society, the bulwark of good government, the source of our truest and noblest earthly happiness." Christians should reject this official sanctioning of immorality, advised a Tennessean; ministers should refuse to marry divorcées, and churches should refuse them membership.[59]

Moral reformers' concern with social decay, focusing on its public display, led to an attempt to extend private, evangelical morality to the public sphere. Nothing better exemplified this than the effort, beginning as early as the 1880s, to regulate sexual morality in the urban South. In 1887 the Methodist *Alabama Christian Advocate* called for a statewide campaign to eradicate red-light districts. Although some of the state's strongest churches were in urban communities, it was there that the "social evil" of prostitution thrived. Like the problem of alcohol, the root cause of this social disease was systemic; it was "much easier to prevent a great social evil than to destroy it when it has once thrust its poisonous fangs into the social life of a community." In brothels, "female abodes of disease and death," satanic vultures fed on "the blighted hopes and ruined prospects of fallen and degraded humanity." The newspaper pledged itself to mobilize against evil by extending private morality into the public sphere. "We intend to make prolonged war upon these dens of infamy," it wrote, "until they are closed forever, or the moral sentiment of the community refuses to support us."[60]

Vice reformers increasingly asked why prostitutes, as victims of a traffic in human souls, were any more culpable than brothel owners or the men who patronized them. Male clients, a Florida minister declared, were "the corrupt fountain from whence this stream flows, the evil tree on which this fruit grows." Rescue work was possible only if the tree was made good and the fountain purified. Organized vice, like other forms of organized immorality, allowed evil to walk in ordinary clothes among good people. Male clients walked the streets, worked in jobs, and led society; some were even church members. "They sing psalms and you sing with them . . . and while the word is yet in their mouth they may have their eyes on a woman, lusting after her in their hearts." Why should society "bless the man and curse the woman"?[61]

Beginning in the 1880s, evangelical reformers mobilized against other forms of moral decline. As early as 1881 the northern Presbyterian divine Theodore Cuyler condemned recreations, such as card playing and gambling, that inflamed "the evil passions of our nature" as "sinful amusement." During the next twenty years he was joined by a chorus of denunciations by other mobilized Christians. Some parents, lamented a North Carolinian, unwittingly abetted sin by playing cards with children at home and thereby creating in them a desire for that kind of diversion. But the problem with acquiescing in the evils of card playing, as this observer and others like him noted, was only partly individual degeneration; the larger problem was the social decline it brought with it. Parents did not realize that it opened the pathway to public card playing and attracted young men toward social idleness, gambling, and vice. Card playing and gambling brought individual decline, observed a Chattanooga Baptist minister in 1884; they provided conditions in which "every rank and vile weed of infidelity" and "every species of evil association" flourished. Drinking, obscenity, cheating, and crime were social, not individual, failings. Gambling existed in "co-partnership" with the saloon and prostitution, according to the *Charlotte Presbyterian Standard*; all three should be "banished" from the city.[62]

On similar grounds reformers also denounced other public amusements. Particularly alarming were the newly introduced urban recreations that existed outside the supervision of the Christian home. Cuyler, who included the theater in his list of immoral public amusements, warned of this loss of control when he observed that most people who frequented the theater went there for "strong passional excitement." Although not all plays were immoral nor all of its audiences "on a scent for sensualities," theater in general was "only a gilded nastiness." Other moral reformers denounced theaters as indecent and corrupt. Describing theaters as existing in opposition to churches, a southern Methodist in 1889 condemned both the "roving bands of men and women" actors and the display of "vulgar posters" that accompanied them. The theater, added an Alabama Baptist, was "the vestibule of the brothel." The theater relaxed the moral constitution, according to Methodist Warren A. Candler, allowing individuals "to take in whatever poison may be about in the surrounding atmosphere."[63]

Dancing, another urban entertainment growing in popularity during the 1880s and 1890s, was condemned for similar reasons. Cuyler described it as a public amusement involving "the promiscuous contacts of the sexes" that was "fraught with terrible peril to purity and Christian character." Dancing's chief deficiency, according to Cuyler and others, was that it encouraged the loss of individual and collective control. It inflamed passions and kindled salacious emotions. It bred extravagant dress, late hours, jealousy, and other lusts that warred against the soul. Promoting self-indulgence, dancing undermined public morality and became a bane of the church.[64]

Across the South, evangelical churches agreed with Cuyler's jeremiad. A Richmond observer described dancing as "the patron and parent of lust," its fruits as "shame and disgrace." Music, excitement, and the spirit of the crowd gave dancing its most potent sway. A "hideous abomination," dancing was accompanied by a train of fearful perils and was something that grew "by that upon which it feeds." Dancing marked a first step toward moral breakdown; dancers should "quit the church of Christ and serve the devil without scruple." Dancing endorsed the worldly over the otherworldly; it belonged, as a South Carolina Baptist explained, "to those who are of 'the world,' as distinguished from those who have been 'chosen out of the world.' "[65]

Moral reformers increasingly concluded, as they did about alcohol, that only public policy could affect social behavior. Where they had the opportunity—entirely in urban communities—reformers pressured local government to enforce existing statutes regulating moral behavior or to enact new laws that ended any official connection with vice. In Louisiana, moral reformers organized a state Anti-Lottery League against the state lottery in the early 1890s. In the case of the lottery, government had entered into a partnership with evil; it was an official institution, according to one reformer, created with "a license to destroy morality and to degrade society"—"a negation of government itself." State sponsorship of the lottery "inevitably" corrupted government.[66]

Nothing, aside from prohibition, mobilized the sentiment of moral reformers more than the issue of Sabbath observance. Not only did the subject of Sunday closing embody the obvious issue of the continuing authority of traditional Protestantism over public policy; it also offered further evidence of moral declension and traditional governance's inability or unwillingness to combat it. Sabbatarianism—the desire to enforce, by law, the biblical proscription against working on Sunday—had powerful resonance as a public issue galvanizing evangelicals in nineteenth-century America. A major local question in the Jacksonian period, the passage or enforcement of Sunday closing laws acquired renewed vitality in the emotionally charged atmosphere of the 1880s. The Sabbath was an essential practice of Christianity; debasing its significance made Christianity's belief system a "meaningless fable" and meant that "practical religion" would become a "thing of the past."[67]

But the protection of the Sabbath had broader implications for social cohesion, according to another evangelical. It provided the basis for "the perpetuity of a pure social life, the glory of our nation and the ultimate triumph of the church of God in this country over the infidelity that is sweeping in upon us from all sections." The end of the Sabbath would bring the decay of religion, the triumph of ignorance and vice, and the end of "communication between earth and heaven." Social disintegration followed nonobservance. Respect for the Sabbath and tolerance of the "grog-shops" were directly antagonistic, said the *Richmond Religious Herald*.[68]

Others detected connections between Sabbath violation and vice—both of which were, moral reformers believed, on the rise. The "twin evils" of public life, according to a South Carolinian, were "liquor selling and Sunday excursions." Saloons were "the greatest menace to the Sabbath," declared a

Baptist minister, because they violated the Lord's day and encouraged others to do the same; the two were "antipodes" and "deadly enemies." While the Sabbath exerted "an elevating, inspiring influence," saloons were "debasing" and "degrading." Sunday had "fallen from its high and holy estate" and had now become "a day for the transgression of laws of the State, of morals and of religion." Protecting the Sabbath safeguarded the moral fabric. Baseball, a "notorious corruptor of morals and religion," had become an "organized national evil" that violated the Sabbath. As a primary violator of the Sabbath, the sport was morally equivalent to saloons in fostering "gambling, whisky-drinking, and the violation of laws sacred and profane." [69]

Events that broke the Sabbath under official sponsorship were especially odious. When the city of Nashville opened its centennial celebration on a Sunday, the *Baptist and Reflector* objected. Such official transgression eroded its sanctity and encouraged the social acceptance of Sabbath violation. Similarly, when the organizers of Chicago's Columbian Exposition announced that it would remain open seven days a week, Sabbatarians around the South objected. The exhibition should never be held if the alternative was a change from the American Sabbath to a European Sunday, complained a Tennessean. Publicly violating the Sabbath belied the reputation of the United States as a Christian nation. By publicly endorsing "godless materialism," Americans defied God and risked the imposition of a divine sentence of condemnation and calamity. [70]

Sabbatarians were particularly concerned about the relationship between immorality and its advertent or inadvertent sponsorship by government. Evangelicals had long opposed the operation of Sunday mail trains and the opening of post offices on the Sabbath. As a South Carolinian said in 1889, God's law prohibited work on the Sabbath as much as it forbade "theft or murder or idolatry." Public violation of the Sabbath rejected the assumption that underlay it: that "all men should assemble for public recognition of the blessings received from the bounty of an indulgent and beneficent God." Almost ten years later, the *North Carolina Presbyterian* objected to Sunday excursion trains operating on state-owned railroads. Not only did the state compel its workers to violate biblical law, it also encouraged further Sabbath desecration on the part of the excursioners. [71]

Some Sabbatarians, while condemning public violations of the Sabbath, drew back from full-scale governmental intervention. As the *Richmond Religious Herald* expressed it in 1883, many of them assumed that people could not be made "good by acts of Congress or Legislatures, however legitimate it is to call on the lawmaker to protect the citizen." Other evangelicals looked to private, family observance of the Sabbath. The increasing number of violations was rooted in the "great influx" of immigrants with alien, Roman Catholic traditions, noted a South Carolina Baptist, but this only partly accounted for this social and cultural transformation. Rather, its source lay in the native-born American home, where parents were careless in ensuring that their children observed the Sabbath properly. Sabbath desecration reflected a breakdown in traditional family structure; a generation earlier, "parents ruled the children and not the children the parents."[72]

Sabbath desecration, to many reformers, was simply part of a larger matrix of public vice. In Birmingham, Alabama, local churchmen in 1887 opposed the playing of Sunday baseball. When a local team played a game on Sunday, apparently in violation of the existing statute, the *Alabama Christian Advocate* condemned the indifference of local authorities as "legal protection to idleness." Less culpable than the players was a social system that "wilfully" abandoned "all former teachings," threw off "all moral restraints," and descended "into a wild mob on the holy Sabbath" to "carouse and bet like bacchanalian heathens." Sabbath breaking, in the instance of baseball, was connected to the larger monster of vice. Where was the headquarters of the baseball club but at the saloon, whose owner controlled not only that sport but also much of the city's gambling operation?[73]

After 1880 Sabbatarians increasingly endorsed public enforcement. In the instance of Sunday baseball in Birmingham, pressure by local ministers resulted in the trial and conviction of the game's umpire in the city's criminal court. In even stronger terms several months later, the *Alabama Christian Advocate* urged a moral role on local government. "Every law that legalizes crime must be repealed," it stated, "every form of lawlessness must be punished by the strong arm of the law." No individuals possessed the moral right to do wrong; government should prohibit and suppress every form of public vice. This was, the newspaper believed, part of the "grandest moral battle" that had "ever been fought on this continent."[74]

Just as liquor traffickers had corrupted the political system and dominated governance, so also had Sabbath breakers gained control of the state. The result was that Sabbath violation had increased "fearfully" and had become a "national sin." Sunday openings had become a routine occurrence in which the wealthy and powerful winked at legalized crime. Public indifference meant that the South was touched by a "hideous stench-emitting and withering octopus" that kept local government in a stranglehold. While the better citizens held their heads in helpless shame and women and children were caught "in the slimy embrace of this blighting beast," city government either tolerated "this open and contemptuous violation of law" or was "*particeps criminis* in the transaction."[75]

The popular mobilization that accompanied the prohibition movement was now linked to a broader mobilization around a new moral agenda. The time was ripe for "*action*," declared an Alabama reformer in 1888; the "fearful issue" of moral reform was "upon us," and every citizen had to show his colors. In this and other characterizations of moral reform, there was no room for neutrality—all must either support or oppose "law and order." The battle between good and evil reaffirmed the urgency of the social and moral crisis. On the one side were the "brewers, the anarchists, and the Sabbath-breakers" who had "unfurled their banners openly and defiantly." On the other side were Christians and responsible citizens who were prepared "to sustain and defend virtue and truth, law and order, home and altar."[76]

In this battle, Christians were obligated to take sides. Among them, biblical law was paramount, observed a Texan, and disloyalty to it was equivalent to a refusal "to repent, believe, be baptized, join the church, eat the Lord's supper, or give of our means to evangelize the world." Christians had no right, either by quiescent consent or by the ballot, to maintain a system whose fruits were evil, wrote another reformer. Too often, however, they were guilty, by action or inaction, of legalizing or making respectable evil and its attendant woes. Once Christians expressed solidarity, evil would be uprooted. They were duty-bound to defend righteousness; by mobilizing politically, they could elect righteous leaders and enact righteous laws. A first step in reform, according to Theodore Cuyler, was "to purify our politics" and to "fasten upon the consciences of all upright citizens their individual responsibility as trustees."[77]

Despite the powerful appeal of moral reformers, their efforts during the 1880s and 1890s to limit, regulate, or abolish the liquor traffic and to impose a new standard of morality were uniformly frustrated. They discovered, as did others, that even the passage of legislation meant little more than moral suasion, given the structure of prebureaucratic governance. Out of this frustration, they emerged earliest among those social reformers who advocated an activist form of governance that would restrict individual autonomy and neighborhood power and, in some undefined fashion, project a new degree of public authority. The emergence of moral reform during the last two decades of the nineteenth century, moreover, provided an emotional language and a rhetoric to a variety of reforms that appeared in the subsequent generation. Moral reformers offered a powerful critique of traditional governance and produced the first organized movement that denounced, in comprehensive fashion, the results of nineteenth-century social policy. In calling for sweeping changes in the nature of individual-government changes, they paved the way for a wider reconceptualization.

PATERNALISM AND REFORM

◆

In the last two decades of the nineteenth century, a consensus emerged among elite southern whites and at least a portion of mass public opinion that their region was confronting a general social and cultural crisis. Seeking a reconfiguration of the social and political order to alleviate it, reformers expressed profound anxieties about the potentially disastrous consequences of worsening racial tensions. Their approach and program of change reflected a commitment to white supremacy; most of them saw the acknowledgment of black inadequacy and the need for white paternalism as basic requirements. Closely tied to this refined sense of racial hierarchy was a concern about the South's fragile social order and the conviction that disorder and conflict among whites comprised the most dangerous threat of the racial powder keg. Against the backdrop of the volatile class and race relations of the 1890s, reformers were guided by the imperatives of restoring social peace and creating a new, harmonious environment for the region's development.

◆ ◆ ◆
CLASS AND REFORM

Most reformers expressed what can be described as, at best, uneasiness with majoritarian democracy. To many of them, working-class and rural whites had become a dangerous, uncontrollable element in the South's new social mix. The "other half of the race peril" was the problem of lower-class whites, according to the Reverend John E. White, an Atlanta Baptist minister and reformer. Perhaps a majority of southern whites lived in conditions of "ignorance, poverty, and irresponsibility"; although native Anglo-Saxons, they had not yet been elevated "to a safe level of civilization" and were therefore unable to resist the "elemental impulse of lawlessness." Reform's obligation was "to make law minister to their development."[1]

Other reformers, like White, feared class conflict and social disintegration. Eugene C. Branson, who became the South's leading pre–World War I rural sociologist at the Georgia State Normal School and then at the University of North Carolina, saw the greatest potential for conflict in rural areas, where, he believed, isolation had brought social degeneracy and decay; the modern South threatened to be overrun by a "crab-apple civilization." In Georgia alone, a million people inhabited one-room cabins in primitive conditions that beggared imagination. The typical "Georgia cracker," as Branson described him, lived "on the edge of a small clearing, with a cotton patch on one side, a pine forest behind him, and a reed thicket or a gallberry swamp in the direction of his spring." Except for occasional trips to town, he existed there in "solitude unbroken." The problems of farm tenancy fostered these conditions, Branson would later write, locking farmers into a cycle of poverty, reducing large areas of the region to social stagnation, and rendering rural southerners "more defenceless" in a modernizing world economy.[2]

Although their fear of the white masses received apparent confirmation in the phenomenon of lynching, reformers qualified their condemnation. Like most whites, they believed that lynching came in response to a real increase in black crime. They were convinced that part of the responsibility for this crime wave lay in the breakdown of the legal system, part in what they believed were declining moral conditions among blacks, and another part in the black community's apparent unwillingness to police its own and condemn the criminal. Reformers approached lynching cautiously, carefully avoiding a defense of the black victims of vigilante justice. When the *Nashville Christian Advocate* in 1899 discussed the case of a black lynching victim in Newnan, Georgia, it expressed little sympathy for him and assumed his guilt of the crimes of murder and rape. "No punishment," the newspaper declared, "could have

Eugene C. Branson.
(Courtesy of the Southern Historical Collection, University of North Carolina
at Chapel Hill Library)

been severe to go beyond his just deserts." Lynching of blacks for the rape
of white women, according to the Presbyterian editor and social reformer,
Alexander J. McKelway, had long been considered a punishment that was not
"too sudden or severe for the crime referred to." It seemed understandable to
him that in rural areas, "where homes must often be left defenceless," white

communities had refused to tolerate legal delays and trial publicity, delivering instead a "swift and terrible justice to the brutal offender." Responding to a particularly barbaric lynching in Georgia in 1899—in which body parts were handed out as souvenirs among the mob—McKelway concluded that this could have occurred in "any community in the South . . . under the provocation of the fiendish crime." The real source of lynching, he said, was a rapidly increasing incidence of black rape of white women, which constituted more of a "manifestation of race hatred" than of "brutal lust" and was an "assault of barbarism upon civilization."[3]

Even those white reformers who criticized lynching saw it as an understandable reaction among rural whites to rising black crime. When Robert Strange, a Methodist bishop of eastern North Carolina, proposed a wholesale crackdown on lynching, in the same breath he maintained that rape should be tried in special courts, where the guilty could be executed speedily and appeals could be limited. The problem of black crime was aggravated, reformers believed, by resistance within the black community to the rule of law. When a meeting of the AME Zion church in Charlotte condemned lynching and endorsed federal intervention, a Richmond reform-oriented newspaper responded that this attitude fostered crime in the black community. It encouraged the notion that "the victims are martyrs and their crimes a badge of honor." All "intelligent and self-respecting" blacks, the newspaper concluded, should denounce "such a piece of incendiarism."[4]

White reformers were most concerned about the class implications of lynching. Rather than focusing on the injustice to the innocent victims of mob violence, they stressed the damage it inflicted on the legal, political, and social fabric. Mobs violated rule by law. It was dangerous to permit the legal system to be weakened in any community, observed an Alabama Methodist. When men neither respected the law nor feared its punishment, a social breakdown resulted. If mob justice was tolerated, the road was open "to the destruction of all government and the enthronement of an awful anarchy." "Absolute obedience to constituted authority" remained a precondition of the "security of republics," declared a North Carolinian, whereas "disregard for law" was the "peril of governments." Mob rule became an issue of power among white people. Lynching opened the way for the "lawless and ruffianly element," warned a Mississippian; ultimately, blacks would not be their only victims. Whites could also "fall under the ban of ruffianism," and civil war and class disorder might follow. Class relations were most fluid and dangerous during periods of turbulence and change. According to the North Carolina prohibitionist Josiah William Bailey, a "mob-spirit" had entered "the blood of our people." Not yet a "fully civilized people," southerners were in the process of "becoming civilized." Some whites were "advanced," others "backward," and in times of stress the "instincts of barbarism" overcame those of order.[5]

Lynching also threatened the foundations of the social system. News of a lynching spread quickly in rural communities and excited "other lustful minds," observed McKelway; imagination was "the food on which lust thrives." A "malicious woman with a small amount of intellect and character" could unleash unspeakable violence "with a word from her lying tongue"; others could "obtain private revenge by organizing a mob to commit murder." Those involved in a "wrathful orgy" of lynching could in the future "do anything that their passions or their prejudices suggest," warned the *Nashville Christian Advocate*. Having flouted the law once, it was scarcely possible that they would "ever again be good citizens." Was anyone "so blind as not to see" that mobs meant "the ultimate destruction of society"? Mob violence, declared a Georgian, unleashed a "Frankenstein of lawlessness and unreason" that would incur a social debt that future generations would have to repay.[6]

Heretofore directed at black victims, mob violence could easily turn against whites. A practice in which night-riding whites violently resisted outside intrusion and administered community justice, *whitecapping* supplied an example, if reformers needed one, of how vigilante justice could turn against the social system. Recent scholars have pointed to its existence in the 1890s and early 1900s as evidence of turbulence and crisis in the upcountry South and have shown that most of the vigilantism was directed against whites. In northern Georgia, whitecappers protested against attempts to impose prohibition and outside regulation on the local whiskey trade. Yet whitecapping extended to a range of issues in which the traditional rights of yeoman whites had changed under law and were subject to attack by outsiders. On the Tennessee-Kentucky border in October 1908, for instance, whitecappers resorted to vigilante justice when real estate developers attempted to limit traditional fishing rights. To reformers, whitecappers represented a more vivid example of the dangers of vigilante justice. The "mob spirit," observed Greenville's *Baptist Courier*, wherever it existed, was similar. If lawbreakers acquired the right to mete out justice once, they could claim that right in every case, and the legal system would be set aside and anarchy would prevail. It was therefore imperative that "respect for law and order . . . be so strong that the lawless element" would "stand in awe of the law and the officers of the law."[7]

Most reformers, believing that the nineteenth-century social and political system was flawed, maintained that both the nature of power and its administration should be altered. Most reformers did not dispute the principle of majoritarian democracy but they questioned whether, in the South, it brought wise and beneficial policies. Edgar Gardner Murphy, a Texan who was active in race, education, and child labor reforms, has been described by his biographer as a "gentle progressive." Yet Murphy favored basic structural changes in the South's social and political system. Leadership would, he believed, come from above: from the region's natural leadership, composed of men of "responsibility" and "family." These were leaders "to whom power had taught those truths of life, those dignities and fidelities of temper," which power always taught men. Under their leadership would emerge a "true basis of an enduring peace between the sections and between the races"; out of the Old South would evolve a wise and responsible leadership for the New South. The old southern aristocracy, leading with the consent and even partnership of the plain people, would exert the "old sense of responsibility toward the un-privileged."[8]

For southern social reformers, social stability among whites depended on racial peace. Rural lynching and urban race riots not only manifested a kind of racial warfare and hatred but also challenged traditional leaders and orderly, legal means of resolving conflict. In this equation, violence among the races also meant class conflict and disorder, a probable end to any hopes for regional development and progress, and continuing isolation and backwardness. For these reasons, reformers viewed the resolution of the racial crisis as the primary ingredient in a larger social and political restructuring.

◆ ◆ ◆
THE RACIAL CRISIS

Closely connected to the social crisis of the late nineteenth and early twentieth century was a racial crisis of dangerously increasing velocity. To some observers, race war was imminent, fueled by a clash of black and white expectations and the loss of what one observer described as the "old friendly relation of the two races." During the years around the turn of the century, declared one particularly insightful observer, there had been a significant increase in racial conflict. In the entrance of the race issue into politics, "a demon in the South" had awakened, bringing on "more hatred of whites for blacks and of blacks for whites than ever before." Both races were trapped in a "torrent of passion."[9]

Other observers acknowledged the seriousness of the crisis. "We cannot blind ourselves to the fact," editorialized the *Atlanta Constitution* in 1907, that race relations were "steadily growing more complicated, more sinister, more pregnant with possibilities of danger to both races and to the entire nation." The problem was pervasive, according to Albert Bushnell Hart. It underlay the social, political, and economic system; it was "stamped on every page of the newspaper"; it began even in casual conversation; and it affected every enterprise. Interconnected with it was an "uneasy sense of a destiny unfulfilled, of a civilization anxious for its own future." Between southern whites and blacks, added the *Alabama Christian Advocate*, there existed "a widening chasm of alienation." The race crisis, wrote Mississippian Belle Kearney, was neither the work of the "old slave" nor the "old master," nor even that of their sons. It was rather the result of a "new element of both races" that warred "one on the other." [10]

Southerners responded to the racial crisis differently. Trinity College historian John Spencer Bassett, in a frequently quoted essay that appeared in the *South Atlantic Quarterly* in 1903, asserted that racial conflict was rooted in a fear of racial amalgamation. Whites had developed an exaggerated fear of interracial sexual relations and then had extended it to most other matters of life. Yet social separation had led to mutual misconception; whites imposed their own images on black people. The popular view of antebellum blacks as either benign old men or mammies was "mythic," and Thomas Nelson Page's nostalgic descriptions of Virginia plantations were "castles in the air." According to Bassett, the solution of the race problem lay with southern whites. Racial animosity was not mutual; it was not "the white man against the negro and the negro against the white man." Whereas blacks would eat, attend church, and frequent the theater with whites, too many whites had open contempt for Negroes. Either progress or regression among blacks resulted in white hostility. The solution lay in a reversal in white attitudes and the adoption of these "children of Africa" into American life. Despite the poisonous racial atmosphere, blacks would, he predicted, eventually win equality. They could not be removed, destroyed, or prevented from advancing in civilization. Although now "very weak," they would some day become stronger; while now ignorant and "passion-wrought," they would someday be "wiser and more self-restrained." It was in the interests of whites to devise a racial solution. [11]

A few other reform-minded whites agreed with Bassett's assumptions. North Carolina educational reformer Charles Lee Coon wrote in 1913 that racial conflict would be resolved once whites rid themselves of their "prejudice, ignorance, and . . . meanness." A racial settlement lay in "peace, toleration, goodwill, and helpfulness"; it would prevail someday, "whether we live to see the day or not." Another white southerner maintained that the sources of racial conflict lay in the white man's conviction that blacks, as a race and as individuals, were his inferior. Yet views such as these, which suggested that the race problem was rooted in racial inequality rather than black inadequacy, were not only rare, but their expression was usually greeted with hostility.

Bassett's essay described Booker T. Washington as "the greatest man, save General Lee, born in the South in a hundred years." Although he also asserted that Washington was atypical and did not "even represent the better class of negroes," the essay so aroused the North Carolina press that Bassett faced a public pillorying that eventually drove him from the state. Similarly, when, in 1909, Coon publicly suggested that gross inequalities existed in black and white schools, he was savaged by the state press.[12]

Few early twentieth-century whites, especially among reformers, were as evenhanded as Bassett or Coon. Rather than assuming equality in ability, most of them believed that the problem of race lay mainly in black inadequacy. Many white reformers accepted the wisdom of contemporary social science: alongside innate race differences existed a hierarchy of racial classifications in which, at its pinnacle, were northern Europeans, and at the bottom, black Africans. Under slavery, according to this view, blacks achieved a rapid racial evolution. In advancing Africans and their descendants from cannibalism to a condition of comparative civilization and Christianity, wrote McKelway, the institution of slavery was "the greatest blessing as an enlightening and evangelizing agency that such large numbers of the African race ever received from the dawn of history until now." In the uplifting of the race, slavery accomplished more for an underdeveloped people than a century of modern missions had achieved for all the heathen races put together.[13]

The notion that slavery had fostered black development became a kind of working assumption for early twentieth-century white racial reformers. Negroes arrived in America as savages, wrote Robert F. Campbell, a racial moderate and Presbyterian minister of Asheville, North Carolina. But under slavery they were "civilized and elevated" by the training that they received in southern homes and plantations. No other economic system in human history compared with southern slavery in creating the "bonds of personal affection between capital and labor" and in linking "the hearts of the two together with hooks of steel." Although Campbell admitted that slavery shackled southern economic development, he asserted that any future "stable superstructure" of racial goodwill needed to be constructed upon a foundation built during slavery.[14]

Development under complete subservience and white control, according to white racial moderates, was essential to racial peace. Blacks served under the "tuition of slavery," Georgia racial moderate Walter B. Hill told a northern audience in 1903; this prepared them for American citizenship. No other "free civilized race" had ever accomplished equal progress in emergence from barbarism in so short a time. Black education, under slavery, was not scholastic. Rather, it disciplined slaves in labor and practical ethics and in the values

Robert F. Campbell.
(Courtesy of the Presbyterian Church [U.S.A.], Department of History,
Montreat, North Carolina)

of order, fidelity, temperance, and obedience. Slavery provided a sort of "compulsory" education that required a restraint and prevented open crime among slaves. Although it failed to stimulate independent manhood, declared Hill, slavery created a system of racial order and control that suppressed blacks' "criminal propensities" and instructed them in values of work and order.[15]

Racial moderates contrasted the benefits of the slave system with what they considered to be the obvious failings of postemancipation race relations. The end of the Civil War, wrote Campbell, brought the "sudden and violent" freeing of blacks from the restraints of slavery and placed them into an alien environment for which they had had little preparation. Their enfranchisement not only alienated them from their former masters, their "life-long and natural friends," but it also permitted a freedom that only encouraged their worst attributes. The implication, for Campbell and others, was clear: blacks could achieve development and progress only under white guidance and patronage.[16]

Most reformers assumed that innate racial differences existed and that white supremacy was likely, even desirable. Few favored equality in any sense of the word. The mixture of whites and blacks in educational, religious, and other public activities encouraged the erosion of all social distinctions, noted one reform-minded southerner; eventually, what he called "the inner life of the private family"—a code for interracial marriage—might even be affected. Although it resulted in "many evils," race prejudice served as a "great bulwark against miscegenation." He concluded that it was difficult, perhaps "useless," to expect outsiders to comprehend the uniqueness of the southern race situation, for in no society except the South had a white and a dark race dwelt together on the same soil.[17]

The alternatives, at least as far as white moderates understood them, were deeply troubling. Their working assumption was a model of black inferiority; they saw black assertiveness as unnatural and destabilizing. Yet contemporaries saw ample evidence of black assertiveness, as the old system of racial control seemed to be eroding.[18] White racial reformers drew clear lessons about the possibilities of both race war and class conflict in the Atlanta Race Riot of September 1906. Throughout the South, the response of newspaper editorialists was similar. The riot occurred because of a collapse in racial etiquette; the riot had the same dynamics as a rural lynching. Because they were moved by a "spirit of racial hatred" to assault "innocent and defenseless white women," declared the *Richmond Times-Dispatch*, lawless blacks had brought the riot and the indiscriminate rampage on themselves. Although it admitted that mob justice was an "evil," the *Macon Telegraph* said that the fundamental causes of the riot were the arousal of "the brute in the negro" and the direction of its fury against white women.[19]

In Atlanta, white racial moderates reacted similarly. Like other southerners, they diagnosed the causes of the riot as misplaced black assertiveness, especially sexual assertiveness with women; the white reaction, although predictable, revealed a troubling strain of disorder and lawlessness. Soon after the riot, a prominent group of Atlantans resolved that "crime breeds crime and lawlessness begets more lawlessness"; they deplored "the crimes of both races which have been committed by their worst elements." The "worst elements" of the white community were clearly the greater threat. Once a mob "tasted blood," wrote the *Atlanta Constitution*, it would become "CARELESS OF RACE AND COLOR in its hunger for further horrible nourishment." The prospect struck fear into the minds of Atlantans. Most blacks lived under what that newspaper called "the white man's protection"; they implicitly trusted the supremacy of law and respected their white employers and sponsors. Under mob rule the racial order became a "tragic farce," a "burlesque of our twentieth century civilization."[20]

Southern social reformers often expressed a strange combination of ideas: a fervent belief in white supremacy along with a belief in the necessity of black progress. As a prohibitionist Presbyterian editor and then as a child labor reformer, Alexander McKelway held firmly to the racial hierarchy. A leader in North Carolina's notorious White Supremacy Campaign of 1898–1900, which enacted the political exclusion of blacks by constitutional amendment in 1900, McKelway endorsed de jure racial segregation. As a child labor reformer, he once publicized photographs that juxtaposed white children working in cotton textile mills with black children walking to school.[21] McKelway strenuously opposed racial equality, which he believed led to racial amalgamation. The violation of the taboo against social equality would lead, he wrote, to "the destruction of the white race itself, the loss forever of the Anglo-Saxon strain," a development against which southerners would "set their faces as a flint." The social circles of white and black, he maintained, should remain distinct and never coalesce into one. The need for racial purity required strict separation. Southern whites permitted blacks inside their homes, but here he drew an important distinction: "entering our families" meant "a crossing of races" that was "abhorrent of the instincts of nature." Thus, social separation was a necessity in order to prevent social equality. God drew "a line in black and white between the two races," although respecting that line did not mean "that our brother in black" was not "our brother."[22]

Yet McKelway also advocated black progress. Thinking whites, he wrote, were obligated to uplift blacks "to the highest possible plane." The key distinction was black political power, the exercise of which depended on a form of responsibility and ability which, he believed, blacks then lacked. In another instance, McKelway made clear that his advocacy of white supremacy did not preclude black development, especially educational development. "No Christian man," he argued in 1899, could believe that "this vast population, dependent upon the stronger race," should be relegated to a permanent condition of ignorance, for the safety of any society depended on the intelligence and morality of its citizens. Although the suffrage should be denied blacks, other avenues of opportunity should be opened.[23]

This combination of refined racism and a belief in black progress was also evident in the case of Edgar Gardner Murphy. He maintained that the South had experienced three stages in the history of its race relations. During the first, slavery imposed a state of "forced interdependence," which was characterized by policed racial peace and absolute white supremacy. With emancipation, black-white relations entered a second phase in which these traditional constraints became "increasingly hateful." Growing black assertiveness brought conflict; both races abandoned their "normal and proper interdependence," and constant racial struggle and competition ensued. A final stage lay somewhere in the future, when these antagonisms would disappear and leave "legitimate participation" for both races and "a reciprocal recognition of the fundamental interests of both." For the present, however, the South confronted a dangerous period and a bleak future, Murphy believed. That the first decade of the new century brought worse, not better, race relations was "obvious enough," for among white and black masses a sense of estrangement had grown and conflict had become increasingly acute. Answering the title of his essay—"Backward or Forward?"—Murphy concluded that progress would likely occur in a "total movement of our social and political changes" rather than in "the familiar antagonism between race and race." He hoped that this social evolution into an environment of "broader margins and happier horizons" would soothe the "chafing and corroding elements" of the early twentieth-century South.[24]

No outside intervention could accomplish a racial solution, many white reformers believed. The source of race conflict, they maintained, lay within the flawed character of southern blacks; the white South, one observer wrote, was "the victim, not the author" of the race problem. Although responsibility for conflict lay in black inadequacy, any solution carried with it a presumption of white supremacy. This was the problem of the southern white; it lay at his door, and upon him fell its menacing shadow. It was whites, not blacks, who would "always determine what Southern standards shall be," wrote historian William Garrott Brown in 1904, for whites controlled "the mass of negroes and fix[ed] the conditions of their lives."[25]

Historians of southern progressivism have shown convincingly that reformers had a darker, racist side to their attitudes and programs. Believers in white supremacy, most reformers were convinced that racial peace, social harmony, and regional progress depended on it. Assuming the innate inadequacy of southern blacks, reformers maintained that the solution of the race problem lay in paternalist uplift; black culture needed to change along lines that whites would dictate. The twin convictions of black inadequacy and white paternalism formed a bedrock for the reform program.

◆ ◆ ◆

REFORMERS AND RACE: TWO EXAMPLES

White moderates' conviction that racial progress could only occur on their terms was evident in their attitudes toward the issues of race and prohibition. Southern prohibitionists had long seen the black vote as an impediment to prohibition, and they believed that disfranchisement was a precondition for reform. McKelway linked prohibition with North Carolina's suffrage restriction amendment of 1900. Blacks were, he wrote, usually the "pawns of the saloon in the political game"; eradicating the saloon depended on their political exclusion. A precondition of the antisaloon movement, he declared another time, was the purification of the electorate "by the elimination of the ignorant and venal element of the voting population." Black disfranchisement meant the "downfall of the saloon, with all its menace to the individual, to society, to the State and to the Kingdom of Christ."[26]

Others asserted that prohibition would help to create a more effective system of racial control. Emancipation had freed slaves but had provided no replacement for slavery's discipline; as a Mississippi white wrote, drink became "a badge of freedom" for emancipated slaves but soon was their "worst curse." In the antebellum period, according to a white North Carolinian, slaves came to taverns "humbly bowing in"; they bought their dram or pint and then "quietly" returned home. Since Reconstruction the freed slaves, who were "untrained, passionate, brutal," saw the "forcible restraints of slavery removed." With "low moral natures unharnessed," they gained access to whiskey. Their passions inflamed by alcohol, they "mistook license for freedom and recklessness for liberty." Most racial conflict was rooted in the indirect results of strong drink, noted the *Nashville Christian Advocate* in 1890. If drunkenness could be suppressed, the problem of race would be "at once half solved." Rum was destroying blacks, wrote McKelway, just as it had "annihilated other inferior races," and a "controlling motive" among prohibitionists was "to keep liquor from the negroes."[27]

This line of reasoning appeared frequently in prohibitionist literature. In years of "careful observation," a white Mississippian wrote, never had there been a case of "outrageous crime" committed by black men against white women in which saloons were not the cause. Nor was there "a single instance" of racial conflict in which they were not the primary "disturbing influence." Drinking destroyed black character and dissipated social restraint; "practically" it returned them to "barbarism." A tenth of the black community was criminal because of the saloon, asserted a Texas prohibitionist; it had done *"more to ruin the negro and make trouble between him and the whites than any other agency since the days of reconstruction in the South."* To others, a strong connection existed between racial disorder and the liquor traffic. The closing of the saloons in Wilmington, North Carolina, during the riot of 1898 precluded further carnage, asserted a prohibitionist in an odd rendition of that event. The presence of alcohol among blacks, he maintained, accounted for the aggressive acts that led to the bloodshed that followed. Regular drinking occurred among blacks who were, according to another prohibitionist, "the street idlers, the law-breakers, the shiftless and wandering." Nothing would accomplish more for the moral development of blacks than to make war on the liquor business; saloons blocked black progress.[28]

The loosening of restraints, argued reformers, could lead to a race war. In Warren County, North Carolina, a white observer complained that "dispensary whiskey" had led to increased harassment of white women by black men; traveling on the roads without a man, he complained, would soon require accompaniment by a Gatling gun. Yet the connections between alcohol and racial disorder became, to many white commentators, even clearer in southern cities, where racial controls appeared to be breaking down and where blacks had easiest access to saloons. Whereas rural blacks were "under the influence of white people" and "immeasurably free from many of the worst temptations," warned the *Alabama Christian Advocate*, black migrants to furnaces, factories, and rail camps escaped "the influence of whites and their own best people." In towns and cities they were exposed to saloons and the accompanying vices, and there thousands were "lapsing into barbarism." Out of this unregulated environment came a new "conscienceless, lawless, fearless brute," who acted upon "his strong animal nature" and, under alcohol's "devilish influences," raped, robbed, and murdered.[29]

White moderates saw no better example of the explosive potential of alcohol and race than the Atlanta Race Riot of September 1906. According to many white contemporaries, the causes of the riot lay in the scores of reports of sexual assaults during that summer and early autumn. These accounts held that blacks lost their restraint because of the prevalence of "dives," or saloons, and the loosening effects of alcohol on black males. The underlying cause of the riot was the saloon, according to one account, "the hotbed of crime," which contained an "array of ignorant human beings" who were "robbed of all their reason" and "under the mastery of animal passion," and whose judgment was "dethroned." In the wake of the riot, reformers pressed for limiting saloons in black neighborhoods or for total prohibition.[30]

The notion that alcohol broke down restraint and thereby destabilized race relations prevailed among reformers. Alexander McKelway asserted that drinking in the early twentieth century had decreased among whites but increased among blacks; the daily proof was that any black could "fill up with mean whiskey and run amuck." In any southern community with a saloon, race war had become, according to John E. White, a "perilously possible occurrence." The danger was particularly acute among what he described as the "lower levels of both races," where "the inflammable fringes hang loose." In an "inverted social pyramid," the lower classes of both races converged at the saloon, which became an attractive social center for the dangerous elements. White maintained that the presence of dangerous and uncontrollable blacks constituted "the most difficult sociological problem any people ever had," a problem that "the Liquor Traffic only tended to complicate."[31]

McKelway wrote two contrasting, but interconnected, vignettes that embodied the strands linking the problems of race and alcohol. One appeared on September 22, 1906, when the statue of Henry Grady at the center of Atlanta was stained with innocent blood spilt by an enraged mob. Juxtaposed against this was a very different image about a year later when, at the Grady monument, another crowd celebrated the passage of statewide prohibition by singing the Long Meter Doxology "with a will." "No thoughtful man," wrote McKelway, "could have failed to connect the two scenes." The passage of prohibition came, not as an expression of "Puritan fanaticism," but as the "deliberate determination" on the part of whites to relinquish a part of their personal liberty in order to protect the "weaker race" from crimes caused by drunkenness.[32]

For suffragists also, reform and the social and political subordination of blacks were directly connected. Most southern suffragists exhibited white supremacist racial attitudes. "Oh how I wish," moaned Louisiana suffragist Kate Gordon, that all blacks would "go north," especially "the jew mulattos who are in evidence everywhere."[33] Although few white women suffragists were as vehement as Gordon, virtually all of them believed in white supremacy. They not only accepted disfranchisement but also endorsed it enthusiastically, while they made the case that the enfranchisement of southern women provided yet another component in racial control.

Suffragists based their argument at least partly on expediency. The anti-suffragists contended that woman suffrage would enfranchise thousands of black women. Suffragists were forced to answer the challenge, and they did so by contending that votes for women would strengthen rather than weaken white supremacy. When Lila Meade Valentine, Virginia's leading suffragist, heard of concern about the black vote in Front Royal, Virginia, she instructed her field agent to respond "immediately with all the figures and arguments at our command." Black women were no "more of a menace" than were black men; constitutional restrictions maintained white supremacy in both instances. Should a federal amendment be ratified, it was clear to her that the legislature would "take all necessary steps to make these restrictions apply to the woman voter." That, she added, was "all we need say."[34]

So concerned were Virginia suffragists about neutralizing the race issue that they provided further, and rather extraordinary, assurances that black women would continue to be excluded. In 1915 Valentine attempted to assure Virginians by pointing to Article 2, Section 30, of the Virginia Constitution of 1902, which provided that the General Assembly could establish a property qualification for voting on the petition of a county. When women acquired the vote, she suggested, this constitutional guarantee would ensure the continued exclusion of blacks if other restrictions proved "insufficient to maintain white supremacy." Excluding white women because of the fear of black rule, argued another suffragist, made little sense. The same restrictions that applied to men would also apply to women, and disfranchisement would eliminate the illiterate and irresponsible women, as they eliminated the illiterate and irresponsible men of both races.[35]

Not all suffragists were comfortable with the contradiction between enfranchisement and exclusion,[36] but few of them expressed doubts about embracing white supremacy. To Mississippi suffragist Belle Kearney, votes for white women would guarantee "immediate and durable white supremacy, honestly attained." There were more white women than black men and women combined, she declared in 1914. Woman suffrage would give "an enormous preponderance to the Anglo-Saxon race" and would permanently secure white supremacy. A North Carolina suffragist described the vote for white women as "the only means of preserving white supremacy" and the one sure way to prevent the return of black political power.[37]

These examples of the views of prohibitionists and suffragists are representative of early twentieth-century social reformers in general. Virtually all

Woman Suffrage Amendment Raises No Race Issue

Of all the specious pleas made against equal suffrage that are wholly without foundation in fact is the alleged menace of the negro-vote. The only change in the Federal law respecting the franchise is striking out SEX QUALIFICATION. There is no other ulterior or possible construction to be applied to language so plain. The amendment reads:

"Section 1. The right of citizens of the United States to vote shall not be denied or abridged by the United States or by any state on account of sex.

"Section 2. The Congress shall have power, by appropriate legislation, to enforce the provisions of said act."

It will be seen from this that the amendment is such as not to disturb our North Carolina qualifications except as it makes them apply without reference to sex, and therefore does not create new conditions in the negro question. The qualifications that now apply to negro men will apply to negro women; those that apply to white men will apply to white women.

WE HAVE BEEN REGULATING OUR FRANCHISE in North Carolina as we see fit for more than two decades, and without interference or attempt at interference by the Federal government.

The Fifteenth Amendment is so clear and explicit as to the negro race that no additional amendment could possibly add to its strength. We have been as much in danger of Federal interference since the adoption of the Fifteenth Amendment, so far as the negro is concerned, as we could possibly be. If the Federal government has not undertaken to upset our present franchise system and if the Supreme Court of the United States has not rendered decision upsetting it all these years, it is because sectional hate no longer exists in America, and, just as the East allows the West to regulate the Jap problem, so the North has accustomed itself to hands off in the negro question.

States are accorded wide latitude in fixing franchise qualifications of local application.

It would be impossible to raise the color issue on the equal suffrage amendment, because there is no mention of color, and color cannot be dragged in by the utmost strain of construction.

Equal Suffrage Association of North Carolina, Raleigh

3

Suffrage broadside, North Carolina.
(Courtesy of the North Carolina Collection, University of North Carolina at Chapel Hill Library)

of them defined "the Negro problem" in terms of the deficiencies of blacks rather than of an increase in racism or racial oppression by whites. According to their intellectual construct, which expressed prevailing cultural and ethnological assumptions, white supremacy, either in morality or political judgment, was a given. The changing variable was the condition of southern blacks and what they believed was their "inferior" stage of development. The task of reform was therefore to accept black inferiority and to adjust southern society to it.

◆ ◆ ◆

THE PATERNALIST MODEL OF REFORM

Blacks, a Texas prohibitionist wrote in 1903, should be permitted "the largest liberty and the greatest incentives to progress that can be given in safety to the white race." They should be instructed, he believed, that hope for blacks lay in education, industry, and sobriety. From whites, the black man should learn "that to be respected by a white man he must be respectable; that to prosper and live in peace he must labor and be law-abiding." This Texan, typical of other reformers, sought a formula for black progress that would reconcile his white supremacist views with a program of purposeful development. White reformers believed that blacks utterly depended on the goodwill of humane southerners. White supremacy, maintained William Garrott Brown, meant that white direction of black affairs was practically complete—"as complete as it can ever be under democracy, with slavery barred." But that control meant a responsibility of the superior toward the inferior, and Brown was "troubled deeply" by the problem of white responsibility and by a "distinct lessening of the intimacy, the freedom and carelessness of daily intercourse and consultation as between individuals of the two races." Still, white indifference and ignorance could not relieve southerners of responsibility, nor could they shield them from the abiding risks of the situation, for a white society that denied justice would soon lose it for itself.[38]

That responsibility, according to Walter B. Hill, required that reformers confront the painful and depressing elements of black inadequacy. Maintaining family life "in unity and sanctity" was the key to black development; the condition of most blacks, a Mississippi reformer wrote, remained hopeless until they acquired "higher moral ground," which she described as the secret of their future.[39] Development meant encouraging the inculcation of modern white values and a leapfrogging of black racial development.

According to Eugene Branson, the key to racial evolution was the "steady and fateful pull and power" of social laws of development that could be discovered and manipulated to accelerate or retard progress. The Negro problem, he wrote, would not find solution through words but rather through purposeful direction. Like most reformers, Branson was deeply suspicious of black urban immigration. In cities, blacks waged a losing battle against drink, drugs, and urban vices and disease. He described blacks as suffering from a "belated" racial evolution, which meant that it was unreasonable to expect them "in any large racial way" to achieve the highest levels of civilization. The best opportunity for blacks, and for their development as a people, lay rather in "the lower levels," where life was less intense and the struggle to succeed was less desperate. The destiny of southern blacks, Branson held, was in the rural South, where, aided by sympathetic whites, they could discover their own salvation. Proper supervision of black development meant stimulating those qualities that, paternalists believed, were most lacking. Only having recently emerged from "jungleism," blacks had moved from "darkness into light in accord with and in obedience to the laws of development." Every step forward racially was marked by struggle; blacks could progress only after they had achieved economic self-sufficiency. That, in turn, Branson said, depended on farm ownership and a "home-owning, home-loving, home-defending instinct." Land ownership would sharpen the powers of the intellect, clarify social vision, and reinforce the strength of conscience. Within the black community would emerge responsible leadership, which would serve as "an efficient moral and social police" against the "idle and vicious" among them. Widespread landownership cured social problems as no legislation could ever do, confirming Branson's belief—and that of most rural sociologists—that patriotism was "rooted in the soil and nourished by it."[40]

Other reformers also assumed that inferior racial development necessitated the inculcation of basic Victorian values. When a Georgia educator sympathetic to reform was asked about black development, he responded that blacks had to be made to understand the real dignity and honor of everyday work. Under slavery, a black worked under compulsion; once freed, he believed that "he would never be called upon to work again." In black schools, accordingly, this educator advocated inculcating "good moral character," which would make each child "a conscious ruler of his own spirit."[41]

Paternalism, in education and elsewhere, required a combination of black autonomy and the development of a fully articulated class system within the black community. There was "no race problem as between the good citizens among the whites and the good citizens of the South among the blacks," observed Walter Hill. Black autonomy needed supervision; interracial contacts, though encouraged, would still follow a paternalist model. Reform without such supervision meant disaster, as one reformer, northern Rockefeller official Wallace Buttrick, discovered in Auburn, Alabama. Although local whites had done little for blacks, they had given them $450 for a new school. To Buttrick's disgust, the whites had left the school's administration to "a group of untutored and inexperienced negroes." The result was a school facility that was "worse than no building at all" and school equipment "that for inadequacy beggars description." Buttrick urged local officials to reestablish contact by hiring a "white man with a deep sense of responsibility for these negroes" to take charge. Buttrick, who made these comments during a tour of southern schools in the summer of 1902, found the lack of white control over black education to be a disturbing example of black development gone wrong. Like most other reformers, he saw racial progress, either in the short or long term, as occurring only through strong white leadership. A black community near Nixburg, Alabama, needed instruction "in right ways" from whites, Buttrick believed. White aid to black education should be "carefully conditioned," with the expenditure of money "watched to the last penny." Even "unusually good negroes" could be spoiled by unconditional grants or by permitting them too much autonomy.[42]

Paternalists embraced industrial education as the primary vehicle for racial reform. In the case of a white superintendent visiting a black school in Mississippi in 1908, these attitudes were reflected in his attempt "to impress upon them the necessity of having a high moral idea in their schools and neighborhoods." Although industrial education permitted exceptional, elite education, it advocated diverting most resources toward what Buttrick called "the immediate practical necessities of rural schools" and toward meeting "conditions as they really exist." This involved a balancing act, for reformers did not, as a South Carolinian explained, favor a system of schools that would perpetuate a permanent kind of racial inequality. Under "our form of government," he wrote, "we cannot have a class of helots, or 'hewers of wood and drawers of water.'" Black education needed adaptation to what these white racial reformers defined as inadequacies in the intellectual and moral makeup of southern blacks. If blacks were "weak industrially" and "poorly adapted," commented this observer, "let proper efforts be made to effect the needed adjustment."[43]

No fuller explication of the paternalist program exists than in the writings of Edgar Gardner Murphy. Although Murphy was active in both educational and child labor reform, his career as a reformer and regional spokesman was tied to his often-arresting ideas about race, which were articulated in speeches, articles, and two important books, *The Problems of the Present South* (1904) and *The Basis of Ascendancy* (1909). Murphy's paternalism implied that white responsibility should accompany white supremacy. Under slavery, white slaveholders had learned about inherent black inadequacy, a "heritage of barbarism" that limited and often doomed black development and progress. Yet southern whites were irrevocably tied to southern blacks under a "bond of slavery," and the future of the two races was mutually dependent. Like other reformers, Murphy combined what he called a "distinct assumption of the

negro's inferiority" with "a distinct assumption of the negro's improvability."
Out of this "double assumption" came a "sense of responsibility" toward
blacks. If blacks were "not peculiarly in need of progress" or "utterly incapable
of progress," the problem would be of little concern and not a special burden to thinking whites. For Murphy, the promotion of black progress under
white leadership was a matter of "supreme self-interest" and an "obligation of
Christian stewardship."[44]

The key to black progress, and southern progress, lay in balancing black
autonomy with white supremacy, according to Murphy. He opposed a static
conception of race relations; regional uplift depended on the rapid improvement of blacks as a race. Moreover, black inadequacy should not mean black
passivity. White southerners had to deal with two black classes. One was
"backward, thriftless, profitless," contributed nothing to its community, created no wealth, lacked any economic skills, and furnished only murderers,
rapists, loafers, and incendiaries. The second class included blacks who were
"quiet, sensible, industrious men and women," who sought "through intelligence and skill to be useful to themselves and to their country." While the first
class was moving backward, the second was moving forward. Whites should
encourage the development of the right sort of black leadership from among
those located in the "scores of little homes through the better negro districts of
our Southern cities"; these blacks were accumulating wealth, educating their
children, and purchasing goods "chiefly from the white man's stores and to
the white man's profit." It was this "efficient" class of blacks that would lead
the race to self-sufficiency and development under white paternalism.[45]

Despite his subsequent pessimism and disavowal of disfranchisement as
a failure, Murphy continued to believe that, over the long run, race relations would improve under the paternalist model. The current decline in
interracial harmony was, he wrote in 1909, "transitory and temporary," for
improvement depended on a long-term evolution of attitudes among both
races. Race was a social problem that would—like most social problems—
never achieve solution "in any mathematical or final sense," but only "in the
sense that their conflicting or complementary elements find a working adjustment to one another." This adjustment, in the case of race relations, would
properly come with "wisdom, right, [and] happiness"—despite the continued
chance of "misconception and with recurrent periods of acute antagonism"—
which would eventually yield "an increasing measure of social peace [and]
individual freedom and happiness."[46]

Paternalism, and a top-down approach to power and decision making, were
fundamental assumptions of reformers like Murphy. This paternalism was
most apparent in their program for black development, yet it also colored their

approach toward the cultural and class differences that separated them from other southern whites. Fearful of social upheaval, they were determined to introduce changes affecting the folkways of the southern white masses. Their attitudes, and the extent to which they were separated from this hinterland white culture, became apparent in their efforts to apply the paternalist model to southern mountain whites.

◆ ◆ ◆

MOUNTAIN MISSIONS AND WHITE PATERNALISM

Between about 1880 and 1920 the southern Appalachian region became a center of mission and settlement house outreach. After Reconstruction, northern Protestants sent missionaries to the mountains to discover an exotic, unschooled people who, they believed, remained ignorant of the ways of proper Christianity and modern civilization. As Henry D. Shapiro shows, the exoticism of Appalachia particularly appealed to those northern Protestants previously committed to freedmen's education, who, after 1880, came to see the southern mountaineers as embodying a pure Anglo-Saxonism. This fascination with Appalachia, in turn, grew in direct proportion to northern reformers' declining commitment to the southern race problem.[47]

Meanwhile, also in the 1880s, southern Protestants began mountain mission work through the establishment of Sunday schools, which operated sporadically throughout the Appalachian region. The early purposes of these missions were evangelical, but soon education became paramount. As one missionary reported, their primary obligation was the creation of schools in every township. Despite disclaimers to the contrary, denominational lines remained well defined in these efforts and included work by southern Presbyterians, Baptists, Methodists, and Episcopalians, who founded mission churches and schools that went well beyond the early Sunday school efforts. In eastern Kentucky, Presbyterian Edward O. Guerrant began missionary and evangelical work in 1881, and he popularized the notion of the saving of mountain souls by Bluegrass missionaries. By 1912 he had organized some thirteen mountain schools and was widely recognized for his expertise in mountain mission work.[48]

In the late decades of the nineteenth century, other southern Protestants established missions in the Appalachians. Andrew J. Ritchie, a native of northeastern Georgia's Rabun County who was a Harvard graduate, returned home in 1904 to what an admirer called a "broader field of activity . . . to elevate to a higher plane of usefulness the derelict and neglected children of the Georgia hills." Ritchie's inspiration, to this observer, was missionary: a zeal that motivated "the worthiest among the ranks of Christian ministers" combined with an enthusiasm for evangelizing.[49]

Robert Fishburne Campbell had a similar experience. Not long after he moved from Piedmont North Carolina to the First Presbyterian Church of Asheville, he became western North Carolina's leading exponent of mission work.[50] In the autumn of 1896 he helped to found a separate Asheville Presbytery, created out of Mecklenburg Presbytery, to coordinate the extension of mountain Presbyterianism. Within two years of its creation, two evangelists, authorized by the new presbytery to visit the eleven westernmost counties of North Carolina, were instructed to "leave railroads and telegraph lines, and the larger valleys behind, and to penetrate into secluded coves and highlands and report what they found." What these Presbyterian evangelists uncovered was perhaps predictable: an impoverished population that offended the standards of middle-class Victorian Protestants. The missionaries reported that large numbers of homes lacked "a lamp, a candle, a comb, a brush, a looking-glass, or similar articles of civilized life." Food was poorly prepared and served under unsanitary conditions; families inhabited small quarters with little privacy. Many of the backwoods mountaineers had never seen a town; even the buggy in which the missionaries traveled was considered a curiosity locally. Most serious, many families, even those "of a more intelligent grade," were found to have no Bible.[51]

Ritchie described what he believed was a similar condition of degradation. Conditioned to poverty and privation, living from hand to mouth, the mountaineers had only one "abundant commodity": their "unused and unvalued time." During their long isolation from modern civilization, an erosion of "moral and civic standards" had occurred, with the result that schools and churches had deteriorated. Those churches that had survived, he wrote, were "moribund"; throughout the Appalachians, the gospel was "seldom heard." The native clergy lacked education and "the moral requisites of acceptable leadership." Descendants of original leading families had degenerated to the "lowest moral levels"; the adult population, he believed, was beyond reclamation. Rather, the "only hope" lay in the region's children: with them, "the work of regeneration must begin."[52]

The most active Episcopal missionary in the southern Appalachians was Frederick William Neve. Beginning his work in 1888, by 1917 Neve had established thirty-seven missions in the mountains west and south of his base in Ivy, in western Albemarle County, Virginia. Neve first arrived from England to take charge of two country parishes, but he soon encountered what he remembered as the "large and neglected" population in the nearby Ragged Mountains. In 1890 he built a church for a community there, about five and a half miles from Ivy. A decade later, in 1900, he opened a school at Simmons' Gap, atop the Blue Ridge; in 1904 Neve helped to create a new archdeaconry, broken into four districts, with one or more clergymen in each district.[53]

By the turn of the twentieth century, mission schools like those operated by Campbell in North Carolina, Ritchie in Georgia, and Neve in Virginia were in evidence across the southern Appalachian region. In 1901 wealthy Presbyterians from Atlanta founded Nacoochee Institute, a mission school in White County, in northeastern Georgia. Beginning with a one-room schoolhouse, Nacoochee missionaries greatly expanded the school plant over the next decade. "Our efforts to reach and help the hundreds of mountain and Valley children . . . *who needed it*," wrote a Nacoochee worker in 1908, "have been so successful that we have been compelled to enlarge, and *enlarge*, and *again enlarge*, and broaden the scope of our work, at great cost, but with wonderful results in increased efficiency and broadened sphere of usefulness."[54]

Many of these missions evolved into or laid the basis for more ambitious settlement houses. In most instances, either direct or indirect ties linked these new southern mountain settlements with their counterparts in the North. Reformers in both northern cities and the southern mountains were attempting to alter the behavior and civilization of underdeveloped peoples mired in poverty; both offered an opportunity for the redefinition and extension of the traditional definition of "missionary." In the case of a struggling mission in Haywood County, North Carolina, in 1900, a connection with northern examples of cultural intervention occasioned a change in its function. When a mission school in that county located in the Fines Creek neighborhood experienced a financial crisis, a wealthy New York City merchant, Walter M. Smith, who was visiting Asheville for rest and recuperation, intervened and made a large contribution. But he also insisted that the mission school model itself after the Water Street Mission in New York City, and he dispatched its superintendent to visit. Smith also donated a "beautiful and sweet-toned bell" so as to "ring out the old, ring in the new" in the expanded role of the Fines Creek Mission.[55]

Settlement houses in northern cities and in the southern Appalachians both offered careers and leadership roles to Social Gospel Protestants and college-educated, middle-class women. Northern settlements sought to transform residents of the city, especially immigrants; southern settlements sought to refashion the behavior of rural mountain whites. Women had previously helped to found early missions and the Sunday schools that often accompanied them. Women from Charlottesville, Virginia, for example, established a mission school in 1901 in the nearby mountains. By their own account, it

Frederick W. Neve.
(Courtesy of the Manuscripts Division, Special Collections Department,
University of Virginia Library)

functioned as both a center of women's club activity and an outpost of modern, Victorian civilization. Traveling periodically and somewhat erratically among the mountain people, they led Bible readings, orchestrated the singing of hymns, and operated an occasionally functioning school. They described it as "a sort of 'club,' serving-school, and literary circle combined."[56]

Women's activism was crucial in the establishment of one of the region's first settlements, the Hindman Settlement School, established in Hindman, Knott County, Kentucky, in 1902. Its roots dated to the mid-1890s, in the activities of Bluegrass women such as its founders, Katherine Pettit and May Stone, and its key supporters, Sophonisba Breckinridge and her sister-in-law, Madeline McDowell Breckinridge. Beginning in 1899, with the support of the Kentucky WCTU and the state Federation of Women's Clubs, Pettit and Madeline McDowell Breckinridge operated a summer tent school in a location that they called Camp Cedar Grove, about forty miles from the nearest railroad. After operating two subsequent summer tent settlements, Pettit and Stone began a permanent, year-round school at Hindman in 1902.[57]

The Hindman school was self-consciously Protestant in its emphasis. When a Hindman supporter wrote General Education Board head Wallace Buttrick in 1902 for a $2,000 contribution, for example, she explained that a tour of eastern Kentucky had revealed a "condition truly appalling": only eight of fifty-six teachers in one county, though "intensely religious," could repeat the Lord's Prayer or identify its location in the Bible. Her response, however, went beyond the usual Sunday school solution; she wanted to create a model school in the settlement that would conduct "every thing from a Kindergarten to a Mother's class." In fact, the purposes of the Hindman school extended beyond the mountain mission work out of which it originally sprang. In addition to the social settlement activities that were directed at the adults of Knott County, Hindman operated the community's public school—which was not, in contrast to most missions, a denominational school—and in the first year it enrolled 164 students. Also in the first year of its operation, local interest was being described to a potential northern benefactor as "very keen," progress as "splendid," and the school's prospects as "most excellent indeed."[58]

By World War I, this mixture of missions and social settlements dotted the southern Appalachians. What they had in common were the driving forces of evangelical humanitarianism and the activism of middle-class women with the objective of remaking mountain civilization in the image of Victorian American culture. Missionaries sought both to extend their standards of culture and to secure their own self-definition. "The time may come," wrote a young John C. Campbell in 1896, when Christians would abandon the security of their "well-established churches" in favor of "a call from those who are nearby our peers, who can almost understand & appreciate us." An opportunity for missionary service awaited those "weary and heartsick in longing & waiting."[59]

The purpose of the early mission workers was the saving of souls through the establishment of denominational footholds.[60] The southern Appalachian region, as Guerrant explained, contained "many people destitute of the Gospel"; mountain people were often "as utterly ignorant of the way of salvation as the heathen in China." By supplying churches and schools, wrote a missionary in Virginia, workers enjoyed a "glorious opportunity" to "redeem a hollow in the mountains to The Christ and His Church." Mission schools, accordingly, had a strong religious component. In one Episcopal mission school in Virginia, pupils repeated the church catechism daily and, during the weekly church services, each child promised to bring at least one person along to participate.[61]

For most of the missionaries, the main tenets of the Social Gospel—the belief that the Kingdom of God could be realized immediately through Christians' ameliorative efforts—guided their actions. Although deeply affected by a Protestant impulse to convert, mountain workers were increasingly viewing conversion in a social, rather than an individual, sense. The imagery of a coming Kingdom was pervasive. Working in "this great Mountain Field" meant "hard work for you brethren," instructed a missionary to potential recruits back north in 1895, but it also meant "great things for the Kingdom." Attaining the Kingdom of God was the first objective of mountain mission work, wrote Frederick William Neve in 1912. Christians, if faithful to their profession, should act as "fellow workers with God." By participating in His church, they were obligated to "identify themselves with the cause, which the Church represents,—the upbuilding, and extension of the Kingdom of God upon earth." As a supporter of the Nacoochee Institute added, its mission school sought to "work for Education, Presbyterianism, and Kingdom of God, in that Mountain Country."[62]

Whether their objectives were overtly religious, as in the case of the missions, or more secular, as in the case of the settlements, they sought in common the alteration of mountain values. In 1913, at an Episcopal mission in Lydia, Virginia, missionaries announced an emphasis on sanitation and health; they promised to circulate pamphlets about flies, hookworms, infant care, sewage disposal, and venereal disease. The same missionaries also pledged to urge mountain families to eliminate widespread hereditary diseases. At the Hindman school, settlement workers tried to organize mountain folk who were "public spirited" and "interested in the improvement of the village." "Improvement," however, usually meant adopting alien urban-industrial values. One of the most important of these was a regimented sense of time, and, when the school established a social club, among its earliest actions was the organization of a movement for the installation of a town clock. For reformers, marketplace values were also important; the Hindman school workers encouraged, among other things, mountain women to sell their crafts for cash to buy "new fashioned things" such as false teeth, cooking stoves, and eye glasses and pay doctors' bills. In Pocosan Hollow, an Episcopal missionary, Susan Preston, described similar objectives in 1914. She operated a mission home that was open to mountain people, as she put it, "morning, noon and night"; they were "always made to feel welcome here." One night each week mountain boys and girls played games at the home— evidently to their great pleasure. Even after a long day in the fields, Preston wrote, "they walk for miles to join in these games at the Mission Home."[63]

Scholars have recently demonstrated that the Victorian Era's fascination with the southern mountains and their people paralleled its attitudes toward southern blacks.[64] Both were regarded as fundamentally different in culture and social structure. These societies were alien to the urban middle-class world that reformers inhabited; both were also regarded as inherently inadequate and inferior. As the reformers' response to both was similar—the assertion of the propriety of their intervention—paternalism once again became a central element in their ideology.

◆ ◆ ◆

THE CLASH OF CULTURES

Missionaries and settlement workers carried heavy cultural baggage. Reformers commonly described their objective as the spread of "civilization"; the missionary educator, according to the *Atlanta Constitution*, was "the advance-agent of civilization and development." The people of the mountains, one southern reformer concluded, had developed outside of the mainstream of civilization and culture. Consequently, their culture had evolved in its own way for decades "without molestation from the progress of civilization." But that separately developing mountain culture had become alien, and in some respects antithetical, to the reformers' own cultural standards. Above all, mountain culture existed with "no law and little religion."[65]

Missionaries saw nothing wrong with replacing what they considered an inferior culture with their own, supposedly superior civilization. Reformers were attempting not just to reach the "isolated and scattered" mountain folk, wrote a Virginia missionary, but also to reform "those in close touch with civilization, who have been left by the wayside in the onward march of progress." These were people whose underdevelopment and lack of Victorian civilization were the results of their social environment—what this observer called "conditions and circumstances beyond their control." Only through a self-realization of the inadequacy of their own civilization and a readiness to accept a new one could reform occur.[66]

Missionaries and settlement house workers, like other reformers, fastened on children. Mountain mission schools, according to one description in 1910, were "centers of Christian civilization" that spread "new and higher views" to mountain children and enabled them "to change for the better the conditions into which they were born." These children would grow into men and women. Having learned in schools how "to make their homes better fitted to be training schools for life for their children than their own homes were for them," missionary-educated mountain children would themselves become advocates of Victorian civilization. In a few generations, this observer predicted, mountain people would improve themselves. To most missionaries, children were malleable, plastic creatures. According to a missionary in Virginia, children lacked "discipline and control exercised over them at home"; under the authority of the mission school they would "become docile and tractable" and would make "little trouble." These children, corrupted only by their environment, were innately blessed with a "brightness and aptness to learn" and were, with strong discipline, "a delight to teach."[67]

For both missions and settlements, paternalism undergirded their sense of cultural superiority and provided a language of uplift. Early missionaries who focused on individual conversions saw improvement along Victorian middle-class lines. The door had opened for one missionary in Glade Springs, Virginia, in 1899, with some recent, "very striking conversions." Both young and old mountaineers had been saved and were "witnesses to the power of Divine grace to save the lost." The gospel, along with schools, was "the real need of the people." Another mission worker in Dillingham, in the North Carolina mountains, was clearer about the motives behind conversion efforts. Having provided a demonstration of Christmas—including a Christmas tree, the exchange of presents, and candy and oranges—mission workers were impressed by their ability to introduce this important example of Victorian civilization. The children, the worker reported, were "very obedient and teachable," and progress was possible if "we can get them out of their idle, thriftless habits," so "characteristic of the people." These were a simple folk who only needed the appropriate training. Uplift and guidance, combined with the assumption of cultural inadequacy, were the principles of mountain workers. Nacoochee Institute sought to provide "a chance to the chanceless" and "a hope to the hopeless," wrote one of its supporters in 1908.[68]

Missionary paternalists regarded mountain people and their culture as malleable. Before the world war especially, reformers often described southern Appalachians in condescending terms. Although they were as "excitable as children," they could be "easily control[l]ed if treated properly." Mountain people were "responsive to good influences," presumably coming from missionary reformers. They were also "adaptive" and "imitative of good examples," which made "work among them generally easy, progressive and successful." Mountain people, according to another account, were "full of kindness" and were "sensitive, silent, suspicious, brave, loyal, and hospitable to a fault." These qualities laid the basis for good character if mountain people could gain access to schoolhouses and churches.[69]

Reformers on forays into the profoundly different world of rural Appalachia found its ways of life baffling and alien. Neve ventured into an isolated Ragged Mountain community known as Shiftlett's Hollow, where lawlessness and extreme individualism seemed to confirm most of the stereotypes held by urban outsiders about Appalachian society. Neve traveled with a terrified friend who was convinced that mountaineers armed with rifles were hidden in the bushes, prepared to warn others of the invaders; to him, recalled Neve, "every habitation we came to was the abode of a moonshiner." These preconceptions of mountaineers were at least partly confirmed when they discovered that a local preacher began services by laying down his pistol on his Bible and telling his congregation that "if necessary he could handle the one as effectively as the other." Neve and his companion encountered no overt hostility, but their visit, as they subsequently learned, aroused the suspicions of the residents of Shiftlett's Hollow. Their arrival had caused "considerable consternation": a young woman whom they visited "nearly fainted away" when she first spotted the outsiders.[70]

Most reformers brought with them exotic notions of mountain society. John C. Campbell's sister-in-law, visiting a mountain community in search of ballads, described herself as "*bustling* with excitement" about native mountain culture, and she was brimming with visions of feuding hillbillies and illicit moonshine stills. After seeing a real still for the first time, she wrote that she had felt "a delicious thrill of excitement" when she sighted the place. She half hoped to discover a Winchester rifle sticking out from behind a log, along with a summons to stop. But, with some disappointment, she rode up to the still unmolested and even took some photographs. The location nonetheless was a romantic spot—"trees and green moss, a sloping hill covered with timber"; as a stage setting, it was perfect—just what she had always imagined. No other experience could approach this "glorious excitement."[71]

This fascination with exotica only thinly masked an assumption of cultural inferiority. A missionary to eastern Kentucky expressed some of these attitudes when he wrote in 1895 of his first encounter with a mountaineer whose dialect, he observed, was "by no means as bad as we have supposed," or at least so he thought. After opening a school, he noted that the children, although "naturally bright," were "inclined to be *lazy*, lack ambition and the aesthetic sense." He also complained that the mountaineers were dirty and that it was impossible to keep his schoolroom clean. When John C. Campbell first visited the southern Appalachians in 1896, he expressed similar attitudes. Everywhere, he noted, were offensive examples of mountain culture—women dipping snuff, children unkempt and dirty—"all about us many things that offend the aesthetic sense." Despite the missionary urge to uplift them, it was difficult not to be repulsed because they were "so common & so dirty." Only through the inspiration of St. Peter's example, who had urged that no man be called "common or unclean," could these impulses be restrained.[72]

Robert F. Campbell was even stronger in his condemnation of mountain culture. Among Appalachian people, he wrote, ignorance and vice abounded. Large sections lacked schools or doctors; profanity was common among men, women, and children. Central ideals of Victorian civilization—the exaltation of work and family—were violated by the realities of mountain society. In contrast to the sentimental bonds of the Victorian family, among mountain folk, wrote Campbell, there was typically "no evidences of affection between different members of the family." Children were controlled merely by force, until they became strong enough to fight; the aged were neglected and despised. Children used tobacco before they could talk; bastardy was common, even accepted. Mountain people lacked any sense of a work ethic. Women and children did most of the work; the men generally spent their time hunting, fishing, or moonshining. In some parts of the mountains, observed Campbell, a young man "reached the summit of his ambition" once he had learned to play the banjo, owned a dog and a pistol, and was ensured of a regular supply of whiskey.[73]

Major cultural differences divided paternalist reformers from traditionalist mountaineers, and clashes between the two cultures occurred with some frequency. Reformers criticized central elements of Appalachian society, such as family structure. Susan Preston, the missionary in Pocosan Hollow, located deep in the Virginia mountains, wrote in 1914 that there was "something appealing and sweet" about the submissiveness of mountain girls and women, but, noting that they carried it to an extreme, she urged greater assertiveness. Preston was also horrified to see women working side by side with their men in the fields, and she longed to inform the mountain people how differently women were treated in the outside world and "how wrong I think it's for them to let women slave so hard." Despite her feelings, she usually was tactful, as changing these customs, at least in a "short while," would be a "hopeless undertaking." Real changes would come only through education and Christianity.[74]

A differing conception of family was mutual: mountain folk regarded the family practices of the outsiders as equally strange. Local residents of Pocosan Hollow described the small child of two mission workers as a "mountaineer pet" because of the attention the infant received. To the community, the child was "a real curiosity." Mountain mothers marveled at her "spotless white clothes"; their children usually wore only a few dark calico dresses. Local women regarded the nursing habits of the outsiders as "very strange"; one mountain mother told how she had raised fourteen children on sweetened coffee.[75]

The clash of cultures between reformers and mountaineers was widely evident. Neve remembered his shock at discovering that women and children were subjected to frequent physical abuse by their husbands-fathers. The children, he wrote, had never been inside a schoolhouse; worse still, they had received no moral training from their parents. Instead, they were used to beatings whenever they displeased their parents, even though the offense might be trivial. This constant dread of punishment made them afraid to tell the truth; as a result, they were habitually deceitful. Reforming missionaries made the alteration of these and other family customs a primary objective. They encouraged the mountaineers to change their homes and to adopt the modern conveniences of Victorian life. In Pocosan Hollow, residents, who had been happy to inhabit one-room cabins that housed a family of ten or twelve persons, were persuaded that it was neither necessary nor best to live in that manner. The missionaries encouraged them to adopt different life-styles by constructing "nice, well-built cottages" and additions to their homes. Everywhere, noted one observer, local people now wanted the "little things" that made homes more comfortable, such as windows, chairs, and carpets. Mountaineers in this way would, he thought, relinquish one of their "most pathetic characteristics"—the "patient endurance of all kinds of hardship and poverty, without any desire to live differently." By adopting Victorian religious and educational practices, mountain people would submit to a "law-abiding" civilization.[76]

Reformers objected to other mountain practices that were an integral part of Appalachian culture. Along with the Victorian church and school, missionaries brought with them new, professional conceptions of public health, and they urged mountain people to abandon traditional folk medicine. The prevalence of superstition and even witchcraft contributed to the benighted state of mountain life, wrote Susan Preston. She related an episode in which a mountain man lost confidence in the local physician and turned to a "hoodoo," or folk, doctor, who treated the man's ailment with a combination of herbs and mysterious incantations to mountain spirits. These hoodoo doctors appear to have been black. Frederick Neve remembered an incident where, after a child fell into a boiling tub for scalding hogs, the parents summoned a "hoodoo doctor," called "Nigger Guy." The folk doctor, who enjoyed the community's general confidence, attempted to save the boy by using charms, but the child died the following morning. Nonetheless, in this instance and others, the parents believed that they had fulfilled their responsibilities by summoning this man.[77]

Perhaps nothing better exemplified the cultural gap between reformers and mountaineers than the different ways in which they observed Christmas. The modern observance of Christmas had come into existence by the middle of the nineteenth century, and reformers sought early on to implant the Victorian Christmas in the southern Appalachians. Typically for mountaineers, Christmas was a time of social sprees and drunkenness. A missionary noted in 1914 that Christmas was over, and he was "breathing freely again." But in spite of the "superabundance of brandy in the neighborhood," the holiday had been a peaceful one. Neve recalled in 1917 that Christmas in the mountains was traditionally observed "in anything but a fitting and seemly manner." After establishing his first mission some thirty years earlier, he had been advised by the locals that holding a Victorian Christmas, with tree trimming and carol singing, would likely bring "trouble" in the community.[78]

The reformers' insistence on changing the observance of Christmas became a symbol of a wider and more significant cultural invasion. In Pocosan Hollow, missionaries wrote proudly that the local population had expressed "great interest" in Christmas preparations; they encouraged this interest by giving the mountaineers the opportunity to do all they could to help. In the period before Christmas, a day was appointed for the decoration of the mission chapel, and the local residents were urged to bring evergreens, garlands, crosses, and stars. Christmas trees, also typical of the Victorian Christmas, were decorated, with the singing of carols and an appearance by Santa Claus. The missionaries declared that this was the "most satisfactory Christmas we have had since we have been in the Mission work." Particularly encouraging was the "good behavior of the people," especially the men and boys—not one of them attended the tree trimming drunk.[79]

In an unusually reflective moment, Robert F. Campbell warned reformers about the implications of their condescending attitudes toward mountain people. Much had been written about the southern Appalachians that "excited bitterness and resentment" among the residents, in part because of what he called "a class appellation" that implied "peculiarity, if not inferiority." Indeed, some outsiders wrote about their mountain trips as if they had "visited a menagerie and were describing what they saw when the animals were stirred up!" Yet, he noted, precisely this sort of condescension had "stirred the animals up still more."[80]

There was great diversity among them, to be sure, but most of these reformers shared common attributes. Almost all of them came from towns and cities; even rural reformers usually owed some connection to the urban nexus. Most, almost synonymously with the latter, were middle class; many of them were women; and most expressed themselves and viewed the world using Protestant missionary language. Together, these social reformers sought a diversity of goals, from prohibition to child welfare to public health reform, but what united them was a certainty about the necessity of what amounted to a cultural invasion of the southern hinterlands.

What Campbell perhaps unwittingly described was typical not just of mountain missionaries but also of most early twentieth-century southern social reformers. Although most of them assumed that their vision of change was the right one for their region, they failed to recognize either the invasive cultural assumptions that underlay that vision or the nature of the conflict that arose when they tried to impose it. If class and culture defined reform efforts in the mountains, race and culture punctuated the attempts to uplift southern blacks. As in the case of mountain whites, however, the attempt at race reform exposed not just amelioration and improvement but a basic assumption of paternalism.

The social reformers of the post-1900 South shared this combination of the impulse to uplift and a certainty of the inadequacy of the uplifted. It became a guiding concept in their attempt to transform the region's social and political institutions. Assuming that control over reform would come at their initiative, they still faced the challenge of changing public opinion, which gave little indication of dissatisfaction with the status quo. It was incumbent on reformers, for this reason, to devise a means of persuading southerners of the need for change and to mobilize political support behind it. To accomplish this, they turned to the most common model of popular organizing in Victorian America, the evangelical crusade.

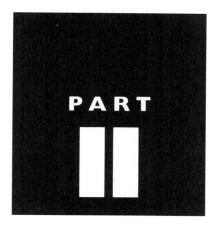

PART II

THE REFORM CRUSADE

SOCIAL PURITY

◆

Imbued with the certainty of paternalism, early twentieth-century reformers sought to remake social and political institutions in such a way as to readjust them to the changing conditions of the market revolution. As a social movement, progressivism manifested itself in every region of the United States, while it affected local, state, and national institutions alike. It refashioned the nature of politics by helping along the decline of political parties, opening access for single-interest pressure groups, and introducing a new degree of interventionism and regulation in the economy. In the South, progressivism was accompanied by the political exclusion of blacks, which was accomplished by constitutional revision in most of the region between 1890 and 1908. While on the heels of disfranchisement came a reformed political system, the creation of the one-party state also paved the way for southern social reformers who together embraced similar methods of popular mobilization.

Among the most important of these social reformers were prohibitionists, who early in the twentieth century launched an ambitious crusade to remake folkways through an unprecedented exertion of public power. The antisaloon campaign became a successful model of publicity and pressure group organization. In Dewey W. Grantham's description, it "may well have been the most dynamic and passionately supported" reform of the Progressive Era

South.[1] Identifying a social problem, prohibitionists rallied public opinion against it and promoted a solution through legislation and reformed social policy. In this sense, the prohibition crusade had wide implications. Offering a powerful critique of passive, diffused governance, reformers argued that only interventionist social policy could serve the interests of the whole community. Meanwhile, moral reformers also adopted new techniques of mass mobilization that a wide array of social reformers eventually embraced.

◆ ◆ ◆

THE PROHIBITIONIST APPEAL

In the euphoria of the new century, reformers were hopeful about the future. Before the century ended, prophesied a Tennessee prohibitionist in 1901, there would not be "a saloon in America, if any in the world." The time was not too distant when it would become a commonplace for saloons to have no more right to exist in a community than a mad dog. Nine years later, Alexander J. McKelway told a North Carolina audience that he foresaw a future in which a crow could fly across the South—from Cape Hatteras, west through Virginia, Kentucky, Tennessee, Arkansas, and Oklahoma, returning through Texas, Mississippi, Alabama, Georgia, Florida, and South Carolina, to the Atlantic Ocean—without seeing anything but prohibition country.[2]

Between the late 1890s and the onset of World War I, southern prohibitionists recorded a series of successes. Before July 1907, only three states—Maine, Kansas, and North Dakota—had adopted statewide prohibition; in most of the North, with the exception of Indiana, Ohio, and Illinois, prohibitionism, according to one observer, was "moribund, if not dead." In contrast, in the South it was "sweeping onward with relentless and irresistible force, gaining new converts and increasing in power every year." Either through local option or statewide prohibition, the great majority of southern territory was at least officially dry by about 1910; according to one estimate in 1907, fewer saloons existed in thirteen southern states than in New York City![3] The South had become a mainspring of the modern American prohibition movement. Rather than provincial and inward-looking, prohibition had emerged as a "great, broad, deep movement," wrote another reformer, of "commanding proportions and with inspiration at its heart." By leading the way, the South had achieved a position of moral leadership in the nation.[4]

The prohibitionists' message carried a new urgency: the battle over prohibition constituted a struggle between the forces of progress and those of backwardness, what one reformer called "two polar principles of right and wrong." "We hate whiskey, we hate the saloon gang, we hate the idea that either are a necessity and must be endured," declared another prohibitionist in 1907. No important moral issue had two sides, according to still another reformer; the matter was "either right or wrong." For expediency's sake, reformers could "minimize the evil," but their ultimate goal should be its destruction. Always vote against what the saloon was for, he advised other reformers, for the issue was "squarely drawn": the moral forces were on one side and "the world, the flesh and the devil" were on the other.[5]

Prohibitionists were willing to tolerate few compromises. According to one North Carolinian, reformers would pursue any legal means, even if it meant an unending struggle, to "supress the eavill of Strong drink." Mobilized by this intense language, the prohibition movement often depicted the struggle against drink in Manichaean terms. Using familiar Jacksonian rhetoric, a South Carolinian described the "deeply entrenched Hydra" that was "the greatest evil of the age." Saloons belonged "to the dark and not to light," added a Texan. On one side stood the supporters of churches, women, schools, and "all the institutions and forces which make civilization." On the other side were "the saloons, the gamblers, the brothels and all the forces which degrade civilization and blast the hopes of humanity." In the struggle for prohibition, wrote a Mississippian, there were "but two sides and no neutral ground." This was a struggle between "the forces of evil, concentrated in the saloon business," added a Floridian, and "the followers of Jesus Christ." In the past, wrote another reformer, temperance legislation had had little effect; the liquor traffic had grown "insolent in its license of power," defying all restrictions. "The only way to save ourselves," he concluded, was "to shoot the thing dead with statewide prohibition."[6]

For prohibitionists as for other reformers, the message that corruption was rampant effectively mobilized grass-roots support behind reform. In the imagery of southern prohibitionists, corruption affected both public and private spheres. The family, according to reformers, was directly threatened because saloons imperiled the home and its purity. A Texas prohibitionist testified that whiskey had wrecked her home, and she was "in the fight . . . to the end." Her children remained unsafe while there was "one drop in this country of ours"; the familiar "foot-prints of the saloon" were everywhere. In the homes of the unsuspecting, the corrupting liquor traffic took bread and clothes from mothers and children "in order to feed and sleep and clothe itself." This "monster parasite" had slipped its "slimy tentacles around almost or quite every phase of life and activity."[7]

Saloons, according to reformers, also corrupted public life. The men behind the liquor traffic, wrote a prohibitionist, used corrupt methods; whatever they touched was polluted by the system's "strong evil influences." Organized

Burying whiskey, Dismal Swamp, Virginia.
(Courtesy of the Virginia State Library and Archives)

alcohol trafficking was a power and a great industry that provided "employment, such as it is, to many men." The saloon was "the mother and the breeder of all anarchy in this and every other country." As what a Georgian called the "principal source of political corruption" and "the creator of hydra headed vice in our cities," the liquor traffic directly affected government. In large urban centers like Birmingham, claimed a reformer, saloons exerted a "grasping and cruel hand"; entrenched and fortified with every safeguard in city government, they were openly defiant. Wielding strong political power, saloons dominated politics and elected officials dedicated to ignoring the law. As the "mightiest combine on the face of the earth," the liquor traffic and government had formed a conspiracy to "defeat law and to rule over the ruins of law, religion, public decency and all good." Such collusion and corruption undermined the legitimacy of government. For these reasons, anything short of statewide prohibition provided "state sanction to a wrong act" and gave "the hydra-headed monster of rum an air of legality." A Texan favored statewide prohibition because the liquor traffic had become a "portentous and continuous menace" to social and political institutions.[8]

The corruption of the saloon had wide implications. Saloons were partners of the gambling den and the house of shame. They filled jails, diminished workers' productivity, and increased taxes on the sober citizen. They were purveyors of a poison that impaired the laborer's ability to work, incited his evil passions, and transformed him into a brute. Everywhere, prohibitionists claimed that outlawing the saloon would help to lower crime and ease social tensions. From Fayetteville, North Carolina, a prohibitionist claimed that, with the end of the saloon, his town had been freed from the drunken brawls that had so commonly occurred. In southern Virginia, a South Boston resident asserted that local option prohibition had meant little or no disorder in that section.[9]

What set prohibitionists apart from their temperance predecessors was their emphasis on collective responsibility. Drunkards were the victims of a physiological problem. Under the destructive grip of alcohol, drinkers underwent a process in which the victim degenerated physically as well as morally and eventually experienced moral delinquency and physical degeneracy. Drunkenness lowered manhood, destroyed self-respect, impaired health, ruined business prospects, and left the victim a "wretched wreck." To the victim's family, it brought untold sorrow; to society, crime and corruption; and to others, injury to person and property. These "poor besotted brutes" were "creatures and products of the open saloon." The liquor traffic had destroyed innocent, ordinary men. Civilized society, declared a Virginian, had rejected the notion that drunkenness was "a manifestation of original sin"; most reformers believed that overdrinkers were "as much a victim of disease as the consumptive." Who was more insane, more lacking in responsibility, than the man who put down his last dime for a drink? Who was more in need of the restraint of organized society than the derelict who had lost his will? [10]

The prohibitionist message advanced these sociological assumptions in order to appeal to a broadened reform coalition. The success of state prohibition in the South after about 1907, according to McKelway, lay in the transformation of a "total abstinence party" into a movement that enjoyed the support of more conservative folk who believed that not all drinking was wrong but were united in antagonism to the saloon. In this transformation, what he called the "economic argument" was paramount. Southerners were attracted to prohibition because they became convinced that saloons bred disorder and crime and demoralized labor. In a key ideological development, they became convinced that saloons represented "everything that was abhorrent in politics and government." [11]

As McKelway suggested, southern prohibitionists realized that their success would depend on the establishment of a coalition that would extend well beyond the political base of the nineteenth-century temperance movement. That coalition would be attracted to a new, revitalized movement through a significantly different appeal, one that stressed the wider sociological implications of excessive drinking and, especially, the determinative effect of the open saloon system. But even more important to the success of this prohibition coalition was its ability to marshal public opinion through a campaign. A crucial link in its organization was the Anti-Saloon League.

◆ ◆ ◆

THE ANTI-SALOON LEAGUE AND THE PROHIBITION CRUSADE

What made the early twentieth-century South so "perpetually interesting," wrote the southern historian William Garrott Brown, was that it offered "a spectacle of transitions." On a tour from Virginia to Texas, he marveled how the region had changed; revisiting the region on another occasion, he found even greater changes. Nothing better illustrated the South's sudden conversion to the idea of change, wrote Brown, than the fact that an "energy of things new or newly freed" had replaced its "once atrophied or baffled" approach to social problems. Southerners, he believed, were now entering a period of governmental activism, particularly in regard to public and private morality. [12]

In southern prohibition, Brown discovered abundant evidence of this "energy of things new or newly freed." Culminating about 1914, this social movement sought to expand on local option legislation enacted between 1880 and 1900 that had created, on paper at least, widespread rural prohibition. By 1908, to cite only three examples, 125 of 145 counties in Georgia, 69 of 76 counties in Mississippi, and 94 of 119 counties in Kentucky were officially dry. Thereafter, through statewide prohibition laws, much of the South underwent a rapid transition. Between 1908 and 1914 what one observer called a "prohibition wave" swept through the South; in the latter year, only South Carolina, Kentucky, Texas, and Florida remained outside the statewide prohibition camp.[13]

Behind the mobilization of southern public opinion was a singularly successful pressure organization: the Anti-Saloon League. Organized in Ohio in 1895, it had spread nationally by the late 1890s and had spearheaded a new campaign for prohibition. The ASL pioneered the mobilization of public opinion and established a model for Progressive Era reform campaigns. Employing a crusade model of popular campaigning, one very familiar to most Victorian Americans, the ASL operated on the assumption that accomplishing a change in public opinion was the most effective means of effecting substantive policy changes. But it also believed that altering public opinion would require a staged manipulation through publicity, communication of a message through pamphlet literature and public meetings, and nearly constant pressure on legislators.[14]

Although the ASL possessed strong national leadership and a centralized bureaucratic apparatus, one of its most prominent operating principles was the importance of local leadership and control. To the extent that the ASL intervened in local affairs, it sought only to create a more effective coalition of local prohibitionists. Yet the ASL required local and state chapters to organize strictly controlled crusades, to focus them on saloons and the liquor traffic, and to obtain a gradual increase in legislative restrictions leading eventually to complete prohibition. Having established nineteen state leagues in 1899, the league made a conscious decision to expand to the South in 1900, and its early organizing efforts there were based on these assumptions.[15]

The league's early activities in Virginia were typical. In late 1900 the ASL sent a field agent to the commonwealth; a state chapter was formally organized in March 1901. As events at this meeting made clear, the league emphasized the cultivation and development of state leadership and the creation of an effective antisaloon coalition. Operating as a nonpartisan, single-interest organization, it focused exclusively on the saloon, employed a businesslike, efficient system of finance, and employed full-time professional organizers. Under the leadership of the Reverend James Cannon, Jr., a Methodist, the Virginia ASL succeeded in forging strong denominational support—especially of Baptists and Methodists—while it also attracted the cooperation of other reform groups. As editor of the *Richmond Christian Advocate*, the state Methodist newspaper, Cannon made it a forum for league activities. In 1909 he began an even more ambitious effort when he helped to establish a daily newspaper, the *Richmond Virginian*. With Cannon as president of the company that published the newspaper and with J. Sidney Peters, a Methodist prohibitionist as editor, the *Richmond Virginian*, which ran until 1917, became the South's leading prohibitionist alternative to the "wet" press.[16] Effective in the use of media, the Virginia ASL was also known for its high-pressure political tactics. After turning to the gallery of observers, a Virginia legislator once commented that it was not often that he had the opportunity to address the Virginia Anti-Saloon League. The league directed the introduction of legislation and then pushed its passage with a barrage of letters, telegrams, and petitions. Cannon, who became a master lobbyist, was often seen at the Virginia House of Delegates in his usual position—the front row of the gallery—or occasionally on the floor of the House itself, taking notes and carefully observing the proceedings.[17]

The organization of ASL chapters elsewhere followed a roughly similar pattern. When the North Carolina league campaigned in 1903 for the passage of the Watts Act, which enacted rural prohibition, the *Raleigh News and Observer* noted that there "seemed to go forth a tacit understanding that the time for definite action had arrived." In fact, the campaign was obviously well organized. Under league direction, every county in the state sent a petition to the legislature supporting the Watts bill. Arriving in big bundles from across the state, they "kept on coming, new ones every day, until something was done." During legislative hearings, the galleries, lobbies, and floor of the General Assembly were crowded with the state's "best people"—clergymen, lawyers, doctors, teachers, and businessmen—all present "for one and the same purpose, temperance legislation." "Never before in the history of North Carolina or perhaps any other State" had a legislature seen such a well-orchestrated campaign.[18]

Because they sustained local enthusiasm and sought to coerce antiprohibitionist communities, statewide campaigns were vitally important to ASL strategists. Timing was crucial; they struck only when the political conditions were favorable. The situation was ripe, a North Carolina campaigner reported before a prohibition referendum in 1908; he was confident that the crusade would "swamp the deck." These campaigns, operated on an evangelical model of mobilization, focused on the single issue of saloons, and the league advanced a new notion of politics: it voiced strong antiparty rhetoric, what one historian has called an "omnipartisan" approach. It stood for one

James Cannon, Jr.
(Courtesy of the Virginia State Library and Archives)

cardinal principle, explained the *Richmond Virginian*—"the elimi[na]tion of the saloon as an institution in American life."[19]

The ASL saw its organization as existing not only outside of but also above party politics. From Franklinville, North Carolina, a rank-and-file ASL worker commented that, although a lifelong Republican, he would desert the party "if the Republican candidate for the legislature don[']t pledge his word and honor" to prohibition. Essential to the league's independence was its almost military organization. In statewide campaigns across the South, the ASL's main purpose was, as a North Carolinian explained, to develop, "out of chaos," "a splendid *regular army*." Marshaling the state's prohibitionist forces through strong organization, the league had, "in a marvelously short time," created a "trained army."[20]

The backbone of that army was the Protestant church, and most of the league's chapters were formed out of an interdenominational base. In North Carolina, McKelway recalled how such a coalition came into existence in Fayetteville in the late 1890s, even before the ASL formalized the alliance. Six men—a Baptist minister and his deacon, a Methodist minister and his steward, and a Presbyterian minister and his elder—met in a Fayetteville church parlor and elected the Baptist deacon to organize a petition campaign to press the legislature to enact a county dispensary law. The campaign was eventually successful.[21]

In most cases, Methodists and Baptists dominated such alliances. McKelway, himself a Presbyterian, noted that by participating in this campaign he violated all the traditions of the Presbyterian ministry, although he had "never yet had the grace to be ashamed." According to William Garrott Brown, Methodist and Baptist members of the ASL were committed to the cause "unreservedly, inside and outside the pulpit," while their congregations provided "the readiest converts" to prohibition. They endorsed local option over dispensaries and high license, and state prohibition over local option. Temperance was a concept they had virtually ceased to preach, demanding instead that government compel all people to become teetotalers. These Methodists and Baptists were ready-made foot soldiers for the prohibition crusade. They preached incessantly about it and made constant visits to their members; they studied their people "as closely as the most observant politician." They were fully aware, as well, of the "ever-widening influence of women." Collectively, they exerted considerable power. If the ordinary people of the white South were to be called "priest-ridden," wrote Brown, "the strongest objection to the phrase would be, that Methodist and Baptist ministers do not consider themselves priests." Together, the two denominations took the lead in the global prohibition movement.[22]

To Brown and others, it was not surprising that the Anti-Saloon League had adopted evangelical methods. He described one prohibition meeting, typical of the crusade, as relying on the "devices of a Methodist revival or 'protracted meeting.'" It employed "rather terrifying and rather coarsely emotional oratory from pulpit and platform," which was "interspersed with singing and praying" and marked by the parading forth of women and children, "drilled for the purpose." In its crusade, the ASL employed ruthless methods, including what Brown called a "sort of persecution, not stopping short of an actual boycott," of those sympathizing with the "wet" cause, as well as intense political pressure on local politicians and the "mobbing" of polls with women and children "singing, praying, and doing everything conceivable to embarrass and frighten every white voter without a white ribbon in his lapel."[23]

Other accounts confirm that the ASL crusade possessed a deeply evangelical Protestant flavor. Reformers never tired of reminding their audiences that they were, as a Tennessee crusader expressed it, "Christian men and women" opposed to "body destroying and soul damning" saloons. Another ASL crusader asked the state league leadership to get "all of the Christians to begin work of a new Sunday" to achieve prohibition. In Southern Pines, North Carolina, a Baptist preacher boasted that he had found "occasion of late" to bring the subject into nearly every sermon he preached. In Greensboro, North Carolina, another Baptist minister reportedly gave a prohibition sermon that "drew blood (and was intended to)." The passage of statewide prohibition legislation in several states was greeted by the singing of the Doxology, often on the floor of state capitols.[24]

The ASL's message was increasingly geared toward convincing southerners of the need to relinquish some individual and community autonomy in exchange for a purer moral and social order. A common analogy was that of the "mad dog," the subject of an editorial that appeared in the *Tennessee Baptist and Reflector* in August 1903. If a meeting were held about the subject, at least one man would claim absolute individual rights of ownership; suspicious of governmental intrusion, he would urge that the dog be left alone. Another man would agree with this position but might endorse instructing his children on mad dogs and how to avoid them. Still others—although they might argue about the amount—would favor taxing the owner of the dog to allow the dog to run loose and bite people. The proper solution, the newspaper suggested, was that the mad dog be shot, just as the saloon should be completely eradicated. Where the mad dog could "slay its tens the saloons will slay and is slaying its tens of thousands." The fact that the saloon was superficially attractive rather than repulsive did not mitigate the danger it posed to the community. If boys enjoyed being bitten by mad dogs, did that justify charging "ten cents a bite?" Should dog owners be licensed to bite people? Why, then, asked the editorialist, license a saloon in any community?[25]

A key objective of the ASL crusade was to generate what McKelway called a "determined moral sentiment" among average white southerners. In North Carolina, he pointed out, there had been two popular referenda on the question of statewide prohibition in the space of almost three decades: in the first, in 1881, prohibition was decisively defeated; in the second, in 1908, it triumphed. The difference in result lay, he believed, in the educational tools of local option and disfranchisement, which excluded the prosaloon black vote. But equally important was a revolution in public sentiment on liquor legislation. Other prohibitionists, viewing reform in similar terms, believed that the most important result of crusading was the general mobilization of new reform opinion. The crusade marked a coalescence of reform sentiment; in this case, it was an expression of public opinion against the evil sway of the organized liquor business in public affairs. To a reformer like John E. White, the uses to which this aroused public opinion could be put were extensive. The Anti-Saloon League, in bringing together a diverse coalition, had succeeded precisely because it had convinced public opinion of the "higher social selfishness" of prohibition. Under the aegis of the league, prohibition had matured as a twentieth-century reform movement.[26]

◆ ◆ ◆

PROHIBITION: THE SHAPING OF A SOCIAL REFORM

When the Anti-Saloon League was first organized in Virginia, skeptics and antiprohibitionists, James Cannon, Jr., recalled, ridiculed it as "another spasmodic effort of the temperance cranks, as another wave of enthusiasm, engendered by the appeals of a few fanatical preachers and hysterical women." Although they perceived correctly that the ASL organization and ideology owed a large debt to the evangelical tradition, those critics were wrong in assuming that, like a typical revival, the ASL campaign would soon blow over and everything would return to the old condition. As time passed, the movement gathered momentum; "the breeze became a rushing wind, and the wind became a gale." This gale had now become a "hurricane" that would bring a "tireless, persistent, deadly warfare" against the saloon.[27]

The prohibition crusade, like other early twentieth-century campaigns for social reform, underwent a crucial transition from a spasmodic and essentially temporary reform movement to a revolution in long-term social policy. Reformers were well aware that either local option or statewide prohibition would bring resistance. Among yeoman white farmers, wrote William Garrott

Prohibition rally, Lowndes County Courthouse, Valdosta, Georgia, 1907. The banner reads:
"Vote as if the Master waited at the door. / Vote as if tomorrow your voting would be o'er. /
Vote as if you met the Master's searching look. / Vote as tho it were his hand your ballot took.
(Courtesy of the Georgia Department of Archives and History)

Brown, hard drinking was extensive. In contrast to Europe, where the peasantry drank heavily but where drunkenness was extremely rare, in the rural
South prohibitionists faced both a better opening and a more serious challenge. That challenge was readily apparent to most prohibitionists. Saloons
that paid a federal excise tax in prohibition districts abounded throughout the

South—a fact that the reformers readily admitted. In Florida, a local group claimed that violations of local option were now troubling their community; under the garb of respectability provided by the federal license, saloons operated freely there. Others acknowledged a systematic effort by liquor sellers to subvert prohibition; the cry that "prohibition doesn't prohibit," ironically, came from the "false prophet" of the "whiskey devil," for there was no whiskey sold in dry territory for which liquor interests were not responsible.[28]

Still, prohibitionists walked a thin line in defending laws that resulted in such extensive violations. In Alabama, Senator John Hollis Bankhead, a Democrat, wrote in 1913 explaining why he opposed statewide and federal prohibition, even though he believed in and practiced temperance. In 1908 Alabama had enacted a law that, according to Bankhead, "all fair minded men" agreed had failed. "Blind tigers and bootleggers" were "everywhere," and illicit distilleries were "in almost every community." Those Alabamians who opposed the open saloon but maintained a liquor supply at home for moderate use and for sickness resisted excessive restrictions and, like Bankhead, saw local option as the most effective vehicle of control.[29]

Unlike Bankhead, most early twentieth-century prohibitionists looked toward statewide prohibition as a comprehensive solution. Although the pattern of legislation differed from state to state, the enactment of statewide prohibition in North Carolina is somewhat typical. Local option legislation provided for township, not county, prohibition; as a result, whereas rural areas prohibited saloons, towns pursued a more tolerant approach. After the mid-1880s prohibitionists began a long campaign to tighten the noose around North Carolina's saloons. The passage of a law permitting county dispensaries in 1897 provided a vehicle for locally organized campaigns to eliminate saloons. Subsequent legislation in 1903 and 1904 confined them to large towns and cities and encouraged these municipalities to enact local option. Yet reformers in North Carolina discovered that the problem of alcohol could not be solved easily. Local option might outlaw saloons in one community while they remained open and available across the county line, or, even more likely, in the nearest large town. For this reason, statewide prohibition, as one Edgecombe County prohibitionist wrote, became "our only hope." Everywhere in this county, restrictions on drinking encountered efforts to evade the law legally. This was evidence of the "desperation of the Whiskey leaders in our County," he thought, but it also indicated the need for an effective statewide policy.[30]

The emergence of support for statewide prohibition elsewhere in the South evolved out of the realization that local solutions were impossible. In Virginia, a reformer conceded that it took only one wet town to nullify the effectiveness of prohibition in six other dry towns and counties. That wet town became a source from which shipments were readily made. The ease with which an invasion of dry territories could occur brought widespread disrespect for the law. Local officials became lax in stamping out local violations, and whiskey dealers became more aggressive in their efforts to procure trade in the dry districts.[31]

Southern prohibitionists' realization that alcohol required a larger policy meant that they endorsed local remedies only until they possessed sufficient strength to enact statewide prohibition. Reformers mobilized public opinion by focusing it, not on consumption, but on saloons, and the new laws reflected this predisposition. Mississippi's law, enacted in 1908, permitted both "medicinal" dispensing of alcohol by druggists and home manufacture of wine. Georgia's law, described by a contemporary as "one of the most drastic in the history of prohibitory legislation," provided similar allowances for consumption. Clearly, however, advocates accomplished their primary purpose, which was the abolition of the legal saloon.[32]

These and other laws were far from completely effective, yet prohibitionists acknowledged that enforcement was a chief priority. Prohibition statutes had first to be "practicable," wrote one southern prohibitionist, and then had to have force behind them. "You never saw a law that would enforce itself," he wrote. "You have got to have somebody enforce it." Prohibition would prohibit, added a North Carolinian, only if popular sentiment was behind enforcement. That violations would accompany even the strictest enforcement, they claimed, did not mean that prohibition was ineffective. The notion that prohibition could never prohibit absolutely was, according to the *Richmond Virginian*, a "man of straw." Violations would always occur. The real test of prohibition's effectiveness lay in its social impact. Rather than the complete eradication of drinking or even of liquor selling, the same newspaper later commented, prohibition had two purposes. The first was to put the "habitual consumer[s]," those who would be "otherwise easy victims to the liquor habit," out of business. The second purpose was to save those who would have been tempted to take a "first step" toward drinking.[33]

Prohibitionists, by removing the environmental sources of excessive drinking and by creating "a new and sober generation," sought a form of social purification. Prohibitionists pointed to the apparent benefits of reform, but rather than focusing on the eradication of drinking or even of saloons, they stressed the positive social consequences. In Birmingham, which enacted municipal prohibition in 1907, observers noted a decline in crime directly attributable to alcohol: aggregate arrests dropped by a third, drunkenness by 80 percent, vagrancy by 40 percent, wife beating by 70 percent, and burglary and grand larceny by a third. Overall, crime, according to the prohibitionists' reading of the data, declined by perhaps as much as half.[34]

But as the *Richmond Virginian* observed, the main social benefit of prohibition was an increased degree of public order and stability. Workers' efficiency grew dramatically; manufacturers noted increased productivity. Workers' earnings, previously lost at the saloon, now went toward savings banks, homes, food, consumer goods, and, most important, their families. Women could now walk on Birmingham streets without fear for their safety or of hearing offensive language or promiscuous profanity. Perhaps the most vivid change was the transformation of public holidays, particularly the Fourth of July, the observance of which had long been an occasion for public disorder but now was a tribute to public order. "In the entire crowds and during the whole day," read one account, "no one could remember to have seen more than two or three men under the influence of liquor, and not a single man in a State of beastly intoxication."[35]

In other southern cities, reformers claimed similar results. Religious and social workers were convinced, according to one account, of the beneficial social consequences resulting from the banishment of the saloon; prohibition had reduced drunkenness, crime, and poverty. In Atlanta, reformers cited declines in drunkenness and disorder after the onset of statewide prohibition in 1908. On Decatur Street, once that city's center of saloons, business life was "being redeemed." A bank had been constructed in place of one of the saloons; in another building, "men who once crowded around the bar to get whisky" now massed around the counter to buy groceries. White and black "loafers" were returning to work, and labor was more plentiful. Throughout the city "a moral tone undreamed of before" prevailed; even the "rumheads" were realizing that prohibition was a good thing.[36]

To many, social stability seemed the chief benefit of prohibition. In 1908 a general review of the impact of prohibition in the South found substantially reduced crime in dry as compared with wet counties and the "increased steadiness" of black labor in states that adopted statewide prohibition. In some small towns that adopted municipal prohibition, such as the North Carolina Piedmont town of Shelby, a local leader and future governor and senator, Clyde R. Hoey, wrote in 1903, reform had brought a change "evidenced in the morals of the people . . . so clearly apparent that no one at all conversant with the conditions here would attempt to argue that closing up the saloons has not wrought mightily for good here." Like other communities, according to Hoey, Shelby enjoyed a greater degree of public order and stability in reduced crime, "the undisturbed serenity of every public gathering," and an increasing number of sober men. Liquor, he believed, was "doomed in North Carolina."[37]

Prohibitionists pursued the alteration of social policy with relentless energy. From local option to national prohibition in 1919, reformers gradually evolved a new definition of the relationship between individual southerners and their government. Intervening in the name of community welfare, prohibitionists pioneered a reconceptualization of governance in which the connections between the regulation of alcohol and the regulation of other aspects of social life became increasingly apparent. In public education, the *Richmond Virginian* pointed out, compulsory schooling legislation had been enacted as a "State-wide Prohibition of the Vice of Ignorance." In public health, legislatures had passed new statutes that permitted the "State-wide Prohibition of the spread of virulent and deadly diseases." If the people had the right, in the name of community welfare, to prohibit "physical and intellectual diseases," then they should also have the power to regulate and abolish the liquor traffic, which shaped the "physical, the intellectual, and the moral life of the State."[38]

Prohibitionists became the earliest and most vigorous advocates of state intervention and a redefined purpose of governance. Since the 1880s, they had opposed the high license system and had called for the severing of any connections with the liquor traffic. Reformers opposed a union of saloon and state as much as they had, several generations before, opposed a union of church and state. The licensing system, a Baptist claimed in 1908, had provided saloons a legal right to "corrupt, debauch, and kill" with the "sanction and protection of the Commonwealth." "Nearly as much evil" existed in the "union of the State with the saloon as there was in [the] connection of church and state."[39]

Most prohibitionists went much further. As "citizens of the Kingdom of Heaven," Christians were compelled to work for social progress, the general secretary of the Virginia Anti-Saloon League told an audience in 1910. Especially in matters pertaining to "the moral welfare of our country," Christians were obliged to belong to a "holy alliance for a destructive and never relenting warfare against wickedness" in all aspects of life. Their consciences compelled moral reformers to "denounce evil and . . . to destroy it." In this instance, the "greatest public enemy of the Church of God" was the "organized traffic in intoxicating liquors." Government, to effect a new moral policy, would not only have to end all forms of compromise with the corruption of the liquor traffic, according to an Atlanta Baptist, but it would also have to "minister positively to the public morality."[40]

In pursuing this radical new departure in public policy, prohibitionists were breaking new ground in several respects. Their organizational methods, ideological appeal, and experiments with public policy provided a model of a reform crusade that other social reformers eagerly adopted. Their ultimate message—a fusion of social betterment and social purification—also gave hope to advocates of other varieties of moral reform. Prohibitionists, with their startling successes, began to break down the traditional wall that regarded civil and moral affairs as, in the words of a Florida Baptist, "totally different spheres." Did it make sense, he asked, to "eschew the moral side of man's nature wholly when we come to make up our minds regarding any great question for the state's betterment?"[41]

◆ ◆ ◆

MORAL REFORM AND SOCIAL PURITY

About the same time that southern prohibitionists achieved their legislative successes, moral reformers organized a powerful social purity crusade. Social purity reformers sought conservative objectives: to replenish and revive the traditional order, as they understood it, among parents and children as well as husbands and wives and, at the same time, to assert Protestant cultural domination. They were suspicious of cities, although most of them lived in them. They were also suspicious of European immigrants and foreigners—a "tide of aliens," as a Tennessee moral reformer once wrote, that was "ceaselessly rolling upon us." Predictably, moral reformers exhibited, like the Protestant culture at large, a strong strain of anti-Catholicism. Like prohibitionists, they believed that only a crusade, rooted in the evangelical culture of the South, would change public opinion.[42]

Moral reformers lived in a world of panoramic social change and, by their lights, decline. They saw a rapid breakdown of family values, traditional sexual roles and sexuality, and the institutions and values that had upheld them. But in contrast to late nineteenth-century moral reformers, who viewed this breakdown in terms of individual sin and responsibility, Progressive Era reformers discerned environmental sources. The *Alabama Christian Advocate* in May 1902 observed several disturbing social trends, including the tendency of couples to put off or avoid marriage entirely for reasons of comfort and congeniality. Similarly, the declining size of families, according to this assessment, was "an evil tendency" that violated divine law and bordered "closely on murder." The Christian family itself was threatened, according to a Virginia Methodist, and whatever eroded its stability was "a menace to civilization."[43]

Reformers' portrayal of the declining family often appeared in sociological terms that laid responsibility outside the individual. Denominational news-papers criticized the overabundance of wealth and its destructive impact on traditional values. A chief manifestation of materialism was evident in the decline of business ethics and the spate of speculation during the Progressive Era. The United States had become a "nation of gamblers"; a craze of busi-ness speculation had possessed and consumed men and had taken them and their society toward an "awful precipice." A passion for Mammon, claimed a group of moral reformers, was a "monster evil" that had become "the ruling passion and supreme aim and ambition of men."[44]

Materialism accentuated the erosion of the social order and family struc-ture, according to a Floridian, in two ways. First, it discouraged marriage because young men were now conditioned to believe that they needed "some thousands in the bank, with prospects of other thousands" in order to marry. Young women, bred to "extravagance in dress and hatred of household work," possessed similar expectations that reinforced the tendency to marry later. Second, materialism created conditions that loosened marital bonds and en-couraged divorce. "In one way or another," said one commentator, most divorces arose out of a "love of display and luxury," financial failure, and resulting immoral behavior.[45]

Although materialism also had baneful consequences for child rearing, moral reformers were of two minds in their response. Most urged parents to create a more moral home environment and exert greater restraint over chil-dren by excluding immoral and "improper associations" that could substitute a peer environment for the home environment. The "ruin of many girls" was caused by parents who were indifferent about their children and the "selection of their friends and companions" and who allowed them to "promenade the streets dressed in clothes immodest to the verge of indecency." At the same time, moral reformers frequently advised parents, as part of a purer home en-vironment, to pay greater attention to sexuality. Frankness and candor about sexuality were an essential part of upbringing, said an evangelical minister. Parents, rather than conveying an attitude of "prudery" to children, should stress the sacredness of the human body; lacking the proper instruction, chil-dren would learn about it through the devil. Through "foolish prudery," ignorance about vital questions of the physical and moral life had encouraged rather than discouraged the spread of vice. Parents were obligated to provide advice and instruction as a "most sacred duty." To this reformer, without parental instruction in sexuality, children might acquire a distorted knowl-edge from "the vilest of men and women" and the "vilest of books." This "distorted knowledge" could, in turn, cause moral ruin.[46]

The most threatening evidence of social decline was the rising incidence of divorce. It was widely denounced. The home was society's "greatest institution" and should be "protected at whatever cost," wrote a reformer; the "divorce monster" was the "arch enemy of society." To a southern Baptist, divorce was "the most gigantic evil," excepting only the liquor traffic, of the modern age; he urged Christians to awaken to "righteousness and put both these curses from them." The sources of what reformers called the "divorce evil" were at least partly found in the erosion of traditional attitudes and values. Flirtation, said a Virginian, frequently led to divorce. If men or women were flirts before marriage they likely would remain so after it. Were there not "as many married flirts as single ones"? Increasingly, Americans were losing their regard for the institution of marriage; divorce, for many, permitted a form of "trial" marriage that enjoyed the aid and connivance of the law and the courts. Divorce was a "virus of contempt for the marriage relation."[47]

Also troubling was the widespread tolerance of divorce. In popular literature, according to a Floridian, novelists claiming "the loftiest moral sensibilities" depicted separation and remarriage upon the slightest incompatibility of temperament. In fiction and the theater, lifelong marriage was ridiculed; women heroines declared that if they saw a man whom "they loved better than their husband they would not hesitate to follow him." What the *Richmond Virginian* called "multiple marriages"—or divorce and remarriage—exerted a baneful influence in the "public eye . . . against the continuity of marriage."[48]

Southern moral reformers had been issuing jeremiads against divorce since the 1880s, but what made their approach so distinctive during the Progressive Era was their reliance on public policy solutions. The loosening of divorce laws was a main source of the problem, reformers believed. "Easy divorce" was the "scandal of our nation," declared James Cannon, Jr.; changes in the law legitimated "legalized adultery." It was up to the law to safeguard, not undermine, marriage, wrote the *Richmond Virginian*; matrimony as an institution should be preserved despite the "personal difficulties" of those spouses "here and there" who made "unhappy alliances." The problem of divorce, the same newspaper later concluded, necessitated "plain speech from . . . moral leaders" and demanded a solution through legislation. The purity of the home and marriage demanded, according to southern moral reformers, different attitudes toward sexuality. Like reformers nationwide, they favored a single standard of sexuality. For some, this meant that women should be held as responsible for vice and impurity as men. The *Richmond Virginian* cited the case of a woman in Bristol, Virginia, who had deserted her husband and ten-month-old child for a man with a wife and several children.

Under the "unwritten law" of honor, the cuckolded husband shot and killed the adulterous man. The newspaper questioned the justice of the result: one man was dead and another "disgraced," while the woman escaped any form of punishment.[49]

For most reformers, however, the most important thing was to eliminate the double standard. What a Richmond Methodist called "one code of ethics for the girl and another for the boy" encouraged an environment of sexual impurity. In the home environment, parents tolerated the "boy of impure lips and life," while they ostracized "the girls of no worse words and life." Critics of the double standard focused primarily on prostitution and the impurity it brought to the institution of marriage. Only by mutual purity before and after marriage, wrote a Presbyterian reformer, could physical health and social happiness be ensured. To this reformer, venereal disease was tied both to the double standard and to the "social evil" of prostitution. The brothel had become a center for the spread of disease; young males everywhere flocked to them. Having visited prostitutes and contracted venereal disease, the husband became the "connecting link between the house of prostitution . . . and the house of happiness called home." Both a moral and a scientific necessity existed for sexual purity and a single standard.[50]

Over time, moral reformers viewed prostitution and sexual immorality with increasing sociological sophistication. Progressive Era reformers freed women from full responsibility and looked instead to male involvement and to the environmental causes and consequences of sexual impurity. A Richmond reformer pointed out that brothels existed only because of male patronage; he described them as evil resorts that gave "a rotten heart to the surface of virtue." Rather than entering prostitution as a matter of personal choice, "fallen" women were portrayed as victims. Poverty and ignorance were primary causes of the "social evil," wrote one reformer, while parental indifference also figured prominently. In large cities, wrote one woman, girls were dragged into the life of the prostitute by low wages and other social conditions.[51]

Moral reformers also perceived a decline in the public standards of morality. The authority of evangelical churches was clearly eroding, complained an Alabama Methodist in 1901. Women attended card parties and neglected their children for the punch bowl. Church members frequented the theater without a "blush of shame." Some Christians engaged in dance and had the audacity to discuss it before a minister. Others committed fraud in business, while still others exhibited a growing tendency to seek entertainment rather than edification at the house of worship. All these developments betrayed "an insidious skepticism in the minds of multitudes" that doubted basic truths and undermined the traditional cultural order. In the "revolt from Puritanism,"

Cannon wrote in 1905, the pendulum had swung too far in the other extreme. Women and men were immodest; public immorality was on the increase. These developments were at least partly the product of a degenerating public atmosphere, most particularly the "indecent pictures" from theaters and films that appeared at every turn and that were a constant temptation, especially to the young, to think and do immoral things. Cannon advocated creating an environment of "modesty and decency" and eradicating those things that "defileth or worketh abomination."[52]

Social purity reformers regarded Sabbath desecration as evidence of this erosion of authority and values. When President William Howard Taft gave an address in 1909 on Sunday morning's "preaching hour," he was roundly criticized for violating the accepted notion that the United States was a Christian nation. Sabbath desecration also suggested secularization and the erosion of church authority, as popular summer resorts were crowded with Sabbath pleasure seekers, open shops abounded in many cities, and the noise of the peddler was heard in the streets. The possibility seemed real that America was on the verge of becoming a "Sabbathless land with all its dire consequences."[53]

The violation of the Sabbath offended other reformers for more than just biblical reasons, for the sanctity of the Sabbath embodied their view of social purity and moral reform. Violations of the Sabbath created public demoralization in a "spirit of lawlessness," wrote a Tennessee Baptist in 1903. Other reformers portrayed the Sabbath as involving something different from, in the words of Cannon, "the strictures of the Puritanical Sabbath." Few supported "all the rigorous exactions of the old New England Sunday." Rather, reformers described the Sabbath with familiar rhetoric: according to one, it was a social convention that permitted an opportunity for rest and recuperation from the daily grind of life. According to this view, the Sabbath was a "law of social hygiene for the promotion of the health of each man who forms a part of the social organism." This Sabbatarian, and others in the early twentieth century, borrowed social scientific language. Primitive societies, he argued, needed the Sabbath less than urbanized and industrial communities. In modern society, a "conventional" Sabbath was absolutely indispensable, for in a highly organized society one had to get his natural rights in convention with others or not at all. Moreover, the greater the degree of social complexity and social interdependence in the social organism, the greater its need for the convention of the Sabbath.[54]

The traditional Sabbath faced competition from commercialized amusements that destroyed "its peculiar sanctity" and encouraged "every other form of violation." Sunday was "fast becoming a holiday" and was no longer recognized as "a holy day as it was originally designed to be." In cities and small towns, beer gardens, theaters, saloons, and other public amusements remained open on Sunday; in many cases, they were more largely patronized on this day by a certain class of persons than at any other time. The problem was most pressing in the case of baseball, which, during the Progressive Era, began to introduce Sunday games. It evoked strong opposition. One newspaper denounced the playing of a World Series game on Sunday in 1910 as an "open desecration of the Sabbath," in which the day of rest was transformed into "an orgy of sport and gambling." It was a serious affront to the followers of a Christian nation.[55]

Sabbatarianism aside, reformers did not like the new urban popular culture. Southern denominational newspapers maintained a steady drumbeat of criticism against baseball, which they regarded as a form of organized vice. A Columbia, Tennessee, Baptist denounced the game as encouraging the "criminal consumption of time" in idleness. "How could we get further from heaven and God," he asked, "than amid the roaring shouts of a Base Ball contest?" Other public amusements, such as carnivals, prizefights, theater, and dancing, were criticized for similar reasons. Public performances brought a loss of control and order. Dancing was described as "purely physical," appealing to "the animal nature," and an "open door to the house of ill-fame." Too often theater performances encouraged a similar degree of cultural and sexual disorder. One Richmonder attacked Sarah Bernhardt's staging of *Camille* in 1911 as "vulgar, obscene, and immoral" and "unhampered by moral scruples." Similarly, a Floridian opposed the arrival of a carnival in town because of the "drunkenness and rowdyism and all sorts of moral filth" that accompanied its visit.[56]

Moral reformers also needed an apparatus to spread their message and to organize and marshal public opinion. For them, the crusade model adopted by prohibitionists seemed perfectly appropriate. It could demonstrate the existence of an evil, such as prostitution, in which public policy colluded and thereby encouraged; a moral crusade could also mobilize public opinion in new directions. Yet these reformers realized that a revival and shaping of public opinion alone would not change moral conditions. That change would come only through the long-term alteration of public policy.

◆ ◆ ◆

VICE CRUSADING AND A NEW MORAL POLICY

Moral change, reformers maintained, would come through a popular mobilization. Only through an infusion "into our politics of righteousness," claimed a Florida Baptist, could the "precious heritage of our free and Christian institutions" be restored. Reform depended on the arousal of Christian opinion, a strong moral sentiment, and the Christian conscience of Protestants. This sentiment would impel "pure and good men" into public office, while it would support journalists who wielded the pen in behalf of good morals. To lead this mobilization, declared the *Alabama Baptist*, reformers needed an outspoken and militant ministry. The role of an evangelical ministry was to denounce the great evils of the day, wrote a North Carolinian, "not as partisans or politicians but as watchmen on the walls of Zion." Evangelical Protestants should not be confined to the institutional church "as cloister and sanctuary for the small company of the sanctified," argued the *Richmond Virginian*. Both religion and government could not avoid the "moral test." [57]

Lacking national, regional, or even statewide coordination, moral reform developed spasmodically in the towns and cities of the pre–world war South. Like other reform groups, it was nonpartisan. "Duty to God," explained an Alabama reformer, came "before duty to party." The primary considerations were "Christian citizenship," "civic righteousness," and the "highest standards of duty." [58] "Civic righteousness" usually meant a crusade to restore public morality. When the Virginia legislature in 1910 met to consider liberalizing its divorce law, moral reformers converged against it. In "an array of moral forces as has rarely been seen in this city of notable meetings," moral reformers condemned what they feared were further threats against home and family. Beginning as a "demonstration against the divorce evil," this marked the onset of what one observer called a "crusade for purity." [59] In many cities, evangelicals pressured municipal governments either to pass legislation limiting public amusements and requiring Sunday closing or, more commonly, to enforce existing statutes more vigorously. In 1905 Birmingham's Pastor's Union held meetings and circulated literature to restrict gambling and liquor selling at the state fair. In the same year, similar campaigns occurred in Selma and Montgomery. In Salisbury, North Carolina, the local ministerial association in 1914 pressured the city government into restricting the performances of movies and vaudeville shows. In a municipal campaign typical of many others across the urban South, Richmond evangelicals in 1910 pressured city government to enact "protective legislation" to restrict the young from attending movie theaters; in the next year, they sought the banning of theaters near churches. Meanwhile, Richmond reformers urged the city government to enact stricter vagrancy ordinances to rid the streets of young toughs of both races. For similar reasons, other localities such as Midland City, Alabama, enacted a new curfew law that applied exclusively to adolescents. [60]

Other reformers successfully lobbied municipal governments to enforce Sunday closing requirements. In 1911 Richmond Baptists launched a campaign to enforce the existing law against sidewalk merchants who maintained fruit, soda water, and candy stands on Sunday.[61] In Tampa, Florida, ministers persuaded local officials to prosecute two aviators who performed in a Sunday air show. While a Lexington, Kentucky, reformer called for the enforcement of that city's Sunday closing laws and the establishment of both "civic righteousness" and a "civic conscience," in Alabama another reformer demanded that the law be enforced. "We do not ask for enactment of new laws," he wrote, "but simply for the enforcement of laws already existing." These local crusades to restrict or end public amusements spilled over into even more ambitious crusades to abolish prostitution. Unlike the Sunday closing campaigns, these enjoyed wider support and participation among social workers and humanitarians. In part, the appeal of this crusade lay in its sociological analysis: prostitution, reformers argued, had become an organized "white slave trade" that coerced, either openly or subtly, the women "inmates" into a life of disrepute.[62]

Among the strongest supporters of antivice crusading were suffragists. The Norfolk, Virginia, Equal Suffrage League registered its objection in January 1913 to the practice of hiring girl ushers in local movie houses because of the "evil effects of late hours for young girls' work." The league sent a delegation to the theater manager, who promised to change his policy. But suffragists were most concerned about eradicating prostitution. Among Birmingham suffragists, ending the red-light district, according to one observer in 1913, was the uppermost issue. The Columbia, South Carolina, suffrage league, after hearing the speech of an antivice crusader, resolved to gain the franchise chiefly in order to express "the will of woman." That will, it declared, included the passage and enforcement of strict antiprostitution legislation. In Lexington, Kentucky, a suffragist began an antivice crusade after learning that black children had to walk past the red-light district to get to school. Under her leadership, suffragists formed a coalition with local ministers to launch the crusade.[63]

Antiprostitution campaigns attracted suffragists for obvious reasons. Eradicating the "social evil" had become part of women's responsibility as "mothers of the race" to "guard, to love and to save," according to the Virginia novelist and feminist Mary Johnston. Antiprostitution campaigns were part of a suffrage agenda that included legally empowering women within marriage, raising the age of consent, and limiting the use of child labor. Most men had ignored these issues, wrote a suffragist. Women enjoyed no protection under male government, which had ignored its "moral responsibility." Vice, according to many suffragists, was the most prominent example of the insufficient protection that the law and the political system extended to women.

Men claimed, under the system of chivalry, that women had adequate protection, yet the law sentenced a jewel thief more harshly than a pimp. Were such laws as these protective?[64]

Suffragists frequently reiterated the theme that organized vice existed because of gender inequalities. When men gave up the notion that women were created principally for their pleasure and need, when women outgrew this idea, when men and women received equal pay and achieved legal equality— only then, concluded one suffragist, would the question of the social evil be solved. Prostitutes were victims of the system. According to Kentucky suffragist Madeline McDowell Breckinridge, it punished women and rewarded men, even though it was even more a man's problem than a woman's problem. Before prostitution could end, a new sense of social responsibility had to develop among men. Most prostitutes, wrote Breckinridge, were not old or middle-aged but "young women, like our own young people, with the eager hopes and desires of youth." A sinister system, "commercialized and organized vice," had ensnared them. Breckinridge endorsed a "war on the red light district, as upon the whole evil of prostitution" that would, no matter "how many times we may stumble and fall," achieve "its ultimate necessary consummation of victory." But, believing that a relationship existed between economic conditions and prostitution, Breckinridge and many other suffragists favored measures such as minimum-wage laws and welfare and industrial commissions to change conditions at home and eliminate prostitution.[65]

Other reformers were also attracted to the antivice crusade. In Goldsboro, Wilson, and Rocky Mount, North Carolina, school and child labor reformer Charles Lee Coon led efforts to compel local authorities to enforce antivice statutes in 1913 and 1914.[66] In 1913 the Austin, Texas, WCTU began an antivice campaign to enforce antiprostitution statutes and to establish a reformatory for former prostitutes. In Asheville, North Carolina, Robert F. Campbell caused a local furor in early 1912, when he called for the "immediate repression and ultimate annihilation" of the city's segregated red-light district. Campbell's objection and logic were, for the early twentieth-century South, unusual. He criticized the segregation of vice in districts that were almost always located within the black community. If brothels were a "necessary evil" for white people, was it therefore "not fair that the residence districts of the white people, near their own homes and churches, should endure this 'necessary evil,' instead of thrusting it off upon the poor black people"? This was akin to directing sewer pipes of the city toward the black community and permitting "them to flood the negro district with their filth and contagion." If Asheville whites were to "sow the wind," he asked, was it "strange that we should reap the whirlwind"?[67]

The response to Campbell's letter suggested the broad range of approval for an antiprostitution campaign in Asheville and elsewhere and the way it intersected with other social reforms. Within the black community, significant support emerged. The *Star of Zion*, a leading North Carolina black publication, agreeing with Campbell, maintained that red-light districts were located near black neighborhoods in nearly every southern city and town. The solution, it believed, lay in demanding for blacks the selfsame protection in public morality that was guaranteed white families. "Let Negroes," it declared, "protest and organize to oppose the location of 'red light' districts in their very doors." Another observer, a white, drew a different conclusion. Race improvement depended on those southern whites who would resolve that blacks should have "an equal chance with themselves to bring up their children in decent surroundings."[68]

The vice crusades, while enjoying wide participation, were led by a solid Protestant core. Although prohibitionists unsuccessfully attempted to shed their denominational image, moral reformers were militantly Protestant. When the suggestion was made that a citywide antivice crusade in Atlanta include Jews as well as Christians, the Protestant-dominated leadership decided against it. According to John J. Eagan, a Presbyterian reformer, the Atlanta leadership rejected the attempt to make the crusade into a "Sociological fight" that would include "Jew and Unbeliever." The reformers instead decided that the crusade could only "be won in the name of Jesus Christ." While non-Christian supporters were welcome, the leaders had to "follow the banner of Christ."[69]

The first effective antiprostitution crusades, while usually attracting wider support, were thus led by clergymen. In 1905 the Reverend J. C. Massee, pastor of Raleigh's Tabernacle Baptist Church, led a campaign in that city to end prostitution. In a sermon that gained wide publicity, he called for action to rid the city of its vice centers. Sporadic campaigns against red-light districts sprang into existence elsewhere about the same time, but a flood of municipal campaigns followed national exposure of the "white slave" traffic after 1910 and the work of successful vice commissions in Chicago and New York City.[70]

In Richmond, a well-coordinated antiprostitution crusade began in the autumn of 1912 and enjoyed the virtually complete support of the city's churches. For several Sundays in September, churches across the city heard sermons denouncing the segregated and officially tolerated red-light district. Eventually, these vice reformers were successful at least partly because they employed the techniques of exposure, publicity, and political pressure pioneered by the prohibitionists. With irresistible logic they insisted that the laws be enforced. Righteousness could not be legislated, declared one minister, but the very existence of the law made a statement about the condition of the public conscience. The campaign culminated with the establishment in 1914 of a city vice commission, which made its report in February 1915. The commission included six ministers, the secretary of the state welfare board, the president of the city chamber of commerce, a social worker, and representatives from both the Jewish and Roman Catholic communities. The commission's report constituted a sweeping and extensively documented indictment that sought to convert the moral crusade into a long-term, concrete policy. The report blamed the moral environment that made prostitution possible; dance halls, motion pictures, automobiles, and soda fountains had all helped to create a declining moral atmosphere. While complimenting local theaters on their physical condition, it claimed that many films and stage performances paved the way to the red-light district through their "suggestive performances." The commission further asserted that economic factors had created a ready supply of prostitutes; poverty had had a decided bearing on the subject. The cycle of depravity continued inside brothels, where taboos against interracial contact and homosexuality were violated.[71]

The white slave trade, according to the Richmond vice commissioners, had permeated municipal government as a result of the city's decision in 1905 to establish a segregated red-light district. Yet this system of official regulation had led to greater abuse and even growth of the system. The commissioners discovered, for example, that 120 brothels existed outside of the district, while the number of prostitutes operating out of it were more than double those working inside of it. Regulation had been an abysmal failure; streetwalkers functioned in a revolving door in which, in order to pay off their fines, they pushed their business more briskly. The fining system amounted to a licensing tax. Finally, the report implicated Richmond's police commissioners, declaring that they enjoyed a profitable relationship with organized prostitution.[72]

The implications of the Richmond Vice Commission—and of vice commissions in other major southern cities—were extensive. The commission's report of February 1915 included several significant recommendations. It said that the existing laws prohibiting prostitution should be immediately enforced; that police administration should be centralized under a more powerful police chief; that a separate department, a Bureau of Public Morals, should be given responsibility over "illicit sexual immorality"; that Richmonders should be encouraged to participate in a continuing antivice program; and that the city should provide rehabilitation for arrested and reformed prostitutes.[73]

Subsequently, most of the commission recommendations became a permanent part of the city's antivice policy. The city council investigated for six months and discovered extensive corruption within the board of police commissioners. Within days of the vice commission's report in February, the mayor ordered the police to close all brothels in the city. After the mayor's announcement, the usually brightly lighted houses in Richmond's segregated district had become a "dimly lit section." It was, according to this exuberant reporter, deserted with a "dead look."[74]

Following Richmond's lead, other Virginia towns and cities in the spring of 1915 announced their determination to enforce the law. A few other cities, such as Atlanta in 1913, had organized similar vice commissions with similarly spectacular results. Still other communities enacted new legislation making enforcement against prostitution more effective. In Guilford County, North Carolina, which contained the growing urban center of Greensboro, the legislature passed a public morals act that made it difficult to rent property for immoral purposes.[75] Many more communities avoided extensive publicity and quietly began more vigorous enforcement of existing statutes.

The successful crusade to achieve greater public control over morality produced significant results. Both the prohibition and antivice crusades mobilized public opinion around reform to an unprecedented extent in the South. The purification advocated by moral reform became a metaphor for a larger social redemption extending to a variety of areas of everyday life; its urgency and fervor, its absolutism and certainty, could be translated into a broader sociological analysis of the South's inadequacies. The crusade, with its techniques of exposure of social problems, its ability to manipulate public opinion around a single issue, and its increasing skill and sophistication in applying pressure on the political system, was also adopted by allied reformers in woman suffrage, child labor, education, and health.

SCHOOLS AND HEALTH

———————————— ◆ ————————————

Although the crusade model of popular mobilization was a familiar fixture in Victorian southern culture, moral reformers had used it to advance new notions about social conditions, to manipulate and mobilize public opinion, and to impress a radically different conception of governance upon it. By the outbreak of World War I, the crusade had become a successful vehicle for activists with different agenda who shared a belief in the need for fundamental changes in the nature and substance of public policy. Among the most vigorous advocates of this approach were reformers in education and health who pioneered, like moral reformers, a new activism to resolve social problems. Although themselves a diverse group, "social efficiency" reformers shared the conviction that southerners, especially rural southerners, were backward, isolated, and provincial. Exposure to outside cosmopolitan influences, they believed, would foster regional progress. The key ingredients of such progress would be regional modernization through the extension of public education and public health.

Social efficiency reformers were far from a monolith. Among them were professional administrators who had long wanted change; they were joined by a wider circle of supporters interested in a new approach to social policy. Yet there was a significant overlap of interests, social characteristics, and organizational methods among educational and health reformers. Both groups also confronted an essentially similar problem: a vast, dispersed rural population that had long defied outside attempts to control it. Both eventually adopted similar methods to overcome these obstacles through centralized, coercive administration and the development of a more extended state apparatus. Both were also bound together by the cord of northern philanthropy, especially Rockefeller philanthropy, that concentrated resources in southern health and education.

◆ ◆ ◆

ORIGINS OF THE SOUTHERN SCHOOL CRUSADE

About the same time that the Anti-Saloon League was organizing the South, a now-legendary crusade for schools began in the region. Its organizers were diverse: professional school administrators who had long advocated change but had remained in the political wilderness, middle-class women, ministers, journalists, and publicists. They all saw schools as vehicles for a regional trans-formation. What brought these varied social types together was the Southern Education Board, first organized in 1901, and the state-based campaigns for educational improvement that it orchestrated across the South during the next decade.[1]

Historians of southern school reform have long questioned the SEB's motives. Recently, scholars have concluded that reformers sought schools as a means of manipulation and that a rhetoric of uplift masked real motives of social and racial control.[2] There is some truth in these assertions. Reform-ers, deeply suspicious of what they believed was the excessive democracy of the late nineteenth century, feared both lower-class white and black disorder while they endorsed disfranchisement and segregation as necessary correctives for a troubled society.[3] For social efficiency reformers, as for others, highly subjective cultural assumptions and a deeply rooted paternalism determined their approach to social problems. Nonetheless, this explanation, relying solely on motives of class and racial domination, is ultimately reduction-ist. A mixture of emotions and feelings guided reformers: sometimes they came together in a coherent, explainable whole, sometimes they did not. Yet understanding the motivations of reformers requires accepting the assumption undergirding the work of recent historians of ideology and rhetoric: instead of masking darker motives, reformers often meant what they said.[4]

For Rockefeller official Wallace Buttrick, for example, the main reason for reform was not crude social control. Rather, as he explained to a group of North Carolina county superintendents in November 1902, he was inspired by an exaltation of childhood. Recalling a discouraging New York City educational rally where opponents seemed to outnumber supporters of reform, he suddenly heard the voices of singing children. There then emerged "a little child followed by children . . . until the stage was filled with the little forms and the halls with the music of their voices." Listening to their singing, he was overcome with "hope and enthusiasm," for before his "enraptured eyes" was a vision of a vast army of children, present and future, who cried out for school reform. "Let us strike hands," he declared, "for this great work of saving the children who are dearer to us than life itself."[5]

Just as moral reformers genuinely believed in the decline of the social fabric and in an impending crisis, so also did school reformers perceive a crisis of culture. That crisis, they believed, was undermining the future development of the South and the solution of its most urgent problems—reintegrating the South into the national mainstream and resolving the region's chronic racial conflict and instability. While some of them saw schools as vehicles for social control, many more expressed and were probably guided by a national ideology of child saving and a new fascination with childhood that swept through educational circles after 1890. Southern children, an Alabama schoolman wrote to Edgar Gardner Murphy, were subjected to "cruel discomforts," but a brighter day lay ahead in which the children of the future would "rise up and call you blessed." The day had now come, maintained Tennessee educator Philander Priestly Claxton, when schools would "educate the children of all the people for all the walks of life." To Claxton, school reform addressed "that great prayer that Jesus prayed for His disciples": that children work with less toil than did their parents. The coming generations, because of modernized schools, faced a different and more hopeful future. The man who turned the clod, he wrote, could "himself be more than a clod"; the man who pounded the anvil could develop "a heart more sympathetic than his own iron." Rural parents, added Amanda Stoltzfus, a Texas school reformer, in their strenuous efforts to make a living had long since forgotten how it felt to want to play. Childhood was a special time; play was "much needed relaxation from heavy work, and a means of regaining fresh vigor for the next task." To a Georgia woman reformer, school reform meant a realization of the home and the priceless value of childhood. Through the quickening of public opinion, parents would turn their hearts toward their children.[6]

To reformers, the problems of southern education were those of rural education. Young southerners offered a clear opportunity; they composed, wrote Stoltzfus, *"the material of which leadership is made."* This leadership, for the South, was sadly absent in rural communities. To reformers, southern rural schools had failed on most counts. With shortened school terms and transient pupils and teachers, asked a Georgian, how could rural schools have much effect? Instead, they existed only as a home to a "grasshopper plague of people and teachers swarming in one year and swarming out the next." The physical condition of rural schools exacerbated the problem. "A community's love for its children and faith in them" could be measured by the schools it provided, added North Carolina reformer James Y. Joyner in 1907. Ideally, attractive physical facilities should inspire "every other district and . . . every passer-by." The reality was quite different. There was no better measure of popular attitudes toward education, wrote a woman reformer in Kentucky in 1906, than the appearance of their schools. In that state, schoolhouses told "a piti-ful and a shameful story"; farmers provided better barns for their stock than they did schools for their children. The shaping of character and the building of future citizens was carried on in buildings that were "tumble-down and dilapidated."[7]

Reformers often registered their shock at the physical conditions of rural schools. Urban women, who provided the backbone of the educational cru-sade, mobilized on the issue of school facilities. Southern club women be-came involved in school politics around the turn of the century. In Kentucky, the state Federation of Women's Clubs began a traveling library program in 1896 and then, three years later, subsidized Katherine Pettit and Mary Stone's famous "tent settlement" school in Hindman County, in eastern Kentucky. But even these Kentucky women discovered that undereducation was not con-fined to their rather exotic conception of mountain whites. Indeed, they were shocked to discover that, in their own Bluegrass counties, illiteracy among whites was a widespread phenomenon. Club women found that ten Blue-grass counties counted only ninety-two fewer illiterates than the entire state of Maine and more than twice as many as in Massachusetts and Nebraska. Out of this realization, wrote one of Kentucky's leading women reformers, came a determined effort to participate in a general school campaign to improve school facilities that would "awaken the families of the neighborhood to a quickened interest in their public school."[8]

Just as the Anti-Saloon League provided models of strategy and coordi-nation for moral reform, so did outsiders help to coalesce southern school reform. The formation of the Southern Education Board in 1901 sealed an emerging intersectional alliance of southern reformers and northern philan-thropists. "Densely ignorant" about the South, most northerners regarded China as "nearer to them than North Carolina," according to one observer. He believed that the SEB might make some impression on "the ignorant edu-cated of the North." School reform might also serve as a mechanism for the healing of old sectional wounds. According to Joyner, the SEB and its parent organization, the Conference for Education in the South, helped to bind the regions together "in a stronger bond of patriotic love." Another northern observer noted the "inspiring and amazing spectacle" at these meetings of veterans of "the conquering armies of the North nobly pleading with the followers of Lee and Jackson" to help with educational reform.[9]

Under the SEB's direction, the strategy and organizational structure of the school crusade emerged. Like the ASL, the SEB was oriented toward results— concrete policy changes through the manipulation of public opinion and the application of pressure on the political system. The SEB addressed itself to the fears of southern white reformers by making significant concessions on racial issues. Northern members of the board who had once possessed feelings of egalitarianism either abandoned or suppressed them in intersectional company. Their temporary abandonment of black education mostly reflected the national racial climate, but it was also partly pure political realism. Southern reformers were well aware of the potential for backlash, and the newspaper campaign emanating from Baltimore's *Manufacturers' Record* in 1903 only confirmed their fears. The attack, which was endorsed by southern newspapers such as the *Charlotte Observer* and the *Charleston News and Courier*, charged that SEB members had dined with blacks; that William H. Baldwin, a prominent northern philanthropist and railroad developer, had once sided with an "impudent negro" over a white conductor; and that the SEB had proposed a gift to the white Catawba College in North Carolina on the condition that it become racially integrated. Southern supporters of the SEB carefully admonished their northern sponsors to take this sort of attack seriously and to act quickly to defuse it. Although the SEB in public campaigns scrupulously avoided black education, it endorsed white supremacy. It openly accepted segregation. As the SEB's executive secretary, Edgar Gardner Murphy, phrased it, the two races "must dwell apart," "must live apart," and "must be schooled apart." This was a closed question, he wrote, and no member of the SEB or its allies wanted "to open it."[10]

The educational alliance that united northern philanthropists and southern white reformers relied on a generation of intersectional contacts developed through black industrial schools and through the Peabody Education Fund, established by northerner George Peabody in 1867. To southern educators, the PEF was attractive primarily because it pursued limited objectives but also provided an alternative to the restrictions of post-Reconstruction school governance. When the PEF was considering ending its activities and dispersing its funds in 1896, North Carolina educator Charles Duncan McIver urged its general agent to maintain the fund's "present method of management." PEF philanthropy had succeeded, he wrote, because it had avoided local control and influence. It had supplied aid to those educators who believed in a broad and liberal system of public education but who faced local prejudices.[11]

The key figure in the PEF was its general agent, Jabez Lamar Monroe Curry, originally of Alabama, who simultaneously enjoyed the support of northern philanthropists and the confidence of southern whites. As an admirer told him, Curry possessed the unique ability to promote school improvement "without unduly antagonizing the southern people." Although he portrayed southern educational conditions "in harmony with northern views," he tempered these descriptions with a "rare discretion to the requirements of local situations." Curry combined opposites. He endorsed common schools and praised aristocratic private schools, he advocated the "regeneration of southern society" and avoided criticizing "the pre-existing conditions of the south," and he made a case for black education without "violently thrusting" it before southern whites.[12]

By the turn of the twentieth century, most northern philanthropists were interested in becoming what Wallace Buttrick described as "silent partners" of white educational uplift.[13] They acknowledged that the construction of a philanthropic empire in black education depended on changed white attitudes. With extensive economic contacts in the South, many philanthropists sought to stabilize southern class and race relations and to improve the investment climate. Yet philanthropists were also motivated by a missionary impulse to uplift humanity. John D. Rockefeller had long devoted a portion of his fortune to philanthropy; as that fortune grew larger in the 1880s and 1890s, he developed a systematic method of distributing philanthropy which his lieutenants, Frederick T. Gates and Wallace Buttrick, then managed. John, Jr., who gradually assumed direction of the Rockefeller philanthropies as a full-time enterprise, was also committed to using the fruits of his family fortunes for human betterment.

Similarly, the founding father of the SEB, Robert Curtis Ogden, who had made his fortune in the New York City department store business, expressed an ideology of evangelical humanitarianism. The "betterment of humanity" was "demanded by Divine authority," Ogden wrote, "through the living purpose clearly revealed in Holy Writ, providential guidance and human consciousness." Like other humanitarians, Ogden was child-oriented in his approach toward school reform. The "fusing power" behind social reform, he once declared, was the notion that "the great social duty of our age is the saving of society." But this salvation depended on saving the child. All progress began "with the little child"; the distance from "the kindergarten of to-day to the university of to-morrow" was "a very short step."[14]

Ogden and his counterparts in the Rockefeller establishment were very different men, with divergent styles and objectives. From its inception in 1902, it was obvious that the General Education Board, which became the main vehicle of Rockefeller involvement with southern education, was a distinct organization. Established by Gates and Buttrick, it operated with streamlined and centralized planning and direction. The GEB intervened in southern education through typical Rockefeller methods: a consistent, rationalized policy that tied the funding of grantees, whether private or public, to the spread of more "efficient" and "businesslike" methods of administration. When Gates butted heads with the railroad magnate and philanthropist William H. Baldwin, a formidable figure, over the powers of the board, there was little doubt about the outcome. Although "Mr. B." was tenacious in his position, Gates reported to John D. Rockefeller, "I was also tenacious in a pleasant way, and by reasoning and persuasion *we finally got our way on every point.*" Buttrick made a similar point early in the board's operation. Although he agreed with the SEB "for the most part," Buttrick told Curry soon after the GEB's creation, "there will doubtless be a very few instances where we shall 'agree to disagree.' "[15]

In contrast to the General Education Board, the Southern Education Board and the Conference for Education in the South were temporary organizations. They were loosely organized, and there was considerable crossover between the SEB and the GEB, which discreetly dispersed some of its funds through the former organization. But where the GEB sought to influence policy over the long term, the SEB sought to alter public opinion, and it was in this sense more an organization that sustained itself on a public crusade. The CES, explained Ogden, was a "purely voluntary association." Its treasury, along with that of the SEB, was "merely a vacancy, a figment of the imagination," and what meager disbursements it made—aside from GEB funding— depended on the generosity of SEB members, especially Ogden and the board's treasurer, southern-born investment banker George Foster Peabody. Both the SEB and the CES lacked a constitution and possessed what Ogden termed an "inorganic character"; their purposes were to provide a social environment of congeniality between reformers of both sections.[16]

Although loosely organized and financed on a shoestring, the SEB had the advantage of having a well-defined purpose: to launch a regional crusade to convert public opinion to better schools across the South. Between 1901 and about 1910, the SEB sponsored and encouraged state-based school crusades that, to their participants, yielded a startling reversal in public attitudes. The success of this crusade gave further evidence of the success of the reform crusade model, but it raised questions about the ability of reformers to translate evangelical rhetoric into concrete policy.

Beginning with the Southern Education Board's organization in 1901, a co-ordinated crusade focused on the improvement and modernization of south-ern schools. Much of this crusade frankly aimed to manipulate southern public opinion about schools. Reformers believed in democratic traditions, but they also thought that the political and social system could no longer function without a trained, educated citizenry. Though they were convinced that changes in schools, and southern society, would come from above, they freely acknowledged the need to persuade the public. The objective of the SEB campaign, wrote Edwin Anderson Alderman in 1907, was to help in that for-mation of southern public opinion that would be "vitalized and increased." [17]

Reformers believed in a democracy in which public opinion reacted to, rather than initiated, policy changes. As Joyner phrased it in 1908, pub-lic opinion needed to be both "informed" and "quickened"—imagery that strongly suggested manipulation—but he combined this phrasing with a re-affirmation of the power of democracy. Other reformers expressed this combi-nation of manipulation and democracy. In the Deep South, wrote Alderman in 1903, the school crusade sought to convert public opinion to the creation of a system of schools adequate for the needs of a free people. Only when public opinion had been aroused could another, "scientific" phase begin. Alderman, as did other reformers, stressed that the purpose of the crusade was a kind of staged manipulation. The "moulding [sic] of public opinion," he wrote, was a "slow business," but it was "splendid and renovating" when it occurred. Reformers needed to "hammer on" until the popular desire for improved schools became a "contagion with the people." [18]

The organizers of the SEB crusades, which by 1905 had spread to most of the former Confederate South,[19] realized that the manipulation of public opinion required a recognition of the social and political realities of the early twentieth-century South. SEB leaders and local organizers alike excluded any mention of black education in these crusades; in their Herrenvolk democracy, they encouraged the widening of black-white school disparities. In Robeson County, in eastern North Carolina, a crusader described a rural community as "hot" for reform if it could "leave the negro out." Although willing to in-crease local taxes—which was the purpose of most of the local crusades—it refused to "divide with the negro." If the county superintendent could "devise some plan for leaving the negro out," the community was eager to proceed. Seeking to cultivate community favor, the SEB leadership tolerated and some-times even encouraged a policy of exclusion. Charles D. McIver, who headed the SEB campaign in North Carolina, cautioned in 1905 against allowing a white woman to speak before a meeting of black women. There was "absolutely no necessity for a mixing of the races in the meetings." It would be "unfortunate," he warned, if the race question were raised at all.[20]

Educational crusaders, as outsiders, operated at a disadvantage, and rural southerners, black or white, often resisted their intrusion. A combination of localism and resistance to the higher property taxes necessary to finance school improvements sometimes frustrated reform. An Alabama official who wrote to Murphy in 1904 and 1905 describing the school crusade there warned that results in his state might worry SEB leaders. The crusade had evoked a hard fight, and reformers had been reasonably successful. But in at least several counties he was dubious about the outcome. In Lee County, voters turned down a tax increase on account of "pure 'cussedness' "; in Lee, as he explained it, things usually went the other way. In Lauderdale County, the vote went "decidedly" against the crusaders, while he expected another difficult battle in Autauga County. These countywide problems often reflected a combination of factors. An eastern North Carolina crusader wrote in 1903 that he was anxious about the prospects for reform; one community whose residents had "differed much in politics" was "now trying to unite in Education." Accordingly, he requested that the state campaign organization send a "strong, *discreet* man." Across the state, in northwestern North Carolina, another glum supporter of the crusade noted that his community had "many kinds of elements."[21]

To accommodate local opinion and yet maintain the integrity of their campaign, then, reformers adapted their program and especially the style of their appeal to the scattered rural communities of the early twentieth-century South. The SEB, as a regional organization, had little direct contact with local campaigns, which were operated by the state committees and the local alliances they formed. School crusaders at the county or community level deliberately lacked an official connection with the SEB. Rather, the board preferred, as Alderman wrote, to encourage a "deep-seated purpose on the part of the people out of their own thinking to establish their school solidly and enduringly." By accommodating to local opinion, reformers hoped to develop public support for better schools and to translate that support into a groundswell for fundamental changes. Although in early forays crusaders attempted to rally whole counties, they eventually focused on single communities. At the local level, as a first step they usually sought higher taxes. Early in the North Carolina campaign, for example, McIver compiled a list of 500 towns and villages of more than 500 persons that paid no local school tax and targeted these communities for educational rallies. In North Carolina and elsewhere, reformers usually had to settle for something less than comprehensive, countywide tax increases. In the wake of the school crusade in North Carolina, for example, the number of special tax districts jumped from only 30 in 1902 to 704 by 1908; of the latter, 600 were described as "distinctly rural." By 1910 the number of special tax districts had increased to 1,077.[22]

Reformers sought spontaneous public enthusiasm. As a Kentucky campaigner put it in 1911, his purpose was to "vitalize and popularize" schools so that rural parents would "be converted to the idea that the school is worth everything to the community."[23] But in reality the crusades were carefully staged and involved considerable coordination. A local supporter from North Wilkesboro, North Carolina, explained his strategy in 1903. He advised an eight months' program of preparation in which reformers would soften up local opinion through publicity in the town's two newspapers. He promised to talk about the matter "quietly and cautiously" himself, and, along with others, to petition the county board of education for an election. Careful advance preparation was common. In Caldwell County, in western North Carolina, a SEB agent visited every schoolhouse in the county, photographed them, and then composed a detailed account of school conditions for local newspapers. Exposure and publicity became an end in itself. One educator in 1905 termed these methods the principal work of the future because they helped local communities realize their true educational conditions and needs.[24]

The centerpiece of the school crusade was a public meeting, often held at the county courthouse or some other community center. The state committees arranged for visiting speakers, but only with assurances from local allies of a good turnout. In Hayesville, North Carolina, a local coordinator promised a "good attendance" for a visiting state school official. Although the county was small, "our people can all come," he wrote, ensuring "every effort possible to get the people out." These rallies bore a striking resemblance to a revival meeting. Singing, entertainment, banners, and even hymns and invocations preceded and followed speeches. According to an SEB agent in Virginia, "large concourses of the country people" attended these meetings. The residents of a mountainous county of Alabama participated in another such rally, which was an all-day event in 1903. In a scene common to many of the school crusade rallies, an observer described how the local community arrived in great numbers from the surrounding countryside. "Many walked, some rode in good buggies and surreys; but many families of from three to twelve persons came in plain farm wagons with straw-covered beds, chairs from the fireside as seats, drawn by a yoke of oxen." These rural Alabamians were "clad in home-woven jeans and cotton; most of them wore shoes, but some, even adults, were barefooted; but all were happy and cheerful and welcomed visiting speakers most cordially."[25]

◆ ◆ ◆

THE SCHOOL CRUSADE AND THE MOBILIZATION OF WOMEN

Like many women of her class and generation, Atlantan Emily Stewart Harrison was attracted to social reform. In determining her lifework, Harrison considered the following facts: she was thirty-four years old, unmarried and lacked prospects for marriage, had no particular claims on her time, and had abilities that she was eager to apply. At present, she worried that her talents were "altogether too small to cope with the work" with which she was presently engaged. In the Progressive Era South, the case of Harrison was not unusual: many middle-class women, married and unmarried, were attracted to reform—school reform in particular. If there was a subject that "closely" concerned a southern woman, wrote a North Carolinian, it was education. Schools affected "her personal interests through her children"; no one was "more competent to join in the educational movement than the mother who has been the valiant foe to ignorance." For many women, participation in school reform became a "sacred duty."[26]

Perhaps the earliest evidence of this new activism came during the school crusades of 1901–10. First in North Carolina, and then in other southern states, urban middle-class women supplied much of the crusade's enthusiasm, organizational skill, and mass support. The entry of women into the public arena was part of a regionwide and nationwide coming of age of women's activism and assertiveness, and their impact on early twentieth-century reform is hard to overestimate. As James Leloudis has shown, southern activist women first became mobilized in school reform through organizations such as the Woman's Association for the Betterment of Public School Houses in North Carolina, founded in 1902.[27] Its creation and subsequent expansion was rooted in the married, middle-class, and mostly nonworking women who participated after the 1890s in the women's club movement. Elvira Evelyna Moffitt, who figured importantly in the Raleigh Woman's Club and later was a leader in WABPS, after 1900 led a campaign to beautify the city, improve cityscapes, and maintain public buildings and streets—all "to be accomplished by the organized work of earnest women." By the early twentieth century, women like Moffitt were seeking a wider vision of social change that would provide women of her class a greater voice in public affairs.[28]

The increased activism of women coincided with the SEB's determination to exploit it. As head of North Carolina's State Normal and Industrial College and, earlier, as a public school administrator and campaigner, Charles D. McIver had achieved a regional reputation as a school reformer. With extensive contacts through college alumna throughout the state, McIver, soon after the formation of the State Campaign Committee, sponsored the organization of WABPS in early 1902. The purposes of the organization were, from the beginning, to mobilize sentiment behind the educational campaign. Along with a state organization, WABPS developed county organizations; local, "branch associations," composed of at least three members, were attached to a school. Meanwhile, McIver's organization and the state SEB organization provided expenses for ten field-workers.[29]

McIver and WABPS leaders agreed that the organization's chief purpose was to focus on the improvement of physical facilities. The *Raleigh News and Observer* described WABPS as a "labor of love undertaken by the patriotic women of the state" whose main purpose was to make schools more attractive. Inside the schoolroom, the reforming women sought to create "happy surroundings" that would instill a vision of "home adornment"; schooled in these surroundings, future generations would beautify their own homes. Outside the school, similarly, the women reformers intended to arrange those "happy conditions" that would be found in any "model home." One of WABPS's primary purposes, wrote another woman, was to nurture "a love for the beautiful" among children. School betterment should reach "the lowliest home and put brightness and sunshine into lives enveloped in gloom and cause them to put forth tendrils that will reach out and take hold of a higher civilization."[30]

Deliberately, the organization's stated purpose meshed well with women's clubs' activities. Given her experience in the Raleigh Woman's Club, Moffitt was no doubt comfortable with these purposes, which she described as beautifying schoolhouses and grounds and thereby "transforming unattractive cheerless School grounds into places of beauty and refinement." Through WABPS, reformers sought to mobilize North Carolina women behind school improvement, McIver disclosed, and "attract or force by public opinion many children into the school who do not now go." When this organization ceased "to be needed in North Carolina," declared a woman reformer, an "educational millennium will have come."[31]

The involvement of women in the school crusade was a clear manifestation of the role they would play in southern social reform. By focusing on the domestic side of school reform, reformers sought to appeal to the Victorian conception of gender but also to push it toward a new limit. Men had done an inadequate job of maintaining existing schoolhouses, wrote McIver; they had the exclusive management of both courthouses and schoolhouses, and

Charles D. McIver.
(Courtesy of University Archives, University of North Carolina at Greensboro Library)

"the marks of masculinity and neglect" were evident on both. For women like Moffitt, WABPS activism expanded areas of traditional autonomy in church, family, and home. Although women were the "Mother of men," they should also, in a "modest & suggestive way," "perform in the World[']s work." Activism in school reform would operate on the "same plane of Churches" and would be a "hand maiden to Church extension." Women possessed, Moffitt maintained, the ability to humanize modern society. With smaller families, women possessed a "fine opportunity to exercise their energy"; this involvement awakened a "torpid power" within them. Women were obliged, first, to improve their own homes and, second, to widen their influence by improving public schools.[32]

Lula Martin McIver, the wife of Charles D. McIver, was another WABPS leader who saw school improvement as a vehicle for increased activism by women. "We seem to have thought that the mother's responsibility ceased at her own front door when she handed her six year old child a primer, kissed him, and pointed the way to the school house," she declared on one occasion. Yet these schools had been constructed by the "men of the community": they chose the furniture, selected the teacher, determined the curriculum, but then "did not darken the doors again unless some child had been punished and family pride had been wounded." Lacking the "loving thought, care and work of a woman," the school was "not a real home for the children"; without community women behind it, the school therefore failed in its essential functions.[33]

WABPS, and the other southern school improvement associations modeling themselves on it, took a grass-roots approach to reform. "We must get out among the people, meet them, and talk to them face to face," insisted one reformer. WABPS workers should demonstrate their earnestness by helping North Carolinians "to see their needs" and prove to them "that we want to work with them for the general uplift of the whole people." But, she contended, reformers should also "learn from them" and not treat "them in any patronizing way." By using "tact and judgment and love," reformers could thus "arouse and set in motion mighty forces throughout the length and breadth of the grand old State."[34]

Although WABPS possessed a state organization, the real work of "tact and judgment and love" went on in towns, villages, and rural communities. Often women teachers took an active part. In Kentucky, a teacher wrote that a rural school near Carlisle with no yard fence, an old stove, and dingy walls benefited from the organization of a school improvement league. Local women renovated the schoolhouse, constructed a new fence, wallpapered inside the

schoolroom, installed a new stove, and built a small library. In North Carolina, the strongest WABPS chapters were located near urban centers: in Wake
County, surrounding Raleigh, and Guilford County, surrounding Greensboro. A Wake County woman expressed her enthusiasm in 1902. She was
interested in education and willing to do what she could to improve it;
although mother to one child, she had "much sympathy for the rising generation." At the local level, these women reformers pioneered the work of
school modernization. "We have planted a good many flowers," reported one
woman; while males of the community donated timber, local women raised
money to buy flowers. In other communities, the women of local WABPS
chapters landscaped the school exteriors, cleansed the interiors, installed sanitary water supplies, provided for new furniture, and purchased brooms and
cleaning equipment. In one school, WABPS reformers adorned the walls with
portraits of Henry W. Longfellow, Robert E. Lee, and Charles D. McIver![35]

WABPS reformers were careful to avoid antagonizing localities by appearing
too intrusive. Moffitt urged organizers to stress "Harmony" and "community
interest." Urban women had to be convinced of the value of rural reform.
"These ladies in the town," wrote one North Carolina woman in 1908, had
to "be made to feel" the urgency of school reform, and it required an effort
"to get these good women aroused." Reforming women encountered an even
more daunting obstacle in the suspicious attitudes of rural North Carolinians
toward outsiders. Although one teacher was interested in WABPS and wanted a
local chapter to improve a "badly arranged and very uncomfortable" school,
she explained that such an effort would be useless. Recruiting was often most
difficult the farther the community was removed from urban centers.[36]

WABPS reformers, stretched to the limit, found more than episodic forays
into rural North Carolina impossible. One field agent described the mixture
of hope and frustration that she faced when she set out to organize rural communities. After meeting with state leaders of WABPS, she spent "two weeks
wondering where to start and how to start, and at the end of that time I found
myself still wondering." Hoping to begin at a local teachers' institute, she
soon realized that no institutes were scheduled to take place nearby. A visit to
the county superintendent, who was new on the job, yielded little information about the local schools. With what he did pass along, the WABPS worker
sent fifty letters to teachers and committeemen but received only six replies.
Concluding that she "must get out among the people and know them and talk
to them," she and a companion ventured into the rural backcountry "almost
as truly explorers as those of the early days, for neither of us knew a foot of
the road on which we started." Soon, however, this woman of extraordinary

energy was meeting rural women at local gatherings in their homes and organizing local chapters. At occasions where she spoke, her fright was replaced by exhilaration. She recalled: "I felt that I was certainly doing nothing unwomanly when I sat in some school house with women and children gathered close around me, and planned means by which that house could be made more comfortable and attractive."[37]

Another field-worker faced similar obstacles but greater frustration. Describing her journeys into the hinterlands as "fatiguing," the WABPS worker complained that the "greatest drawback" to her efforts was the "lack of efficient leadership." Rural North Carolinians seemed "willing to work" but were "timid about taking the initiative, one waiting for another." Involvement in women's clubs or WABPS assumed the existence of leisure time, which many rural women did not typically possess. Even affluent rural women— the sort that WABPS hoped to attract—were reluctant to participate. Women with larger families had no time to take an active part in any social work, explained one woman, for their first duty was at home. In a number of chapters, consequently, WABPS leaders complained of local indifference and low attendance.[38]

In other states of the South, women reformers were also mobilized around the issue of school reform. Wherever the SEB crusade was well under way, vigorous women's school improvement associations were established and modeled on the WABPS. In Virginia, the Co-Operative Education Association was created in 1902; led by Richmonders Mary Munford and Lila Meade Valentine, it created a network of school improvement leagues across the state. By 1906 there were active women's associations in South Carolina, in its Women's Association for the Improvement of Public Schools; in Georgia, in its School Improvement Club; and in Alabama, in its Federation of Women's Clubs.[39]

Although all of the South could claim such organizations by the outbreak of World War I, in the latter stages of the school crusade, these school improvement associations lost their momentum as school modernization came under control of state bureaucratic agencies. Thereafter, women turned in earnest to anti-illiteracy campaigns, the first of which occurred in Kentucky at the instigation of Cora Wilson Stewart. As superintendent of schools for Rowan County, Stewart established "Moonlight Schools." Organizing a teachers' club that included almost every teacher in the county, she won their agreement to keep their schools open on moonlit nights for a special six-week session. The Moonlight Schools, uniquely, were directed at adult illiterates between the ages of eighteen and one hundred. This effort, as Stewart wrote, was directed at an "imperative human need": the emancipation of "those who were enslaved in the bondage of illiteracy" and wanted "to improve their store of knowledge." Opening on September 5, 1911, the Moonlight Schools initially sought to reach about 300 people. They received an unexpectedly enthusiastic response when more than 1,200 persons, ranging in age from eighteen to eighty-six, enrolled. Whole families turned out: children during the day, parents and older children at night. "Not only men and women of mature years," wrote one observer, "but the aged have shown a yearning for this opportunity to learn." This was a "scene to bring tears to the eyes," wrote Stewart, with "hoary-headed old people" and "robust young people" alike studying together and writing their names on the blackboard "for the first time with joy and pride."[40]

In the next two years, Moonlight Schools achieved significantly larger turn-outs. In 1912 they enrolled more than 1,600 students—the oldest student was eighty-seven—while in the following year, in an attempt to wipe out illiteracy in the county, they enrolled 2,500 people. So successful were these campaigns that, according to Stewart, more than 600 persons in the county learned to read and write and only 23 remained illiterate. Thereafter, the campaign spread across the South. In Kentucky, eight other counties opened Moonlight Schools in 1912 and twenty-five did so in 1913. By 1915 nineteen states had adopted this model for an anti-illiteracy campaign. Moreover, in Kentucky and elsewhere, the establishment of state illiteracy commissions— Kentucky had the first in 1914—made these efforts a permanent part of the school apparatus. This model became a standard. "It was tried in tobacco districts," wrote Stewart; "it was tried in the mining camps, and miners embraced the opportunity with eagerness." In isolated farming sections, rural Kentuckians traveled for miles to attend class and could hardly be persuaded to go home when the hour for dismissal arrived. In the mountains, people crowded to the schools in throngs.[41]

The anti-illiteracy campaigns were largely carried on and continued to be dominated by women. The state illiteracy commissions were heavily influenced by women and, more important, the field-workers were largely female. Inspired by the example of the Stewart Moonlight Schools, for example, South Carolinian Wil Lou Gray began "Opportunity Schools." Like Moonlight Schools, these operated only at night for illiterate adults. The Opportunity Schools, receiving strong support from the state's illiteracy commission during and after World War I, focused especially on reaching illiterate adults of the textile belt. The campaigns by Stewart, Gray, and others employed the crusade model of organizing. Much of the success of her program, advised Stewart in 1912, depended on exhorting teachers and school officials to undertake the work of "campaigning with zeal"; no half-hearted methods would do, and they must enter the crusade with "whole hearts." The appeal of the campaign would rest on "a plea none can resist": a "missionary spirit" that would free illiterates from ignorance and "bring to them long-armed usefulness and power." Once teachers realized this need, Stewart predicted, their hearts would be "overflowing."[42]

Along with a rhetoric of evangelicalism, Stewart urged hard-nosed, grassroots organizing. Campaigners should enroll in writing all who were willing to come. Enrollees should be pressed to attend regularly, and, she advised, canvassers should point out to potential students the names on Stewart's list of those who would "have an influence with others." The "half-educated" should be included on these lists along with the total illiterates; the "most intelligent and influential persons" should be granted leadership roles. The scheduling of the classes, she warned, was crucial, and "the finest moonlight night in the month" should be chosen, as dark and rainy nights discouraged attendance. The schools themselves should be as attractive as possible—in particular, they should be well lighted with "plenty of clean, well-trimmed, bright lights." Classes should be limited to two hours, with a short opening talk, a "stirring song," at least one rapid drill, and simple lessons in history and geography. All students should have one lesson to complete; it would be enough to make them hungry for more.[43]

Whether women or men, school reformers discovered that the way to break the grip of traditional governance on public opinion was to adopt the crusade model of popular mobilization. Using modern forms of media, they successfully dramatized the obvious deficiencies in the post-Reconstruction school system. Fanning popular outrage through a careful manipulation of newspapers and other organs of opinion, they also successfully employed the vehicle of a revival-style mobilization. In these crusades, reformers often recognized the powerful potential of local opposition and adapted their strategy to it. As a result, rather than a single, centralized crusade, they developed a decentralized campaign, adjusting timing and style to local opinion. As an SEB official noted in 1907, the board's strategy acknowledged the fact that state and local conditions were individual and different.[44]

Fresh from this successful crusade, educational reformers eventually were forced to confront its policy consequences. Crusades were effective in rallying public opinion; other skills were needed to effect real changes that would have a local impact. As early as 1905, a North Carolina school crusader faced this reality. "The educational campaign," he wrote, had "largely passed away from the stage of oratory to that of plain discussions of plain business propositions." This, it appeared to him, "should be our policy in the future, except perhaps in a few counties in which no campaign has yet been carried on."[45]

◆ ◆ ◆

ORIGINS OF THE ANTIHOOKWORM CRUSADE

When it ended in 1915, only slightly more than five years after it began, the participants in the southern antihookworm crusade were deeply moved by the experience. Many of them complained that the crusade was ending just as its significant work was beginning; almost all paid tribute to its importance. The antihookworm campaign, wrote one reformer, was the "greatest work for human redemption the world has ever seen." To another, the memories of the crusade's accomplishments were "bright and precious" and thinking about them brought a lump into his throat.[46] Modeled closely on the school crusade, the antihookworm campaign also sought to reform social policy by altering public opinion. In an ambitious effort to eradicate hookworm disease in the South, reformers attempted, through public health, to alter folkways and mass behavior. To a greater extent than was true of the southern school crusade, the antihookworm crusade enjoyed external coordination and planning, for the Rockefeller philanthropic officials who operated it were applying almost a decade's worth of experience in southern school reform.

There was, indeed, an unusual affinity between Progressive Era educational and health reform.[47] The Rockefeller Sanitary Commission for the Eradication of Hookworm Disease was created in late 1909 after it received the support of key figures with experience mainly in school crusading. Many of its members, such as Walter Hines Page and James Y. Joyner, also sat on the Southern Education Board. Although the commission had come into existence at the urging of medical zoologist Charles W. Stiles, who was appointed its scientific secretary, he took little part in the antihookworm crusade and was mistrusted by a wide range of reformers. Not hesitant to promote his views, Stiles often became embroiled in controversy, and state health officials learned to resent his insistence on a single approach to public health. They were also deeply suspicious of what one state official described as his "notorious and sensational methods," which substituted for "a generous exercise of modesty, tact and policy."[48] Still other reformers resented Stiles's contention that industrialization improved the living conditions of children because it removed them from a hookworm-infested environment.[49] Effective power over the new commission went instead to its administrative secretary, Wickliffe Rose. Significantly, Rose's chief skills were organizational rather than

Hookworm rally, Lutcher, Louisiana.
(Courtesy of the Southern Historical Collection, University of North Carolina
at Chapel Hill Library)

technical. Possessing no public health experience, Rose had close connections to Rockefeller philanthropy. He also possessed, as a professor of education at George Peabody College for Teachers in Nashville, and then as executive secretary of the SEB, extensive experience and contacts with the southern education crusade.

Rose's first important decision was to sponsor a conference of southern public health officials in early 1910; all but two states, Arkansas and Florida, were represented.[50] Rose and the officials attending reached a consensus about the antihookworm campaign. They established a regional coordinating organization, the Rockefeller Sanitary Commission, which dispensed ideas, suggested strategy, and provided a message of reform. Unlike either moral or school reformers, however, antihookworm campaigners enjoyed the formidable financial support of the Rockefeller philanthropic empire. Backed by a one-million-dollar endowment, the commission eventually secured the participation of every southern state; the exception was Florida, which operated its antihookworm program independently. For the remaining states that did participate, the RSC established terms for receiving Rockefeller funds. The campaign would operate under the auspices of state health officials. In a tacit understanding with them, the Rockefeller name rarely appeared. It would "be well to omit all reference to the Rockefeller Commission," Rose advised an Arkansas antihookworm crusader. Such discretion was necessary, he explained, to stimulate the development of the state health bureaucracy and to create the impression "that this work is altogether the work of the State." But another motive was to avoid the appearance of outside interference bearing the name Rockefeller.[51]

The RSC nonetheless retained control over the state antihookworm campaigns, which operated under the state health bureaucracies but in reality were responsible to the RSC national office. Rose took great care in appointing directors to head these campaigns; they were usually men with little experience with or allegiance to the state health officials. Rose also highly valued initiative, enthusiasm, training in modern public health methods, and skill in the art of public relations. Perhaps Rose's most successful appointee was John A. Ferrell, of North Carolina, who had trained at medical colleges in North Carolina and at Johns Hopkins and then had served as a county health officer in Sampson County, in the eastern part of the state. Ferrell brought unusual skills to the antihookworm crusade. Thoroughly acquainted with the doctrine of modern public health, he was an effective administrator, bureaucratic infighter, and public relations organizer.[52]

Most southern state health officials greeted the arrival of the RSC with unrestrained enthusiasm. Long isolated from each other and frustrated by penurious state legislatures, they saw the commission as an opening wedge toward greater expansion of their powers. For them, therefore, the appearance of Rockefeller philanthropy could not have been more timely. Working with an invigorated state health bureaucracy, the RSC, during its first year of operation, laid the groundwork for a regionwide health crusade. The state directors, under the supervision of Rose, hired local agents or field directors. Paying careful attention to organizational and communication skills, Ferrell recruited a staff of five field directors in North Carolina, composed of young, recently trained physicians who were generally underpaid and overworked. To his subordinates, he stressed a methodology of precise record keeping and systematic investigation, and, as central goals, exposure and publicity rather than immediate eradication of the parasite.[53]

During 1910 and 1911 the campaign experimented. Much of the early work sought to expose the problem and to convince the public that hookworm disease existed. Yet what reformers found genuinely appalled the sanitarians. The report of field director C. F. Strosnider to Ferrell about one North Carolina community in August 1910 is illustrative. Surface privies, he wrote, that exuded a "very foul odor" were "common"; as a rule, rural people lacked basic sanitation. The mill villages that dotted the Piedmont boasted no better health conditions. While Strosnider described an industrial community near Wilson as "low, weedy and very wormy," another field director, Benjamin W. Page, concluded that there was "a great deal of work for us to do in these mills." Benjamin Earle Washburn, finding similar conditions in the textile communities of Alamance County, judged conditions there to be "most backward," primarily because the county lacked any effective local public health regulations. The county's backwardness manifested itself in the "greatest evil against the public health"—the "dirty, loathsome, unsanitary, open-back privies found in so many homes." Nine-tenths of the homes in the county, according to Washburn, possessed unsanitary privies.[54]

These accounts and others betray paternalistic attitudes on the part of reformers. They believed that the solution to widespread ill health would come from outside the rural South, from professional, modern medicine. They viewed the object of reform—the culture and society of the rural South—condescendingly, and their efforts to change local conditions often ran squarely against long-standing traditions of rural independence and autonomy. Typically, field-workers for the Rockefeller Sanitary Commission felt isolated and alienated from the largely rural communities in which hookworm prevailed. "This is a God forsaken place," moaned one operative, "& I will be glad to get out of here." A wide gap existed between the reformers' perceptions and those of rural communities.[55]

As a preliminary to the crusade, Rose instructed state secretaries to survey the extent of hookworm infection. Conducting these examinations on an unscientific and random basis, the state directors were able to demonstrate widespread infection. In North Carolina, Ferrell and his agents uncovered hookworm disease across the state. Benjamin W. Page reported in August 1910 that an infected man, about forty-eight years old, had been suffering from the anemia and general weakness that came with the parasite. Having neglected his farm because of his feeble condition, he was "very proud" to learn that a cure was possible. In Ramseur, Page found the town "fairly well 'Hookwormized'" and its residents interested. Although these early examinations were, as one campaigner admitted, "more educational than practical," they succeeded in their original intention: to demonstrate the prevalence of hookworm infection across a wide spectrum of North Carolina society. By the autumn of 1910, the commission's survey had detected hookworm disease in all but two counties.[56]

Along with exposure and demonstration, the state campaigns employed various approaches to publicize the extent of hookworm infection among southerners. The skills required of campaigners were more related to public relations than to public health. In North Carolina, crusaders disseminated information through the public schools. In the summer of 1910 field directors lectured at county institutes to convince teachers of the need for sanitation and public health. In the eastern part of the state, Page visited nineteen institutes between July and September and lectured to almost 1,400 teachers. At these meetings, the campaigners found that spectacular methods yielded the best results. Visiting a teachers' institute in Brunswick County, Strosnider brought forward a typical hookworm sufferer, a twenty-seven-year-old who was "dwarfed mentally and physically." Presenting the victim as an example of the devastating potential of the parasite, Strosnider made a "lasting and stimulating impression" on the teachers.[57]

During 1910 and 1911 other state campaigns also employed high visibility tactics. The Georgia campaign similarly emphasized work in schools. In Arkansas, the state director toured the state, lecturing before county medical societies and local women's organizations. While working in schools, the campaigners sought to create district and county associations that would spearhead a grass-roots crusade. In Louisiana and Tennessee, RSC officials, obtaining the cooperation of the railroads, operated a "Health Train" that toured the states to promote the gospel of sanitation. In Louisiana, the railroads lent several cars—including a Pullman car that housed the campaigners— to the Health Train, and thirty-one different lines provided free transportation. Throngs of people from the countryside often greeted the Health Train, which was filled with traveling exhibitions on modern sanitation. "All along the line," reported state director Sidney Porter, local people seemed to display great interest, arriving from long distances in the country at an average of a thousand persons daily. Things were "humming along the line," he later wrote.[58]

In Tennessee, the Health Train yielded similar success. Under an arrangement similar to that in Louisiana, the Tennessee train toured the state to raise public consciousness about health matters, especially sanitation. Space was limited to half a car, which contained exhibits on hookworms as well as on tuberculosis, pure food, floor cleaners and dustless dusters, and nursing bottles. RSC officials installed a working laboratory that was capable of conducting microscopic examinations; they also squeezed in a model privy. Health officials aboard the train were "preaching, preaching, preaching," according to state director Olin West, and everywhere the crusade had received "fine attention" and "great interest."[59]

Yet the first year of the antihookworm crusade also brought frustration. Rose, concerned about the different tacks that the state campaigns were taking, groped for some regionwide standard. State directors, meanwhile, expressed concern about their inability to have a more significant impact on public opinion, primarily because of opposition or potential opposition. Arkansas provided one extreme example. Because the state lacked any health bureaucracy, RSC officials found themselves at a great disadvantage. Even when state director Morgan Smith in 1911 persuaded the legislature to establish a state health bureaucracy, no funds were provided. Characterizing his first year of operation as "far from satisfactory," Smith complained that he had as yet failed to strike "the right chord." Although there was "wide spread and progressively growing interest," the lack of a public health organization remained a serious handicap. Other antihookworm campaigners reported a comparable sense of frustration during 1910 and 1911. Georgia state director A. G. Fort wrote in October 1910 that he was not accomplishing as much as he would like, although he was "pushing" the work all he could. Six months later, he wrote that he felt "very blue" about the prospects of the campaign. Despite their public relations triumphs, the Health Train in Louisiana and Tennessee overextended resources and yielded few long-term results. On one occasion Porter described the Louisiana work as "very strenuous"; on another, he noted that his hands were full. "Every minute of our time on this Train," he subsequently complained, was "occupied and we work about sixteen hours daily including Sundays." Olin West went further. The Tennessee Health Train, he wrote, was a "disappointment."[60] Although health reformers were committed to the crusade method, many of their early experiments in organizing public opinion on hookworm were frustrating. Although they overcame popular hostility toward public health, they lacked a spectacular event that could rally public opinion and draw the rural masses toward reform. Then, very quickly, all of this changed with the introduction of the county dispensary as the central tool of the antihookworm crusade.

◆ ◆ ◆

THE DISPENSARY CAMPAIGN, 1911–1913

The county dispensary, the best-known feature of the antihookworm crusade, originated partly in response to the deficiencies of its early experiments. In a scattered, undirected manner, free demonstration clinics—or dispensaries—first opened their doors in Mississippi in 1910 and in Louisiana a year later. Yet Wickliffe Rose regarded these dispensaries with some skepticism, and not until mid-1911 did they receive the RSC's full support. As an instrument of public health reform, dispensaries were most successful in Alabama, Kentucky, and North Carolina and least effective in Arkansas and Florida. The states where the dispensary succeeded most dramatically possessed a leadership that could organize and exploit a well-coordinated public relations campaign. In dispensaries, crusaders openly borrowed from other social reformers. The stump speeches at courthouse days and in small villages, the attempt at mass conversion through moral persuasion, and the use of new forms of media such as displays and even stereopticon and slide shows: these were all techniques that early twentieth-century educational crusaders pioneered. The dispensaries became instruments for adult education. Drawing upon earlier Rockefeller-financed programs, such as county agricultural extension, the dispensaries sought to expose the problem of hookworm infection and to bring about an evangelical-style mass conversion to public health.[61]

In Alabama, Rose discovered a program that addressed the weaknesses of the Mississippi and Louisiana experiments. As early as June 1911, state director William W. Dinsmore had devised a dispensary procedure. After the state campaign made an initial contact with local physicians, it then attempted to persuade them to join in a petition campaign to cajole the county commissioners to appropriate funds for the incidental expenses of the dispensary. If the appropriation was granted, a field representative then mapped an itinerary that identified three to five "points" in the county and located a traveling dispensary in them once a week for a period of three to six weeks. After receiving encouraging reports about the operation of Alabama's dispensaries, Rose visited the state in June 1911. In Florala, Alabama, he described a dispensary that in one day treated 118 persons. Hookworm sufferers came from the surrounding countryside, from distances of up to twenty miles. From nine in the morning until four in the afternoon, a "throng" gathered around the dispensary. According to Rose, "they lingered; gathered in groups around the table of exhibits; exchanged experiences, listened to stories of improvement of persons who had been treated; and returned home to tell their neighbors what they had seen and heard." By the end of June 1911, three field-workers, operating in seven Alabama counties, had treated 11,466 persons.[62]

Rose quickly adopted the Alabama dispensaries as a model for the entire region. In North Carolina, Ferrell in February 1911 suggested that the field directors extend free medicine to the poor through a system of traveling field hospitals. Run by a field director, the hospitals would consist of two large tents that provided overnight facilities for infected men and women. These new facilities would serve as a base for mass education about hookworms and provide a location for demonstration, public lectures, and the dissemination of literature. Ferrell hoped that such a field hospital, operating under field director C. L. Pridgen in Columbus County in southeastern North Carolina, would furnish a workable model for the rest of the state. Combining treatment and demonstration, Pridgen began work in July 1911, supplied with four army tents and twenty-three cots. Rotating his location in the county, Pridgen pitched camp for a week in a single location and then moved on, depending on local demand. Early on it became obvious what Pridgen's emphases

Dispensary scene, Hals Fork, Leslie County, Kentucky, ca. 1914.
(Courtesy of the Rockefeller Archive Center)

would be. After treating two cases in the hospital, the field director exhibited them before an assembled group and, as the crowd "gathered & marveled," displayed some of the hookworms found in their intestines. Pridgen reported an overwhelming response. "We have gotten in the habit of breaking records down here" was his comment from Tabor; droves of rural folk thronged to the hospital tent, and he found that a majority of them were infected.[63]

Yet Pridgen's field hospital had problems. Because of the unexpected community enthusiasm it generated, its staff and resources were inadequate to run both a demonstration clinic and a residential hospital. Twice during July Pridgen complained of overwork. He admitted that he was worn out, as he had had such "early & late hours . . . without [a] chance to sleep." "Have had but little rest," he observed on another occasion, and "need help badly." "Don[']t think I can stand the strain every day to do the writing, get up reports at night & run hospital too." By August Pridgen was warning Ferrell that, although the Columbus County populace was "enthused" and the work doing "great good," the responsibility weighed heavily, and he feared that by ignorance or carelessness some serious mistake would be made.[64]

It was therefore not surprising when the field hospital experiment came to a close in Columbus County at the end of 1911.[65] Along with overwork, there were two further reasons for its demise. First, Rose and the Rockefeller Sanitary Commission headquarters exerted pressure to require all operating dispensaries to follow a standard model. Second, the field hospital emphasized treatment over mass education, and Ferrell correctly divined that the commission approach would lean more toward the latter than the former. Clearly, the greatest benefits of the dispensary would be in public relations.[66]

While Pridgen led a failed experiment in Columbus County, other dispensary campaigns, operating on the Alabama model, began in Robeson, Sampson, and Halifax counties within a hookworm belt that extended across eastern North Carolina. As in Columbus County, the dispensaries attracted large crowds. The first month-long campaign in these counties, Ferrell claimed, had achieved remarkable results. During the first week, the dispensaries attracted 1,000 people; by the final week, they were drawing 3,000. For the month, they claimed 12,500 participants. After almost two years of sometimes unpopular investigation, commission agents were stunned by the enthusiasm. "Our work is becoming very, very popular," C. F. Strosnider wrote from Sampson County; the dispensary's ability to attract participants had exceeded his wildest expectations. Even local physicians, who were usually suspicious of any experiment in indigent care, were providing aid in every way possible. "As in days of old," he concluded, " 'the Harvest is Ripe, but the Laborers are few.' "[67]

News of these successful dispensaries soon reached Rose. After visiting North Carolina in the summer of 1911, he discovered an expanded version of the Alabama dispensaries. The scene Rose described in Sampson County was vivid. As he approached the dispensary, he encountered a trail of buggies and wagons loaded with departing rural families. Reaching the dispensary, he counted thirty-three buggies nearby and about a hundred people waiting to be examined. Inside, Strosnider and his microscopist worked "to the limit of their capacity." Not even stopping to each lunch, he treated 136 cases that day.[68]

Largely based on the success of the dispensary in Alabama and North Carolina, Rose pressed all the state campaigns to adopt it—or to modify existing dispensary programs. During the next three years, the large number of enthusiastic reports about dispensaries that flowed through Rose's Washington offices became almost monotonous in their regularity. In Alabama, a campaigner described a sanitary revival that had occurred in one community. Another North Carolina field director reported that the hinterlands were "fermenting with hookworm enthusiasts." "Should you have skeptics about the dispensary work," he wrote Ferrell, "please send them to us for conversion." In Texas, which did not begin a dispensary campaign until 1913, a fieldworker described his dispensary as "completely swamped." In Mississippi, a local official characterized the dispensary as "the finest work that has ever been done in our County," while in Kentucky Rose found its results "interesting and inspiring" and public opinion "aroused."[69]

At dispensaries, campaigners dramatized the before-and-after results of modern science. They received numerous letters of thanks from parents whose children had been treated for hookworm. An Alabama woman related that, as a result of the treatment, her children were "looking so much Better and can work without tire." She thanked the antihookworm campaign "for my dear ones"; she knew God's mercy "sent you within my reach when I look over them now." Testimonials like this, no doubt genuine, were frequently publicized by the RSC organization and used to dramatize its success. In other instances, antihookworm crusaders reminded their audiences of the immediate economic value of public health. Families that had been "objects of charity," explained a Mississippi public health worker, were discovered to have nothing wrong but hookworm infection. Their inability to work and their proclivity for idleness, rather than being a product of "indifference and real laziness," was a sign of parasitic infection. In Tennessee, reformers provided another instance of a startling physiological and psychological change that followed the discovery of hookworm infection. An eighteen-year-old youth in Pickett County had been a slow learner, "listless and inattentive," and emotionally and physically underdeveloped. After three doses of thymol to kill the worms, he experienced an "immediate and marked" improvement; he not only gained weight and height but also was enjoying normal mental and emotional development.[70]

Hookworm infection thus became an ideal disease around which to organize a mass mobilization. It had an easily identifiable cause and an equally identifiable solution, and it could be cured almost immediately, as quickly and suddenly as the religious conversion experience that the secular dispensary sought to emulate. In those states where the dispensary was the most successful, the state campaigns enjoyed political support and a strong base in the state health bureaucracy, as well as employing state directors with administrative ability. Under the leadership of Arthur T. McCormack, the crusade in Kentucky reaped visible benefits after it adopted the dispensary in 1912.[71]

Yet the accomplishments of the crusade were less the eradication of hookworm disease than a conversion of public opinion to its dangers. In Kentucky, a field director's description of a Jefferson County dispensary—which McCormack passed along to Rose—could have been written by either Ferrell about North Carolina or Dinsmore about Alabama. His characterization of the dispensaries as revivals would have had obvious appeal to RSC officials. "I have never seen the people at any place," he wrote, who were "so wrought up and so full of interest and enthusiasm." The dispensary was like a "big, old-time camp meeting," and the local population talked "of nothing but hookworm and hookworm disease." In Christian County, McCormack described another successful dispensary. At the town of Crofton, sixteen miles from the county seat, about 1,500 people listened for six hours to health lectures by physicians, county officials, and state health officials. To sustain the crowd, the meeting offered the barbecue of fourteen sheep and six shoats. "We certainly are writing big pages," concluded McCormack, "in the health history of Kentucky these days."[72]

Whether in Kentucky or North Carolina, effective campaigning, reformers discovered, depended on careful planning. A single "marvelous cure" in a community, observed one crusader, did more to educate rural North Carolinians along "Hookworm and Sanitary lines" than did six months of constant lecturing. By the fall of 1911 North Carolina field directors were following a carefully prescribed approach. They first sought endorsements from the county health and school superintendents and local opinion shapers, whose support was considered essential. Next, campaigners called on the county commissioners and asked them to contribute two hundred to three hundred dollars to help pay for drugs and specimen tins, printing and advertising, and the travel expenses of a microscopist. Field directors visited the commissioners before any meeting, sometimes exerting subtle or even direct pressure to get their support. In Duplin County, the field director found a "lever" to pressure a reluctant commissioner—his political connections with a banker who supported the antihookworm campaign. In other situations, campaigners were more blunt. In at least one instance, Ferrell warned commissioners that if they failed to make an appropriation, it was likely that they would lose political support in the state legislature.[73]

At meetings the county commission was often greeted by a large turnout of prodispensary forces. If and when the commissioners appropriated the money requested, they were asked to identify five locations, or "points," in the county where dispensaries could be conducted one day a week for four to six consecutive weeks. During the ensuing campaign, the dispensary became a vehicle of mass persuasion. Ferrell strongly emphasized publicity. He advised the field directors to spare no effort in advertising and urged that campaigners use it vigorously, even if it exhausted "every cent" of the county appropriation. The field directors spent the first weeks before and during the campaign in elaborate preparations. A campaigner who followed the "usual methods" in Alamance County, North Carolina, recounted how leading roads were plastered with placards and small handbills detailing the examinations and dispensary locations. Typically, a thousand circular letters were distributed to leading citizens of the county, and lectures were given to soften up public opinion.[74]

Campaign literature verged on the sensational and helped to create a circus atmosphere designed to attract large crowds. "See the Hookworms and the various intestinal parasites that man is heir to," read one handbill. Parents who neglected to treat infected children, warned another, stood "squarely across their offspring's future, condemning them ofttimes to an early death or a life of misery, which may result in making them a public charge." It was no disgrace to have hookworms, admonished a Mississippi campaigner, but it was a "disgrace for a man to allow it [to] be in his family any longer that [than] it would take him to find it out and give the treatment." Otherwise, he wrote, it was a modern-day case of the sacrifice of "the blood of their children to unknown gods."[75]

Once inside the dispensary, participants came to expect the spectacular. An essential part of any successful dispensary was an exhibit that included pictures of worms and detailed how infection occurred. Charts, which often illustrated an accompanying lecture, demonstrated further details, while bottles containing hookworms, roundworms, and other parasites provided alarming evidence to the visiting rural folk. One of the most popular parts of the dispensary was the microscope, before which eager participants queued in order to view the developing hookworm eggs. Along with the public lecture often came the singing of hymns.[76]

What had begun ostensibly as a campaign to eradicate hookworm became a program of mass education. With the use of dispensaries and the ensuing public enthusiasm, the complicated and foreboding problem of southern public health became simplified and solvable. As early as 1911, Rose was describing dispensaries as effective educational agencies that would teach southerners "how to recognize the disease, how to get it cured, and how to prevent getting reinfected." As Ferrell observed, for educational purposes hookworm provided greater opportunities than did any other disease for "a quick, successful, easily comprehended and concrete victory over a single disease distributed over every County of the State." Hookworm was an almost ideal disease for spreading broad doctrines of public health to the mass of North Carolinians. The parasite was prevalent throughout the state, and its chronic, degenerative character made it available for demonstrations. Because its cause was simple and obvious to the naked eye, it could be prevented and cured by methods whose simplicity appealed to everyone. The results of this massive adult education effort were "so prompt and emphatic" that they could be compared to miracles recounted in the New Testament.[77]

The heart of the antihookworm crusade lay in the dispensaries, but even its most enthusiastic advocates admitted that it brought unexpected consequences. Although the dispensary campaigns produced an "immense amount of good . . . in so many different ways," declared Platt W. Covington, a North Carolina crusader, many of these benefits "were not anticipated at the inauguration." Indeed, the chief result of the campaign, it had now become clear, was not eradication, which reformers were acknowledging as a multigenerational problem. Rather, the real benefit of the dispensary campaign was the enthusiasm found among rural southerners for public health.[78]

◆ ◆ ◆

THE LIMITS OF THE ANTIHOOKWORM CRUSADE

For John A. Ferrell, the success of the North Carolina dispensaries virtually made his career and professional reputation. Brought to the attention of Rose and the Rockefeller Sanitary Commission, he became Rose's lieutenant in the commission's national headquarters in 1913. But even in states such as North Carolina, where the dispensary yielded spectacular results, there were limits to its role as a model of public health reform. Some critics of Ferrell and the dispensary approach, such as future state health officer Charles Laughinghouse of Greenville, complained that publicity took precedence over sound medicine; dispensary physicians, Laughinghouse suggested, were too hurried and sloppy in their diagnosis and treated their patients ineffectively. Although he admitted that the dispensaries had generated great enthusiasm, Laughinghouse questioned whether they could be translated into long-term public health measures. Once the dispensary became a memory, rural North Carolinians might well lose interest and prove not so responsive.[79]

Other public officials expressed similar concerns. The antihookworm campaign's "present mode of warfare," wrote one sympathetic critic, resulted in "raids into the enemy's country." But once the invaders had left, the favorable impression gradually evaporated and rural folk soon became more or less indifferent. The dispensary might sweep through a community, generate widespread enthusiasm, but then be unable to sustain a follow-up program. Dispensaries had little effect on the building of sanitary privies, an essential part of any long-term program of public health reform. Despite the Rowan County, North Carolina, school board's enactment of a sanitary privy ordinance for schools in 1910, enforcement did not follow, as one field director put it, "as rapidly as we like." Another agent reported "rather discouraging" results in privy building. In the enthusiasm of the moment, the community often professed its commitment to the establishment of sanitary privies, wrote one Rockefeller official, but in most cases if the privies were not constructed before the field director left the county, they were never built.[80]

Others, such as the North Carolina state health officer, Watson Smith Rankin, criticized the dispensary's emphasis on the spectacular and sensational. In one instance Rankin defended dispensaries because they reached those people attracted by "big headlines and with pictures," but he conceded that their unorthodox methods alienated the "dignified, modest, retiring, professional habit" of most physicians. On other occasions, he was less equivocal. When a Georgia public health official declared that dispensaries "misrepresented" the problem of hookworms and failed to eradicate the parasite, Rankin responded that he was "thoroughly in accord" with these views, adding that the problem of hookworms was "not nearly so important as the advertising being given it would indicate." The campaign in North Carolina, he complained in a letter to Charles W. Stiles, inaccurately depicted hookworm infection as a "monster . . . out of proportion to other diseases of great importance" and created the impression that public health work only amounted to talking about hookworm and dispensing thymol.[81]

The limitations of the dispensary were even more obvious in states where its achievements were more problematic. In Georgia, a weak state health bureaucracy and tepid political support slowed its progress. In South Carolina, the state director informed Rose that, while dispensaries worked in some counties, in adjacent counties they were clear failures. Still another antihookworm campaigner complained that "conservatism" among Tennesseans prevented the success of dispensaries.[82]

The experience in two states, Arkansas and Florida, vividly demonstrated the limits of dispensaries. In Arkansas, Rockefeller agents found virtually unceasing frustration. Without a health bureaucracy to deal with, early organizers were at a significant disadvantage. About a year after the campaign began, the state attorney general ruled that counties had no legal authority to dispense funds for the dispensary campaign. Subsequently, campaigners attempted to circumvent this obstacle by obtaining private appropriations, and in February 1913 the assembly enacted new legislation that permitted county appropriations for dispensaries. Into 1913 and 1914 RSC agents enjoyed few successes. Many of them encountered local resentment at outside interference. A newspaper editor wrote that his county regarded dispensaries as "another way for the rich to spend their money in so-called philanthropic work" without "any beneficial results to humanity." A field director, complaining that he faced "every obstacle to overcome before accomplishing anything," told of local health officials who "showed no courtesies to us" and opposed the dispensaries. Consequently, the opening of the dispensary points in the county was met with "a spirit of resentment, jest or contempt"; in some communities "we barely escaped personal insult."[83]

Whereas RSC agents in other states typically concluded their glum reports with some statement of success, an aura of depression prevailed in Arkansas. The dispensaries operating in that state, admitted state health officer C. W. Garrison in June 1913, were not "arousing the enthusiasm as was anticipated," although he expected soon to have dispensaries like those in North Carolina. By October RSC headquarters received still more pessimistic news from Arkansas. "I realize that we are not getting the results in this State as in some of the other States," Garrison wrote, but the failures of the dispensary, rather than the product of a "lack of energy and effort" or of an inadequate "system and methods," was the result of "conditions that could not be met."[84]

Facing defeat, Rose dispatched W. P. Jacocks to Arkansas. One of several Ferrell protégés who served as a roving troubleshooter in states making little progress—a "general utility man," according to his own description—Jacocks arrived in September 1913. Yet even as experienced a crusader as Jacocks found Arkansas deeply frustrating. In Monroe County, he persuaded a county court to appropriate funds for a dispensary but then discovered that payment would come only in scrip worth thirty-five cents on the dollar. Jacocks decided, after consultation with Garrison, to depart Monroe until its scrip was "more or rather worth par." Subsequently, matters improved but little. Although Jacocks wrote in November that local communities were "just as interested as any I saw in N.C.," Garrison described him as having "hard luck" in his chief responsibility—securing appropriations. By January 1914, facing impatience with the meager funds he had obtained from both state officials and RSC headquarters, Jacocks described the "poorest week's work I have done since joining the force"; one point was apparently "hopeless." Reporting indifference and slow progress, he later expressed discouragement and doubts about his ability to arouse public opinion and blamed himself for the failure of rural folk to respond. By the end of 1914 the RSC had withdrawn Jacocks from Arkansas and apparently admitted defeat.[85]

In Florida, state officials had refused to cooperate with the RSC in 1910 because their own antihookworm control program had been in place since 1908. Under this program, which began in earnest in the summer of 1909, the State Board of Health paid attending physicians three dollars—including the cost of thymol to kill the worms—for each indigent patient treated; the state also provided containers and forms and supplied a free microscopic examination. Meanwhile, the state assigned two roving agents to canvass the state, meeting as far as possible, every sufferer and having a personal talk.[86]

Wickliffe Rose.
(Courtesy of the Rockefeller Archive Center)

The Florida campaigners uncovered extensive infection. Hookworms were found in all but one county—Monroe—in which Key West is situated.[87] As was true for the rest of the South, infection was heaviest among children, especially rural white children. One physician described the case of his six-year-old grandson. Since birth, the boy had been "very pale & anaemic & has other symptoms common to the complaint, enervated, & showing some bloat." His appetite was "very variable and often entirely nil." Complaining of "ground itch," he was in altogether a precarious condition and the usual remedies had failed "to add much to his health or appearance."[88]

Nonetheless, the Florida program was strapped for funds and, in the end, was probably ineffective. Unlike the RSC campaign, the Florida program eschewed publicity. In May 1910 a state health official urged crusaders to "work in the quietest possible way[,] giving the least publicity to the subject," and to avoid any attempts to "stigmatise an individual, or a community, or a state." Without any public relations techniques to promote it, Florida's campaign depended on mass treatment to be successful. But the avalanche of complaints that poured in from both sanitarians and patients during 1910 suggested failure. Calvin T. Young, field agent for the state board, claimed in April 1910 that the program lacked clear direction, organization, and administration and was "upon anything but an established basis." Because physicians were granted considerable leeway, they had developed their "own remedy, method of administration, and dosage. All were equally at sea, floundering in a misty understanding of the limited experience of a few who have rushed into print." Young recommended stopping and reorganizing the campaign. Then, once a foundation was established, the crusade could proceed with the superstructure.[89]

Others, including Florida's state health officer, Joseph Y. Porter, agreed. Although health officials were conducting an "active" campaign that sought to reach each county "systematically," limited staff and funds had slowed the work. A central flaw in the Florida system was its reliance on physicians. Some were tireless in their efforts, others expended little more energy than that necessary to collect their three-dollar fees, and still others actively opposed the program because they feared losing their patients. Other participants in the program complained of local noncooperation. From one part of the state came the report of a physician who found a large number of children in his territory infected but claimed that people there were indifferent. A significant number of rural Floridians did not trust physicians. An Avon Park resident complained that a "good many people here treat the whole idea as a joke, thinking it some new scheme of doctors to make money."[90] Despite their independence from the RSC crusade, Florida officials found themselves gravitating toward its methods, in part because of loose administration in their own program and because of rural opposition to it. Most important, however, was the fact that the indigent program appeared to have failed. As a health official later noted, under this program sanitary conditions in rural homes and schools generally did not improve and in nine out of ten cases hookworm sufferers became reinfected shortly after treatment.[91]

Out of this failure, Florida officials groped for alternatives. As early as July 1912, in a conscious imitation of the RSC crusade, Florida field agents began operating dispensaries. By that fall the indigent program had been abandoned and Porter announced that the field agents would run a statewide dispensary campaign in different sections of the state with the treatment of hookworms "pushed in that way." Closely resembling the RSC approach for dispensaries, the new Florida program conducted an intensive publicity campaign before-hand, offered treatment after physical and microscopic examinations, pro-vided thymol to all suspected of infection, and told chronic sufferers to return for further treatment. Other participants in the dispensary received a heavy dose of adult education, learning about the parasite through lectures and exhibitions, and were able to view hookworms under the microscope.[92]

Joseph Porter pronounced these dispensaries as "the most successful" of Florida's various antihookworm efforts. Still, familiar problems persisted. One field agent described many disagreeable features connected with the fieldwork. The other agent, who had served in the same position for six years, resigned because of overwork. The hookworm assignment was "very unat-tractive," with frequent absences from home and family, according to the departing agent; remaining in the job would result in "my complete medical deterioration, rusting out as it were." These agents expressed a continuing problem: the overextension of the meager resources of the Florida health bureaucracy in light of the overwhelming health needs of rural areas. The dispensary program only made clear the inability of the crusade to alter local conditions.[93]

For educational and health reformers, the crusade became the most impor-tant way to mobilize public opinion. In this instance, popular mobilization followed a familiar pattern: reformers exposed the existence of a long-standing problem, attracted large public support for a rather vaguely defined reform, and then went to the state legislatures for a significant alteration of public policy. Other reformers, following in their footsteps, embraced their methods. For humanitarian reformers seeking fundamental changes in the traditional family structure, the path was well cleared.

FAMILY

◆

Among no other group of social reformers did new impulses to change southern folkways throb more strongly than child labor and woman suffrage crusaders. For both, the primary purpose was uplift and reform of the family
structure through the radical alteration of traditional attitudes and practices
regarding childhood and gender, and they were motivated by the very different forces of Protestant humanitarianism on the one hand and feminism
on the other. Advocating child nurture and the sentimental bonds of family,
child labor reformers articulated the new ideas of the child-saving movement,
the chief objective of which was to remove children from the adult, workaday
world and segregate them in protective institutions such as schools. Woman
suffrage reformers, meanwhile, sought not only the extension of the franchise, but also, as a broader objective, a new public role for women. Yet both
groups were united by a common challenge: to persuade an often indifferent
and even hostile public to endorse radically different notions of childhood,
family, and marriage.

In 1915 a native of the North Carolina mountains and a child labor reformer, W. H. Swift, traveled through the Appalachian South. An experience in what he called this "beautiful land, the home of a strong people" had a striking effect. While his train stopped in a mountain industrial community, he saw several boys, who he was certain were no older than eleven, emerge when the mill whistle blew at noon. Contemplating the fact that these boys, along with "thousands of my neighbor's children," worked in conditions of industrial labor, the reformer rededicated himself to reform. Was there "any possible way," he asked an audience of humanitarians, "to free these white boys and girls . . . from premature and racking toil?" [1]

As David L. Carlton has shown in his study of South Carolina, child labor reform had urban, middle-class origins. Seeking to redefine the conception of childhood among working-class families, reformers emphasized child nurture over child exploitation. According to Carlton, they viewed the issue of child labor through tinted lenses: reform, requiring the imposition of a version of family upon a culture that correctly regarded it as alien, sought to extend the control of the town class over the working class by restricting parental control over their children. Reform thus served as a vehicle of class stabilization. [2] In making this argument, Carlton underestimates the power of ideology. The reformers' vision of missionary uplift, directly focused on children, was more important than class. In the case of the South's leading humanitarian, Alexander J. McKelway, child labor reform had Protestant roots. As a Presbyterian minister in Johnston County and Fayetteville, North Carolina, during the 1890s, he had become an avid prohibitionist. After he became editor of the *North Carolina Presbyterian* in 1898, however, his primary interest was child labor reform, which for McKelway was an expression of a Christian humanitarianism. All Christians, he once said, should hear the "call to social service" as the "insistent appeal of our time." Like other advocates of the Social Gospel, McKelway held what he called a "two-world theory of life": an other world "to which we are bound" and the immediate world, which Christians should make "more sanitary, more humane, more kind hearted, more brotherly." The amelioration of social problems was crucial in the building of the Kingdom of God; whatever brought about the Kingdom, he wrote, was "the chief business of the Church." The Kingdom would arrive by way of the child; toward the impending Golden Age, "a little child shall lead." Entrance into the Kingdom would occur "by the way of childhood, and those who have left childhood before entering in must become as little children again." [3] McKelway viewed the child as a "central figure" in the coming Golden Age. Once human society reached the point where it exerted "energies of mind and heart for his advantage," the "dawning of a brighter day" and a "more glorious sun" would occur.[4]

The exaltation of childhood was a central part of the thinking of McKelway and others. One reformer maintained that the most important issue facing Americans was "the physical, the intellectual, the moral and the spiritual good of the children." Reforming the structure of society so as to ease the burden of children, added another reformer, was part of a "larger social vision, a deeper sense of brotherhood." In contrast to the selfishness and greed behind industrialization, there would be an awakened public opinion that would protect children. The assumption here and elsewhere among reformers was implicit: the middle classes to whom they were appealing would realize that children "must not be allowed to climb to luxury and ease upon the labor-bent backs of other children." Children were the basis of society, wrote one reformer, upon whose shoulders rested global destiny; the "boy of today" became "the man of tomorrow." "Plastic, impressionable, aspiring, recurring," childhood was a precondition of progress and a center around which social reform efforts turned. By solving the problems of childhood, he maintained, "you have solved all social problems."[5]

Reformers were horrified by any exploitation or abuse of children. A Virginia reformer explained that he was attracted to the child labor cause because a deep emotion had stirred within him; the conditions of working children appealed directly to his conscience. "Surely no one with a human heart," he declared, could be aware of these conditions "without shuddering many times, without blushing often for shame, without being stirred to the depths, and without coming forth a consecrated soul, determined to put forth every effort possible to wipe out this damning blot on our alleged Christian civilization." As McKelway put it, this was "essentially a humane question" in which the appeal of "helpless childhood" touched a "deeper chord than any commercial consideration" and made a more powerful appeal than any social condition affecting adults. This clash between the commercial and the humane involved a struggle between "moral and humane forces" and the "power of greed." Eventually, Americans would realize that their chief social asset was their children, the hope of the future.[6]

To reformers, child nurture would replace child labor. Instead of a life of monotonous industrial labor, children needed a "life of joyous activity" that was an "uplifting, an outsifting, a refining, an organizing, an interpreting and enriching" experience. Childhood, commented an Alabama reformer, was "sacred." Accordingly, it should not "be despoiled of its golden bloom if manhood is to reap the rich harvest of life." This reconsideration of childhood was based partly on Victorian notions of child nurture and partly on the new emphases of child and adolescent psychologists on the protection of the formative years of human development. The premature shortening of childhood brought disastrous social consequences. Children should be protected against too early toil, McKelway maintained, because it led to a "stunting of the body," "dwarfing of the mind," and "spoiling of the spirit." Citing medical authorities, he maintained that the "toxin of fatigue" in factories amounted to a "wholesale poisoning of children." Children were "plastic"—malleable and changeable, in whom adult personality and behavior were fixed. Childhood, he told a group of social workers in 1911, should become a special growth stage for both body and mind. To save a child now was to save society for the future; the longer a society prolonged childhood, the more truly civilized it was.[7]

To reformers, the spectacle of working children was appalling. Factory work, they believed, dulled or stunted development. With "bones but partly formed, and muscles undeveloped," child factory workers suffered an insidious physical degeneration for which society would pay heavily in the future. For children who worked in Gulf Coast canneries, "exhausting toil" and "monotonous activity" blunted their sensibilities, stifled their minds, and placed "the unnatural burdens of industry on their weak shoulders." Factory work of a monotonous, mechanical kind, observed an Alabama reformer, dwarfed minds, stunted growth, and broke health. "The pinched, pitiful weariness of old age" was on their faces "when they should be in the bloom and buoyancy of life's morning."[8]

Deeply influenced by humanitarianism and by child saving, many reformers saw the shaping of children as instrumental to future social progress. The conservation of childhood became an imperative that united reformers; children working in factories violated that imperative. McKelway's "Declaration of Independence" for children encapsulated this new view of childhood. Childhood, the "Declaration" read, was endowed with certain rights that included "the right to play and dream," the right to sleep rather than work at night, and the right to schooling "that we may have equality of opportunity . . . in us of mind and heart." Further, children were "helpless and dependent" and were entitled to nurturing and protection; because of this fact, they deserved the "restoration" of their rights through the abolition of child labor.[9]

ALEXANDER J. MCKELWAY AND THE SEARCH
FOR SOCIAL STABILITY

Powerful ideological forces drew reformers into the child labor movement and held considerable appeal for middle-class urban southerners. Exposés of child labor in southern industry, which became common fare in many newspapers and periodicals, thinly masked an appeal to middle-class sensibilities and emotions by portraying working children as helpless victims of an oppressive, degrading system. "Picture a little child, a girl just twelve years old," read one account in the *Child Labor Bulletin*, the chief mouthpiece of the National Child Labor Committee. "Imagine this little girl, in the winter months, arising at five o'clock in the morning, eating a poorly cooked meal . . . wending her way in the darkness to a mill, working not for one hour or two hours, but for six hours steadily at one continuous task (a task which does not in any way elevate), a monotonous, invariable, nearly incessant, grind." Deprived of the joy of conversation because of a deafening work environment, breathing a polluted and badly ventilated atmosphere, this child worker possessed few rights. She had become a mechanized robot and an "illiterate, helpless, maltreated human."[10]

Such images resonated with the central ideals of Victorian culture, but this essentially sentimental appeal did not exhaust the child labor reformers' arsenal. Like other reformers, they contended that child labor was the product of a corrupted social environment and, in turn, was helping to erode the possibility of social stability in the South. Humanitarian reformers were imbued with the same degree of paternalism and racism that influenced other white southerners of the Progressive Era. The views of McKelway, although not necessarily typical, are at least representative of the cultural imperiousness of child labor reformers. Although he became increasingly sympathetic to the culture of southern textile workers, McKelway was attracted to reform for paternalistic reasons. In his version of uplift, the recipients of reform played a passive role, yet his program of reform often conflicted with the desires of working-class southerners. The contradictions of paternalism became exemplified in an experience within his own family. In 1896, after the death of a daughter, McKelway and his wife adopted an orphan girl, of what he described as "common stock," whose siblings worked in cotton mills. In a metaphor for the larger issue of child labor reform, the adopted daughter proved difficult to handle. Sending her to boarding school, McKelway found her untruthful and unreliable; during a summer trip to the mountains she was

Alexander J. McKelway.
(Courtesy of the Presbyterian Church [U.S.A.], Department of History,
Montreat, North Carolina)

unruly and disobedient, and it became impossible to "have her in our home under the former conditions." Consequently, the adopted daughter was sent from relative to friend in an unhappy search for a solution.[11]

McKelway sought to uproot a child from her cultural surroundings in the same way that he attempted to impose an alien conception of childhood on rural southerners who comprised the textile working class. Along with other reformers, McKelway was deeply suspicious of an independent, and potentially dangerous, southern proletariat. He often referred to the new "cotton mill type" as a phenomenon in which the social maladjustment of child labor figured prominently. Because of excessive reliance on child workers, southern white workers were, McKelway and others claimed, experiencing a racial degeneration. Citing the case of England—which had depended on child workers and had, he maintained, apparently experienced a racial decline among the working classes—southern child labor threatened Anglo-Saxon vigor. The South was going the way of England, he warned.[12]

Other reformers made a similar argument. As an Alabamian put it, working in mills debased childhood, retarded the proper growth of children, and produced a population that was plagued by "ignorance and physical degeneracy." To McKelway, although southern mill families came from what he believed was the "purest Anglo-Saxon stock on the Continent" and were "superior physically, mentally and morally to their fellows in any part of the world," the industrial environment fostered a degeneration of these qualities. Because of child labor, a depreciation of the "purest American stock on the Continent"— white southerners—had occurred. And since Anglo-Saxons were the world's "dominant race," their integrity had to be preserved as the only safeguard of America's greatness.[13]

By interrupting the prolongation of childhood, McKelway maintained, child labor frustrated "the race in its upward progress" and turned it "towards degeneration and extinction." Those races that protected childhood achieved progress, he told a Texas audience in 1910; those that debased childhood became "degenerate, the nation a dying nation." Preserving native-born American white qualities, he said on other occasions, meant saving southern children, as immigrant children in the North already enjoyed protection. The protection of southern children required the preservation of the vigor of the region's Anglo-Saxon stock, he wrote. While no child of American stock had been found in the sweatshops of New York City, young native-born southerners were threatened with degeneration in southern mills.[14]

Shorn of its obviously racial underpinnings, McKelway's analysis had extensive sociological ramifications, perhaps the most important of which was the defining of a debased, degenerate "cotton mill type." It was common knowledge, he wrote, that child labor in southern mills had created a "factory type" that was "easily distinguished by their pallor and a certain sallowness of complexion." Early employment led to a loss of parental restraint, early marriage, and unstable families; the consequences were an intergenerational cycle of poverty and what McKelway called "racial degeneracy." "We are brought face to face with the fact that the depreciation of our racial stock has already begun," he told a meeting of the National Child Labor Committee in 1906, and "a cotton mill type, easily recognizable," already existed. Reformers were only beginning to "learn the lesson about the defiling of the stream of our common life through the propagation of the mentally defective, adults in body, children in mind," he wrote on another occasion. These "defectives" should be taken "out of the stream of life, so that that stream may gradually clarify itself." So also, by prolonging childhood and preventing premature work by children, reformers should purify this stream of life at its source.[15]

In expressing these attitudes, McKelway and other reformers revealed how deeply racial and class paternalism pervaded their thinking. But even if paternalist, their humanitarianism was firmly rooted in a broader intellectual construct: child protection meant a greater degree of social stability. Depriving a young worker of a proper childhood was not just an affront to middle-class sensibilities, it was also a threat to social development. Ultimately, either in the present generation or the next, child labor would create an "army of tramps and paupers and criminals" from the ranks of those "whose lives have been embittered by too early toil, by the loss of childhood itself." Having robbed the factory child of his childhood, society had sowed the seeds of rebellion against all law and order.[16]

Child workers were potential criminals in part because they lacked training, provided in the public schools, for modern citizenship. The chances for working-class children to become an effective part of the civic life of the state would increase a thousandfold, wrote a reformer, if they could "spend their childhood in the fresh air of the playground . . . instead of imprisoned in the unhealthy atmosphere of the factory." The "childhood of today" would become "the citizenship of the morrow," warned McKelway. How confident could Americans be of the "well-being of the Republic itself" if public affairs were decided by the votes of children who were educated and trained in factories? That environment was "the poorest place in the country for the training of citizens of a democracy."[17]

The social instability that child labor engendered would ultimately produce greater political instability. Child workers held in ignorance and bondage would eventually grow into voters who might inflict "everlasting hurt" on democratic institutions, warned McKelway. For patriotic reasons, therefore, it was essential to abolish a system "under which large and continually increasing masses of our people are led into a bondage from which there may be no escape, save by way of a social revolution." To Edgar Gardner Murphy, the child labor system was at war with democratic institutions because it fostered the perpetuation of a nonparticipant class of southern whites whose arrested development imperiled the political order. Child labor also undermined the social institutions of church, family, and school. The long work day made the proper religious instruction of children impossible. By reversing the natural relationship of parent to child—by making the child the breadwinner—child labor undermined familial stability by creating an "unnatural independence" on the part of children. The impact on the normal development of girls was, according to McKelway, "pitiable" because they grew up completely ignorant of the ordinary duties of homemaking.[18]

Fractured by its social environment, the mill family, according to this analysis, was a debilitated institution. Child workers married at a young age and wives continued to work, but their marriages and motherhood lacked "naturalness" and "sensitiveness." Working children knew only a routine of "work and sleep," observed another reformer, without learning "how to live." He knew of "no population apparently so joyless and helpless as that surrounding the ordinary mill." Within the family, according to McKelway, the natural order was "reversed, and with it the whole ideal of family life." Children became adults "too soon" and consequently developed as "irreverent" and "independent." Fathers, in a cruel mockery of the "natural" family structure, were often unemployed "dinner toters" who became vagrants and idlers while the rest of the family worked in the mill.[19]

Child labor further undermined the family by helping to perpetuate a cycle of poverty and underdevelopment. Industrialization had debased work and depressed wages, but child workers only continued to suppress wages. Child labor, argued McKelway, actually was "one of the creators and perpetuators of poverty." By providing cheap labor, it depressed the general wage scale and forced the entire mill family to work in order to make ends meet. Child labor in this sense meant family disintegration. Working children made the "manhood" wage scale equivalent to the "childhood" wage scale: the whole family worked while living on a subsistence wage. But in an increasingly technological world this system would perpetuate and extend poverty.[20]

Child labor ran squarely against the modern public school as the primary agency of socialization. Schools and mills were in direct competition for the attention of the child in a struggle, according to McKelway, that was not unlike "the battle between Satan and the Archangel for the body of Moses—the one for its deeper burial, the other for its lifting into a larger life." The general practice in mill villages, claimed a North Carolina reformer, was "to shut the school house and open the mill door, and send every child from the home into the mill." As a former school superintendent for about nine years, he estimated that only nine pupils in his mill district ever went to high school. Children working in factories constituted a "fatal obstacle" that blocked educational progress, and, not surprisingly, illiteracy among mill children was high. Unchecked by a "stern" child labor law, the demand for child labor emptied the schools of children. True child labor reform meant transferring children and adolescents from factory to school. A compulsory education law would end child labor "by placing the children in the schoolroom and the playground" and out of the factory, a group of Georgia women petitioned to the legislature. Without an end to child labor, mill communities would never possess adequate schools, and any notion of effective compulsory education remained a pipe dream. Reformed, modernized schools would become a "substitute" for child labor, argued one reformer. Particularly in what he called the "second infancy"—adolescence—the school taught the essential principles by which pupils would be guided in their adult lives. "Send them to school," urged a North Carolina reformer writing about mill children, "where heart, mind and body may be trained."[21]

◆ ◆ ◆

THE MILL COMMUNITY AND THE NEED FOR REFORM

The characteristics and results of child labor, reformers such as McKelway came to conclude, were part of a larger problem: the emergence of a southern industrial proletariat that was alienated from the rest of society and threatened to become a permanent underclass. Put to work prematurely and denied access to educational opportunities, the cotton mill population had become a "class apart," the mill villages pockets of "feudalism, sometimes benevolent, sometimes otherwise." This feudalism embodied the permanency and future threat of the mill village. In the "feudal" village, workers were "helpless" while employers wielded near-absolute power as lords of the manor. Extending the metaphor, McKelway could describe children as "slaves" to this system.[22]

The mill village system aggravated pressures on the family. Transiency among mill workers—which McKelway described as "the only freedom yet retained by these helpless people" to change "their feudal lords"—further eroded family and social stability. Children were "the worse sufferers" in the "roving disposition among the mill employees." With the intense demand for labor, especially child labor, the industrial system's effects radiated outward throughout the rural South, disrupting its stability by attracting farmers off the land. Mill recruiters scoured the countryside for workers. They sang a sweet siren song, but among Appalachian recruits it meant a "shipwreck" to their lives, "both to those who are induced to leave their mountain homes from a desire for a change, or because of the increasing stress of life." [23]

Such popular movement, reformers believed, had a devastating effect on those rural communities of the Piedmont and Appalachia that supplied most of the mill workers. In 1906, in the middle of a major expansion that drew thousands of new industrial recruits, McKelway rode on a train from Memphis to Spartanburg filled with new workers bound for South Carolina mills. Aboard with him was a minister and child labor reformer, who deplored the disintegration of mountain families. Another traveler, a schoolteacher who was "intimately acquainted with the life of the people," complained that "it was nothing short of calamity for the children to be removed from their mountain farms to the cotton mills." A businessman, expressing himself "in two languages, English and the profane," warned of the scarcity of labor in the Appalachian South. A train conductor, joining the discussion, testified that he had seen "these people leaving their native hills in the full tide of vigorous manhood and womanhood, with rosy-cheeked children," only to return "broken in health and spirits, the fair pictures that had been painted for them by the agent blotted out in the tears of disappointment." Only the businessman favored the mass migration, stressing the material benefits the immigrants, children included, would enjoy in mill villages.[24]

Reformers were not opposed to child labor per se, as their persistent defense of children working on farms confirms. On farms, McKelway maintained, children experienced a fundamentally different sort of labor. It was a "known fact," he wrote in 1905, that open-air farm work, if not too taxing, was "beneficial in developing a strong physical constitution." Seasonal farm work did not necessarily interfere with school attendance and was "beneficial in the direction of physical development." Constantly under the watchful eye of supervising parents, a "large majority" of rural children, he maintained, engaged in harmless work that was helpful in their development. Behind the defense of rural child labor lay an articulation of the superiority of rural life over the mill village. Charles Lee Coon, an educational reformer and secretary of the North Carolina Child Labor Committee, maintained that farm children progressed better than did mill children. Whereas children from farms became "our best citizens and leaders in all walks of life," factory children failed to graduate "from the factory to any higher occupation." The argument that the mill village actually improved the standard of living for children was a central question, because it obviated "any reform in our child labor laws." [25]

Mill owners frequently responded to reformers' attacks, wrote McKelway, by "setting up the factory as a sort of earthly paradise in comparison with the farm." Mill owners liked to portray themselves as philanthropists who operated—instead of factories—health resorts, orphan asylums, juvenile reformatories, and industrial schools "rolled into one." Although this was an attractive picture, replied a Georgian, the condition of mountain people was not "so hopeless as you might think." Appalachian southerners were "healthy" in "body, in mind, and in heart." The "extremest type of the little hut" in the mountains was still a home, McKelway added, while the four-room house in the mill village, with child labor and debased family labor, was not.[26]

When Charles W. Stiles suggested in 1909 that hookworms were more present in rural than in industrial settings—implying that conditions in mill villages marked an improvement—he crashed into a hornet's nest. Child labor reformers universally condemned this position. One reformer, disputing the notion that all mill villages were better than farms, urged that standards be raised in mill towns and mountains alike. John C. Campbell, the mountain reformer, noting in 1910 that the controversy had evoked more heat than light, maintained that Stiles's assertion mistakenly suggested that "if the hookworm could be eliminated, all the industrial problems and all wrong social conditions in the mill centers would be solved." According to Campbell, "the possibilities of life in the mountains" were superior to the "possibilities in the mill centers."[27]

The controversy with Stiles provided reformers with an opportunity to restate their view of how factories were corrupting childhood and the rural family. Even if the "mill pallor" was the product of hookworms, wrote McKelway, children nonetheless retained a special claim for protection against the known consequences of child labor. In spite of Stiles's contentions, he said, "about the most wholesome place for bringing up a child" was on "the average farm." By implication, the reformers' refutation of Stiles reaffirmed that rural conditions were not "immoral and indifferent or degenerate," but that the social problems of the mill village were the product of an enervating social environment. The "heart of the question" remained whether children in the mills were "better off when the fullest exploitation of their toil" was permitted. Clearly, an environment that was "humid, heated, [and] lint-filled" was corrupting; work in the open air of the farm was not.[28]

Reformers advocated strong measures. Most realized that child labor reform struck at the heart of southern society and its desire to industrialize, and they anticipated the difficulty of effecting so radical a change. Reformers deeply committed to the cause, McKelway once observed, sometimes grew "sick at heart" when they considered the fierce opposition they met and the abuse and ridicule to which they were subjected. Although public opinion usually sympathized with children, it did so only when the costs were low. In the South, to challenge the "curse of child labor" risked the label of "an extremist, an agitator." The whole modern industrial system, he ruefully concluded, was "built on child labor."[29]

One of the chief obstacles to reform was the attitude of mill-worker parents. Reformers generally held the parents in low esteem and blamed them for allowing their children to work. With considerable exaggeration, they cited the instances of parents who lived on the wages of their children. According to John C. Campbell, it was common for Appalachian fathers to "put their children into the mills and live off of the proceeds." "The heartless greed and often the laziness of the parents" were largely at fault, said an Augusta, Georgia, school superintendent in 1912. Parents insisted, he claimed, on the employment of the entire family—children as well as adults. The "unprotected child" was "caught between the cupidity of his parent and the apprehension of the mill-owners," and his life was "ground into a joyless, hopeless, pitiable existence." An Alabama reformer discovered what he called the "utter perversion of parental obligations," in which "thriftless and dissipated" fathers lived off the earnings of their families and squandered them in saloons and gambling dens.[30]

Although most reformers blamed mill parents, others minimized their responsibility. "Who are interested in perpetuating this child labor system?" McKelway asked. Not parents, "if only they knew," for "parental nature" was "not so different a thing among the poor from what it is among the well to do." Although they were caught in a system that consumed children, the children themselves preferred to work in mills than to attend school—hence the contradiction inherent in the "great problem of saving the children [is] that frequently the child himself prefers the mill to the school." McKelway instead stressed that the problem of child labor was systemic, beyond the control of children, parents, and even mill managers. He used the image of the "child slave" with some effectiveness. The mill village system placed numerous temptations in the way of "ignorant, indifferent or poverty-stricken parents." Wherein did responsibility, then, truly lie?—with parents, or properly with their employers? Who was more responsible for the institution of slavery, McKelway asked, the "African chief who sold his people, already slaves to his lordly will, or the British or New England slave-trader who bought them and transported them?"[31]

The emphasis on environmental sources of social problems, along with the utter futility of voluntarism, led McKelway and other reformers toward public policy solutions. The issue could not be left to sensible Christians, wrote a North Carolinian, because "all of us know that many parents are neither

John C. Campbell.
(Courtesy of the Southern Historical Collection, University of North Carolina
at Chapel Hill Library)

sensible nor Christian." Only state intervention, if need be in violation of the parent-child relationship, could end the evil. Southerners had entered an era in which government was exercising "a much wider function than we formerly believed." With a duty to children, the state was obligated to provide for their protection. According to this reformer, there was a right of "state guardianship" in which the rights of children superseded parents' rights.[32]

The solution to child labor, reformers eventually concluded, lay in state intervention. Government should "step in between the child on the one hand and the parents and the mill owners on the other" to prevent children "from being broken on the wheel of exploitation." Rather than paternalism or excessive governmental intervention, according to this reformer, a better description was "maternalism," or the "conservation of human assets by a sovereign State." If the home atmosphere was demoralizing and degrading, argued another reformer, government possessed the right to "declare the authority of such inhuman parentage forfeited." Short of this extreme solution, the state had an "imperative duty and moral obligation" to "guard and watch" children and to enable them to become "honest, decent, and useful citizens."[33]

◆ ◆ ◆

THE CHILD LABOR CRUSADE

Child labor reformers found that the crusade was the most effective means of translating their objectives into policy. Like moral reformers and social efficiency reformers, they sought, as an Alabama reformer put it, to ignite the "fires that have illuminated the disgraceful conditions found in every nook and corner of this land of prosperity." As had other crusaders, they would achieve their ends by converting public opinion through mass mobilization and then riding an irresistible groundswell of sentiment. Child labor reformers depended on well-worn techniques of exposure and the effective use of modern media. The arousal of southern public opinion, wrote McKelway, would sound a "trumpet call to battle to protest against such outrage upon helplessness." Imagery of a crusade and a societal conversion was common. For McKelway, a "few years into the future" lay a society without child workers. In the early mornings, according to his vision, "a great army of children" rested in the "deep sleep of childhood," undisturbed by the whistles of industry. Roused from sleep, these children would go off to school, no longer breadwinners but as children should be—carefree, with a "right to play."[34]

The instrument of this change, and the coordinating agency of the crusade, was the National Child Labor Committee. As was the case with the Anti-Saloon League, the Southern Education Board, and the Rockefeller Sanitary

Commission, the NCLC was an outside pressure group that sought to organize and coordinate a regional campaign to effect policy change. Its structure was modeled on other successful single-issue, pressure groups. Formed in 1904, the committee turned out literature, sent out investigating agents, held national conferences, lobbied in Washington, and helped to organize state committees. State committees, in turn, ran local campaigns and lobbied state legislatures.[35]

The state committees brought together child labor reform groups that had existed before the NCLC's formation. In the cotton textile belt that extended from the Carolinas to Alabama, local reformers had already organized themselves and engaged in an attempt to have restrictive legislation enacted. Local reformers were spurred on by the activities of Irene Ashby, who toured twenty-five mills in Alabama in 1900–1901 and other mills elsewhere in the South thereafter at the behest of the American Federation of Labor.[36] As a young English girl of good social standing, Ashby had, as she remembered it, a "life of garden parties, theaters and balls." Convinced that the only way to help the masses was by living with them, she decided to work in the West London Social Guild, a settlement house. Suffering from poor health, she traveled to the United States, where she met Samuel Gompers, president of the AFL. At his suggestion, Ashby traveled to the textile belt. After visiting a South Carolina mill where conditions were "too horrible for belief," she helped to organize local reform forces.[37]

Reformers, especially women, were impressed with Ashby, whom they found to be "so young & pretty & charming & so unlike a labor agitator." Emily Stewart Harrison, the Atlanta reformer, remembered her as "blond and fair and petite" whose blue eyes were "steady," looking "you straight in the face," sometimes dancing with merriment, other times "serious with thought." Ashby was what Harrison described as a "new woman." Pioneer women reformers of an earlier generation were not "lovely to look upon"; they took life seriously, with "too many errors to combat, too many wrongs for them to right." No thought could be given to gowns or banquets. Reformers like Ashby, in contrast, were part of "a great and growing class of young men and women who today, with hearts aflame over existing economic injustice and industrial wrongs," were attracted to a new conception of social service. En route, however, they could "trip lightly along" and "pluck by the way the fragrant blossoms of love and happiness."[38]

While Ashby helped to mobilize social reformers, especially women, the National Child Labor Committee offered the advantages of single-interest organization and planning. Over time, the NCLC's political skills became well honed. The experience of Mississippi provided an example of the benefits of regional coordination and the NCLC's political expertise. In that state, child labor reform concerned the few cotton textile mills of its central region and the shellfish canneries of the Gulf Coast. Reform was first suggested at the annual meeting of the King's Daughters in 1902. Appointing a committee to consider the question, the women's group proposed new regulations at the state legislature two years later. But the women reformers received a rude introduction to political realities when they discovered the "ignorance" and "general indifference" of the legislators toward the issue, and the bill never emerged from committee. With the aid of the NCLC, the reformers tried a different approach. Branching out to include other interested reform organizations, they learned the importance of first educating the public and launched an extensive public relations campaign.[39]

Nonetheless, the efforts of the NCLC to organize a crusade throughout the South proved frustrating. In spite of an ambitious plan, the campaign remained top-heavy, with a well-supported national organization matched by poorly structured and largely ineffective state committees. The state committees were especially weak in the cotton textile belt—a fact that is evident in the absence of surviving records of these organizations. In North Carolina, where prohibition, school, and health crusades received an enthusiastic response, the state NCLC remained unorganized until 1909, when it began an ambitious campaign of general education over the next four years. Seeking a higher age limit for child workers (from twelve to fourteen), a reduction in the maximum number of hours (from sixty-six to sixty), the abolition of night work, and factory inspection, the campaign employed stereopticon lectures, newspaper articles, and speeches to "arouse the people who are at present ignorant of these conditions." With the campaigns in both Carolinas working in coordination during 1910, the national office also supplied a state agent, W. H. Swift, whose salary was paid out of its coffers.[40]

The North Carolina campaign could claim few victories. A major reason was the mutual suspicion that existed between state- and national-level reformers. This tension was perhaps unavoidable, given what many southerners perceived as northern domination of the organization. In contrast to other reform groups, it never achieved a true intersectional character. On the other hand, NCLC officials generally believed that the state committees were too cautious and reluctant to risk controversy. In a letter to the North Carolina secretary, Charles Lee Coon, the national executive secretary, Owen R. Lovejoy, acknowledged that NCLC aggressiveness had in the past "aroused considerable antagonism," which was "an obstacle to our work." Yet he was concerned that a policy of providing aid "in quiet ways" would result in "harmful delay" by the state committee.[41]

Lovejoy and other NCLC officials were also concerned about what they perceived to be a nonconfrontational, even cozy relationship between the state committee and the cotton textile industry. That perception was rooted in the reality that a number of millmen endorsed and even participated in the reform leadership. But in order to obtain this support, the NCLC national leadership claimed, the state committee had made too many concessions. Although he realized that the committee did not wish to appear radical and to show the manufacturers that the committee was "as sane and conservative as they," Lovejoy wrote in May 1912, the result was that in its legislative agenda the campaign was "tied . . . hand and foot." Although legislation enacted by the North Carolina General Assembly yielded what Coon called the "small gains" of a reduced age limit while it lowered the maximum hours, Lovejoy believed that on the crucial point—factory inspection—the law was weak. Manufacturers could now claim, with "considerable justice," that they had coopted the movement for reform and had themselves written the new law. Future changes, he thought, would come with greater difficulty. Millmen could "make an impressive appeal to the people not to be led astray by theoretical reformers to the ruin of their one great industry, but continue to trust to the judgment and unselfish philanthropy of the cotton manufacturers."[42]

Even among members of the North Carolina NCLC committee, suspicion of outside intervention continued to rankle. Clarence Poe, editor and publisher of the *Progressive Farmer* and a member of the committee, complained in April 1911 that the campaign would enjoy "better success here in North Carolina if we run our shebang entirely without outside aid or interference." About a year later, he wrote that McKelway, as a national NCLC official, could "do us no good, but a lot of harm" by visiting the state, and he urged that "only residents of the State should participate in our North Carolina fight."[43] Although Coon, as state secretary, tried to steer a middle course, others, including state Baptist editor and prohibitionist Josiah W. Bailey, were equally suspicious.[44]

In part because of its frustrating experience with state campaigns, the NCLC after 1910 conducted its own investigations independent of the state committees. What the NCLC discovered added grist to its mill. In the cotton textile belt, predictably, investigation confirmed the ever-presence of young workers in the mills. NCLC investigators reported that most children were employed in the spinning room and were generally concentrated in the unskilled phases of production. Most doffers were boys between the ages of twelve and fourteen. Boys also worked as spinners, band boys, and sweepers; girls were spinning-frame tenders. Few of the workers were socially mobile. NCLC investigators further concluded that the social and psychological consequences of child labor in mills were devastating. Several agents reported that workers who had entered the factory as children appeared to be "all worked out" by their twenties or thirties. In Athens, Georgia, an agent described a thirty-four-year-old woman who had started in the mill as a nine-year-old. She "hated the very thought of working in the mill and from all appearances was ready for the scrap heap." Now a "worn-out person," she wished that she could escape to a place "where she could never hear the whistle blow."[45]

At the same time, these field reports dispelled some of the reformers' illusions about the mill village. Indeed, they brought home the complexity of the child labor issue. Numerous accounts told of how whole families were employed in mills, but, at least according to the mill managers, the labor scarcity and a high rate of transiency during the Progressive Era permitted workers to insist on family labor. In Alabama, a mill superintendent said he made a "special effort" to obtain family workers because he would then possess "a greater hold on them as they can't move about from place to place so readily." A Georgia mill owner explained to an investigator that he preferred not to hire underage children but "he did not understand how the large families and the widows would get along without the help of children."[46]

The pressures that transiency exerted on mill managers provided incentives for them to hire child workers, especially after age twelve. In many instances, violations of the law were as much the result of parental evasion as they were of owner connivance. According to a North Carolina reformer, many owners preferred not to hire children but were forced to do so because they were unwilling to challenge the signed statements of parents about their children's ages. The complexity of the problem often baffled reformers. In Moultrie, Georgia, a NCLC investigator followed three boys, employed as frame tenders, who appeared to be underage and learned that they were from the same family. Posing as a salesman offering "free" insurance, the agent asked for the children's ages and discovered that they were all in violation of the law. Even hardened and jaded NCLC investigators found the rate of turnover and a constant interchange of farm and mill sobering. This "moving habit" made systematic investigation difficult, especially if one desired to get below the surface, and made the prospects for real reform daunting. Mill people were "very independent in their attitude toward an employer, often too much so for their own good," wrote an owner. Because of "mere restlessness" and as a "wholesome check" on managers, they did not "hesitate when dissatisfied to move from mill to mill or back to farm work." As one superintendent explained, boys were hired early, even though their work was "irregular," so that they could acquire "the training necessary to do their work more quickly."[47]

Almost everywhere that cotton mills existed, investigators found that small children were hired as "helpers." In Columbus, Mississippi, an eight-year-old boy accompanied his sister to help with spooling because, she explained, he had nowhere else to go. The practice was tolerated, according to another worker in the same mill, because management "ain't strict here." Not far away, in West Point, a mother justified having her daughter as a "helper" because it kept her "out of mischief." Child labor, NCLC investigators demonstrated, was woven into the fabric of working-class life. Thus, when a mill closed in Mississippi, parents were disappointed, but the "greatest hardship," according to one observer, was on the children because they would now have to attend school.[48]

The field investigations muddied the waters in other respects. While most of the NCLC reformers concentrated their attention on cotton textiles, their investigators demonstrated that child labor permeated the southern economic system and that the abuse of childhood was not confined to the mill village. In 1911 and 1913, when NCLC agents Lewis W. Hine, Edward F. Brown, and Harry M. Bremer visited the Gulf Coast states, especially Mississippi, they found that shellfish canneries depended on a system of transient, migratory families who picked berries and tomatoes and shucked oysters in the Chesapeake basin states of Delaware and Maryland during the summer months and then moved to Mississippi for the winter packing season.[49]

In urban communities, as well, investigators noted that child labor was a well-established part of the social fabric. Night messenger services, which existed in all southern cities, were staffed by young boys, who came into regular contact with the world of urban prostitution. Often serving as messengers to arrange assignations, night messenger boys were witnesses to debauches, according to one agent, "of such a nature that they can neither be written or spoken, with propriety." And in the rural South, where most child labor reformers tended to glorify the social environment of the farm, investigators were forced to concede that a strong affinity existed in the child labor culture of farm and mill.[50]

The net results of the NCLC state campaigns were meager. In North Carolina, for example, the legislature in 1903 banned child labor for age twelve and under. Thereafter, reformers met with a series of frustrations; their scant accomplishments included, in 1907, an age limit of fourteen—except for "apprentices" ages twelve and thirteen—and, four years later, a reduction in the maximum allowed hours for children from sixty-six to sixty. By 1912 North Carolina had stubbornly but successfully resisted regulation; it remained one of five states in the nation with an age limit under fourteen and one of three states, along with Florida and Arkansas, with no provisions for factory inspection. By the beginning of World War I, no state in the region had enacted what most reformers would have considered an adequate child labor law. More important, the existing legislation, especially in the cotton textile states, lacked the means of effective enforcement. Georgia's law, which was fairly typical of the Southeast, prohibited workers under twelve but exempted them if they had a widowed mother or a "dependent" father. The result, according to one account, was that the law was "absolutely useless." Even when the law was adequate, it was unlikely to be enforced in textile communities. As a reformer conceded in 1905, restrictive laws for child workers were "constantly [and] easily violated."[51]

Reviewing state laws in 1910, McKelway noted that, although some states had made a beginning, the effectiveness of southern child labor legislation was "farcical." In no state did limits on hours and ages compare to those in northern industrial states. Alabama's law was enforced by its inspector of jails and factories, with only one assistant; Tennessee had a single official who lacked travel funds or clerical help; North Carolina, Florida, Georgia, Mississippi, and Arkansas had no such official at all. Violations of the law occurred in an "open and shameless and innumerable" fashion across the South. Child labor crusaders were the most frustrated social reformers of the early twentieth-century South, and the causes of their frustration helped to distinguish child labor reformers from other social reformers. In contrast to the latter, child labor reformers found the formation of alliances with the objects of their reforms—in this case, workers and managers—exceedingly difficult, and they remained outsiders to the inhabitants of the mill village. The fact that the reformers relied on investigators rather than on rallies or locally based crusades suggests that they met a united front. The NCLC field agent for North Carolina, W. H. Swift, noted that reformers faced a "determined opposition" that compared to the antebellum South's response to abolitionism. Both owners and workers understood an unwritten code, what one agent called a "gentlemen's agreement," that "neither I nor any one else should go to the mill operatives themselves to put the matter square to them."[52]

Hostility was not unusual. One NCLC agent, described as a "lovable and gentle Christian minister," visited a Georgia mill village, about two miles from a railroad. After he inspected the mill school and took photographs, the president of the mill learned of his visit and ordered him out of the town. The agent then discovered that he was also forbidden entrance to the local hotel and was warned to leave the village limits. In Mississippi, Alexander Fleisher, another NCLC inspector, was harangued by the president of the Stonewall Cotton Mills during a visit in early 1912. He claimed that the agent "had been sneaking around the town without letting him know." The agent "explained this away" by claiming that he had sought to avoid interfering with the marriage of the mill president's daughter. The president, apparently accepting this untruth, "calmed down" and proceeded to describe himself as "a benefactor of the community through the charity of allowing the children to work." NCLC agents often had to use extraordinary ingenuity to uncover examples of illegal child labor, and they usually pushed to the limit whatever rules and restrictions the owners had established. When Lewis Hine was told by a Kosciusko, Mississippi, mill superintendent that he could take photographs of the mill but not of the workers, he photographed them "when the boss was not around."[53]

In other communities, mill owners portrayed NCLC agents as outside invaders and, with some success, as the greater threat to the mill village. What was needed, instead of "cheap criticism," argued one South Carolina manufacturer, was "an accurate knowledge of mill and mill-village conditions and influences as they really exist, and an intelligent discussion by the public at large." Mill owners, with some justification, also pointed out the vast cultural gap that divided middle-class reformers from the cotton textile proletariat. They maintained that there was little difference between working children in the mills and working children on the farms; to limit the labor of their children meant taking the potentially explosive step of encroaching on the traditional parental authority of rural southerners. Rural children began working on the farm at "the tender age of eight years, toiling under a burning June and July sun," wrote a Gastonia, North Carolina, manufacturer. Singling out workers for "legislation which they do not solicit" meant informing them that "you are ignorant, . . . you know not what you need, you are a class entirely different from us, who have the trained mind and who desire to be your guardians." The result might well be the sowing of seeds for "a revolution right here in the South." Why should this "interference" take place on behalf of "satisfied, contented people whose conditions have been so greatly improved?"[54]

In these circumstances, child labor reformers could expect an unenthusiastic response from the mill village. An exception to this generalization occurred in Atlanta, where a bitter strike in 1914 prompted workers at the Fulton Bag and Cotton Mills Company to attempt to forge an alliance with social reformers in that city. Announcing that they endorsed the elimination of all child labor under the age of fourteen, the strikers briefly attracted the support of downtown reformers and attempted to exploit the divisions between the Jewish owners of the mill and the WASP reformers.[55] But even in this instance, cooperation between workers and reformers was fleeting and tenuous. Elsewhere, it was even rarer, largely because of the mutual suspicions stemming from a gap in cultural perceptions.[56]

The child labor crusade yielded the most meager results among all the

Laurel Cotton Mills, Laurel, Mississippi, 1911: Father with two sons in front row.
Photograph by Lewis W. Hine.
(Courtesy of the Mississippi Department of Archives and History)

southern social reform crusades. Unlike other reformers, child labor reformers faced formidable obstacles. They were seeking, on the one hand, a policy change that struck at the heart of the cheap labor advantage of the southern cotton-textile industry. Consequently, the attempt to abolish child labor encountered powerful opposition from factory owners of the Piedmont South. But reform also enjoyed little enthusiasm among workers, primarily because it assaulted a conception of family and the role of children that was alien to them.

◆ ◆ ◆

ORIGINS OF WOMAN SUFFRAGE

Southern suffragists shared with other American women activists a heritage that dated back to the nineteenth century. Woman suffrage had occupied a prominent place on the national agenda since the Civil War, and suffrage organizations existed in the South from the 1890s onward. To be sure, woman suffrage was both a political and a social movement. Yet it is impossible to separate the strands completely, because the movement to enfranchise women grew inevitably out of their participation in social reform. It can be argued that in the South, and probably in the rest of the country, there would have been no movement for woman suffrage without a prior large-scale entry of women into the public arena via the side door of social reform. Virtually all suffragists were social reformers—in the South and elsewhere. In addition, suffragists adopted new attitudes toward gender and gender roles precisely because of their experiences in and knowledge gained from campaigns for moral and social reform. Finally, suffragists justified their cause on the ground that only female participation could ensure the triumph of moral and social causes.

The suffrage cause remained isolated and ineffective until after the turn of the century, however, and not until about 1910 did southern suffragism emerge as a potent force. The energizing and growth of the suffrage movement in the South—and across the nation—reflected profound social changes occasioned by urbanization. In most states, Progressive Era suffragists began their movement in urban centers that tolerated and sometimes nurtured different conceptions of gender. In Virginia, the early suffrage organizations were established in Richmond and other cities. In Alabama, the first organization and the center of the movement was in Birmingham; in Georgia, it was in Atlanta; in Texas, it was in Houston. "New" suffragists such as Madeline McDowell Breckinridge of Kentucky, Pattie Ruffner Jacobs of Alabama, Lila Meade Valentine of Virginia, and Minnie Fisher Cunningham of Texas came from urban backgrounds.[57]

Southern suffragists were also from elite urban families and, not surprisingly, appealed to urban elites. Suffragists consciously sought to attract elite support. Their "greatest grip" in Birmingham, according to one account, was in the homes of society's leaders and "most exclusive women." The movement there and in Alabama generally was completely organized and promoted by women of "old and aristocratic families" whose "culture, high social position and wide personal influence" made them a "powerful factor" in the success of the movement. Birmingham suffragists emphasized the social qualities of the movement; "Meet Me at Headquarters" was their official slogan. Meanwhile, the committee work and leadership structure was dominated by women who were prominent in education, philanthropy, and other social areas.[58]

Hailing from the "best" families, suffragists were usually well educated and very articulate. Minnie Fisher Cunningham of Houston—known by contemporaries as "Minnie Fish"—graduated from the School of Pharmacy at the University of Texas Medical School in 1902 and then married B. J. Cunningham, a Galveston insurance man. She ran for the U.S. Senate in 1928 and for the governorship in 1944. Pattie Ruffner Jacobs was a member of an influential West Virginia family; her first cousin, William Henry Ruffner, served as Virginia's first superintendent of public instruction. Described by

Suffrage parade, Georgia.
(Courtesy of the Georgia Department of Archives and History)

her biographer as her family's "most stimulating and original thinker," she attended preparatory school in Nashville and teachers' training school in Birmingham, took voice lessons in Paris, and studied art in New York City. Married to a wealthy Birmingham railroad man in 1898, she devoted herself to local causes. In 1911 she helped to found the Birmingham Equal Suffrage Association and, a year later, the state suffrage organization.[59]

Suffrage leaders elsewhere in the South were also women of exceptional talents. Madeline McDowell Breckinridge's speaking abilities were legendary and made her widely sought after by suffragists around the country. Probably only second to Breckinridge in her regional and national reputation was Virginia suffragist Lila Meade Valentine, who, like Jacobs and Breckinridge, possessed superb speaking abilities and served as a unifying figure for the state organization. When the Equal Suffrage League of Virginia was organized in 1909, she was characterized by Ellen Glasgow as the only woman who combined the requisite courage and intelligence with "the inexhaustible patience of which victors and martyrs are made."[60]

Suffragists were "strong minded women," according to Alabama suffragist Virginia Tunstall Clay-Clopton, a characteristic that antisuffragists liked to use as their "favorite reproach." Yet suffragists, she thought, would do well not to pretend that they were "simpletons or imbeciles." These "strong minded women" usually saw the suffrage as the natural extension of a collective reaching out; suffragists were cosmopolitan and wanted a greater role in the wider world. Jessie Stokely Burnett, in her thirties during most of the suffrage struggle, was raised on a mountain farm near Newport, Tennessee. Although her mother was widowed at the age of twenty-nine with four children, Jessie studied at Yale and Smith colleges and taught at the University of California, where she became a suffragist. Moving to South Carolina to teach at Furman University, where she married a physician, she continued to lead suffrage and women's causes in South Carolina.[61]

Whether married or unmarried—and suffrage ranks certainly included both—suffrage women were activists. On one level, they enthusiastically accepted contemporary mores, especially on class and race, and their appeals were couched in language that fellow southerners could readily understand. But whereas they vigorously defended the status quo of race and class relations, in the last analysis suffragists were willing to test traditional definitions of gender in southern culture. For most married, white middle-class women, the suffrage issue had little direct or immediate relevance; the great majority of them, after all, were traditionalists who did not venture much into the world of public affairs. Yet economic change for working women has always affected women who do not work outside the home in subtle, indirect ways. Moreover, as historians have noted, an even more important consideration for middle-class women was the transformation of woman's role inside the family. This changing role, suffragists contended, was not accompanied by a new political role for women. Twentieth-century women suddenly wanted the vote, Breckinridge told the Virginia legislature in 1913, because of "changed conditions" that had extended the role of women outward into the world. This new role did not mean the destruction of married women's status in the family; rather, it meant its exaltation. The changes affecting the roles of men and women were subtle and "interfered little with the home or with industry." By demanding the vote, women were not abandoning their sphere as much as "demanding a share" of the management of public policy.[62]

To suffragists, women's political role should reflect their position within the Victorian home. This role redefinition involved articulate, educated women of the upper middle-class family especially. Jessie E. Townshend, a Norfolk suffragist, explained that, at age fifty-two, she possessed "more time, leisure, money, brains[,] health and strength to study and handle the question[s] of the day than ever before." Although materially secure and intellectually equipped to help solve "the many perplexing problems of these days," she faced a government that excluded her because of her gender. The lack of political representation meant nothing to many southern women, but others found it deeply frustrating. To Valentine, disfranchisement for women meant that they remained in a condition of "guardianship," as if they were minors or incompetents. Those women who "passively" accepted political conditions "as if they were decrees of Providence" retarded "the progress of the race." Because they were mothers of both genders, passivity of this sort, she warned, could be passed on genetically; sons of "undeveloped" mothers might also lack independence, initiative, and the ability to seize opportunities. Among women of the middle class, psychological "flabbiness" had resulted from an inbred "disuse of . . . God-given faculties." Women should stand forth as mothers of their country, declared Laura Clay, and not be "bounded by the walls of the home," sacred though they were. Women laboring for the "elevation" of their gender also worked for the "the unity of the race."[63]

◆ ◆ ◆
SUFFRAGISTS AND SOCIAL REFORM

Prohibition, education, public health, and child labor were all social reform movements in which women played a major role, and a revitalized southern suffrage movement emerged on the heels of these crusades after about 1910. Women were attracted to these reforms at least partly because they protected their status; enfranchising women, said suffragists, would provide them even greater self-protection. Although the long-run objective of the suffrage movement was to improve society generally, wrote a Texas suffragist, its immediate aim was to secure for woman two things that the political system denied her: self-respect and self-protection.[64]

Legislatures, suffragists frequently pointed out, rarely if ever enacted legislation raising the age of consent for sexual intercourse. It was clear that the legal code was "dictated solely by men," wrote a Georgia woman, when legislators honored themselves and their constituents by protecting little girls only to the age of ten. When the Mississippi legislature in 1914 refused to raise the age of consent from twelve to eighteen, a suffragist concluded that there was no stronger argument for woman suffrage than "this disgraceful fact." Without the vote, many women increasingly realized, it would be impossible to achieve equal legal status. No group had ever "legislated with perfect justice, or approximate justice to another class," explained Breckinridge. Mothers possessed "no standing in court in our male autocracy" because men asserted that they would, at their pleasure, "perfectly protect them." Nonetheless, every suffragist understood that the vote would bring women greater legal and economic security.[65]

Yet achieving the vote also represented the culmination of a broader agenda. The vote would feminize the previously all-male world of politics and policy and make possible, as Josiah W. Bailey put it, "a new and better point of view" that would end the "sort of politics that the professional politicians cultivate."[66] Woman suffrage would unite men and women for the general welfare, wrote a Texan, bringing neither "smoking car politics" nor "petticoat government" but, instead, "a state and national home, where good fathers and mothers are alike indispensable." Equal suffrage, argued the Birmingham suffragist and lawyer Isadore Shapiro, added the "penetrating voice of women's votes" to the political sphere. Ellen Evans Cathcart, a South Carolina suffragist, acknowledged that votes for women would not usher in the millennium, yet she predicted that they would vote "in terms of humanity" rather than in "terms of special privilege." By "long habit" men thought in terms of "dollars & cents," whereas women thought about "husbands, children & unborn babies."[67]

Inadequate protection led women toward social reform and, ultimately, the suffrage. Men had paid little attention to those aspects of governmental activity that affected the home, wrote Alabama suffragist Bossie O'Brien Hundley in 1915. The home was not men's business; adherence to the adage that politics was "the business of men" had led to negligence and indifference regarding the domestic issues of childhood, education, and public health. What man ever ran for public office on a platform of pure food, clean water, and pure milk? she asked. "What set of men ever required it?" Alabama women were "quickly learning that watchfulness, a desire to control their homes and their children" was hopeless without the power that possession of the ballot guaranteed them.[68]

A Georgia suffragist in 1915 recited the case of a woman living in a small town in that state. The woman was married to a drunkard, and her life had been "one long, hard grind." In only a few days, her husband was able to lose her savings through drinking and gambling; she nonetheless ran a hotel until she could free her husband of his debts. Despite local prohibition, he easily found liquor, and so she pressed for national prohibition to overcome local indifference toward enforcement of the law. Her conclusion was that the inadequacy of local prohibition and of the protection of women under the law reflected masculine government. In her case, indifferent enforcement was a matter of her "very existence." "If the wives and daughters and sisters of these men," wrote the suffragist, "had a voice in the selecting of these officers of the law," prohibition would be enforced.[69]

Suffragists were confident that including women in politics would allow women of their class to exert "their influence" to bring "better days" for the South. States that had woman suffrage, they pointed out, tended also to have compulsory education, industrial welfare commissions, protective legislation for women, equal guardianship legislation, a higher age of consent, restrictions on prostitution, statewide prohibition, and child labor restrictions. States that inadequately protected women and children and codified male supremacy within the institution of marriage were working "contrary to the requirements of society," maintained the Richmond artist and suffragist Adele Clark. Woman suffrage was "a working force for the betterment of society." "Just give to women this right of representation," an anonymous woman wrote in 1915, and "we will tell you how we want to be represented." Such a woman's program would include an eight-hour law for men and women, widows' and mothers' pension laws, child labor and school reform, public health improvements, and an end to political corruption.[70]

Suffragists contended that the expanding functions of government in morality, education, health, and child welfare were a result of the expanding power and influence of women. A group of interests existed, argued Valentine, that belonged particularly to women and were associated with the expanding functions of government. Women had already involved themselves in the public affairs of southern life. In caring for the infirm, dependent, and helpless, wrote Breckinridge, southern women played so important a role that their abrupt departure from public affairs would result in "sudden and widespread calamity." In a "higher conception of the word," southern women were already "political" in the "carrying on of that public business on which private life depends, in civilized society."[71]

As mothers, voting women would humanize society. Women specialized in child welfare and were "primarily the custodians of these home interests." Wherever mothers had a voice in government, children had a better chance. Guardians of the home, women were obliged to participate in politics. In order to protect the home, argued a Texas suffragist, the "mother's duty" of women compelled them to "enter the struggle against the combined forces of the professional politician and commercial corruptionist." According to the Virginia novelist and feminist Mary Johnston, the entire civilized world was attempting to "clean house," and women everywhere were entering "into the larger world" in a "great social home." Describing this new role for women as "social motherhood," Johnston asserted that they would stand "shoulder to shoulder" for reform: "for a far more general, truer and nobler education, for health, for temperate living, for world peace, for economic betterment, for equalization of opportunity, for a high freedom and responsibility for each human being, man as well as woman, woman as well as man." To Atlanta suffragist Eleonore Raoul, the vote was a "broom that will sweep clean, or let us say cleaner, the dirty streets and the dirty houses of our ring-ruled city."

Woman suffrage was a "disinfectant" that would help to purge the social germs afflicting society. It would not only serve as the "protecting arm" to save the lives of their own babies, but it would also be a vehicle of uplift for other people's babies.[72]

In many instances, reformers and suffragists were mutually nurturing. Early urban women's organizations, such as the Portia Club and the Equal Rights Association Club of New Orleans, considered social reform and suffrage as interrelated. The Portia Club, formed in 1884, was superseded by the ERA, which was organized in 1896 as a broad, reform-oriented women's club. For most of its history, according to a Louisiana suffragist, the ERA undertook civic reform, with suffrage a "secondary consideration." According to one of its most prominent members, suffragist Kate Gordon, the club was responsible for "every bit of civic advancement in New Orleans." Its main purpose, explained another account, was to make women "Triumphant Citizens" by pressing for social legislation. Early on, the ERA took a particular interest in leading a local effort to restrict the "moral cancer" of prostitution.[73]

Yet the turn toward suffrage, especially after 1910, reflected a sense of frustration. In Alabama, the Birmingham Equal Suffrage Association—whose formation preceded the state suffrage association—was organized after the National Child Labor Committee met in that city in March 1911. As one suffragist recalled, those who heard the speakers at this meeting "became convinced that if the child labor problem could be solved the mother[']s voice must be heard politically." Similarly, in South Carolina one of the founders of the state's Equal Suffrage League remembered that its formation resulted from the legislature's unwillingness to restrict prostitution and provide for compulsory education. In a political scene dominated by Governor Coleman L. Blease—whose antireform working-class appeals were obviously repugnant—women had a "greater responsibility" to aid the "good men," who were in a minority, to bring about "drastic reforms." Another suffragist in the same state remembered that suffrage leaders were less concerned about a mass movement than they were guided by a belief that having the vote would provide an opportunity to enact social reform.[74]

The case of Kentucky provides another example of the relationship between women's role in reform crusades and their eventual conversion to suffrage. There, suffragists emerged directly from the mountain settlement, education, and child labor reform activities of the state's women's organizations.[75] There was an especially strong affinity between the school reform crusade and the campaign for votes for women. The connection became immediately apparent in 1907, when the legislature passed a county school board act that established the rudiments of a consolidated, centralized system of school gov-

Eleonore Raoul.
(Courtesy of the Special Collections Department, Emory University Library)

ernance and was designed to replace the locally controlled district system. At the same time, the new legislation so altered the law as to forbid women to vote in school elections, a privilege that they had enjoyed in limited form since 1838.

This stunning defeat for Kentucky women's organizations, which mobilized in 1907 against the passage of the act, brought home a contradiction: women educational reformers were expected to participate in the school crusade without, according to Breckinridge, also enjoying "an equal share in government with men." For these women, the "most important education" in this setback "had been of ourselves." After 1907 Breckinridge insisted that participation in educational reform could occur only on a basis of equality, as she along with others had concluded that it was "not dignified to work for the schools without a voice in their government."[76]

Over the next five years, reinstating school suffrage for Kentucky women became the dominant issue for suffragists. Because it had already existed and fell short of full suffrage, school suffrage could be portrayed as a conservative reform; moreover, it was, as the state General Federation of Women's Clubs resolved in 1909, part of the "vital interest of the mother sex in the education of children." The attempt to enact school suffrage was, according to Breckinridge, connected to school reform; women emerged "to shelter and protect the great brood of Kentucky children" who were growing up in ignorance. But school reform depended on granting school suffrage to women. Indifferent men, "too largely absorbed in business," neglected schools; "more interested" women would provide better supervision. Although men nominally ran the schools, in fact they were "supported both from the inside and the outside by the mother sex."[77]

The passage of legislation in 1912 providing for school suffrage in Kentucky marked the beginning of a campaign for full suffrage in the state. Its "triumphant enactment," according to the president of the General Federation of Women's Clubs, was the product of the mobilization and "intense interest in the subject" of Kentucky women. Clearly, as Breckinridge declared soon after this victory, the law affirmed that all women "had a duty to perform in the interest of education of the child"; it meant that, rather than a rigid conception of a woman's sphere, "her sphere led wherever the child goes."[78]

◆ ◆ ◆

WOMAN SUFFRAGE AND THE EMERGENCE OF FEMINISM

The twentieth century, declared Mary Johnston in 1910, was the "Woman's Century." It deserved such a description because it was "producing and will produce more and more a very noble type of woman—free women and noble." For the first time in thousands of years, women would achieve power in "all the more specifically sociological, humane and educational aspects of human society." Women, she predicted, would become artists, administrators, writers, scientists, historians, and poets. Eventually achieving economic independence, women would also, in time, gain political freedom. This would be a "great" and "revolutionary" century after which a "new era" would commence.[79]

As an offshoot of early twentieth-century reform crusades, the woman suffrage campaign adopted familiar ideological imagery. Like other reformers, suffragists argued that American society had experienced a total transformation to which present institutions were ill adapted. Favoring an alteration of social and public institutions to reflect these changes, they believed that enfranchising women would create a new constituency for reform that did not exist within the male political culture. Like other reformers, they expressed paternalist attitudes; in particular, they believed that votes for women would reinforce white supremacy. Most suffragists would have agreed with the Louisiana woman who complained in 1918 that "common, unskilled, even illiterate" workers, along with blacks, possessed the vote, while "intelligent, educated, and in many cases college trained women" did not have it. Because women, according to Mary Johnston, were "mothers of the whole world," those who deprived them of their rights were birds that fouled their own nests. Even women who did not marry or bear children, with a "potentiality of motherhood," retained a maternal instinct, a "great and gracious thing" that made them also "godmothers of the race."[80]

For Johnston, *race* had both a general and a specific meaning. Although in this instance the term referred to the human race, in other cases it had to do with the concept of racial hierarchy. Like other reformers, Johnston combined a vision of human uplift with a pseudoscientific notion of eugenics. The improvement of women was tied to "the welfare of the present race" and a "nobler, finer, higher human type," for from an "undeve[l]oped mother" a "developed race" could not emerge. Through woman suffrage and broader political participation, Johnston said, white women could protect their race from "racial poisons" such as alcohol and venereal disease. It would not be possible to achieve a "super race," she wrote on another occasion, "until you get your super woman." Superior intellectual and emotional qualities— preconditions of racial development—were connected to the uplift of womankind "to the strength and stature of angels." Those thinkers who endorsed women's elevation were, she concluded, feminists.[81]

Suffragists advocated what was, for the early twentieth-century South, a new departure. As a precondition to the feminist vision of Mary Johnston, the enfranchisement of women paved the way for a transformation of gender roles. The most basic reason for the vote was that women, as disfranchised as "Chinese co[o]lies," sought "self protection, self government, [and] self-realization," all parts of a quest for political liberty. Women sought equality with men, asserted Virginia Clay-Clopton. In the Garden of Eden—a state of nature—womanhood, symbolized in Eve, was endowed with a "gift of Life" and with "physical and mental faculties" that were "keenly alive" to the realization that she was "capable of *thinking* and *speaking* and *acting*." Here, no inequality existed; a ban of inferiority came from men, who "assumed it without authority from God."[82]

Although suffragists disagreed about its meaning and implications, most of them moved toward a fuller conception of equality. In general, they avoided a direct challenge to either the South's gender role differentiation or its chivalric code. "Many feminists and certainly thousands of women suffragists" would "flatly deny" that their goal was for women to assume masculine roles, Eleonore Raoul declared in 1915. Most women suffragists had "no desire to live as men do": what they sought was "a certain enlargement of their sphere." Women were "essentially and fundamentally different from men"; although "admittedly different from men mentally, physically and nervously," women should be represented in government and policy making.[83]

Mary Johnston also arrived at a restricted definition of equality. She wrote that woman suffrage, rather than breaking down chivalry, would extend it; those who claimed otherwise would be "hard put" to provide a correct definition of chivalry. The characteristics of chivalry, she maintained, transcended gender: "gentleness of heart and courtesy, quickness to see injustice and to right it, good manners and good will" would not evaporate when women voted and were "politically free." Women could also be chivalrous; women such as Jane Addams and Florence Kelley were "very good knights."[84]

Other women offered a more precise definition of equality. For many suffragists there was an explicit connection between economic status and the vote: political representation brought greater opportunity. When women entered business, wrote a Birmingham suffragist, survival required submission to "all manner of humiliation." Once there was competition between men and women, the male chivalric code would be "a secondary consideration." Only when women possessed a "voice in government and a hand in the making of just laws for her sex" would this "aristocracy of men" appreciate the shoulder-to-shoulder march of women in industry and mark the way with justice to the other sex. Disfranchised women in the work force, maintained a Texas suffragist, were "outside the pale both socially and industrially, and are fair prey in both capacities." Thus to "talk of freedom for women without the ballot" was a "mockery." Sympathy "as a civil agent" was only "vague and powerless until caught and chained in logical propositions and coined into law."[85]

Other women challenged the notion of absolute male supremacy and even separate spheres. Modern women, argued a Louisiana feminist, were a "different asset in the home" as companions and close friends of husbands. Under her conception of a companionate marriage, wives were "no longer the doll, the weakling, the clinging vine." Women, with the suffrage, would enjoy equal spheres rather than separate spheres. No man should rightfully limit a woman's activity, argued a southern suffragist in 1908, for God had "designated both in the beginning—unequivocally." God assigned an aerial sphere for birds, an aquatic sphere for fish, and a land sphere for animals. All existed without regard to gender. God placed women within "the same spheres with man." The chief charm of modern women lay outside a restricted sphere that classified them with "idiots, insane and criminal[s]." Rather, their role was, through political equality, to advocate and achieve "the protection of women & children." The old doctrine of separate spheres, a suffragist wrote in 1918, was nothing but a "thread bare excuse." Women's sphere lay "in the unlimited field of effort and endeavor in whatsoever work human hands may do, and human brains achieve."[86]

Challenging patriarchy in the family, an ultimate objective for many suffragists and feminists, meant replacing it with an equal, companionate conception of marriage. Suffrage and the political equality it symbolized would not mean the destruction of the home—far from it. "Duty to home" was always "first with suffragists," wrote a Norfolk activist, but because of this duty they pleaded for better health, education, and housing legislation. "Neglected" homes were "not those of the suffragists"; divorce courts were not "filled with suffragists." "Drinking girls and women in cafes and rathskellers" were "never suffragists." Indeed, she declared, states that had equal suffrage boasted a record of more marriages, fewer divorces, more births, and a lower death rate.[87]

In this way, suffragists tested the boundaries of reform. Baptized in the social reform crusades that emerged in southern cities, suffragists confronted the eternal dilemma of reformers: how to impose reform on an indifferent or unwilling population. Woman suffrage, they initially believed, provided a partial solution of this dilemma because it would enfranchise greater numbers of white women of their class and cultural orientation and thereby provide a constituency for change. Yet increasingly suffragists were drawn to a different vision, best articulated by Mary Johnston, of women's consciousness and fuller equality, not only politically, but also within the institution of marriage and in the workplace.

Until the twentieth century, Johnston argued, women had experienced a "long, slow, painful struggle" toward equality of opportunity, education, and the twin realizations that only political freedom could bring economic freedom and that "self protection, self government, self development, [and] self-realization" all depended on political liberty. The suffrage broadened the experience of women and lifted "a roof that was too low." With the vote, women heard the voice of the world. The vote, Johnston believed, created a new collective sisterhood among enfranchised women. "Too long, too long have women held apart from women," she told a sympathetic audience in 1910. United by a broad maternal instinct in the acquisition of the franchise, voting women would realize a "new feeling, impulse, motive, possession"— an "instinct of sisterhood."[88]

The creation of sisterhood came not just through the vote but in the struggle to acquire it. In the Equal Suffrage League of Virginia, which Johnston played a prominent role in founding in 1909, women had discovered a "feeling of friendliness and sisterhood" that was "remarkable." Suffragists included married women and single women. Some had children, others did not. Suffragists pursued a variety of dissimilar occupations. Some taught, some sewed, some were secretaries; others were store clerks, bookkeepers, and journalists. Suffragists also included a variety of religious faiths—Protestant, Roman Catholic, Jewish, Unitarian, "and just plain pagan."[89]

◆ ◆ ◆

ORGANIZING A CRUSADE

On the same day that the House of Representatives passed the Nineteenth Amendment in 1919, Lila Meade Valentine recalled how, almost a decade earlier, a "handful of forward-looking women" had gathered to "consider ways and means for securing the enfranchisement of women." In organizing the Equal Suffrage League of Virginia, they faced what then seemed a "hopeless" task. This "little band of women" succeeded in constructing a mass movement, and, shunned by a "blind, intolerant public," Virginia suffragists by 1919 had attracted a following of almost 32,000 supporters. It was a far cry from the days when it was considered "indecent for women to speak in public, to march in processions with their brothers, to serve the community in the many ways now deemed essential to the welfare of the state."[90]

As Valentine suggested, public attitudes toward suffragists had changed radically between about 1909 and 1919. Before the onset of World War I, wrote the Charlottesville, Virginia, suffragist Roberta Wellford, women were largely "indifferent" to the vote. By the end of the war southerners inhabited a different world, one in which it was considered irrational to keep women disfranchised when their work was recognized as more necessary than ever before.[91] Like other reformers, suffragists sought reform through a revival-style popular mobilization. Experienced in crusading, they adopted this model of reform. As part of this mobilization, the intervention of an outside, coordinating group—the National American Woman Suffrage Association—was crucial. NAWSA provided resources, leadership, and organizational skill for statewide campaigns.

Under NAWSA sponsorship, a renewed effort was made to revitalize state suffrage movements during the early decades of the twentieth century. Yet the real focus and energy of the suffrage campaign, in the South and elsewhere, came after 1909. In Kentucky, the school suffrage fight, along with the new leadership of Madeline McDowell Breckinridge, stimulated the growth of the existing NAWSA chapter, the Kentucky Equal Rights Association. In Virginia, prominent Richmond women—including Lila Meade Valentine, Mary Johnston, and Ellen Glasgow—organized themselves into an informal suffrage group in 1909. They then formed an Equal Suffrage League and held its first statewide meeting in 1911. That meeting, which representatives from some of the larger towns and cities of the state attended, was addressed by NAWSA president Anna Howard Shaw. In Louisiana, the New Orleans social reformers and sisters, Kate and Jean Gordon, both of whom were linked to NAWSA, helped to organize a statewide suffrage organization in 1913. In Florida, a group of Jacksonville women met in a private home to form a local suffrage league in 1912; in the next year, a newly created statewide Equal Franchise League affiliated with NAWSA.[92]

Organizers from these states fanned out to establish suffrage organizations elsewhere in the South. The South Carolina Equal Suffrage League was organized in March 1914 after a visit by Valentine, who had been invited by a group of Columbia women who had banded together to study the suffrage issue. In Georgia, suffragists worked in close coordination with Madeline McDowell Breckinridge of Kentucky to form a state group in 1914. In the wake of the NCLC meeting in Birmingham, local reformers organized a suffrage movement. Following a speech by Jean Gordon urging reformers to endorse equal suffrage, a few women met privately, according to a participant, to study the suffrage question. These women organized a Birmingham Equal Suffrage League—"with a capital S," remembered Pattie Ruffner Jacobs—in November 1911. After similar organizations sprang up in other Alabama cities, a statewide group was formed at Selma in January 1913.[93]

In still other states, outside prompting by NAWSA organizers helped to revive moribund state suffrage groups. Although a Texas Equal Rights Association had been organized in 1893, it was defunct by 1896 and subsequent attempts to revive it failed. Then, after Anna Shaw visited the state in 1908, a new chapter was established in Austin; under its leadership, the statewide Texas Equal Suffrage Association was formed in 1913. With vigorous direction and tight coordination with NAWSA, the Texas movement grew rapidly thereafter.[94]

These new statewide organizations depended on an urban core of leaders and constituents. In Virginia, Richmond supplied most of the leaders of the movement and continued to dominate the state organization throughout its history. At its peak in 1919, membership reached 32,000, of whom some 12,000 were from Richmond and 3,000 from Roanoke. In Alabama, the social reformers who had first established a state suffrage organization supplied its ablest leaders, women such as the president of the state organization, Pattie Ruffner Jacobs, or fellow Birmingham resident Bossie O'Brien Hundley. In Georgia, early organizational efforts focused on recruiting in towns and cities. The last city to organize was Savannah; the women who met there in November 1914 included one hundred of the "best people of the city."[95]

Like other reformers, southern suffragists relied on an outside coordinating agency—NAWSA—for funds, lecturers, newspaper copy, organizational skills, and overall strategy. The South became a NAWSA stronghold. Although Alice Paul's Congressional Union emerged as a rival national suffrage association in 1914, later becoming the National Woman's Party, all the southern statewide organizations remained NAWSA loyalists. In 1915 Valentine wrote that she was "overwhelmed with work and perplexities about this Congressional Union business," which made her "sick at heart." Yet despite the state suffrage organization's refusal to allow them to organize their members, Congressional Union recruiters surreptitiously used its facilities to create their membership rolls—a "very unscrupulous method" that Valentine described as "dishonorable in the extreme." When the National Woman's Party formed, the mainline state suffrage association condemned it. The executive committee of the Alabama Equal Suffrage Association denounced the NWP when it picketed the White House in 1917 and warned of its "deleterious [sic] effect on suffrage in Alabama." The NWP's arrival in the state, the committee resolved, was "uninvited." The committee urged the public not to associate "thousands of peaceful Alabama suffragists" with the "acts of a handful of militant interlopers."[96]

The CU/NWP made few inroads, as most southern suffragists rejected its militancy and feared its impact. Southern suffragists were interested in the

English suffragettes and drew on them for inspiration in their own locales. In 1910, for example, Lila Meade Valentine visited London, where she was obviously impressed with the accomplishments of the movement in England. The situation, she wrote, was "intensely interesting," and she was confident of the success of these "wonderful women." Yet when English suffragettes used militant methods, southern suffragists became dubious. "We believe in Democracy," Breckinridge told the Virginia legislature, "not only for ourselves but for the other fellows." She promised not to "hammer" the suffrage "into our heads as English women have had to hammer it." Similarly, Alabama suffragists responded to a proposal in 1913 to invite the English suffragette Emmeline Pankhurst to speak by voting "emphatically no."[97]

In June 1917 the executive committees of the southern suffrage organizations received a letter from NAWSA president Carrie Chapman Catt outlining a plan for organizing each state for the ratification of a federal suffrage amendment. Catt recommended a specific strategy: in each congressional district, names should be gathered on petitions that included "influential signers," and a "complete history and record" should be kept of each member of Congress. NAWSA not only supplied strategic and organizational skills, but it also provided traveling speakers who beat the bushes to organize local suffrage leagues throughout the South. In Alabama, for example, NAWSA "lent" the state suffrage association an organizer for two months in 1917, and she managed to visit all but one county that had not been previously organized.[98]

By 1919 the results of the suffrage crusade in the South were impressive. Virtually all of the southern states had suffrage organizations that orchestrated attempts to enact the suffrage, first at the state level and then by federal amendment. Whether they succeeded or not—and they usually failed—southern suffragists, over time and with greater experience, were undeniably becoming more effective. In Virginia, the Equal Suffrage League managed to get the question of state suffrage before the legislature in 1912, but the House of Delegates defeated it by a vote of 89 to 12. In the next legislative session, in 1914, suffragists reintroduced the measure, and the House again defeated it by a similar margin, 74 to 13. By 1916, however, the margin of defeat had declined to 51 to 40. Similarly, when South Carolina suffragists first suggested the vote for women by state enactment in 1914, a "ripple of laughter ran over the House." But in the next year, when Valentine spoke before the legislature, she was greeted by cheers. By 1916 the House only narrowly defeated a woman suffrage measure. In Alabama, the attempt by suffragists to introduce legislation in 1914 was postponed in committee; two years later, although the measure failed in a full vote, suffragists made a large showing at the state capitol. As one of their leaders expressed it, this legislative effort also gained "many recruits to the cause" through intensive publicity and lobbying.[99]

In other states, suffragists brought their campaign to a more successful conclusion. In Texas, suffragists in 1915 were able to bring a state suffrage law to a vote in the House but watched its defeat by a wide margin (90 to 32). But when a measure for a state constitutional amendment came before the same body two years later it passed, only failing the necessary two-thirds margin. During the next year, suffragists won a major victory when the legislature enacted woman suffrage in political primaries. In 1919, although suffragists were defeated in a statewide referendum that combined woman suffrage with the disfranchisement of aliens—the latter measure directed at Mexican immigrants—the legislature ratified the Anthony amendment.[100]

In the child labor and woman suffrage crusades, reforming humanitarians came of age in the South during the Progressive Era. Facing similar obstacles that confronted other reformers, they turned to a crusade model of popular mobilization that was beginning to have an impact by the end of World War I. Yet there were also clear limits to the crusade, for child labor reformers, suffragists, and others: although it could marshal public opinion for the passage of legislation, crusading meant little in the implementation of a permanent policy. For that, reformers found that the best tool to maintain control over a reluctant rural population was the instrument of bureaucracy.

PART III

SOCIAL POLICY AND COMMUNITY RESISTANCE

◆

BUILDING THE SOCIAL

EFFICIENCY STATE

◆

Educational and health reformers shared the conviction that governmental intervention would provide a purposeful evolution out of underdevelopment. They believed that better schools and better health would reshape public attitudes in such a way as to replace backwardness and poverty with a fresh determination to achieve regional modernization. Properly structured schools would refashion attitudes and correctly socialize young southerners; public health, in another way, would transform the habits and increase the performance and efficiency of millions. Through education and health, reformers sought to attain a new standard of social efficiency and to transmit new values that, modernizing officials believed, would foster self-actuating development among southerners. They sought to end the provincialism and isolation of their region and replace it with what they often called a "wide-awake" attitude toward a more cosmopolitan world.

Following the achievements of their crusades, reformers looked for ways to translate rhetoric into policy. They realized that nineteenth-century state and local officials were ineffective but that, in the twentieth century, they were gaining greater power. The success of the reform crusades was a mandate; reformers interpreted it to mean more power to intervene in local affairs. Interventionism became a sine qua non of educational and health policy in the social efficiency state, while governance experienced far-reaching changes. A new degree of centralized state power, employing bureaucracy and a new administrative state, sought to replace a locally controlled, decentralized system.

◆ ◆ ◆

PUBLIC SCHOOLS AND PUBLIC HEALTH

Reporting on conditions in northern Florida in 1919, a health inspector confirmed what southern school officials had already discovered: there was an intimate connection between the modernization of public education and of public health. Schools, he urged, should become "models" of modern public health; they should provide a lesson in "sanitary teaching" that would "stand forth as beacon lights to educate the youth in . . . better and more wholesome living." Not only should this be accomplished through healthier facilities, but also children should learn new habits of healthy living through an "influential environment." The public health problem was primarily a question of education, observed the North Carolina school reformer Charles L. Coon. When children and their parents learned "to clean up around their homes" and provide proper sanitation, common health problems disappeared. The rub came in convincing rural southerners that any health problems existed; there were still people in Coon's county who refused to believe in the germ theory or that mosquitoes caused chills and fever. Because of these attitudes, which Coon attributed to ignorance and carelessness, some form of compulsion was necessary. Although the introduction of public health into schools ideally should have been grounded in "the love of our fellowman," reformers needed a legal mandate "to force some people to learn who will not learn otherwise that they have no inalienable right to do as they please about anything."[1]

Health reformers sought far-reaching structural changes in southern rural schools. A major goal of public health reform was ensuring that every schoolhouse in the South had a sanitary privy, which became a symbol of rural school modernization. Health reformers advocated the construction of sanitary privies and the education of rural southerners about their proper use and maintenance. At the urging of reformers, communities often sought outside help in privy building. In Cherokee County, in southwestern North Carolina, the county board of education in December 1914 petitioned state health officials for their help in installing privies to correct the "unwholesome conditions" that existed near schools. "In our opinion," the board declared, "every School should have proper means for caring for and disposing of the bowel movements and other body excrements in a way that will prevent disease." In mountainous Yancey County, conditions were about the same six years later, when another group complained of two "old fashioned open, fly-breeding, disease-spreading" privies that served a community school. In Florida, another observer in 1919 described the schools of one probably typical county as "very primitive, grossly insanitary."[2]

Yet the widespread construction of sanitary privies in the rural South depended on the commitment of the health and educational bureaucracy, a commitment that varied from state to state. In both West Virginia and Arkansas, state inspection of rural schools began to include provisions for the maintenance of two "well kept and clean" outhouses for both sexes. In Georgia, state school officials encouraged local officials to build outhouses by offering the designation "standard" to any rural school that would build privies; by 1913 the state had thirty-nine such schools. But Georgia school officials characteristically relied on suasion and voluntary compliance. In 1911, for example, the State Department of Education circulated a publication, entitled "Better Rural School Buildings," describing sanitary toilet and outhouse facilities, but the state did not require all schools to have privies.[3]

At the opposite end of the spectrum were those states such as Louisiana, Virginia, Florida, and North Carolina whose boards of education by 1914 required the construction of sanitary privies. The North Carolina state superintendent of public instruction ordered all school districts to include provisions for sanitary privies in their plans for new school construction. The Virginia State Board of Education enacted the most sweeping regulation of its kind in the South in 1912. After that year, it required that all schoolhouses have two outhouses and that communities with water and sewerage have water closets in the schools. Moreover, it empowered the State Board of Health to enforce this regulation.[4]

In the wake of higher state standards for sanitation came other structural changes in southern rural schools. Many school and health authorities began to require disease- and parasite-free water supplies. In Florida, a teacher asked state health officials to help in getting "the old time water bucket and dipper out of the school." The local community, she complained, did not realize the necessity of each child having an individual drinking cup. The state health officials promised to assist.[5]

The threat of polluted or unsanitary water became apparent in Progressive Era school surveys, which demonstrated the prevalence of tainted water and of unsanitary methods of drinking. According to a survey of one northern Florida county, over half of its schoolchildren were drinking water of a potentially dangerous nature or else were using common drinking cups. A consensus existed, observed another health reformer, that ensuring the purity of water was "the most important single sanitary measure in a climate like ours." As it turned out, the antihookworm campaign coincided with and encouraged what one contemporary called a regional and national "revolt" against the common drinking cup and impure water in schools. By 1915 most of the southern states had acted. Some border states addressed the problem directly—for example, the common cup was declared illegal in the public schools of Kentucky, Maryland, and West Virginia. Health authorities in Louisiana issued a blanket prohibition against it in all public places. In Virginia, health officials promulgated new regulations requiring that water receptacles be scoured and sanitized daily.[6]

Other health-related innovations also required changes in the environment of public education. The discovery that mosquitoes transmitted diseases such as malaria led to the screening of schoolroom windows. In an age when tuberculosis was pervasive and ever-present, public health officials stressed the importance of fresh air and ventilation; they judged rural schools, on this as on other public health standards, to be deficient. Breathing badly ventilated air, wrote one educator, made children "irritable, nervous, restless, and unstudious," whereas proper breathing and respiration were indispensable parts of the educational environment.[7]

Another structural change in southern rural schools was a new emphasis on health education in the curriculum. In Virginia, schoolchildren recited a "health catechism," prepared by the State Department of Education. It contained lessons about the germ theory of disease, the nature of specific diseases, and the principles of sanitation. Hookworm "quizzes" were given in some states, and teachers were supplied with bulletins written in collaboration with state health and Rockefeller commission officials. In Alabama, teachers were provided with a bulletin that discussed the "main facts" about hygiene and sanitation. Its purpose was frank: to alter attitudes about health and disease. "If every child who attends schools be regularly taught the principles of hygiene and see them in effect each day at the school," the bulletin explained, "he will leave with a bias in favor of hygienic principles and will become a focus for the dissemination in favor of public-health movements and measures."[8]

By 1914 most southern teacher training, especially in state normal schools, emphasized instruction in health and hygiene even at the elementary level. Thomas Jackson Woofter's *Teaching in Rural Schools* (1917), a standard manual in southern normals, urged teachers to inculcate proper health practices among children at an early age. Teaching physiology and anatomy in rural schools, he wrote, was less important than instruction in "how to care for and preserve the body and bodily health." Woofter urged teachers to stress the basics—care for the child's body, including eyes, teeth, ears, nose, and throat, and nutrition, exercise, proper breathing, and personal hygiene. Woofter wrote that teachers should not just instruct about good health, they should also be aware of the physical abnormalities and illnesses of their students and should isolate the "mentally defective" from other pupils.[9]

The early success of these bulletins and manuals persuaded educators of the value of health instruction as a permanent part of the curriculum. Many southern states had already introduced the study of physiology at the high school level; by 1914, however, the study of health had replaced it. This new discipline was meanwhile rapidly becoming a prerequisite for teacher certification. In 1911, for example, health officials spoke to students in every teachers' institute in Kentucky; within two years, health instruction in the state's teacher training program was commonplace. The director of the anti-hookworm campaign in Georgia, A. G. Fort, undertook to distribute *Talks on Health for Georgia Teachers* across the state. This circular included a "Health Creed" in which students pledged adherence to values of health and good sanitation, promised to keep clean and germ free, forswore unhealthy habits like drinking alcohol and spitting, and acknowledged the value of fresh air and open windows. In other states, educational officials began to require instruction in health as a condition of certification. In North Carolina, the state examination for elementary schoolteachers beginning in 1911 required some knowledge of hygiene and sanitation. In the examination of 1913, for instance, teachers were asked to explain the prevention of disease, the advantages of exercise, and the benefits of good ventilation in the schoolroom. Still another question asked applicants how they might improve the sanitation of their locality.[10]

The state departments of education also began to include health texts on state-approved lists. The most popular of these was John W. Ritchie's *Primer of Sanitation* (1910), which by 1914 was used in eight southern states. Ritchie's *Primer* discussed the germ theory of disease and the nature of various diseases, such as typhoid fever, intestinal tract infections, malaria, and smallpox. Ritchie emphasized disease prevention and the necessity of governmental control over public health—a control that would give public health officials the power to coerce. "Only some one with authority over all the people can guard the health of a community," he wrote, "and public health officials are absolutely necessary if sanitary measures are to be enforced." With regard to sanitation, the "ignorant and careless" should be forced, if necessary, "to live so that they will not be a source of danger to those about them."[11]

Implementing these structural changes required more than the moral suasion on which southern school officials had long relied. Educational and health modernizers realized that change depended on their ability to persuade and cajole, and, when necessary, to require southern rural communities to adopt these innovations. The variety of changes made in southern public education in the era of World War I—such as the creation of high schools, the consolidation of rural schools, and the standardization of teacher certification—constituted models for state intervention.[12]

By 1915, when the Rockefeller Sanitary Commission had ceased its activities in the South, the main feature of state intervention in pupil health was regular medical inspection of schoolchildren. Here, as in other forms of school hygiene, southerners followed national and international trends. In Europe, the introduction of compulsory education by the middle of the nineteenth century brought early forms of medical inspection of pupils, but only after the turn of the century did the practice spread to the United States. By 1914 some twenty states and four hundred cities had begun health inspections of schoolchildren.[13]

Rural school modernizers in the South eventually embraced medical inspection as the central component of public health regulation in schools. The reaction of the North Carolina state superintendent was typical of other educators. Giving his blessing to the passage of a new medical inspection law, he offered his help to state health officials. "Command me at any time for any cooperation in this valuable work," he wrote. In the future, he promised, health officials would receive the hearty cooperation of the county superintendents and teachers in the counties where the work had been inaugurated.[14]

In popular educational manuals, medical inspection became a regular part of the program of the reformed rural school. Some parents ignored the physical welfare of their children, wrote Eggleston and Bruère, "not through malice or indifference" but because of ignorance. Therefore, children should not be allowed to enter school until they had undergone medical inspection, argued a North Carolina antihookworm reformer. Disease prevention would come through the school rather than through the home, since so many parents remained unconcerned because of ignorance or indifference. Just as the weaving of cotton cloth depended on the physical condition of the yarn, so too the building of a stable society depended on the good health of its children through regular, compulsory medical inspection. Extending the analogy, the reformer concluded that many human threads were "defective, weak, or knotty"; the school should assume responsibility for watching the loom, unraveling the knots, and relieving the tension so that threads would not break.[15]

County nurse conducting a medical inspection of schoolchildren, Maysville Consolidated School, Mason County, Kentucky, 1922.
(Courtesy of the Rockefeller Archive Center)

The main duty of the medical inspector was to examine pupils. Through regular visits to schools and systematic record keeping, inspectors identified disease, malnutrition, parasites, or any other "defects"—and directed pupils to local physicians. Reformers believed that some, and probably most, of these "defects" could be easily cured. According to North Carolina health official Benjamin Earle Washburn, the most prevalent ailments were the result of bad teeth, and free dental clinics were made available for North Carolina children.[16] In other states as well, medical inspectors examined children not only for dental defects, but also for deficiencies in eyesight and parasitic infections.[17]

In most southern states, medical inspection was introduced at the county level either by school or health authorities. Thus in 1913, a local county health officer described as "wideawake" in his attitudes began a program in which county physicians agreed to deliver lectures and conduct rudimentary inspections in each of the county's schoolhouses.[18] In 1917 North Carolina enacted the strongest legislation of its kind. According to this law, a physical examination of each pupil was mandatory every three years. Teachers arranged for the examinations and sent the results to the county medical inspector, who was chosen by the county board of education. The law required that teachers obtain family and disease histories for each child; record information on height, weight, chest expansion, condition of teeth, vision, and hearing; and note the presence of dangerous diseases or parasitic infection. Only students who were seriously diseased—"impaired" or "defective," in the language of the inspectors—were sent to the county health physicians. Florida had enacted a similar law in 1915. According to its provisions, however, local physicians were responsible for conducting the examinations and reporting their findings to an appointed county medical inspector.[19]

Both the Florida and North Carolina laws contained obvious defects. Florida's statute made little provision for enforcement; the state health officer admitted in February 1916 that it was impossible to state accurately to what extent medical inspection was actually occurring. Local reports suggested that nonenforcement was the rule. In one county, a health officer admitted that no examinations occurred because it was too large a task for him to undertake personally. In another part of Florida, an inspector wrote of "grave difficulty" in enforcing the law. In North Carolina, a health official similarly complained of nonenforcement in 1923. In a western county, she wrote, school officials made little effort to keep up their records or anything else having to do with the law; teachers rarely "bothered themselves about filling the cards." In the same year, a North Carolina public health nurse was "a bit discouraged" because of local apathy about medical inspections.[20]

Recognizing these and other difficulties, most advocates of medical inspection by 1918 favored substituting teachers and visiting nurses for doctors. Physician inspectors were frequently greeted with antipathy on the part of the poorer classes, observed one southern health official. In contrast, a tactful visiting nurse could "enter the home and accomplish her purposes where the physician would be considered to have exceeded his authority." In those states where the hold of modernizing educational officials was weakest—Alabama, South Carolina, Louisiana, and Mississippi—responsibility for inspection lay with visiting nurses.[21]

In contrast, the southern states that were dominated by modernizing school officials tended to rely on teachers as substitute inspectors. Beginning in 1917, Virginia's requirements for teacher certification included instruction in preventive medicine, first aid, and physical inspection. Accordingly, the physical inspection of schoolchildren became the responsibility of teachers, and when teachers discovered "defects," they referred the affected pupils to public health physicians.

Modernizers considered the diagnosis of health problems to be a central part of a successful medical inspection program. Curing inflamed adenoids and tonsils and otitis, reported one southern inspector in 1914, had brought "new life" to children and removed one of the "great burdens" in schools. Frequently, "dull, stupid children . . . have been awakened into a new world by the removal of adenoids and tonsils whose presence had not been appreciated by the teacher or the mother." In other instances, inspectors classified children as belonging to the more problematic category of "mentally defective."[22]

The duties of the medical inspector, like those of the Rockefeller hookworm agents, included supervising the relationship between school hygiene and community health. Medical inspectors became boosters of the cause of public health. In North Carolina, beginning in 1915, the newly created State Bureau of Sanitation supplied lecturers who spoke on school health and in many communities organized a special health day. These lecturers also helped found the first Adenoid and Tonsil clubs, in which families pooled resources and arranged—at savings of from 25 to 75 percent—for public health physicians to remove tonsils and adenoids, often performing the surgery in school buildings. In North Carolina and other states, state health officials also sponsored dental clinics at schools.[23]

In addition, medical examiners were responsible for the physical transformation of schools. They inspected and regulated school sanitation. If necessary, they required mosquito-infested swamps to be drained; proper ventilation, heating, and lighting to be installed; and standards for cleanliness inside the schoolroom to be met. Most important, the health officer ensured that schools had unpolluted drinking water and sanitary disposal of human wastes. Through medical inspection, the southern school projected itself into the community as a center of healthiness. No longer "a place for the exchange of disease," it would now become a model of new health practices for the entire rural community, a center where the means of preventing disease were taught and the teachings put into practice.[24]

The modus operandi of a Florida school inspector in 1922 typified the new power of the state over the school environment. On a visit to a rural school, he inspected the grounds and its "sanitary arrangements." The toilets, he wrote, were "absolutely filthy," "simply shacks" that were "sickening." After his inspection, the official gathered the local trustees and insisted that these conditions be changed. Informing them that they were in violation of state health ordinances, he said that he would furnish standardized plans for the construction of sanitary privies. Unless these plans were followed, he warned the chairman of the school board, state officials would close the school.[25]

By the 1920s medical inspection of schoolchildren was offering clear evidence of the new alliance between school and health modernizers—and the strength of the social efficiency state in the South. The growth of medical inspection paralleled the expansion of centralized, bureaucratic school governance. The responsibilities of the progressive school now also included preparation for life through socialization, instruction in responsible political behavior, and training in vocational skills. As a key part of the transformed function of public education, maintained an advocate of rural school modernization, the state should now possess the power to coerce, especially in instances where localities ignored the interests of the community.[26]

It was only natural that a loose association emerged between educational and health reformers in the early twentieth-century South. Their alliance came into being in part because common problems confronted anyone seeking to impose state bureaucratic power on backwoods rural communities. Unlike other social reformers of their generation, educational and health reformers needed to organize larger numbers of southerners and to determine their exact compliance with state policy. Both soon turned to bureaucratic methods, about which they learned more through the growing influence of northern philanthropy. Northern philanthropists played a determinative role in shaping the new social efficiency state. They had figured prominently in both the school crusade and the antihookworm crusade. Now, through the judicious use of their funds, they continued to shape educational and health policy.

◆ ◆ ◆

NORTHERN PHILANTHROPY AND THE BUREAUCRATIC STATE

Rockefeller philanthropy was particularly aggressive and effective in promoting bureaucratic governance. The General Education Board, established in 1902 as the first Rockefeller philanthropic organization directly involved in the South, was initially concerned with the subsidization of the school crusade and investigations into the causes of southern educational underdevelopment. By 1905, however, the GEB had begun a more concerted and systematic effort. In that year, it hired high school agents to promote secondary education among southern whites. The position of these agents typified GEB and Rockefeller involvement. Although their salaries were paid by the GEB, the agents were part of the southern educational hierarchy and held posts as professors of secondary education—but taught no courses—at the public universities of the South. GEB sponsorship of these positions seemed to suggest that the board could shape the evolution of southern public education. The agents served as evangelists of high schools, but their main purpose was to directly influence policy: to persuade communities to finance schools, to lobby legislatures for the approval of greater expenditures, and to persuade educational officials to intervene more aggressively, as needed, to promote high schools.[27]

As time passed, the GEB regarded these agents less as itinerant evangelists than as part of a permanent school bureaucracy. Accordingly, their most important function lay outside the world of the university and inside the growing school bureaucracy. By the outbreak of the war, the GEB had shifted its focus from southern state universities to the state departments of education and transferred control over the agents from university presidents to state superintendents of education. The agents, as a result, came to identify with the state educational bureaucracy. One high school agent wrote that he feared that a close association with the University of Arkansas would bring him "into the sphere of the University politics" and make him "a dependent of the politicians who controlled the University." In order to protect himself from these pressures, he transferred his offices from Fayetteville, where the university was located, to Little Rock, the state capital. Eventually, in Arkansas and elsewhere, control was completely shifted to state educational officials.[28]

GEB intervention through high school agents provided a model for even more ambitious involvement. Beginning in 1914, the GEB financed the salary of rural school agents for both races in all the southern states; by the 1920s every southern state had taken advantage of Rockefeller largesse. From the start, the agents followed a familiar pattern. Working within the existing bureaucracy, the rural school agents reported directly to the GEB. Although their salaries were paid by the GEB, state educational officials considered them essential parts of their supervisory force, and they provided the manpower for the earliest attempts by school officials to intervene in local school affairs.

The role that the Alabama agents for white rural schools played in the expansion of the educational bureaucracy was typical. The agent in 1916, J. B. Hobdy, was involved in virtually continuous travel around the state for about nine months out of the year. His duties were broad. He cajoled localities into consolidating rural schools, promoted new school construction, encouraged the raising of new local revenues and lobbying for greater state financing, sponsored teacher training for rural schools, and supervised other forms of state standardization. With a restricted staff, the state superintendent, William F. Feagin, considered Hobdy essential. "I am compelled to rely greatly upon him," he wrote, "to look after matters of importance to the school interests of the various counties."[29]

Other GEB activities stimulated bureaucratic involvement. In Tennessee, along with supplying the white and black school agents, the General Education Board sponsored an agent who specialized in the supervision of mountain schools. Meanwhile, between 1917 and 1922 the GEB also sponsored a model organization plan in Montgomery County, Alabama, to establish a modern school system in a single county as a demonstration. Headed by Feagin, the Montgomery program had an ambitious agenda, including comprehensive school consolidation, systematic supervision, and the construction of "teacherages," or teachers' homes, for rural schoolteachers.[30]

The GEB's intervention in southern public education was supplemented by a growing intervention in public health. The Rockefeller Sanitary Commission adhered to the general pattern that the GEB had already established. The primary objective of Rockefeller philanthropic involvement, either in schools or in health, was the stimulation of state bureaucratic development. The Rockefeller Foundation's attack on ill health became an "entering wedge," according to a Rockefeller official, by which the South "could be induced to build up permanent machinery to take care of the whole problem of public health."[31]

When the Rockefeller Foundation was organized in 1913, the International Health Commission—which three years later, in June 1916, became the International Health Board—became its primary agency of public health. The IHC's and then the IHB's main agenda was less to end disease or ill health, which it acknowledged was a long-term problem, than to encourage coercive state power. John A. Ferrell, who had run the RSC campaign in North Carolina and later headed the IHB's domestic operations, explained the Rockefeller strategy on several occasions. The control of a specific disease, although "easily justifiable on its own account," he wrote, was "much more important as a means to a larger end." That "larger end" was arousing popular interest in public health and, as a by-product, stimulating "the development of permanent agencies for the control of . . . preventable diseases." Ultimate control over public health should remain governmental, Ferrell stressed in a different context. The IHB's work was only temporary; responsibility properly lay with state agencies.[32]

The IHB, although exerting considerable influence over southern public health, shunned the high visibility tactics of the antihookworm campaign. On one occasion, when reviewing a draft of a public health publication, Ferrell urged state officials to avoid quoting IHB reports or alluding too frequently to the Rockefellers. Rather, he wrote, emphasis "should be placed upon the state boards of health and what they are doing." In general, it was IHB policy, as he later remarked, "when working with, through and in the name of a State Health Department, to avoid emphasizing the Foundation's name." In this instance, he urged state officials to use the letterhead of the state health department rather than the IHB's.[33]

Although always discreet, the IHB aggressively promoted the expansion of coercive government in southern public health. The IHB's usual instrument was the expenditure of its funds, over which it exerted strong control. It refused to provide funds to states that did not meet its standards of administration; Florida, for example, remained outside the IHB nexus until the early 1920s. In those states whose administrative and bureaucratic standards were insufficient, the IHB often provided troubleshooters, the most effective of whom was Platt W. Covington, another of several veterans of the North Carolina antihookworm campaign who became part of Ferrell's operation.[34] In states receiving Rockefeller funding, IHB officials did not hesitate to threaten a cutoff of funds if the states did not strictly adhere to their standards.[35]

Rockefeller involvement in public health was supplemented by the activities of other northern philanthropies whose operations were, by comparison, limited. The Commonwealth Fund, as part of a nationwide attempt to improve child health, sponsored child health demonstrations in two southern communities, Rutherford County, Tennessee, and Clarke County, Georgia, between 1924 and 1927. Later in that decade, the Rosenwald Fund, which had previously focused exclusively on the construction of black rural schoolhouses, expanded into a broader program of public health for blacks.[36]

But Rockefeller philanthropy dominated southern public health. It sponsored an identification of interests between education and health and a push toward similar policy approaches. It faced similar obstacles in the limited power of state officials and the resistance of local communities toward change. Its solutions were the use of coercive power and centralized state governance. Under Rockefeller sponsorship, then, the beginnings of the southern social efficiency state began to emerge.

◆ ◆ ◆

THE IHB AND THE BUREAUCRATIZATION OF SOUTHERN PUBLIC HEALTH

The goal of expanding bureaucratic control is perhaps most apparent in the IHB's early efforts to transform the administration of rural public health. Rockefeller officials viewed a successful county health program as essential to the creation of the permanent agencies for the control of preventable diseases that Ferrell had advocated earlier. County health would reach the grass roots; it would become the rural equivalent of emerging urban public health systems. And because it would require financing by local and state authorities, along with initial IHB funding, it would foster public support for coercive governance.

The county health program emerged in the aftermath of the RSC's campaign. As part of its commitment to what they called the "final stage" in hookworm eradication, IHC officials inaugurated a program then known as *intensive community work*. Begun in the late stages of the dispensary crusades, intensive community work sought, at least initially, universal examination and treatment. The earliest programs in this antihookworm effort began in states that had already completed dispensary crusades. The first such attempt to eradicate hookworm in a single community occurred in coastal northeastern North Carolina. There, on Knotts Island, a fishing village in Currituck Sound, a RSC-IHC team in the summer and autumn of 1913 treated nearly all of the island's population, composed of only 567 people, 93 of whom were found to be infected. Along with systematic examination of the population, commission agents sought to establish sanitary privies for all residents. Once finished, the program claimed that practically all residents were free of hookworm infection.[37]

The results of the Knotts Island experiment were encouraging enough to provide IHC officials with a new model for rural public health. As the director of the program, J. D. Maynard, wrote in April 1914, this sort of community health work was *"the thing to do"* in order to achieve the objective of eradication.[38] Further experiments in British Guiana in March 1914 reportedly yielded extremely successful results in both the physical examinations and privy construction, the lessons of which were eventually applied to the Caribbean basin and the American South. In the wake of these findings, in the spring and summer of 1914 the commission supported five similarly organized programs in eastern North Carolina. In these early "intensive" community health programs, the object was the same as it had been at Knotts Island: universal examination and treatment for hookworms, systematic establishment of sanitary privies, and eradication of the parasite.[39]

These experiments in local health led directly to attempts to establish systematic and bureaucratic county health systems. In the autumn of 1914 North Carolina state health officer Watson Smith Rankin and John A. Ferrell, now an associate director of the Rockefeller Sanitary Commission in Washington, agreed to provide a joint program of rural public health for North Carolina. Ferrell modified the "intensive" community health programs begun in eastern North Carolina by accepting the stipulation that they continue under the control of newly established, professionally run county health systems; Rankin consented to Rockefeller participation but reserved ultimate authority for the state. Both Rockefeller agents and state health officials also agreed that state and county authorities (the latter on a voluntary basis) would make significant financial contributions. During the next three years, the intensive community model was introduced throughout the South, and the IHC embraced it as the central component of its program—and as the essential link between the RSC's exclusive focus on hookworm and the IHC's broader conception of public health.[40]

In the intensive community campaigns, IHC officials were forced to adapt their original objective to local circumstances. Seeking to eradicate hookworm within a defined geographic unit—usually a community of between 1,000 to 15,000 people—they began by mapping out a geographic and demographic profile. They then conducted microscopic examinations of the entire population, treating those infected and providing follow-up examinations. But IHC directors increasingly acknowledged the difficulty of universal examination and treatment. By 1919, as Ferrell acknowledged, there was "no record" of complete eradication in any community except on Knotts Island. Health officials instead came to emphasize rural sanitation through the construction of privies.[41]

By 1916 the IHC's program of rural public health was well established in the Carolinas, Virginia, Louisiana, Mississippi, Alabama, and Tennessee. Fairly typical was the arrangement struck between the IHC and state health officials in Louisiana in early 1915. Although run by a state director nominated by the local parish but approved by both the state health director and the IHC, the program was to exist under the control of the state health officer, who provided central offices, clerical support, and office supplies. The intensive rural health program would be established only in parishes where the conditions were considered "most favorable" for local financial support. The IHC provided a portion—between a quarter and a half—of the costs of the program, expecting equal contributions from both the state and the parish governments. The purpose of the program primarily concerned soil pollution; it was to run a comprehensive, grass-roots schedule of examination, treatment, and popular education.[42]

Nonetheless, well into the 1920s some states avoided participation in what was now the IHB's intensive community health work. In Florida and Arkansas, the RSC crusade had failed to penetrate fragile health bureaucracies, which remained resistant to IHB involvement. Other states, such as Georgia and Texas, possessed health officials who, as Ferrell explained in July 1915, were "very anxious" to have IHC support but were unable to attract sufficient state or local funds.[43] As for rural public health in general, the IHC confirmed that hookworm infection was only part of a larger pattern of ill health, and a transition from the temporary, rotating intensive community health units into a structure of permanent rural public health occurred naturally. This transition happened earliest in North Carolina, the scene of innovative leadership during the RSC campaign and the first state to develop a full-scale intensive rural health program.

The man chosen to lead the program, Benjamin Earle Washburn, was a native Tar Heel and a veteran of antihookworm campaigns in North Carolina and the Caribbean. In the late summer of 1916 the IHB and Rankin agreed to a formula in which Washburn, with the sponsorship of the state health department, operated a full-time, modern health department in Wilson County, in the state's eastern tobacco belt. The state health officer had long sought a comprehensive county health program and, in the late stages of the antihookworm crusade, had proposed converting the dispensary crusade into a permanent program of rural health. Earlier, North Carolina had been the scene of sporadic local attempts, mostly in urbanized counties, to inaugurate modern county health systems. The first professionalized county health system was begun in Guilford County, surrounding Greensboro, and the health officer there, George F. Ross, had run an ambitious program of school inspection, inoculation, screening, and vital statistics.[44]

For the most part, however, the IHB required the construction of a local health bureaucracy that would be responsible to state officials from the bottom up. The description of local health officials in Rutherford County, Tennessee, provided by a Commonwealth Fund official in 1924 was typical of the rural South. In Rutherford County, health matters were only theoretically "cared for" by the health officer in the county seat, who was employed at a part-time salary and whose main responsibilities were the care of the indigent sick. The law that created the town's health department, wrote the official, "bristled with words such as 'miasmatic'" and regarded diphtheria and membranous croup as separate diseases. Needless to say, "no health work was done under such a regime," and although local health officials were obligated to control infectious diseases, "in actual practice smallpox was the only disease feared."[45]

The IHB's inauguration of systematic county health in 1916 sought to alter these conditions fundamentally. As one observer put it, the "whole time health officer" could not just be "any doctor." Instead, he needed to be a physician who was thoroughly acquainted with new ideas about public health and sanitation, preventive death, and the spread of diseases. In addition, the modern county health officer needed to possess political skills; invaluable was "a pleasing personality" and an ability to "not mind kicks." Finally, he needed to secure the support of the county's doctors and to transform them "into an organization for better sanitation and health in the county."[46]

This was a tall order, but IHB officials were confident that a successful demonstration in a single state would enable a model of bureaucratic rural public health to spread elsewhere. In North Carolina, the demonstration in county health that began under Washburn's direction in 1916 embodied the same approach as the intensive rural health programs—universal hookworm treatment and local-state-IHB financial cooperation—and Washburn used the Wilson County program to provide preliminary training for IHB workers abroad. Within the first year of operation, Washburn's experimental program in eastern North Carolina had developed into a full-fledged, IHB-sponsored program that encompassed ten participating counties. In 1917 the state formalized the relationship by appropriating regular state funds and by agreeing to a long-term plan of expansion.[47]

By the 1920s the IHB program in North Carolina had established a model for the development of bureaucratic rural health. Those counties that cooperated with the program submitted to bureaucratic state control. As Washburn explained, participation meant having "their work directed" by state officials, who assumed responsibility for formulating a plan of attack. The county health officer was appointed by the state board of health and reported directly to Washburn, the state director of county health. Based on this plan, "model health units" were inaugurated in several townships, generally those communities that had remained unaffected by previous health campaigns. County health officials continued the antihookworm efforts primarily by privy building and limiting the problem of soil pollution. They participated in hookworm resurvey efforts to measure the effectiveness of parasitic control. They were also responsible for health education, the promotion of medical inspection of schools, quarantine, and infant hygiene. By 1919 the fourteen counties that were participating in the IHB program were also introducing an IHB program of "life extension" that sought to inoculate residents against preventable diseases.[48]

Other states followed North Carolina's lead. By early 1917 South Carolina and Alabama had both begun modest county health programs in three counties and two counties, respectively. Over the next decade, county health programs along IHB lines spread across the South. In Louisiana, for example, a parish health program began in 1919 out of a rural sanitation program in Caddo Parish, where a program funded by IHB, state, and parish money built privies and extended sanitation to seven communities. Within two years these program had expanded, as five parishes—Beauregard, Caddo, De Soto, Natchitoches, and Ouachita—appropriated the necessary matching funds to qualify for IHB support, while in a sixth parish—Washington—the U.S. Public Health Service and the state supplied the parish's contribution. By 1925 a total of twelve parish health programs existed, and they performed a variety of functions, including—along with rural sanitation—infectious disease control, reduction of maternal and infant mortality, medical inspection of schoolchildren, malaria control, and inspection of water and milk supplies.[49]

So complete was the transition from the earlier, ephemeral dispensary campaigns to the experimental intensive rural health demonstrations, and, finally, to permanent, state-funded and controlled county health programs that in 1920 the IHB was able to proclaim an end to its antihookworm program in the South. Although the region was not freed from the parasite—far from it— the IHB had helped and was continuing to sponsor state bureaucratic development. As the general director of the IHB reported, a foundation had been laid for a tax-supported health service—state and local—to control hookworm and other preventable diseases.[50]

By the late 1920s the IHB could claim encouraging results in the establishment and expansion of state and local health bureaucracies in North Carolina, South Carolina, Alabama, and Mississippi. For the South as a whole, 150 counties had established permanent, professionalized county health programs by 1920. A number of states delayed participating, mainly because of their legislature's refusal to enact enabling legislation. Although Tennessee had earlier participated in the intensive community health program, for example, not until the legislature passed a bill permitting the establishment of permanent, full-time county health departments could counties join the IHB program.[51]

In other states as well, the success of the county health program converted the dubious and persuaded them to join hands with Rockefeller philanthropy. States that were out of the IHB nexus eventually joined it by the late 1920s. The last to enlist was Florida. Under the leadership of Joseph Y. Porter, one of the late nineteenth-century South's leading sanitarians, Florida developed an aggressive state public health apparatus. But in the first decades of the twentieth century it ventured no further than the control of epidemic disease, and, with the end of the RSC campaign, in which it did not participate, Florida was increasingly isolated from other states. Even communities that wanted an expanded local health bureaucracy were frustrated. Although the appointment of a county health officer had the support of local government and the county medical society in Lakeland in 1914, for example, the state refused to provide any funds on the ground that state law forbade financing any program that did not serve the whole state. For the remainder of Porter's tenure, state health officials refused to aid, and worked vigorously to block, the development of local health bureaucracies, preferring instead to support an eight-district statewide system that was responsible directly to the State Board of Health. Because these district inspectors dealt almost exclusively with towns, Florida's rural communities lacked virtually any form of public health.[52]

After Porter's retirement, a succession of inept partisan hacks followed him; the IHB, despite frequent attempts, failed to penetrate the state health bureaucracy. Not until Calvin T. Young, a Porter protégé, became state health officer in 1921 did Florida participate in the IHB's rural health program. After considerable negotiation, Florida inaugurated a "health units program" that closely resembled the IHB county health programs elsewhere in the South. Under a compromise reached with the IHB, these "health units" could include more than one county, but the eventual emphasis was to be on the county. The program, which began in counties willing to make a $5,000 appropriation, included public health education, epidemiology, immunization, rural sanitation, life extension, child hygiene, and school inspection.[53]

Further bureaucratic expansion followed in the wake of other IHB antidisease programs. During the late teens, the IHB sponsored, or jointly sponsored with the U.S. Public Health Service, experiments in malaria control in selected towns in Arkansas and rural communities in Mississippi. By the early 1920s, based on these findings, it had articulated a program that would be accompanied by further administrative centralization and bureaucratization. As part of this program, the IHB in the 1920s insisted on the formation of separate, state-level antimalaria bureaus—or bureaus of communicable diseases—that would operate according to IHB standards and cooperate with local county health departments. As one Rockefeller official announced in 1921, malaria control could take place only within the local administrative structures of county health, "as part of the permanent county health scheme," supported by "state, county, and local funds; and . . . under the direction of the county health officer."[54]

Throughout the 1920s the IHB continued to support those public health programs that promoted bureaucracy. Even research programs of the sort that the IHB was increasingly funding in the twenties usually had some direct value for bureaucratic public health. When the IHB established a training station in Covington County, Alabama, in 1922 and operated it more or less outside the control of state health authorities, its primary purpose was to develop a model county health program. Headed by Wilson G. Smillie, who had developed a wide reputation as an IHB official in Brazil, the station both trained public health workers and conducted programs to develop practical means of combating malaria and hookworm.[55]

In whatever program it sponsored, the IHB insisted that state authorities eventually assume the responsibility for public health; in fact, they usually did so. Programs in which county and state authorities did not participate to a substantial degree, explained one Rockefeller official, were not likely to succeed. Permanent local and state authorities would have to bear the cost of the work "gradually but steadily" and, ultimately, "the entire burden of direction and expense." This necessitated, first, the growth of a health bureaucracy at the local level, and, second, the subsequent expansion of central authority— what one observer described as a "central or guiding bureau to give special attention to county health departments." [56]

By 1927 the IHB had increasingly adopted a strategy that at least partly reversed its initial approach. Instead of focusing on the development of rather scattered experiments in local health, it spurred the consolidation and rationalization of state health departments. Across the country, but mainly in the South, it sponsored interregional visits and conferences among southern health officials, promoted the development of more elaborate bureau structures, and encouraged the creation and expansion of state health officials' research capabilities. Meanwhile, the IHB gradually withdrew its support from county health programs and attempted to wean health officials from their dependence on Rockefeller funds. [57]

By the time that the IHB, and the Rockefeller Foundation, underwent a major reorganization in 1927, philanthropy had already had a significant impact on southern public health. The development of a bureaucratic structure occurred earliest in North Carolina. In 1913 Watson S. Rankin divided the state health department into bureaus, each headed by a bureau chief who reported to the state health officer. The chiefs held equal rank and had no official connection with each other. By the 1920s, under IHB prompting, most of the southern state health departments had adopted a bureaucratic structure similar to North Carolina's. Tax support for state-directed public health expanded steadily. Whereas eleven southern states spent $255,395 in 1910, a decade later that figure had risen over 500 percent. The increase was even greater in states like North Carolina, where public health expenditures grew from $18,200 in 1910 to $102,000 in 1918. Because the IHB had early earmarked it, the South emerged as the first region in the United States to develop a permanent, bureaucratic system of rural public health. As one observer expressed it in 1922, the most "notable advances made in the improvement of local [rural] health administration" were found "exclusively in the Southern States." [58]

Under outside stimulus, the powers of southern public health authorities expanded exponentially during the decade after 1915. Under the umbrella of bureaucratized county departments, southern public health workers assumed responsibility for a broad definition of preventive public health. In part because of Rockefeller philanthropy's strong interest in hookworm, southern sanitarians first concentrated on sanitation. These efforts enjoyed their most substantial results in towns and cities. Urban health officials required the regular testing of drinking water, and, by the 1920s, state health departments had secured and were exerting authority over water supplies in the urban South. State health officials sponsored and often directed clean-up campaigns that were designed to heighten local awareness of public health. These campaigns focused on privy inspection, the banning of spitting, the limitation of livestock pens, the regular cleaning of stables, the drainage of mosquito-breeding bodies of water, the regulation of food markets, and the sanitary disposal of garbage. State officials worked with local urban allies to sanitize public facilities. Courthouses, which, according to one observer, had no pretensions "whatever to cleanliness," were often scrutinized, as were county jails.[59]

Some of the most spectacular urban health campaigns focused their energies on the fly. At the suggestion of Joseph Y. Porter, the Florida health officer, Jacksonville in early 1915 inaugurated an antifly campaign. Local residents, advised Porter, should be "stirred up by a fusillade of conspicuous newspaper articles of 'Swat the Fly.'" The Jacksonville antifly campaign was matched by similar efforts across the South. After a local campaign to reduce its fly population, for instance, the North Carolina state health officer in August 1916 declared Greensboro as "the most flyless city in North Carolina."[60]

Health officials also sought new controls over rural public health, and it was here that they faced their greatest challenges. Despite the efforts of some late nineteenth-century health officials, the failure to collect accurate vital statistics—which was a precondition to a modern public health system—had remained a frustrating symbol of the health bureaucracy's impotence. During and after World War I, however, the southern states gradually introduced the systematic collection of health data, and most of the region had effectively enforced laws in place by the late 1920s.[61]

Working through county health departments after 1916, sanitarians inaugurated an ambitious program to improve rural health. In North Carolina's Life Extension Program, county health workers conducted physical examinations to detect preventable sources of early death; as one worker put it in 1917, its

Schoolchildren in county health campaign, Montgomery County, Tennessee, 1921.
(Courtesy of the Rockefeller Archive Center)

purposes were "to prolong life and make it more useful." As part of this new
responsibility to prolong life, health officials frequently paid greater attention
to nutrition, to nutritionally related diseases such as pellagra, and to what one
sanitarian described as the "deplorable lack of milk and green foods" in the
average southern diet.[62]

State health officials also introduced more effective means of disease control through centralized reporting procedures and better use of the quarantine. Despite some advances against smallpox, southern health officials
had failed to establish adequate quarantine procedures, except in the case
of direst emergency, when it was usually too late to stem the sweep of epidemics. Under W. S. Rankin's aggressive regime, North Carolina became the
first southern state to attempt the efficient regulation of infectious diseases.
Using county health officials to enforce reporting and quarantine procedures
more effectively, Rankin also launched frequent inoculation campaigns, especially against typhoid, and vigorous efforts to distribute diphtheria antitoxin.
In a campaign conducted during the summer of 1921, for example, North
Carolina health officials administered over 70,000 typhoid vaccinations and
distributed over 10,000 doses of antitoxin. At Rankin's insistence, the state
legislature in 1917 enacted a much tougher quarantine law that compelled
physicians to report all diseases and empowered the State Board of Health to

write regulations governing the local management of disease. State officials were also granted powers to remove quarantine officers on grounds of negligence or incompetence, while the state epidemiologist acquired the ability to supervise local quarantine officials.[63]

Under the stimulus of federal funds, county health officials expanded their activities to include maternal and infant care. In 1922 the passage of the Sheppard-Towner Act provided federal money for child welfare, which became a primary focus of rural health efforts. Child welfare meant infant welfare, which focused on prenatal and postnatal care for mothers. Sheppard-Towner funds stimulated the formation of separate bureaus of child welfare within the health bureaucracies. In Florida, for example, the infusion of federal funds in 1922 resulted in the organization of a Division of Maternal and Infant Hygiene. Under its program, a single black nurse and three white nurses supervised midwives and attempted to educate the public about hygiene.[64]

Operating across the South during the 1920s, child welfare workers discovered conditions of childbirth that, they became convinced, caused high rates of maternal and infant deaths. Many southerners, especially blacks, had limited access to modern medicine because of poverty. As a black woman explained in Macon County, Alabama, a "heap of people" could not afford to pay doctors, who refused to see indigents "less you got the cash or will pawn something." For many, then, midwives remained the primary care givers; they had long served the mass of southern women. Although reformers acknowledged their abundant folk wisdom, they criticized their ignorance of modern sanitation. Their "calling" as midwives granted to them "prestige in their community," noted one official, along with "change enough to supply them with tobacco for a long time." Yet they often wondered "why anyone should have such new-fangled things as clean sheets, pads, etc., when an old quilt on the floor would answer all purposes." One midwife, to her listener's horror, recounted this experience. During a birth she was without a pair of scissors so she went to the woodpile and borrowed a knife from her husband, who took the precaution of wiping it on his trousers before handing it to her.[65]

As a central part of infant and maternal hygiene, health officials inaugurated a program of regulating midwives. By the end of the war, most southern states had enacted legislation requiring midwives to obtain a license from health officials. With Sheppard-Towner funds, state health officials possessed the supervisory force to regulate midwifery. In Virginia, where 9,500 midwives were registered in the mid-1920s, state officials inaugurated a midwife education program that required them to attend countywide instructional sessions on public health. A traveling nurse from the state health department

Instruction in infant health, Boyd County, Kentucky, 1925.
(Courtesy of the Rockefeller Archive Center)

described one such meeting. At the appointed hour, about twenty-five mid-wives turned up, and the meeting opened with the singing of spirituals and a prayer. The sea of faces before the nurse revealed "all ages, flappers to great-grandmothers, all sizes, all shades, arrayed in clothes of every description and every color." Much to the nurse's surprise, the meeting was a success. During the 1920s state officials gradually tightened these standards of licensing by requiring further education and examination and the submission of regular reports by midwives. In most states, midwives were required to attend demonstrations and lectures designed to acquaint them with modern gyneco-logical methods. In Florida, for example, midwives were informed by letter through local registrars to report to district nurses for "instruction." At these meetings, midwives learned the basics of sanitation during a week-long visit by the district nurse, and free silver nitrate was distributed to prevent infant blindness.[66]

State officials involved in child welfare preferred to work through county health departments if they existed. North Carolina's Bureau of Infant Hygiene, established in 1919, maintained nurses in county health departments that participated in the IHB program. These nurses conducted prenatal classes for pregnant mothers, encouraged the formation of mothers' clubs, conducted home visits, gave demonstrations on baby care, and lectured on sanitation. But states with weak county health departments had to rely on outside aid. Thus in Florida in 1921, state health workers established, in conjunction with the U.S. Public Health Service, two traveling child welfare units. Meanwhile, other child welfare workers toured the state, founding maternity prenatal care centers, supervising birth registration, administering silver nitrate, and establishing child health centers to provide medical supervision for infants and children not under a physician's care.[67]

The Florida child health workers discovered, as did health officials across the South, widespread ill health. When public health workers operated eight child welfare clinics at "progressive" communities in Escambia County in June and July 1922, they were shocked at what they saw. Physicians at the clinics examined 533 infants, preschoolers, and schoolchildren in search of health defects. What they found exceeded their worst fears. Of the children examined, three-fifths were underweight by 10 percent or more. Almost half of the children had never used a toothbrush; a similar proportion experienced serious tooth decay. Over half had impaired vision. Finally, almost three-quarters were confirmed to have hookworm infection.[68]

Southern health officials also employed bureaucratic methods to address the ancient scourges of malaria and venereal disease. A malaria control program developed out of joint federal-philanthropic intervention. Under the sponsorship of the IHB and the U.S. Public Health Service, investigations were conducted in a number of towns across the South after 1916. By the early 1920s southern health bureaucracies had developed and adopted a program of urban malaria control that curbed the mosquito through drainage, screening, the oiling of breeding areas, and even the use of mosquito-eating fish. At the same time, the IHB began an experiment in malaria control in rural areas in the Mississippi Delta involving the isolation of patients and the use of quinine.

During the twenties malaria control became a basic part of southern public health programs. In 1913 Rankin undertook a project in North Carolina after seeing an impressive program in the Canal Zone. Concluding that the problem in his state was simple compared to that in Panama, he concentrated his efforts in towns and cities. Rankin encouraged localities to begin a program of mosquito control in the autumn of 1913.[69] With the help of the Public Health Service, several surveys were made of eastern North Carolina towns.[70] The control program that followed in selected urban areas emphasized mosquito eradication. In October 1913 Rankin visited Roanoke Rapids with R. H. Von Ezdorf, the Public Health Service's expert on malaria. They recommended mosquito control through drainage, the oiling of mosquito breeding places, screening, and the use of mosquito canopies over beds. Subsequently, Von Ezdorf inspected other eastern North Carolina towns, where he spoke before local doctors. He also visited schools and obtained blood samples from the children. The solutions offered by Von Ezdorf and the Public Health Service resembled those pioneered in the Canal Zone and then applied in Roanoke Rapids: the elimination of mosquito breeding by draining poorly drained ravines and ditches and standing pools of water, along with other methods.[71]

By the 1920s a more permanent program had superseded these early experiments. In 1919 the Public Health Service and the IHB offered a full-scale antimalaria program for southern towns. Under its terms, PHS sanitary engineers, whose expenses and start-up costs were paid by the IHB, were attached to the state departments of health. These sanitary engineers visited participating towns, conducted a survey, and made specific suggestions about malarial control.[72] By the mid-1920s, moreover, state health officials were promoting malarial control programs through the bureaucratized county health departments.[73]

Southern public health bureaucrats in the 1920s also mounted an attack on venereal disease. Two considerations influenced their efforts: strong pressure from moral reformers to eradicate prostitution and, during the war, the more clinical objective of eradicating disease among American soldiers. For southerners at home, the real impact of the antivice and anti-VD campaign was felt once the war was over. In Tennessee, for example, state officials joined with Public Health Service and federal officials to control VD but were unable to obtain the necessary legislation to detain infected prostitutes until 1919.[74] North Carolina's anti-VD program, which began in earnest in 1919, was more ambitious. Aided by federal officials, state health workers conducted a campaign to educate the public. Meanwhile, they also instituted coercive measures that included quarantining prostitutes, "educating" local officials to methods of repression, targeting men as well as women, and supplying local governments with model ordinances to control prostitution and VD. The PHS and the federal antivice agency, the Interdepartmental Social Hygiene Board, financed this campaign, but it operated under a newly created state agency, the Bureau of Venereal Disease.[75]

Its director, Millard Knowlton, initiated a vigorous effort to eradicate vice and VD. Sponsoring "soft" measures such as traveling motion pictures that warned of the dangers of unrestrained sexuality, Knowlton also created a network of undercover agents who conducted "vice surveys" and then turned over the results to the local police. After a six-month tour of North Carolina's cities, Knowlton reported his findings to Watson S. Rankin. With the exception of Charlotte and Asheville, he wrote, the moral conditions were "bad"; in five towns, red-light districts were openly tolerated. In Raleigh, one of his agents informed on men and women cohabitating in the city's red-light district and arranged for their arrest.[76]

Similar programs were adopted in other southern states. In Florida in January 1921, the State Board of Health began a program jointly sponsored by the Interdepartmental Social Hygiene Board and the Public Health Service. As in North Carolina, both of these agencies freely lent staff and financial resources to state health officials. Conducting a state survey of prostitutes, agents of the Florida Bureau of Venereal Disease estimated that the state had about 100,000 cases. Along with free treatment clinics, a major part of their program was to sponsor the organization of community social hygiene committees to eradicate prostitution. But the Florida campaign also involved educational activities. The American Social Hygiene Association lent state officials a large motor field truck. Used as a "healthmobile," the truck was equipped with movies and an electric lighting system and served as a stage for lectures and exhibits. Meanwhile, the program also sponsored clinics to treat VD victims. By the 1920s anti-VD programs had become widespread across the South, but increasingly they emphasized education and treatment rather than repression. With PHS participation, state boards of health operated VD clinics in major towns. PHS agents also attempted to visit and educate physicians and to convert the community through a public relations campaign with local religious and cultural leaders. These activities mushroomed into a broader effort to control VD in the rural South, usually through state bureaus and county health departments.[77]

The disproportionate share of all these public health efforts benefited whites. Not until the mid-1920s did southern health bureaucrats pay attention to the health of blacks; they did so then only because of the interest of philanthropic agencies.[78] In 1926 the Julius Rosenwald Fund, which had exclusively supported the construction of rural black schools, began a modest black health project. At the suggestion of JRF field agent Samuel L. Smith and E. L. Bishop, a former IHB agent and then the Tennessee state health officer, the Rosenwald Fund financed the training and expenses of black public health nurses in selected rural communities. Over the next two years the Tennessee program acquired permanency. Modeled on IHB procedures, the JRF agreed to a formula, which became available to any county in the South, in which it paid a quarter of the costs of the black public health nurses over five years, provided the state and county authorities agreed to fund the balance. By the late twenties the JRF black health project was well established in selected counties in Tennessee, Kentucky, Louisiana, Mississippi, North Carolina, Virginia, and Georgia.[79]

The Rosenwald Fund also inaugurated anti-VD research and demonstration programs in black communities. In North Carolina in late 1929, the JRF financed, with the support of the PHS, an anti-VD program in a single county.[80] In Georgia, it allied itself at the same time with the PHS in a similar project. But the fund's most ambitious project was in Macon County, Alabama, operated in cooperation with the Public Health Service. This project sought to reach the great mass of rural blacks afflicted with VD but untouched by public health resources. The director of the project, O. C. Wenger, was a veteran of PHS anti-VD programs in postwar black-belt Mississippi that, he was convinced, had had virtually no impact on plantation blacks. In parts of Mississippi, he found that the infection rate for syphilis among rural blacks in the 15–40 age group was about 25 percent.[81]

Wenger's project sought a precise measurement of infection in Macon County and the development of a comprehensive treatment program for the county's entire black population. He chose Macon County because of its high percentage of blacks and because of the known extent of VD, as well as malaria, pellagra, tuberculosis, and malnutrition. Operating through the county health department, Wenger established examination and treatment clinics throughout the county. But he found that rural blacks were suspicious of white public health workers. According to Wenger, Macon blacks invariably responded to questions however it would "please the questioner"— whether their answer was truthful or not. Consequently, Wenger took the extraordinary step of hiring only black physicians to perform the medical work in the field. At the same time, a team of investigators, headed by Fisk University's black sociologist Charles Spurgeon Johnson, conducted an intensive community study of the county to search for the environmental sources of infection.[82]

If anything, the JRF's rather brief experience in black public health confirmed what other public health workers had already discovered about the rural South: the problems of health were overwhelming and could be solved, if at all, only after several generations. As was true for rural whites, poor health was directly linked to poverty. Wenger reported the dire poverty of the southern black peasantry. Their typical housing was a shanty; inside, blacks lived in "neglect, poverty, and ignorance." Their water supply came from an open well and was often polluted. Sanitation, he wrote, was a word that did not exist among them. Their diet, composed of cornbread, salt meat, and molasses, with some summer vegetables, caused malnutrition, especially among children. "One wonders," concluded Wenger, "how any of these children ever reach the age of adolescence." The problem of VD was linked to a wider and interconnected socioeconomic environment of ill health. It was, he said, useless to attempt to cure syphilis without a concurrent attempt to address the diseases that surrounded it and the conditions that caused it.[83]

The public health policy that was firmly in place by the end of the 1920s relied heavily on bureaucratic management and state intervention. Yet the more public health workers explored the social environment of the South, the more they discovered the array of diseases and nutritional deficiencies that plagued ordinary people. With health problems so urgent, their measures seemed temporary and minor, and most of them saw an even greater need for centralized control over health affairs. These frustrations were paralleled by the experiences of modernizing educational officials, who also uncovered an appalling social problem—undereducation—whose roots lay in a dispersed and underdeveloped rural society.

◆ ◆ ◆

THE BUREAUCRATIZATION OF SOUTHERN PUBLIC SCHOOLS

In 1927, reviewing a generation of educational change, veteran school reformer James Hardy Dillard described a division between old-timers, who believed that schools had strayed too far from their classical traditions, and reformers who, viewing the system itself as "an old-timer," wanted greater "free expression" in the classroom. Yet larger trends were overshadowing these two positions, he believed. The great mass of educators regularly attended professional conventions and were "serried hosts of the system." This army of educators remained completely loyal to the school bureaucracy. Moreover, the public generally endorsed this system, voted for it, provided ample funds, and was generally proud of it from the first grade to the university. Consequently, the system marched "on valiantly, worrying little over the occasional onsets of either the old-timers or the radicals."[84] As Dillard suggested, the bureaucratic evolution of southern public schools had acquired a life of its own. Like the health bureaucracy, its expansion was stimulated by northern philanthropy, especially the General Education Board. By the onset of the Great Depression, schools had become remarkably uniform regionwide.

As part of this transformation, the state superintendent's office evolved into a new center of power. The nineteenth-century state superintendency had been a symbolic office, lacking any real coercive power. After about 1910, the office's role and authority began to change. In Tennessee, for example, the General Education Act of 1909 established state normals, mandated that a set percentage of state revenue be allocated to schools, and established an equalizing fund for extending the school term. Four years later, the state acquired control of teacher certification, while subsequent legislation further expanded the state role. Other states followed this general pattern. Early on, state officials acquired power over teacher certification, and by World War I, they had the exclusive right to administer exams and issue licenses, often through state boards of examiners. Through a policy of "rigid examination" of teachers, the Kentucky state superintendent explained in 1911, the "old back numbers" of teachers were "down and out," while new teachers demonstrated "a strong work and professional spirit."[85]

State officials responsible to the superintendent's office also exerted greater control over curriculum through the development and implementation of required courses of study for both elementary and secondary schools. A school inspector in 1915 described a uniform curriculum in Nicholas County, Kentucky. Over the past four years, he proudly reported, it had been followed "almost to the letter." Every school in the county opened on the same date and began and closed at the same time every day. Each school adhered to the same daily program; the same classes were recited "all over the county at the same time, so far as they can have the same time."[86]

Greater state power, in turn, reflected a greater reliance on the bureaucracy. GEB funds provided the first rural school supervisors; northern philanthropy pioneered the implementation of bureaucratic school supervision. With the latter came a supervisory force, controlled by the state superintendents' office, that had the power to inspect schools and ensure that centrally determined criteria were implemented locally. "While some mistakes have been made," as a Kentucky school official admitted in 1915, the establishment of a supervisory force had brought "real efficiency" to the state school system, particularly rural schools.[87]

School supervisors performed a variety of functions, but their main role was to represent state power at the local level. When communities requested state financial aid, the supervisors ensured adherence to state requirements, and they tied local compliance to state funding. Tennessee's state rural school agent, O. H. Bernard, visited a Giles County community in 1927. He found irregularities in schools so serious that he warned that state funding was "impossible . . . until the corrections were made." The school's building committee received specific instructions as to the corrections required; local leaders assured Bernard "that every irregularity would be corrected before the building would be opened for occupancy."[88]

Supervisors became an essential communication link between local communities and the state superintendent's office. In Kentucky, a supervisor described his work in a rural county. For him, supervision meant visiting a school "until the whole business" was systematized. Centralization, he wrote, was impossible as long as local teachers and school officials did as they pleased "regardless of the splendid and competent supervisory advice coming from the [State] Department of Education." For this supervisor, a school visit began with taking "inventory" of the school. He asked the teacher about the curriculum and observed the class; based on these observations, he took notes and offered the teacher advice. As part of his job, he required teachers to maintain uniform report books. "We are sticklers," he wrote, "for system, efficient work, co-operation and supervision." These four principles brought sure and lasting results.[89]

Not all inspectors were unsympathetic to local conditions. Wil Lou Gray, who served as a supervisor for the Laurens County, South Carolina, rural schools, recounted in 1915 how experience with rural school supervision had formed the most important and enjoyable part of her work. After three years' exposure to rural schools, she developed what she called a bond of sympathy that motivated her to improve local facilities and conditions. Yet the case of Gray was probably an exception; where she experienced fulfillment, others more often confronted frustrating circumstances. When a supervisor in the Arkansas Ozarks reported to his GEB superiors in 1925, he described a society that was removed from the world, whose habits and customs and ideas were "as fixed and stable as the rocks themselves." Perhaps because of this rural conservatism, he confessed "a vein of disappointment in the things not achieved."[90]

Overcoming the formidable cultural and geographic obstacles of the rural South, bureaucratizing school officials discovered, depended on centralized county school systems. In every southern state, postwar officials first regulated and then tried to eliminate altogether the semiautonomous school districts that had dominated public education since the nineteenth century. The ultimate objective of modernizing educators was to draw these community schools into countywide systems that were directly accountable to the state school bureaucracy. With the encouragement of state officials, county superintendents and boards of education often took the initiative in administrative centralization. In July 1915 the Halifax County, North Carolina, superintendent wrote the state superintendent for advice about how to expand his power. The state superintendent, James Y. Joyner, responded by suggesting that he increase his staff and appoint a supervisor as an assistant county superintendent. Preferably, he advised, the post would go to a woman because a "good woman" could organize local women in school improvement work and reach local women teachers.[91]

As the latter account suggests, women played a central role in the extension of state authority. Although most of the supervisory force tended to be male, women figured prominently in supervision, partly because of the supposedly feminine nature of education. In most southern states, state and county superintendents were exclusively male. But in both Tennessee and Kentucky, there were frequent instances of women superintendents. According to one report to the GEB, women superintendents were peculiarly well suited to bureaucratic supervision. Of those Kentucky counties seeking school modernization, observed the veteran black educator W. T. B. Williams in 1915, the "best chance" for success lay in those counties that had women superintendents. They were "conscientious and sympathetic" and usually knew "more about their colored schools than the men."[92]

As time passed, state officials acquired a more direct stake in the running of county school systems. New statutes consolidated school finance and required counties—and, through them, the states—to centralize control. By the 1920s, local financial authority in district-based systems was sharply curtailed.[93] In North Carolina, for example, county school boards, in sweeping legislation enacted in 1919, acquired virtually complete control over school finances. State funds composed a large share of these county funds—along with special "equalizing" funds to extend the school term—and provided bureaucratizing officials with additional leverage.[94]

Meanwhile, state officials, by imposing educational requirements and certification procedures and by mandating that their offices be full-time and professional, stimulated professionalism among county superintendents. State officials supplied supervising officials and other technicians to assist the county superintendents, and their aid usually solidified state control over county operations. Where they could, state officials promoted the transfer of authority over teacher hiring from community to county control. In one North Carolina community in 1926, a teacher obtained the approval of the local board and community—which, only a decade earlier probably would have ensured her the job. In this case, however, the county superintendent turned her down on grounds of incompetency.[95]

While constructing a bureaucratic school system based on county-level administration, state officials aggressively prosecuted violations of their standards. Fentress County officials challenged a Tennessee school supervisor; by his account, they questioned his right to investigate local affairs and asked whether his board of education had requested that it be done. Eventually, local authorities acquiesced in the investigation, and the supervisor, finding financial irregularities in the county, succeeded in bringing the local officials up to standard. In an eastern Tennessee county, a supervisor found a pattern of maladministration and systematic corruption. Twenty-three teachers were uncertified, while funds were administered irregularly, with excessive amounts going to the county school board. Most important, the county board was defying state policy on pupil transportation, teacher hiring, and financial administration. In response, the State Department of Education, in an action that would have been unthinkable a decade earlier, brought legal proceedings against the county school board.[96]

Although state officials often provided county superintendents with a road map for school modernization, the progress of the county superintendents was regularly reviewed. A Florida state official reported to the state superintendent that his supervision of a county superintendent had caused him to give more of his time to the schools and to "stiffen his back bone" and begin to organize his schools. In some states, as further evidence of the extension of centralizing influences, members of the county school board were no longer elected but appointed by the state legislature. Increasingly, the state school bureaucracy directly financed the operation of the schools and determined how they would operate. Although state superintendents could and did claim that local school affairs were in local hands, in fact they were exerting decisive and even direct control.[97]

As part of the centralization of school governance at the county level, southern state legislatures established the county unit and abolished the power of local school districts. Alabama's law of 1915 provided for the appointment of county boards of education, which in turn appointed county superintendents and district trustees. The act also empowered boards to redistrict according to "convenience, efficiency, and economy." Not only did the North Carolina legislature abolish the district system but also, after 1923, it granted counties the power to achieve a countywide consolidation. Under the terms of the law, counties, with the participation of state officials, had to conduct a county school survey and prepare a countywide plan for administrative and school reorganization.[98]

Other important changes were made in the heretofore community-based school system.[99] On the eve of the war, southern schools were in the midst of a major physical transformation. In most communities, school improvement was greeted with enthusiasm, and new or improved schoolhouses came to be symbols of local pride. After "great progress" in constructing new school facilities, according to a school official in Kentucky in 1911, school building was met with considerable "favor." In every district where better buildings and better facilities became available, wrote a school supervisor in southeastern North Carolina in 1912, communities were "responsive, and the schools have been well attended." Other districts, seeing the advantages that their neighbors enjoyed, were "clamoring for better buildings." [100]

Modernized school facilities further undermined community control.[101] To begin with, backed by popular sentiment for modern schools, state officials succeeded in changing the traditional arrangements of school construction. Offering the incentive of state funds, they required that localities submit to standard architectural plans.[102] In many states, schoolhouse standardization affected all schools. In North Carolina, by the mid-1920s the county school system was required to build any schoolhouse according to plans provided by the state. Uniform requirements specified size, ceiling height, light, heat, ventilation, toilets, and water. Classrooms also had to adhere to a "standard unit." In instances where old structures were remodeled, state officials were equally specific about building design. In Benton County, Tennessee, a state supervisor visited a one-story, four-teacher frame building that was poorly lighted, laid out, and constructed. The supervisor recommended that the building be razed, but the local committee refused to tear it down. The supervisor then proposed that the community construct a one-room addition and remodel the old building according to "definite instructions" from the state; this time the committee accepted the official's suggestion.[103]

There were also new measures to regulate community education. Compulsory attendance, rare before World War I, was enacted by most of the southern states by the early 1920s, along with provisions for its enforcement. Hand in hand with new school construction went requirements for rural school consolidation. After experiments in small-scale school consolidation before the war, school consolidation began in earnest during the twenties. Changes in technology—the availability of trucks and buses to transport children and the construction of better roads—made consolidation possible after 1920. But equally important was the new degree of power that state officials wielded through county school systems.[104]

State officials were not loathe to advertise the advantages of consolidation. They pointed out that newer school buildings were only possible in large districts, that better paid and better qualified teachers would teach in the schools, that they could sustain more diverse curricula, and that attendance would become more regular through pupil transportation.[105] To a certain extent, public opinion sustained this view and endorsed school consolidation as the main vehicle toward the modernization of southern rural schools. After a successful consolidation in Grant County, Kentucky, in 1919, "nearly all the people" in the district were "delighted"; meanwhile, other districts nearby asked for state help in achieving consolidation. "The demand of the rural people," as the North Carolina state superintendent phrased it in 1926, was for "more consolidations" so that their children could "be given better advantages in these large centers." State officials, working through the counties, were "firmly committed" to countywide consolidation and a comprehensive system of pupil transportation. Popular demand for pupil transportation, he added on another occasion, was "now . . . so great in many counties" that it was very difficult to meet it.[106]

Either in conceiving or planning school consolidations, state school officials usually played an instrumental role. Often that role was to advise and urge consolidation, but the primary incentive or threat was usually money. When making an argument in favor of consolidation, explained a Mississippi county superintendent in 1922, he frequently stated that "if we show that we are willing to do this, the State will help us with funds." By maintaining firm control over the purse strings in school construction, state officials exerted veto power over consolidations, and few occurred without their blessing. A Tennessee supervisor described a consolidated structure in 1927 in Kittrell, in Rutherford County. The building was a brick veneer, eight-teacher building, "possibly the best school building that has yet been constructed in Rutherford County." It had a modern furnace, desks, opera chairs, and blackboards.[107]

In the 1920s state officials also began to exert greater control over secondary school development. Early experiments in the prewar era had led to a profusion of scattered high schools, which were characterized by their great diversity: there were large central high schools, district high schools, community high schools, and agricultural high schools.[108] During the 1920s high school expansion came under strict state control. High school inspectors scrutinized them and, as did rural school inspectors, enforced a state standard governing facilities, teachers, and curriculum. In a typical example, the Tennessee high school inspector, W. A. Bass, recommended better equipment and facilities, more books for the library, and closer certification of teachers after visiting the Maynardsville High School in 1925. Bass and other high school inspectors operated with clear but imperious authority. After observing a high school in Manchester, for example, he informed the principal that "your school is in need of more room." The school's standing with the state, he warned, would be endangered unless better facilities were provided.[109]

The areas of health and education provide perhaps the best examples of the expansion of centralized state involvement in local affairs. Although state officials had made significant inroads into the direction of local affairs by the end of the war, they were increasingly forced to adapt. Central state control did little to change the social pathology, with its array of staggering problems, and modernizers were forced to confront the culture behind these problems.

The new social policy in health and education also had to adapt to a sizable popular resistance to outside intervention; the degree to which it succeeded depended on the ability to defuse community opposition. Meanwhile, post-war reformers began to face the problems inherent in the troublesome area of race.

THE LIMITS OF

PATERNALISM

◆

In 1910 a northern visitor to the South described a central contradiction among white reformers. On the one hand, the welfare of the South depended on the progress of African-Americans. As "children of the soil," blacks and their labor were "necessary for the prosperity of the section"; they possessed both a social organization of their own and growing economic resources. On the other hand, he saw the spread of a corrosive racism. Blacks, he said, were "distrusted by nearly all the whites, despised by more than half of them, and hated by a considerable and apparently increasing fraction."[1] However, the attitudes of southern reformers were beginning to change by the end of World War I. In the 1920s the intellectual and cultural underpinnings of paternalism in race and culture started to erode as reform underwent a larger redefinition.

PATERNALISM, EDUCATION, AND THE
EMERGING RACIAL POLICY

Historians have pointed out, often with some surprise, that prewar reformers not only accepted but also often enthusiastically endorsed white supremacy. An assumption of black inadequacy and white superiority typified not only reformers but also the modernizing officials who subsequently executed their policies. A survey of North Carolina state educational and welfare officials in 1929 revealed an arresting degree of racism. The statement of the superintendent of welfare in Appalachian Jackson County, who believed it "only fair to give the negro his chance" by providing equal education, was exceptional.[2] In Anson County, the superintendent of welfare admitted that she did not "push" compulsory school attendance among black students. Because of a "racial difference" that had made and would always keep blacks "inferior to the white race," she said, only exceptional blacks gained much from school; too much schooling made most of them "biggety."[3] These attitudes were not unusual. A welfare superintendent in Beaufort County pronounced blacks to be "racially inferior" to whites, while the Bertie County superintendent of schools declared that blacks had their "place" and "should be helped to fill it better."[4]

Both reformers and policymakers accepted the premise that blacks occupied a defined, generally inferior "place" and that it was the duty of whites to "help" them to fulfill that function more efficiently. Yet reformers succeeded in blending the objectives of white supremacy and Christian uplift. Many white reformers saw the problem of race in Social Gospel terms. In 1913 a reformer described black uplift as both "a missionary enterprise" and "a matter of self-protection." Eugene C. Branson told a group of southern liberals meeting at Blue Ridge, North Carolina, in August 1917 that Christianity could provide a model for race relations. But a Christian approach meant something other than equality before God. The "Master's way of life" required Christians to help blacks to bear their burdens, to provide a "friendly lever" under their boot straps, and to help them in their struggle for "liberty and security." As he more candidly wrote on another occasion, Branson believed that black development depended on the "upward pull" of "surrounding superior masses."[5]

During the years just before the war, reformers often agonized over the growing alienation between whites and blacks. Whites knew little about the world of southern blacks, wrote one observer; their true personality lay in an "inner man," unknown to whites, and their environment was one of poverty, violence, and family disarray. Blacks were "everywhere with the whites, but not of them." A different truth seethed "in the soul of the Negro deep down below the surface," wrote Branson in 1916. Southern whites only knew blacks "superficially." Through what he called a "self-protective hiding instinct," the "real Negro . . . cunningly" withdrew from sight and masked his true feelings. Blacks knew whites "far better" than whites knew blacks.[6]

Reformers searched for a new basis of racial stability. Through organizations such as the Southern Sociological Congress and the University Commission on Southern Race Questions, both formed in 1912, and the Southern Publicity Committee, organized in 1918, they pursued two objectives. The first was to educate whites about blacks and to encourage the spread of "sympathetic," that is to say paternalist, attitudes. A second objective was to instill appropriate values and objectives within the black community by encouraging the evolution of a class structure that existed parallel to the white social hierarchy. The solution to the race problem, as a leader of the Southern Publicity Committee put it, lay in encouraging better contacts among "the better class of Negroes." The latter appeal fell on receptive ears among black leaders. At a meeting of the University Commission in Asheville in 1916, for example, black leaders of that city explained that a "gradual evolution of social distinctions among negroes" had occurred. Whites present applauded these sentiments; attitudes like these, they declared, appealed "to the sympathy of the white man" and enabled "co-operation in helping the negro in his struggles."[7]

The best revelation of the white reformers' program before and after the war came in black education. Louis R. Harlan has demonstrated that the SEB crusades encouraged greater general public neglect of black schools and that the mass of black children remained untouched by modernization.[8] Black educational reform followed about a decade after the whites-only crusade, with the organization of the Jeanes Fund's teacher supervision program in 1907, the General Education Board's and Slater Fund's program in rudimentary secondary education and bureaucratic supervision in 1910, and the Julius Rosenwald Fund's massive program of rural schoolhouse construction in 1914.[9]

The involvement of northern philanthropy in black education was deeply influenced by school and health crusades and by the subsequent development of a social efficiency bureaucracy. Yet philanthropists proceeded cautiously. Given the low level of public enthusiasm for black education, the GEB limited its support, according to Wallace Buttrick, to those "very few" counties that could yield "the largest permanent results." GEB funds supported a limited number of black schools conducting a demonstration of industrial education.

The philanthropists' primary objective was to ease the race crisis through education. Successful reform in black schools, observed a GEB agent, meant that the races could "live together in peace"; instead "of feeling antagonistic toward each other," a "spirit of sympathy and respect for each in his sphere shall be evidence." Black educational reform, wrote another GEB agent in Alabama, had "opened the eyes of all citizens—both white and black—as to the new meaning of education."[10]

In attempting to assure whites that their programs posed no threat to them, paternalists displayed a caution that was well founded. When the GEB proposed to finance separate state school supervisors for black schools after 1914, Louisiana at first rejected the GEB offer of support outright; others accepted it only on significant conditions. As late as 1928, a GEB official complained that it was still extremely difficult—and in some states practically impossible—to obtain state funding for the black rural school agent. It was even more problematical if the agent was black.[11]

There were already scanty public resources for black schools; a backlash would limit them even further. As a GEB official explained it, the social and political conditions as they actually existed in Kentucky meant that black school improvement could occur only under white direction; to do otherwise would be "suicidal in our work." In Florida, the state superintendent reported in 1917 that it was impossible to obtain any money to improve black education in the state. Although he was able to persuade the legislature to finance a single white state school supervisor, no one seemed to care for "the poor negro and his neglected schools." A Georgia educator in 1914 described a "feeling of fear" among whites that blacks would overtake them in wealth and education. This anxiety that conditions would "then suddenly become unbearable for the white man and his children" severely limited public support for black schools. School officials in that state avoided open support for black uplift out of fear of criticism from their white constituents. These attitudes, most reformers assumed, would change only in the distant future; in the meantime, they accepted them as a fact of life.[12]

Blacks greeted the infusion of philanthropic and public funds enthusiastically, and this only confirmed many of the paternalists' assumptions. A Jeanes official in Kentucky who organized blacks into school leagues reported that black communities without strong, industrially oriented schools were slovenly and backward and were "accomplishing nothing." A white official in Georgia agreed in 1916. In those communities where white reformers intervened, black teachers and parents were attracted to "a higher vision of life," one that encouraged them to realize the duties and responsibilities of citizenship, higher social standards, and the "sacredness of moral obligations." White reformers were soon exposed to the inadequacy of black school facilities. They found the condition of black schools, especially in rural areas, appalling, though they often blamed their condition on the poverty of surrounding black homes and family life. Spreading a gospel of uplift and self-improvement among blacks, wrote GEB agent Leo M. Favrot, was impossible when the vast majority of schools were "scattering in their aims, wretched in their squalor, utterly inadequate and inefficient as to methods and results." With inadequate facilities, he concluded, neither teachers nor officials could hold a vision of "the broad field of opportunity," particularly regarding industrial education and community betterment.[13]

After about 1914, much of the paternalist program for southern blacks focused on school improvement. In schools, reformers found an arena for racial change; they saw black children, like white children, as malleable, improvable objects that held the key to the future. Improving black schools would produce long-term benefits in the development of attitudes that were appropriate to a modernizing society and in the acquisition of "industrial" skills that most blacks supposedly lacked. Black educational reform offered another significant advantage. It required a large measure of cooperation between the races, for either complete white control or total black autonomy would manifestly fail. By providing a model of interracial cooperation, black education attracted the attention of northern philanthropists interested in southern reform.

◆ ◆ ◆

PHILANTHROPY AND THE DEVELOPMENT OF BLACK EDUCATION

Although northern philanthropists cooperated in an alliance for black educational reform, they had a distinctly different agenda. The General Education Board stressed secondary education and other structural changes within the school bureaucracy. The Jeanes Fund pursued primarily pedagogical objectives in the introduction of curricular changes and industrial education. The Rosenwald Fund focused entirely on the construction of modern schoolhouses. Each of these philanthropies also differed in outlook. The GEB, the most conservative, stressed accommodation and white control; the Rosenwald Fund, the most liberal, encouraged black control and leadership. Nonetheless, there was an obvious partnership and a sense of mutual helpfulness among the philanthropists. The Rockefeller philanthropic structure, as it often did elsewhere, coordinated this diverse program. GEB largesse provided a stimulus for the cooperation of the educational bureaucracy, and the state agents of black rural schools coordinated a three-cornered relationship between state officials, black communities, and northern philanthropists.

State agents for black schools headed all black educational supervision and provided the necessary bureaucratic commitment. The GEB-sponsored bureaucracy worked closely with the supervising Jeanes teachers, who acted as field agents for the state agents. Financed in a government-philanthropic partnership, Jeanes teachers spread industrial education to public schools through "practical" skills such as sewing, cooking, basketry, crafts, and agriculture. They also emphasized cleanliness, hard work, and hygiene. Eventually, because of the realities of black education, Jeanes teachers became advocates of the improvement of schools and their facilities.[14]

The development of county training schools, which were an early form of rural black secondary education, was an important example of northern philanthropists' involvement in black education. Sponsored by the Slater Fund and the GEB, almost four hundred county training schools came into existence by the late 1920s. Supported by philanthropy, state officials, and county governments, they also depended on black initiative, local white cooperation, and state interest.[15] Upon local white support usually hinged the necessary financial resources from county authorities. In Hempstead County, Arkansas, for example, "a prominent white gentleman," who served as president of the board of a local black school, guaranteed the support of local officials. "His name alone," according to one report, "carried more weight . . . than would have the petitions of many Negroes." White support for the Uchee Valley County Training School was "on the increase" in Russell County, Alabama, according to one account in 1918. Local whites realized that unless better opportunities for black education were made available, the county's blacks would emigrate. In Louisiana, local whites, described as "very anxious" to have a black parish school, were "willing to help put over the movement." In Tennessee, a school official stated that the "good, wholesome sentiment" of the white people of one community was crucial to the success of a county training school.[16]

If white support was crucial, black enthusiasm was essential. In central Alabama, the Cottage Grove Training School, in Coosa County, became the first such institution in the state when a local black donated one hundred acres of land and two buildings to the state. The school was located twelve miles from the railroad, near the center of the county's black population. It charged tuition and boasted a faculty of five, whose courses included instruction in home economics, agriculture, and training for rural teachers. Once established, the school continued to rely on black enthusiasm as well as community support. After a training school opened in De Ridder, in Beauregard

Parish, Louisiana, in 1921, a mass meeting was held at the new school building in which every black family was represented. At the meeting, according to one account, the people pledged their support by organizing a School Improvement League; they promised that the school would "take first rank among the Training Schools." Meanwhile, other committees were organized to scour the community for additional funds for the future support of the school.[17]

The county training schools had modest but realistic objectives, and they emphasized the development of school facilities.[18] A black educator working for the GEB described the new Wake County Training School, near Raleigh, North Carolina, as "nicely kept" and equipped with "fairly good" facilities. Local blacks, he reported, although timid in the face of white opposition, were pressing for greater support from the county. Most training schools stressed an industrial curriculum. Rather than seeking to send students to "some university North," the schools, a GEB agent told black supporters of the Cottage Grove School, should supply their own county with graduates to live "useful lives upon finishing school." For many blacks, the training schools only whetted their appetite for secondary education. One group of black teachers protested that they were "painfully conscious" of the inability of black children in North Carolina to study beyond the seventh grade. The teachers "urgently" prayed that state officials would provide such high schools to meet "the growing need."[19]

After the war, North Carolina undertook the most ambitious program of black secondary education in the South. In 1918 North Carolinians approved a constitutional amendment that expanded state funding for black education and provided a basis for expanded high schools. State officials in the 1920s began a reorganization of black education that sought to establish a black high school in every county with a substantial black population. By 1928, in a development that a state official called "truly remarkable," the state financed fifty-six accredited black high schools, with another seventy-five that were moving rapidly toward that status.[20]

In North Carolina and elsewhere, black high schools often evolved out of county training schools. After the war the issue of facilities came to overshadow curriculum, in part because of black resentment toward the racist assumptions of industrial education. Many black communities engaged in deliberate subterfuge.[21] In East Carroll Parish, Louisiana, a state agent in November 1916 discovered that the Jeanes teacher was teaching "like one of the regular teachers"; when asked to produce evidence of industrial work by students, she could only manage to show "soiled" work that revealed "a lack of system." The boys meanwhile "had nothing to do." According to the agent, the chief problem was that the local community "had no conception" of industrial education. In 1917 Leo Favrot was shocked to find a rural black teacher with a copy of *The Crisis*, the magazine of the NAACP, containing an article by W. E. B. Du Bois that ridiculed industrial education. Although Favrot informed the teacher that Du Bois was "out of sympathy with some of the work she was trying to do"—and his GEB superiors noted approvingly what "a good fellow Mr. Favrot" was—the disturbing message was that rural black teachers never fully accepted the Hampton-Tuskegee model.[22]

By the 1920s black opposition to the industrial program surfaced more openly. When a philanthropist told a Winston-Salem group in 1927 that the "inevitable lot" of black children necessitated industrial training, W. A. Robinson, a black teacher, took sharp exception. In reality, he said, the so-called industrial training was "anemic" and succeeded only in preventing children from learning the "rudiments of reading, writing, and figuring." He denounced any effort, through schooling, "to perpetuate the present industrial, economic and social status." "American ideals of democracy and human justice" contradicted a dual pedagogy.[23]

In general, there was greater black enthusiasm for the Rosenwald program. Between 1914 and the mid-1920s, Rosenwald agents sponsored the construction of thousands of new schoolhouses for southern rural blacks. The success of the program, as James D. Anderson shows, was rooted in black support.[24] Contemporaries would agree. According to Favrot, the Rosenwald program stimulated unity, pride, and autonomous development in black communities. Rosenwald schools united people, "regardless of denominational difference," around "a common cause." In this way they fostered a "community spirit" among blacks.[25]

Rosenwald schools openly encouraged black self-help and autonomy. In Autaugaville, in black-belt Alabama, community support became contagious. After a woman who had "only one copper cent" donated it toward the cause, "a great commotion" ensued in which $200 was given, in denominations ranging from $20 to one cent. Over the next month, clubs were formed to raise more funds. "I have never seen greater human sacrifices made for the cause of education," remembered the Rosenwald agent. Shoeless children donated from fifty cents to $1; old women, "whose costumes represented several years of wear," gave $1 to $5; men offered to pawn their livestock and pledged their future crops. When the campaign ended, the community had raised $1,300.[26] In one community in Wood County, Texas, where children attended what was described as "a shack that could scarcely be called a school house," local blacks decided to raise funds by planting a crop of cotton, while another black community agreed to sell communally held pine forests to finance the Rosenwald school. In Fayette County, Tennessee, some 1,200 members of local black lodges agreed to contribute a dollar each. On a rainy day, representatives of the lodges trudged into a meeting of community leaders and presented 936 one-dollar bills; subsequent contributions raised a total of more than $2,000. Others who could not give cash donated eggs, chickens, corn, potatoes, and cotton.[27]

Although the first Rosenwald schools, built during the war, were modest one-room structures, they became larger and more elaborate in the twenties. By the end of the decade, fewer one-room schools were constructed in favor of three-room or larger structures, and school consolidation became a condition of financial support. In North Carolina, the Rosenwald program began to promote black school consolidations in the early 1920s; they soon were common elsewhere. In White County, Tennessee, local blacks in 1926 received Rosenwald aid only after they had agreed to a consolidation that created a five-room school. The building was constructed according to Rosenwald standards and included facilities for industrial instruction and "suitable grounds for recreation, etc." For the state as a whole, only six of the forty-nine schools built were one-room schools in 1928.[28]

Rosenwald officials gradually ended their school construction program in the late 1920s. In its place, they began other programs designed to modernize black education. In June 1928 they inaugurated a school term extension program that provided for aiding a maximum of ten black rural schools and thirty teachers in each of fourteen southern states. According to the terms of the program, Rosenwald financed over several years a declining share of the costs of a nine-month school term.[29] In the next year, Rosenwald offered support for bus transportation.[30] In the early 1930s the Rosenwald Fund began to divert its resources toward public health, social science, and the broader implications of race relations.[31]

The results of these northern philanthropic programs were significant. Working closely with the newly invigorated school bureaucracies, philanthropists succeeded in fostering a degree of white commitment to black education. After 1920 black school facilities improved measurably, especially compared with their rather dismal condition even as late as 1910. Moreover, white involvement in black education had a kind of multiplier effect. While it brought renewed attention to the problem of black underdevelopment, it also blazed the trail for a more general search for justice within the Jim Crow system.

Not long after the United States entered World War I in April 1917, a GEB agent wrote from Kentucky about a white man from Chicago who was causing "agitation" among blacks in Fayette County. Although local black leaders reassured him that the troublemaker's efforts were "entirely fruitless," the agent sounded a clear note of anxiety. In 1920 a white educational official expressed similar anxiety about "agitators" who were apparently attempting to "stir" blacks "to excitement or urge them to deeds of violence," or "to come among them and make [them] suspicious of the white people of the state." One interracialist in North Carolina warned against labor recruiters who enticed "the negroes to move north or west by holding up shining prospects of wealth and social advantages." These promises were empty ones for southern blacks, he claimed.[32]

The anxieties voiced by the white official were rooted in a troubling race crisis before, during, and immediately after the war. The outbreak of hostilities in 1914 had ended European immigration to the United States and set in motion the beginning of a monumental demographic transformation: the migration of what would become millions of southern blacks to northern cities. But as the black immigrants filled jobs and neighborhoods that once had been all white, as they began to exercise unprecedented freedoms of the franchise and cultural life, and, above all, as blacks served as part of a conscript army created in 1917, virtual race warfare erupted across the nation in riots and lynchings. During the years 1917 to 1920 especially, the race crisis grew so intense that, at least among opinion shapers, there were profound fears about the future of race relations.

Most white racial moderates agreed that the war years had irreversibly altered black-white relations. Yet this period created not only uncertainty but also new opportunities. In 1917 Eugene Branson described black migration to the North and Midwest as "a race exodus very like the exodus of Israel out of Egypt"; it marked "a new era in negro history in America." He predicted that the Great Migration would "immensely better" the status of rural blacks by raising income and wages and increasing home ownership. The "stay-at-home negro," he wrote, possessed "close to the largest chance he is ever again likely to have to own a home or farm of his own." Other white reformers pointed to black migration as the best evidence of the need to ameliorate the Jim Crow system. According to one of them, the Great Migration provided a chance "to improve conditions for those who remain," and black leaders could make the case that the root problem was the failure to address the "removable cause of the migrations." Will Winton Alexander's assessment of conditions in Mississippi in 1924 was similar. He believed that the improvement of the economic and legal status of blacks in the state was linked to black migration, which furnished "an opportunity for some fundamental education and constructive building of far-reaching and permanent value." [33]

The changed perceptions evoked by the war gave rise both to fear and to heightened expectations. "One of the clearest and most unmistakable results of the war," wrote one observer in 1920, was the central importance of race and "the considerable feeling of unrest on the part of the Negro." The war, remembered another perceptive commentator, "had a marked effect on the race situation in the South." By providing blacks a chance to demonstrate "their power and value in an hour of national crisis," it lifted them "into a new consciousness" of their worth. But this self-consciousness "greatly heightened" their resentment toward "the many handicaps" thrown in their path. Whites, in contrast, emerged from the war with a mixture of feelings. Some, particularly those who saw blacks "from long distances and through a fog of rumor," feared an unknown future. Others, who saw blacks at "close range and in relation to other racial groups," believed that the race problem offered both a "new challenge" and a "new obligation." [34]

The war and the black exodus, and the racial turbulence they created, began a process that culminated in the founding of the Commission on Interracial Cooperation. Racial tensions within the armed forces during the war's late stages had become so severe that Woodrow Wilson in 1918 sent Tuskegee principal Robert Russa Moton and Thomas Jesse Jones, educational director of the Phelps-Stokes Fund, to France to investigate the situation. Based on its findings, the Moton-Jones mission proposed the creation of biracial committees to ease the transition of black soldiers back into southern society. In Atlanta, black and white ministers had participated in prewar groups such as the all-white Men and Religion Forward Movement and the biracial Committee on Church Cooperation. Out of these was organized the Christian Council, which served as a committee sponsoring cross-racial communication. In December 1918 a group of white reformers met to discuss the wartime race crisis. The group convened at a larger, more formal meeting in Atlanta during January 1919 to study race relations. Its charge was to investigate "what the negro wanted," establish a "minimum program" of white-black cooperation, and devise a means for securing the support of interracial leadership. [35]

This group—which by March 1919 was calling itself the Committee on After-War Cooperation—operated under white domination: the Atlanta meeting was all white. The core was composed of educators: Wallace Buttrick, James Hardy Dillard, and Thomas Jesse Jones. But a significant num-

Will W. Alexander.
(Courtesy of the Library of Congress)

ber of liberal Protestants sympathetic to the paternalist program also were present. YMCA official and racial liberal Willis Duke Weatherford attended this early meeting, as did a core of representatives of Atlanta liberal Christianity: another YMCA official, Richard Hayne King; philanthropist and liberal Presbyterian John J. Eagan; Meredith Ashby Jones, pastor of Ponce de Leon Baptist Church and special adviser on the black church to the War Department; and, most important of all, Will Winton Alexander.[36]

After the meeting the Atlanta group outlined the beginnings of an interracialist program. Establishing a card index of "sympathetic and intelligent" white southerners, it was, within six months, reaching out to include blacks such as Morehouse College president John Hope, Tuskegee principal Robert Moton, and black Methodist bishop Robert Elijah Jones. During 1919 and early 1920 the group organized "training schools" that were located in segregated facilities: for whites, at the YMCA's Blue Ridge Assembly in western North Carolina and, for blacks, at Gammon Theological Seminary in Atlanta. The training schools operated, as Will Alexander noted, "without publicity"; those in the Atlanta group plus the members of "one or two other small groups" were the only men who knew of this program. Out of these and other conferences came the Commission on Interracial Cooperation, which was formally organized, with black and white membership, in February 1920.[37]

Financed by a $75,000 grant from the YMCA's National War Work Council for a "preliminary experiment," the CIC attempted during 1919 and 1920 to organize the eight hundred counties in the South that possessed more than 10 percent black population. The training schools and other meetings had concluded, according to one account, that the war completely altered "the whole status of race relationships" and the duty of the local committees was to explore the basis for a new racial stability. These early biracial committees were designed, for the short term, to deal with the immediate crisis and instability caused by the war and to aid in the transition to a postwar situation. Their immediate purpose, as Alexander explained it, was to sponsor local plans for cooperation among blacks and whites of "intelligence and good will."[38]

By the early 1920s the CIC had secured more stable financial support. The National War Work Council had provided virtually all of the funds required for the extensive efforts before 1922 to organize the local interracial committees; its contribution between 1919 and 1921 totaled over $600,000. Support from other quarters filled the breach thereafter. A small amount, $25,000 in 1922, was raised from the boards of the mainline Protestant denominations; in the same year black organizations donated about $10,000. But the largest contributors were northern foundations. The Phelps-Stokes Fund usually contributed about $2,000 annually, although in one year it gave $20,000. The Laura Spellman Rockefeller Memorial provided $25,000 during 1922 and 1923; for the rest of the decade it contributed $40,000 annually. Beginning in 1924, the Carnegie Corporation supplied $10,000 a year, while in the late 1920s the Rosenwald Fund contributed the same amount.[39]

The CIC operated as a multilevel organization. It met regularly at its Atlanta headquarters, but most of its work and policy came from Will Alexander, the director, and other staff, which included, by the mid-1920s, directors of women's work, research, student work, and publicity. Headquarters staff conducted public relations campaigns, mainly aimed at altering white attitudes. Under the direction of R. B. Eleazer, the CIC orchestrated a massive effort to supply copy to and shape the editorial policies of newspapers. In the year 1924, for example, Eleazer's news service supplied a total of 50,000 pieces of material to all southern daily newspapers.[40] Much of this publicity supported an educational and legal campaign against lynching. CIC officials pressured sheriffs to prosecute lynchers, recognized and publicized the names of sheriffs who did so, lobbied for greater state enforcement, and in some cases even supplied undercover detectives to gather evidence on mob violence. By 1926 the CIC was committed to a "special emphasis" in the antilynching campaign that would seek a "final drive . . . with every possible means" toward the eradication of that evil.[41]

Alexander and CIC reformers saw particular potential in southern universities. After the war, in conjunction with the student department of the YMCA, the CIC sponsored annual conferences that encouraged the study of race in the higher education curriculum.[42] Alexander worked with sympathetic academics, especially Howard Odum, to foster the study of social science and the sociology of race at southern universities, where it was typically either absent or inadequately supported. The CIC also offered a program to educate white college students to different views on race. People rarely changed their fundamental attitudes after age thirty, Alexander once wrote; thus, young people, especially college students, presented "the best opportunity for creating better racial attitudes." On some campuses, leading blacks, such as Robert Russa Moton and George Washington Carver, spoke; the objective of these appearances, as Alexander explained, was to expose "one generation" of white college students to prominent black leaders. By 1922 black educators had, under CIC sponsorship, lectured at some forty white men's colleges in Kentucky, North Carolina, Virginia, Tennessee, and South Carolina. Meanwhile, the commission also sponsored annual summer conferences of white college students, with black speakers, at Blue Ridge, North Carolina, and Hollister, Missouri.[43]

Promoting direct contacts with black leaders, white interracialists experimented with new models of racial etiquette. Hollister, Missouri, one location for interracial conferences, was an isolated community in the Ozarks that had long boasted "of not allowing a Negro to stay overnight." When Moton appeared at the meeting and "delighted" an audience of white students, the conference leaders, without any publicity, integrated the dining hall to the "nine cheers" of the students. A student participating in the conference later remarked that this was the first time that he had eaten with a black; he declared that he and his peers were "not going to stand for anything but fair treatment for a man of Major Moton's calibre." He was "proud of the fact that the college men of the Southwest have come to the day when they can appreciate a man although he is black." Although Alexander kept the incident secret, he judged it indicative of a change in public sentiment that predicted "tremendous results" in the future.[44]

Meanwhile, the CIC constructed a network of state and local interracial committees. The National War Work Council largesse sent CIC organizers across the South, and by November 1920 state committees had been organized in twelve southern states. The state committees encouraged interracial contacts as well as racial moderation in the press, lobbied for favorable legislation, and coordinated improvements in public services for blacks. In many states, CIC committees also lobbied for antilynching legislation and, at the local level, held sheriffs accountable for the protection and fair trial of black defendants. While they lobbied at state capitols for the apprehension and prosecution of lynchers, the state committees promoted expanded contacts between national and regional welfare officials and local interracial committees, which served as "a clearing house and point of contact" for black welfare work.[45]

The "chief emphasis" of the interracial movement, according to a CIC official in 1922, was on local interracial activity; by 1930, according to the CIC's assessment, local interracial committees had become "an accepted fact" in many communities. Yet local committees, composed of separate black and white members who met both separately and together, varied considerably. In smaller communities, explained one observer in 1922, the committees, neither "formal" nor "elaborate," met infrequently. In larger communities, the committees organized themselves more formally, with black and white churches represented. In both large or small communities, however, the white and black sections of the local interracial committees met separately, often weekly. Perhaps as often as once a month, the two sections came together, considered the general racial situation, and examined signs of racial conflict. In "friendly conference," the leaders of the two races attempted "to clear it up."[46]

But the frequency of these meetings depended entirely on local initiative. A white leader in Asheville, North Carolina, explained in 1923 that the local committee met only infrequently "because of the good feeling . . . between the races in this Community." The city's interracial committee was, as Woodrow Wilson described the initiative and referendum, "like a shotgun behind the door," which was "ready for an emergency." The most active biracial committees were in those communities in which the threat of mob violence and racial crisis loomed large. Although this responsibility fell especially heavily during the tense months after the armistice, committees were most active when race war seemed imminent. In 1924, for example, a white mob formed in Madisonville, Kentucky, in pursuit of a "drug-crazed" black who had allegedly murdered a sheriff. When it became apparent that the mob might turn its fury on the black section of town, the local committee met and declared that "the guilt was that of an individual and not that of a class." Local black leaders joined in the search for the culprit and, through the interracial committee, "deplored" his crime. Through the committee's intervention, the murderer was apprehended, tried, and legally executed. But the larger result, as the CIC noted approvingly, was that "race war" had been averted.[47]

The members of the local committees were all male, but women figured prominently in the committees' activities. In April 1920 a meeting of the white Methodist Women's Missionary Council in Kansas City called for an interracial effort. Will Alexander, who attended the Kansas City meeting, had already recognized the potential in the WMC, which he described on one occasion as "the most progressive and constructive religious group in the South."[48] He urged the Methodist women to lay aside prewar paternalist assumptions and approach race relations "as though it were a new problem." The WMC responded by appointing a Commission on Racial Relations, with the Georgian Carrie Parks Johnson as its chair. Meanwhile, with the support of YWCA women, who were committed to interracial organizing, and at the urging of Lugenia Burns Hope, wife of Morehouse president John Hope, a conference took place in June 1920 at Tuskegee in Booker T. Washington's study. The participants included ten leading black women, Carrie Johnson, and Nashville reformer and YWCA leader Sara Estelle Haskin.[49] Described as somewhat "ill at ease," the interracial group issued a resolution stating that the black woman's "world of pain" could be healed only when shared with her white sister. Although tensions continued, as did important differences on objectives, a meeting of white and black women's leaders in Memphis in October 1920 was successful. In its wake, a Women's Committee, headed by Johnson and later by Texan Jessie Daniel Ames, became a permanent part of the CIC headquarters staff. Alexander actively encouraged these groups, serving as an unofficial male adviser; as a link to the CIC, he was a vigorous advocate of continued support.[50]

The Women's Committee, subsequently known as the Department of Women's Work of the CIC, constantly encountered the boundaries of early twentieth-century gender roles. Women interracialists functioned within a gender-segregated organizational structure, operating in tandem with the all-male interracial committees. Just as the male committees joined together the "best" people, the women's committees, according to one account, brought "little groups of interested white women . . . in the closest touch with the Negro women of their community." Among both races, the representation was to be well balanced among the religious denominations. The committees were also intended to represent women's club organizations, "to touch practically," according to one account, "all the women who make the sentiment of the South."[51]

Yet at every level of the CIC, women bristled at male domination. While some of the commission's early organizers hesitated to include women because of the possibility of publicly mixing with black men, others, as Alexander remembered, feared that "emotionally women couldn't be trusted." When the CIC field agent, R. W. Miles, first organized Mississippi in 1924, he relied heavily on a Methodist bishop to assemble the first meeting of the state's interracial committee. But, according to Carrie Johnson, the bishop invited "the wrong people, all men." She believed that this incident typified how the Methodists limited women's participation; the bishop was sure "that the men will meet and work out what they want and pass it on to the women." Even at CIC headquarters, women expressed frustration. Jessie Daniel Ames described Will Alexander, whose support and patronage had been crucial in the early organization of the CIC women, as both "as fine a man as I ever knew" and as "so unsatisfying." Ames considered her coworkers as neither men nor women, just competent or incompetent. Her long experience of "fighting every step of the way" made her forget Alexander's "lovely consideration of me as a woman." She said that she was unsure whether he had "spoken freely when he talks with me," and she had the "general idea" that his support was weaker than it might have been if she were a man.[52]

Constrained by limits both inside and outside of the CIC, the women's committees focused on the intersection of race and the traditionally feminine category of morality. Framing their appeal in the name of "chastity," women interracialists often endorsed, as a group of Texas women declared, a "single standard of morality among this race as well as among our own." Justice was impossible, agreed a Tennessee group of women, until there was a "single standard of morals for all, and a sentiment for the equal protection of women." Chivalry among white men was meaningless unless it also included "the integrity of the Negro home," which needed to be "no less sacredly respected and safeguarded by the men of both races." This conception of race-blind chastity eventually led interracialist women to oppose lynching, that "black spot on America's soul," as one group put it, which "as women, as the mothers of men, we protest." [53]

Despite some success in reducing postwar racial tension, neither the local nor the state committees fulfilled the expectations of interracialists. The sharply reduced budgets of 1922 fell especially hard on fieldwork. In 1920 and 1921 the CIC supported one full-time white and one full-time black agent for each state, but by 1922 the number of field operatives was reduced to eight (four black, four white). By 1934 the CIC could only manage one full-time agent. For most of the twenties state committees were active only in Georgia, Kentucky, Tennessee, Texas, North Carolina, and Virginia. But even in those states, progress at the state and local levels was slow. From Greensboro, North Carolina, James Dudley, president of the local state black college and chairman of the black section of the city's interracial committee, complained that the committee had not "occupied the place in the community-life that it should have." He added that this problem of nonactivity was typical of the rest of North Carolina. In New Bern, in the eastern part of the state, another observer wrote that the local interracial committee had never functioned "as a unit" and had never established itself as more than a "paper" organization. Howard Odum complained in 1921 that white Tar Heels exhibited a most progressive and wholesome spirit of cooperation with Negroes, but that their "rather upstanding and independent way of working and thinking" sometimes worked against the progress of interracialism. [54]

Elsewhere progress was slow. According to Carrie Johnson, as of 1924 in no state in the South were CIC women's groups "sufficiently organized" nor had they achieved "results commensurate with the time and money expended." Among club women, whose leadership originated the movement, Jessie Daniel Ames reported that interracialism was "not generally popular." Many were "indifferent," others "openly antagonistic." As late as 1927, a field agent complained to Ames: "If all your Committees have functioned as inadequately as the one you asked me to work on I feel sorry for you." In Deep South states like Alabama, the complaint of one interracialist about the director of the state committee, who continually promised to call a meeting but actually did nothing, was not unusual. After an initial burst of enthusiasm, local interracial committees functioned erratically and were, in the understated language of one historian of the CIC, of "a very loosely constructed nature."[55]

◆ ◆ ◆
THE EMERGENCE OF INTERRACIALISM

In 1920 Will Winton Alexander told of his return to his home place in rural Georgia. Visiting his grandparents' graves, he noticed that Ike and Mary—two former slaves who had figured importantly in his father's childhood—lay in unmarked graves; Alexander's relatives knew nothing of what had become of their children. His family's indifference to formerly closely connected blacks suggested that the gap between the races had widened rather than narrowed since emancipation. Although southern whites often said that "We know the Negro," in reality they knew "little about the Negro[,] . . . as little as any one." There was "absolute ignorance" on the part of "the best white people" about black discontent and suffering.[56]

Behind Alexander's observations was the realization among postwar white liberals that the war and the social changes accompanying it had affected the caste system. One of the approaches that white reformers embraced in response to this new situation was interracialism. Best exemplified in the CIC, it encompassed a diverse leadership, constituency, and program. Some of its features challenged racial hierarchy; others confirmed it. But what seemed to hold the CIC together was a consensus supporting racial "cooperation"—the development of regular, institutionalized contacts between the races. Interracialists sought, as a Kentucky group explained in 1922, the development of "a wholesome atmosphere" for cross-racial understanding by providing an environment for a spirit of goodwill and cooperation between the races. Sympathetic whites would provide a "ready and frank admission" of "injustices and handicaps" and make known to black leaders "their desire to know the facts" in order to devise "ways and means by which these injustices may be corrected and these handicaps removed."[57]

These goals were vaguely stated—and deliberately so. Most interracialists endorsed some variety of white supremacy. At a North Carolina interracial conference, state school superintendent Eugene Clyde Brooks advised blacks to stop "complaining" about Jim Crow and instead "show gratefulness for the many blessings bestowed in Educational and other matters." Rather than labeling segregated railroad cars as "Jim Crow," he urged blacks to call them "separate" facilities. Denouncing Bolsheviks and rapists, Brooks urged black leaders to repudiate "foreign organizations," such as the NAACP, which sought to interfere in local affairs. Other white reformers held similar attitudes. In 1920 white Louisiana interracialists described blacks as "not fully awakened to their opportunities." White leaders had an "obligation," as members of a "ruling and . . . dominant race, to exercise such guardianship and to furnish such guidance as will prove helpful in raising standards of living, conduct and efficiency" among blacks. Describing themselves as endowed with "the greatest earthly powers," a group of Arkansas whites felt obligated to help their black inferiors. The "test of character in an individual or race" was how they treated those who were "helpless" and whose opportunities were limited.[58]

The interracialist movement displayed a strong Protestant flavor, yet not all southern white Christians were impelled toward racial uplift. Most church people, noted one interracialist, had "only a slight conviction as to the implications of Christianity in this field, and even less ability to formulate these implications into a plan." For interracialists, along with a small number of well-informed, socially minded liberal Protestant ministers, the real impact of the Social Gospel interracialists should be on the lay public. A concern for "justice and good will" toward blacks, according to Will Alexander, strongly affected whites of the urban middle classes, and the ingredients of humanitarianism and elitism were much in evidence among interracialists. Alexander declared that he believed "not in the white race, but in the justice of humanity." But true humanity and justice would occur when "the best white people" understood "the difficulties" of race relations.[59]

Among the most prominent of "the best white people" was John Joseph Eagan, Atlanta philanthropist and Social Gospel adherent, who led efforts to Christianize race relations. Born in Georgia, Eagan used an inheritance to buy the American Cast Iron Pipe Company in Birmingham, Alabama, which, during World War I, manufactured almost a fifth of all cast iron pipe in the country. He subsequently became an early practitioner of Christian labor relations. Observing what he claimed was the golden rule in business and labor practices, he implemented profit sharing, guaranteed employment, and extended medical and retirement benefits, and he constructed recreational facilities for his workers. He even insisted that one member of his board of directors be elected by the Federal Council of Churches. In 1913 Eagan helped to secure black participation in Birmingham's YMCA building campaign; he also was an organizer of the Atlanta Christian Council, an early interracial organization. Through the YMCA's National War Work Council he emerged as an advocate of new approaches to race relations, and from the formation of the CIC he served as chairman until his death in 1924.[60]

But the most important figure in postwar racial liberalism was Will W. Alexander. A graduate of Vanderbilt University, Alexander took a Methodist church in Nashville, where he discovered, as his biographers put it, the "tightening grip of need" among the city's working class and the reality of deprivation among the city's black residents. After witnessing a vicious beating by a white of a young black boy, Alexander denounced the man in a sermon, an experience that he later remembered as his "first instruction in the race problem." Later, Alexander left the pastorate to work with the National War Work Council at Fort McPherson, Georgia, and then in Atlanta, where he came to conclude, as he wrote in his reminiscences, that "illiterate whites were the product of poverty and these Negroes were the product of poverty plus discrimination."[61]

The Social Gospel provided a language and rationale for racial cooperation, yet its message was interpreted differently. In Atlanta, the CIC headquarters staff embraced a relatively egalitarian view of race. Outside Atlanta, the Social Gospel translated into a cautious reaching out to blacks, with careful observance of existing racial taboos and etiquette. Upon the church must be placed the major responsibility for solving the problem of race, declared a Tennessee group of whites in 1922; here was a "colossal opportunity" to apply Christian principles. Yet, at the same time, the group suggested a cautious tack: only when Christians learned "His principle" and applied "His rule" would the problem of race disappear.[62]

Many interracialists feared a future conflagration. Interracial committees in South Carolina, denying rumors of "race friction" in 1919, reported "a certain amount of nervousness" about the explosive potential of postwar black-white relations. According to a resolution of the Southern Baptist Convention in 1920, which endorsed the formation of the CIC, one of the "unmistakable results of the war" was the "considerable unrest" among blacks. That unrest did not, however, mean that there could be "any change in the fixed separation of the two races"; no such change was "possible," nor was "any change desired by the thoughtful [leaders] of either race." Nonetheless, there was both "an urgent need and an open door" for better interracial understanding "and a more sympathetic attitude of each toward the other." White public opinion, explained a group of Arkansas women in 1922, had been too long influenced by prejudice, passion, indifference, and ignorance. Those attitudes could only be changed by "facts and better understandings advanced by courageous souls."[63]

Impelled by Christian humanitarianism and concerned about the specter of race war, white interracialists developed a program of "cooperation," which meant the establishment of formal interracial contacts. As Eagan expressed it in 1921, whereas the CIC provided blacks "a forum" for venting their "troubles, misunderstandings and fears," it offered whites an opportunity to express their "fault-findings." This "common platform of good will" supplied "the best insurance for the work already done for the Negro in the South." But such cooperation could succeed only if it operated with a minimum of publicity. "Our work," as Alexander explained it, was "entirely in the background"; its chief function was to "stimulate other organizations to incorporate our ideas in their own programs of work for Negroes." According to another advocate, the CIC offered a platform on which "the best white and negro citizens came together . . . quietly, without advertising." The *Nashville Tennessean* assured its readers that interracialism in the state sought "nothing radical"; its efforts were "directed largely toward the eradication of the various causes of irritation and friction."[64]

CIC officials were cautious in yet another respect: "cooperation" meant primarily and usually exclusively contacts among the "better" classes of southern whites and blacks. According to a Texan, interracialism fostered association among "the sane, conservative element in both races" with "common interests, common hopes, common aspirations, and common aims." The "sober-minded" of both races needed exposure to each other at "closer range." Among "the best white and the best Negro men and women of the South," asserted one white, there was "little communication or understanding." As a result, a gulf existed between them; it kept better whites from knowing the aspirations and capabilities of the best class of Negroes. Interracialism would bridge the gulf between "intelligent white and Negro men and women."[65]

This implied, at least to whites, an acceptance of segregation: interracialists, rather than advocating the demise of Jim Crow, favored softening its worst features. Their enthusiasm for racial segregation varied. In Louisiana, a group of white reformers viewed the state's segregation laws as "passed in the interest of both races and . . . wise and proper." Segregation merely confirmed "the satisfying of a natural instinct," and the task of reform was to "assist the Negro in every way possible in maintaining his racial integrity and developing pride of race." In North Carolina, Eugene Brooks declared that Jim Crow railroad cars were "better under the circumstances in the South for both races." Separation of the races, he reasoned, avoided the close contact that would "unquestionably result in racial friction." Under "proper management," moreover, separate facilities would eventually become more equal. Other whites, such as Howard W. Odum, expressed their support for segregation only with considerable qualification. The color line permitted independent, autonomous development among blacks, Odum believed. In public schools, for example, black performance at segregated facilities—if those schools were "of the most modern and up-to-date"—brought "good results" among black children.[66]

In accepting the continued existence of segregation for the foreseeable future, white reformers promoted, as a conference of Methodists phrased it in 1918, a "real sympathetic cooperation between the leaders of the two races." By institutionalizing contacts between the leadership classes of the two races, a "frank interchange" of views on housing, transportation, education, and moral and religious conditions could occur. White and black leaders, believed interracialists, would determine the sources of "bad feeling and open friction" and seek to ameliorate the system to contain it.[67]

By fostering interelite communication, the interracialist program sought to transform community racial attitudes. These could be changed, Alexander maintained, only if the focus was on the community rather than the individual. But the creators of community attitudes were the black and white elites, and they remained isolated from each other. The result, argued Alexander, was a kind of inverted pyramid: whereas lower classes of both races experienced frequent, often daily contact, interracial elites knew little of each other. At the top of the social pyramid, "where there was intelligence, good-will, moderation, and self-control," he told the American Missionary Association in November 1922, "the races were far apart." But as both races "began to drop in intelligence, in opportunity, in self-control, in religion, their contacts were multiplied." Among the lower rungs of the social order, the races freely mingled, yet at this level the cross-racial contacts frequently led to social disorder and violence.[68]

Seeking to attract the leadership elite of both races, the CIC deliberately kept its programs diverse and vaguely defined. Although the commission attracted the "best people of the community," wrote a Rockefeller official in 1923, for some it was "not moving fast enough," while for others it proceeded "too fast." He quoted a white leader in Savannah, who described the CIC as a "life preserver in a torrent." It provided a "rallying point," but, of necessity, included a wide spectrum of opinion. His advice, which CIC officials generally took, was to "move very slowly and with great caution."[69] With substantial differences among interracialists, the CIC waged a frustrating battle for amelioration of the Jim Crow system.

THE LIMITS OF PATERNALISM

The organization of the Commission on Interracial Cooperation and the popularity of interracialism among white liberals revealed subtle but significant attitudinal changes. World War I was in many respects a watershed. The notion of black inadequacy, and the assumptions that accompanied it, strongly influenced the ideas of prewar reformers; black uplift, went their reasoning, depended on white initiative and leadership. During the 1920s several developments began to erode paternalism's underpinnings. The changing composition of the black population and the Great Migration to northern and midwestern cities brought change and uncertainty to the white South. Meanwhile, the intellectual support for racism and paternalism further eroded because a consensus of social scientists rejected the prewar assumptions of white supremacy.

A major factor in the erosion of paternalism lay in the posture of blacks toward it. Although blacks saw it before the war as a temporary, stopgap program that would bring some benefits, they became increasingly critical after the war. When white opinion makers were exposed—most of them for the first time—to the true feelings of blacks during and after the war, they discovered widespread dissatisfaction. Many whites found their image of black contentment and docility permanently exploded. If it took a century for working people to achieve a "complete stage of class consciousness," observed a CIC member, "the Negro attained it during the War." Among blacks there was a new spirit of impatience that the war amplified. As Will Alexander observed, some black leaders were resentful of handicaps and openly rebellious, defiant, and contemptuous of any program that fell short of "immediate action."[70]

White interracialists who asked what black people wanted received an often-surprising response. Blacks wanted "the chance to be men," to have access to resources "with the minimum of impediment in their way," Alexander told an integrated audience in 1920. Particularly at interracial meetings where black leaders could speak with candor, white reformers were exposed to multidimensional individuals who found white supremacy humiliating and debasing. The Women's Interracial Conference that convened in Memphis in 1920 offered prominent blacks an opportunity for frank talk. Elizabeth Ross Haynes, who in 1908 had become the first black secretary of the YWCA, told of the daily humiliation of Jim Crow streetcars, which, she maintained, kept the races in a state of permanent alienation. It affected everybody: men, women, children, the young, and the old. It affected "people when they are going to work, when they are going to church, when they are going to bury their dead." Very few thinking blacks who entered a segregated streetcar were able to "keep themselves feeling well balanced." Although this was not a personal criticism of the white women present, she said, "I am telling you how it is for us, how we feel and think about it."[71]

Other conferees, such as the North Carolina black educator Charlotte Hawkins Brown, spoke with similar candor. She told of how she had been harassed, en route to Memphis, by a group of whites who objected to her occupying a sleeping car berth on the train. "Put yourself in my place," she said, and "just be colored for a few moments." She told how the whites forced her to leave the sleeping car for the Jim Crow coach, how she felt "crushed and humiliated."[72] The statements of what one white woman called the "unrestrained frankness" of the black women at Memphis began to expose the limitations of the paternalist racial system. According to Alexander, who heard Brown's address, this was the final act that clinched the determination of the white women to embrace the interracialist cause. As Carrie Johnson later remembered it, many white women present experienced "the pulsing desire" of the black women, who "helped us to see some things in a different light" and to bridge, at least momentarily, the "gulf of distance, of mistrust and suspicion" that divided the races. When the black women told of their "aching hearts and unspeakable fear" at Memphis, said Johnson, "my heart broke, and I have been trying to pass the story on to the women of my race." The black women were "surprised," as Brown recalled, that white women could say such things.[73]

Whenever they had the chance, blacks sought to dispel the notions of white interracialists. It was impossible, Charlotte Hawkins Brown told a CIC meeting in October 1921, "to help a people without knowing the environment and conditions under which they live." White reformers, benevolent though they might seem to be, could not help her people without understanding what she represented, and there was only one way to understand it. White reformers needed to be directly confronted with black life. They should enter black homes, watch families at the dinner table, and observe their daily life. In doing so, whites might discover that, after all, the idea of social equality was "a bugbear."[74]

At another such meeting, held in Oklahoma in November 1920, an integrated audience heard a strong indictment of Jim Crow. "We don't want any social equality," one black physician said, "but we want justice." He did not understand why whites thought that Negroes were brutes. Some blacks complained of the "jeering" attitudes of even the "best" white men toward the most careful and prudent black women. Most black spokesmen at the gathering called not for an end to segregation but for equalized facilities. If separate railroad cars were supposed to be equal, asked one black, why did conductors commit the injustice of supplying no step stools for black passengers? "We are not asking for an annulment of the separate coach Bill," declared a black woman of Cadde County, Oklahoma, "but if we can have a clean place, if we can have a comfortable car, . . . we will be thankful." Another black speaker, of Muskogee County, maintained that he had "no complaint against the separate coach law"; his objection was to its "manifest workings." Whether confronted with a "gross and ill bred" streetcar conductor or cramped into a Jim Crow compartment—when the white coaches had ample room—he felt a powerful, perhaps even criminal impulse to protest. So long as black people were "subjected, segregated, and humiliated," predicted another spokesman from McCurtain County, there would be "dissatisfaction in the Negro."[75]

As these comments suggest, blacks often expressed ambivalent feelings toward interracialism: on the one hand, they were repulsed by de jure segregation; on the other, they regarded contacts with white reformers as a vehicle toward what an Alabama black leader called a "fairer and more considerate manner of dealing with the humbler folk of all groups and races." Other black leaders were attracted to a system that recognized, and gave official sanction to, an existing black class structure. Most whites knew "nothing whatever" about the black community, declared the *Savannah Tribune* in 1924. About blacks in business and the professions—"our talent, our endeavors, our ambition and our desires for betterment"—the average white knew little. Nor were whites aware of "our social life, our churches, our homes." Interracialism at least provided an opportunity to educate whites about the black community.[76]

Nonetheless, the erosion of paternalism became only partly clear to contemporaries. Late in life, in 1923, GEB director Wallace Buttrick, a paternalist who favored little essential change in the status quo, described a visit to a South Carolina school that, he believed, pointed to an important change in the nature of black education. The school was located on attractive grounds and looked well from a distance, but a closer look revealed severe deterioration: the steps had rotted, windows were broken, and there were other indications of a general "lack of care." When Buttrick asked local trustees why a community that "would have had interest enough to build so nice a school" would not maintain it, a trustee told him "in a grieved tone" that a Chicago philanthropist had donated the money for the building but would not "keep it up."[77]

Other white liberals, from different perspectives, came to recognize the limits of paternalism. Cautioning against optimism, Alexander wrote in 1928 that "the greater task" in racial progress lay ahead. Even in parts of the South where the CIC had made inroads not much more than a beginning had been accomplished, while the most difficult and ultimately most important aspects of the situation continued to be unaddressed. Political empowerment and economic improvement would need increasing consideration in the years just ahead. Most whites remained convinced of the "essential inferiority" of blacks; even among most blacks, the notion was "quite general." Especially in the remote areas of the rural South, most southern blacks lived in a world in which educational, social, and economic opportunities were at the barest minimum; in these communities, little or nothing had been accomplished.[78]

Where Alexander's critique of paternalism was subtle, others were more direct. The Atlanta liberal minister M. Ashby Jones wrote in the opening issue of the *Journal of Social Forces* in 1922 that the assumption that the "better" classes of whites treated blacks more fairly—a key assumption behind the paternalist system—was simply wrong. Although upper-class whites had "inherited a benevolent feeling toward the individual Negro," they expressed a "social and political fear of the race en masse." This dehumanization of blacks among the "better" classes of southern whites was responsible, he thought, for "the unspeakable record of barbarities committed against this weaker race." In 1926 a Tennessee white interracialist, E. L. Orr, attacked another assumption behind the paternalist system: innate racial differences. He declared that classification by race was now acknowledged as "a difficult, even an impossible, thing." There were no longer, if indeed there ever had been, any absolutely pure races. If anything, the traditional definition of race purity could be applied to "the very lowest types of people." In fact, the notion of "distinctive races," he maintained, was "fading out," for standards of "color, language, geographical location, custom &c" broke down under close scrutiny. If anything, there was "greater racial differentiation within races than among races." A group of Texas women put it more directly. The "universal existence of prejudice among people of different races" was inevitable. Yet, they contended, blacks should have a hearing on their own behalf; whites should not be content simply with being kindly disposed to blacks, but rather they should extend "justice in all things and opportunities for living the best possible life."[79]

Subtle changes in attitudes, in the case of Buttrick, or more pronounced shifts in strategy and objectives, in the case of Alexander and Orr, suggest a larger reorientation in which older assumptions about black inadequacy and white control were evaporating. As the bankruptcy of paternalist assumptions became clear, the approach of Alexander, Orr, and liberal interracialists superseded that of Buttrick and moderate paternalists. In place of the Victorian sociology of race to which Buttrick subscribed, Alexander had adopted the clinical, empiricist language of postwar social science. Rejecting the traditional, and scientifically unproved, assumption of innate racial differences, postwar social scientists emphasized social environment.

Alexander and other interracialists, adopting the language of social scientists, saw the problem of race in terms of "discrimination"—language itself that suggested a fundamentally different approach. "Race prejudice and race discrimination," wrote Alexander in 1924, were "interwoven with elements that are in no sense racial." Those elements included, above all, "bad economic and civic conditions"; these so complicated the problem of race that it was "not always possible to know to what extent the various forces" were responsible. Yet purely economic and social forces had played a large part in the present racial antagonism. To Alexander, racial prejudice, poverty, and legal and political discrimination made the solution of the problem of race exceedingly difficult, a long task that was multigenerational. A group of Texas women interracialists reached a similar conclusion. "Prejudice," they declared, was "universal . . . among people of different races." They found paternalist assumptions of white control anachronistic. The exposure of paternalism led these women to endorse "personal and racial justice in private life and in the courts of the land."[80]

The implication of these new assumptions was that the dominant attitudes of prewar white racial reformers were eroding. In 1925 one CIC pamphlet expressed it this way. Whites, it declared, possessed a peculiar obligation to be both just and generous in their treatment of blacks. While repeating the paternalist language of uplift, the pamphlet then arrived at a strikingly different conclusion: the obligation to help blacks also required whites to recognize the "infinite worth" of blacks. This meant a respect for the integrity of blacks' personality and an assumption of their humanity. Whites should no longer think of blacks in terms of their own convenience, as a race divinely doomed to remain in perpetual servitude. Rather, whites were obliged to extend to them a "fair opportunity for self-development."[81]

A knowledge of, and a belief in, the "infinite worth" of blacks did not necessarily mean that white interracialists favored ending the color line. Those that foresaw an integrated society spoke of it as a long-term, but also remote, objective. But it did mean, as Alexander said as early as 1920, that the old program of paternalistic uplift should be abandoned in favor of "real brotherhood." Perhaps the clear verdict on the early years of the CIC came from John Hope in 1928. He characterized the commission's approach as "quite different from those of a number of other efforts in behalf of Negroes." The traditional approach was, he wrote, paternalistic: the habit of white racial liberals was "to think out what was best for Negroes and do that." The interracialist program, in contrast, operated on the assumption that no program for racial uplift could work without the participation and consent of black people. In "a strange search of the heart" and "a frank penetrating look into their own civilization," a small number of CIC liberals sought "a new interracial gospel."[82]

Into the 1920s white racial reformers were increasingly forced to confront inherent contradictions in their approach. Like the approaches of other reformers, it was based on the paternalist model of uplift. Assuming cultural superiority of their urban white civilization, racial reformers believed that the solution to racial problems would come under their control and direction. With the interracialist program, some of them slowly realized that progress depended on a degree of equality; immersed in the problems of southern blacks, they began to develop a degree of empathy toward black culture. Yet there were clear limits to this empathy, and in the end reformers were unable to resolve the conflict between their desire to uphold Jim Crow segregation and to promote black progress. At the root of this failure, and at the root of early twentieth-century southern reformers' larger frustration, lay their inability to acknowledge the integrity of the culture they sought to remake in their own image.

SCHOOLS, HEALTH, AND

POPULAR RESISTANCE

◆

Historians of the Progressive Era have said more about the reform crusades and the policy changes that they stimulated than they have about the social` context of reform.[1] Crusades in prohibition, education, health, and, to a lesser extent, child labor and woman suffrage created a popular mandate for change. But when that mandate was translated into policies, especially when it involved centralization and coercion, the popular response was quite different. Few ordinary southerners fully comprehended the price of reform, and when they did, reform was strongly resisted across the region. Reformers in health and education, and the ambitious policy changes that they sought, soon discovered this reality. Their challenge in creating a policy was more formidable than that of the other reformers. They had to create and then maintain administrative systems capable of reaching millions of long-isolated people accustomed to little outside intervention. Perhaps inevitably, these new administrative systems quickly became coercive and centralized, and they removed decision making from the community. Not surprisingly, the community response was often hostile, and by the late 1920s there was a kind of standoff between centralizing officials and traditional localists.

◆ ◆ ◆
RESHAPING THE SCHOOL INTERIOR

Centralized bureaucratic control over schools often evoked communal re-assertion of power. Teachers, bombarded with a new professional ethos that stressed allegiance to the school bureaucracy, needed standing within the community, and a struggle between competing views of teacher-parent relations frequently ensued. A North Carolina teacher attempting to impose regularity on the age of entry into school in 1912 met strenuous parental objections and was forced to back down. Teachers seeking to adhere to a centralized curriculum also encountered community opposition.[2]

Conflicts frequently arose about the traditional right of rural parents to fire unpopular teachers, either through pliant school officials or through intimidation and boycott. In November 1925, when a teacher near Marion, Tennessee, used corporal discipline to impose order in his schoolroom, one father appeared "in a menacing way" and, according to the teacher, "acted like he might use a pistol on me."[3] In 1929 a teacher in Cape Hatteras, North Carolina, described a school composed of the "roughest, most selfish, most deceptive, unappreciative children I ever saw"; "illiterate and childish" trustees dominated the school board. When the teacher disciplined a local girl, she and two boys vandalized the teacher's car. A controversy ensued. Some parents withdrew their children because they believed they were wrong-fully accused, others left because they did the vandalizing. Still another student, the daughter of the Dare County School Board chairman, attempted to set fire to the school and "openly refused obedience." After the teacher whipped her, the pupil refused to attend class. Her father then blocked payment of the teacher's salary.

But the teacher's ordeal was not over. Her opponents brought charges, which she claimed were trumped-up, that she used profane language and that she began and ended school either too late or too early. Especially galling to the teacher was the claim that she had lost control of the school and that "disorder" prevailed in the classroom. "That is false," she wrote, "because the children that have stopped, stopped because they were punished." Meanwhile, little official response was made to the charges. The campaign against the teacher came to a head when a mob of some twenty parents and children appeared at the schoolhouse door. One parent pledged that the teacher "shan't teach another day" and "shan't live here." Pleading for help, the woman informed state officials that she was "scared" because there was "no officer here." With such discouraging prospects, the teacher fled the community.[4]

Community pressure usually transcended race; if anything, because of white neglect, the black community exerted considerably more power than its white counterpart. In April 1927 three black families in a rural Forsyth County, North Carolina, community attempted to drive a teacher out "without any cause whatever," although the root of the conflict lay in her decision to change her boarding place. As was true of the Hatteras teacher, the black teacher proved difficult to dislodge. As one observer noted, this was not the first teacher the community had tried to run off, but it seemed that she was a little harder than most. When opposing parents boycotted the school and pressured the county superintendent to fire the teacher, she informed the attendance officer of the pupils' nonattendance. But he announced that he "would not fool with these niggers"; local school officials cared little "whether the colored have any school or not."[5]

Much of a community's power over teachers lay in its ability to withhold children from school. Despite the passage of compulsory education legislation during and immediately after World War I, regular attendance, especially in rural areas, depended on parental consent. Without an enforcement officer, as a southeastern North Carolina teacher asked in January 1918, "how in the world" was it possible to get the children to go to school if their parents said that they were "not agoing to send their children to school until they have to?" In 1920 a mother, complaining about the lack of "much system about our schools now," noted that the superintendent rarely visited the school in her area and ignored the compulsory attendance law. Local committeemen charged with enforcement often simply lied. Given the conditions present in rural Georgia, the compulsory attendance law there was declared in 1929 to be "almost impossible" to enforce. In Cherokee County, in North Carolina's southwestern corner, an investigator for the Laura Spellman Rockefeller Memorial found that observance of compulsory attendance laws occurred "only in sporadic instances," chiefly because local officials were "as interested in finding reasons why the child should be excused from school" as they were in serious enforcement. In western North Carolina, another observer complained that "a very poor officer" who had "only done enough to draw his pay" was responsible for enforcing the attendance law.[6]

The situation was no different in Tennessee. There, a General Education Board official claimed in October 1912 that the compulsory education law remained unenforced. Teachers, who were required to report nonattendance, were excused "for almost anything"; the county board accommodatingly allowed any other excuses. In Campbell County, he reported, the law had been ignored so long that it was forgotten.[7] Although the legislature strengthened the compulsory education law during the next decade by providing for truant officers, complaints continued. In January 1926 a Benton County teacher wrote that there was no truant officer and, consequently, many children remained out of school.[8] In those Tennessee counties where truant officers were employed, often little consideration was given to competency. In Cocke County, in the eastern part of the state, the school board hired the wife of one of its members. She was described as "a good woman" who had "done nothing to inforce [sic] the attendance." By the late 1920s the problem of nonenforcement was serious enough for the state superintendent to consider penalizing counties that did not enforce the law.[9]

Yet nonenforcement was a symptom rather than a cause: local officials skirted the law because of community opposition. Securing regular attendance, as a South Carolina county superintendent explained, was a difficult matter, primarily because of parental attitudes. Some thought it was useless to put their children in school at the beginning of the session, while "these same thoughtless parents" would withdraw their children two or three weeks before the close of the session. "Valiant knights" across the South who were prepared "to do battle for the so-called rights of a free people" grew "hysterical over the word 'compulsory'" and were "exceedingly anxious" about it. An eastern North Carolina teacher who attempted vigorous enforcement in December 1925 was assaulted by the county school board chairman, who also threatened his life.[10]

Community opposition to compulsory education reflected long-standing social, economic, and geographic factors. Bad weather and poor transportation often kept students from remote communities out of school. How could school authorities expect children to attend "in all kind of weather Such as rain and snow"? a North Carolina parent asked state officials. No law should compel attendance, she believed, "under unreasonable disadvantages." In Randolph County, North Carolina, a white woman wrote on behalf of a black tenant farmer, whom she described as a "fine man . . . tho. black," whose children had to walk seven miles to school.[11]

As improved transportation penetrated the rural South, however, the preeminent reason for nonattendance remained the labor demands of the agricultural economy. In Kentucky, a survey in 1917 concluded that work was the primary reason for nonattendance. In a community in a southwestern portion of the state, two white boys, aged nine and eleven, who worked in the tobacco fields with their father missed forty-five out of seventy-four school days because of the need for their labor. In most of rural Kentucky, the compulsory education law remained a "virtually dead letter," the report went on, and non-attendance was "winked at by the authorities." In the struggle between work and school attendance, the odds favored work.[12]

Any attempt to enforce attendance struck at the heart of the rural labor system and threatened the economic security of the family. As an informed student of the subject wrote, the problem of farm work and nonattendance was a stubborn sociological phenomenon. For most working families, children were a necessity. In 1924 school authorities attempted to force a North Carolina woman to send her fourteen-year-old-daughter to school. The mother appealed to the state superintendent, claiming that she was "afflicted with an awful Kidney trouble and 10 acres of cotton to House." Local officials enforcing the law had "a Rock Heart" and cared little "for a mother at all." How, she asked, was it possible in a "free country" for outsiders to "compel us to do as [they say]"?[13]

Most parents whom reformers often casually described as recreant kept their children out of school for reasons of poverty. "I have got to have some help, and I cant hire any . . . that is the Reasun he is not at School," explained one parent to an attendance officer in 1920. He had two children attending daily, and "if I could do with out Melvin he wood be going to[o]." Another farmer voiced the same sentiments. He kept his boys out of school to help him work because he and his family had "to live by [the] Sweat of our face." To this parent, with a family of seven and a scarcity of labor, it was a question of survival. In Wayne County, North Carolina, in 1918, patrons asked school officials for permission to keep their boys—about twelve years old—at home to plow. Labor was very scarce, and it was "important that a big crop be made." In these circumstances, county officials allowed "the boys to go to the field." State officials rarely contested such acquiescence. In 1927 the state superintendent encouraged county officials in western North Carolina to suspend school for "a week or two" if it promoted better attendance later on. In other states, schools opened in the summer months so that they could be closed during periods when there was a heavy demand for labor.[14]

A Laura Spellman Rockefeller Memorial study found that compulsory attendance laws were simply ineffective in North Carolina in the 1920s. Between 1924 and 1927, the LSRM sponsored a project to create a model county welfare program in four counties. Based on the results, state officials concluded that the failure to enforce compulsory attendance—which in North Carolina was the responsibility of the county superintendent of public welfare—constituted one of the most serious failings of the welfare system. In the Piedmont counties of Orange and Chatham, teachers and officials paid little attention to the problem and exercised their authority inconsistently. Even after the county welfare demonstration program, teachers and officials were reluctant to enforce the law. County officials saw little possibility of resolving the conflict between school and home; if a parent "declared that his child had been needed on the farm or in the home, it was generally felt that there had been sufficient excuse for the child's absence" and the rights of the family were "practically accepted as inviolable." Consequently, enforcement was "very difficult."[15]

The problem of compulsory attendance remained one of the chief obstacles to extending modernized public schools to the southern rural masses. The failure of reform here was emblematic of similar failures elsewhere, with similar causes. Reformers discovered that enacting legislation and altering policy was not enough to change the environment of schools. Winning the struggle for control over the school interior, best exemplified in the problem of compulsory attendance, depended on more wholehearted community cooperation, which, at least until the next generation, was not forthcoming.

◆ ◆ ◆
CONSOLIDATION AND TRANSPORTATION

Reformers also faced a struggle with local communities over the control of school exteriors, including physical facilities, their location, financing, and administration. Transforming the school exterior would wrench it from its social context, but that, they believed, was the primary cause of undereducation. As part of this transformation, they sought to close community schools and replace them with modern, permanent structures that projected the new power of the bureaucratic state.

Few contemporaries, either reformers or localists, disagreed that the traditional schoolhouse inadequately served southern children. Indeed, in an era of rapid educational expansion, most communities sought their fair share. In one locality, a group of petitioners complained in 1917 that a promised school building had not yet materialized. They described their present schoolhouse as "a very small building and not by no way's comfortable for winter." What this group sought, rather than "a fine expensive building as some have," was "a warmly comfortable building." As in this case, local opposition often erupted not so much over the construction of new facilities, but over which communities would directly benefit from them. In Avery County, in western North Carolina, for example, a number of communities objected when a new school was constructed outside their locality. The chief source of the controversy, according to the state superintendent—who personally investigated the situation—was a "lack of cooperation and harmony among the people and between the people of those districts."[16]

Intercommunity conflicts usually arose over questions of location and administrative control. In the nineteenth century, schools symbolized the community, and their dispersion ensured local autonomy. Under most programs of school modernization, the small, dispersed schools were replaced by more centralized, consolidated school facilities that were no longer singularly associated with the local communities. The increasing emphasis that modernizers placed on a hierarchy of grades, with elementary and secondary schools, only raised the stakes further and heightened antagonisms.

Communities responded with a mixture of emotions toward the centerpiece of school modernization, the consolidation of rural schools. Although they often welcomed the improvement of facilities that accompanied consolidation, they opposed the loss of control and the erosion of autonomy that went with it. Early experiments with consolidation usually met with some community opposition. In South Carolina, a woman supervisor visited two schools in Dorchester County with poor facilities. The schools, unpainted and located directly in front of the road, had no grounds, outbuildings, or water; they also had cracks in the front door through which one could see passers-by. Despite these primitive conditions, these two communities steadfastly refused to consolidate. Elsewhere in the state, the same supervisor found "so many miserable short-term schools" whose only remedy was consolidation. If only, she wrote, they could "be brought to see this."[17]

But efforts to consolidate almost always met opposition. Although a county school official in 1902 said that most people in Greene County, Georgia, were "satisfied" with consolidation, he admitted that there was usually "one man [who] took a notion that he wanted a school of his own, [and] wanted it near by." In some instances, such opponents could withdraw their support of the consolidated school. Another Georgia school official was more frank. School consolidation, he declared, was a subject that caused "a great deal of trouble all over the state." Most communities possessed their own "little one-horse school they have had for 25 or 30 years," and it was "the hardest work imaginable to get these people to believe that there can be any better school in the world." In the countryside, such opposition came down to a single "very great difficulty": that the typical parent preferred "a poor school at his back door to a good one two miles distant." Everyone in his county favored school consolidation, still another Georgia official noted sarcastically, "provided the school is located next door."[18]

Localism made other southern parents resist school consolidation. In Craven County, in eastern North Carolina, the efforts of the superintendent to encourage consolidation apparently alarmed some citizens. They had attached a "sanctity" to the school's previous location because some of their kinsmen had participated in its founding, which, he observed sardonically, was "incidentally near their homes." In the Appalachian community of Jonas Ridge, residents agreed that their three districts provided inadequate schools, but intercommunity divisions over location blocked consolidation. Every time representatives met to discuss the question, they squabbled over location.[19]

Before the end of the war, modernizers moved hesitantly to implement a comprehensive system of consolidation, as one Georgia superintendent explained, because of the "peculiarity of the geography . . . & the opposition of the patrons." The Florida state superintendent "heartily" approved of consolidation on "general principles," but he acknowledged that this was a subject that usually created "more or less dissatisfaction." It was therefore a matter that had "to be handled very wisely." Consequently, state officials insisted that local officials initiate consolidations, and, perhaps predictably, local efforts moved slowly. Practically nothing had been done to amalgamate Kentucky schools, a county superintendent explained in 1911, because "our people simply fight consolidation from start to finish."[20]

School consolidation was entangled with high school expansion. Especially in the pre-1920 period, a large number of new schools described themselves as high schools, often receiving state aid for that purpose. But creating a high school usually meant establishing a consolidated school, as most pre-1920 high schools educated pupils from the elementary grades onward. Even so, the new high schools frequently competed with each other for students and resources.[21]

More ambitious attempts to implement a regular program of school consolidation occurred when the war ended. New, favorable conditions—the construction of a network of hard-surfaced roads and the availability of school buses during the 1920s—made centralized governance and state-directed consolidations quite common. Yet opposition persisted throughout the decade, especially against state intervention. When the state rural school agent for Kentucky visited Carroll County and urged consolidation, local residents vented their fury, charging that a "forced consolidation would be attempted." Although the agent tried to assuage these misgivings, which he characterized as a "misunderstanding," opposition continued. He hoped that a full explanation would eliminate it. In North Carolina, as elsewhere, state officials worked through county authorities. In one community, neighboring districts were, claimed a trustee, "trying to pull us over them," while county officials acted without any regard for his district. But the state superintendent responded unequivocally. Consolidation by county school officials was perfectly legal, he wrote, if they located the school within reasonable walking distance from the children's homes or provided "adequate" transportation. A Tennessee county superintendent explained in 1925 that opponents of school consolidation had said "many bitter things" against him. But the tide had turned, he claimed, when the state rural school supervisor intervened and "came to the rescue." Even with the increasing force of state authority behind consolidation, the struggle between centralizers and localists continued. Despite the new facilities that a consolidation offered one North Carolina community, parents objected in 1925 to the school's increased distance from their homes, a factor that made it "unconvenient" for their children. The new location favored a neighboring community, one patron claimed, and "should be near the center." He suggested that school authorities revert to the traditional school arrangement.[22]

The location of consolidated schools continued to set communities against each other. When one community was passed over for another, charges of unfairness and favoritism were fairly common. An Iredell County, North Carolina, parent objected when a consolidated school was located, she claimed, outside the center of the district. Despite inspections by state supervisors, the county superintendent, who had made only a perfunctory visit, urged an unpopular location because of its "political pull." Unhappy with this decision, a group of parents appealed it, apparently to little avail. It was "their business to look after the cause of education, and not any one neighborhood," a parent lamented, and if "they had been looking out for the convenience and benefit of the largest number of pupils" they would never have reached the decision that they did. In another county, trustees arbitrarily removed a school "without our consent"; this led to a sharp drop in attendance from their community. Despite the consolidation, patrons continued to object. With a schoolhouse "large enough to accomidate these puples," one patron failed to "see why we are not entitled to our school." Instead, they were the victims of "a crooked deal pulled over us by the Local Board and the County Supt." While one group of parents depicted the decision to consolidate and close their community school as the result of school officials "defrauding us out of our school," another community objected to the efforts of school officials to "tare up" their school without "the consent of the patrons of this District."[23]

Other southerners objected to allegedly unresponsive school officials, but high-handed control by outsiders was particularly rankling. Without its knowledge, the Brasstown neighborhood, in southwestern North Carolina, was divided in the 1920s in a rearrangement of the border separating Cherokee and Clay counties. Traditionally, the community, although composed of two separate valleys, had sent its children to a single school, located at the confluence of the Big and Little Brasstown creeks, which, according to one observer, always had been the intersection of the "educational, civic, and religious life of the people living in these two valleys." Accordingly, both valleys refused to consolidate with other schools in their respective counties. "I do not believe," wrote the observer, "that a school can prosper which is dependent upon strong arm methods of obtaining pupils."[24]

An important factor behind the opposition to school consolidation was parental fear about their children walking to distant schools. From Henderson County, a North Carolina parent described the treacherous roads of that mountainous region. The present route, he argued, was "very dangerous" and "unsafe for a grown person to walk." He had had "some narrow escapes." Appeals to the county school board had been futile, he maintained, because the chairman had "no relatives on this road" and therefore had little concern for "the Life of our little one[s]." Frustrated by this unresponsiveness, he took his case to the governor as "a Democrat & a man that voted for you . . . to see that we get this Bus for the protection of our little ones."[25]

Yet even the provision of publicly financed bus transportation provoked parental objections about the unequal and politically motivated distribution of resources. While some communities enjoyed the benefits of publicly financed school buses, others complained that their children were forced to walk. How was it, asked a northwestern Piedmont, North Carolina, parent in 1924, "that some districts have the trucks and others don[']t"? In the same year another community questioned "the right of the county Board to descrimanate [sic] against us in the matter of transportation." Such complaints persisted throughout the 1920s. A group of Tennessee parents protested that the driver of a school wagon transported "the children on his place" while neglecting others. Whereas some schools had their students transported, other pupils were "left to walk," wrote a North Carolina parent in 1929. Some families "of all grades [were] being Halled [sic] and others walking Regardless of [the] distan[ce] to school." Understandably, the parent wanted to know why school buses were available for some children but not for his own: "As I am a tax payer of this Poticular county and have been for 16 years I want to no for what Reason I cannot Receive the sam[e] as others does." Despite the fact that he and about ten other neighboring families had complained to school officials for the past two years, the officials were able to produce "some excuse to put our Community off."[26]

At the same time, mass transportation aboard school buses raised new fears. Many parents, probably with good reason, had little confidence in either the roads or the drivers. A group of parents in Claiborne County, Mississippi, charged that school buses were "old and worn out" and the drivers "reckless." A mother doubted that "little tots of six and seven years old" were "as capable of looking out for themselves on trucks driven by young boys." These buses, she claimed, traveled on inadequate and sometimes dangerous roads. Her six-year-old son had sustained a concussion in a bus accident that left him "desperately ill for days." Another parent complained that the buses picked up his children only after they had walked two miles on a dangerous highway.[27]

Rural parents also objected to the long hours of riding to which their children were frequently subjected. Consider what the children endured, wrote a North Carolina mother, "leaving home early in the morning, some at 7 A.M. and even earlier, returning at 4:30 and *much* later; whereas in town small children go at 9 A.M. and get out at twelve." During the dark winter months, complained a western North Carolina mother, her children left before daylight, with a ten-minute walk with lanterns and flashlights to the bus stop. "We feel," she wrote, that "our children cannot do their best work and compete with the other students under such conditions."[28]

Parents often expressed frustration that their complaints evoked little sympathy from school officials, who regarded school consolidation and transportation as the central features of their long-term program of change. Moreover, by the late 1920s the officials had little reason to alter this policy, aside from minor adjustments, for the balance of power was clearly shifting in their favor. School officials only responded to community objections with stiffened confidence. A. T. Allen, the North Carolina state superintendent, told one dissenter that he could not see "how hauling a child to and from a public school would in any way interfere with his liberties or the liberties of his parents." Rather, school consolidation and transportation offered "a great service" to the children of this and other communities.[29]

◆ ◆ ◆

CENTRALIZATION AND COMMUNITY RESISTANCE

If consolidation and transportation were the centerpieces of rural school modernization, both of these changes depended on a new conception of power and decision making. Modernizers realized that effecting change hinged on relocating the lines of authority and transfiguring a localized into a highly centralized system. These administrative changes did not, however, pass unnoticed.

Many of the most important administrative issues concerned the interrelated questions of districting and finance. For much of the early twentieth century, reformers sought to infuse funds into community schools by persuading districts to raise taxes voluntarily. Although this was the usual objective of the earlier school crusades, it often ran aground because of rural opposition to higher taxes. When local authorities in a Mississippi community agreed to raise school taxes in 1908, for example, they received twenty-five petitions from outlying rural areas against it. "No doubt it will be beaten," lamented a school supporter. In North Carolina, school campaigners sought to improve school finances either by creating special tax districts with higher levies or by persuading existing districts to increase taxes. Yet keeping local revenues high required a constant struggle. In Cana, for example, voters approved a higher district tax, but opponents remained "fierce, tho' few in number," and for the next four years they continued to press the county board to rescind the tax.[30]

The campaign to raise school revenues in North Carolina and elsewhere often resulted in higher taxes, but reformers realized that it frequently encouraged the localism and intercommunity squabbling that they were trying to overcome. The creation of special tax districts in North Carolina accelerated the profusion of more gerrymandered districts. In Wilkes County, supporters and opponents of higher taxes split into two oddly shaped school districts. According to one account, schoolchildren attending the two schools passed each other going to and from the two schools, and school administration and finance were "much out of place."[31] In Appalachian Jackson County, gerrymandering worked in favor of the supporters of higher taxes; school officials faced such strong opposition that they redrew district lines, excluding opponents and including the entire property of the Southern Railroad. The resulting district was five to six miles long and slightly over a mile wide.[32]

The profusion of school districts produced by reform crusades in North Carolina typified much of the rest of the South. In a mountainous Tennessee county, a GEB agent reported in 1917 that the disagreement of two communities on the question of a tax increase led to bitter partisanship. When the communities, from two counties located next to each other in a remote region, were consolidated into a single special school district, one community brought suit and appealed the consolidation to the state supreme court. The fight between the two communities became embittered; members of one faction boycotted the school when a girl from the other faction played the organ at the local Methodist church.[33]

Increasing district taxes also gave new legitimacy to the localists. The levying of taxes in South Carolina, complained the state superintendent in 1911, tended to "multiply small districts and thus to retard consolidation." The result was deep-seated localism and continuing community autonomy. When school authorities sought to consolidate school districts, as they did with increasing frequency, they often faced well-entrenched opposition. After two school districts in western North Carolina consolidated in 1912, opponents, sensing higher taxes, called for the reinstitution of two separate schools, while those favoring higher taxes wanted one, consolidated school. In a community in Durham County, a similar conflict arose when opponents of a district consolidation wished to secede and establish a separate tax district. But, as the state superintendent noted, that would have resulted "in breaking up the consolidation and decreasing the efficiency of both schools." This pattern persisted into the 1920s, especially in remote counties. In 1928 a Mitchell County, North Carolina, district that objected to higher taxes and where parents, according to a hostile account, knew "very little and don[']t seem to care [whether] their children know any thing or not," sought to "vote off" a school tax after it had consolidated with a neighboring district. According to a state official, the district still possessed this right.[34]

The issue of districting and taxing offered a focus for community resentment at the wholesale changes coming to southern schools. In Tennessee, the efforts of modernizers to merge school districts and provide for a larger and expanded tax base met sharp resistance. In one community in 1927, disgruntled Tennesseans formed a Taxpayers' League, which a school official said was made up of a small element of "disgruntled, sore heads," who were against everything and had nothing constructive to offer. Their campaign, which opposed a centralized financial system, was "without merit," assaulted "the very heart" of educational improvement, and was, he believed, "prompted by petty, malicious politics." In Kentucky, the legislature passed a county unit act in place of a district system in 1908. But considerable opposition soon emerged, as one reformer noted, based on resistance to administrative centralization. By abolishing the offices of about two-thirds of the 15,000 white trustees and all of the several thousand black trustees, the new law evoked popular ire, even in sympathetic areas such as the prosperous Bluegrass area.[35]

By the 1920s reformers were seeking to establish a countywide administrative system, believing that administrative centralization would eventually be irresistible. Yet throughout the decade opposition continued. What right did an eastern North Carolina county school board have, asked one parent, "to throw a school out . . . without consulting the patrons of the school"? After another county centralized administrative power in 1923, a wave of school consolidations occasioned community resentment. There was "much talk of contention" over the issue, according to one account; the majority of the county's population was in opposition. In the same year, after an administrative consolidation in Mecklenburg County, a parent asked whether county authorities possessed the authority "to break up a School without the consent of the people." The state superintendent ruled, unequivocally, that the county's new power was virtually unlimited.[36]

In some instances, however, the invigorated county authorities abused their new powers. As residents of the county, superintendents occasionally made the mistake of identifying themselves with or showing favoritism toward one faction over another. In Pickett County, Tennessee, two state rural supervisors reported a clash between the county superintendent and a high school principal, with two factions formed around each side. The conflict reinforced divisions in the community, and the two sides were willing to fight a war "to the death," even if it meant sacrificing the school system. According to the supervisors, the quarrel was "one of the many manifestations of the feud spirit" in this county; the superintendent and the principal had come to represent "the two factions that have existed in the community for years." In another community in eastern Tennessee, a parent complained that the county superintendent and school board were exchanging teaching certificates for political favors. In another Tennessee county a member of the school board, according to one complaint, used his official authority for his own personal benefit and that of his relatives. During the last year, he had arranged for his brother to be appointed truant officer; the brother was later found to be a bootlegger.[37]

An important instrument of expanded bureaucratic power was the use of rural school supervisors; some were attached to the county superintendents, whereas others were solely responsible to state officials. Few communities accepted this kind of intervention without objection. A law in North Carolina requiring that teachers attend county institutes before they could be certified often aroused opposition.[38] Supervisors said that their most time-consuming and difficult duty was the administration of teachers' exams. Although some states established separate teachers' examiners, who administered the exams, others relied either on county officials or on the already overworked rural school supervisors. Among the supervisory force any supposed uniformity was "a beautiful fiction," wrote the South Carolina state superintendent in 1910. Some county boards were rigid in their examinations; others followed their own, peculiarly local standards. Many officials worried about cheating. In Florida, the state superintendent said that cheating was so persistent that, in 1916, he assigned his rural school supervisor to investigate. About a year later, his fears were confirmed when he uncovered a cheating "ring": thieves stole and prepared the questions, then sold them to teaching candidates.[39]

Given the frequency with which supervisors intervened in local affairs, it is not surprising that the hostility they aroused often translated into political problems. In North Carolina in 1915, opponents of legislation granting greater state control over teacher certification aroused opposition in the legis-

Thomas Settle, a Virginia school inspector.
(Courtesy of the Southern Historical Collection, University of North Carolina at Chapel Hill Library)

lature because of excessive centralization and discrimination against poor teachers with limited opportunities. Opponents further claimed that the bill would only help an aristocracy of the profession and would work a hardship on the rank and file. Four years later, the South Carolina state superintendent experienced what he called the bitterest opposition he had ever encountered in the legislature because of aversion to state supervision of local schools. Faced with this sort of legislative response, he doubted the wisdom of provoking "such bitter personal and official antagonism."[40]

The possibility of this kind of political opposition led state officials to proceed carefully. Most of them, like the South Carolina state superintendent, expanded bureaucratic intervention only if their political moorings were secure. In Florida, according to the report of a GEB official, county school officials feared encountering a boomerang if they supported politically unpopular positions on higher taxes and consolidated high schools. Accordingly, they treated these subjects "rather timidly." These fears were no less pronounced for the Florida state superintendent about a decade later. Facing similar attempts to abolish rural school supervision in the legislature and mindful of his own need to survive politically, he instructed the state rural school inspector to inspect schools cautiously. In one county, the state superintendent warned, too many schools were visited "to leave proper impress." He advised not visiting over two schools a day and remaining long enough to make some impression. "An impression must be made in many counties," he wrote, "or the Legislature will abolish the position."[41]

◆ ◆ ◆

PUBLIC HEALTH AND POPULAR RESISTANCE

In a satire of a representative southern community—which he called "Miasma County"—Rockefeller agent Benjamin Earle Washburn described the obstacles that blocked progress in public health. In Miasma, he wrote, the hookworms were of a "ferocious type," open-surface privies prevailed, and malaria was prevalent. The rural residents simply took ill health for granted. Because of indifference and poverty, the people of Miasma had little conception of public health. The revered community physician, Old Doc Richards, who mostly dispensed "what is Technically Known as Hot Air," was suspicious of and hostile to sanitary reform. Permitting its onset, he warned, would threaten the county's "Rights and Personal Liberty," and he knew "the county Much better than an Outsider could ever know it." Public health meant higher taxes; it also implied that a "Rank Outsider" would intervene without understanding Miasma and its ways. When Miasma finally adopted a county health system, it appointed Richards as the county health officer. Needless to say, little was accomplished. The hookworms and mosquitoes, wrote Washburn, "didn't keep their contract with Doc; and Typhoid Fever was as Gay As Ever and Infant Diarrhea acted like it had never heard of a Health Officer." The local authorities, claiming all public health efforts were futile, abolished the office of the county health officer. The result, according to Washburn, was that Miasma County returned to "the Good Old Times when each family took care of itself without having the County or State Meddle with Its Personal Affairs."[42]

Washburn's story typified the situation that public health reformers encountered across the South. Although health officials rarely expressed themselves with Washburn's candor, they often communicated a general pessimism about the prospects for reform. Olin West, the director of the Tennessee antihookworm campaign, who later served as state health officer, often commented on the futility of changing public attitudes. "Just when I get a notion in my head that perhaps we are gaining ground and getting on a solid basis," he lamented in 1915, some new frustration would appear on the scene. Sanitary reform always encountered an underlying current of opposition in the collective mind, noted a Louisiana health official, and it was "very difficult to arouse interest in health, either individual or public." In 1917 an Arkansas health official tried to be optimistic by describing the state's citizens as eager for public health, but he advised that more "cultivation" was necessary before "the greatest return" would be realized.[43]

Washburn's tale suggested two further considerations: the reformers' obvious frustrations and the degree of community opposition they confronted. Health modernizers faced obstacles that were essentially similar to those that often stalled educational reform. Like school reformers, public health advocates attempted to construct a centrally controlled bureaucracy, which provoked vigorous community efforts to preserve autonomy and deflect outside domination. Constructing a centralized bureaucracy, health workers often discovered, required considerable patience. The involvement of several philanthropies, such as the International Health Board and the Commonwealth Fund, as well as the federal government through the U.S. Public Health Service, frequently caused competing rivalries.[44] In some cases state health officials and their IHB sponsors were at odds about proper lines of authority, although, as a general policy, Rockefeller philanthropy encouraged the extension of state authority.[45] In Florida, state officials long resisted what one state health officer in 1920 called the IHB's "inelastic and inadequate plan" and "stereotyped rules" of public health.[46] Even in more cooperative states, such as North Carolina, clashes arose over state bureaucracies and the IHB.

Watson S. Rankin, the strong-minded state health officer, had his own ideas about the proper direction of public health, ideas that sometimes conflicted with IHB objectives. In 1919 Washburn, who directed the IHB-financed county health program in North Carolina, protested that Rankin was so intent on dominating the program that it was drifting "farther away from our plan as time goes by." Rankin's attitude toward the IHB was "peculiar": the board, he believed, had to support whatever projects the state "will allow," rather than vice versa.[47]

In spite of such occasional intrabureaucratic skirmishing, these officials agreed on the need for a centralized bureaucracy. Yet they also knew there was a potent rural opposition. Although one approach was to begin "at the top" and trickle down in health work, wrote the Mississippi state health officer in 1915, it was essential to build up sanitation from the bottom up. Based on his experience, he believed that it was frequently much easier to get the "poor class of people" to accept public health than it was those who claimed "to be much more highly civilized." Existing southern health bureaucracies, well into the 1920s, intervened in local affairs with great caution. The Florida State Board of Health, explained the state health officer in 1916, was "not a judiciary body" and possessed "no power to imprison or exert police authority." Rather, it was "an advisory body"; its "good work" came through "persuasive methods and persistent effort."[48]

In many southern states weak bureaucratic infrastructures reflected a low level of popular support. Across the South, health officials fended off attacks from legislatures that regularly imperiled their existence. From Alabama, the state health officer reported in 1915 that assaults on the State Board of Health from many different sources had grown to such "enormous proportions" that it "required the combined energies and efforts of all concerned to overcome the fight." Health officials, fighting for their professional survival, expended little political capital in pressing for higher appropriations. In Kentucky, opponents of public health twice mounted serious if unsuccessful attempts, in 1918 and 1924, to gut the State Board of Health. In Tennessee, public health advocates exhausted themselves beating back attempts to abolish or weaken the State Board of Health. As late as 1926, an IHB official wrote that in much of the South there was "considerable unsettlement and uncertainty" about prospects of political support for public health.[49]

Two states with weak health bureaucracies during the early years of the twentieth century, Arkansas and Florida, both possessed entrenched political opposition to public health. In 1911, after both houses of the Arkansas legislature enacted an ambitious public health bill, the measure was "lost" before reaching the governor's desk. So acrimonious were feelings in the legislature that conflict between proponents and opponents was inevitable. Although the bill was eventually signed, opponents in subsequent legislative sessions continued to describe the State Board of Health as "excess baggage" that could be cut from the state budget. During the next two decades, state health officials lacked strong political support.[50]

In Florida, the state health bureaucracy made significant strides against an epidemic of a tropical disease chiefly through the efforts of Joseph Y. Porter, the state health officer between 1889 and 1917. But on his retirement, the weakness and vulnerability of the state health bureaucracy became exposed. Porter's successor was described, in one report, as a "rather obscure rural practitioner"; in another, as having a "disinclination to pay any attention to the routine or details of the work." Under the post-Porter regime, the state public health system became a main source of political patronage, and the state health officer had practically no authority in the conduct or management of health affairs.[51] Over the next five years, if anything, Florida's health bureaucracy seemed to weaken. In 1921 an official complained that the State Board of Health's budget had been "crippled" by budget cuts in the legislature. In that session and others, legislators considered abolishing the body; the state health bureaucracy had "drifted along the same old rut for thirty years." Two years later, when an IHB official visited the state, he said it was "ready for advance" but characterized the state health bureaucracy as "very weak."[52]

Although Florida and Arkansas were the only states where bureaucratic penetration stalled, in most of the South health officials faced some frustration. One of their most daunting challenges—and one of the most severe tests of their bureaucratic effectiveness—was their ability to collect accurate vital statistics. Despite efforts by nineteenth-century officials—such as the ill-fated attempt by health officials in Alabama to enforce the vital statistics law—the collection of accurate vital statistics was virtually impossible without bureaucratic governance. Centralizing health officials made it a chief priority and, although much of the South was admitted into the U.S. Census Office's Registration Area during the 1920s, some states continued to fail its stiff standards. In Georgia, despite an aggressive effort by state officials, effective vital statistics enforcement foundered during the mid-1920s for lack of sufficient financial support by the legislature. In other states, public health officials encountered opposition, much of it from physicians and undertakers, who refused to implement new reporting requirements for births and deaths.[53]

Often physician opposition reflected fears that public health would reduce practices. The mission of public health workers was to stamp out disease, noted one official, "thereby depriving the physician of his means of livelihood." Despite early hopes to mobilize the medical profession behind an antihookworm program, many physicians viewed Rockefeller intervention suspiciously. A Tennessee antihookworm campaigner was not surprised to see that the crusade had aroused antagonism from local doctors. "We have not," he explained, "been overwhelmed with help from this source heretofore." Physician resistance continued. In response to the operation of free tonsil and adenoid clinics for schoolchildren by North Carolina state health officials, the Guilford County Medical Society objected in 1920 to "curative medicine" on the part of state authorities and described such programs as unnecessary expenses that reflected badly on local physicians. Physician opposition to this form of indigent medicine appeared in western North Carolina about three years later. "Before I could get howdy out of my mouth," reported a public health nurse, a rural doctor had "launched upon a violent attack on the State Board and said unless I had more influence in this county than he did there would be no clinic." The problem, she explained, was that local physicians were pursuing "selfish interests." [54]

Health officials, especially at the local level, faced other, often insuperable obstacles. In Wilson County in 1917, a Rockefeller agent working in rural public health wrote that continuous wet weather and impassable roads greatly handicapped his work. Without coercive legal power, health officials primarily operated through moral suasion. It was difficult "to get a neighbor [to] take out papers against his neighbor," explained a North Carolina county health officer in 1915, "as he would forever make his enemy." As health officer, he wrote, he possessed no legal status in the community. [55]

When county health officials were too aggressive, they could risk serious consequences. Alvin E. Keller, the modernizing county health officer of Covington County, Alabama, ran afoul of the local community in 1927 and was harassed by a Ku Klux Klan chapter. Local opponents of centralization took advantage of the fact that Keller was a Jew, and within several months he had fled the county. Although the work in Covington was "progressing satisfactorily," he explained, he had "not felt exactly right down here," and, because of "the question of religion," he was operating "under tension." He had come to a firm decision: "I have thoroughly made up my mind to get out of this County." Either he moved, warned Keller, or he would "have to get out of Public Health[,] which I do not want to do." [56]

Behind all of these problems lay a cultural gap separating the reformers from the reformed. Reformers discovered that southerners, often perceiving the issue of health differently, were not easily persuaded. The enforcement of public health regulations in rural Virginia was a problem, according to one sanitarian: laws could not be enforced without public sentiment behind it, and this was lacking. In 1917 Benjamin Earle Washburn expressed feelings of ennui and frustration in dealing with rural ignorance. Although he sometimes favored outright coercion, he admitted that such a method would not get results. A Louisiana health official was even franker about his differences with local communities. It would take "a world of education to induce our rural population," he observed, "to put into effect [the] most necessary sanitary reforms." [57]

To many southerners, public health loomed as a perilous threat, and what reformers characterized as ignorance was often deeply rooted antagonism either to professional medicine or to state intervention. Microbes and threats to health were simply an "imaginary being invented by doctors to scare people out of dying a natural death," declared a North Carolinian in 1913. Microbes provided a pretext for physicians to "multiply serums, add to the fears, subtract you from your money and divide all the profits among the doctors." The germ theory and public health were merely inventions to generate more medical business. This wariness extended to forms of state medicine. Many southerners, for good reasons, feared medical practitioners and resisted treatments such as vaccinations or the administration of drugs. Early attempts by health officials to immunize a community against smallpox often ran afoul of local opinion. In Jefferson County, Florida, a health official reported in 1904 that "much concealment" was occurring in a smallpox-infested community. It was "next to an impossibility for anything to be radically done to get the disease stamped out." In another part of the state, an official wrote of *"stiff resistance"* among blacks; vaccination took place only "at the point of my pistol." As the state health officer later wrote, vaccination almost always aroused popular opposition, "for there are always some that like to be 'agin the Government,' no matter who the Government may be. In North Carolina, when a teacher in 1924 refused to allow unvaccinated children to enroll in school, a parent complained to the state superintendent that the state could "not make law to take the liberties [sic] away from the people and make them take medicine and vaccine when it is not necessary." Such "martial laws" as vaccination imposed medicine "regardless of need or cause." [58]

Popular suspicions of vaccination were partly based on traditional resistance to outside intervention in the family sanctum. But they also reflected real fears about the adverse effects of public health medicine. Smallpox vaccinations caused reactions harmful enough to instill widespread popular apprehension about the procedure. Other forms of public health were also greeted warily. The occasionally negative consequences of public health measures reinforced community suspicions. In North Carolina, a man inoculated for typhoid subsequently died. A local health official noted that "it was a very unfortunate coincidence" because the "ignorant public" would link the death to the vaccination.[59]

Antihookworm crusaders discovered that the poison used to kill the parasites could sometimes cause the same reaction in patients. Thymol, which was used in the Rockefeller Sanitary Commission campaigns, was a highly toxic substance that could have fatal results if administered on a full stomach.[60] Even after hookworm specialists switched to other poisons, such as carbon tetrachloride and chenopodium, fatalities were possible. In one case in 1923, a man participating in the Hookworm Field Research—which was part of the IHB's County Training Station at Andalusia, Alabama—died after drinking a large quantity of whiskey before and after his treatment. The impact of such episodes, which were usually rare, reinforced popular suspicions of state-imposed medicine. "You can hardly know the distress that this case has caused me," wrote station director Wilson G. Smillie. He and his program were blamed for the death, particularly by the rural people whom he desired most to reach.[61]

Subsequent incidents related to hookworm treatments resulted in fatalities and public suspicion. When a black child of Orange County, Virginia, died as a result of hookworm treatment, according to a health official, the black community became "considerably exercised over this unfortunate occurrence." Rather nervously, he hoped that the episode would not have "a bad effect" on the program. In 1925 physicians at the Andalusia station in Alabama diagnosed a child who was extremely weak and could hardly walk to the table for meals as having hookworm infection. The parents, who were urged to begin treatment, were described as "very ignorant" and their home life was "unfavorable." The treatment involved taking sodium bicarbonate three times a day for three days. On the fourth day, fifteen grains of thymol were administered at 6:00 A.M. and fifteen grains two hours later; a dose of Epsom salts was given at 10:00 A.M. This treatment was repeated twelve days later and then two weeks after that. But the child, who had apparently eaten ice cream, began vomiting after the last treatment and died of cardiac arrest. After hearing about the incident, neighboring parents refused to participate in the treatment of their children.[62]

In subsequent antihookworm efforts at Andalusia, IHB workers encountered significant suspicion and noncooperation. They were often confounded by the Alabama country folk's willingness to submit to examination but their reluctance to participate in follow-up treatment. Even among those who agreed to treatment by thymol or some other medication, suspicion lingered. In other instances, rural southerners participated in examinations but resisted or sabotaged treatment.[63]

♦ ♦ ♦
THE FRUSTRATION OF POLICY

The implementation of a centrally controlled, bureaucratically administered policy of public health ran into serious obstacles when it was first introduced during and after World War I. Because rural communities believed that public health would reduce or even eliminate familial and community control over health, modernizers almost always faced some degree of noncooperation or opposition. In an era before the complete triumph of bureaucratic authority, community resistance succeeded in stalling the onset of state medicine in the South.

Wherever bureaucrats sought to introduce the new health policy they often found an unwilling local population. The Commonwealth Fund's two child health demonstrations in Athens (Clarke County), Georgia, and Rutherford County, Tennessee, both yielded disappointing results. During its first year, the Athens program, concentrating on cotton textile mill children, reported objections and inertia on the part of the community, which displayed "a lack of appreciation of its need for such a program." Such opposition was attributed to hostility to higher taxes and a misunderstanding of the purposes of the program. One of the fund's earliest efforts involved a public relations campaign to gain community support. Three years later, however, the Athens workers reported continuing local resistance.[64]

The CF program operated at an even greater disadvantage in Rutherford County, Tennessee. Unlike Athens, where a county health department already existed, Rutherford lacked any bureaucratic infrastructure. Constructing such a county health apparatus was in "itself a considerable undertaking"; establishing it as part of a specialized child health program was "a still greater undertaking." After inspecting the program in 1924, CF official Courtenay Dinwiddie reported formidable obstacles. The "chief striking weakness" he found was a "lack of strong community leadership interested in intelligently following a plan for the future of the Demonstration." Long distances, intense isolation, and the "apathy and inertia of the rural population" were the greatest obstacles to successful implementation of the program. Dinwiddie also observed a lack of enthusiasm among local officials. The chairman of the county school was, he wrote, "indifferent and somewhat evasive" about supporting the school health program.[65]

These were not, according to the local director of the Rutherford County program, unusual problems. This same indifference could be found in any comparable area of the agricultural South where poverty and isolation were primary causes of ill health. CF officials eventually concluded that the results of the program in Tennessee were disappointing. Although "greatly encouraged" about its progress, Dinwiddie reported in late 1925 that problems such as inadequate hospital facilities, the lack of local tax support, and local opposition by physicians were hampering the program. Another assessment in the same year was even gloomier. Most of the work in Rutherford County was "undeveloped." Even an additional commitment of a few years would probably prove "inadequate," and anything less than a long-term involvement would yield only negligible results. "Very little of a definite nature" had been achieved, although this was not "the fault of those in charge but rather because of the difficulty of the problem."[66]

The difficulties encountered by the Commonwealth Fund's child health demonstration in two southern counties became even more evident in the more ambitious, regionwide programs of Rockefeller philanthropy. Most Kentuckians, according to a Rockefeller agent, were unaware of the basic rules of modern sanitation. Their ignorance had little to do with education; even those with advanced education defied "the plain lessons of sanitation as wilfully as our more ignorant neighbors." The average audience attending the dispensaries of the RSC campaigns denied the existence of hookworms and other parasites; even if infected, they did not believe it—"nor that we could cure them if found." Rather than "aggressive in their disbelief," as were "the anti-vaccination people," they were "in a passive state of negation."[67]

When the IHB assumed the remnants of the RSC's antihookworm campaign by financing dispensary crusades in states that had not yet experienced them, Rockefeller officials discovered the limits of reform in the rural South. In Georgia, there were numerous examples in January 1915 of county reluctance to finance sanitary campaigns. While the treasury in one county was too bankrupt to make the necessary appropriation, in another the opposition of local physicians doomed the campaign. In still another county, an appropriation was made and then withdrawn without explanation. In Tennessee, the state director Olin West wrote letter after letter expressing his pessimism about the dispensary campaign's prospects. Western Tennessee, he reported in March 1915, preferred "to keep its hookworms and traditions" rather than finance dispensaries. In heavily infected Bledsoe County, the dispensary was "almost a complete failure." About a month later West wrote that the Bledsoe dispensaries had been "very disappointing," largely because residents were of "that peculiar type which we might class as Tennessee conservatives." In other parts of the state, funds were tight among county governments, and they were "not disposed to open the strongbox."[68]

The experimental programs that evolved during the IHC's intensive anti-hookworm community campaigns also encountered resistance. When IHB official John A. Ferrell visited an IHC site in Aiken County, South Carolina, he described the response of one "extremely backward community" as not "so large or spontaneous" as in other parts of the county. A similar reluctance was evident elsewhere. In Tennessee, West reported in the spring of 1915 that political opposition to rural public health had already emerged in the state legislature, as well as in some county courts. He had been feeling out a few counties and discovered "to my sorrow" that county authorities preferred new schools and roads to better health. In other counties where state health officials sought support, the county courts overwhelmed them with negative votes. County officials, fearing adverse public opinion, were "positively afraid of their shadows," West declared. There would be "no easy road to travel" in implementing the intensive community plan, partly because this approach to public health was "decidedly ahead of the times in this state" and the majority of its rural population was neither "sufficiently interested nor adequately instructed to offer any very decided cooperation."[69]

Elsewhere the IHC encountered local opposition. From Georgia, a state with a weak public health bureaucracy, Rockefeller operative A. G. Fort complained in June 1915 that, despite a meeting in Muscogee County, he had heard nothing; he suspected failure. Other counties also turned a deaf ear. By August Fort was reporting a "condition of inactivity" throughout the state. "I must confess," he later wrote, "that the attitude of our S[tate] B[oard] [of] H[ealth] and our Gen[.] Assembly, and all public health activities has considerably upset my plans and shaken my confidence just a *little bit*." Arkansas proved even more frustrating to an IHB field worker, who, not long after his arrival in 1917, reported to his superiors that his work had been "an utter failure." Although he described the people favorably, he declared that conditions were "simply intolerable." He was willing to accept a demotion if only he could be reassigned to another state.[70]

Health officers felt the same everywhere. Progress was slow; for every step forward, public workers took two steps backward. Platt W. Covington, a legendary troubleshooter whom the IHB sent to particularly difficult states, described his introduction to rural public health in Texas in 1916. Along with the state health officer, he visited five counties to persuade local authorities to appropriate matching funds for the IHB program. Although three of the five counties agreed to provide the necessary eight hundred dollars, one of them subsequently reneged. In many localities, opposition to higher taxes lay behind this reluctance. In one community, the most "prominent men" opposed the program, with a local judge predicting "trouble" if the IHB pressed its cause. Similar tightfistedness was the case in other southern states. As the Kentucky state health officer put it in 1916, it was difficult for his field-workers to "have to scrap around to collect money for their own support." As a result of their need to raise funds, they were unable to expend much energy on behalf of public health.[71]

Even in North Carolina, despite its reputation as a success story, public health workers met local opposition. Benjamin Washburn, who inaugurated the intensive community health program and then supervised its transition into a full-fledged county health system, described the Rock Ridge community in rural Wilson County, in the eastern part of the state. Many of its inhabitants were Primitive Baptists, who strenuously opposed any form of medical intervention and were "more influenced and interested in what Moses and the Prophets have to say than they are in Osler and Koch and their views." Members of the local opposition to public health, Washburn later wrote, were "more numerous and difficult, perhaps, but are just as varied and as interesting as any found in the West Indies."[72]

By the 1920s, when the IHB's community health program had evolved into a more permanent county health program, local opposition persisted. More realistic public health workers acknowledged that establishing a modern bureaucratic county health apparatus was a herculean task. Washburn, after a visit to Alabama in 1919, made this point in no uncertain terms. Alabama health officials had a good opportunity to institute a county health program, but he warned that they were risking everything by acting too quickly. This, he believed, was a familiar problem throughout the South. State health officers were "not content with definite worked-out problems and gradual expansion." Instead, they expected field-workers to do all kinds of things and to expand their activities too rapidly.[73]

In fact, the IHB county health program, rather than sweeping through the South, grew despite local opposition. And, because of the IHB's stipulation that its support was contingent on local matching funds, penurious local governments remained a major obstacle.[74] Platt Covington, who had developed a reputation for his ability to deal with stingy local governments in North Carolina and Texas, was dispatched to Louisiana in the spring of 1921 to persuade police juries in the state's parishes to appropriate the necessary matching funds. There he discovered extensive local resistance to outside intervention. In De Ridder Parish, the parish health officer led the opposition because of his concern that the IHB program threatened his job. Although the police jury appropriated the funds nonetheless, Covington feared that the disgruntled official might "yet find some way of defeating the appropriation." Subsequently, Covington reported that, because the bad feeling persisted, opponents had succeeded in sabotaging the inauguration of the program. Elsewhere, Covington observed, Louisianans were "annoying in their insistence that this one or that one be selected for the various posit[i]ons on the staff from that of Director on down." Many, probably most, of those concerned had "some ax to grind."[75]

As an outsider, Covington found that the challenge of penetrating the cultural gap between reformer and reformed was daunting. Within several months of his arrival in Louisiana, he wrote that several parishes that had originally appropriated funds were now rescinding their decisions. This was "quite discouraging" and reminded him of the frog that, in an effort to leave a well, jumped four feet forward while he fell three feet back. Typically, Covington made successful appearances before police juries; the members then returned home and received "considerable criticism" from constituents, who urged them to renege.[76]

This sort of guerrilla warfare between centralizers and localists became a familiar part of the attempt to inaugurate county health during the 1920s. In Tennessee, health officials in June 1922 reported rather glumly that only three counties were participating in the county health program, chiefly because of local noncooperation. Despite a determined effort in one county, opposition from the county judge, out of a "misguided spirit of economy," and from the health officer, to protect his job, doomed the program. In other counties, efforts to secure appropriations failed in the face of opposition that was "all but impossible to overcome." Public health work in Tennessee, ruefully concluded an IHB worker, was becoming "less attractive than formerly."[77]

Despite success with the dispensaries during the RSC campaign, Kentucky also encountered problems inaugurating bureaucratized county health during the 1920s. In 1922, after failing to persuade local authorities to appropriate the necessary funds, the IHB dispatched Covington. Covington soon reported that a general desire statewide to economize hindered the IHB campaign, as counties were rescinding previous appropriations for county health programs. Local reluctance in this instance was justified because of the hard times of the early twenties, but even during the general prosperity of the mid-1920s health officials frequently encountered difficulties.[78]

Despite the formidable array of governmental power that modernizers were able to bring to bear, communities were at least partly successful in resisting the erosion of their autonomy in school and health affairs. For most of the postwar era, localists fought a rearguard, guerrilla war against the intrusion of outside bureaucratic power. Before the full advent of nationalizing tendencies in media, culture, and the federal government, they were able to hold wholesale change at bay. And in areas outside of education and health, particularly in the attempt to redefine the nature of the southern family, reformers faced similar frustration.

THE FAMILY AND

THE STATE

◆

Reformers assumed the merits of a new relationship between families and government that sought to change the traditional, autonomous rural family. This redefinition of governance endorsed a new role for women that granted them an important position in public affairs and, at least implicitly, gave impetus toward gender equality. It challenged familial control over children, not only by asserting the power of the modern school but also by attempting to restrict child labor. And it attempted to interpose the power of state government in matters of morality, most obviously in the restriction of drinking. As was the case in every other instance of Progressive Era reform, however, the introduction of this new kind of governance met strong resistance.

◆ ◆ ◆

THE FRUSTRATION OF SOUTHERN SUFFRAGISM

Despite the jubilation that accompanied the ratification of the Nineteenth Amendment on August 26, 1920, southern suffragists faced a rather disquieting reality: of the thirty-six states that ratified, only four were from the former Confederacy. The ratifying southern states—Tennessee, Kentucky, Arkansas, and Texas—included no states from the Southeast and only one from the Gulf Coast area, while of the ten states that refused to ratify or to consider ratification, only one, Delaware, lay above the Mason-Dixon line.[1]

The reasons for the defeat of southern suffragism are not to be found in the absence of a well-organized and well-led suffragist movement. Indeed, southern suffragists such as Madeline McDowell Breckinridge of Kentucky, Lila Meade Valentine, and Minnie Fisher Cunningham of Texas were articulate participants in the national movement, and in their states they helped to construct a genuinely vibrant mass movement. Moreover, the movement had close ties with reform campaigns in education, public health, and especially social welfare, and the suffrage crusade that sprang into existence all over the South after about 1910 attracted the support of urban middle-class women, many of whom had long experience in social reform.

Rather, the reasons for the overwhelming defeat of woman suffrage in the South lay in the hostility to it. Opposition, even among otherwise reform-minded southerners, was a potent force soon after the equal suffrage movement began following the Civil War. There was, for example, a limited and, at best, ambivalent response to the proposed vote for women in the denominational press, which led the way, after the 1880s, in social purity campaigns. When the national WCTU endorsed the suffrage in the 1880s, the prohibitionist press clearly separated the issues of moral reform and suffrage.[2] In an argument that had considerable saliency to many southerners during the ratification battle, opponents of woman suffrage contended that the vote would end the moral monopoly that women held in American society. Women would no longer be "queen in the home circle," wrote an Alabama Methodist, leaving it so that they could "rival man in the endeavor for prominence in the world." In charge of domestic life and morality, women possessed "a scepter more potent than the sword," declared the Methodist *Alabama Christian Advocate* in 1888. But if women departed "the sacred temple in which she had been enshrined," she would face "the hard and bitter struggle for standing-room, which engages all the rugged strength of manhood."[3]

Throughout the South, formal opposition to suffrage—through either political opposition or an organized antisuffragist movement—coalesced during the ratification battle. Much of the political establishment, including the male leadership of the state Democratic parties, opposed the Nineteenth Amendment. The suffrage movement, contended one Democratic leader, had been "fastened & pushed by a few hundred women who would have been much better off trying to teach the people to be contented, & to look upon women as som[e]thing too good, too pure, & too sweet" to be involved in politics. Many politicians felt threatened by woman suffrage; some claimed that it would raise taxes by increasing the cost of elections. Others contended that it threatened a way of life. Henry Watterson, Kentucky newspaper editor and Democratic leader, described woman suffrage as a Trojan Horse that was being "trundled along into the very Holy of Holies by people who were but just now proclaiming death and destruction to all things Southern."[4]

Other objections by male southerners were more directly connected to political and ideological realities, and their anxieties embodied fears about new forms of governance. Among the most effective thrusts against ratification was the contention that federalization of woman suffrage was an opening wedge that would tip the balance toward national dominance of local affairs. Adoption of the Nineteenth Amendment, argued a Louisianan, would "*set a precedent* for Federal interference in State Franchise." If this "slight pretext" for intervention in an area of heretofore near-total state autonomy could exist, he asked, "how many more or less weighty reasons may be urged in the future [for] the ultimate breaking down of all State control, and our consequent destruction"? While American boys resisted autocracy abroad, wrote a male opponent of the suffrage, Virginians would oppose it "to the uttermost . . . at home."[5]

Not far behind in importance were anxieties about the security of white supremacy. When woman suffrage was joined with federal control, wrote one Democratic opponent, it became "instantly submerged by the unanswerable question of the relationship between the races." The suffrage amendment, a Louisiana constituent wrote to his senator, "was written by Thad Stevens, Frederick Douglas[s], [and] the negro & the radicals of that time in order to destroy white supremacy in the south forever." To some, the Nineteenth Amendment threatened disfranchisement of blacks. In 1915 the *Richmond Evening Journal* predicted the loss of white political control if women obtained the vote. The literacy test, it believed, would not restrict voting by black women; the "hard fact" was that almost a third of the commonwealth's counties would be "in serious peril" of black rule. The passage of the Nineteenth Amendment, declared Edward J. Gay, senator from Louisiana, would again open "an old sore" and "revive questions pregnant with dangerous consequences to the South." In time, it might also expand the "power of Federal control to male suffrage and cause a most serious situation."[6]

For others, these racial fears reached a complex convergence, as apprehension about sexual and political control intersected in the controversy over woman suffrage. In Virginia, Henry St. George Tucker, a member of a distinguished family of lawyers and politicians, a former congressman and candidate for governor, and a leader in the Southern Education Board's school crusade, led the opposition to ratification in the General Assembly during the summer of 1920. At a crucial moment in the legislative battle, an anonymous pamphlet, which suffragists believed Tucker wrote, circulated and had a considerable impact. It asserted that NAWSA president Carrie Chapman Catt advocated free love and racial equality, and it ran a picture of her side by side with Frederick Douglass.[7]

◆ ◆ ◆

SOUTHERN WOMEN AND OPPOSITION TO SUFFRAGE

"In the mass," the Virginia novelist and suffragist Mary Johnston wrote in 1910, southern women were "yet strongly held by the traditions and customs, the manners, the habits of the past." As idealists, they attached themselves to the principles of chivalry and had "merely reversed direction, and placed their ideal in the past rather than in the future."[8] Southern women, added a North Carolina woman, did not "like to mingle in politics." Rather, they preferred to leave "the men to manage the government to their own way, . . . feeling glad to be free from a responsibility" that interfered with more congenial duties. Women were "not made that way" and cared little about exercising their "talents in any such manner."[9]

In fact, much of the opposition to woman suffrage came from women. Prominent women's organizations, such as the WCTU, approached the subject gingerly, and, unlike their counterparts elsewhere, backed away from endorsing the suffrage.[10] Among other women, as Belle Kearney wrote, there were many who had a "belligerent attitude toward the movement that was instituted especially for their well-being." By the time the struggle for ratification of the Nineteenth Amendment began, formal organizations that were loosely united in their opposition to woman suffrage had already come into existence. It was safe to assume, declared an antisuffragist pamphlet in Virginia, that the majority of Virginia women did not desire suffrage for themselves individually, "nor for womankind." Most women, it maintained, were "intelligent enough to ask for what they need." A small minority should not be allowed to impose legislation upon "the large majority of women, who do not wish it."[11] "Antis," as the suffragists called them, claimed to represent a hidden majority. Most Virginia women opposed equal suffrage, wrote one woman in 1919, and did not feel "competent to vote on the intricate affairs of state." This majority would "love and honor" their men if they saved them from having to do something they did not know how to do properly.

The antis have led a shadowy historical existence. Although most scholars have ignored them, they played a crucial role in the defeat of the suffrage amendment in the South. Their strength, as Madeline McDowell Breckinridge once noted, contradicted their assertion that women should refrain from political activism. Many of them, she declared, traveled thousands of miles to tell audiences that "woman's place is in the home—and many of them do prove it, . . . by the ridiculous figure they cut on a platform." Although many antis echoed the argument about the threat of suffrage to white supremacy, they more frequently repeated fears that enfranchisement might cause a displacement of gender roles. "God forbid" the day woman suffrage arrived, a Texas antisuffragist asserted. It would see "women turned loose upon the nation" who would be "unsexing themselves to the detriment of the home and all social and domestic relations." Voting women would be required to serve on juries, where they might be confronted with the seamier details of murder, prostitution, and whiskey, the Alabama Association Opposed to Woman Suffrage warned in 1920. Women would become exposed to "profanity, obscenity, and the detailed narration of the immoral acts and doings of the lowest type of humanity." "How would you like for your mother, wife, or daughter," Alabama antisuffragists asked, "to be locked up all night in a jury room, filled with men, white or black?" This might "suit Colorado, but would it suit Alabama"? Antis maintained that woman suffrage violated the orderly, and secure, system of gender relations. It was a "*fatal* thing to add or to take from the laws of God or nature," warned a Louisiana woman in 1918. The involvement of women in politics was "the most abnormal, abhorrent thing the imagination can conceive." With women in the political sphere, the social "equilibrium" would be destroyed and chaos would follow.[12]

The more important reason for the frustration of suffragists was the cultural gap dividing them from the rural and small-town communities that they attempted, with little success, to convert to their cause. On the other hand, suffragists found urban areas most hospitable to their campaign. The case of the suffrage movement in Virginia was typical. There, chapters emerged in the commonwealth's largest towns and cities; the most active were in Charlottesville, Lynchburg, Roanoke, Norfolk, and, above all, Richmond. In fact, Richmond dominated the movement in terms of its leadership, financial support, and mass following.[13]

In the hinterlands, in contrast, the movement remained unorganized. Outside urban areas, suffragists frequently felt isolated. Although reporting "fine progress in our work in North Carolina," a suffragist admitted in 1915 that the campaign was "sadly handicapped by [a] lack of workers." A year later, a Texas organizer complained that, "in the small places," few people were "up on the subject of Woman Suffrage"; most women believed that it was "a freakish fad of a few women who don't appreciate their homes, and want to get before the public." A Virginia suffragist, writing from a plantation region in 1917, complained that it seemed "almost impossible to go ahead or accomplish anything." Although there were many true believers, there was also "such a strong sentiment here against it" that many women lacked "the courage to come out & declare themselves in favor of this glorious work." Although rural women signed petitions, observed another activist, they would not contribute money or effort to a lobbying campaign. "Anybody with one eye and half sense," a suffragist reflected many years later, should have realized that powerful opposition doomed the cause.[14]

Many organizers dispatched by the Richmond headquarters encountered a gap between their urban values and a hinterland political culture. Small-town suffragists often felt out of touch with Richmond, as one organizer explained it in 1919. Few Virginians from the rural Shenandoah Valley counties would attend a forthcoming state suffrage convention, she predicted: that region, it was commonly believed, was too "far removed from Richmond." In most counties, complained an activist in 1917, there was no chairman, "not even a suffragist who is known to our officials at State headquarters." Meanwhile, among active county chairmen, there was little, if any cohesion, and regular teamwork was unknown.[15]

The organizers sent into the field by the Virginia Equal Suffrage League and the National American Woman Suffrage Association to obtain public support for ratification in 1919 and 1920 often accomplished nothing. In the autumn of 1919 Mary Elizabeth Pidgeon, a NAWSA organizer assigned to Virginia, traversed the commonwealth. She was obviously frustrated by the end of her tour. From the Shenandoah Valley, she reported in October that she "was not satisfied" with the enrollments in the local leagues. A trip to Clifton Forge in December was "fruitless," with "*few* enrollments," while organizing in Wadesville was "very discouraging." Later in the month an expedition to Bedford, in the Virginia Piedmont, was "quite a fizzle." Meanwhile, during her organizing efforts, Pidgeon experienced considerable trouble navigating the complex and often Byzantine geography of rural Virginia.[16]

Like other Progressive Era social reformers, suffragists faced an uphill struggle in persuading rural southerners to accept reform. Despite the considerable impact of the antis, suffragists confronted a more daunting, if diffuse and unorganized, resistance throughout the rural and small-town South. In one Virginia county, a suffragist complained in 1912, the women were largely opposed to equal suffrage because country people stuck to old traditions and were very conservative. "I do not believe that the Suffrage movement would be considered favorably here at this time," an early southern suffragist wrote from eastern Virginia. Local people, she maintained, had never "thought of it and really don[']t think they know anything about it." In 1914 a suffragist wrote from a mountain county that, despite the existence of an organized league, "hard-working country women, living far apart, with little time of their own," lacked "an adequate idea of suffrage work." "We are doing the best we can," lamented another suffragist a year later. Although the dawn was "reddening," the movement constantly met "an apathetic public."[17]

In their frustration, suffragists often betrayed the cultural gap between themselves and the women of the rural South. An organizer near Paducah, Kentucky, complained that she was disgusted with the response to the local Equal Rights Association's campaign. The women were "hopeless" and "wooden heads" when it came to equal rights; the surrounding counties were "something terrible." In West Virginia, a Georgia suffragist campaigning on behalf of NAWSA complained about the lack of popular enthusiasm; she pointed to the "absolute ignorance" of her audiences, which were mostly composed of "a very plain class of people." A Virginia suffragist made a similar characterization, describing local rural women as "backward" and lacking in leadership. One village that she visited was "little and *cliquey*"; in another community, her suffrage speech "made an impression—they had never 'heard tell' of the matter before." Suffragists were working very hard, but it was almost impossible to reach the rural districts, explained a Georgia woman in 1915, because country folk were so "ignorant & hopeless." Other reformers exuded condescension toward rural conditions. Vowing not to go on another suffrage tour, one Atlanta campaigner in 1915 described accommodations in the small towns of Georgia as "holes" where "the wash basins & pitchers hadn't been washed in a month & the matting in the floor looked as if it were old matting put over still more venerable matting." In the hotels of these backwoods communities, nothing as advanced as a water closet existed, while the favorite diet consisted of cold vegetables on plates an inch thick.[18]

The reformers' appeals for gender equality were greeted with a mixture of reserve and almost pornographic curiosity. From southwestern Kentucky in 1910, a campaigner for school suffrage described local women as "a conservative set." She estimated that only a few members of the women's club would join the cause; for this reason, she urged that the campaign "proceed cautiously." A Kentucky organizer reported in 1913 that women in one town were "rather afraid of Woman Suffrage." They regarded the suffragist "as an unsacred being." In the 1930s two Virginia suffragists recalled similar resistance. The members of the Essex County Equal Suffrage League, they wrote, made themselves unpopular and generally disagreeable by persisting in the face of strong sentiment against them. According to another woman from the same league, the movement was held together by a slender thread because there was so much opposition by both men and women. With little local support, "we were always few in number." At a meeting where Adele Clark, a state lecturer from Richmond, spoke, local suffragists were humiliated when, in spite of a vigorous effort, they could get only about a half-dozen women to hear her.[19]

Even more widespread than active opposition was rural indifference. During the early days of the suffrage campaign in South Carolina, a suffragist recalled more than half a century later, indifference, rather than open hostility, was the main problem. In Texas, a suffrage organizer named inertia as the chief obstacle to success. Although women generally did not oppose the movement, she wrote, they were often content "to sit still until the vote drops into their hands." The president of a women's club in Kentucky said that local women were lukewarm about suffrage in 1910; a year later a Virginia organizer commented on the "dense mist of 'chivalry' " that enveloped "womenkind in its malarial haziness."[20]

The extent of local hostility to suffrage often became apparent at public meetings in courthouse towns. A Kentucky organizer, who spent only two hours in the village of Falmouth, observed that this time was "quite sufficient"; " 'God forsaken,' " she declared, "doesn't express it." She was greeted by an audience of about ninety people who were "visibly *unsympathetic* as I glanced them over before beginning." A local judge, hostile to equal suffrage, gave a forty-five-minute introduction of the suffragist in which he described her as a "Suffragette (only he pronounced it '*get*') Agitator." The judge then announced that she would be allowed only fifteen minutes to speak. When Belle Kearney spoke before the Brookhaven Woman's Club in Mississippi, she was greeted by a "dazed expression" among its members, "as if I were talking to them in Sanscrit about Nirvana." A Virginia suffragist conducting a speaking tour in 1918 had a similar experience in Appomattox Courthouse. Greeted by a "splendid crowd," suffragist Elizabeth H. Lewis was preceded on the platform by a local judge, whom she described as "courtesy itself," and the local congressman, Harry D. Flood, who introduced Lewis by announcing his opposition to woman suffrage.[21]

With rural public opinion at best indifferent and at worst openly hostile, votes for ratification were often scarce. Wavering or sympathetic legislators could justify their opposition on the ground that most of their constituents, even women, opposed woman suffrage. In Kentucky, P. J. Beard, a legislator from Shelbyville, explained in 1911 that, in the past, he had nearly voted for school suffrage. The chief difficulty, he said, was that so few women appeared interested in it. The great majority of women, he said, were "content to govern us in the future as they have in the past—with that delightful form of Despotism which can be intrusted to women only."[22]

Elsewhere in the South, suffragists elicited the same response. Meeting with a woman lobbyist in 1912, a legislator informed her that he was "in quite a quandary on the subject of suffrage." Although "favorable to it," he said, the women in his county were against it, and he did not like to vote against their wishes in the matter. "Whenever the majority of the white women of this State" made clear their support for suffrage, an Alabama legislator stated, he would support it. But he was convinced that a minority was "trying to wield the majority." Whether they were unalterably opposed to suffrage or, perhaps more commonly, only wavering, the argument that the "women do not want it" carried a great deal of weight with male legislators. This might well have been a rationalization after the fact; informing suffragists of such opposition became a graceful way of justifying a negative vote. But there is abundant evidence that it was the perception of most southern politicians that women did not want the vote, indeed opposed it.[23]

◆ ◆ ◆

CHILD LABOR AND THE FAMILIAL TRADITIONALISM

A similar dialogue between reformers and the reformed occurred in the attempt to restrict the hours of children participating in the industrial work force. Imbued both with a conception of childhood and with paternalistic attitudes toward the culture of the southern proletariat, reformers were usually frustrated in enacting effective child labor laws. When such laws were passed, moreover, they experienced even greater difficulty in enforcing them.

To many southerners inside and outside the mill village, child labor legislation smacked of unnecessary governmental interference and of obnoxious paternalism. Early in the child labor crusade, the most perceptive reformers were well aware of community opposition. In any modernizing society, wrote one observer, social reformers usually encountered "apathy and indifference in the public mind toward the program of reform." In the South especially, prejudice against concentrated outside groups such as labor unions, antipathy toward government, and the inability of states to provide for compulsory education accentuated popular opposition. In a region where local autonomy had been "most jealously guarded for generations at the cost of blood and treasure," it was natural "that there should obtain also a higher theory of the rights of the individual." Beneath this stubborn opposition to child labor laws lay a traditional antipathy to anything that even hinted of governmental coercion. This observer predicted that the "storm centre" of the fight against child labor, rather than the passage of legislation, would be the "efforts to make the laws more effective."[24]

Into their second decade of crusading, the reality of extensive opposition dampened reformers' optimism. At the outset of the campaign, Alexander J. McKelway had been "hopeful and sanguine" about its success. He remembered his first visits to North Carolina mills, when, looking at the faces of twelve-year-old workers, he believed that it would be possible through legislation to "save these children from the maw of the mill." Even so, he wrote in 1914, reformers were "still far from reaching, in most of the states, the standard of legislation which has been established by the verdict of our generation." McKelway's pessimism reflected his realization that state laws regulating child labor were woefully ineffective. Soon after the first spurt of state legislation, McKelway reported to the National Child Labor Committee that "almost no machinery" in the South existed for the enforcement of these laws. In many states, it had become common knowledge that the statutes were flagrantly violated. Americans had the habit of regarding the passing of a law as the remedy for every abuse, and the southern states had accomplished little either to vindicate their authority or to protect children from exploitation.[25]

Immediately before and during the war, NCLC inspectors, either openly or secretly, sought evidence of child labor in southern factories. The most successful was Lewis W. Hine, who traveled across the South between 1910 and 1916 on behalf of the National Child Labor Committee. Hine's findings were documented by pioneering sociological photography, which often required unconventional methods. On his arrival at Birmingham's Avondale Mills in 1910, Hine was told that he needed the authorization of the owner, former Alabama governor Braxton Bragg Comer, to enter the facility. But instead of seeking Comer's permission, Hine, as he explained it to the NCLC, went off on a little tour of his own and found a rear entrance where workers entered and congregated. Spending two days there, Hine obtained a number of striking photographs and interesting data to go with them, and he discovered that most of the child workers seemed almost conditioned to respond that their age was twelve—the legal limit. Only after he sneaked into the spinning room and took more photographs did he obtain official permission to visit the mill.[26]

Elsewhere Hine employed similar investigative techniques. After inspecting Mississippi cotton textile mills in the spring of 1911, he admitted that enforcement of the law had improved in that there was now "universal recognition" of the twelve-year-old age limit. But, he asserted, violations continued. As had been the case in Alabama, the chief difficulty he found was in working children who were posing as "just past twelve"; this became a "monotonous and discouraging . . . stereotyped answer." Returning to the state about five years later to investigate child labor in the Gulf Coast canneries, Hine reported systematic evasion of the law. "The actual conditions as to the enforcement of the child labor law over five years of child labor agitation," he maintained, could not be "much worse." [27]

The problem that reformers faced in Mississippi, Hine discovered, was the product of weak enforcement. After interviewing the state factory inspector, David McDowell, Hine concluded that the official position toward enforcement was lax at best. McDowell's approach was to prosecute only as a last resort on the assumption, as he put it, that "you can *lead* these people; you can't drive 'em." By "keeping on good terms with them," they would cooperate. But McDowell's cozy relationship with the canneries, based in part on his need for their political support to secure his appointment, rendered enforcement ineffective. The canneries considered his visits a "great joke," according to one Biloxi resident; often with advance notice, they dismissed all of the working children before he arrived. McDowell's apparent collusion with factory owners was compounded, according to several accounts, by gifts of free oysters. [28]

Other observers agreed with McKelway, who concluded that there "was never a greater farce enacted" than the law in Mississippi, where the situation "would be ridiculous if it were not tragic." The method of enforcement, which according to legislation enacted in 1912 required county sheriffs to inspect factories at least twice a year, had made the law "a dead letter"; it fell "below the standard which reason dictates and humanity requires." NCLC investigators discovered that county sheriffs, out of neglect or lack of time, frequently ignored the law. In 1914 an NCLC agent related that, for the state as a whole, "not a single county sheriff had inspected the factories once a month, as required by law." Only two had inspected the factories at all, and none knew what the law's actual requirements were. When an NCLC agent asked the sheriff of the town of Columbus about the law, he admitted that he had never been in a factory and had taken the owner's word on the subject of child labor. In Tupelo, the sheriff, who apparently knew nothing about the work permits and employment certificates required by law, described the owner of the local textile mill as "a *nice* man" who "wouldn't do nothing in violation of the law." Even when the law was amended in 1914 and the office of state factory inspector was created, widespread nonenforcement remained the rule. [29]

Nonenforcement was, in fact, the pattern across the South. In Alabama, a woman reformer complained in 1913 that mills showed "great laxity" about enforcing an eight weeks' school requirement and in ascertaining proof of age. In general, to both mill operators and the inspectors, the parents' word

Child workers at oyster plant, Bay St. Louis, Mississippi, 1911. Photograph by Lewis W. Hine.
(Courtesy of the Mississippi Department of Archives and History)

was "all that was necessary." A year later McKelway declared that the law was "habitually violated" in Alabama. NCLC inspectors also suspected that under-age child workers were coached to state their age as twelve. In Kentucky, with only one labor inspector for the state, McKelway judged regulation to be "entirely inadequate to the task"; in West Virginia, the law was a "failure." In Georgia, an understaffed State Department of Labor enforced the law, but effective inspection proved impossible. In 1914 the office had a staff of two—the state commissioner and one assistant—who were unable to conduct much fieldwork. Appeals for additional funds and staff, according to one account, were "as pitiful as they were futile." In Virginia, enforcement was also under a commissioner of labor, who confessed similar difficulties. The two inspectors who enforced the child labor law admitted that they could at best "secure by prosecution a few convictions as a deterring example to other violators of the law."[30]

Violations were even more common in the heart of the textile belt, the Carolinas. In 1910 an NCLC organizer in South Carolina charged that exemptions to the twelve-year-old age limit for widows and disabled fathers had led to abuses and "practically, nullification." About two years later, Hine found that enforcement in the same state had improved significantly, but, he said, many violations and evasions persisted; these were perpetrated by the few mill managers and many of the workers who dodged the law wherever possible. Violations were even more common in North Carolina. On one occasion, McKelway deemed that state's child labor law, enacted in 1903, to be "ineffective"; on another, he stated that its restrictions were "notoriously violated." Despite the passage of new legislation in 1913 providing for factory inspection—by the already overtaxed county superintendents of education—there were reports of what one observer called "frequent violations of our very poor laws." As late as 1914, McKelway found that the evidence in North Carolina was "overwhelming and incontestable" that underage children were regularly employed and that the local enforcement machinery remained ineffective.[31]

Nonenforcement, reformers acknowledged, reflected community sentiment. As was the case with other innovations in social policy, child welfare reformers met stiff resistance, much of it from management. In Mississippi, textile mill owners defeated passage of a law in 1906 by claiming that the bill was the work of New England mill owners who sought to reduce the state's competitive labor advantage. Despite the organization of a state NCLC committee, the law ran aground two years later because of owner opposition. Not until 1912 did the state enact its first child labor.[32]

Reformers frequently blamed the failure of legislation on owner opposition. Despite North Carolina's reputation as a sociological laboratory, reformers acknowledged that owner domination of the political system blocked child labor legislation. Among millmen, indeed, the efforts of reformers were often ridiculed. The *Charlotte Observer*, then a reliable owner mouthpiece, once described reformers as "weepy-eyed philanthropists" who had suddenly become "much concerned about the welfare of the poor people in the Southern cotton mills." Among the stock arguments of millmen, claimed reformers, were the "glowing" references to the new church and school facilities of model mill villages and the assertion that an improvement in workers' standards of living accompanied the move from farm to mill. In the end, the "indifference" of mill owners was such that they did not "take kindly to the *Authority of Law* over them." This kind of "feudal" thinking, which wrapped the mill community's welfare in a mystique and discouraged state intervention, became what Charles Lee Coon called "the greatest hindrance to child labor legislation."[33]

Yet millmen were probably only slightly more opposed to enforcement than were mill workers. On the farm, family labor, especially that of children, composed the bulk of the labor force, and, as recent historians have shown, mill workers transferred these traditions to the industrial setting of the Piedmont South. "i am going to make a Change," a Union, South Carolina, mill worker wrote to a prospective employer in Atlanta in 1913, noting that he had

"Five Hands For the Mill." Another parent from Gainesville, Georgia, who wanted to change jobs, boasted of two boys who were "good doffer[s] too." Rather than recalcitrant owners, NCLC investigators more commonly complained of noncooperating parents. Although reformers often suggested that parental obstruction reflected the domination of owners, it was the workers who most strenuously insisted that their children should work. When Coon complained to a mill superintendent about an underage child worker, the superintendent responded that the child had been employed because "his Mother wanted us to give him work[,] as she was in great need of money and we supposed he was over 13 years old."[34]

Other reformers blamed violations on parents. The laws in the South were a "dead letter," complained one agent, because of the "shiftlessness and heartlessness" of parents. The chief reason why the law was unenforced in South Carolina, charged the *Columbia State*, was "lazy" and "lying" parents. Children would not attend school of their own volition; they preferred play, "even play in the gutter." Parents who ignored their responsibility and bound young children to work could not "be expected to have sufficient interest in their welfare to require them to attend school." Mill parents, reformers claimed, lacked real control over their children; the mill family was incapable of providing proper direction and reform-minded nurture. In April 1913, when an NCLC investigator visited a mother at the Enterprise Mill in Augusta, Georgia, he asked why she did not send her children to school instead of having them work in the mill. The investigator was shocked to hear that she "could not get them to go." As late as 1929, a reformer in the same state told of "ignorant or vicious" parents who lied about their working children's ages; although owners might be "morally certain" that they were underage, they had "no recourse" but to hire them.[35]

Resistance to child labor reflected the independence of mill worker culture. When members of the U.S. Commission on Industrial Relations visited Fulton Bag and Cotton Mills in 1915, the mill's owner, Oscar Elvas, warned them that the workers were likely to resent the intrusion of outsiders. As a general characteristic, he wrote, mill workers lived "without regard to [the] wishes of others." They were "proud and independent in spirit," resented "outside interference," and were "suspicious of the motives and intent" even of owners with whom "they have been associated to a greater or less extent for a period of years." All this meant that the "handling" of the mill proletariat was "an exceeding vexatious daily problem."[36]

At the root of the matter lay conflicting conceptions of the family. The traditional rural family was structured as an economic and productive unit. It was geared more toward the "protection of men and property," wrote a Georgia reformer, "than for the protection of children." Children had no property rights, and they were under the absolute domination of the father-husband. Tyrannical and unloving fathers, the reformer observed, could transfer custody against the will even of mothers. The law not only protected parental control of child labor but also permitted parents to abuse their children. In the traditional rural family, fathers could and often were "careless at best." They were "forced by law to feed their mules and horses, but not their families." Under this system, the child became a "pawn of fate."[37]

Needless to say, reformers found enforcement to be an exceedingly complex business. In a society with little formal child care, working mothers and management agreed on a "helper" system in which small children accompanied their parents to the factory. McKelway said that this system was "so well recognized" in North Carolina that labor recruiters used it as a device to lure farm families to the mill villages. NCLC investigator Harvey P. Vaughn reported that, despite the public posting of the child labor law, a large number of small children worked in the Augusta Cotton Mill. One little girl worked with her mother, according to the mill superintendent, because "there was no other place to leave her." In order to get the mother's help, he had to tolerate her bringing the child. In a similar scene a year later, NCLC agent Herschel Jones, visiting a Mississippi textile factory in January 1914, found an underage child shifting bobbins at the same frame with her mother. But her mother explained that she was not employed; she "only helped her mother." Her father claimed that the girl was too sick to attend school, and that he and her mother brought her to the factory "where it was warm."[38]

Reformers also encountered strong resistance from mill parents in the struggle to enact new legislation. Reformers tended to discount workers' petitions as indicative of their opposition to reform; they claimed that mill owners coerced their workers into signing them. McKelway regarded antireform petitions as sufficiently important to denounce them as "the most pitiful example of . . . feudalism." Nonetheless, while these petitions offer evidence of opposition, there is no similar record of significant worker support for reform. Indeed, if anything, the mandate seemed to run against reform. "From present appearances," the NCLC agent in South Carolina gloomily observed in 1911, the hardest obstacles to be overcome were the very large number of employees' petitions that were diligently circulated. The impact of these documents was often quite dramatic. From Georgia, Lewis Hine described petitions containing thousands of names, or crosses marked next to them, in which mill operatives instructed legislators to vote against child labor legislation. This outpouring was usually hard to counter in the legislature. "Are you trying to do these things for these people that they *themselves* do not want?" legislators would ask reformers. Hine admitted that the conclusion was inescapable: workers should be left undisturbed. The only thing to do was to wait until the workers themselves said, "Come over and help us."[39]

◆ ◆ ◆

COMMUNITY RESISTANCE AND THE FAILURE OF PROHIBITION

When Virginia suffragist Jessie E. Townshend visited London in the autumn of 1924, she was struck by, according to her, the major difference between British and American life: the continuing presence of alcohol. The saloon existed in London as it used to exist in the United States. There were the swinging doors that "disclosed the same sordid lot of men, emitted the same offensive odors," and contained women "in every state of wantonness." It was a sight that made her "blood boil." How could anyone contest the success of prohibition, Townshend asked, "when it has rid us of such cesspools as this"?[40]

Townshend was living in a dream world. The prohibition experiment met determined and wide-ranging opposition, perhaps nowhere stronger in the United States than in the South. Although reformers were generally successful in securing gradually increasing controls leading to the Eighteenth Amendment in 1919, these restrictions met persistent community resistance. Many critics of prohibition predicted its failure. "So long as the delicate green nectar, with its fine frost of summer, can suffuse the soul of man with melody and brotherhood," predicted the *Richmond Times-Dispatch* in 1910, "so long will prohibition fail to prohibit." Although many had died of thirst, it asked, "who ever died from mint juleps"? Other critics maintained that the fatal flaw of prohibition was unnecessary and intrusive governmental interference. Statewide prohibition, in vogue in the South, was a measure of "constraint" rather than "self-restraint," according to one critic in 1907. Instead of the southern political traditions of self-government and local autonomy, it "substituted government of one section by another." The burden of enforcement was placed "upon people who do not believe in a law." The crucial distinction, he believed, was between a society in which the strong yielded "a measure of personal liberty for the sake of those to whom such liberty is full of irresistible peril" and a society in which "those who make their own conscience the rule for others' conduct."[41]

Serious doubts about prohibition enforcement were rife long before the passage of the Volstead Act in 1919, even among enthusiastic advocates of restriction. The federal government's powers were insufficient "to control . . . local affairs," North Carolina Baptist editor Josiah William Bailey wrote in

1907. To institute national prohibition, he said, meant "not only a China-like centralization, but a China-like power to behead, and, moreover, a practical constabulary occupation of the country." While he called federal prohibition a "delusion," Bailey determined that the evidence was "overwhelming" that state prohibition was equally ineffective. In the case of North Carolina, the state was worse off with it than it would be without it.[42]

The difficulty of enforcing liquor restrictions had become apparent long before national prohibition. In many backwoods communities, the production of moonshine was an accepted part of the local economy. After vigorous efforts by revenue agents led to the destruction of a number of stills in a North Carolina community in 1906, the complaint circulated of a "whiskey famine." According to a local politician, his constituents were unable "to get even enough whiskey to alleviate the pangs of snake bite and child birth." Consequently, they were "feeling very sore over the situation."[43]

Even federal agents were not immune to the corruption of high profits. In 1912 an Appalachian moonshiner produced illicit whiskey for markets in Virginia, the Carolinas, Tennessee, and Georgia. He claimed that three U.S. marshals cooperated in the illicit trade and received a tenth of his profits. Although these marshals made perfunctory raids and destroyed a few stills, they permitted them to be repaired quickly. Prohibitionists often found themselves working at loggerheads with revenue agents, who sought not the end of whiskey distilling but the payment of the excise tax. Indeed, throughout the Progressive Era distillers continued to pay the tax in dry areas of the South.[44]

Regionwide hostility to outside intervention was pronounced when federal agents tried to tax illicitly produced moonshine during the late nineteenth century. Throughout the South, the popular aversion to state intervention persisted; as an Alabamian wrote, such intervention was "antagonistic [to] the pusinall Liberty of the people at Larg[e]." The Founding Fathers, wrote a Mississippian in 1887, established a system of government that exalted personal liberty. The world already suffered from too much government; there was no need for an "invasion into private and domestic affairs on the plea of paternal care for the morals and good order of the people." As William F. Holmes has shown, resistance to the enforcement of the federal whiskey tax culminated in whitecapping—vigilante violence directed at federal revenue agents. The economic importance of corn whiskey for the isolated counties of the South combined with the popular traditions of republicanism and political independence meant that moonshiners often enjoyed strong community approbation.[45]

Whitecapping occurred sporadically throughout the South, usually because of the moonshiners' unwillingness to submit to any outside regulation.

In a Pitt County, North Carolina, neighborhood that was, according to a newspaper account, "scandalized and debauched by moonshine stills," two local men sought to end the illicit trade by informing on the moonshiners. When they discovered this apparent treachery, whitecappers visited one of the men and "whipped him severely," apparently causing his wife to suffer a nervous collapse. But when whitecappers visited the second informer, he was ready with a pistol, and they fled. The informer brought charges against the whitecappers, but although half a dozen were indicted, no local juries would convict them.[46]

Open conflict between moonshiners and federal revenue agents became a common scene in the Progressive Era South. Throughout the southern mountains, IRS agents sought out illicit stills, often at great risk, and the prevalence of moonshiners added to the exotic legends of the region. Enjoying local support and approval, moonshiners sometimes emerged as community heroes, and the attempts of outsiders to apprehend them could backfire and rally local unity. The most sensational instance of violence occurred in Carroll County, in southwestern Virginia, in 1912. Floyd Allen, a prominent moonshiner, had just been convicted of assault when his nephew, Thornton Massie, shot and killed the judge. Other members of the Allen clan opened fire, killing the sheriff and the commonwealth's attorney. Two jurors, the clerk of court, a spectator, and Floyd Allen were wounded. The governor dispatched a force of forty special constables to apprehend Allen and his gang. After a mountain battle, the constables shot and killed the wife of Allen's brother Sidney; even in death, she grasped the trigger of a Winchester. Although Floyd Allen and two sons and nephews were eventually apprehended, convicted of murder, and electrocuted, Allen, the patriarch, became a hero to the people of Carroll County. In prison awaiting execution, he was showered with flowers, delicacies, and cigars. "All maudlin sympathy," to the disgust of a Richmond newspaper, was "turned toward the jail," and Floyd's "thoughts of the death chair" were tempered "by the more palpable contemplation of how much he was applauded."[47]

In spite of the popular impression that moonshine was produced exclusively in the mountains, it existed wherever there was the opportunity to evade detection. If anything, well before prohibition—and perhaps in response to it and other restrictions—moonshining became more prevalent. As one federal revenue official wrote in 1917, illicit liquor manufacturing had increased in his district, for "in the degree that it is made difficult to obtain liquors by shipment, in that degree moonshining is encouraged." Within three years, the same agent reported an "alarming" increase in illegal stills.[48]

The problems inherent in federal enforcement of the excise tax, which

involved merely the regulation of the liquor trade, were much more pronounced in efforts by state and local governments. The dispensary system
of South Carolina, the boldest experiment in a state alcohol policy during
the post-Reconstruction period, exposed the limits of state involvement. Led
by Governor Benjamin R. Tillman, South Carolina adopted a dispensary
law in 1892 that sought a middle ground between prohibition and the traditional high license system. Under the law, a state commissioner purchased all
liquors legally sold in the state. South Carolinians could then buy alcoholic
beverages in sealed packages of between one-half pint and five gallons upon
written application at local dispensaries; no alcohol could be consumed on
the premises.[49]

Defenders of dispensaries portrayed them as a compromise between the
license system and absolute prohibition, but even this limited state regulation encountered popular opposition. Between July and mid-November 1893
alone eighty-eight violations were tried in the courts. Tillman responded with
a hard-fisted policy of enforcement. He withdrew dispensary funds, which
financed public schools, from communities that were delinquent in enforcing
the law and established a special force of constables with wide-ranging powers.
After reports that the upcountry town of Darlington was openly violating the
law, Tillman dispatched four constables, who began raiding suspected violators. The use of special constables aroused popular indignation—fanned by
the anti-Tillman press—and coalesced opposition to his program. Opposition
to the constables in Darlington and the dispensary system was expressed in
a language of republicanism: the constables, composed entirely of outsiders,
represented a military force with the power to violate personal liberty. Fear
of outside intervention became a rallying issue, as rumors spread among the
townspeople of spies arbitrarily searching the belongings of innocent women.
Groups of armed men soon appeared, prepared to shoot the constables if they
violated the sanctity of Darlington's homes.[50]

When Tillman threatened to send militia reinforcements, a disturbance—
known as the Darlington Riot—erupted. A mob, including "some of the best
men in the State," convened at the Darlington courthouse and endorsed an
anticonstable resolution and resistance to the execution of the law. Meanwhile, the citizenry of nearby towns poured into Darlington, armed and spoiling for a fight. In early April 1894 a shoot-out between eighteen constables
and a local mob left six dead and others wounded. When Tillman summoned
the state militia to suppress the "Whiskey Rebellion," as he called it, all of the
state's militia units refused to serve. Facing civil war, Tillman issued a "peace
proclamation" that eventually restored order. But the lesson was clear: heavy-

handed, coercive government violated traditional sensibilities about the role of government in South Carolina.[51]

In South Carolina and elsewhere, southern state and local officials walked a tightrope in enforcing aggressive social policy. Even after the Darlington Riot, South Carolina's dispensary system was plagued both by violations and lax enforcement. Blind tigers, or illegal saloons, operated through a loophole in the law that, after an 1898 court case, permitted out-of-state imports of liquor for "personal" consumption. In 1903 Charleston began fining blind tigers twenty-five dollars every three months, and this soon became a significant source of revenue for that city. A full-scale investigation in 1905 revealed widespread corruption in the administration of the dispensary system. In the next year's gubernatorial campaign an antidispensary candidate, Martin F. Ansel, was elected; in 1907 the legislature abolished the system.[52]

The increasing number of localities and states that attempted prohibition met stiff, often crippling, resistance. The enactment of local option prohibition in Knoxville, Tennessee, was greeted by widespread noncooperation in 1908. Just before the law became effective, liquor dealers sold out their stock to private consumers. There then emerged sophisticated methods of evading the law, such as purchasing liquor from dealers in Kentucky, who advertised widely in the local newspaper. Bootleggers became a common sight, although arrests were said to be frequent. Many former saloons meanwhile became, according to one account, "innocent 'soft' resorts" but were "suspected of concocting mysterious drinks."[53]

Widespread violations were the case in Birmingham, which became dry upon statewide prohibition in Alabama in 1908. Two years later a prohibitionist visitor, who was a correspondent for the *Richmond Virginian*, claimed that the city had the "best enforcement" in the nation. He described a toothless enforcement, however. Beer could be easily obtained by the bottle, costing twenty or twenty-five cents; whiskey was also available, albeit in only two or three inferior brands. At small hotels, as well as at one or two "pretentious" larger hotels, the management made it a regular practice to sell beer in large coffee cups and whiskey in demitasse cups. At private suppers in many hotels, whiskey was served "on the boards" in quart sauce bottles.[54]

Wherever it was adopted, statewide prohibition encountered stiff resistance. In North Carolina, which became dry in 1908, a prohibitionist claimed in 1912 that the popular will was flouted, especially in towns and cities, and that corrupt public officials conspired with liquor dealers "to bring the law into reproach." Strict enforcement of prohibition was "impossible," added a resident of Salisbury, although he pointed out that that locality was "in no worse plight than other towns and cities" of the state. Although these accounts suggest that most violations were urban, in the same year another observer from Durham wrote that although that city "rigidly enforced" the law, the authorities in outlying rural areas experienced "great difficulty in enforcing it." Other states experimenting with prohibition found enforcement equally daunting.[55]

Violations of statewide prohibition were rampant across the South. Dealers and consumers alike exploited every conceivable loophole: they purchased liquor in large quantities through mail-order, interstate express companies that before 1914 lay outside the law, they manufactured the allowable limits of cider and fruit brandies that many of the state laws permitted, or they sold liquor for "medicinal" purposes. Through the latter loophole, complained a Virginian in 1910, "nearly every drug store in the State" had become "a licensed bar, selling whiskey without a license." He cited one instance where a man regularly purchased ten gallons of whiskey a week on prescription![56]

Each application of governmental power, reformers discovered, met a determined enough response to require the exercise of additional power. In the space of twenty years between the 1890s and World War I, reformers moved from local option, to statewide prohibition, to national prohibition by constitutional amendment. With each alternative frequently violated by what one reformer described as "the persistent and aggressive efforts of the liquor traffic . . . to flood the dry territory with liquor,"[57] the ultimate solution lay in complete and unqualified prohibition. With the ratification of the Eighteenth Amendment and the enactment of the Volstead Act in 1919, then, radical reformers began an unprecedented experiment in social policy.

◆ ◆ ◆

THE FAILURE OF PROHIBITION:
THE CASE OF VIRGINIA

No state made a more honest effort to enforce prohibition than Virginia. Although the commonwealth did not enact statewide prohibition until 1914— and did not put it into effect until two years later—at the urging of prohibitionists led by the Reverend James Cannon, Jr., Virginia created elaborate machinery to enforce the law. In 1916 the legislature established a Prohibition Commission, appointing as its head J. Sidney Peters, a Methodist minister and Cannon lieutenant. The Prohibition Commission was granted broad police powers, including the authority to remove noncooperating local officials.

Under Peters's leadership, Virginia mounted an aggressive campaign to enforce the state law and the Eighteenth Amendment, which went into effect in January 1920. In many communities, according to early reports trickling into the commissioner's office, his enforcement campaign effectively ended the liquor trade. Predictably, support was strongest in dry communities. In a Buchanan County community that had been dry for sixteen years, bootleggers apparently had gone out of business, "as they could not get it to sell." Although moonshiners were reported in neighboring Craig County, a Prohibition Commission agent who "used every plan to locate intoxicants" could uncover "none" because the area was "dry . . . good and plenty." Even cider production had ceased because of "threats and warnings from certain citizens around there." Nine months later the same agent said that another southwestern community lacked enough violators of the law "to disturb a prayer meeting." [58]

Nonetheless, even under the tireless administration of J. Sidney Peters, violations continued. Within a year of taking office, Peters discovered the existence of smuggling networks that imported liquor from the Midwest to the Shenandoah Valley, from Maryland to the Eastern Shore, and all along the Chesapeake Bay. In April 1917 Peters heard that there was a vast amount of illicit distilling and selling of "ardent spirits" in the mountainous part of Franklin County, south of Roanoke. Taking this report seriously, he sent out a general alert to law officers to uproot the "lawlessness." [59]

These accounts were not isolated, for soon after taking office Peters had begun to receive a steady stream of bleak reports. From Portsmouth a woman married to a drunkard complained that there was nothing any easier to get in Portsmouth than whiskey. In Lebanon, a procession of people appeared in the shop of a local merchant to purchase vanilla extract, which was 52 percent alcoholic. Even those originally sympathetic to prohibition now opposed total restriction, particularly farmers who sought to convert surplus fruit production into marketable ciders and brandies. Could farmers "squeeze or press, or have squeezed or pressed, the juice from blackberries, dewberries, strawberries, and grapes?" asked one Valley farmer. The wine produced, he promised, was for "the purpose of tickling the palates, gratifying the stomachs, and warming the cockles of the hearts, of themselves and families." He believed that he had a right to make wine for his own use, from fruit grown on his own land. Peters responded by stating that it was lawful to produce for home consumption. [60]

Clearly, however, the line between home consumption and sharing the product with one's neighbor was often blurred, and it was here that Prohibition Commission agents found enforcement so difficult. When a farmer of Comorn, Virginia, told Peters that he was producing sweet cider that contained a low alcoholic content, he crossed a thin line. Although he was a "strong advocate of Prohibition" and had "always voted for it," he insisted that he possessed the right to produce cider. He was anxious to get some little profit from the waste of his apple crop, so long as he could do so under the provisions of the prohibition act. Although Peters was equally insistent that the farmer had to obey the law, it was apparent that the energies of his office would be exerted in other directions.[61]

In fact, the Prohibition Commission was soon concerned with more obvious violators, who seemed to grow bolder as time passed. A Jeffress woman claimed in March 1919 that "every man (almost)" was aware of illegal whiskey selling "just as well as they know that Lee surrendered or that Germany surrendered." Moreover, "everybody here, men and women (*including* the *Justice of Peace*)" endorsed the practice, and it was "almost impossible to get anything done against it." Bootleggers were "making and selling liquor here and keeping our community in a continuous turmoil," a group of petitioners wrote in July 1922 to Peters's successor, Harry B. Smith. They had become very brazen and were openly defying the law. Violations of the law were growing "worse all the time," wrote a woman from Salem; local bootleggers had become "very bold about it too." By 1923 reports were streaming in to the hapless prohibition commissioner. Bootleggers were "selling whiskey here on most every corner," read one; another said that liquor was being consumed "very freely" in the community and that drunkenness was becoming quite common.[62]

This extensive, almost systematic violation of prohibition occurred despite vigorous efforts. Early on J. Sidney Peters hired undercover agents to detect violators and make arrests. He also enjoyed the support of the Anti-Saloon League, which organized Law and Order leagues and helped to finance raids on bootleggers. One Prohibition Commission agent, E. C. Payne, visited a community in 1916 and purchased a gallon of cider—"plain old hard cider" that would make "a man as drunk as a dog"—and grape juice, which was a combination of wine and whiskey that would make "a jack rabbit spit in a bull dog[']s face." After buying the drink, Payne made the arrest. Another undercover agent, E. H. Staley, followed a smuggler from wet Hagerstown, Maryland, in October 1917; when he crossed the border into Virginia he arrested him with sixteen quarts of illicit liquor. Not long afterward he kept an agent for an express company under surveillance in Waynesboro, Virginia, and watched him receive and distribute smuggled alcohol.[63]

Often the enthusiasm of the Prohibition Commission's agents provoked a violent reaction. In Shenandoah County, Staley led a force consisting of the sheriff and six deputies to break up a whiskey ring near Woodstock in July

1917. A shoot-out between the law officers and the bootleggers followed in the nearby mountains. Staley reported that "they were shooting so close to us that we were compelled to lay flat on the ground." Staley and his men were unable to capture the lawbreakers in their hideout. The "moonshine work" had become so dangerous, wrote one anxious Prohibition Commission agent in September 1917, that small arms would no longer do. "We cannot risk our lives with small pistols," he said; it was "nothing but right" that the government furnish agents with high-powered rifles and repeating shotguns.[64]

The vigor with which the Prohibition Commission orchestrated assaults upon the illicit liquor trade was met by a growing and increasingly violent resistance. In another clash in 1919, after bootleggers were apprehended in a car loaded with whiskey, they opened fire on the officers. The ensuing battle resulted in the killing of the two bootleggers, but it also so inflamed a nearby community that Peters sought a change in venue at the subsequent hearing of the officers. Despite federal-state cooperation in raids, prohibition agents faced growing community resentment and, often, physical danger. In the southwestern mountains, bootlegging developed what one agent called about as perfect a system of defense against the law "as the German Secret Service."[65]

In the 1920s, despite sporadic federal participation, authorities were unable to end the spreading liquor traffic. In one southeastern Virginia community, the home of a local Baptist prohibitionist was dynamited in February 1921 in retaliation for his antigambling and antidrink campaigns. After bootleggers visited another crusading minister in Louisa County in June 1922 and unsuccessfully tried to bribe him, they shot him and left him for dead. A well-armed mob greeted a raid on a rural still near Gretna, in Pittsylvania County, in 1922. The agents destroyed a large still and confiscated 1,500 gallons of mash, but, as one of them put it, they were resisted by "a great number of men seeking our lives." Wisely, the officers decided to get out while they could, as the bullets whistled close to their faces. Although a "disgrace to our beloved State," these bootleggers had for years freely supplied "the whole Country." Conditions in a county near Norfolk, reported another local official during the same year, were "worse than in Mexico." "Respectable" citizens were "afraid to leave home without arms," for local bootleggers kept the county in a "reign of terror."[66]

The key to the success of prohibition was enforcement, which depended on cooperation among local, state, and federal authorities. But if enforcement was too zealous—or if the local community so perceived it—the consequences could be disastrous. When Virginia first attempted to enforce statewide prohibition in 1916, the agents of the Prohibition Commission were sometimes overenthusiastic. In September 1916 the *Richmond Times-Dispatch* complained about "rum hounds" who were "as keen on the scent of liquor as ever was the bloodhound on the trail of a fugitive." It objected in particular to the agents opening baggage, particularly of single women travelers. These complaints continued. In February 1917 a local shipper objected to the high-handed manner of a commission agent. Two years later, in a letter to the governor, a Virginian described the "humiliating scene" of innocent citizens "having their baggage unceremoniously searched, or else, be forced to pass through the nerve-racking ordeal, of being 'held up' by armed agents on the public highways."[67]

But these were isolated incidents. Actually, from the outset Peters and his successors were hobbled by the lack of an adequately funded or staffed force. As early as January 1917, Peters complained that the modest funding provided by the commonwealth made it "absolutely impossible" for him to cover the state completely and effectively. His limited resources, he noted later that year, rendered his office utterly unable to field a police force that would "meet one-tenth of the demands upon the office." Without sufficient funds at his command, he explained to the governor in April 1918, he was unable to hire enough agents to stop the inflow of liquor from other states.[68]

Yet the high point of public support for state enforcement of prohibition had already been reached. State officials often enjoyed only limited cooperation from local authorities who, along with their communities, resented the intrusion of outsiders, and local enforcement was usually anemic. Moreover, if community support for prohibition was weak, local authorities were often totally indifferent. In Franklin County in 1917, for example, "a considerable number" of these officials expressed ignorance about their responsibilities in enforcing the law. In Charlottesville, neither the local commonwealth's attorney nor the county's magistrates were in sympathy with the law, according to a Prohibition Commission agent in the same year. Meanwhile, local juries refused to indict local violators. After a counterattack by Virginia wets in January 1920 that stressed dry excesses and made a case for governmental economy, the General Assembly voted to end the Prohibition Commission's administrative autonomy; beginning in September 1922, it became subordinate to the state attorney general's office. Meanwhile, Harry B. Smith, a Culpeper businessman, replaced Peters by a vote of the legislature.[69]

In some cases, local authorities participated in the liquor traffic. In Covington in August 1916, a prohibitionist advised Peters that, "as a matter of precaution," Prohibition Commission agents should operate "secretly and independently of the town authorities." In Leesburg, in northwestern Virginia, the commonwealth's attorney was described as "an x-booze artist" who was "in league" with local bootleggers. In Madison, on the edge of the northern mountains, the "Whiskey crowd" exerted "full sway," apparently unmolested by local law officers—many of whom had been seen publicly drunk—who were "either in with them or afraid of them." While prohibitionists were "intimidated by threats of bodily and personal injury," wets openly sold liquor and seemed "delighted in getting as many as possible drunk." In still another community, a "bootlegging ring" ran affairs because the local authorities were "mixed up in this thing."[70]

State officials discovered that removing noncooperating officials was difficult, despite the ouster law that had been enacted in 1916. In fact, that law never fulfilled the original expectations, primarily because of the hesitancy of state officials to take on local law officers in a frontal assault. Yet, given the degree of community hostility to a stringent interpretation of the law, even enthusiastic prohibitionists had become realistic about the limits of enforcement. The problem, as one prohibitionist wrote in 1918, was more than just negligent local officials. Sheriffs had to sleep sometime, he wrote; with effective enforcement, they would "have to be on duty every hour out of the last twenty-four." Small-town police were unable to monitor automobile traffic; when they tried, they risked the uninviting prospect of meeting desperadoes who might "ruthlessly run over the officer, run over his machine, fire upon him and do him any hurt they can."[71]

By the early 1920s it had become clear that the new moral policy of southern state governments, embodied in prohibition, was a failure. Instead of applying flattering unction to their souls by claiming that conditions were improving, wrote one observer in 1921, Virginians should face the fact that they were growing worse. Liquor was plentiful enough for those who had the price to pay and the stomach to stand the stuff that passed under the name. Any thirsty Virginian who took the trouble could easily obtain a drink. The sad reality, this man observed, was that "a standing army of a half million could not suppress the traffic within striking distance of the point of execution."[72]

As was the case elsewhere, reformers seeking to reshape the relationship between the family and public morality found often crippling obstacles to the implementation of policy. Suffragists, intent on either subtly or openly reshaping the role of women within the family, discovered a wide cultural gap between themselves and the hinterlands that they needed to convert. Humanitarians seeking to restrict child labor had even less success penetrating mill communities. Moral reformers learned that rallying public opinion against alcohol was one thing, and that enforcing prohibition was entirely another. In all of these areas, reformers were more often than not perceived as interlopers and outsiders, who deserved resistance rather than cooperation.

Epilogue: Legacies

◆

Reviewing the results of public welfare during the 1920s, the prominent southern sociologist Howard W. Odum concluded that rural social work in North Carolina had yielded "substantial and successful beginnings" but suffered from "marked limitations." By 1926 no county in the state was organized satisfactorily or had sufficient personnel and resources. Consequently, county superintendents of public welfare had no real power, while county boards were ineffective, community support was inadequate, and there was no professional rural casework. Against this gloomy picture, Odum offered some small hope of progress: efforts at establishing rural social work were "an experiment of great promise."[1]

In many respects, Howard Odum and other southern social reformers faced conditions unique to their region: poverty, a dispersed and largely isolated rural population, and a political culture that stressed individualism and reinforced localism. Probably more than reformers elsewhere in the country, southern progressives who preceded Odum, as well as those who followed him, operated in a restricted political environment, a condition that they were able to use to their advantage: the political conformity and consensus achieved through the one-party state and disfranchisement helped to advance reform. The lack of political competition permitted sweeping changes in social policy; without a political system that encouraged dissent, either at the local or state level, it became possible to advocate and advance unpopular innovations. Southern reformers also confronted different problems and posed different solutions. Southern social reformers were seeking to invigorate the habits and attitudes of the southern masses so as to lift the region out of poverty; northern social reformers also sought social stability, but through the amelioration of the social pressures resulting from industrialization. Not the least important was the factor of race, which more than any other illustrated the central tensions in reform and distinguished the South from the rest of the country.

Although southern progressivism was a distinctive development, it was part of a larger movement that reflected and embodied national trends. In most of the United States, similar, even duplicative movements occurred, sometimes with similar, sometimes with very different results. Together they were part of a dispersed but also nationalized reform movement—the first truly national reform movement in American history. In no sense could southern reformers either have devised or operated a regional program of policy changes had these nationalizing influences not also been present. In one way or another, all of the turn-of-the-century crusades possessed important national connections: prohibitionists were affiliated with the Anti-Saloon League, educational reformers with northern philanthropy, health reformers with both federal and philanthropic influences, suffragists with the National American Woman Suffrage Association, and child labor reformers with the national child-saving movement.

The origins and fruition of southern progressivism are in this sense consistent with reform elsewhere. As was true in much of the United States, reform had originated in the late decades of the nineteenth century, when moral reformers mounted an effective critique first of the system of alcohol distribution, then of the sociopolitical environment that made it possible. Moral reform provided the tone for a wider social critique and array of social reformers. These reformers, the crusades that followed them, and the changes in social policy that they effected shared the value of paternalism, along with the certainty that reform would transform "alien" folkways. Although in the South paternalism was manifested in efforts to change African-American and rural white folkways, it was also a force nationwide and shaped the functioning of early twentieth-century reform elsewhere.

In the reform crusades and the changes in social policy that followed, the contradictory character of reform unfolded: the clash between a rhetoric of uplift and democracy and the evident need to control and even to coerce. Most reformers subscribed to a tradition of democratic republicanism: they believed in, even revered, majoritarian democracy. Yet events forced them to abandon it out of a greater necessity: the need to persuade an otherwise contented, largely rural population of the urgency of reform and of the need to end the traditional means of governance. Reformers were in the minority; they faced the challenge of convincing a large populace of the necessity for change. For centuries, the prevailing principle of government—for southerners and other Americans alike—had been local autonomy. In important categories of government such as public education, isolated and dispersed communities exerted complete control over standards, administration, and the daily operation of schools. Moreover, rural southerners guarded the tradition of local control jealously, and they resisted the intrusion of outsiders.

Lacking extensive powers, reformers and then practitioners of a new southern social policy waged a frustrating battle with localists. This was so in part because of an inadequately developed bureaucratic administrative structure and because of the enormity of the social environment of the rural South. But it was also so because of a paradox internal to reform: that combination of democracy and hierarchy, of humanitarianism and coercion, and of racism and paternalistic uplift that lay behind a cultural invasion of southern communities. Despite a coherent social critique and, frequently, an acute understanding of the nature of social conditions, reformers failed to comprehend the integrity of southern communities. This failure meant, in turn, that reformers never enjoyed significant support among those portions of the southern population they they sought to uplift.

Thereafter, in the post–1930 South, new generations of reformers would confront unique problems of their region. In 1938 Franklin D. Roosevelt's description of the South as "the Nation's No. 1 economic problem—the nation's problem, not merely the South's" exemplified the increased attention the region received from social scientists, both regionally and nationally.[2] Poverty, underdevelopment, and undereducation concerned a generation of New Dealers who sought to rehabilitate the southern social and economic system. Working through bureaucratic structures of governance created during the Progressive Era, New Dealers endorsed most of the diagnoses and policy solutions offered by early twentieth-century reformers. In many instances, however, they went beyond these solutions and, in the three decades after 1940, further expanded central control over local communities.

In public health, for example, centralizers extended a more effective reach into localities. Earlier public health measures in sanitation, disease control, and prenatal and postnatal care continued, often through much stronger compulsory measures. At the same time, in states such as North Carolina, public health enthusiasts embarked, between the 1930s and the 1960s, on a coercive sterilization and birth control program that expanded the structure and assumptions of Progressive Era public health policies to a logical, if morally ambiguous, conclusion.[3]

Post–New Deal southern social policy brought another significant change, for the balance of power now lay with centralizers rather than localists. Although local communities continued to wage a rearguard action, centralizers gained the weapon, during and after the New Deal era, of federal power over state and local affairs. The federalization of social policy tipped the balance. The passage of the Social Security Act in 1935 resulted in federal dominance and the nationalization of standards, thereby decisively shaping state health and welfare bureaucracies. Three decades later, in public education, the development of Great Society federal aid to education imposed a new degree of standardization that southern communities found impossible to resist.

At the same time, southerners after 1930 were operating in a new social environment. The transformation of southern agriculture through mechanization and a modern enclosure movement forced millions of black and white rural southerners off the land; they took familiar problems of poverty and underdevelopment to northern and southern cities.[4] The development of southern urban centers that became magnets for New South prosperity might have fulfilled the reformers' vision, but it also contrasted with the persisting pockets of underdevelopment throughout the region. Nonetheless, these were social forces that were unleashed by governmental policies, especially federal policies, which created a conflicting pattern of development and stagnation. These policies encouraged economic development, and in the South that development became largely dependent on federal largesse. Yet southern poverty and the marginalization of a large part of the southern population continued to elude policymakers.[5]

Into the 1980s and 1990s the distinctive social problems of the South again became apparent. In the mid-1980s the Southern Growth Policies Board, an interstate compact organization that coordinated the planning and policies of twelve southern state governors, convened a Commission on the Future of the South. Issuing its report in 1986, the commission described the region as "halfway home and a long way to go." Despite the appearance of "coming home to the national family," the South, according to this report, had reached a crossroads. It now appeared that the "sunshine on the Sunbelt" was "a narrow beam of light, brightening futures along the Atlantic Seaboard, and in large cities, but skipping over many small towns and rural areas." Meanwhile, millions of southerners remained in poverty because of obsolete jobs and economic underdevelopment. Why, the report asked, had it taken so long for southerners to be comfortable in the "modern global village"? What had stalled "the New South's transformation into the Promised Land it always seemed"?[6]

The SGPB's answer, as it had been to an earlier generation of reformers, focused on rescuing those left behind. These were people, according to the report, who were neither strangers nor "people too lazy to work." Yet reform did not mean charity; it meant "greater parity to bring forward all the South's neighborhoods at once." Reform would also come in the final abandonment of the tradition of localism: it was today "urgent" that southerners realize "their interdependence with one another and with the world." Few southerners realized how the Mason-Dixon line had been "effaced by lines of latitude and longitude expanding outward from the South around the globe, the way water ripples used to spread across the old swimming holes." The leaders of the New South were "lifting their eyes from that safe, local waterhole to view with some shock the economic panoramas beyond the Atlantic and Pacific."[7]

Three-quarters of a century after the Progressive Era, the fulfillment of that period's reform program remains qualified. If somehow magically transported to the South of the 1990s, early twentieth-century social reformers would confront what had become, in some respects, a completely alien landscape. Although a powerful force in southern life, localism has receded politically and culturally; the power of coercive governance and the invasion of television and the media have partly smoothed over local differences. What passes for localism is expressed by a population absorbed in network television and surrounded by interstate highways. The South has emerged as a center of economic growth in key sectors of industry and finance, and it has also fostered high-tech centers joined with higher education, the federal government, and finance. Still, it is clear that, despite the development of the post-1945 South and its altered physical landscape, underdevelopment and its attendant characteristics remain prominent, perhaps frustrating another generation of the region's liberal reformers.

NOTES

---◆---

ABBREVIATIONS IN NOTES

ADAH   Alabama Department of Archives and History, Montgomery

ADE   Alabama Department of Education Records, ADAH

ADPH   Alabama Department of Public Health Records, ADAH

AESA   Alabama Equal Suffrage Association Records, ADAH

AHC   Austin History Center, Austin Public Library, Austin, Tex.

Annals   *Annals of the American Academy of Political and Social Science*

BESA   Birmingham Equal Suffrage Association Records, ADAH

BFP   Madeline McDowell Breckinridge Series, Breckinridge Family Papers, LC

BPL   Archives and Manuscripts Department, Birmingham Public Library, Birmingham, Ala.

BTH   Eugene C. Barker Texas History Center, University of Texas, Austin

CF/CHD   Commonwealth Fund Records, Child Health Demonstration Series, RAC

CFP   J. L. M. Curry Family Papers, ADAH

CIC   Commission on Interracial Cooperation Records, Atlanta University Library, Atlanta, Ga.

CWS   Cora Wilson Stewart Papers, KUL

DUL   Manuscript Department, Duke University Library, Durham, N.C.

EJG   Edward J. Gay Family Papers, LLMV

ESH   Emily Stewart Harrison Papers, EUL

EUL   Special Collections Department, Emory University Library, Atlanta, Ga.

FBCM   Fulton Bag and Cotton Mills Records, Special Collections Department, Georgia Institute of Technology Library, Atlanta

FDE   Florida Department of Education Records, FSA

FSA   Florida State Archives, Tallahassee

FSBH   Florida State Board of Health Records, FSA

GDAH   Georgia Department of Archives and History, Atlanta

GDE   Georgia Department of Education Records, GDAH

GEB   General Education Board Records, RAC

HF   Presbyterian Church (U.S.A.), Department of History, Montreat, N.C.

IHB   International Health Board Records, Rockefeller Foundation Archives, RAC

JCODC   John C. and Olive Dame Campbell Papers, SHC

JMW   Josephine Matheson Wilkins Papers, EUL

JRF   Julius Rosenwald Fund Archives, Special Collections Department, Fisk University Library, Nashville, Tenn.

JYM   Jane Yelvington McCallum Papers, AHC

327

KUL   Special Collections and Archives, University of Kentucky Library, Lexington

LC   Library of Congress, Washington, D.C.

LDE   Louisiana State Department of Education Records, LSA

LLMV   Louisiana and Lower Mississippi Valley Collections, Louisiana State University Library, Baton Rouge

LSA   Louisiana State Archives, Baton Rouge

LSRM   Laura Spellman Rockefeller Memorial Records, RAC

MDAH   Mississippi Department of Archives and History, Jackson

MDE   Mississippi Department of Education Records, MDAH

NAW   *Notable American Women.* 3 vols. Edited by Edward T. James, Janet Wilson James, and Paul S. Boyer. Cambridge: Harvard University Press.

NCBH   North Carolina Baptist Historical Collection, Wake Forest University Library, Winston-Salem

NCDAH   North Carolina Division of Archives and History, Raleigh

NCDHS   North Carolina Division of Health Services Records, NCDAH

NCDPI   North Carolina Department of Public Instruction Records, NCDAH

NCDSS   North Carolina Division of Social Services Records, NCDAH

NCLC   National Child Labor Committee Papers, LC

NOPL   New Orleans Public Library

RAC   Rockefeller Archive Center, North Tarrytown, N.Y.

RFP   Eleonore Raoul Series, Raoul Family Papers, EUL

RGNS   Rabun Gap–Nacoochee School Records, Rabun Gap–Nacoochee School, Rabun Gap, Ga.

RSC   Rockefeller Sanitary Commission Records, RAC

RWCTU   Richmond, Va., WCTU Records, UVA

SCDAH   South Carolina Department of Archives and History, Columbia

SCDE   South Carolina Department of Education Records, SCDAH

SCL   South Caroliniana Library, University of South Carolina, Columbia

SEB   Southern Education Board Papers, SHC

SHC   Southern Historical Collection, University of North Carolina at Chapel Hill Library

TCE   Tennessee Commissioner of Education Records, Archives Branch, TSLA

TDPH   Tennessee Department of Public Health Records, Archives Branch, TSLA

TSL   Archives Branch, Texas State Library, Austin

TSLA   Tennessee State Library and Archives, Nashville

UVA   Manuscripts Department, University of Virginia Library, Charlottesville

VHS   Virginia Historical Society, Richmond

VPC   Virginia Prohibition Commission Records, VSLA

VSLA   Archives Branch, Virginia State Library and Archives, Richmond

VWSP   Virginia Woman Suffrage Papers, VSLA

WABPS   Woman's Association for the Betterment of Public School Houses Papers, University Archives, University of North Carolina at Greensboro Library

PREFACE

1. For a fuller discussion of this historiographical conflict, see William A. Link, "The Social Context of Southern Progressivism."

2. For the best treatment of southern progressivism generally, see Grantham, *Southern Progressivism*.

CHAPTER ONE

1. See Wyatt-Brown, *Southern Honor*; and Ayers, *Vengeance and Justice*, pp. 9–33. For a portrayal of social policy in one state, see Wallenstein, *From Slave South to New South*. On welfare policies, see Wisner, *Social Welfare in the South*.

2. Kearney, *A Slaveholder's Daughter*, p. 84; Richardson, *Christian Reconstruction*.

3. Speer, "Contagion and the Constitution," p. 14; Warner, "Local Control versus National Interest." On the evolution of southern state health bureaucracies, see Speer, "Contagion and the Constitution," p. 14, and Legan, "Evolution of Public Health Services in Mississippi," pp. 24–25.

4. Medical Association of Alabama, *Report of the Board of Health . . . for . . . 1883 and 1884*, pp. 9–20; "Will the Legislature Please," *Florida Health Notes* 1 (April 1907): 145–466. In 1889 the Florida legislature mandated that the State Board of Health should receive ¼ mill per year; ten years later this was raised to ½ mill. See Joseph Y. Porter to E. M. Hendry, August 21, 1901, RG 894, ser. 46: Correspondence, box 2, folder 2, FSBH.

5. For discussions of the licensing system, see Whitener, *Prohibition in North Carolina*; James Benson Sellers, *The Prohibition Movement in Alabama*; Pearson and Hendricks, *Liquor and Anti-Liquor in Virginia*, pp. 152–66; Isaac, *Prohibition and Politics*, pp. 1–11.

6. Clark, *Deliver Us from Evil*, pp. 14–24; Rorabaugh, *The Alcoholic Republic*; Davis, "Attacking the 'Matchless Evil.'"

7. For a fuller discussion of the operation of governance in the instance of public education, see William A. Link, *Hard Country*, pp. 24–44.

8. McCormick, "The Party Period and Public Policy."

9. Olive Dame Campbell Diary, typed copy, October 1, 1908, box 4, JCODC.

10. Hart, "Conditions of the Southern Problem," pp. 644–45.

11. Ibid., pp. 646, 649; Hart, *The Southern South*, p. 59.

12. Hart, *The Southern South*, p. 23; Branson, "The North Carolina Scheme of Rural Development," speech given at the National Conference of Social Work, June 1919, box 3, folder 125, Eugene Cunningham Branson Papers, SHC (hereafter cited as Branson Papers).

13. Branson, "The North Carolina Scheme of Rural Development" and "Our Carolina Highlanders," speech given at the Conference of Southern Mountain Workers, Knoxville, Tenn., March 29, 1916, box 2, folder 52, Branson Papers.

14. Branson, "Our Carolina Highlanders"; John E. White, "Prohibition," p. 135.

15. John C. Campbell, "Confidential Report of the Activities of the Southern Highland Division of the Russell Sage Foundation, September 30, 1913–September 30, 1914," Southern Highland Division Records, sec. 169T, Russell Sage Foundation Papers (unprocessed), RAC.

16. Coon, "The Need of a Constructive Educational Policy for North Carolina," address as president of the North Carolina Teachers' Assembly, Raleigh, May 30, 1911, Charles Lee Coon Papers, SHC (hereafter cited as Coon Papers).

17. J. Y. Porter to Walter Wyman, August 8, 1901, ser. 46, box 2, folder 1, FSBH; Swearingen, *Report on [Texas] Quarantine for 1883–4*, p. 4.

18. Campbell to John M. Glenn, March 10, 1909, box 1, folder 14, JCODC.

19. Alderman, "The Southwestern Field," p. 291; S. D. Booth to W. S. Rankin, February 4, 1913, NCDHS.

20. R. B. Maury to J. D. Plunket, November 6, 1878, February 7, 1879, ser. 14: Epidemics, box 31, folder 2, TDPH; Chase P. Ambler to R. H. Lewis, September 7, 1905, and Lewis to Ambler, September 8, 1905, NCDHS.

21. Legan, "Evolution of Public Health Services in Mississippi," pp. 35–38.

22. J. Y. Porter to the Mayor of Quincy, Fla., August 8, 1904 (box 8, folder 2), Porter to Thomas D. Coleman, June 17, 1903 (box 6, folder 2), Porter to E. Lartique, September 25, 1902 (box 2, folder 4), and September 8, 1901 (box 2, folder 3), ser. 46, FSBH. Even when, in another instance, a local physician asked for help in containing an outbreak of scarlet fever, he was told that financial strains and limited powers meant that the State Board of Health could assist "only in an advisory and recommendatory way." J. T. Sturkes to Porter, September 2, 1901, ser. 46, box 2, folder 3, FSBH.

23. According to one account, only Kentucky and Arkansas had compulsory attendance laws that were "general and effective." Claxton, "A Substitute for Child Labor."

24. James Yadkin Joyner to George P. Deyton, March 2, 1912, ser. 5: General Correspondence of the Superintendent, box 12, NCDPI.

25. County superintendents, according to one account, were rare in Arkansas. The establishment of the office depended on a majority vote of the county, and local approval was the exception rather than the rule. A reformer described the lack of county superintendents in Arkansas as "one of our biggest problems." See Leo Favrot, monthly report, June 9, 1913, and J. L. Bond to Wallace Buttrick, December 31, 1914, ser. 1.1, boxes 25–26, folders 219–20, GEB.

26. Charles Lee Coon, "N.C. School Organization," 1907, Coon Papers.

27. Medical Association of Alabama, *Report of the Board of Health . . . for . . . 1883 and 1884*, p. 32. See also "Report of President," in Mississippi State Board of Health, *Biennial Report . . . , 1880–1881*, p. 6.

28. Florida State Board of Health, *Eleventh Annual Report*, p. 143; "Report of Dr. W. B. Sanford, Chief Health Officer [Alcorn County, 1890]," in Mississippi State Board of Health, *Biennial Report . . . , 1890–1891*, p. 19.

29. M. H. Lane to Solomon Palmer, September 24, 1889, Correspondence, 1868–1916, box 1, ADE; N. D. Hathorn to Solomon Palmer, October 30, 1888, box 4, ADE; James Yadkin Joyner to F. A. Edmondson, September 28, 1915, ser. 5, box 46, NCDPI; "Confidential Report of Mr. [Courtenay] Dinwiddie's Visit to the Rutherford County, Tennessee, Child Health Demonstration, November 22–23, 1924," box 2, folder 39, CF/CHD (unprocessed).

30. Eugene Clyde Brooks, "The Public School Question," *Raleigh News and Observer*, January 5, 1902; Coon, "The Need of a Constructive Educational Policy for North Carolina"; J. M. Anderson to J. Y. Porter, June 23, 1911, ser. 46, box 21, folder 4, FSBH.

31. Report of Blount County health officer for 1883, in Medical Association of Alabama, *Report of the Board of Health . . . for . . . 1883 and 1884*, p. 177; B. F. Rea to Jerome Cochran, August 11, 1890 (box SG6401: Chambers County), J. L. Granberry to W. H. Sanders, February 26, 1900 (box SG6401: Choctaw County), and L. J. Simpson to Jerome Cochran, September 26, 1889 (box SG6399: Autauga County), ADPH.

32. George M. Lynch, monthly report, July 1908, ser. 1.1, box 35, folder 318, GEB; S. M. Vick to James Yadkin Joyner, July 28, 1913 (box 5), and R. S. Graves to Joyner, February 29, 1912 (box 13), ser. 5, NCDPI.

33. W. R. Anderson to Solomon Palmer, 1889, box 1, ADE; Brooks, "The Public School Question," *Raleigh News and Observer*, December 1, 1901.

34. Petition to the State Superintendent, December 1873, Correspondence of the Superintendent, LDE; C. W. Grant, Report for Habersham County, Ga., 1902, GDE.

35. M. D. Louvorn to Solomon Palmer, September 5, 1889, box 1, ADE; R. C. Ayby to Thomas W. Conway, June 30, 1871, LDE; N. N. Mizell, Report for Catoosa County, Ga., 1902, GDE.

36. A. J. Beck, Report for De Kalb County, Ga., 1902, GDE; Frances Sage Bradley to Margaret Bradley, July 1, 1923, Frances Sage Bradley Papers, EUL.

37. See William A. Link, *Hard Country*, pp. 21–23.

38. Coon, "N.C. School Organization," 1907, Coon Papers; Olive Dame Campbell Diary, October 28, 1908, box 4, JCODC.

39. Eugene C. Brooks, "The Public School Question," *Raleigh News and Observer*, December 1, 1901; John Weaver to Perry L. Harned, July 14, 1924, ser. 2, box 103, folder 20, TCE.

40. John Weaver to Perry L. Harned, July 14, 1924, ser. 2, box 103, folder 20, TCE; Richard Parker to James Yadkin Joyner, April 5, 1912, and Joyner to Parker, April 10, 1912, ser. 5, box 14, NCDPI.

41. "Annual Report of the Secretary of the State Board of Health," MS, 1913, NCDHS.

42. Lewis Whaley to Jerome Cochran, October 17, 1885, box SG6400: Blount County, ADPH.

43. G. W. Foster to Jerome Cochran, November 10, 1886, and W. C. Maples to Cochran, June 20, 1886 (box SG6409: Jackson County), and Joseph Darling to Cochran, November 12, 1887 (box SG6404: Dallas County), ibid.

44. T. J. Kennedy to W. H. Saunders, June 9, 1904, box SG6409: Bibb County, ibid.

45. L. J. Simpson to Jerome Cochran, July 4, 1889, J. U. Ray to W. R. Brasswell, January 21, 1898, and W. J. Nicholson to Cochran, September 11, 1889, box SG6399: Autauga County, ibid.

46. F. H. Hudson to W. H. Sanders, January 27, 1898 (box SG6400: Blount County), and L. J. Simpson to Jerome Cochran, December 4, 1889 (box SG6399: Autauga County), ibid.

47. J. W. Weisinger to Jerome Cochran, March 16, 1885 (box SG6404: Dallas County), B. F. Rea to Cochran, March 12, 1895 (box SG6401: Chambers County), L. J. Simpson to Cochran, June 22, 1889 (box SG6399: Autauga County), M. H. Collins to Cochran, November 30, 1887 (box SG6400: Blount County), and R. B. Carr to Cochran, January 13, 1886 (box SG6401: Choctaw County), ibid.

48. Benjamin H. Riggs to Jerome Cochran, March 21, 1885 (box SG6404: Dallas

County), W. B. Smith to Cochran, February 8, 1886 (box SG6409: Jackson County), and W. B. Trent to Cochran, March 17, 1885 (box SG6401: Chambers County), ibid.

49. T. H. Willoughby to the Board of Commissioners of Blount County, January 28, 1882, S. H. Estell to Jerome Cochran, January 18, 1882, and H. H. Bryars to Cochran, February 23, 1895, box SG6400: Blount County, ibid.

50. J. Thigpen to Jerome Cochran, February 7, 1884, box SG6400: Butler County, ibid.; Medical Association of Alabama, *Report of the Board of Health . . . for . . . 1887*, p. 19.

51. P. G. Allredge to Jerome Cochran, March 15, 1884, box SG6400: Blount County, ibid.

52. F. P. Clarke to W. H. Sanders, February 2, 1897, box SG6401: Choctaw County, ibid.

53. C. W. Hunt to W. S. Rankin, January 12, 26, 1912, and Rankin to Hunt, January 23, 1912, NCDHS.

54. M. Turner to Jerome Cochran, February 6, 1883, box SG6401: Choctaw County, ADPH; Rankin to Lydia Holman, September 18, 1913, NCDHS; "Midwife Work in Virginia," from an unsigned, undated MS (probably ca. 1928) entitled "Midwives Tales," box 224, folder 5, JRF. For an example of typical physician hostility toward midwives, see C. W. Hunt to Rankin, January 12, 1912, NCDHS. On southern midwives, see Gardner, "Medical Men versus Granny Women."

55. "Report of Dr. G. W. Purnell, Chief Health Officer [Copiah County; 1880]," in Mississippi State Board of Health, *Biennial Report . . . , 1880–1881*, p. 37; "Report of Dr. Carroll Kendrick, Chief Health Officer [Tishomingo County; 1880]," ibid., pp. 58–59; Arthur M. Greene to Rankin, September 8, October 14, 1912, and Rankin to Greene, September 11, 1912, NCDHS. For another example of the impotency of state officials to affect quarantine, see William Edward to Richard Henry Lewis, October 7, 1905, and Lewis to Edward, October 9, 1905, NCDHS.

56. "Report of President," in Mississippi State Board of Health, *Biennial Report . . . 1880–1881*, pp. 6–7; R. M. Swearingen, *Annual Report on [Texas] Quarantine for the Year 1882*, p. 9; Thomas F. Klinge, "Boys of the 90's," MS autobiography, ADAH.

57. James M. Davison to Jerome Cochran, August 12, 1893, box SG6409: Jefferson County, ADPH; "Biennial Report of the President," in Mississippi State Board of Health, *Biennial Report . . . , 1884–1885*, p. 5; V. McR. Schowalter to W. H. Sanders, January 12, March 30, 1905, box SG6399: Baldwin County, ADPH; Texas State Board of Health, *Report of the State Health Officer . . . for . . . 1891 and 1892*, pp. 3, 5–8.

58. H. D. Stewart to Richard Henry Lewis, December 14, 1905, and James C. Elliott to W. S. Rankin, March 16, 1912, NCDHS. For another incident concerning quarantine, see C. W. Hunt to Rankin, March 4, 1912, and Rankin to Hunt, March 7, 1912, ibid.

59. C. P. Wilcox to J. Y. Porter, February 12, 1907, ser. 46, box 13, folder 2, FSBH.

60. M. Griswold to John A. Ferrell, October 26, 1917, ser. 1.2, box 40, folder 613, IHB; J. A. Elliott to W. S. Rankin, February 1919, NCDHS; T. H. Willoughby to Board of Commissioners of Blount County, Ala., January 28, 1882, box SG6400: Blount County, ADPH.

61. —— to Porter, October 8, 1901, Frank Cole to State Board of Health, October 7, 1901, Chief Clerk to Cole, October 1, 1901, and Chief Clerk to Isaac Reed, October 1,

1901, ser. 46, box 2, folder 5, FSBH; Roswell E. Flack to W. S. Rankin, February 16, 1915, C. F. Strosnider to John A. Ferrell, August 4, 1910, and Benjamin W. Page to Ferrell, October 22, 1910, NCDHS; Edo. Andrade to Joseph Y. Porter, September 3, 1904, and Porter to C. H. Smith, September 5, 1904, ser. 46, box 8, folder 3, FSBH; William C. Warren to Rankin, September 1, 1910, and Mrs. James H. Allen to Rankin, October 8, 1915, NCDHS.

62. J. R. Sams to James Yadkin Joyner, November 22, 1915, ser. 5, box 50, NCDPI; Caroline L. Dickinson Diary, November 20–23, 1911, in "Leaves from a Supervisor's Notebook," MS, ser. 1.1, box 131, folder 1198, GEB; M. Griswold to John A. Ferrell, December 20, 1917, ser. 1.2, box 40, folder 613, IHB; Amanda Stoltzfus, March 10, 1917, Amanda Stoltzfus Papers, BTH; B. P. Jordan, Report for Columbia County, Ga., 1902, GDE.

63. A. F. Sharpe to Eugene Clyde Brooks, June 12, 1919, ser. 5, box 73, NCDPI; James L. Sibley, monthly report, February 28, 1914, ser. 1.1, box 17, folder 145, GEB.

64. When authorities relocated a South Carolina school, the community protested their "right to interfere with our district." Alabama parents claimed that the county superintendent was diverting funds to larger schools, which was "of course death to the Short Termed Schools, and poor people who can't run by a 3 mo. school are kept from sending." J. M. Armstrong to Solomon Palmer, April 9, 1889, box 1, ADE. In North Carolina, patrons claimed that resources were unfairly allocated. Their well-attended school had "proven beyond reoson [sic] of a doubt that we deserve to be treated as good as the west half of the district." It was "unjust" to provide their district with inferior school facilities; they explained that they "don[']t ask but for half" of the school funds. John H. Nichol to James Yadkin Joyner, May 15, 1912, ser. 5, box 13, NCDPI. And in Mississippi, a group of patrons claimed in 1908 that a "school trouble" was the result of the machinations of a "small minority" that was able to convince school authorities to move a "centrally & conveniently located" school to a site that was "unsuited and inconvenient." Hugh D. Cameron to J. N. Powers, September 10, 1908, MDE. Another group of petitioners made the same complaint. Primarily because of geography—creeks that had to be crossed—it was "inconvenient," they wrote, for their children to attend the new school a mile from the old one. J. N. Carter, W. M. Bullock, and J. N. Barnes to J. N. Powers, August 11, 1910, MDE. See also S. C. Steele to Powers, September 18, 1907, MDE.

65. E. B. Chattin to Solomon Palmer, September 18, 1887 (box 3), and M. D. Louvorn to Palmer, September 5, 1889 (box 1), ADE. On Alabama's educational system, see Hunt, "Organizing a New South," p. 50.

66. D. C. Camp to Solomon Palmer, August 10, 1887, box 3, ADE; J. J. Beck, Report for Calhoun County, Ga., 1902, J. L. Magill, Report for Catoosa County, Ga., 1902, Unidentified school superintendent, Report for Elbert County, Ga., 1902, and W. A. Reid, Report for Jasper County, Ga., 1902, GDE; J. O. Freeman to W. D. Mayfield, September 23, 1893, SCDE; C. K. Thompson to James Yadkin Joyner, August 23, 1910, ser. 5, box 5, NCDPI; L. A. Morris to Solomon Palmer, August 20, 1889, box 1, ADE.

67. J. C. Burnett, Report for Appling County, Ga., 1902, GDE; P. S. Vann to James Yadkin Joyner, April 11, 1910, ser. 5, box 5, NCDPI; D. H. Laws to P. L. Harned, December 9, 1925, Creed Rollins to Harned, December 8, 1925, Affidavit of Fate Toffer, December 7, 1925, Affidavit of Jesse Laws, December 7, 1925, Affidavit of Columbus Rollins, Decem-

ber 7, 1925, Roy T. Campbell to Harned, December 20, 1925, and Harned to Campbell, December 24, 1925, ser. 2, box 103, folder 19, TCE.

68. Wiebe, *The Search for Order*.

CHAPTER TWO

1. Zimmerman, "Penal Systems and Penal Reform," p. 186; Taylor, "The Convict Lease System in Georgia."

2. Rodgers, "In Search of Progressivism," pp. 121, 123.

3. "The Temperance Reformation," *Richmond Religious Herald*, March 16, 1882.

4. G. J. J., "Present Status of the Temperance Reform in Our Country," *Florida Baptist Witness*, August 6, 1885.

5. For this perspective on prohibition, see particularly Clark, *Deliver Us from Evil*, and Rorabaugh, *The Alcoholic Republic*. See also Tyrell, *Sobering Up*.

6. James Benson Sellers, *The Prohibition Movement in Alabama*, pp. 15–19; "Champion," "A Drunken Christian," *Raleigh Friend of Temperance*, September 4, 1868.

7. *Clinton Argus*, October 1, 1883; John A. Thompson, "Prohibition," *Alabama Christian Advocate*, January 20, 1886.

8. Thomas H. Hammond, "Evil Effects of Alcohol," *Florida Baptist Witness*, March 13, 1901; Report of the Committee on Temperance, E. R. Hendrix, Chairman, Meeting of the Methodist Episcopal Church, South, St. Louis, Mo., in *Raleigh Friend of Temperance*, November 8, 1871.

9. "The Makers and Sellers of Intoxicating Drinks," *Tennessee Baptist*, February 3, 1883; "Intemperance in the Church," *Raleigh Friend of Temperance*, November 22, 1871; "Drunkenness—How to Deal with It," *North Carolina Baptist*, February 11, 1891; "Be For or Against," *Raleigh Friend of Temperance*, September 20, 1871.

10. Committee on Temperance report, St. Louis, Mo., in *Raleigh Friend of Temperance*, November 8, 1871; John Harral, "When Is a Man Drunk?," *Tennessee Baptist*, March 27, 1886.

11. "The Report on Temperance," *Nashville Baptist and Reflector*, October 30, 1890.

12. "The Temperance Society and the Church," *Raleigh Friend of Temperance*, August 23, 1871; Whitener, *Prohibition in North Carolina*, pp. 22–28; James Benson Sellers, *The Prohibition Movement in Alabama*, pp. 20–21, 32–39, 43.

13. Whitener, *Prohibition in North Carolina*, pp. 28–31; James Benson Sellers, *The Prohibition Movement in Alabama*, p. 44; Leab, "Tennessee Temperance Activities," pp. 53–56; Beattie, "Sons of Temperance." See also Tyrell, "Drink and Temperance in the Old South," and Eslinger, "Antebellum Liquor Reform in Lexington."

14. James Benson Sellers, *The Prohibition Movement in Alabama*, pp. 22–24; Record of the Sons of Temperance No. 45, Bennettsville Division, S.C., 1869–81, entry for June 22, 1867, WPA typescript, SCL; Launcelot Minor Blackford Diary, March 17, 1848, SHC; "Ulna Vox" to the Editor, n.d., *Clinton Argus*, April 15, 1884; "Resolution—Pledge," *Raleigh Friend of Temperance*, February 28, 1872; A. K. Barlow to James J. Phillips, April 23, 1849, Ivan Proctor Battle Papers, SHC.

15. "The Moderate Drinker," *Raleigh Friend of Temperance*, September 13, 1871; J. T. W., "Intemperance in the Church," ibid., November 22, 1871.

16. J. W. McNamara to the Editor, *Florida Baptist Witness*, October 15, 1885; "The Moderate Drinker," *Raleigh Friend of Temperance*, September 13, 1871.

17. Record of the Sons of Temperance No. 45, Bennettsville Division, S.C., entries for February 23, March 2, 1867; "Civicus," "Principle vs. Policy" (April 9, 1869), and "The Reason We Don't Prosper" (June 2, 1869), *Raleigh Friend of Temperance*.

18. "Decently Drunk," *Raleigh Friend of Temperance*, May 26, 1869; Thomas Cameron, address before the Council of the United Friends of Temperance, Black Hawk, Miss., March 31, 1881, *Clinton Argus*, May 15, 1883.

19. "Friend" to the Editor, *Raleigh Friend of Temperance*, April 9, 1869.

20. "Cold Water," ibid., June 23, 1875; *Clinton Argus*, October 15, 1883.

21. "The Prohibition Outlook—No. 2," editorial, *Baptist Courier*, October 13, 1892; Address to the citizens of Pike County, Miss., November 19, 1883, *Clinton Argus*, December 1, 1883.

22. "Mad Dogs," *Raleigh Friend of Temperance*, June 2, 1869; "The Rumseller's Proposal of Co-Partnership to the Devil," *Greensboro Battle Ground*, June 8, 1881; "Riding in His Carriage," *Raleigh Friend of Temperance*, June 2, 1869.

23. "The Temperance Reformation," *Richmond Religious Herald*, March 16, 1882; "A Friend" to the Editor, *Raleigh Friend of Temperance*, October 2, 1868.

24. The social consequences of drink were most severe for the family, wrote a Chattanooga Baptist. How could he "fail to be opposed to intoxicating liquors?" With destruction of individuals came the destruction of families and the "many mothers and sisters" who were "crushed under their sorrow." Rev. J. T. Christian, "A Sermon for Young Men," *Tennessee Baptist*, February 2, 1884.

25. "What Has Become of the Children?," *Alabama Christian Advocate*, June 25, 1896.

26. *North Carolina Baptist*, January 28, 1891; "Wine-Drinking and Drunkenness," *Richmond Religious Herald*, July 3, 1879; "Civicus," "A Drunken Son," *Raleigh Friend of Temperance*, October 2, 1868. "The dram-sellers stand with effusive smiles waiting for your boys and mine," wrote another prohibitionist. "They will lure them in with music and games and jolly fellowship and send them reeling back to us to shatter our hopes, mock our prayers and break our hearts." "Must It Be Prohibition?," *Baptist Record*, November 30, 1893.

27. William Walton Hoskins, "Philip Raymond: A Plea for Wife and Home," William Walton Hoskins Papers, MDAH. In a description provided in 1881, a Mississippi prohibitionist portrayed the typical drunkard as a "wretched victim," enticed to "a ruin worse than death," whose "last penny" had been "filched." With "bloated face and bloodshot eyes," the drunken father staggered home to his "miserable hut"; if the mood so struck him, he might abuse both "the wretched wife he promised at the altar to protect" as well as the "shivering starving ones" that called him father. To this reformer, alcohol undermined the "quiet and harmony of society" by crushing "the hearts of helpless, sorrowing women" and ruining "the future of innocent childhood." Thomas Cameron, address before the Council of United Friends of Temperance, Black Hawk, Miss., March 31, 1881, *Clinton Argus*, May 15, 1883.

28. *Clinton Argus*, October 1, 1883.

29. Jessie Mary Branch, speech before the Columbiana Temperance Union, ibid., March 1, 1884; Alice Randolph, "Married to a Drunkard," *Florida Baptist Witness*, September 5, 1888; Rev. C. H. Spurgeon, "Filling with the Spirit, and Drunkenness with Wine," sermon, *Nashville Baptist and Reflector*, October 23, 1890.

30. Thomas C. Amick, "The Temperance Cause," *North Carolina Prohibitionist*, January 28, 1887.

31. "Wipe Out the Evil" (January 23, 1882) and "The Saloon Evil" (June 27, 1894), *Raleigh Spirit of the Age*.

32. Ownby, *Subduing Satan*, pp. 204–8.

33. As early as 1871 the *Raleigh Friend of Temperance*, a Sons of Temperance newspaper, complained that every year "fearful defection" had occurred from "the ranks of Temperance men" along with "increased apathy in the public mind and an immense increase of the army of drinkers recruited from our noble young men." Without a "change of tactics, or an increase of devotion, some stupendous providence, or the uprising of some new champions for this cause," there was "but a poor prospect of overcoming the enemy." "A Revival Needed," *Raleigh Friend of Temperance*, September 20, 1871.

34. W. E. Williams to the Editor, n.d., *Clinton Argus*, May 1, 1883; *Clinton Argus*, February 2, 1883.

35. Citizens of Beat No. 11, Madison County, Ala., to the Governor, September 20, 1880, Alabama Governor's Papers (1878–82: Cobb), box SG6454, folder 14, ADAH; *Florida Baptist Witness*, May 21, 1885; Rev. J. W. Hawthorne, speech at Atlanta temperance meeting, November 8, 1885, *Tennessee Baptist*, January 23, 1886; W. Drury Smith, "To All Friends of Prohibition in Cumberland County," *North Carolina Baptist*, June 24, 1891. On the crisis that lay behind the sudden surge of prohibitionism, see Harvey H. Jackson, "The Middle-Class Democracy Victorious," esp. pp. 465–66.

36. "The Saloon Business," editorial, *Nashville Baptist and Reflector*, March 9, 1899; J. E. Sibley to Warren Akin Candler, April 29, 1892, Warren Akin Candler Papers, EUL.

37. J. M. White, "The Liquor Power," *North Carolina Baptist*, April 4, 1894; "Prohibition Address," *Columbia Journal*, May 26, 1894, clipping, Lysander Childs Papers, SCL.

38. J. P. Kincaid to the Editor, April 27, 1888, *The Baptist* (Memphis), May 19, 1888; "Nemo," "Prohibition and Politics," *Alabama Christian Advocate*, October 13, 1887.

39. "Associate" to the Editor, *Raleigh Friend of Temperance*, June 14, 1871; "Odessa," *Clinton Argus*, October 15, 1883; Jessie Mary Branch, speech before Columbiana Temperance Union, n.d., *Clinton Argus*, March 1, 1884; "Women and the Prohibition Movement," *Clinton Sword and Shield*, September 26, 1885.

40. Women were therefore fully justified in their "active efforts" to free themselves and their communities "from this blighting curse." " 'Scourge the Preachers Back to the Pulpit,' and the Women to the Kitchen," editorial, *Alabama Christian Advocate*, September 15, 1887.

41. G. P. Keyes, "Woman Suffrage" (January 19, 1888), and "M. S.," "True Women," Gadsen, Ala., January 24, 1888 (February 9, 1888), ibid. See also Thomas Dabney Marshall, "The Possible and Probable Influence of Women on Party Politics," *Clinton Sword and Shield*, September 26, 1885.

42. On the WCTU, see Anne Firor Scott, *The Southern Lady*; Friedman, *The Enclosed Garden*; Epstein, *The Politics of Domesticity*; Sims, " 'The Sword of the Spirit.' "

43. Minutes, September 25, 1882, March 19, May 6, 1883, February 4, 1884, RWCTU. See also Hoge, "Organization and Accomplishments." In Mississippi, Belle Kearney remembered that the WCTU was a "a benediction to the girls of the South"; it served as a "quickening, uplifting agency of love for humanity" that transformed "their slumberous lives and raised them up to God." Kearney, *A Slaveholder's Daughter*, pp. 166–67.

44. Whitener, *Prohibition in North Carolina*, pp. 61–67; James Benson Sellers, *The Prohibition Movement in Alabama*, pp. 55–62.

45. *Clinton Argus*, April 15, 1883. Less than a year later a statewide Prohibition Union endorsed local option prohibition campaigns. Ibid., January 1, 1884.

46. Pearson and Hendricks, *Liquor and Anti-Liquor in Virginia*, pp. 183–84.

47. James Benson Sellers, *The Prohibition Movement in Alabama*, pp. 73, 88; Hendricks, "The South Carolina Dispensary, Part I," pp. 176–77; Leab, "Tennessee Temperance Activities," pp. 57–60.

48. O. P. Fitzgerald, "The Southern Race Problem," address at the National Reform Association, Washington, D.C., April 3, 1890, *Nashville Christian Advocate*, April 19, 1890; *Clinton Argus*, May 15, October 1, 1883.

49. *Clinton Argus*, February 2, 1883; Report from *Louisville Courier-Journal*, republished in *Clinton Argus*, April 15, 1883.

50. *Clinton Argus*, September 15, 1883; "Moral Suasion," *Alabama Christian Advocate*, November 10, 1887; George B. Eager, Steward McQueen, et al., petition, "A Memorial in Behalf of the Dispensary Law," *Alabama Christian Advocate*, January 26, 1899; *Clinton Argus*, May 1, 1883.

51. "The Makers and Sellers of Intoxicating Drinks," *Tennessee Baptist*, February 3, 1883.

52. W. B. Clifton, "Prohibition," *Tennessee Baptist*, May 28, 1887; "The Makers and Sellers of Intoxicating Drinks," ibid., February 3, 1883.

53. "A Plea for the Saloon," *Nashville Christian Advocate*, April 19, 1900; "What the Liquor Dealer Wants by License," *Raleigh Friend of Temperance*, May 10, 1871; "Licensing Vice," editorial, *North Carolina Baptist*, September 5, 1900.

54. N. N. Burton, "Church Members as Dispensers," *Baptist Courier*, October 5, 1893; Hendricks, "The South Carolina Dispensary System," p. 178; "The White Ribboners Win," *Columbia State*, undated clipping (ca. 1891), Lysander Childs Papers, SCL.

55. "A Lawless Business," *Nashville Christian Advocate*, January 5, 1889; "The Devil Over-reaching Himself," editorial, *Charlotte Presbyterian Standard*, February 2, 1899; "The Real Question," editorial, *Baptist Courier*, June 14, 1900.

56. George A. Lofton, "That Report on Temperance," *Nashville Baptist and Reflector*, November 6, 1890.

57. Reagan to Davis, July 29, 1887, in *Tennessee Baptist*, September 10, 1887; "Should Drinking Saloons Be Licensed?," editorial, *Baptist Courier*, January 8, 1885; "Temperance and Prohibition," editorial, *Alabama Christian Advocate*, September 1, 1887.

58. *North Carolina Baptist*, January 28, 1891; V. I. Masters, "The Growing Disregard for Authority," *Baptist Courier*, April 16, 1903.

59. "Dr. Landrum on Divorce," sermon by W. W. Landrum, First Baptist Church,

Atlanta, Ga., *Florida Baptist Witness*, September 14, 1898; "Divorce," editorial, *Nashville Baptist and Reflector*, June 24, 1897; "The Scriptural Law of Divorce," editorial, *Nashville Baptist and Reflector*, January 12, 1893.

60. "Protection of Morals by the Law," *Alabama Christian Advocate*, August 18, 1887.

61. J. B. Moody, "To Banish the Effect, Remove the Cause," *Florida Baptist Witness*, April 5, 1899.

62. "Dr. Cuyler on Amusements," *Tennessee Baptist*, January 29, 1881; "Card Playing," editorial, *North Carolina Baptist*, October 24, 1894; Rev. J. T. Christian, "A Sermon for Young Men," *Tennessee Baptist*, February 2, 1884; "Gambling in Charlotte," editorial, *Charlotte Presbyterian Standard*, January 11, 1900. See also Ownby, *Subduing Satan*, pp. 116–17.

63. "Dr. Cuyler on Amusements"; "Theaters versus Churches," editorial, *Alabama Christian Advocate*, October 10, 1889; "Theater-Going," editorial, *Alabama Baptist*, December 13, 1905; "The Theatre," *Nashville American*, October 10, 1887, clipping, Candler Papers, EUL.

64. "Dr. Cuyler on Amusements."

65. "The Dancing Mania," *Richmond Religious Herald*, February 28, 1884; "The Dance," editorial, *Baptist Courier*, November 10, 1887.

66. *The New Delta* (New Orleans), October 1, 1890, clipping, Woman's Anti-Lottery League of New Orleans Papers, NOPL. In July 1891 women in New Orleans organized the Woman's Anti-Lottery League of New Orleans, which was modeled on the Louisiana league. Minutes of the Woman's Anti-Lottery League, June 25, July 14, November 16, 1891, NOPL.

67. "Base Ball vs. the Sabbath," editorial, *Alabama Christian Advocate*, May 23, 1889.

68. "The Holy Sabbath," editorial, ibid., October 3, 1889; "Sunday Laws," *Richmond Religious Herald*, September 12, 1879.

69. "Truth" to the Editor, n.d., *Baptist Courier*, June 6, 1892; Edgar E. Folk, sermon, June 25, 1899, *Nashville Baptist and Reflector*, August 10, 1899; Rev. W. T. Young, "Sunday Amusements and the Secular Press," *Nashville Baptist and Reflector*, May 7, 1891.

70. "The Sabbath" (July 1, 1897) and D. S. Martin, "A Great Peril and a Great Emergency" (August 21, 1890), *Nashville Baptist and Reflector*.

71. "Sunday Trains," editorial, *Baptist Courier*, May 16, 1889; "The Sabbath and the State," *North Carolina Presbyterian*, October 13, 1898.

72. "The Sabbath Question," *Richmond Religious Herald*, October 4, 1883; Rev. C. H. Wetherbe, "Sabbath Observance," *Baptist Courier*, January 8, 1885.

73. "Sunday Base-Ball," editorial, *Alabama Christian Advocate*, August 25, 1887.

74. "'Blue Stockings vs. the Sabbath-Breakers,'" editorial, ibid., September 15, 1887; "Philo," "Sabbath Desecration," ibid., March 8, 1888.

75. "Philo," "The Holy Sabbath," and "Sabbath Desecration," ibid., March 8, 15, 1888; "Base Ball vs. the Sabbath," editorial, ibid., May 23, 1889.

76. "Philo," "Sabbath Desecration," ibid., March 15, 1888.

77. M. V. Smith, "Evils of the Sale and Use of Liquors," *Florida Baptist Witness*, June 22, 1898 (quotation); E. S. Herbert, "The Press and Temperance," *Baptist Courier*, February 8, 1900; Theodore L. Cuyler, "Christianity and the Ballot Box," *Florida Baptist Witness*, October 2, 1885.

CHAPTER THREE

1. John E. White, "Prohibition," p. 136.

2. Branson, "The Real Southern Question," *World's Work* 3 (March 1902): 1889, and "Farm Tenancy: The Problem of Problems in the Southern States," 1912, box 1, folder 7, Eugene Cunningham Branson Papers, SHC (hereafter cited as Branson Papers).

3. "The Mob at Its Worst," *Nashville Christian Advocate*, May 4, 1899; "Lynch Law and Its Logical Outcome," editorial, *North Carolina Presbyterian*, March 10, 1898; "Lynch Law and Race Hatred," editorial, *Charlotte Presbyterian Standard*, May 4, 1899.

4. Strange, in "Some Thoughts on Lynching," pp. 349–51; *Richmond Virginian*, May 11, 1912.

5. "The Tendency of a Mobocracy," editorial, *Alabama Christian Advocate*, September 29, 1904; Kearney, *A Slaveholder's Daughter*, p. 95; Bailey, in "Some Thoughts on Lynching," p. 353.

6. "Lynch Law and Its Logical Outcome," editorial, *North Carolina Presbyterian*, March 10, 1898; "The Mob at Its Worst," *Nashville Christian Advocate*, May 4, 1899; "The Law and the Church," editorial, *Atlanta Constitution*, November 21, 1906.

7. Ayers, *Vengeance and Justice*, pp. 255–64. See also Holmes, "Whitecapping"; "The Reign of the Mob," editorial, *Baptist Courier*, October 29, 1908.

8. Murphy, *Problems of the Present South*, pp. 10–11, 16–17.

9. "Lynch Law and Its Logical Outcome," editorial, *North Carolina Presbyterian*, March 10, 1898; Bassett, "Stirring Up the Fires of Race Antipathy," pp. 297, 304. On the racial crisis and white reaction to it, see Luker, *Social Gospel in Black and White*.

10. "Is It Just to Either Race?," *Atlanta Constitution*, January 2, 1907; Hart, "Conditions of the Southern Problem," p. 644; "Not an Academic Question," editorial, *Alabama Christian Advocate*, March 19, 1903; Kearney, *A Slaveholder's Daughter*, p. 95.

11. Bassett, "Stirring Up the Fires of Race Antipathy," pp. 298, 300, 304.

12. Coon to W. S. Hagans, March 18, 1913, box 4, folder 43, Charles Lee Coon Papers, SHC (hereafter cited as Coon Papers); Ewing, "The Heart of the Race Problem," pp. 389–94; Thurston T. Hicks to Coon, October 17, 1909, Coon Papers; Bassett, "Stirring Up the Fires of Race Antipathy," p. 299. About Washington, Bassett further noted in the same paragraph: "He is an exceptional man; and, endowed as he is, it is probable that he would have remained uneducated but for the philanthropic intervention of white men. The race, even the best of them, are so far behind him that we cannot in reason look for his reproduction in the present generation. . . . To expect it is to insure disappointment."

13. "Up to Slavery," editorial, *Charlotte Presbyterian Standard*, April 22, 1903; "Social Equality and Purity," editorial, ibid., November 6, 1901.

14. Campbell, *Some Aspects of the Race Problem in the South*, pp. 5–6, 10, in Robert Fishburne Campbell Papers, HF (hereafter cited as R. F. Campbell Papers).

15. Hill, "Negro Education in the South," pp. 321–22; "Southern Question," *Outlook*, p. 190.

16. Campbell, *Some Aspects of the Race Problem*, p. 16.

17. Tillinghast, "Race Heterogeneity," pp. 154–56.

18. When, for example, a Mississippi community of blacks organized itself, at least according to a white account, into well-armed secret societies in 1902, it did not seem sur-

prising to the *Raleigh News and Observer* that violence would erupt between the "lawless" blacks and local whites. "Blacks Leagued against Whites," *Raleigh News and Observer*, August 23, 1902.

19. *Richmond Times-Dispatch*, quoted in *Atlanta Constitution*, September 26, 1906; *Macon Telegraph*, quoted in *Atlanta Constitution*, September 26, 1906.

20. "Law Abiding Citizens Denounce Rule of Mob," *Atlanta Constitution*, September 26, 1906; "An Appeal to Conservative Atlanta," editorial, ibid., September 25, 1906.

21. Betty Jane Brandon, "Alexander Jeffrey McKelway," p. 29. McKelway was in most respects a typical white racial moderate. As a Presbyterian newspaper editor, he denounced lynching on several occasions. He also supported the establishment of a separate "African" synod of the Presbyterian Church of the United States—the southern Presbyterian church. His reaction to the Wilmington Race Riot of 1898 and the Atlanta Riot of 1906 revealed similar moderation, although he endorsed, in North Carolina, the White Supremacy campaign of 1898 that made the former event possible. See Hugh C. Bailey, *Liberalism in the New South*, pp. 60–65; Kirby, *Darkness at the Dawning*, pp. 78–79.

22. "Social Equality and Purity," editorial, *Charlotte Presbyterian Standard*, November 6, 1901; "Our Duty to the Negro," editorial, ibid., November 25, 1903.

23. "Our Duty to the Negro"; "The State's Duty to the Negro," editorial, ibid., February 23, 1899.

24. Murphy, "Backward or Forward?," pp. 21–27.

25. "Not an Academic Question," editorial, *Alabama Christian Advocate*, March 19, 1903; William Garrott Brown, "Of the North's Part," p. 418.

26. McKelway, "Some Changes in North Carolina in Twenty Years," address at Smithfield, N.C., May 21, 1910, and "The Anti-Saloon Movement in the Southern States," undated book MS, Alexander Jeffrey McKelway Papers, LC (hereafter cited as McKelway Papers/LC); "The Devil Over-reaching Himself," editorial, *Charlotte Presbyterian Standard*, February 2, 1899. For further discussion of the connections between race and prohibition, see Washington, "Prohibition and the Negro"; Walton, "Another Force for Disfranchisement"; Walton and Taylor, "Blacks and the Southern Prohibition Movement"; and Walton, "The Negro and the Prohibition Movement: Georgia and Alabama."

27. "A Study of Prohibition in the South," *The New Voice in Mississippi*, February 6, 1902, Belle Kearney Papers, MDAH (hereafter cited as Kearney Papers); W. D. Morton to the Editor, "The Saloon and the Rum-Crazed Negro," *Raleigh News and Observer*, February 22, 1903; "The Race Problem," *Nashville Christian Advocate*, January 11, 1890; McKelway to Nolan R. Best, October 6, 1907, Alexander J. McKelway Papers, box 2, HF (hereafter cited as McKelway Papers/HF).

28. J. B. Lehman, quoted in "A Study of Prohibition in the South," *The New Voice in Mississippi*, February 6, 1902, Kearney Papers; Granville Jones, "The Saloon and the Race Problem," speech at Amarillo, Tex., December 12, 1903, Prohibition Scrapbook, BTH; John McLaurin, "Ten Days of Prohibition," *North Carolina Presbyterian*, December 1, 1898; J. H. Gambrell, "Is Slavery Ended?," *Dallas Home and State*, February 28, 1914, Prohibition Scrapbook, BTH.

29. "Vicious Outrage," *Raleigh News and Observer*, December 18, 1906; "Prohibition in the South," editorial, *Alabama Christian Advocate*, September 3, 1903.

30. Dan Hammack to the Editor (Coleman, Ga.), September 26, 1906, *Atlanta Consti-*

tution, September 27, 1906; "Atlanta Counts Death Harvest," *Raleigh News and Observer*, September 26, 1906; "Death Knell to All Dives," *Atlanta Constitution*, September 26, 1906; "All Licenses for Saloons are Revoked," *Atlanta Constitution*, September 27, 1906; "A New Start for the Saloons," editorial, *Atlanta Constitution*, September 28, 1906.

31. McKelway, "The Anti-Saloon Movement in the Southern States," undated MS, McKelway Papers/LC; John E. White, "Prohibition."

32. McKelway, "State Prohibition in Georgia and the South," n.d., McKelway Papers/ LC.

33. Kate M. Gordon to "Massie," July 18, [?], photocopy, in Pattie Ruffner Jacobs Papers, BPL (hereafter cited as Jacobs Papers). On suffragists and race, see especially Wheeler, "New Women of the New South."

34. Valentine to Mary Elizabeth Pidgeon, October 11, 1919, VWSP.

35. See Valentine to Jessie E. Townshend, April 10, 1915 (two letters), and Adele Clark to the Editor, *Richmond Times-Dispatch*, December 21, 1919, clipping, VWSP. The text of Article 2, Section 30, can be found in Brenaman, *History of Virginia Conventions*, app., pp. 7–8. The notion that black women would immediately learn to read and write was "farcical," Valentine wrote on another occasion. Indeed, the notion was "unreasonable in the extreme to subject the women of the South to an indefinite, if not perpetual postponement of their enfranchisement because of the presence of the negro race." Valentine, speech at 7th annual convention of the Equal Suffrage League of Virginia, Richmond, November 12–14, 1917, Lila Meade Valentine Papers, VHS.

36. During the battle for ratification of the Nineteenth Amendment, a field-worker wrote that everyone "who advanced the negro objection" was met with the standard suffragist response, but she "did not want to bring that question up to those who did not ask it." Mary Elizabeth Pidgeon to Lila Meade Valentine, October 14, 1919, VWSP.

37. Kearney, "Race Problem in South," *Augusta* (Ga.) *Tribune*, April 22, 1903, clipping, Kearney Papers; "Statutory Suffrage for the Women of Mississippi," *Jackson Daily News*, February 11, 1914, ibid.; Josiah William Bailey, "In Behalf of Ratifying the Anthony Amendment by the Special Session of the [North Carolina] Legislature," July 21, 1920, Josiah William Bailey Papers, box 102, DUL (hereafter cited as Bailey Papers).

38. Granville Jones, "The Saloon and the Race Problem," speech at Amarillo, Tex., December 12, 1903, Prohibition Scrapbook, BTH; William Garrott Brown to Robert Fishburne Campbell, open letter printed in *Asheville Citizen*, January 11, 1912, clipping in scrapbook, R. F. Campbell Papers.

39. Hill, "Negro Education in the South," p. 323; Kearney, *A Slaveholder's Daughter*, pp. 101–2. "The word home," Kearney added, was "as foreign to the negro's vocabulary as to the Frenchman's."

40. Branson, "Negro Farm Ownership: The Facts and Their Significance," address at Presbyterian Assemblies Country Life Conference, Atlanta, May 18, 1913, box 1, folder 9, Branson Papers.

41. J. D. Gwaltney (Floyd County, Ga.), quoted in Wallace Buttrick, itinerary and report of conference with county school commissioners of Georgia, September 10–12, 1902, box 3, folder 16, CFP.

42. Hill, "Negro Education in the South," p. 329; "Secretary [Buttrick's] Southern Trip, June 30–July 11, 1902," box 3, folder 16, CFP.

43. C. F. McKee to J. N. Powers, August 14, 1908, MDE; Wallace Buttrick to Curry, October 8, 1902, box 3, folder 15, CFP; "Consideration of Race Problems," *Baptist Courier*, February 8, 1900.

44. Murphy, *Problems of the Present South*, p. 7.

45. Ibid., pp. 84–86.

46. Murphy, "Backward or Forward," pp. 23–24, 34, and *Problems of the Present South*, p. ix.

47. Shapiro, *Appalachia on Our Mind*, pp. 43–58. For a fascinating compendium of Progressive Era perspectives on the southern mountains, see John C. Campbell, *The Southern Highlander*. Campbell's rather romantic views should, however, be contrasted with another, differing social reality: Appalachia's incorporation into a wider market economy. See Pudup, "The Limits of Subsistence"; Dunn, *Cades Cove*; Waller, *Feud*.

48. Shapiro, *Appalachia on My Mind*, pp. 56, 145–46; Ogden E. Edwards to R. F. Campbell, June 16, 1899, box 5, R. F. Campbell Papers; Whisnant, *All That Is Native and Fine*, pp. 37–38.

49. "For Georgia's Mountain Boys and Girls," *Atlanta Constitution*, June 21, 1907, clipping, RGNS. See also in RGNS: Andrew J. Ritchie, "At Rabun Gap, in the North Georgia Mountains," ca. 1922; interview with Mrs. Walter Neville, May 5, 1972, Dillard, Ga.; Isma Dooly, "Story of Georgia's Mountain Folk Told by Prof. Ritchie, One of Them," *Atlanta Constitution*, May 13, 1906, clipping, RGNS.

50. See, for example, his *Classification of Mountain Whites*, copy in box 3, R. F. Campbell Papers, which types mountain whites into three "grades": those who lived in towns; Scotch-Irish, who were "hardy, . . . honest and intelligent" but were "too far from the highways of civilization to have kept pace with their more fortunate kinsmen in education and the conveniences of modern life"; and the descendants of English, German, Dutch, and Scottish settlers, who consisted of "degenerates" who composed the "worst elements" of mountain society (pp. 4, 8).

51. Campbell, "Three Years of Home Mission Work in Asheville Presbytery," printed report in box 3, R. F. Campbell Papers, and "Mission Work among 'The Mountain White' in Asheville Presbytery, North Carolina," *Charlotte Presbyterian Standard*, April 6, 1899.

52. Dooly, "Story of Georgia's Mountain Folk Told by Prof. Ritchie."

53. Neve, "Genesis of Mountain Missions in the Diocese of Virginia," *Our Mountain Work* 1 (March 1909): 1, "Twenty-Five Years Work in the Mountains of Virginia," *Our Mountain Work* 2 (June 1913): 1–3, *Our Mountain Work* 2 (December 1912): 1, *Our Mountain Work* 6 (March 1917): 1, and "Memoirs of Frederick William Neve," MS typescript, ca. 1914, Frederick William Neve Papers, UVA (hereafter cited as Neve Papers); Dooly, "Story of Georgia's Mountain Folk Told by Prof. Ritchie."

54. C. I. Stacy to Walter L. Lingle, November 16, 1908, Walter Lee Lingle Papers, HF (hereafter cited as Lingle Papers). A key contributor to the Nacoochee Institute was the Atlanta benefactor, John J. Eagan.

55. Robert F. Campbell, "Three Years of Home Mission Work in Asheville Presbytery."

56. Marelle Davis to R. F. Campbell, February 18, 1901, box 5, R. F. Campbell Papers.

57. For a fuller account of the Hindman school, see Whisnant, *All That Is Native and Fine*, pp. 17–103.

58. Frances Beauchamp to Wallace Buttrick, April 17, August 11, 1902, and C. F. Huhlein to William H. Baldwin, September 15, 1902, ser. 1.1, box 73, folder 630, GEB.

59. John C. Campbell, report, 1896, box 1, folder 5, JCODC. For Campbell's first missionary appointment, see C. J. Ryder to Campbell, March 22, 1895, ibid.

60. See, for example, the "Report of Sub-Committee of Home Missions for Western North Carolina to the Committee of Home Missions of Mecklenburg Presbytery," October 1894, box 2, R. F. Campbell Papers, which stated that the primary concern of early missions was to establish and maintain new Presbyterian churches.

61. Edward O. Guerrant, "A Message from Kentucky," *North Carolina Presbyterian*, January 6, 1898; "Mountain Missions," *Our Mountain Work* 1 (May 1909): 2, box 2, Neve Papers; M. M. P., "Blackwell's Hollow," *Our Mountain Work* 2 (December 1912): 1, box 5, ibid.

62. C. J. Ryder to John C. Campbell, March 22, 1895, box 1, folder 5, JCODC; Neve, "The Kingdom of God—First," *Our Mountain Work* 1 (June 1912): 1, box 2, Neve Papers; C. I. Stacy to Walter L. Lingle, November 16, 1908, box entitled "Correspondence, 1902–1911," Lingle Papers. On the origins of Nacoochee, see Wade and Wade, *Our Life Story*, pp. 312–39. According to a woman who attended the institute in 1913–15, Nacoochee students were required to memorize Bible verses, sometimes whole chapters; they would then appear before the school's founder, John Knox Coit, who would quiz them. Unidentified interview of Nacoochee alumna, 1972, RGNS.

63. L. A., "Education in Hygiene at Lydia," *Our Mountain Work* 2 (May 1913): 2, box 5, Neve Papers; Report of Hindman Settlement School, January 1906, enclosed in Katherine Pettit to Robert C. Ogden, January 26, 1906, ser. 1.1, box 73, folder 631, GEB; Susan Preston, "Life in Preston Hollow," ca. 1914, Neve Papers. A similar routine is described in Katharine Latham, "A Daughter of the Confederacy Visits the Rabun Gap School," undated clipping, and in Interview with Mrs. Sutton Shirley, Gainesville, Ga., 1972, RGNS.

64. Klotter, "The Black South and White Appalachia"; Shapiro, *Appalachia on My Mind*, pp. 47–48.

65. "A Rich Field for Philanthropy," *Atlanta Constitution*, May 15, 1906, clipping, RGNS; extract of an essay read at Virginia Seminary by G. V. B., "Virginia Mountain Missions," *Our Mountain Work* 2 (February 1911): 1, box 2, Neve Papers.

66. "Mountain Missions," *Our Mountain Work* 1 (May 1909): 2, box 2, Neve Papers.

67. "The Hope of the Future," *Our Mountain Work* 1 (January 1910): 2, and "West Blue Ridge Missions," *Our Mountain Work* 3 (March 1914): 3–4, ibid.

68. William W. Wales to R. F. Campbell, July 14, 1899, and Margaret Allison to R. F. Campbell, January 26, 1899, box 5, R. F. Campbell Papers; C. I. Stacy to Walter L. Lingle, November 10, 1908, Lingle Papers.

69. "West Blue Ridge Missions," *Our Mountain Work* 3 (March 1914): 3–4, Neve Papers; "A Helper," "Some Characteristics," *Home Missionary Monthly* 14 (December 1899): 27, box 3, R. F. Campbell Papers.

70. "Memoirs of Frederick William Neve," MS typescript, ca. 1914, Neve Papers.

71. "Daisy" to Family, typed copy, January 16, 19, 1910, box 1, folder 18, JCODC.

72. Morrison E. Meriam to John C. Campbell, August 29, 1895, and Campbell, report, 1896, box 1, folder 5, JCODC.

73. R. F. Campbell, "Mission Work among 'The Mountain White' in Asheville Presbytery, North Carolina," *Charlotte Presbyterian Standard*, April 13, 1899.

74. Susan Preston, "Life in Pocosan Hollow," ca. 1914, Neve Papers.

75. Ibid.

76. "Memoirs of Frederick William Neve," and F. T. M., "The Pocosan Work," *Our Mountain Work* 2 (January 1913): 4, Neve Papers.

77. Preston, "Life in Pocosan Hollow"; "Memoirs of Frederick William Neve."

78. E. E. W., "Christmas Services," *Our Mountain Work* 3 (January 1914): 1–2, and Frederick W. Neve, "Is It Worth While?" *Our Mountain Work* 5 (January 1917): 1, Neve Papers.

79. F. T. M., "Christmas Celebration at Pocosan," *Our Mountain Work* 2 (February 1913): 3, ibid.

80. R. F. Campbell, "Mission Work among 'The Mountain White' in Asheville Presbytery, North Carolina," *Charlotte Presbyterian Standard*, April 6, 1899.

CHAPTER FOUR

1. Grantham, *Southern Progressivism*, p. 160.

2. "In the Twentieth Century," *Nashville Baptist and Reflector*, January 10, 1901; McKelway, "Some Changes in North Carolina in Twenty Years," address at Old Home Coming Week Celebration, Smithfield, N.C., May 20, 1910, Alexander Jeffrey McKelway Papers, LC (hereafter cited as McKelway Papers/LC).

3. Foxcroft, "Prohibition in the South," p. 627; Corrigan, "The Prohibition Wave in the South," p. 328.

4. John E. White, "Prohibition," p. 131; "Moral Dignity of Prohibition." For a general discussion of southern prohibitionism, see Grantham, *Southern Progressivism*, chap. 6.

5. "Too Much Temperance Talk," *Alabama Baptist*, January 16, 1907; Heriot M. Clarkson, "Perseverance—The Duty of Temperance Advocates," MS, 1904, Heriot M. Clarkson Papers, SHC (hereafter cited as Clarkson Papers).

6. W. A. Gaines, "Strong Drink," *Baptist Courier*, May 1, 1902; M. S. Profitt to Josiah William Bailey, July 25, 1904, box 102, Josiah William Bailey Papers, DUL (hereafter cited as Bailey Papers); J. B. Gambrell, "Prohibition in Texas," *Florida Baptist Witness*, September 24, 1902; "Along the Line," *Clinton Sword and Shield*, May 2, 1885; "The Ocala Saloons Must Go," *Florida Baptist Witness*, June 22, 1898; A. J. Harris, Letter to the Editor, *Fort Worth Record*, March 26, 1911, Prohibition Scrapbook, BTH.

7. McCormick, "The Discovery That Business Corrupts Politics"; W. P. Lovejoy, "The Fight for Prohibition in Georgia," *Nashville Christian Advocate*, January 4, 1900; Rosa Collins to John Hollis Bankhead, April 2, 1917, subject files, box 40, folder 7, John Hollis Bankhead Papers, ADAH (hereafter cited as Bankhead Papers); "A Monster Parasite," editorial, *Florida Baptist Witness*, July 14, 1910.

8. Christensen, "The State Dispensaries of South Carolina," pp. 84–85; "George Stuart Electrifies Great Audience at Ft. Worth," *The Home and State*, May 14, 1908, Prohibition Scrapbook, BTH; editorial, *Georgia Bulletin*, October 27, 1911, Georgia WCTU Records; "A Great Victory for Civic Righteousness," editorial, *Alabama Baptist*, November 6, 1907; Gambrell, "Prohibition in Texas"; James Cannon, Jr., "The Dispensary," speech given at the annual conference of the Virginia Anti-Saloon League, *Baltimore and Richmond Christian Advocate*, December 13, 1906; A. J. Harris, letter to the Editor, *Fort Worth Record*, March 26, 1911, Prohibition Scrapbook, BTH.

9. "The Corruption of Politics by the Saloon," *Charlotte Presbyterian Standard*, July 16, 1902. See also Josiah William Bailey, "The Political Treatment of the Drink Evil," pp. 109–10; "A Plea for the Saloon," *Nashville Christian Advocate*, April 19, 1900; W. H. Flowers to Q. K. Nimocks, April 5, 1905, box 2, folder 70, John Alexander Oates Papers, NCBH (hereafter cited as Oates Papers); *Richmond Virginian*, February 7, 1910.

10. *Richmond Virginian*, September 6, 1911; William W. Smith, "The Saloon a Menace to the Young," January 21, 1905, *Baltimore and Richmond Christian Advocate*, February 2, 1905; *Richmond Virginian*, August 21, 1911, April 21, 1912.

11. McKelway, "Local Option and State Prohibition."

12. Brown, "The South and the Saloon," pp. 462–63.

13. Corrigan, "The Prohibition Wave in the South"; Foxcroft, "Prohibition in the South," pp. 627, 629, 631. In 1908, 22 Alabama counties were dry by special legislative enactment, 15 had dispensaries, 21 allowed licensed saloons, and 9 had both dispensaries and saloons. In West Virginia, 33 of 55 counties, in Virginia 46 of 100 counties, and in North Carolina 62 of 97 counties were dry. Similar figures for South Carolina were 17 of 41 counties; for Florida, 34 of 47 counties; for Arkansas, 58 of 75; and for Texas, 145 of 243 counties.

14. The best and most recent account of the ASL is Kerr, *Organized for Prohibition*.

15. J. C. Jackson, "Anti-Saloon League," pp. 483–94.

16. Hohner, "Prohibition and Virginia Politics," pp. 89–90, and "Prohibition and Virginia Politics, 1901–1916," pp. 13–17. On Cannon, see Virginius Dabney, *Dry Messiah*. See *Richmond Virginian*, March 3, 1910, for a description of the circumstances of that newspaper's creation. On Peters, see "Mrs. J. Sidney Peters," *Baltimore and Richmond Christian Advocate*, January 29, 1903.

17. Hohner, "Prohibition and Virginia Politics, 1901–1916," pp. 37–38. See also Hohner, "Bishop Cannon's Apprenticeship" and "Prohibition Comes to Virginia."

18. "Watts Bill and Other Temperance Legislation," *Raleigh News and Observer*, March 22, 1903.

19. R. L. Davis to Oates, January 1, 13, 1908, box 2, folder 69, Oates Papers; Hohner, "Prohibition and Virginia Politics, 1901–1916," pp. 13–17; *Richmond Virginian*, October 5, 1911.

20. J. S. Jordan to Bailey, July 21, 1904, box 102, Bailey Papers; Heriot Clarkson to Oates, June 5, 1908, box 2, folder 68, Oates Papers.

21. Sellers, *The Prohibition Movement in Alabama*, pp. 102–3; "Review of the Contest," editorial, *Charlotte Presbyterian Standard*, March 11, 1903.

22. Hohner, "The Prohibitionists"; "Review of the Contest," editorial, *Charlotte Pres-*

byterian Standard, March 11, 1903; Brown, "The South and the Saloon," pp. 464–65.

23. Brown, "The South and the Saloon," pp. 464–65.

24. "Saloon Men Organizing," editorial, *Tennessee Baptist and Reflector*, August 27, 1903; B. F. Keith to Oates, May 20, 1908, box 2, folder 73, Oates Papers; William T. Tulford to Bailey, July 19, 1904, and Henry W. Battle to Bailey, July 25, [1903?], box 102, Bailey Papers; "Prohibition in Alabama," *Outlook*. For other examples of denominational involvement, see C. H. Anderson to Oates, December 16, 1907, and T. S. Blair to Oates, December 16, 1907, box 2, folders 66–67, Oates Papers; "The Policy of the Liquor Crowd," editorial, *Florida Baptist Witness*, December 1, 1910.

25. "A Mad Dog," editorial, *Nashville Baptist and Reflector*, August 20, 1903.

26. McKelway, "State Prohibition in North Carolina," p. 272; "The South and Liquor-Selling," *Outlook*, p. 943; John E. White, "Prohibition," pp. 134–35.

27. "Blowing a Hurricane," editorial, *Baltimore and Richmond Christian Advocate*, April 25, 1907.

28. Brown, "The South and the Saloon," p. 465; "'Blind Tigers' in License Territory," editorial, ibid., November 1, 1906; "The Government and Blind Tigers," editorial, *Alabama Baptist*, February 21, 1906; W. D. Turnley et al., resolution from Dade City, Fla., August 17, 1906, *The Southern Witness*, August 23, 1906; "Why Prohibition Doesn't Prohibit," editorial, *Florida Baptist Witness*, July 22, 1909.

29. Bankhead to C. D. Carmichael, January 31, 1913, subject files, box 40, folder 6, Bankhead Papers.

30. Josiah William Bailey, "The Political Treatment of the Drink Evil," pp. 120–21; McKelway, "The Dispensary in North Carolina," pp. 820–21; G. T. Lumpkin to John Alexander Oates, November 18, 1907, box 2, folder 73, Oates Papers.

31. *Richmond Virginian*, May 30, 1911.

32. Davis, "Attacking 'The Matchless Evil,'" pp. 252–53; Foxcroft, "Prohibition in the South," pp. 627–29. For laws in Virginia and Alabama, see Hohner, "Prohibition and Virginia Politics, 1901–1916," pp. 164–65; *Richmond Virginian*, March 4, 1910; Sellers, *The Prohibition Movement in Alabama*, pp. 101–89. On Oklahoma's curious combination of prohibition and a state dispensing system, see "Billups' Booze Bill," *Outlook*, p. 311. On Kentucky, see Appleton, "'Like Banquo's Ghost.'"

33. "Billups' Booze Bill," *Outlook*, p. 312; R. F. Beasley to John Alexander Oates, November 5, 1903, box 2, folder 67, Oates Papers; *Richmond Virginian*, February 22, 1911, March 9, 1912. Georgia's statewide prohibition law was "sometimes violated just as all other laws," wrote a WCTU leader, but that it was violated emphasized "the need of it": if there were "no violations there would be no need for the law." The drinking habit had been with society for almost two thousand years; the wonder was that the law was as well enforced as it was. Address of president of WCTU, Mrs. T. E. Patterson, October 1911, *Georgia Bulletin*, October 27, 1911, Georgia WCTU Records, EUL.

34. *Richmond Virginian*, August 21, 1911, March 5, 1910. Booker T. Washington provided these statistics in "Prohibition and the Negro," pp. 587–88.

35. *Richmond Virginian*, March 5, 1910. "With the saloon will go its allies, the gambling den and kindred evils beneath its wings," commented the *Alabama Baptist* about Birmingham's prohibition. "A Great Victory for Civic Righteousness," editorial, *Alabama Baptist*, November 6, 1907.

36. *Richmond Virginian*, August 21, 1911; "Georgia's Example to the Nation," p. 162. According to one account, there were 6,508 arrests in Atlanta for drunkenness in 1907; two years later, these had declined to 1,120. Whereas there were 12,265 arrests in 1907 for disorderly conduct, the figure for 1909 was 9,770. *Richmond Virginian*, November 29, 1910. On Memphis prohibition, see Modey, "The Struggle over Prohibition in Memphis."

37. Foxcroft, "Prohibition in the South," pp. 631–32; Hoey to Oates, November 6, 1903, box 2, folder 67, Oates Papers.

38. *Richmond Virginian*, February 4, 1910.

39. "Separate the Saloon from the State," editorial, *The Southern Witness*, July 30, 1908. For similar arguments, see J. B. Gambrell, "For Separation of Saloon and State," *Baptist Courier*, July 16, 1908; William W. Smith, "The Saloon a Menace to the Young," January 21, 1905, *Baltimore and Richmond Christian Advocate*, February 2, 1905; F. A. Hendry, "Saloon vs. Dispensary," *Florida Christian Advocate*, excerpted in *Florida Baptist Witness*, March 26, 1902; E. S. Herbert, "The Press and Temperance," *Baptist Courier*, February 8, 1900.

40. J. D. McAllister, *Richmond Virginian*, September 9, 1910; John E. White, "Prohibition," pp. 130–31.

41. "Rendering unto Caesar," editorial, *The Southern Witness*, November 21, 1907.

42. T. W. Young, "What Becomes of the Young Men Who Go from the Country to the Cities?," *Tennessee Baptist and Reflector*, January 28, 1902. Congressman Edwin Yates Webb of North Carolina warned that the question would soon be, "Shall foreigners who come here be Americanized or shall Americans be foreignized?" Webb to Kelly Hook, John M. McGailliard, and G. G. McKesson, February 5, 1908, box 1, folder 3, Edwin Yates Webb Papers, SHC.

43. "Some Tendencies of Our Day," editorial, *Alabama Christian Advocate*, May 1, 1902; *Richmond Virginian*, September 16, 1912.

44. "Some Tendencies of Our Day," editorial, *Alabama Christian Advocate*, May 1, 1902; "The Money Craze," editorial, *Florida Baptist Witness*, May 15, 1901; "A Gigantic and Growing Evil," *Florida Baptist Witness*, August 12, 1903; Report of the South Florida Baptist Association, First Baptist Church, St. Petersburg, November 23, 1904, *Southern Baptist Witness*, November 30, 1904. See also "The Root of Evil," editorial, *Florida Baptist Witness*, March 20, 1901.

45. "The Root of Evil," editorial, *Florida Baptist Witness*, March 20, 1901.

46. *Richmond Virginian*, September 13, 16, 1912.

47. Ibid., February 10, 1910; "A Leading Evil," editorial, *Florida Baptist*, February 8, 1905; "Persedas" to the Editor, November 12, 1911, *Richmond Virginian*, November 16, 1911; *Richmond Virginian*, November 4, 1910.

48. Claude W. Duke, paper read before Ministers' Association of Tampa, Fla., *The Southern Witness*, December 6, 1906; *Richmond Virginian*, June 14, 1912.

49. "Legalized Adultery," editorial, *Baltimore and Richmond Christian Advocate*, April 26, 1906; *Richmond Virginian*, March 28, 1910, September 19, 1913.

50. Henry C. Pfeiffer, Central Methodist Church, South Richmond, in *Richmond Virginian*, September 16, 1912; Stewart R. Roberts, "The City and the Social Evil," address delivered at the Memphis Convention of the Laymen's Missionary Movement, Presbyterian Church in the United States of America, box entitled "Correspondence, 1912–1915,"

Walter Lee Lingle Papers, HF (hereafter cited as Lingle Papers).

51. *Richmond Virginian*, August 10, September 16, 1912; Mrs. D. E. Hooker to the Editor, ibid., September 28, 1915.

52. "The Love of the World in the Church Is Increasing," editorial, *Alabama Christian Advocate*, March 21, 1901; James Cannon, Jr., "In Defense of Decency," editorial, *Baltimore and Richmond Christian Advocate*, March 2, 1905.

53. "Sabbath Desecration in High Life," editorial, *Florida Baptist Witness*, November 11, 1909; "Are We Being Robbed of Our Sabbath?" *The Southern Witness*, August 10, 1905; "Sunday Laws and Sunday Observance," editorial, *The Southern Witness*, September 6, 1906. Moral reformers continued to oppose the running of Sunday freight trains. "Sunday Freight Trains," editorial, *Alabama Baptist*, June 12, 1907.

54. William D. Nowlin, "The Two Sabbaths and Their Proper Observance," *Tennessee Baptist and Reflector*, March 26, 1903; "Sunday in the Cities," *Baltimore and Richmond Christian Advocate*, July 11, 1901; A. J. Dickinson, "The Sabbath Is a Social Problem," *Alabama Baptist*, February 20, 1907.

55. "Sunday in the Cities," *Baltimore and Richmond Christian Advocate*, July 11, 1901; "The Sabbath," editorial, *Alabama Baptist*, November 15, 1905; *Richmond Virginian*, October 24, 1910. For other attacks on Sunday baseball, see *Richmond Virginian*, September 7, 11, 1911; "The Devil Never Sleeps," editorial, *Florida Baptist Witness*, May 19, 1911. For an attack on baseball in general, see J. A. Baber, "Match Games of Baseball in Colleges," *Tennessee Baptist and Reflector*, July 28, 1904.

56. W. T. Ussery, "Ethics of Base Ball," *Tennessee Baptist and Reflector*, October 22, 1903; James J. Cannon, Jr., "In Defense of Decency," editorial, *Baltimore and Richmond Christian Advocate*, March 2, 1905; James E. Avery to the Editor, *Richmond Virginian*, February 13, 1911; "The Debauching Influence of the Carnival," editorial, *The Southern Witness*, January 25, 1906. For similar assaults on cigarette smoking and the moral decay of youth, see *Richmond Virginian*, October 19, 1911; on card playing, see "Card Playing," August 28, 1901, *Florida Baptist Witness*, August 28, 1902; on gambling and bookmaking, see *Richmond Virginian*, April 10, 18, 1911; on prizefighting, see *Richmond Virginian*, March 30, 1910, April 15, 1911.

57. "The Christian Principle in Civil Government," editorial, *The Southern Witness*, April 5, 1906; "The Churches and Civic Righteousness," editorial, *Florida Baptist Witness*, March 18, 1909; J. Randolph Belcher to the Editor, Petersburg, Va., *Richmond Virginian*, September 29, 1910; "Preachers Should Be Leaders," editorial, *Alabama Baptist*, October 13, 1909; John Alexander Oates to C. H. Anderson, December 17, 1907, box 2, folder 66, Oates Papers; *Richmond Virginian*, November 5, 1910.

58. "The Christian in Politics," editorial, *Alabama Christian Advocate*, September 4, 1902.

59. *Richmond Virginian*, February 10, 1910. The proposed law would have allowed both parties to a divorce to remarry after three years; the existing law allowed only the injured party to remarry.

60. "A Fight for Civic Righteousness," *Alabama Baptist*, November 15, 1905; Minutebook of the Salisbury-Spencer Ministerial Association, November 2, 1914, DUL; *Richmond Virginian*, May 31, August 8, 1910, October 3, 1912, January 7, 1913.

61. *Richmond Virginian*, February 6, 8, 1911. The same newspaper had endorsed such

a campaign some months earlier. Acknowledging the "difficulty and complication" of enforcement in a city the size of Richmond, it maintained that to ignore enforcement would be "demoralizing." Any community that winked "at the breaking of one law is in a sense jointly indictable morally with those who break other laws. The spirit is one to beget crime and to suggest anarchy." Ibid., May 28, 1910.

62. Ibid., February 18, 1911; Nowlin, "The Two Sabbaths and Their Proper Observance," *Tennessee Baptist and Reflector*, March 26, 1903; "Facts Concerning Public Playgrounds Opened on Manchester St.[,] Lexington, Ky.[,] June 17, 1901," bound book, June 17, 1901, BFP; "The Sabbath," editorial, *Alabama Baptist*, November 15, 1905.

63. Minutes of the Norfolk Equal Suffrage League, January 28, 1913, VWSP; Ethel Armes to Agnes Ryan, June 26, 1913, Pattie Ruffner Jacobs Papers, BPL; Minutes of the Columbia Equal Suffrage League, November 12, 21, 1914, Ida Salley Reamer Papers, SCL; Linda Neville, "Vice in Lexington in 1911," 1911, Linda Neville Papers, KUL. See also H. Augusta Howard, "A Stinging Rebuke for Atlanta's Pharisees," *The Woman's Tribune*, RG4/SG2/S46/file II: Subjects, box 105, Georgia Department of Archives Records, GDAH; Mary L. McLendon, "Report for 1911–1912," box 1, folder 5, Georgia Woman Suffrage Collection, GDAH; Minnie Fisher Cunningham to Mrs. Wendell Spence, November 6, 1917, pt. 1, box 14, folder 1, JYM.

64. Johnston, undated speech, box 27, Mary Johnston Papers, UVA; William Clayton Torrence to the Editor, *Richmond Times-Dispatch*, unpublished letter, February 26, 1912, and A. Dooley to the Editor, *Richmond Times-Dispatch*, undated clipping, VWSP. On the contradiction between chivalry and social reality, see Roberta Wellford, "The Lustre of Womanhood," undated, Roberta Wellford Papers, UVA.

65. Susan Look Avery, March 1, 1898, Laura Clay Papers, Special Collections and Archives, KUL; Breckinridge, "A New Hope," undated speech, BFP.

66. "Are we going to be too chicken hearted to deal with vice as our laws direct us?" he asked. Coon, "Dead Cats and the Law," 1914 (box 4, folder 47), Coon to O. P. Dickinson, April 1, 1913 (box 4, folder 43), and Coon et al., petition to the Wilson Board of Commissioners, May 27, 1913, Charles Lee Coon Papers, SHC.

67. Mrs. F. W. Crane, notes of Austin WCTU meeting, July 10, 1913, Prohibition Scrapbook, BTH; Campbell to the Editor, *Asheville Citizen*, January 1, 1912, clipping in scrapbook, box 5, Robert Fishburne Campbell Papers, HF (hereafter cited as R. F. Campbell Papers). Campbell was responding to an editorial entitled, "Should Be Investigated," *Asheville Citizen*, December 31, 1911, clipping, ibid. This editorial had described prostitution as a "necessary evil" that should be regulated. "We must not by silence and inactivity encourage the spread of these dens of vice into the very center of city life," it declared. For an account of an antivice campaign in one Florida community, see McGovern, " 'Sporting Life on the Line.' "

68. "A Welcome Voice," editorial, *Star of Zion*, January 4, 1912, clipping, and "Race Problem and 'Social Evil' Combined," editorial, *Harper's Weekly* 56 (March 2, 1912): n.p., clipping, box 5, R. F. Campbell Papers. According to one account, the problem persisted. See C. B. Dusenbury to the Editor, *Asheville Citizen*, June 27, 1915, clipping, ibid.

69. Eagan to Walter Lee Lingle, April 21, 1913, box entitled "Correspondence, 1912–1915," Lingle Papers.

70. "The Pastor's Place in Civic Righteousness," editorial, *The Southern Witness*, July

20, 1905; "Enforcing the Law against Crime," editorial, *Florida Baptist*, February 8, 1905. On antiprostitution reform, see D'Emilio and Freedman, *Intimate Matters*, pp. 208–15; Ruth Rosen, *The Lost Sisterhood*; Boyer, *Urban Masses and Moral Order*. In Roanoke, Va., a local campaign in 1911 brought heightened city enforcement of antiprostitution laws. *Richmond Virginian*, June 24, 1911. For a similar campaign in Birmingham, see "Licensing, Regulating, or Segregating Vice," editorial, *Alabama Baptist*, January 11, 1910.

71. *Richmond Virginian*, September 12, 1912, January 9, February 6, 1915.

72. Ibid., February 6, 10, 16, March 3, 1915.

73. Ibid., February 6, 1915.

74. Ibid., February 10, 26, March 3, September 30, October 1–2, 6, 8, November 26, 1915.

75. Ibid., February 13, 1915; "A Law Curbing Immorality Which Should Be State-Wide," *Social Service Quarterly* 1 (December 1913): 61.

CHAPTER FIVE

1. See William A. Link, *Hard Country*, chap. 4, for a discussion of the origins of this crusade. For a more general view, see Theodore R. Mitchell, "From Black to White."

2. See esp. James D. Anderson, *The Education of Blacks in the South*; Kousser, "Progressivism—For Middle-Class Whites Only"; David Carlton, *Mill and Town in South Carolina*; Leloudis, "Social Reform in the New South."

3. See William A. Link, "The Social Context of Southern Progressivism."

4. Pocock, *The Machiavellian Moment*, represents perhaps the best statement of this approach, but see Appleby, "Value and Society."

5. Buttrick, "Dr. Wallace Buttrick to the County Superintendents," *Raleigh News and Observer*, November 16, 1902.

6. Isaac Hill to Murphy, June 18, 1904, box 127, ADE; Claxton, "A Model School," p. 245; Amanda Stoltzfus, "The Boy's Opportunity for Play and Sociability," n.d., Amanda Stoltzfus Papers, BTH; Constance Schley, commencement address, Georgia State Normal School, Columbus, June 17, 1912, box 1, folder 8, Eugene Cunningham Branson Papers, SHC. See also Emily Stewart Harrison, "The Esthetic Value of Nature Study," undated clipping from *Southern Educational Journal*, ser. 5, box 15, folder 5, ESH.

7. Stoltzfus, "The Boy's Opportunity for Play and Sociability"; Schley, commencement address; Joyner, "Educational Progress of the Past and Educational Outlook of the Future," August 6, 1907, James Yadkin Joyner Series, SEB; Mrs. Herbert W. Mengel, "Public Schools of Kentucky," *Report of the Education Committee of the Kentucky Federation of Women's Clubs at Mt. Sterling, June 21, 1906*, p. 12, BFP. For a description of an ideal schoolhouse, see Claxton, "A Model School," p. 246.

8. Madeline McDowell Breckinridge, "The Educational Work of the Kentucky Federation of Women's Clubs," June 1908, BFP.

9. Editorial, "Lessons Taught by the Southern and General Educational Boards," *Raleigh News and Observer*, April 19, 1903; Joyner, "How the Southern Education Board

Has Helped and Can Help the South," October 12, 1908, Joyner Series, SEB; Hamilton W. Mabie, quoted in George T. Winston, "The Conference Marks a New Era," *Raleigh News and Observer*, April 27, 1902.

10. Murphy, speech at Washington and Lee University, December 1902, quoted in "The Real Animus against the Southern Education Board," *Charlotte Presbyterian Standard*, April 22, 1903.

11. McIver to J. L. M. Curry, May 27, 1896, box 3, folder 13, CFP.

12. L. H. Jones to Curry, January 7, 1896, ibid.

13. Buttrick, "Dr. Wallace Buttrick to the County Superintendents," *Raleigh News and Observer*, November 16, 1902.

14. Ogden, "The Conference for Education in the South," pp. 272–73.

15. Gates to Rockefeller, ca. 1902, The Messrs. Rockefeller Records, box 15, folder 146, RAC; Buttrick to Curry, September 14, 1902, box 3, folder 15, CFP. On the GEB, see Fosdick, *Adventure in Giving*.

16. Ogden, "The Conference for Education in the South," pp. 271, 278. The two boards, declared Buttrick, were "distinct and separate" organizations. He noted that most SEB membership was southern; its management was "entirely in their hands." Buttrick, "Dr. Wallace Buttrick to the County Superintendents," *Raleigh News and Observer*, November 16, 1902.

17. Alderman, paper submitted to Robert C. Ogden, ser. 1, box 6, folder 3, SEB.

18. Joyner, "How the Southern Education Board Has Helped and Can Help the South," October 12, 1908, Joyner Series, box 32, folder 19, SEB; Alderman, "The Southwestern Field," pp. 287, 291.

19. On these crusades and their chronology, see Harlan, *Separate and Unequal*; Charles William Dabney, *Universal Education in the South*; William A. Link, *Hard Country*, pp. 98–115.

20. R. F. Beasley to E. C. Brooks, September 9, 1903, Joyner Series, box 32, folder 9, SEB; McIver to Joyner, December 5, 1905, ibid., folder 10.

21. H. C. Gunnels to Edgar Gardner Murphy, September 27, 1904, October 27, June 19, 1905, box 127, ADE; John Alexander Oates to E. C. Brooks, September 8, 1903, and S. J. Honeycutt to Brooks, September 1, 1903, Joyner Series, box 32, folder 9, SEB.

22. Alderman, "The Southwestern Field," p. 291; R. D. W. Connor, memorandum, December 1, 1905, Joyner Series (box 32, folder 10), McIver to Brooks, September 1, 1903 (box 32, folder 9), Joyner, "Educational Progress in North Carolina," 1908 (box 32, folder 13), and C. H. Mebane, untitled report, June 30, 1910, Bourland Series (box 6, folder 7), SEB.

23. T. J. Coates to A. P. Bourland, May 29, 1911, box 7, folder 12, SEB. Earlier, Bourland had written that Kentucky needed "a spiritual awakening" to effect reform. Bourland, "The Work in Kentucky," box 6, folder 2, SEB.

24. S. J. Honeycutt to E. C. Brooks, September 1, 1903 (folder 9), and R. D. W. Connor, memorandum, December 1, 1905 (folder 10), Joyner Series, box 32, SEB.

25. G. M. Fleming to E. C. Brooks, September 1, 1903 (box 32, folder 9), and Robert Frazer, "Annual Report of Robert Frazer, Field Agent for Virginia, of the Southern Education Board," December 12, 1905 (box 6, folder 2), SEB; Graham, "Current Problems in Alabama," p. 37.

26. Harrison to Emily Hendree Park, January 6, 1908, ser. 5, box 15, folder 1, ESH; Mrs. Lillie Archbell to the Editor, "Woman's Problem," *Raleigh News and Observer*, March 9, 1902.

27. Leloudis, "School Reform in the New South," and "'A More Certain Means of Grace,'" pp. 259–96.

28. "To Make Raleigh Beautiful," *Raleigh News and Observer*, November 13, 1904, and ibid., October 15, 1904, clippings in box 5, vol. 12: Scrapbook of the Raleigh Woman's Club, 1904–5, Elvira Evelyna Moffitt Papers, SHC (hereafter cited as Moffitt Papers). In 1904 Moffitt, along with fourteen men, sent a petition to the county commissioners complaining about conditions in the Wake County jail. See Moffitt et al., petition to the Wake County Commissioners, June 1904, box 1, folder 7, Moffitt Papers.

29. McIver, "Current Problems in North Carolina," p. 297.

30. Editorial, "For Attractive School Houses," *Raleigh News and Observer*, September 7, 1907; Mrs. W. R. Hollowell, "What Women are Doing for School Betterment," ibid., August 13, 1905, clipping, box 4, WABPS.

31. Moffitt, address to patrons and pupils of Reddish School House, Wake County, N.C., 1904 (folder 7), and McIver to Moffitt, June 20, 1902 (folder 5), box 1, Moffitt Papers; Lula Martin McIver, speech to North Carolina Teachers Association, n.d., box 1, WABPS.

32. McIver, "Current Problems in North Carolina," p. 297; Moffitt, "Outline for Talks on the Object of the Wake [WABPS] Association," 1902 (folder 5), and Address to patrons and pupils of Reddish School House, Wake County, N.C., 1904 (folder 7), box 1, Moffitt Papers.

33. Lula Martin McIver, undated speech (ca. 1909), box 1, WABPS. She also stated: "The school house must be the best planned, best built, best furnished, best kept and most beautiful structure in the community, the grounds must be both ample and beautiful, and the teachers must be of the highest character, loftiest aims, thoroughly trained and well paid if they are worthy to be entrusted with our most precious possession." Ibid.

34. Leah D. Jones, "Better School Houses," undated clipping, box 4, WABPS.

35. Lila E. Gardner to Madeline McDowell Breckinridge, February 24, 1912, BFP; J. N. Carpenter to Elvira Evelyna Moffitt, September 6, 1902 (folder 5), and Mrs. L. P. Sorrell to Edith Royster, February 3, 1902 (folder 6), box 1, Moffitt Papers. See also M. A. Adams to Royster, January 9, 1902 (folder 5), and Anna G. Yates to Moffitt, March 26, 1904 (folder 7), Moffitt Papers; Mrs. Henry Hunter, report for Betterment Association of Sunnyside, N.C., March 6, 1912, Mary Lou Stamey, report for Betterment Association of Cleveland County, Fallston, N.C., ca. 1912, and Lula Martin McIver, "Work to Be Done," n.d., box 1, WABPS.

36. Moffitt, "Outline for Talks on the Object of the Wake [WABPS] Association," 1902, box 1, folder 5, Moffitt Papers; Annie E. Johnson to Lula Martin McIver, September 22, 1908, box 1, WABPS; Lela B. Pool to Edith Royster, February 9, 1903, box 1, folder 6, Moffitt Papers.

37. Leah D. Jones, "Better School Houses," undated clipping, box 4, WABPS.

38. Mrs. J. W. Baucom to Moffitt, October 30, 1902 (folder 5), Mrs. L. P. Sorrell to Moffitt, March 11, 1904 (folder 7), and Anna G. Yates to Moffitt, March 26, 1904

(folder 7), box 1, Moffitt Papers; Reports of Viola Boddie, September 17, 1903, August 24, 1904, box 2, WABPS.

39. Memoranda for the Meeting of the SEB Budget Committee, December 21, 1906, A. J. Bourland Series, box 6, folder 3, SEB.

40. T. J. Coates, quarterly report, June 30, 1911, Bourland Series, box 7, folder 12, SEB. Wickliffe Rose to Wallace Buttrick, November 21, 1911, Joyner Series, box 33, folder 35, SEB; Cora Wilson Stewart, "Moonlight Schools," ca. 1915, "Other Materials" Series, box 45, CWS. On Stewart, see Nelms, "Cora Wilson Stewart"; Estes, "Cora Wilson Stewart."

41. Cora Wilson Stewart to James Y. Joyner, February 6, 1914, Joyner Series, box 33, folder 40, SEB; Stewart, "Moonlight Schools"; Report of Tobias Huffaker, Adair County, in Superintendent of Public Instruction of Kentucky, *Biennial Report . . . for the Two Years Ending December 31, 1917*, p. 303.

42. Cora Wilson Stewart, "Organizing a County for Moonlight Schools," May 1912, "Other Materials" Series, box 45, CWS.

43. Ibid.

44. Alderman, paper presented to Robert C. Ogden, SEB Series, box 6, folder 3, SEB.

45. R. D. W. Connor, memorandum, December 1, 1905, Joyner Series, box 32, folder 10, SEB.

46. William W. Dinsmore to Wickliffe Rose, March 18, 1915 (box 1, folder 3), and Olin West to Rose, March 18, 1915 (box 4, folder 70), ser. 1.2, IHB. For a discussion of southern public health, see Beardsley, *A History of Neglect*.

47. See William A. Link, "Privies, Progressivism, and Public Schools." For discussions of the southern hookworm crusade and public health, see Glasson, "The Rockefeller Commission's Campaign"; Grantham, *Southern Progressivism*, pp. 310–18; Ettling, *Germ of Laziness*.

48. Calvin T. Young to Hiram Byrd, May 6, 1910 (folder 5), and Watson Smith Rankin to Byrd, July 7, 1910 (folder 9), box 18, ser. 46, FSBH.

49. Alexander McKelway maintained that "the wholesale emigration of the people from the farms to the mills is not necessary to cure them of this parasitic disease, nor being at the mills, is it necessary to work immature children twelve hours a days, or even ten hours a day, in order to cure them of the hookworm." McKelway, "Southern Aspects of the Child Labor Problem," address at Woman's Club, Richmond, April 11, 1910, Alexander Jeffrey McKelway Papers, LC.

50. Florida's hookworm program was already established and state officials resisted efforts to incorporate it into the RSC program. Nonetheless, there was some coordination with the RSC. In the spring of 1910, for example, RSC officials visited Florida to observe; other southern public officials did the same. John A. Ferrell to Hiram Byrd, April 8, 1910, and Byrd to Ferrell, April 11, 1910, ser. 46, box 18, folder 3, FSBH; "The Conference for the Eradication of the Hookworm Disease," *Florida Health Notes* 5 (January 1910): 25–28. In Arkansas, the weakness of its State Board of Health seemed to have been the main factor. See Rose to George B. Cook, March 7, 1910, ser. 2, box 1, folder 57, RSC.

51. Wickliffe Rose to Morgan Smith, May 12, 1910, ser. 2, box 1, folder 57, RSC.

52. Ferrell, "The North Carolina Campaign against Hookworm," p. 129. For the ap-

pointment of the state director for Alabama, see W. H. Saunder to Rose, September 3, 1910, ser. 2, box 1, folder 51, RSC.

53. Washburn, *History of the North Carolina State Board of Health*, pp. 8–37. On post-Reconstruction health policy, see Warner, "Local Control versus National Interest." On the recruitment of field-workers, see Claude L. Pridgen to Ferrell, May 11, 1911, T. E. Hughes to Ferrell, August 21, 1911, and Benjamin W. Page to Ferrell, October 27, 1911, NCDHS. During the first year the North Carolina campaign staff consisted of four field directors; a fifth was added in the autumn of 1911.

54. Strosnider to Ferrell, August 4, 9, 1910, NCDHS; Washburn, *The Hookworm Campaign in Alamance County*, pp. 6–8. For a similar view, see *Bulletin of the State Board of Health of Kentucky* 2 (March 1912): 56–57.

55. Pridgen to Ferrell, November 8, 1911, NCDHS; Washburn, *The Hookworm Campaign in Alamance County*, pp. 13, 23; Pridgen to Ferrell, November 21, 1913, ser. 2, box 7, folder 129, RSC.

56. Page to Ferrell, August 1, September 10, 1910, NCDHS; Washburn, *As I Recall*, p. 5; Ferrell to Rose, October 29, 1910, ser. 2, box 5, folder 115, RSC; Ferrell, "The North Carolina Campaign against Hookworm," pp. 129–31.

57. Page to Ferrell, September 21, 1910, and Strosnider to Ferrell, August 2, 1910, NCDHS.

58. A. G. Fort to Rose, August 16, 1910 (box 2, folder 69), and Morgan Smith to Rose, May 13, July 12, 1910 (box 1, folder 57), ser. 2, RSC; Louisiana State Board of Health, *Biennial Report . . . , 1910–1911*, pp. 27–31; Porter to Rose, November 18, December 7, 1910, ser. 2, box 3, folder 94, RSC.

59. West to Rose, October 23, November 15, 1911, box 8, folder 147, RSC.

60. Smith to Rose, January 21, June 9, August 28, 1911 (box 1, folder 58), A. G. Fort to Rose, October 27, 1910, April 18, 1911 (box 1, folders 69–70), Porter to Rose, November 29, December 7, 1910, January 17, 1911 (box 1, folders 94–95), and West to Rose, October 23, 1911 (box 8, folder 147), RSC.

61. W. S. Leathers, "The Report of the Director of Public Health and Sanitation," in Mississippi State Board of Health, *Report . . . from September 30, 1909, to June 30, 1911*, pp. 84–86; Rose to Ferrell, March 9, 1911, ser. 2, box 5, folder 116, RSC. On Louisiana, see "Resolution of the Police Jury of Lincoln Parish—Ruston, La., April 14, 1911," ser. 2, box 4, folder 95, RSC. On dispensaries generally, see Ettling, *Germ of Laziness*, pp. 152–77.

62. Dinsmore to Rose, June 1, 1911 (box 1, folder 51), and Rose to Ferrell, July 18, 1911 (box 6, folder 117), ser. 2, RSC.

63. Porter to Rose, May 13, 1911 (box 4, folder 95), "Meeting of Field Representatives with Dr. Ferrell," February 1911, and Ferrell to Rose, March 10, June 15, 1911 (box 5, folder 116), and Rose to Frederick T. Gates, August 14, 1911 (box 6, folder 117), ibid.; Ferrell to Pridgen, May 13, 1911, NCDHS; Ferrell to R. H. Duffy, circular letter, May 16, 1911, ser. 2, box 5, folder 116, RSC; Pridgen to Ferrell, July 14, August 3, 1911, NCDHS.

64. Pridgen to Ferrell, July 13, 17, August 7, 1911, NCDHS. See also Pridgen to Ferrell, July 10, 1911, ibid.

65. Pridgen apparently modified the field hospital dispensary model, but it had sig-

nificant variations. Then, in October 1911, Ferrell required that it follow the statewide standard. See Ferrell to Pridgen, October 22, 1911, ibid.

66. Ferrell to Rose, July 17, 1911, box 5, folder 117, ser. 2, RSC.

67. Ferrell, circular letter to field directors, August 10, 1911, NCDHS, and "The North Carolina Campaign against Hookworm," p. 133; Strosnider to Ferrell, July 20, 16, 22, 1911, NCDHS.

68. Ferrell to Strosnider, July 19, 1911, NCDHS; Rose to Frederick T. Gates, August 14, 1911, ser. 2, box 5, folder 117, RSC. See also Strosnider to Ferrell, June 30, July 13, 16, 1911, NCDHS.

69. J. Fraser Orr to Dinsmore, typed copy, September 9, 1913 (box 1, folder 52), O. H. Judkins to M. H. Boerner, February 28, 1913 (box 9, folder 155), W. S. Leathers to Ferrell, August 2, 1913 (box 5, folder 108), and Rose to Gates, October 17, 1912 (box 3, folder 88), ser. 2, RSC.

70. Louisa Pace to C. A. Grote, typed copy, December 19, 1913 (box 1, folder 52), and W. S. Leathers to Rose, January 19, 1912 (box 5, folder 107), ibid.; Tennessee Department of Public Health, *Hookworm Disease*, p. 17.

71. McCormack to Rose, July 31, 1912, ser. 2, box 3, folder 87, RSC. For similar enthusiasm, see McCormack to Rose, August 3, 9, November 25, December 7, 1912 (box 3, folder 88), and McCormack to Rose, September 22, 1913 (box 3, folder 90), ibid.

72. W. W. Richmond to McCormack, December 7, 1912 (box 3, folder 88), and McCormack to Ferrell, August 21, 27, 1913 (box 3, folder 90), ibid. For another account of Kentucky dispensaries, see "Report of the Educational Work for 1913, by the State Board of Health of Kentucky," ibid.

73. P. W. Covington to Ferrell, November 4, 1911, NCDHS; Ferrell, "The North Carolina Campaign against Hookworm," p. 133; C. L. Pridgen to Ferrell, November 26, 1911, and Ferrell to Pridgen, November 29, 1911, ibid. See also C. F. Strosnider to Ferrell, November 22, 1911, ibid.; Washburn, *As I Recall*, pp. 9–10.

74. Ferrell, "The North Carolina Campaign against Hookworm," pp. 133–34; Washburn, *As I Recall*, pp. 10–12. Rose describes the technique of P. W. Covington, one of the most effective campaigners in North Carolina, in Rose to Frederick T. Gates, August 14, 1911, ser. 2, box 5, folder 117, RSC.

75. Ferrell to Strosnider, October 5, 9, 1911, and Handbill, Nash County, May 1912, NCDHS; Washburn, *The Hookworm Campaign in Alamance County*, p. 16; R. N. Whitefield, circular letter, Houston, Miss., June 7, 1913, ser. 2, box 5, folder 108, RSC.

76. Washburn, *As I Recall*, pp. 18, 20; Ettling, *Germ of Laziness*, pp. 159–60.

77. Rose to Ferrell, July 18, 1911, ser. 2, box 6, folder 117, RSC; Ferrell, "The Relation of Hookworm Eradication to the Eradication of Other Preventable Diseases," ca. 1910, and "What the Rockefeller Sanitary Commission Can Do to Build Up County Health Work," ca. 1912, NCDHS.

78. Covington to Ferrell, January 22, 1914, ser. 2, box 6, folder 120, RSC.

79. Ferrell, circular to district directors, January 27, 1912, NCDHS.

80. K. P. Battle to Rose, carbon copy, January 18, 1912, B. W. Page to Ferrell, January 6, 1911, and T. E. Hughes to Ferrell, December 22, 1911, ibid.; Benjamin E. Washburn, "Criticisms of the Work of the Hookworm Commission in North Carolina and

Suggestions as to Township or Community Work as [a] Means of Eradicating Hookworm Disease," ca. 1914, ser. 2, box 5, folder 120, RSC.

81. Rankin to Malcolm Boton, January 10, 1912, Claude A. Smith to Rankin, June 12, 1912, Rankin to Smith, June 15, 1912, and Rankin to Stiles, August 10, 1912, NCDHS. The mountain mission reformer John C. Campbell came to a similar conclusion. He claimed that the dispensary campaign's effects were "greatly over-exaggerated." Campbell to John M. Glenn, March 26, 1913, box 5, folder entitled "So. Mountain Conference—1913–1919," JCODC. Another critic wrote that the dispensary "looked more like a patent medicine fake than any thing else." Malcolm Bolton to Rankin, January 4, 1912, NCDHS.

82. A. G. Fort to Rose, September 8, 21, 27, October 11, 1911 and Rose to Fort, September 25, 1911 (box 2, folder 71), J. LaBruce Ward to Rose, August 3, 1912 (box 7, folder 71), and Olin West to Rose, August 2, 1911 (box 8, folder 147), ser. 2, RSC. On Tennessee opposition, see also Tennessee Department of Public Health, *Hookworm Disease*, p. 23.

83. Morgan Smith to Rose, August 28, 1911 (folder 58), and C. W. Garrison to Rose, July 13, 1912, February 22, 1913, Rose to Garrison, February 27, 1913, R. J. Estes to C. W. Garrison, typed copy, January 6, 1913, and T. M. Fly to C. W. Garrison, typed copy, September 10, 1913 (folders 59–61), ser. 2, box 1, RSC.

84. Garrison to Rose, June 11, October 1, 1913, folders 60–61, ibid.

85. Jacocks to Ferrell, August 22, October 6, November 7, 1913, January 25, February 4, 8, 1914, and Ferrell to Jacocks, September 27, 1913 (box 6, folder 119; box 1, folders 61–62), and Garrison to Ferrell, October 11, 1913, November 27, 1914 (box 1, folders 61–62), ser. 2, RSC.

86. Florida's involvement dated back to 1903, when Hiram Byrd, assistant to state health officer Joseph Y. Porter, observed the prevalence of the disease and communicated his findings to local physicians. After 1908 physicians and teachers collaborated in a statewide campaign. Florida State Board of Health, *Twenty-first Annual Report* . . . , 1909, pp. 20–24; Porter to F. E. McClane, April 18, 1910; Porter to Henry Gatrell, ser. 46, box 18, folder 3, FSBH.

87. Coastal counties, where the soil was shell, and the northwestern part of the state, which was clay, had the lightest infection, while the interior counties of the peninsula had the heaviest infection. Porter to Wickliffe Rose, November 30, 1910, ser. 46, box 19, folder 7, FSBH.

88. G. H. Symmes to Porter, April 8, 1910, box 18, folder 3, FSBH.

89. Hiram Byrd to Charles W. Stiles, May 5, 1910 (folder 5), and Young to Joseph Y. Porter, April 15, 1910 (folder 3), box 18, FSBH.

90. Porter to Andrew Allen, May 9, 1910 (box 18, folder 5), Calvin T. Young to Porter, September 30, 1910 (box 19, folder 4), O. F. Green to Porter, October 14, 1910 (box 19, folder 6), George M. Floyd to State Board of Health, May 10, 1910 (box 18, folder 5), and B. Hinkley to Florida State Board of Health, June 26, 1911 (box 21, folder 4), FSBH. There were patients, wrote one physician, who felt that "you are scandalizing them when you say they have hook worms [. . . when another doctor] greets them with a smile of sarcasm and tells them that his good friends so & so are a little to[o] inthusiastic [*sic*] along that line." J. M. Anderson to Porter, June 23, 1911 (box 21, folder 4), FSBH.

91. *Florida Health Notes* 11 (February 1916): 53.

92. Calvin T. Young to Porter, August 27, 1912 (box 24, folder 3), Ernest W. Diggett to Porter, annual report for 1912, January 1913 (box 25, folder 4), and Porter to B. V. Elmore, October 9, 1912 (box 25, folder 6), FSBH; Florida State Board of Health, *Twenty-fourth Annual Report* . . ., 1912, pp. 89–90, 92–93.

93. Florida State Board of Health, *Twenty-fourth Annual Report* . . ., pp. 33, 94; Ernest W. Diggett to Porter, typed copy, January 1, 1913, and Calvin T. Young to Porter, January 1, 1913, ser. 46, box 25, folder 4, FSBH.

CHAPTER SIX

1. Swift, transcript of comments before proceedings of the National Child Labor Committee, 1915, San Francisco, NCLC.

2. Carlton, *Mill and Town in South Carolina*. See also Davidson, *Child Labor Legislation*; Newby, *Plain Folk in the New South*, chap. 17; DeNatale, "Bynum"; Locke, "The Struggle for the Mind."

3. Brandon, "Alexander Jeffrey McKelway," pp. 5–12; McKelway, "The Needs of the Cotton Mill Operatives," address at Berry School, Rome, Ga., March 25, 1909, and "Some Changes in North Carolina in Twenty Years," May 21, 1910, Alexander Jeffrey McKelway Papers, LC (hereafter cited as McKelway Papers/LC); McKelway, "The Church and Child Labor Reform," n.d., box 2, Alexander J. McKelway Papers, HF (hereafter cited as McKelway Papers/HF). The child was "the savior of the race," he wrote in another setting, and was "the harbinger of the Golden Age, when, as it has been pictured to us, the forces of greed and the forces of violence and the forces of cunning shall walk together in peaceful procession, while 'A little child shall lead them.'" McKelway, "Child Labor in Southern Industry," p. 436.

4. "The Child and the Golden Age," editorial, *Charlotte Presbyterian Standard*, February 1, 1905.

5. Philander P. Claxton, "A Substitute for Child Labor," *Child Labor Bulletin* 1 (June 1912): 7; John C. Campbell, "From Mountain Cabin to Cotton Mill," *Child Labor Bulletin* 2 (May 1913): 83–84; Alexander W. McAlister, "Is the Child Safe?" *Social Service Quarterly* 4 (April–June 1916): 29.

6. John C. Granbery, "Child Labor in Virginia," *Baltimore and Richmond Christian Advocate*, September 26, 1907; McKelway, "The Economic Fallacy of Child Labor," address at Child Welfare Exhibit, New York City, March 1, 1911, transcript of speech at Cooper Union, February 16, 1905, and "Some Changes in North Carolina in Twenty Years," address at Smithfield, N.C., May 21, 1910, McKelway Papers/LC.

7. Claxton, "A Substitute for Child Labor," p. 10; "Child Labor Reform," editorial, *Alabama Baptist*, February 9, 1910; McKelway, "Child Labor in Southern Industry," p. 436, "Child Labor and Democracy," *Child Labor Bulletin* 1 (June 1912): 123–24, and "The Conservation of Manhood, Womanhood, and Childhood in Industry," address at Delaware State Conference on Social Welfare Work, Wilmington, December 7, 1911, McKelway Papers/LC.

8. Charles Lee Coon, untitled MS, March 16, 1912, box 3, folder 48, Charles Lee

Coon Papers, SHC (hereafter cited as Coon Papers); Edward F. Brown, "Neglected Human Resources of the Gulf Coast States," *Child Labor Bulletin* 2 (May 1913): 115–16; "Child Labor," editorial, *Alabama Christian Advocate*, September 11, 1902.

9. McKelway, "Child Labor and Citizenship," n.d., McKelway Papers/LC. For a valuable discussion of child saving, see Hogan, *Class and Reform*, pp. 25–46, 51–60.

10. W. H. Oates, "Child Labor and Health," *Child Labor Bulletin* 2 (May 1913): 117.

11. McKelway to Rev. Dr. Laird, February 23, 1906, McKelway Papers/LC.

12. McKelway, "The Menace of Race-Degeneracy in America," undated MS, ibid. McKelway frequently compared the South's "decline" with England's. See, for example, "The Child Labor Problem—A Study in Degeneracy," paper read at the American Association for the Advancement of Science, New Orleans, January 1, 1906, and Statement before the North Carolina Legislation Committee, North Carolina House of Representatives, February 1905, ibid., and "The Child Labor Problem—A Study in Degeneracy," *Annals* 27.

13. "Child Labor," editorial, *Alabama Christian Advocate*, September 11, 1902; McKelway, "Child Labor and Citizenship," n.d., McKelway Papers/LC, and "The Child Labor Problem—A Study in Degeneracy," *Annals* 27, p. 313.

14. McKelway, "Child Labor in Its Relation in Education," undated MS, "Child Labor," address delivered at Texas State Conference of Charities, November 28, 1910, and "Conditions of Factory Labor in the South, and the Child Labor Question," address delivered before Conference on Southern Problems, University of the South, Sewanee, Tenn., July 5, 1909, McKelway Papers/LC; McKelway, "Child Labor in Southern Cotton Mills," *Annals* 27.

15. McKelway, "The Child Labor Problem—A Study in Degeneracy," pp. 324–25, speech in MS proceedings, NCLC, Third Annual Convention, Cincinnati, December 13–15, 1906, and undated conference address, NCLC.

16. McKelway, "Conditions of Factory Labor in the South, and the Child Labor Question"; "Child Labor and Democracy," *Child Labor Bulletin* 1 (June 1912): 125–26. See also McKelway, "The Relation Between Compulsory Education and the Restriction of Child Labor," undated address, McKelway Papers/LC; "Cheap Bodies, Cheaper Souls" and "Blooded Cattle, Bloodless Children," *Alabama Baptist*, February 1, 1907.

17. Anderson, "Child Labor Legislation," p. 500; McKelway, "Child Labor and Citizenship," n.d., McKelway Papers/LC, and "Conditions of Factory Labor in the South, and the Child Labor Question."

18. McKelway, "Child Wages in the Cotton Mills: Our Modern Feudalism," *Child Labor Bulletin* 2 (May 1913): 15–16; Murphy, *Problems of the Present South*, pp. 123–24; McKelway, "Child Labor and Citizenship," n.d., McKelway Papers/LC.

19. John C. Campbell to John M. Glenn, March 9, 1910, box 1, folder 14. JCODC; Charles Lee Coon, untitled MS, March 16, 1912, box 3, folder 38, Coon Papers; McKelway, "Conditions of Factory Labor in the South, and the Child Labor Question."

20. John Porter Hollis, "The Consequences of Child Labor," *Columbia State*, December 20, 1910; McKelway, "Child Labor—A Challenge to the Church," n.d., box 2, McKelway Papers/HF, and "Child Labor," address at Texas State Conference of Charities, November 28, 1910, McKelway Papers/LC.

21. McKelway, "Child Labor in Its Relation to Education," undated MS, and "Com-

pulsory Education and Child Labor Legislation," n.d., McKelway Papers/LC, and "Child Labor and Democracy," *Child Labor Bulletin* 1 (June 1912): 123–24; Mary L. McLendon et al. to the Georgia General Assembly, Georgia Department of Archives Records, GDAH; McKelway, "Child Wages in the Cotton Mills: Our Modern Feudalism," *Child Labor Bulletin* 2 (May 1913): 16; Claxton, "A Substitute for Child Labor," pp. 8–9; M. W. to the Editor, "Appeal of a Noble Woman," *Raleigh News and Observer*, February 5, 1903.

22. McKelway, "Child Labor in the South," "Child Wages in the Cotton Mills: Our Modern Feudalism," pp. 10, 11, "Child Labor and Democracy," *Child Labor Bulletin* 1 (June 1912): 125, and "The Fight to Save Children," *Alabama Baptist*, July 3, 1907; "Child-Slavery," editorial, *Charlotte Presbyterian Standard*, September 3, 1902.

23. McKelway, "Child Wages in the Cotton Mills: Our Modern Feudalism," pp. 11, 77; McKelway to Charles P. Neil, November 8, 1906, McKelway Papers/LC.

24. McKelway, "Child Labor in Southern Cotton Mills," *Annals* 27, pp. 259–60.

25. "Some Facts about Child Labor," editorial, *Charlotte Presbyterian Standard*, January 4, 1905; McKelway, transcript of a speech at Cooper Union, February 16, 1905, McKelway Papers/LC, and "Child Labor in Southern Cotton Mills," p. 262; Coon to William Louis Poteat, January 30, 1911, box 3, folder 31, Coon Papers.

26. McKelway, undated, untitled address, and "The Fight for Child Labor Reform in the Carolinas," undated speech, McKelway Papers/LC; W. A. Covington, quoted in McKelway, "Child Labor and Citizenship," n.d., ibid. See also McKelway to S. F. Parrott, January 8, 1909, and McKelway, "Child Labor in the South," undated speech at Buffalo, N.Y., ibid.; M. W. MacDonald, Reidsville, N.C., quoted in Coon, untitled MS, March 16, 1912, Coon Papers.

27. John M. Glenn to John C. Campbell, February 11, 1909, and Campbell to Glenn, March 2, 1910, box 1, folder 14, JCODC. See also Campbell to Glenn, March 9, 1910, ibid.

28. McKelway to the Editor of the *Baltimore Sun*, typed copy, April 30, 1910, McKelway Papers/LC; McKelway, untitled speech, ca. 1912, and "The Mill or the Farm," n.d., ibid.

29. McKelway, "Child Labor," address at Texas State Conference of Charities, November 28, 1910, ibid.

30. Campbell to John M. Glenn, March 2, 1910, box 1, folder 14, JCODC; Lawton Evans, quoted in Coon, untitled MS, March 16, 1912, box 3, folder 48, Coon Papers; A. H. Shannon, "Child Labor," *Alabama Christian Advocate*, September 11, 1902.

31. McKelway, "Child Labor—A Challenge to the Church," "Child Labor versus Industrial Education" (undated MS, McKelway Papers/LC), and "Our Modern Feudalism," p. 10.

32. W. H. Swift, "The Last Stand," *Child Labor Bulletin* 2 (May 1914): 87.

33. Hollis, "The Consequences of Child Labor"; Alexander W. McAlister, "Is the Child Safe?," *Social Service Quarterly* 4 (April–June 1916): 31; McKelway, "Duty of a Rich Nation to Take Care of Her Children," n.d., McKelway Papers/LC.

34. "What Are You Doing to Abolish Child Labor?," editorial, *Alabama Baptist*, July 3, 1907; McKelway, "The Curse of Child Labor," address quoted in *Nashville American*, January 29, 1906, box 2, McKelway Papers/HF, and "The Abolition of Child Labor," address at the National Conference of Charities and Corrections, June 13, 1912, McKelway Papers/LC.

35. On the NCLC campaign, see Grantham, *Southern Progressivism*, pp. 191–99; Davidson, *Child Labor Legislation*; Trattner, *Crusade for the Children*.

36. Grantham, *Southern Progressivism*, p. 181; Davidson, *Child Labor Legislation*, pp. 18–51. For the results of Ashby's efforts, see Ashby, "Child-Labor in Southern Cotton Mills"; MacFayden, "Child Labor in the South." See also similar efforts by Leonora Beck Ellis in her "Child Labor Legislation in the South," "Child Operatives in Southern Mills," "Educating Southern Factory Children," and "Factory Children of Georgia."

37. Emily Stewart Harrison, "Irene Ashby: A Type of the New Woman," ser. 3, box 13, folder 12, ESH.

38. Irene Ashby Macfayden to Nina De Cottes, March 22, 1902, W. P. Browne Collection, ADAH; Harrison, "Irene Ashby: A Type of the New Woman."

39. Mrs. E. L. Bailey, "Mississippi," *Child Labor Bulletin* 2 (May 1913): 129. For a similar effort in Alabama, see "A Better Child Labor Law Needed," editorial, *Alabama Baptist*, February 6, 1907.

40. Owen R. Lovejoy to Charles Lee Coon, April 21, 1909, Coon to A. M. Scales, October 4, 1910, Coon to Swift, January 19, 1912, McKelway to Coon, October 12, 1910, December 9, 1911, Coon to McKelway, October 13, 1910, Coon to NCLC Board of Trustees, December 1, 1911, Lovejoy to Coon, December 8, 1911, and Lovejoy to McKelway, December 21, 1911, box 3, folders 29, 36–37, Coon Papers. To my knowledge, none of the state NCLC committees' records have survived or exist in manuscript repositories. Moreover, the records of the national offices of the NCLC suggest little activity at the state level.

41. Lovejoy to Coon, April 21, 1909, ibid.

42. W. H. Swift, circular letter, January 2, 1913, Owen Lovejoy to Swift, May 21, 1912, and Coon to NCLC Board of Trustees, December 1, 1911, boxes 3–4, folders 36, 39, 42, ibid. "The result of making concessions in the past," wrote Coon, had "been to keep any effective legislation off the statute books." Coon to Edwin Mims, October 20, 1910, folder 29, ibid. Later, Coon was even more direct. In 1913 he declared that he was "ready to make a straight fight from now on, or I am ready to resign from this committee. I do not care to be longer connected with the movement, unless we can get rid of the policy of asking mill men what we may do." Coon to Swift, March 10, 1913, box 4, folder 43, ibid.

43. Poe to Coon, April 27, 1911, and Poe to Swift, May 16, 1912, box 3, folders 33, 39, ibid. Coon disagreed, stating that if the state committee accepted outside funds, it must acknowledge the outsider's influence. Coon to Poe, May 21, 1912, box 3, folder 39, ibid.

44. See Coon to Poe, April 28, 1911, Coon to Bailey, September 19, 1910, and Coon to Alexander J. McKelway, September 19, 1910, box 3, folders 29, 33, ibid.

45. "Reports of George Z. Owen of Georgia Cotton Mills, March 1915," entry dated March 9, 1915, NCLC; George F. Ross, "Extending Medical Inspection from Schools to Mills," *Child Labor Bulletin* 1 (June 1912): 7; Harvey P. Vaughn, "Child Labor in Georgia," April 1913, and Lewis W. Hine, "Report on Child Labor Conditions in the Oyster Industry in Some of the Southern States," February 10, 1911, NCLC.

46. Lewis W. Hine, "Alabama Investigation," November 1910, and Harvey P. Vaughn, "Child Labor in Georgia," NCLC.

47. Coon, untitled MS, March 16, 1912, Coon Papers; "Reports of George A. Owen of Georgia Cotton Mills, March 1915," entry dated March 9, 1915, and Lewis W. Hine,

"Child Labor in the Cotton Mills of Mississippi," May 1911, NCLC; Thomas F. Parker, "The South Carolina Cotton Mill," pp. 331–32; Vaughn, "Child Labor in Georgia."

48. Lewis W. Hine, "Child Labor in Mississippi," November 1913, NCLC.

49. Hine, "Report on Child Labor Conditions in the Oyster Industry in Some of the Southern States," Mrs. E. L. Bailey, "Mississippi," pp. 132–33, Brown, "Child Labor in the Gulf Coast Canneries," March 1913, and Bremer, "Report of Investigation of Shrimp Canning Factory at Houma, La.," March 11, 1914, NCLC; McKelway, "Child Labor in Mississippi," n.d. (ca. 1911), McKelway Papers/LC.

50. Herschel H. Jones, "Night Messengers in Louisville, Ky.," December 1913, and Harry M. Bremer, "Night Messengers of Virginia," November–December 1913, NCLC; Edward F. Brown, "The Demoralizing Environment of Night Messengers in Southern Cities," *Child Labor Bulletin* 2 (May 1913): 139–40; "Reports of George Z. Owen of Georgia Cotton Mills, March 1915," entries dated March 10, 22, 1915, NCLC; Mrs. W. L. Murdoch, "Conditions of the Child Employing Industries in the South," *Child Labor Bulletin* 2 (May 1913): 125.

51. McKelway, "Child Labor in North Carolina," undated address, McKelway Papers/ LC; "Can Georgia Do It?," *Outlook*; McKelway, "Child Labor in Southern Industry," *Annals* 25, p. 435.

52. McKelway, "The Present Status of Child Labor and Its Regulation in the Cotton Mills," ca. 1910, McKelway Papers/LC; R. F. Campbell to Coon, September 28, 1910, and J. J. Hall to Coon, September 29, 1910, box 3, folder 29, Coon Papers; W. H. Swift, "The Campaign in North Carolina: The Mountain Whites—By One of Them," *Child Labor Bulletin* 2 (May 1913): 96, 99.

53. McKelway, "Our Modern Feudalism," p. 13; Fleisher, "Investigation of Cotton Mills, Stonewall, Mississippi," January 2–4, 1912, and Hine, "Child Labor in Mississippi," November 1913, NCLC.

54. Thomas F. Parker, "The South Carolina Cotton Mill," pp. 336–37; Few, "Constructive Philanthropy," pp. 82–85; L. F. Groves to Coon, February 25, 1913, box 4, folder 42, Coon Papers.

55. "Strikers Want Children under 14 Yrs. Kept Out," unidentified clipping, box 1, folder entitled "Press Coverage, Men & Religion, Union Activity (1914–1917)," FBCM.

56. When Coon discovered, for example, that a Reidsville, N.C., worker was willing to report on mill conditions, he eagerly wrote for details. The worker, a Mr. M. W. McDonald, who claimed to represent the "Better Class of the Mill People," asserted that workers opposed child labor and endorsed legislation to regulate it but noted that there would be "objections" to any attempt to raise the age limit above twelve. Coon subsequently used McDonald to document the existence of "dinner toters"—fathers who lived off the income of their children—in North Carolina mills. Yet, betraying an uneasiness about the worker's reliability that suggested important cultural differences, Coon later wrote to find out what "kind of man" McDonald was. He wanted verification about his "credibility" and whether he was "all right morally and other wise." Coon to S. G. Harden, February 20, 1911, Coon to M. W. McDonald, February 14, 1911, and McDonald to Coon, February 15, 17, 19, 1911, box 3, folder 32, Coon Papers.

57. Constance Ashton Myers, notes on Elisabeth Perry Collins Interview, Constance Ashton Myers Papers, SCL (hereafter cited as Myers Papers). On the background of south-

ern suffragists, see Wheeler, "New Women of the New South"; Goodman, *Bitter Harvest*; Talmadge, *Rebecca Latimer Felton*; Taylor, *The Woman Suffrage Movement in Tennessee*; Johnson, "Kate Gordon."

58. Clipping, *St. Louis Globe-Democrat*, June 22, 1913, Scrapbooks, Pattie Ruffner Jacobs Papers, BPL (hereafter cited as Jacobs Papers); Goodrich, "Romance and Reality"; Allen, "The Woman Suffrage Movement in Alabama," *Alabama Review* 11. See also A. Caswell Ellis, "Why Men Need Equal Suffrage for Women," ca. June 1918, box SP362, Alexander Caswell Ellis Papers, BTH (hereafter cited as Ellis Papers).

59. Cunningham died in 1962 at age eighty-two. "Noted Suffragette, 'Minnie Fish,' Dies," undated clipping, Jessie Daniel Ames Papers, TSL. Jacobs offered dynamic leadership. According to a contemporary, she was regarded as "a woman of exceptional accomplishments and mental capacity" who was a "splendid and convincing talker." Lee N. Allen, entry in NAW, 2:266; *Montgomery Advertiser*, June 7, 1919, clipping, Alabama Equal Suffrage Association Records, ADAH.

60. After a speech to a Kentucky mountain town in 1919, Valentine's audience was "filled with tears." A "grim-faced mountaineer" remarked that she was "the best I've ever heard, man or woman, and I'm for her." Anne Firor Scott, entry in NAW, 1:233, quoted from Sophonisba P. Breckinridge, *Madeline McDowell Breckinridge*, p. 235. For a fuller treatment of Breckinridge, see Porter, "Madeline McDowell Breckinridge"; Hay, "Madeline McDowell Breckinridge"; Klotter, *The Breckinridges of Kentucky, 1760–1981*. On Valentine, see Lloyd C. Taylor, Jr., entry in NAW, 3:504; quoted from Glasgow, *The Woman Within* (1954), pp. 185–86. On the occasion of her fifty-fourth birthday, a fellow suffragist wrote a poem extolling Valentine's virtues: "If your years of life were numbered / By the good deeds you have done, / By the kind words you have spoken / And the warm friends you have won, / Then your birthdays would be countless / As the green leaves on the trees, / As the bright stars in the heavens / And the white sands of the seas." Alice Overbey Taylor, February 4, 1919, VWSP.

61. Clay-Clopton, undated, untitled address (#1 in folder), Clement Claiborne Clay Papers, DUL; Constance Ashton Myers, notes on Jessie Stokely Burnett (b. 1882) Interview, April 6, 1974, Myers Papers.

62. Breckinridge, speech before Virginia legislature, 1913, BFP.

63. Townshend to Edwin Yates Webb, March 1, 1914, and Valentine, speech, September 7, 1916, VWSP; Clay to Josephine Henry, October 27, 1891, box 1, folder 3, Laura Clay Papers, KUL.

64. Erminia T. Folsom, "Woman Suffrage," n.d., box 1985/119-1, folder 15, Erminia Thompson Folsom Papers, TSL (hereafter cited as Folsom Papers).

65. H. Augusta Howard, "A Stinging Rebuke for Atlanta's Pharisees," *The Woman's Tribune*, December 5, 1891, clipping, file 2: Subjects, box 105, Georgia Department of Archives Records, GDAH; clipping in the *New Orleans Item*, 1914, box 3, folder 2, Ethel Hutson Papers, Manuscripts Department, Tulane University Library, New Orleans (hereafter cited as Hutson Papers); Madeline McDowell Breckinridge, speech reported in the *Lynchburg Daily Advance*, May 14, 1913, clipping, BFP.

66. Bailey, "In Behalf of Ratifying the Anthony Amendment by the Special Session of the [North Carolina] Legislature," July 21, 1920, box 102, Josiah William Bailey Papers, DUL. Texas male suffragist A. Caswell Ellis wrote that votes for women would "protect

us and our government from our own one-sided masculine view of life." Women were "by nature more concerned than men with these vital questions of personal relation and human welfare, and when women have adequate voice in our government we can hope for wiser and more speedy solution of these grave problems." Ellis, "Why Men Need Equal Suffrage for Women," ca. June 1918, box SP362, Ellis Papers.

67. Folsom, "Woman Suffrage"; Allen, "The Woman Suffrage Movement in Alabama," M.S. thesis, p. 44; Cathcart, notes for a speech, ca. 1920, Ellen Evans Cathcart Papers, SCL (hereafter cited as Cathcart Papers).

68. Hundley, letter to the Editor, *Greene County Democrat*, July 12, 1915, clipping, Bossie O'Brien Hundley Scrapbook, BPL.

69. "Woman's Sphere in 1915: One Woman's Story," box 1, folder 15, Georgia Woman Suffrage Collection, GDAH.

70. Mary Pollard Clarke, "Report of the Chairman of Political Study and Research of the Equal Suffrage League of Virginia," 1916, "Brief for Federal Suffrage Amendment," 1918, Adele Clark, reply to the *Roanoke Times*, ca. January 1913, and "Unrepresented" to the Editor, *Richmond Virginian*, ca. 1915, VWSP.

71. "Unveiling [*sic*] of the Lila Meade Valentine Memorial," October 20, 1936, VWSP; Madeline McDowell Breckinridge, "The Prospect for Woman Suffrage in the South," address at the National Suffrage Convention, Louisville, October 29, 1911, *Lexington Morning Herald*, June 14, 1912, clipping, BFP.

72. "Ten Reasons Why Mothers Should Have the Vote," 1919, VWSP; A. Caswell Ellis, "Woman and the Home," Austin *Texas Democrat*, May 2, 1919, box SP88, Ellis Papers; Mary Johnston, undated speech at Lynchburg entitled "Speech III," box 27, Mary Johnston Papers, UVA (hereafter cited as Johnston Papers); Eleonore Raoul to the Editor, *Atlanta Journal*, July 9, 1915, clipping, Letter and Personal Papers, ser. 1, subser. SS12, box 33, folder 1, RFP.

73. "Outline of Progress of Women in Louisiana, 1900–1917," MS, ca. 1917, box 2, folder 2, Hutson Papers; Columbia, S.C., Equal Suffrage League Minutes, February 9, 1915, Ida Salley Reamer Papers, SCL (hereafter cited as Reamer Papers); Judith Hyams Douglas, speech before ERA, 1910, folder 20, and unidentified newspaper clipping, February 12, 1910, Judith Hyams Douglas Scrapbook, Judith Hyams Douglas Papers, LLMV (hereafter cited as Douglas Papers); Clipping from *New Orleans Item*, February 22, 1913, box 3, folder 1, Hutson Papers.

74. Clipping from *Birmingham News*, September 26, 1915, BESAH; clipping in unidentified newspaper, June 24, 1914, South Carolina League of Women Voters Records, SCL; Myers, Collins Interview, Myers Papers. On the NCLC meeting, see Allen, "The Woman Suffrage Movement in Alabama," M.S. thesis, p. 18.

75. Madeline McDowell Breckinridge, "The Educational Work of the Kentucky Federation of Women's Clubs," photostat from General Federation of Women's Clubs, *Ninth Biennial Convention Proceedings*, June 1908, p. 294, BFP.

76. Ibid., pp. 295–97.

77. Resolution, handwritten draft, June 1909, Madeline McDowell Breckinridge to J. A. Sullivan, circular letter, November 26, 1909, and Breckinridge, "A Mother's 'Sphere,'" n.d., BFP.

78. *Lexington Morning Herald*, March 25, 1912, clipping, BFP.

79. Johnston, speech before Woman's College alumnae, May 31, 1910, box 27, Johnston Papers.

80. Mary C. Sumner to Edward J. Gay, December 13, 1918, box 50, folder 432, EJG; Johnston, speech at Philadelphia, November 1911, and undated speech, box 27, Johnston Papers.

81. Johnston, undated speech before Woman's College Alumnae, undated, untitled speech, and "Speech III," n.d., box 27, Johnston Papers.

82. Johnston, speech before Woman's College Alumnae, May 31, 1910, ibid.; Clay-Clopton, undated, untitled address, Laura Clay Papers, KUL.

83. Raoul to the Editor, *Atlanta Journal*, July 9, 1915, ser. 1, subser. 12, box 33, folder 1, RFP.

84. Johnston, speech before Woman's College Alumnae, May 31, 1910.

85. Mrs. Sidney M. Ullman, "Equal Pay for Equal Work—Why Not?," *Birmingham Age-Herald*, August 19, 1915, BESA; Erminia T. Folsom, "Women and Work" and "The Ballot," both undated speeches, and "Women's Bondage," undated speech, box 1985/119-1, folder 15, Folsom Papers.

86. Joan P. Bentley to Edward J. Gay, December 16, 1918, box 50, folder 433, EJG; Judith Hyams Douglas, speech, 1908, and "Women and Ancient Custom," undated speech, folder 20, Douglas Papers.

87. Jessie E. Townshend, "President [of Norfolk Equal Suffrage League] Outlines Summer Work for the League," n.d., VWSP.

88. Johnston, speech before Woman's College Alumnae, May 31, 1910, and speech at a suffrage rally, May 26, 1910, box 27, Johnston Papers.

89. Johnston, speech at suffrage rally, May 26, 1910.

90. Valentine, address at annual meeting of Richmond Equal Suffrage League, January 7, 1919, VWSP.

91. Wellford to Thomas Staples Martin, draft letter, February 15, 1918, Robert Wellford Papers, UVA (hereafter cited as Wellford Papers).

92. "Report of the Kentucky Equal Rights Association for the Year 1912–13," *Report of the Twenty-fourth Annual Convention of the Kentucky Equal Rights Association Held at Louisville, Kentucky, November 20, 21 and 22, 1913* (Louisville: N.p., n.d.), BFP; Mary Johnston, speech at suffrage rally, May 26, 1910, box 27, Johnston Papers; MS history of the Virginia Equal Suffrage League, August 7, 1920, Wellford Papers; Spiers, "The Woman Suffrage Movement in New Orleans," pp. 25–27; Johnson, "The Woman Suffrage Movement in Florida," pp. 29–33.

93. Mary Hohnes Martin to the South Carolina Equal Suffrage League, June 15, 1920, Reamer Papers; "Equal Suffrage League Thrives," *Columbia State*, April 19, 1914, clipping, Cathcart Papers; Emily McDougald to Breckinridge, October 7, 1914, BFP; *Birmingham News*, September 26, 1915, clipping, BESA; Jacobs, speech at the first annual meeting of the Birmingham Equal Suffrage Association, in Amelia Worthington, ed., "Woman Suffrage: A Department Conducted by the Birmingham Equal Suffrage Association," *Birmingham News*, June 1, 1913, Scrapbooks, Jacobs Papers; Alabama Equal Suffrage Association Minutes, January 29, 1913; *Birmingham News*, May 9, 1915, clipping, and President's Report, Alabama Equal Suffrage Association, February 12, 1917, AESA.

94. Taylor, "The Woman Suffrage Movement in Texas," pp. 194–97, 200–204.

95. MS history of the Virginia Equal Suffrage League, August 7, 1920, Wellford Papers; "Brief for Federal Suffrage Amendment," 1918, VWSP; Allen, "The Woman Suffrage Movement in Alabama," M.S. thesis, p. 26. As a Georgia suffragist explained, leaders proposed to focus on "their more benighted neighbors in the Country Districts." Emily McDougald to Breckinridge, October 7, 1914, BFP.

96. Valentine to Jessie E. Townshend, May 29, 1915, VWSP; Minutes, Executive Committee, October 17, 1917, AESA.

97. Valentine to Mary Johnston, July 17, 1910, box 7, Johnston Papers; Breckinridge, speech before Virginia legislature, 1913, BFP; Minutes, Executive Committee, Alabama Equal Suffrage Association, October 12, 1913, AESA.

98. Minutes, Executive Committee, Alabama Equal Suffrage Association, June 9, 1917, AESA.

99. MS history of the Virginia Equal Suffrage League, August 7, 1920, Wellford Papers; *Birmingham News*, ca. 1917, clipping, BESA; Bossie O'Brien Hundley, "Report of the Chairman of the Legislative Committee of the Alabama Equal Suffrage Association," 1916, AESA.

100. Taylor, "The Woman Suffrage Movement in Texas," pp. 208–15.

CHAPTER SEVEN

1. George W. Simons, Jr., "Report of Health Campaign in Escambia County [Fla.] Conducted by Sanitary Inspectors of the Bureau of Engineering, State Board of Health, 1919," ca. November 1919, ser. 46, box 36, folder 1, FSBH; Coon, address at organization of Wilson County, N.C., Anti-Tuberculosis Association, 1910, box 3, folder 30, Coon Papers.

2. W. A. Plecker to Allen W. Freeman, January 11, 1911, RSC; petition, Cherokee County Board of Education, to State Board of Health, December 5, 1914, NCDHS; T. M. Young to State Board of Health, July 22, 1920, ser. 5, box 75, NCDPI; George W. Simons, Jr., "Report of Health Campaign in Palm Beach County Conducted by Sanitary Inspectors of the Bureau of Engineering, State Board of Health, Jacksonville, Florida, November 1919," and "Report of Health Campaign in Escambia County Conducted by Sanitary Inspectors of the Bureau of Engineering, State Board of Health, 1919," ca. November 1919, ser. 46, box 36, folder 1, FSBH.

3. Rockefeller Sanitary Commission, *Fifth Annual Report*, pp. 22–23; *Bulletin of the North Carolina Board of Health* 25 (December 1910): 427; Ferrell, *The Rural School and Hookworm Disease*, p. 41; Georgia Department of Education, *Annual Report*, 1911, pp. 99–106.

4. *Bulletin of the North Carolina Board of Health* 25 (December 1910): 414–15; Dresslar, *Rural Schoolhouses*, p. 141; Cochran, *History of the Public-School Education in Florida*, p. 172. See also Ettling, *Germ of Laziness*, p. 219.

5. Evelyn B. Russ to Florida State Board of Health, August 21, 1916; Porter to Russ, August 22, 1916, ser. 46, box 30, folder 6, FSBH.

6. George W. Simons, Jr., "Report of Health Campaign in Escambia County [Fla.]

Conducted by Sanitary Inspectors of the Bureau of Engineering, State Board of Health, 1919"; Woofter, *Teaching in Rural Schools*, pp. 39–41; Freeman, "Rural Sanitation," p. 870; Florida Superintendent of Public Instruction, *Biennial Report, 1912–1914*, p. 268; Cook, *Schoolhouse Sanitation*, pp. 27–28.

7. Louis Leroy, comment in Barbour, "Importance of Medical Inspection in Schools," p. 188; Woofter, *Teaching in Rural Schools*, pp. 297–98.

8. Quoted in Ferrell, *The Rural School and Hookworm Disease*, p. 23. On the distribution of a similar hookworm catechism, see Ettling, *Germ of Laziness*, 147. For examples of a hookworm quiz, see Freeman to Rose, February 17, 1912, RSC; North Carolina Superintendent of Public Instruction, *Biennial Report . . . for . . . 1912–1913 and 1913–1914*, p. 19.

9. Woofter, *Teaching in Rural Schools*, pp. 298–305 (quotation, p. 298). See also Eggleston and Bruère, *Work of the Rural School*, p. 35.

10. Ferrell, *The Rural School and Hookworm Disease*, p. 24; Georgia Department of Education, *Annual Report, 1911*, pp. 107–39; North Carolina Superintendent of Public Instruction, *Biennial Report . . . for . . . 1912–1913 and 1913–1914*, pp. 25–26.

11. Ritchie, *Primer of Sanitation*, pp. 170–73 (quotations, p. 173).

12. William A. Link, *Hard Country*, chaps. 2, 6.

13. On medical inspection, see Chapin, *A Report on State Public Health Work*, p. 155; Orr, *History of Education in Georgia*, p. 271; *As I Recall*, pp. 40–41. The best account of the impact of medical inspection nationally is Burrow, *Organized Medicine in the Progressive Era*, pp. 93–95.

14. James Y. Joyner to George M. Cooper, July 22, 1918, ser. 5, box 63, NCDPI.

15. Eggleston and Bruère, *Work of the Rural School*, p. 27; *Bulletin of the North Carolina Board of Health* 26 (June 1911): 174–75.

16. Jones, "Medical Inspection of Children in Rural Schools," pp. 199–200; Washburn, *History of the North Carolina State Board of Health*, p. 51. These dental clinics were operated for both blacks and whites. As director of the North Carolina program, George M. Cooper wrote: "We look on negroes as people exactly like we do whites"; disease did not "make a distinction between attacking whites and blacks." Cooper to N. C. Newbold, December 20, 1923, and Newbold to Cooper, December 18, 1923, NCDHS. On the dental clinics, see Margaret McQueen to Cooper, December 29, 1923, NCDHS.

17. Report of H. O. Snow, Tampa, January 1, 1919, in Florida State Board of Health, *Thirtieth Annual Report . . .*, 1918. Also see Report of the Assistant Commissioner of Health (app. 1), *Annual Report of the Health Commissioner to the Governor of Virginia for the Year Ending September 30, 1915*, pp. 71–81.

18. W. S. Rankin to R. L. Daniels, March 15, 1913, NCDHS.

19. W. S. Rankin, Annual Report, 1917, NCDHS; comment by Ennion G. Williams in Pope, "Factors Involved in Medical Inspection," p. 209; Cooper, "Local Health Work," p. 555, and Cooper, "Medical Inspection of Schools in North Carolina," pp. 112–14; Joseph Y. Porter, February 2, 1916, ser. 46, box 30, folder 1, FSBH.

20. Joseph Y. Porter to Oliver J. Miller, February 2, 1916 (box 30, folder 1), Calvin D. Christ to Porter, October 9, 1916 (box 31, folder 2), and Elsie Louise Forrest to Porter, October 2, 1916 (box 31, folder 2), ser. 46, FSBH; Flora M. Ray to George M. Cooper, November 30, 1923, and Geneva Sykes to Roy C. Mitchell, July 27, 1923, NCDHS. Porter

was opposed to the Florida school inspection law in 1915 because he believed it could not be enforced effectively. See Florida State Board of Health, *Twenty-seventh Annual Report . . .*, 1915, pp. 38–39.

21. Barbour, "Importance of Medical Inspection in Schools," p. 187. For more on visiting nurses see Dodd, "Opportunities of the Rural Public Health Nurse," p. 659; Flannagan, "Rural School Inspection," p. 113; Pope, "Factors Involved in Medical Inspection," pp. 207–9; Katherine C. Devine to T. H. Harris, May 15, 1923, LDE; T. B. Attmore to George M. Cooper, February 12, 1923, and Cooper to Attmore, February 17, 1923, NCDHS.

22. Barbour, "Importance of Medical Inspection in Schools," p. 186.

23. The Adenoid and Tonsil clubs paid the surgical expenses of at least two indigent children per community. Washburn, *History of the North Carolina State Board of Health*, pp. 50–51; *North Carolina Health Bulletin* 37 (October 1918): 105–6. On the clubs, see James Y. Joyner to George M. Cooper, September 25, 1916, ser. 5, box 52, NCDPI; Cooper to Watson Smith Rankin, April 4, 1922, Birdie Dunn to J. S. Mitchener, June 10, 1923, Geneva Sykes to Roy Mitchell, December 12, 1923, and Sykes to Cooper, March 4, 1924, NCDHS. On dental clinics, see T. H. Harris to Joe Farrar, March 6, 1922, LDE.

24. Quotation from *Bulletin of the North Carolina Board of Health* 27 (June 1912): 104. See also Flannagan, "Medical Inspection of Rural Schools," pp. 125–26; Carl A. Grote, "Full Time Health Officer Work in Walker County [Ala.]," *Southern Medical Journal* 8, no. 12 (1915): 1061.

25. W. B. Keating, monthly report for February 1922, ser. 46, box 38, folder 2, FSBH.

26. Dresslar, "The Duty of the State," pp. 257–64 (quotations, p. 258).

27. See Fosdick, *Adventure in Giving*; William A. Link, *Hard Country*.

28. B. W. Torreyson to Abraham Flexner, ser. 1.1, box 22, folder 191, GEB. For the gradual shifting of this office from university to state control, see John C. Futrell to Wallace Buttrick, April 8, 1916, ibid. For a dissenting voice in the transition from university to state bureaucratic control, see E. C. Branson to Buttrick, memorandum, July 1919, box 3, folder 127, Eugene Cunningham Branson Papers, SHC (hereafter cited as Branson Papers).

29. "Summary of Reports of Mr. J. B. Hobdy[,] State Agent for Rural Schools in Alabama[,] July 1, 1915 to January 1, 1916," in Hobdy to Abraham Flexner, May 16, 1917, and Feagin to Flexner, April 21, 1916, ser. 1.1, box 18, folder 155, GEB.

30. J. L. Bond to Abraham Flexner, July 16, 1916 (box 26, folder 233), and Flexner to W. H. Smith, December 11, 1914 (box 97, folder 233), ser. 1.1, GEB. On the Montgomery County demonstration program, see Feagin to Wallace Buttrick, June 9, 1917, Flexner to Feagin, June 12, 1917, May 24, 1918, March 1, 1919, May 28, 1920, Feagin to Flexner, October 1, 1917, April 27, November 12, 1918, April 16, 1919, Jackson Davis to Flexner, May 9, 1918, Flexner to A. F. Harman, March 28, 1921, Harman to Flexner, April 7, 1921, E. C. Sage to Harman, March 2, 1922, and Harman to Sage, March 10, 1922, box 18, folders 156–57, ibid.

31. Fosdick, *Story of the Rockefeller Foundation*, p. 32.

32. International Health Board, Report of the General Director, *Rockefeller Foundation, Annual Report*, 1920, pp. 109–10, and 1922, p. 100.

33. Ferrell to Platt W. Covington, January 9, 1923 (box 67, folder 953), and Ferrell to Marshall C. Balfour, September 27, 1927 (box 112, folder 1528), ser. 1.1, IHB.

34. Working in states and localities across the South, Covington's specialty was in arousing local sentiment to endorse sufficient public funding of health activities. Ferrell described his role in 1922 as "assisting states which have not yet organized county health work, and those which do not have state directors." Ferrell to P. E. Blackerby, January 19, 1922, box 129, folder 1725, ibid.

35. See, for example, C. B. Crittenden to Ferrell, February 27, March 7, 1923, and Ferrell to Crittenden, March 3, 1923, box 157, folder 2057, ibid.

36. "Confidential Report of Mr. [Courtenay] Dinwiddie's Visit to the Rutherford County, Tennessee, Child Health Demonstration, November 22–23, 1924," and "Report, Athens Child Health Demonstration, 1924," box 2, folder 25, CF/CHD, p. 39; "A Rosenwald Nurse," ca. 1929, box 224, folder 5, JRF.

37. International Health Commission, Report of the Director General, *Rockefeller Foundation, Annual Report*, 1913–14, pp. 13, 15–16; Ferrell to Rose, January 6, 1912, ser. 2, box 5, folder 118, RSC; Ferrell, "What the Rockefeller Sanitary Commission Can Do to Build Up County Health Work," ca. 1912, NCDHS; Julian D. Maynard to Ferrell, July 26, 1913, Ferrell to Pridgen, September 22, October 1, 1913, and Pridgen to Ferrell, November 21, 26, 1913, ser. 2, box 5, folder 129, RSC; William A. Link, "'The Harvest Is Ripe'"; International Health Board, Report of the Director General, *Rockefeller Foundation, Annual Report*, 1916, p. 79.

38. Nonetheless, Maynard advised future community health programs to avoid selecting "an ignorant community as I did to do your first work" because health officials would need "all the support and backing you can possibly get from the community." Maynard to G. F. Leonard, April 8, 1914, NCDHS.

39. M. K. Gilliam to E. L. Flanagan, April 6, 1916, ser. 1.2, box 28, folder 427, IHB; fragment of press release, 1914, Merrill E. Champion, circular letter, 1914, Covington to B. W. Page, circular letter, 1914, and Rankin, "The Community Aspect of the Health Problem," NCDHS; Pridgen to Ferrell, April 3, 1914, G. F. Leonard to Ferrell, May 7, 1914, and Ferrell to Rose, July 1, 1914, ser. 2, box 5, folders 120, 122, RSC.

40. Rankin to George M. Cooper, typed copy, September 24, 1914, Ferrell to Rankin, September 22, 24, 1914, Ferrell to Cooper, typed copy, September 22, 1914, and Rankin to Ferrell, September 24–26, 1914, ser. 2, box 5, folder 121, RSC. Following the successful experiment at Knotts Island, the IHC during 1914 extended the intensive model to five other communities in North Carolina, one in Virginia, three in Louisiana, and two in South Carolina—all states that had successfully completed dispensary campaigns. In 1915 the program was extended to two Mississippi communities. On the latter, see W. S. Leathers, "The Report of the Director of Public Health," in Mississippi State Board of Health, *Report . . . from June 1, 1913, to June 30, 1915*, pp. 23–24.

41. Ferrell to Benjamin E. Washburn, January 6, 1919, NCDHS; International Health Commission, Report of the Director General, in *Rockefeller Foundation, Annual Report*, 1915, pp. 55–61, 100–102.

42. Ferrell to W. W. Dinsmore, July 1, 1915 (ser. 1.2, box 1, folder 3), and Ferrell to Wickliffe Rose, June 16, 1916 (ser. 1.1, box 14, folder 222), IHB; Louisiana State Board of Health, *Biennial Report . . ., 1914–1915*, pp. 19–20; "Proposal by the Louisiana State Board of Health for a Demonstration of Intensive Measures in Rural Sanitation," enclosure in Ferrell to Oscar Dowling, January 12, 1915, ser. 1.2, box 2, folder 25, IHB. For an

overview of the emerging partnership between the IHC and southern state boards of health, see Ferrell to Rose, memorandum, July 1, 1915, ser. 1.1, box 3, folder 49, IHB. For other examples of similar arrangements, see Ferrell to Dinsmore, July 1, 1915 (ser. 1.2, box 1, folder 3), W. S. Leathers to Ferrell, February 26, 1916 (ser. 1.2, box 24, folder 381), and Rose to A. G. Fort, March 31, 1916 (ser. 1.2, box 24, folder 364), IHB.

43. Ferrell to Rose, memorandum, July 1, 1915.

44. Washburn, *As I Recall*.

45. Harry S. Mustard, "Report [of the] Child Health Demonstration[,] Rutherford County[,] Tenn.[,] January–September 1924," folder 34, CF/CHD.

46. E. C. Branson, "Whole Time Health Officers and Public Health Nurses," May 13, [1917?], Branson Papers.

47. Washburn, "The Wilson County, North Carolina, Campaign against Soil Pollution," 1917, NCDHS; Ferrell to Washburn, July 14, 31, 1916, ser. 1.2, box 26, folder 399, IHB; International Health Board, Report of the Director General, *Rockefeller Foundation, Annual Report*, 1916, pp. 56–57, 84–85. According to the Rural Sanitation Act of 1917, the General Assembly appropriated $15,000 on the condition that it be matched by IHB funds. The state sought a goal of adding six to ten counties during the first year, two to five more the second year, and four to five the third year. Rankin, Annual Report, 1917, NCDHS.

48. Washburn, "Summary of Co-Operative County Health Work in North Carolina," ca. 1917, Field Office Files, ser. 1, box 1, folder 4, Benjamin Earle Washburn Papers, RAC (hereafter cited as Washburn Papers); Washburn, "The North Carolina Plan of County Health Work," paper read at the Southern Medical Association meeting, Memphis, November 13, 1917, "Objects and Methods of County Health Work," address delivered at State and County Council, University of North Carolina, September 18, 1919, "The Wilson County, North Carolina, Campaign against Soil Pollution," 1917, Washburn to George E. Vincent, October 25, 1919, and John Lee Hydrick to W. S. Rankin, May 3, 1922, NCDHS; Washburn, "Present Status of County Health Work in North Carolina," ca. 1919, Field Office Files, ser. 1, box 1, folder 4, Washburn Papers.

49. Washburn, "Report of Wilson County Health Campaign for April [1917]," NCDHS; "Memorandum of Conference between J. A. Hayne and Dr. J. A. Ferrell, Columbia, South Carolina," April 1, 1917, ser. 1.1, box 21, folder 373, IHB; Louisiana State Board of Health, *Biennial Report . . .*, 1918–1919, p. 18, 1920–1921, pp. 11–12, and 1924–1925, pp. 83–85.

50. International Health Board, Report of the General Director, *Rockefeller Foundation, Annual Report*, 1920, pp. 111–12.

51. Ferrell to Calvin T. Young, June 28, 1921, ser. 1.2, box 105, folder 1448, IHB; Roy H. Beeler to E. L. Bishop, April 6, 1933, Tennessee Department of Public Health Records, Series 1: Commissioners' Correspondence, box 1, folder 3, TSLA.

52. See Platt W. Covington to Ferrell, April 15, 1921, ser. 1.2, box 107, folder 1468, IHB; R. R. Sullivan to Porter, July 16, 1914, E. J. L'Engle to Porter, July 20, 1914, and Porter to Sullivan, July 22, 1914 (all in box 27, folder 8), Porter to Frank A. Bryan, August 31, 1916 (box 30, folder 6), W. P. Crigler to Porter, September 13, 1913, and C. H. Dobbs to Porter, September 13, 1913 (both in box 26, folder 6), and Maurice E. Heck to Porter, July 10, 1914 (box 27, folder 8), ser. 46, FSBH.

53. Ferrell to Young, June 28, 1921, and Raymond C. Turck to Ferrell, August 30, 1921, ser. 1.2, box 105, folder 1448, IHB; George A. Dame, monthly report, October 1921, ser. 46, box 37, folder 5, FSBH.

54. International Health Board, Report of the General Director, *Rockefeller Foundation, Annual Report, 1921*. For other examples of the convergence of the antimalarial program with the increasing emphasis on bureaucracy, see Ennion G. Williams to Ferrell, February 11, 1921, and Roy K. Flannagan to Ferrell, March 29, 1921 (both in box 112, folder 1523), and Ferrell to S. W. Welch, September 22, 1921 (box 104, folder 1436), ser. 1.2, IHB.

55. Smillie to Ferrell, September 27, 1922, and Smillie, "Demonstration County Health Unit," 1922, ser. 1.2, box 126, folder 1699, IHB. After graduating from Colorado College, Smillie attended Harvard Medical School, where he received the M.D. and doctor of public health degrees in 1912 and 1916, respectively. He served briefly with the Rockefeller Institute for Medical Research in 1916–17 before joining the IHB staff in August 1917 and spent the years 1918–22 in Brazil. In May 1922 he returned to head the Andalusia (Covington County) Training Station. See Wickliffe Rose to Committee on Admissions, Harvard Club, New York City, October 17, 1922, ibid.

56. International Health Board, Report of the General Director, *Rockefeller Foundation, Annual Report*, 1922, pp. 139–45, and 1923, pp. 89–92.

57. International Health Board, Report of the General Director, *Rockefeller Foundation, Annual Report*, 1924, pp. 93–103; Oscar Dowling to Ferrell, September 12, 1925, ser. 1.2, box 212, folder 2711, IHB; George A. Dame, monthly report, November 1921, ser. 46, box 37, folder 5, FSBH; Smillie to P. E. Blackerby, June 30, 1926 (box 244, folder 3122), Ferrell to S. W. Welch, September 16, 1926 (box 240, folder 3076), and C. W. Garrison to Ferrell, January 6, 1927 (box 279, folder 3538), ser. 1.2, IHB.

58. "Minutes of the Chiefs of Bureaus, N.C. State Board of Health, August 20, 1913," NCDHS; Joe L. Earman to Ralph N. Greene, October 9, 1919 (box 35, folder 1), George A. Dame, monthly report, October 1921 (box 37, folder 5), ser. 46, FSBH; Louisiana State Board of Health, *Biennial Report . . .*, 1920–1921, p. 7; Tennessee Department of Public Health, *Biennial Report . . . for the Fiscal Years 1926–1927*, pp. 10–11; International Health Board, Report of the Director General, *Rockefeller Foundation, Annual Report*, 1917, pp. 168–70, fig. 31; L. A. Riser, "Twelve Years in Rural Health Work," 1922, ser. 2, box 18, folder 105, IHB. For a discussion of the early stages of this development in North Carolina, see North Carolina State Board of Health, "Department of Public Health Work in North Carolina," 1914, NCDHS. The budget of the North Carolina State Board of Health grew from $200 in 1881 to $40,500 in 1913.

59. Francis Womack to W. S. Rankin, September 28, 1912, Rankin to Womack, September 28, 1912, Rankin to Thomas Chears, May 21, 1913, and Benjamin E. Washburn, "Report of the Nash County Health Officer for July 1914," NCDHS; Joseph Y. Porter to J. N. Fogarty, February 27, 1907, ser. 46, box 13, folder 3, FSBH; Rankin to E. C. Branson, February 19, 1918, box 3, folder 94, Branson Papers; Joseph Hyde Pratt and W. S. Rankin, "The Attitude of the State toward Its Prisoners, Convict Camp, and Prison Sanitation," 1915, NCDHS. Rankin described pigpens as "unsightly places [and] psychologically depressing" that "psychically suggest and encourage other insanitary compromises."

60. Porter to C. M. Wilder, January 9, 1915, ser. 46, box 28, folder 6, FSBH; Rankin to Thomas D. Murphy, August 31, 1916, NCDHS.

61. On the North Carolina law, see W. S. Rankin to R. L. Daniels, March 15, 1913, Rankin to L. B. McBrayer, March 12, 1913, Rankin to F. L. Siler, March 14, 1913, and Rankin to Clifford A. Peacock, March 29, 1913, NCDHS.

62. "Report of the Vance County Life Extension Campaign," 1917, "Life Extension in Alamance," 1917, and Rankin, circular letter to county health officers, March 17, 1922, NCDHS. On pellagra and the effort to eradicate it, see Etheridge, *Butterfly Caste*; Rankin to H. F. Harris, July 18, 1912, and James M. Judd to Rankin, July 20, 1914, NCDHS. On the involvement of the PHS in antipellagra efforts, see Rupert Blue to Joseph Goldberger, memorandum, February 7, 1914, folder 16, Joseph Goldberger Papers, SHC.

63. Washburn, "Report of the Nash County Health Officer for July 1914," Rankin to D. C. Absher, April 15, 1915, Rankin, circular letter, January 26, 1922, and Rankin, Annual Report, 1917, NCDHS.

64. Laurie Jean Reid, Monthly Report of the Bureau of Child Welfare, October 1922, ser. 46, box 38, folder 2, FSBH.

65. Wife of Frank Jerriedor, Harday, Macon County, Ala., ca. 1931 (box 556, folder 6), and "The Board Lady Has Her Settings," from undated, unsigned MS entitled "Midwives Tales," ca. 1928, and "Midwife Work in Virginia," from "Midwives Tales" (both in box 224, folder 5), JRF.

66. "Midwife Work in Virginia"; Laurie Jean Reid, "Regulations Governing Midwives for the Protection of Maternal and Infant Life and the Prevention of Blindness in the Newborn," 1924 (box 40, folder 7), and Reid, "Biennial Report, Division of Maternal and Infant Hygiene, Bureau of Child Welfare, Florida State Board of Health for Period July 1st to December 31st, 1922," January 1923 (box 39, folder 5), ser. 46, FSBH.

67. "Duties of the Infant Hygiene Nurse," 1919, NCDHS; W. B. Keating to Raymond C. Turck, monthly report for October 1921, and Keating to Turck, memorandum, August 29, 1921, ser. 46, box 37, folder 5, FSBH.

68. W. B. Keating, monthly report, July 1922, ser. 46, box 38, folder 2, FSBH.

69. Rankin to J. Howell Way, July 30, 1913, and Rankin to Henry R. Carter, September 18, 1913, NCDHS.

70. Henry R. Carter and R. H. Von Esdorf were the PHS officials who participated. See Carter to Rankin, September 16, 26, 1913, Rankin to Carter, September 24, 1913, Rupert Blue to Rankin, September 26, 1913, and Rankin to Margaret C. Brown, September 24, 1913, ibid. While in Tarboro, a PHS investigator described malaria as "prevalent here, very prevalent, but . . . not a bad type"; in Roanoke Rapids, he found a "bad state of affairs," estimating that three quarters of the population experienced chills for most of the summer. Carter to Rankin, September 16, 1913, and T. W. M. Long to Rankin, September 29, 1913, ibid.

71. Rankin to T. W. M. Long, October 3, 1913, Von Ezdorf to Long, October 15, 1913, Long to Rankin, October 18, 1913, Rankin to M. T. Edgerton, Jr., April 19, 1915, and Rankin to R. D. Val Jones, October 17, 1913, ibid. See Report of F. E. Harrington, August 9, 1915, and "Report on the Trip Taken by Drs. Hegner and Root through Certain of the Southern States for the Purpose of Study Malaria and Soil-Pollution," ibid. In

Greenville, N.C., a health official described a "deep ravine" located within three blocks of the Pitt County courthouse. It was, he wrote, "very poorly drained—& with resulting marsh—stagnant water every where—extending about 300 to 400 yrds & about 150 feet wide with one or two small lakes thrown in for good measure." The previous summer "many of the people in the Vicinity had chills & fever." Edgerton to Rankin, April 17, 1915, ibid.

72. For the inauguration of this program in Florida, see George W. Simons to Ralph N. Greene, August 6, 1919, L. D. Fricks to W. H. Cox, July 31, 1919, Rupert Blue to Ralph N. Greene, August 2, 1919, and Ferrell, "Memorandum of the Tentative Plan for the Extension of Malaria Control Measures," June 17, 1919, typed copy, ser. 46, box 34, folder 3, FSBH. For the functioning of the program in other states, see Louisiana State Board of Health, *Biennial Report . . ., 1920–1921*, pp. 10–11; L. D. Fricks to Rankin, September 15, 1922, NCDHS.

73. Tennessee Department of Public Health, *Biennial Report . . . for the Fiscal Years 1926–1927*, pp. 12–13; J. A. Morris to K. E. Miller, May 30, 1922, John A. Ferrell to W. S. Rankin, July 11, 1922, Rankin to Wilson G. Smillie, August 7, 1922, H. A. Taylor to Rankin, August 23, 1922, and Taylor to Rankin, July 21, 1923, NCDHS.

74. For a general discussion of the national anti-VD campaign, see Brandt, *No Magic Bullet*. On Tennessee's rather sporadic antivice program, see Olin West to municipal and county health officers, February 20, 1918, R. L. Lillard to T. C. Rye, May 8, 1918, Frank M. Thompson to West, January 8, 1919, George A. Hays to Thompson, March 25, 1920, and West to Thompson, July 26, 1920, ser. 1, box 2, folder 9, TDPH; Tennessee Department of Public Health, *Biennial Report . . . for the Fiscal Years 1927–1929*, pp. 57–64.

75. Millard Knowlton to Rankin, memorandum, October 8, 1919, Knowlton to Rankin, memorandum, October 14, 1919, and "Memorandum of Conference between Dr. Rankin and Mr. Miner," 1919, NCDHS.

76. Knowlton to Rankin, October 14, November 12, 1919, memorandum, W. J. Hughes to Knowlton, October 18, 1919, "Field Agent's Report on the Repression of Prostitution, May 1st to October 31st, 1919," and Josephine Washington, monthly report, May 1920, NCDHS. The five towns were Goldsboro, Hendersonville, Raleigh, Salisbury, and Wilson.

77. George A. Dame, circular letter to boards of county commissioners, July 14, 1921 (folder 3), and Dame, "Educational Activities Directed toward the Control and Eradication of Venereal Disease," enclosure in Dame to Raymond C. Turck, June 22, 1921, Dame, monthly report, October 1921, and Dame, "Florida's Program for the Control and Eradication of Venereal Diseases," April 25, 1921 (all in folder 5), ser. 46, box 37, FSBH; "Tentative Suggestions for Rules and Regulations for the Control of Venereal Disease," December 1919, "Proposed County Plan for Venereal Disease Control in North Carolina (Dictated December 9, 1919)," Knowlton to Rankin, November 1, 1919, memorandum, and J. S. Kitchener to Rankin, March 16, 1922, NCDHS.

78. On the problem of black health generally, see Beardsley, *A History of Neglect*.

79. S. L. Smith to Alfred K. Stern, June 19, July 31, 1926, and E. L. Bishop to Smith, typed copy, July 27, 1926, box 225, folders 1–2, JRF; Smith to Edwin R. Embree, May 11, 1928, Bishop to Smith, May 11, 1928, Edwin R. Embree to Bishop, June 4, 14, 1928,

and Smith to W. N. Porter, June 12, 1929, box 224, folder 2, JRF; Charles O'H. Laughinghouse to Smith, April 5, 1928, and Embree to Laughinghouse, June 4, 21, 1928, box 223, folder 3, JRF; C. V. Akin to Michael M. Davis, April 13, 1929, Akin to Embree, "Memorandum Relative to Full-Time Colored Public Health Nurses for Louisiana," February 27, 1929, Davis to Embree, memoranda, March 13–14, 1929, and Embree to Akin, March 22, 1929, box 222, folder 5, JRF; Felix J. Underwood to Embree, August 27, 1928 (folder 8), Embree to T. F. Abercrombie, October 4, 1928 (folder 1), and Stern to Will W. Alexander, July 18, 1927 (folder 3), box 222, JRF; "A Rosenwald Nurse," ca. 1929, box 224, folder 5, JRF. Edward H. Beardsley notes that there were only twenty-nine black public health nurses by the end of the decade, but this compared with virtually none four years earlier when the JRF program began. Beardsley, *A History of Neglect*, p. 114.

80. JRF contributed $10,000 to the North Carolina program. Laughinghouse to Michael M. Davis, December 7, 1929, box 231, folder 6, JRF.

81. T. F. Abercrombie to Davis, December 20, 1929, box 231, folder 1, JRF. Wenger estimated that the rate may have been as high as 50 percent. Wenger to Davis, typed copy, August 13, 1929, box 556, folder 2, JRF.

82. Wenger, "The Macon County Alabama Demonstration for the Control of Syphilis among the Rural Negro Population, April 16–May 24, 1930," box 556, folder 2, ibid.

83. Wenger, "The Macon County Alabama Demonstration," and Michael Davis to H. L. H., October 1, 1920, memorandum, ibid.

84. Dillard, "High-Class Samples," *School and Society* 26 (July 2, 1927), reprint enclosed in Dillard to Perry L. Harned, October 2, 1929, ser. 1, box 31, folder 13, TCE.

85. James A. Roberts, "Progress in Elementary Schools," ca. 1927, ser. 1, box 14, folder 4, TCE; "Brief Outline of School Legislation Enacted by the State Legislature of Kentucky, at the Session 1912, and the Recent Session 1914," enclosed in McHenry Rhoads to W. W. Brierly, July 11, 1914, and Rhoads to Wallace Buttrick, March 23, 1920, ser. 1.1, box 77, folders 672–73, GEB; James Y. Joyner to H. F. Wilson, August 20, 1912, ser. 5, box 17, NCDPI; Kentucky Superintendent of Public Instruction, *Biennial Report . . . for the Two Years Ending June 30, 1911*, p. 17.

86. F. C. Button to Barksdale Hamlett, August 9, 1915, ser. 1.1, box 80, folder 699, GEB. For a defense of the concept of supervision, see Kentucky Superintendent of Public Instruction, *Biennial Report . . . for the Two Years Ending June 30, 1913*, p. 264.

87. Button to Hamlet, August 9, 1915.

88. "Report of O. H. Bernard, State Rural School Agent for Tennessee, September 1927," ser. 1, box 31, folder 23, TCE.

89. Button to Hamlett, August 9, 1915.

90. Report of Wil Lou Gray, January 1915, Wil Lou Gray Papers, Incoming Correspondence, SCL; W. E. Halbrook to Wickliffe Rose, July 21, 1925, and Halbrook to Wallace Buttrick, July 22, 1925, ser. 1.1, box 26, folder 233, GEB.

91. Joyner to A. E. Akers, July 10, 1915, ser. 5, box 44, NCDPI.

92. Williams to F. C. Button, January 9, 1915, ser. 1.1, box 79, folder 693, GEB.

93. In North Carolina in 1912, for instance, each county was required to levy a two-mill tax on all property; the law permitted counties to supplement this with an additional three-mill tax. Any school district, on petition, could hold an election to vote a district tax of up to three mills. But, before 1910, counties had no power to levy taxes, and school

authorities were forced to push school improvements through local tax districts. James Y. Joyner to H. J. Willingham, August 14, 1912, ser. 5, box 21, NCDPI.

94. W. H. Pittman to L. Berge Beam, March 25, 1919, and Pittman to W. D. Cox, September 17, 1919 (box 69), and A. T. Allen to M. S. Pittman, October 13, 1927 (box 103), ser. 5, box. 21, ibid.; "Report of J. A. Roberts, State Rural School Agent for Tennessee, June, 1926," ser. 1, box 14, folder 2, TCE.

95. W. H. Pittman to James Y. Joyner, September 25, 1912, Joyner to Pittman, October 3, 1912, A. F. Sharpe to Joyner, April 17, 1915, and Joyner to Sharpe, April 22, 1915, ser. 5, box 50, NCDPI; Roberts, "Progress in Elementary Schools," ca. 1927, ser. 1, box 14, folder 4, TCE; Elizabeth Hodnett to A. T. Allen, November 29, 1926, ser. 5, box 97, ibid. On the duties of county supervisors, see Kentucky Superintendent of Public Instruction, *Biennial Report . . . for the Two Years Ending June 30, 1913*, pp. 269–75. In North Carolina, the state paid half the expenses of supervisors in county schools after 1919. L. Berge Beam to E. C. Brooks, February 4, 1919, ser. 5, box 69, NCDPI.

96. James A. Roberts to Perry L. Harned, April 23, 1927 (ser. 1, box 14, folder 4), and Roberts to Harned, October 16, 1924, and Harned to Cocke County Court, December 23, 1924 (ser. 2, box 103, folder 20), TCE.

97. Shelton Philips to W. N. Sheats, November 17, 1917, ser. 249b, box 3, FDE. For North Carolina, see Howard F. Jones to Eugene C. Brooks, June 30, 1919, ser. 5, box 71, NCDPI. For Alabama, see "Summary of Reports of Mr. J. B. Hobdy, State Agent for Rural Schools in Alabama, July 1, 1915 to January 1, 1916," ser. 1.1, box 18, folder 155, GEB. In Tennessee, after receiving a complaint about consolidation and transportation, the state commissioner of education's office responded that the matter was in local hands while, at the same time, promising that a state inspector would visit the community. Chief Clerk of Commissioner's Office to J. E. Gatley, January 30, 1929, ser. 1, box 27, folder 10, TCE.

98. "Summary of Reports of Mr. J. B. Hobdy," January 1916, W. H. Pittman to Claude C. Falls, May 12, 1923, A. T. Allen to J. J. Blair, July 9, 1923, Robert W. Isley to Allen, May 7, 1924, C. B. Garrett to Allen, August 19, 1925, and Allen to Garrett, August 27, 1925, ser. 5, boxes 88, 93, NCDPI.

99. For the impact of these changes in one state, see William A. Link, *Hard Country*, chap. 6.

100. Kentucky Superintendent of Public Instruction, *Biennial Report . . . for the Two Years Ending June 30, 1911*, p. 18; W. Catlett, report to New Hanover County Board of Education, July 1, 1912, ser. 5, box 15, NCDPI.

101. In Jackson County, Fla., school officials in 1913 installed new desks in many of their rural schools and promised to pay half the cost of constructing new schoolhouses. These improvements, noted a rural school supervisor, made county school officials popular with local communities. But it also upset the traditional arrangements, typical of most rural schools, under which communities operated: "that if you people will put up for yourselves a school house we will agree to place in that house a teacher, and you may also look out for seats for your children." Shelton Philips to W. N. Sheats, September 1, 1913, ser. 249b, box 3, FDE.

102. See, for example, "Report of O. H. Bernard, State Rural School Agent for Tennessee, October, 1925," ser. 1, box 14, folder 1, TCE.

103. A. T. Allen to George Davis, November 12, 1926, ser. 5, box 97, NCDPI. "Report

of O. H. Bernard, State Rural School Agent for Tennessee, April 1928," ser. 1, box 31, folder 23, TCE.

104. Edward N. Clopper, "Farmwork and Schools in Kentucky," *Child Labor Bulletin* 5 (February 1917): 191; W. A. Graham to A. T. Allen, July 14, 1924 (box 92), and *Rules and Regulations Governing Compulsory Education, State of North Carolina Board of Education* (Raleigh, 1919) (box 69), ser. 5, NCDPI. A North Carolina official predicted in 1912 that the time was "ripe for it and we are planning at once a definitive and systematic campaign" for consolidation. L. C. Brogden to J. Y. Joyner, January 16, 1912, Joyner Series, ser. 4, box 33, folder 36, SEB. On consolidation, see Joyner to Edwin A. Alderman, November 11, 1907, box 32, folder 15, Joyner Series, SEB; T. J. Coates, "Steps to Be Taken on Consolidating School Districts," October 1914, ser. 1.1, box 81, folder 710, GEB; J. R. Sams to Joyner, September 11, 1915, ser. 5, box 50, NCDPI; J. B. Hobdy to Abraham Flexner, March 31, 1917, ser. 1.1, box 18, folder 155, GEB.

105. This argument, among others, was made in W. H. Pittman to Novella F. Lloyd, November 8, 1919, ser. 5, box 71, NCDPI.

106. Kentucky Superintendent of Public Instruction, *Biennial Report . . . for the Two Years Ending June 30, 1919*, p. 215; A. T. Allen to E. W. Glazier, April 19, 1926, and Allen to Erwin Heller, November 15, 1926, ser. 5, box 97, NCDPI. For one petition in a southern Piedmont North Carolina community, see J. C. Allen et al., petition, November 1926, ser. 5, box 97, NCDPI.

107. G. L. Martin to A. G. Gainey, September 2, 1922, box 203, MDE; "Report of O. H. Bernard, State Rural School Agent for Tennessee, September 1927," ser. 1, box 31, folder 23, TCE.

108. For problems with high schools, see W. J. Jenkins to Joyner, August 4, 1914 (box 41), and W. E. Finley to Joyner, June 19, 1912 (box 15), ser. 5, NCDPI. A GEB agent described conditions in a typical rural high school in Kentucky. It was doing good work in languages, mathematics, and history, but in science, "it was not doing so well." Because the equipment was "practically nothing" and there was only one teacher, the school offered an inferior education. McHenry Rhoads to D. H. Starns, April 13, 1912, ser. 1.1, box 77, folder 671, GEB.

109. Bass to J. C. Davis, November 13, 1925, and Bass to John H. Laming, October 29, 1925, ser. 1, box 12, folder 5, TCE. For another example, see Bass to B. H. Gaultne, October 26, 1925, ibid.

CHAPTER EIGHT

1. Hart, *The Southern South*, p. 91.

2. The same official added that the attitude of whites was to treat most blacks as "servants," an attitude that he believed was "wrong." The court system, he added, was "unfair" to blacks. "Attitudes toward the Negro, Jackson County," memorandum of meeting for Negro Child Welfare Study, 1929, Commissioner's Office: Subject Files, 1891–1952, box 6, NCDSS.

3. The Anson County school superintendent expressed similar attitudes. He maintained that black parents did not realize the value of education and were "lazy" and lacked ambition. If officials pushed attendance too hard, moreover, white landowners might force

black parents to keep children out of school altogether. "Attitudes toward the Negro, Anson County," memorandum of meeting for Negro Child Welfare Study, 1929, ibid.

4. "Attitudes toward the Negro, Bertie County," memorandum of meeting for Negro Child Welfare Study, 1929, ibid.

5. Branson, "Liberty and Security of Life, the Basis of Economic Progress," Conference on Race Relations, Blue Ridge, N.C., August 4, 1917, and Branson to Warren H. Wilson, February 24, 1916, box 2, folder 57, Eugene Cunningham Branson Papers, SHC (hereafter cited as Branson Papers).

6. Hart, *The Southern South*, pp. 91, 124–25, 187–88; Branson, "A Study of Orange County Negroes," June 1916, box 2, folder 57, Branson Papers.

7. Burrows, "Commission on Interracial Cooperation," pp. 14–16; Ann Wells Ellis, "Commission on Interracial Cooperation," pp. 3–4; Dykeman and Stokely, *Seeds of Southern Change*, p. 58; Weatherford, *Interracial Cooperation*, p. 24; "Race Conference Notable Gathering," *Asheville Times*, September 2, 1916, clipping scrapbooks, box 5, Robert Fishburne Campbell Papers, HF.

8. Harlan, *Separate and Unequal*.

9. For the best account of black educational reform, see Anderson, *The Education of Blacks in the South*.

10. Buttrick to Leo Favrot, September 18, 1913 (box 24, folder 213), George D. Godard to Buttrick, April 30, 1914 (box 67, folder 591), and "Special Report of Jas. L. Sibley, State Agent [for] Colored Rural Schools for Alabama," December 1915 (box 17, folder 145), ser. 1.1, GEB.

11. Favrot to Buttrick, January 14, 1913, and Buttrick to Favrot, January 14, 1913, box 24, folder 213, ibid.; Leo M. Favrot, "The State Agents of Rural Schools for Negroes and Their Relation to Outside Funds Stimulating Negro Public Education," enclosed in Favrot to S. L. Smith, February 14, 1928, box 202, folder 16, JRF. The position of white agents was somewhat tenuous. Favrot explained in 1915 that GEB reports should refer to the agents as "Agents of Negro Rural Schools" instead of "Rural School Agents (Negro)" so as not to "convey the impression that the Agent is a Negro." Favrot to Abraham Flexner, November 9, 1915, ser. 1.1, box 24, folder 214, GEB.

12. T. J. Coates to F. C. Button, January 1, 1913 (box 79, folder 692), W. N. Sheats to Abraham Flexner, November 12, 1917 (box 36, folder 326), and George D. Godard to Wallace Buttrick, April 30, 1914, and Godard, monthly report, September 1915 (box 67, folder 591), ser. 1.1, GEB.

13. E. D. Tard to F. C. Button, February 14, 1916 (box 79, folder 694), George D. Godard to M. L. Brittain, April 3, 1916 (monthly report) (box 67, folder 592), Favrot to Abraham Flexner, November 9, 1915 (box 24, folder 214), ser. 1.1, GEB; Favrot, *Aims and Needs in Negro Public Education in Louisiana*, Louisiana Department of Education Bulletin No. 2 (n.p., 1918), p. 4; Favrot, monthly report for Louisiana, November 1916 (box 81, folder 774), ser. 1.1, GEB.

14. When, in 1914, Leo Favrot described a successful Jeanes program in Jefferson County, Arkansas, he reported that its premises had "all been neatly whitewashed" and walks built to the outhouses. All these exteriors were "spotlessly clean," with flowers planted, basin and towels out for better sanitation, and sash curtain made for the windows. The students proudly reported how they had done all of this work themselves. Favrot,

"Report on State Supervision of Negro Schools, Month of March, 1914," box 25, folder 220, ibid.

15. On county training schools, see Anderson, *The Education of Blacks in the South*, pp. 137–47; William A. Link, *Hard Country*, pp. 189–91.

16. "Monthly Report, Leo M. Favrot, State Agent [for] Rural Schools for Negroes [in Arkansas], February 1916" (box 25, folder 221), and J. S. Lambert, monthly report, October 1918 (box 17, folder 147), ser. 1.1, GEB; B. T. Crawford to A. C. Lewis, February 18, 1922, LDE; "Report of O. H. Bernard, State Rural School Agent for Tennessee, June, 1926," ser. 1, box 13, folder 20, TCE.

17. James L. Sibley, monthly report, December 1, 1913 (folder 143), monthly report, December 1, 1914 (folder 145), and William F. Feagin to Abraham Flexner, March 8, 1915 (folder 148), ser. 1.1, box 17, GEB; Y. A. Lenoir to Leo M. Favrot, August 10, 1921, LDE.

18. See, for example, "Monthly Report, Leo M. Favrot, State Agent [for] Rural Schools for Negroes [in Arkansas], January, 1916," ser. 1.1, box 25, folder 221, GEB.

19. W. T. B. Williams, Report on the Wake County Training School, March 24, 1915, Division of Negro Education Series, General Correspondence Subseries, box 1, NCDPI; James L. Sibley, monthly report, December 1, 1913, ser. 1.1, box 17, folder 143, GEB; Resolution of the State Teachers' Association, June 17, 1921, enclosed in James B. Dudley to Eugene Clyde Brooks, June 17, 1921, ser. 5, box 80, NCDPI.

20. E. C. Brooks, "A Declaration of Principles," 1919, and Eugene Clyde Brooks to James Hardy Dillard, March 14, 1919 (ser. 5, box 69), and "Division of Negro Education," speech at conference with German educators, May 26, 1928 (Division of Negro Education Series, Articles and Speeches Subseries, box 1), NCDPI.

21. An Arkansas Jeanes teacher complained that on return visits to black rural schools, she discovered that in her absence "no work" had been completed. Favrot, "The Industrial Movement in Negro Rural Schools," June 9, 1913, ser. 1.1, box 25, folder 219, GEB.

22. Favrot, monthly report, November 1916 (box 81, folder 774), and Favrot to Jackson Davis, January 22, 1917, and E. C. Sage to Davis, January 29, 1917 (box 24, folder 215), ser. 1.1, GEB. Hampton Institute and Tuskegee Institute both followed an "industrial" curriculum, which stressed manual training and sought racial elevation through rigorous work discipline. See William A. Link, *Hard Country*, pp. 173–89.

23. Robinson to Alfred K. Stern, typed copy, January 17, 1927, box 311, folder 1, JRF. Stern described Robinson as "a bright young chap" but a poor leader for the teachers whose "radicalism" was "not a good thing." Stern to S. L. Smith, July 19, 1927, ibid.

24. Anderson, *Education of Blacks in the South*, chap. 5; Hanchett, "The Rosenwald Schools."

25. Favrot to J. S. Stone, March 19, 1923, LDE.

26. Following this campaign, a prominent white farmer contributed another $1,000, which put the fund drive over the top. M. H. Griffin, MS report on the history of the Rosenwald program in Alabama, ca. 1927, box 76, folder 2, JRF.

27. G. F. Bludworth, MS history of the Rosenwald program in Texas, May 17, 1927, and Samuel L. Smith, "A Story of the Julius Rosenwald Fund in Tenn. from the Beginning to July 1, 1920," box 76, folder 72, JRF.

28. S. L. Smith to W. F. Bond, August 17, October 6, 1920, box 340, folder 2, JRF; L. J.

Bell to M. C. Newbold, July 28, 1922, ser. 5, box 86, NCDPI; "Report of O. H. Bernard, State Rural School Agent for Tennessee, October 1926" (box 13, folder 20), "Report of O. H. Bernard, State Rural School Agent for Tennessee, July, 1927" (box 31, folder F23), and S. L. Smith to Perry L. Harned, May 3, 1928 (box 36, folder 1), ser. 1, TCE. For discussions about consolidation and location, see "Report of O. H. Bernard, State Rural School Agent for Tennessee, October, 1925," ser. 1, box 14, folder 1, TCE.

29. Samuel L. Smith to William D. Gresham, June 16, 1928, box 331, folder 11, JRF.

30. The fund paid one-half of the per pupil cost in a declining ratio over three years; at the same time, it offered to pay one-half of the purchase price of the buses. William B. Harrell to Samuel L. Smith, March 14, 1929, box 336, folder 1, JRF. On an earlier interest in consolidation and transportation, see Alfred K. Stern to Smith, December 27, 1926, ibid.

31. For an early discussion of this change, see Edwin R. Embree to Jackson Davis, April 10, 1928, box 202, folder 16, JRF.

32. "Report of F. C. Button, State of Rural Schools for Kentucky, for the Month of April, 1917," ser. 1.1, box 80, folder 701, GEB; E. C. Brooks, "A Declaration of Principles," 1919, ser. 5, box 69, NCDPI.

33. Branson, "Liberty and Security of Life, the Basis of Economic Progress," Conference on Race Relations, Blue Ridge, N.C., August 4, 1917, ser. 5, box 69, NCDPI; "A General Survey of the Work of the Commission on Interracial Cooperation for 1922–23" (folder 974), and Alexander to Frank B. Stubbs, May 16, 1924 (folder 975), ser. 3.8, box 96, LSRM.

34. "Action of the Southern Baptist Convention in Washington, May 15, 1920," typed copy, in "Endorsement of the Work and Policies of the Commission on Inter-Racial Cooperation, by Denominational Agencies," ca. 1921 (reel 3, frame 6), and Will W. Alexander, "An Effort to Create Racial Good Will," ca. 1922 (reel 4, frame 922), ser. 1, CIC.

35. Ann Wells Ellis, "Commission on Interracial Cooperation," pp. 7–9, 11; Weatherford, *Interracial Cooperation*, pp. 63–64; W. S. Richardson, "Appeal of the Commission on Interracial Cooperation, Richmond, Virginia," January 24, 1922, ser. 3.8, box 96, folder 974, LSRM.

36. Alfred V. Bliss, "Progress in Dealing with the Negro Problem," *Congregationalist*, July 6, 1922, ser. 1, reel 4, frame 1113, CIC; Burrows, "Commission on Interracial Cooperation," pp. 45–55; Dykeman and Stokely, *Seeds of Southern Change*, p. 63.

37. Alexander to Howard W. Odum, September 14, 1920, box 1, folder 3, Howard Washington Odum Papers, SHC (hereafter cited as Odum Papers). On the training schools, see Burrows, "Commission on Interracial Cooperation," pp. 45–55. The Blue Ridge and Gammon training schools accommodated 100 participants at a time for five days; the total attendance at each location was over 1,000. "The Development of the Interracial Commission," enclosed in Trevor Bowen to Alexander, November 7, 1933, ser. 1, reel 4, frames 892–94, CIC. On the origins of the CIC, see Ann Wells Ellis, "Commission on Interracial Cooperation," pp. 7–19, but for the best account, see Pilkington, "The Trials of Brotherhood."

38. W. S. Richardson, "Appeal of the Commission on Interracial Cooperation, Rich-

mond, Virginia," January 24, 1922, ser. 3.8, box 96, folder 974, LSRM; "The Development of the Interracial Commission"; Alexander, "An Effort to Create Racial Good Will."

39. The Rosenwald Fund actually contributed more than this for additional projects. On the financing of the CIC, see Burrows, "Commission on Interracial Cooperation," pp. 146–49; Alexander to Howard W. Odum, September 14, 1920, box 1, folder 3, Odum Papers; Alexander to James Hardy Dillard, October 1, 1921, W. S. Richardson, "Appeal of the Interracial Commission," Richardson to Alexander, February 16, 1922, Beardsley Ruml to Alexander, December 31, 1923, December 23, 1924, February 23, 1926, January 25, December 4, 1928, and "Commission on Interracial Cooperation: Auditor's Report, December 31, 1924," in Alexander to Leonard Outhwaite, January 30, 1926, ser. 3.8, box 96, folders 974–75, LSRM; Alexander to Edwin R. Embree, November 14, 1928, William B. Harrell to Alexander, January 3, 1929, and Embree to Alexander, January 3, 1929, box 186, folder 1, JRF.

40. "The Development of the Interracial Commission," enclosed in Trevor Bowen to Alexander, December 7, 1933, ser. 1, reel 4, frames 898–99, CIC; Ann Wells Ellis, "Commission on Interracial Cooperation," p. 226.

41. "The Development of the Interracial Commission," enclosed in Trevor Bowen to Alexander, December 7, 1933; Alexander to Leonard Outhwaite, January 30, 1926, ser. 3.8, box 96, folder 975, LSRM. CIC officials also were involved in similar efforts to improve the status of housing and the legal condition of blacks. See Clark Foreman, monthly report, April 1, 1925 (frames 848–49), and Foreman, "Report on the Case of Ed. White, formerly of Thomaston, Ga.," ca. April 1925 (frames 850–51), ser. 7, reel 48, CIC.

42. An earlier course on race relations was offered in four colleges in Louisiana: LSU, Louisiana Industrial Institute, Louisiana College, and Tulane University. Offered for seven weeks, with one lesson per week, it stressed the economic value of blacks, the "possible cause of the recent and still threatening migration," and the impact of the war and its "new ideal of World Democracy on race relationships." "Monthly Report of Leo M. Favrot, State Agent of Rural Schools for Negroes, Louisiana, February 1918," ser. 1.1, box 88, folder 775, GEB.

43. "A General Survey of the Work of the Commission on Interracial Cooperation for 1922–23," Alexander to James Hardy Dillard, October 1, 1921, and Alexander to W. S. Richardson, August 17, 1922, ser. 3.8, box 96, folder 974, LSRM; "[The] State as of October First of the Work of 1922 of the Commission on Interracial Cooperation," ser. 1, reel 4, frames 417–19, CIC.

44. Alexander to W. S. Richardson, August 17, 1922, ser. 3.8, box 96, folder 974, LSRM.

45. "Statement as of October First of the Work for 1922 of the Commission on Interracial Cooperation," ser. 1, reel 4, frames 413, 415, CIC. See also Clark Foreman to Alexander, January 31, 1925, ser. 7, reel 48, frames 835–36, CIC; "Report of the Texas Commission to the General Commission on Interracial Cooperation, April 8, 1926," box 3, folder 23, Jessie Daniel Ames Papers, SHC (hereafter cited as Ames Papers).

46. Alfred V. Bliss, "Progress in Dealing with the Negro Problem," *Congregationalist*, July 6, 1922, clipping, ser. 1, reel 4, frame 1113, CIC.

47. R. F. Campbell to R. W. Miles, October 28, 1923, ser. 1, reel 26, frame 160, CIC;

"Better Race Feeling," *Louisville Times*, ca. 1924, clipping, reel 4, frame 1125, ibid.

48. Alexander to Mrs. Fitzgerald S. Parker, May 4, 1921, reel 3, frame 69, ibid. For an account of the origins of the Woman's Interracial Committee, see Hall, *Revolt against Chivalry*, pp. 59–106; McDowell, *Social Gospel in the South*, pp. 88–93.

49. Ann Wells Ellis, "Commission on Interracial Cooperation," pp. 25–27; Rouse, *Lugenia Burns Hope*, pp. 91–111.

50. Ames, "The Memphis Conference," Estelle Haskin, "Report of the Commission on Race Relations to the Women's Missionary, MECS," 1925–26, and Carrie Johnson, "Women and Their Organizations," October 7, 1921, all in box 1, folder 1, Ames Papers. At the Memphis conferences, the white women refused to adopt a resolution drafted at the Tuskegee meeting that called for the suffrage, condemned lynching unequivocally, and urged equality in strong terms. See Ann Wells Ellis, "Commission on Interracial Cooperation," pp. 29–32.

51. "The Development of the Interracial Commission"; "Statement as of October First of the Work for 1922 of the Commission on Interracial Cooperation," ser. 1, reel 4, frames 425–26, CIC.

52. Alexander's "Reminiscences," quoted in Ann Wells Ellis, "Commission on Interracial Cooperation," p. 24; Johnson to Ames, April 28, 1924 (folder 21), and Ames to Johnson, September 8, 1924 (folder 22), box 3, Ames Papers. On the tension at headquarters, see Hall, *Revolt against Chivalry*, p. 65.

53. Jessie Daniel Ames, Maggie Barry, et al., "Findings, Women Members—Texas State Inter-Racial Committee, Dallas, Texas, March 21, 1922," and Mrs. Arch Trawick, Estelle Haskin, et al., "Findings, Woman's Section, Tennessee State Inter-Racial Committee," 1922, ser. 3.8, box 96, folder 974, LSRM. "The protection of white women had always been offered in the defense for lynching," wrote an early historian of the CIC. "Once these white women faced that fact they felt a responsibility in the matter and proceeded to array themselves uncompromisingly against all forms of mob violence." "The Development of the Interracial Commission," enclosed in Trevor Bowen to Alexander, December 7, 1933.

54. Burrows, "Commission on Interracial Cooperation," pp. 86–101; "Statement as of October First of the Work for 1922 of the Commission on Interracial Cooperation," ser. 1, reel 4, frame 413, CIC; James Dudley to Will W. Alexander, typed copy, July 12, 1921, box 1, folder 9, Odum Papers; Robert I. Johnson to R. W. Miles, March 29, 1926, North Carolina Interracial Committee Papers, SHC; Odum to Alexander, July 19, 1921, box 1, folder 9, Odum Papers. For other evidence of weak local committees during the 1920s, see Alexander to R. W. Miles, May 19, 1926, and W. A. Robinson to W. T. Andrews, March 19, 1928, North Carolina Interracial Committee Papers, SHC.

55. Johnson to Ames, September 18, 1924 (folder 22), and Ames, "The Memphis Conference," and Virginia L. Kelly to Ames, March 14, 1927 (folder 24), box 3, Ames Papers; Mrs. J. H. Crawford to Johnson, December 17, 1921, ser. 1, reel 3, frame 140, CIC; Burrows, "Commission on Interracial Cooperation," p. 101.

56. Comments of Alexander, in "Result of Conference of Inter-Racial Meeting, Called by Governor J. B. A. Robertson, Tuesday, November 23, 1920," ser. 7, reel 53, frames 1115–16, CIC.

57. James Bond, *Progress in Race Relations in Kentucky: Report of the Director of the*

Kentucky Commission on Race Relations for 1922 and Minutes of the Third Kentucky Inter-Racial Conference, December 15–16, 1922, p. 1, reel 52, frame 831, ibid.

58. Brooks, notes for a Negro conference, ser. 5, box 69, NCDPI; *Negro Welfare in Louisiana: Program Adopted by a Conference of White Citizens*, June 16, 1920 (reel 52, frames 1169–71), and "Findings, Women Members, Arkansas State Inter-Racial Committee, Little Rock, Arkansas, April 14, 1922" (reel 3, frames 147–52), ser. 7, CIC.

59. "A General Report of the Work of the Commission on Interracial Cooperation for 1922–23," ser. 3.8, box 96, folder 974, LRSM; comments of Alexander, in "Result of Conference of Inter-Racial Meeting."

60. Obituary of Eagan, from CIC release, in *Jackson News*, April 27, 1924, clipping, ser. 7, reel 4, frame 1162, CIC; Burrows, "Commission on Interracial Cooperation," p. 112; Dykeman and Stokely, *Seeds of Southern Change*, pp. 62–63. For an overview, see Ronald C. White, Jr., *Liberty and Justice for All*.

61. Dykeman and Stokely, *Seeds of Southern Change*, pp. 23–29, 31–34, 45–48.

62. Mrs. Arch Trawick, Miss Estelle Haskin, et al., "Findings, Woman's Section, Tennessee State Inter-Racial Committee," 1922, ser. 3.8, box 96, folder 974, LSRM.

63. Jackson Davis to Abraham Flexner, August 4, 1919, ser. 1.1, box 131, folder 1200, GEB; "Action of the Southern Baptist Convention in Washington, May 15, 1920," in "Endorsement of the Work and Policies of the Commission on Inter-Racial Cooperation, by Denominational Agencies," ca. 1921 (reel 33, frame 6), and "Findings, Women Members, Arkansas State Inter-Racial Committee, Little Rock, Arkansas, April 14, 1922" (reel 3, frames 147–52), ser. 1, CIC.

64. Eagan to Raymond B. Fosdick, December 13, 1921, Alexander to James Hardy Dillard, October 1, 1921, and W. S. Richardson, "Appeal of the Commission on Interracial Cooperation, Richmond, Virginia," January 24, 1922, ser. 3.8, box 96, folder 974, LSRM; *Nashville Tennessean*, January 17, 1929, enclosed in James D. Burton to Perry L. Harned, January 3, 1930, ser. 1, box 31, folder 9, TCE.

65. "Inter-Racial Meetings Helpful," *Texas Freeman*, November 17, 1925, clipping (frame 264), and George Madden Martin, "Race Cooperation," *McClure's* 54 (October 1922): n.p. (frame 43), ser. 4, reel 26, CIC.

66. *Negro Welfare in Louisiana: Program Adopted by a Conference of White Citizens*, June 16, 1920, reel 52, frame 1172, ibid.; Brooks, "A Declaration of Principles," 1919, ser. 5, box 69, NCDPI. The schools that Odum was referring to were in Philadelphia. Odum to Bolton Smith, December 27, 1920, box 1, folder 5, Odum Papers.

67. Resolution of the Quadrennial Session of the Methodist Episcopal Church, South, May 1918, "Endorsement of the Work and Policies of the Commission on Inter-Racial Cooperation, by Denominational Agencies," ca. 1921, ser. 1, reel 3, frame 2, CIC.

68. Alexander, *The New Inter-Race Relations in the South*, printed address at the American Missionary Association annual convention, November 8, 1922, reel 14, frame 599, ibid.

69. Frank B. Stubbs to Beardsley Ruml, November 12, 1923, ser. 3.8, box 96, folder 975, LSRM.

70. "Development of the Interracial Commission," enclosed in R. B. Eleazer to Trevor Bowen, April 5, 1934, ser. 1, reel 4, frames 908–9, CIC.

71. Comments of Alexander, in "Result of Conference of Inter-Racial Meeting," ser. 7,

reel 53, frame 116, CIC; "Extracts from Mrs. George Hayne's Speech, Memphis Interracial Conference, October 6–7, 1920," box 1, folder 1, Ames Papers.

72. "Last night I prayed and poured out my soul to God, and I want to tell you that it was a struggle, but finally I said, 'God forgive those young men for I believe they were lacking in soul.'" Brown, speech at Women's Interracial Conference, Memphis, October 8, 1920, box 1, folder 1, Ames Papers.

73. Johnson, "Women and Their Organizations" (report to the CIC, October 7, 1921), "The Memphis Meeting as Related to Miss Abigail Curlee by Dr. W. W. Alexander," and "Women and Their Organizations," ibid.; Ames, quoting Johnson, in "The Memphis Conference," ibid. See also Johnson to Mrs. Archibald Davis, October 26, 1920, and Dudie M. Rowland to Johnson, October 12, 1920, ser. 1, reel 3, frames 35–37, CIC.

74. Brown, "Negro Women and Race Relations," speech before CIC meeting, Atlanta, October 7, 1921, box 1, folder 1, Ames Papers.

75. Comments of Dr. C. B. Chambers, L. L. Henderson, Mrs. A. V. Watkins, R. E. Stewart, and G. W. Dallas, in "Result of Conference of Inter-Racial Meeting . . . Tuesday, November 23, 1920," ser. 7, reel 53, frame 116, CIC.

76. *Birmingham Reporter*, quoted in *Progress in Race Relations: A Survey of the Work of the Commission on Interracial Co-Operation for the Year 1923–24* (n.p., n.d.) (frames 481–82), and "Racial Qualities Extolled," *Savannah Tribune*, ca. 1924 (frame 134), ser. 1. reel 4, CIC.

77. Buttrick, "Notes Made at Hampton, Virginia, Conference of State Agents, May 6 to 9, 1923," box 188, folder 4, JRF.

78. "Review of Ten Years' Work," 1928, ser. 3.8, box 96, folder 976, LSRM. A similar note of pessimism was sounded in "Commission on Interracial Cooperation, Brief Statement of Work for 1927 and Brief Suggestions for 1928," ibid.

79. Jones, "Approach to the South's Race Question"; Orr, "The Church and Race Relations," speech given at the meeting of the Tennessee State Interracial Committee, May 11, 1926, ser. 1, box 12, folder 18, TCE; Jessie Daniel Ames, Maggie Barry, et al., "Findings, Women Members—Texas State Inter-Racial Committee, Dallas, Texas, March 21, 1922," ser. 3.8, box 96, folder 974, LSRM.

80. Alexander, "Building Racial Good Will," *The Intercollegian*, March 1924, ser. 1, reel 4, frame 1142, CIC; Woman's Committee of the Texas Commission on Race Relations, Minutebook, March 20, 1922, box 3, folder 20, Ames Papers. For an elaboration of similar views, see Alexander, "Southern Christians and Their Negro Neighbors," n.d., and *The Crux of the Home Mission Enterprise*, pamphlet, November 1928, ser. 1, reel 14, frames 525–27, CIC.

81. *America's Obligation to the Negro*, pamphlet, ca. 1925, ser. 5, reel 29, frame 890, CIC.

82. Alexander, address at Kansas City, April 1920, quoted in Ann Wells Ellis, "Commission on Interracial Cooperation," p. 24; Hope quoted in Dykeman and Stokely, *Seeds of Southern Change*, p. 77.

CHAPTER NINE

1. William A. Link, "The Social Context of Southern Progressivism."

2. C. J. Everett to James Y. Joyner, October 10, 1912, T. C. Henderson to Joyner, November 9, 1912, and Joyner to Henderson, November 12, 1912 (box 19), and C. B. Woltz to Joyner, November 11, 1912, and Joyner to Woltz, November 13, 1912 (box 21), ser. 5, NCDPI.

3. The state superintendent backed up the teacher. B. A. Vaughn to Perry L. Harned, November 24, 1925, and Harned to Vaughn, November 25, 1925, ser. 2, box 106, folder 3, TCE.

4. Sallie Bryan Hartley to A. T. Allen, April 4, 1929, ser. 5, box 109, NCDPI.

5. J. Letcher Duncan to A. T. Allen, April 21, 1927, box 97, ibid.

6. F. L. Jernigan to Joyner, January 19, 1918 (box 65), and Mrs. Viola Gouge to Joyner, August 5, 1920 (box 75), ibid.; Report of the Children's Code Commission to the Georgia General Assembly of 1929, Georgia Children's Code Commission Records, ser. 2, box 10, folder 6, JMW; Kate Burr Johnson to Beardsley Ruml, January 4, 1928, ser. 3.7, box 106, folder 1076, LSRM; J. W. Gudger to Eugene C. Brooks, July 6, 1920, ser. 5, box 75, NCDPI.

7. Harry Clark to Brown Ayres, October 10, 1912, ser. 1.1, box 143, folder 1323, GEB.

8. J. Martin Butler to Perry L. Harned, January 13, 1926, ser. 2, box 103, folder 12, TCE. In response to the complaint, State Superintendent Harned suggested that the teacher call on local patrons and persuade them to abide by the law. This approach, he wrote, "often gives better results than an officer can get." Harned to Butler, January 18, 1926, ibid.

9. John Weaver to Harned, January 25, 1926 (box 103, folder 21), and Harned to Mrs. F. B. Thornton, February 8, 1927 (box 22, folder 1), ibid.

10. Report of E. S. McKown, superintendent for Cherokee County, "Forty-second Annual Report of the State Superintendent of the State of South Carolina, 1910," in *Reports and Resolutions of the General Assembly of the State of South Carolina Regular Session Commencing January 10, 1911* (Columbia, S.C.: N.p., 1911), pp. 868–99; W. H. Hand, "Need of Compulsory Education in the South," *Child Labor Bulletin* 1 (June 1912): 79; Peter Carver to A. T. Allen, December 21, 1925, ser. 5, box 93, NCDPI.

11. Fannie Askew to Joyner, January 7, 1916, and C. E. McIntosh to Askew, January 15, 1916 (box 52), and L. E. Bird to A. T. Allen, October 8, 1925 (box 93), NCDPI.

12. Edward N. Clopper, "Farmwork and Schools in Kentucky," *Child Labor Bulletin* 5 (February 1917): 187, 200–201.

13. Ibid., p. 201; Mrs. H. V. Kennedy to A. T. Allen, July 18, 1924, ser. 5, box 92, NCDPI.

14. J. T. Wrenn to P. H. Fleming, April 13, 1920, and Monroe Simpson to P. H. Fleming, April 1920, box 88, NCDSS; E. T. Atkinson to Joyner, February 26, 1918 (box 63), and A. T. Allen to R. E. Price, September 3, 1927 (box 103), ser. 5, NCDPI; Clopper, "Farmwork and Schools in Kentucky," p. 187.

15. "Preliminary Report of County Demonstration of Public Welfare Conducted Jointly by the North Carolina Board of Charities and Public Welfare and the School of Public Welfare of the University of North Carolina, July 1924 to January 1927," enclosed in

Howard W. Odum to Beardsley Ruml, February 12, 1927, ser. 3.6, box 75, folder 787, LSRM.

16. W. P. Palrick and A. Chesson to Joyner, August 25, 1917 (box 61), and Joyner to Avery County Board of Education, April 2, 1918 (box 63), ser. 5, NCDPI.

17. Caroline L. Dickinson, diary entry, December 1, 1911, in "Leaves from a Supervisor's Notebook," MS, and Dickinson to W. K. Tate, December 28, 1911, ser. 1.1, box 131, folder 1198, GEB.

18. Wallace Buttrick, itinerary and report of conference with county school commissioners of Georgia, September 10–12, 1902, box 3, folder 16, CFP; T. H. Robertson, Report for Hall County, Ga., Special Reports from County School Commissioners, 1902, GDE.

19. S. M. Brinson to Joyner, April 13, 1912 (box 12), and T. L. Sigmon to Joyner, May 14, 1918 (box 67), ser. 5, NCDPI.

20. M. O. Berry, Report for Whitfield County, Ga., Special Reports from County School Commissioners, 1902, GDE; W. N. Sheats to E. B. Currie, May 8, 1919, ser. 249B, box 3, FDE; Report of Leonard Cassity, superintendent of Bath County, Ky., in Kentucky Superintendent of Public Instruction, *Biennial Report . . . for the Two Years Ending June 30, 1911.*

21. Visitors to a Louisiana high school in Sabine Parish could not help but feel "disappointment and regret" about its close proximity to another high school nearby, wrote a GEB official in 1916. The patrons of these two schools had allowed their "petty differences and prejudices to stand in the way of their building up a strong consolidated rural high school." "Inspection of Public Schools, Sabine Parish, La.," October 1916, box 81, folder 744, GEB.

22. "Report of R. H. Hopkins, State Agent for Rural Schools in Kentucky," March 11, 1921, box 81, folder 713, ibid.; E. R. Cotten to A. T. Allen, October 20, 1925, and Allen to Cotten, October 21, 1925, ser. 5, box 93, NCDPI; K. P. Banks to Perry L. Harned, December 9, 1925, ser. 2, box 103, folder 13, TCE; Carlie Carril to Allen, January 26, 1925, ser. 5, box 93, NCDPI.

23. Ora Elsie Sharp to A. T. Allen, April 28, 1924 (box 92), Robert H. Lewis to North Carolina State Board of Education, March 15, 1924 (box 92), H. A. Holder to Allen, August 15, 1926 (box 97), and A. J. Blevins to Allen, July 8, 1923 (box 88), ser. 5, NCDPI.

24. John H. Dillard to A. T. Allen, July 10, 1926, box 97, ibid.

25. E. H. Goodman to O. Max Gardner, September 1, 1929, box 109, ibid.

26. H. W. Mayhew to A. T. Allen, September 8, 1924, and A. G. Patterson to Allen, December 5, 1924, box 92, ibid.; J. E. Gatley et al. to Perry L. Harned, January 24, 1929, ser. 1, box 27, folder 10, TCE; Fred Hill to Allen, ca. September 10, 1929, ser. 5, box 109, NCDPI.

27. J. Mack Jones to W. F. Bond, October 31, 1927, box 204, MDE; Mrs. B. B. Bell to A. T. Allen, May 25, 1925 (box 93), and Erwin Heller to Allen, November 14, 1926 (box 97), ser. 5, NCDPI.

28. Mrs. B. B. Bell to A. T. Allen, May 25, 1925 (box 93), and Mrs. Mercedes Pressley to Allen, July 2, 1927 (box 103), ser. 5, NCDPI.

29. Allen to J. H. Robertson, February 14, 1927, ibid. See also Robertson to Allen, February 10, 1927, ibid.

30. F. T. Carmack to J. N. Powers, October 28, 1909, box 1, MDE; J. W. Etchinson to James Y. Joyner, March 16, 1914, ser. 5, box 37, NCDPI. Often these districts followed their own geographic definition. One proposed district was delineated as follows: "It includes the residence and farm of the two Lawrences on the west side of the Stewards creek and John N. Daws and including lands of the Cox place, and then across the river to the railroad bed then down the railroad bed to the Clayton place near the water tank, and then back north to the Terry land, and then west to the Roberts' land going north to Ararat River, and then from the Ararat River to the mouth of Stewards Creek and up Stewards Creek to the railroad bridge." Joyner to J. H. Allen, January 23, 1915, ser. 5, box 44, NCDPI.

31. On the controversy, see C. C. Wright to Joyner, January 7, 1914, C. F. Fields and R. L. Proffit, "State to the State Brd.," January 1914 (enclosed in latter), Joyner to Wright, January 15, 1914 (enclosed in Wright to J. H. Joines, January 19, 1914), and C. F. Fields to Joyner, January 22, 1914, ser. 5, box 39, NCDPI.

32. "Statement as to the School District for Special Taxes in Barkers Creek Township, Jackson County, to Be Voted on, on Saturday, January 4, 1913," box 22, ibid. See also I. N. Glover to Joyner, June 8, 1916 (box 54, ibid.) for another example of a district seeking to gerrymander a portion of its district. In Joyner to Glover, June 19, 1916 (box 54, ibid.), it was made clear that such a process could not occur arbitrarily, but only after a districtwide election.

33. Harry H. Clark to Brown Ayres, October 31, 1917, ser. 1.1, box 143, folder 1326, GEB.

34. South Carolina Superintendent of Education, *Forty-second Annual Report* . . . , 1910, pp. 836–40; James Y. Joyner to S. A. Perry, November 21, 1912 (box 20), and Mrs. J. H. Davis to A. T. Allen, February 21, 1928, and Allen to Davis, February 24, 1928 (box 105), ser. 5, NCDPI.

35. J. M. Davis to Perry L. Harned, February 14, 1927, ser. 1, box 20, folder 2, TCE; J. A. Sullivan to Breckinridge, July 13, 1909, BFP.

36. C. G. Pullin to A. T. Allen, April 19, 1924 (box 92), and M. E. Cansler to Brooks, April 30, 1923, Kathleen Barnhardt to Allen, September 19, 1923, and Allen to Barnhardt, September 20, 1923 (box 88), ser. 5, NCDPI.

37. James A. Roberts and T. W. Hunter to Perry L. Harned, October 26, 1925 (ser. 1, box 14, folder 2), John Weaver to Harned, January 25, 1926, and Harned to Weaver, January 27, 1926 (ser. 2, box 103, folder 21), and R. M. Adkins to Harned, June 30, 1927 (ser. 1, box 22, folder 7), TCE.

38. Some teachers who had been "importuned by the patrons of different schools," wrote one North Carolina supervisor in 1912, wanted their certification even though they had missed the institutes. The state superintendent advised the supervisor to use his "judgment in this matter" and do "what is best for the school." W. I. Shaw to Joyner, October 22, 1912, and Joyner to Shaw, October 24, 1912, ser. 5, box 21, NCDPI. In other communities, there were complaints about the county institute requirement. T. A. Carpenter to James Y. Joyner, September 4, 1912 (box 15), J. O. Carr to J. A. Biven, August 13, 1912, and Joyner to Carr, August 19, 1912 (box 15), and R. P. Johnson to Joyner, November 6, 1912 (box 19), ibid.

39. South Carolina Superintendent of Education, *Forty-first Annual Report . . .*, 1909, pp. 768–69; W. N. Sheats to Shelton Philips, August 29, 1916, Philips to Sheats, June 13, 1917, and Sheats to Philips, June 14, 1917, ser. 249B, box 3, FDE.

40. James Y. Joyner to W. H. Hand, January 5, 1915, ser. 5, box 54, NCDPI; J. E. Swearingen to E. C. Sage, March 6, 1919, ser. 1.1, box 131, folder 1200, GEB.

41. George Lynch, monthly report as GEB high school supervisor, May 1908, ser. 1.1, box 35, folder 318, GEB; W. N. Sheats to Shelton Philips, August 15, 1916, June 5, 1917, ser. 249B, box 3, FDE.

42. Washburn, "The Dog in the Manger: Not a Fable," ca. 1917–18, NCDHS.

43. West to Ferrell, May 3, 1915, ser. 1.2, box 27, folder 414, IHB; Oscar Dowling, in Louisiana State Board of Health, *Biennial Report . . .*, 1910–1911, pp. 34–35, and *Biennial Report . . .*, 1916–1917, p. 28; Don M. Griswold to Ferrell, December 10, 1917, ser. 1.2, box 40, folder 613, IHB.

44. For tensions with the PHS, see S. W. Welch to H. S. Cumming, March 30, 1923, with Ferrell's marginal notation, ser. 1.2, box 149, folder 1969, IHB.

45. See the case of Arkansas in 1925, where the IHB-financed director of county health, Kelly E. Miller, objected to state budget practices but backed down after a confrontation with the state health officer. Miller to Ferrell, September 25, 1925, Miller to C. W. Garrison, August 31, September 8, 14, 1925, and Garrison to Miller, September 4, 12, 1925, box 212, folder 2713, IHB.

46. Ralph N. Greene to Edwin R. Embree, February 17, 1920, box 88, folder 1241, IHB. Greene further objected to the notion, on IHB's part, that there was "no one in the employment of the State Board of Health of Florida who has the intelligence to properly admin[i]ster health affairs." In response, Ferrell pointed out that the sticking point in these negotiations was Florida's refusal to contribute funds for rural sanitation work in some equal measure. Ferrell to Greene, March 15, 1920, ibid.

47. Washburn to Ferrell, May 6, August 19, 1919 (marked "confidential"), box 76, folder 1079, ibid. In 1925 Rankin introduced a bill in the North Carolina legislature that would have raised his salary from $5,000 to $7,500, but it attracted significant opposition. When Rankin suggested that the IHB might finance the difference, John A. Ferrell torpedoed the idea. Rankin to Ferrell, April 3, 1925, box 214, folder 2741, ibid.

48. W. S. Leathers to Ferrell, May 21, 1915, box 2, folder 36, ibid.; Joseph Y. Porter to Elsie L. Forrest, October 4, 1916, ser. 46, box 31, folder 2, FSBH.

49. W. W. Dinsmore to Ferrell, September 20, 1915 (box 1, folder 3), P. E. Blackerby to Ferrell, January 29, 1924 (box 180, folder 2333), Olin West to Ferrell, March 16, 1915 (box 4, folder 70), and Ferrell to S. W. Welch, August 2, 1926 (box 240, folder 3076), ser. 1.2, IHB.

50. Morgan Smith to Wickliffe Rose, January 21, 1911 (folder 58), and W. P. Jacocks to Ferrell, November 16, 1913 (folder 61), ser. 2, box 1, RSC. For more on the political problems of the health bureaucracy in Arkansas, see C. W. Garrison to Ferrell, May 21, 1915 (box 209, folder 2677), and Kelly E. Miller to Ferrell, August 31, 1925 (box 212, folder 2713), ser. 1.2, IHB.

51. C. H. Dobbs to Ferrell, January 22, 1917 (box 40, folder 619), and Calvin T. Young to Ferrell, March 4, 1918 (box 58, folder 840), ser. 1.2, IHB. Young had served as a Porter lieutenant earlier, then continued under his successor, W. H. Cox. But in view of the

decline of the health bureaucracy, he wrote, he could not "see any future to it" and quit.

52. Calvin T. Young to Ferrell, June 20, 1921 (box 105, folder 1448), and Wilson G. Smillie to Ferrell, April 2, 1923 (box 149, folder 1975), ser. 1.2, IHB. However, Smillie did note that the Florida public health system possessed "a good nucleus around which a splendid organization could be built." See also Raymond C. Turck to Ferrell, September 19, 1923, box 151, folder 1990, ibid.

53. W. A. Davis to Platt W. Covington, June 25, 1925, (box 211, folder 2693), Davis to Ferrell, May 3, 1926 (box 243, folder 3106), and Mr. ———— Lackey to W. H. Davis, October 7, 1925, enclosed in C. W. Garrison to Ferrell, October 31, 1925 (box 209, folder 2677), ibid.; Cressy L. Wilber to Porter, September 11, 1911, ser. 46, box 22, folder 4, FSBH. For problems of understaffing and vital statistics in South Carolina, see C. Wilson Miler to Ferrell, August 6, 1925, ser. 1.2, box 218, folder 2782, IHB.

54. W. B. Barham, "Some Obstacles in the Way of More Efficient Public Health Service and the Remedy," *Virginia Health Bulletin* 3 (December 1911): 199; Olin West to Ferrell, June 6, 1915, ser. 1.2, box 4, folder 70, IHB; *Greensboro Daily News*, November 29, 1920, clipping, and Birdie Dunn to George M. Cooper, December 21, 1923, NCDHS. Stanly County physicians protested the free clinics when they appeared in their county in 1924; they bluntly complained that the clinics competed with their practices. J. Clegg Hall to George M. Cooper, May 13, 28, 1924, NCDHS.

55. Benjamin E. Washburn, "Report of the Wilson County Public Health Campaign for February 1917," and Russell Flack to W. S. Rankin, February 16, 1915, NCDHS.

56. Keller to W. G. Smillie, March 21, 1927, ser. 1.2, box 278, folder 3531, IHB.

57. Ray A. Moore, "Difficulties of a Rural Health Officer," *Virginia Health Bulletin* 3 (December 1911): 204; Washburn to Ferrell, January 5, 1917 (box 43, folder 657), and Oscar Dowling to Ferrell, December 14, 1916 (box 24, folder 373), ser. 1.2, IHB.

58. Unidentified clipping, enclosed in E. T. Cutland to W. S. Rankin, October 27, 1913, NCDHS; Porter to R. L. Durrance, October 6, 1904 (box 8, folder 4), R. F. Godard to Porter, December 1, 1904 (box 8, folder 6), and Porter to E. L. Stewart, October 27, 1906 (box 12, folder 4), ser. 46, FSBH; K. W. King to A. T. Allen, November 7, 20, 1924, ser. 5, box 92, NCDPI.

59. J. S. Kitchener to W. S. Rankin, January 5, 1922, NCDHS.

60. "I have often to resort to strategy in order to get a suspicious patient to take the treatment at all," wrote a Virginia public health worker during the RSC campaign. R. L. Raiford, *Virginia Health Bulletin* 3 (December 1911): 197.

61. The impact, he predicted, would "doubtless be widespread"; tongues would wag, saying that he had "treated a man . . . and killed him." Smillie to Ferrell, March 11, 1923, ser. 1.2, box 149, folder 1925, IHB.

62. R. W. Garnett to Ennion G. Williams, enclosed in Williams to Wickliffe Rose, April 6, 1916 (box 28, folder 424), and E. H. Downe to Wilson G. Smillie, 1925 (box 4, folder 28), ser. 1.2, IHB.

63. Writing to thank Smillie for her examination and for the hookworm medication, Thelma Mitchell, an Alabama eighth grader, explained that she did not "take it because I did not need it." Thelma Mitchell to Wilson G. Smillie, September 14, 1923, ser. 1.2, box 4, folder 28, IHB. See also T. G. Worley to Smillie, September 14, 1923, folder 29, ibid.

64. Although initially mill workers were interested in the program, the CF staff discovered that in most cases they could not maintain "a sustained interest." Perhaps, one of the health officials speculated, this reflected an initial "curiosity" about a possible health panacea, which in a "few visits would be good for all time." But when the mill workers found that participation in the CF program took more sustained effort "under our supervision," interest lagged. "Report, Athens Child Health Demonstration, 1924" (folder 25), and "Annual Report, Athens-Clarke County Child Health Demonstration, January 1st, 1927 to December 31st, 1927" (folder 28), box 2, CF/CHD.

65. Draper, "The Rutherford County Demonstration," January 4, 1926 (folder 40), and "Confidential Report of Mr. Dinwiddie's Visit to Rutherford County, Tennessee, Child Health Demonstration, November 22–23, 1924" (folder 39), ibid.

66. Harry S. Mustard, "Report [of the] Child Health Demonstration, Rutherford County, Tenn., January–September 1924" (folder 34), and Barney Smith, memorandum, December 30, 1925, Courtenay Dinwiddie, "Confidential Report of Visit to Rutherford County Child Health Demonstration," December 7–16, 1925 (folder 40), and L. T. Royster, "Rutherford County, Tenn., Child Health Demonstration," July 21, 1925 (folder 40), ibid.

67. "Report of the Educational Work for 1913, by the State Board of Health of Kentucky," 1913, ser. 2, box 3, folder 90, RSC.

68. A. G. Fort to John A. Ferrell, January 9, March 15, 1915 (box 1, folder 13), and West to Ferrell, March 4, 16, April 10, 1915 (box 4, folder 70), ser. 1.2, IHB.

69. Ferrell, "Visit to Aiken County, South Carolina, April 27, 1915," ser. 1.1, box 3, folder 48, IHB; West to Ferrell, May 25, 29, June 6, July 6, 1915 (folder 70), and West to Wickliffe Rose, August 30, 1915 (folder 71), ser. 1.2, box 4, IHB. For West's continuing pessimism, see West to Ferrell, September 13, October 6, 1915, folder 71, ibid.

70. Fort to Ferrell, June 14, September 20, 1915 (box 1, folder 16), Rose to Fort, August 23, 1915 (box 1, folder 17), and M. Griswold to Ferrell, December 29, 1917 (box 40, folder 613), ibid.

71. Covington to Rose, February 25, 1916 (box 27, folder 418), Dr. Buckner to Covington, December 19, 1916, Covington to Ferrell, December 22, 1916 (box 27, folder 421), and A. T. McCormack to Ferrell, May 25, 1916 (box 24, folder 372), ibid. For Mississippi, see W. S. Leathers to Rose, February 12, 1916, box 24, folder 381, ibid. For Georgia, see M. F. Haygood, report for 1918, January 10, 1919, ser. 2, box 8, folder 46, ibid.

72. Washburn to Ferrell, November 2, 22, 1916, ser. 1.2, box 26, folder 400, ibid.

73. Washburn to Ferrell, May 7, 1919, box 76, folder 1079, ibid.

74. See, for examples in Georgia, Mississippi, and Virginia, "Report of the Division of County Health Work [of Georgia] for the Year 1920" (box 8, folder 46), and L. J. Petritz, Report of County Health Work for Mississippi, August 1, 1920 (box 14, folder 78), ser. 2, ibid.; Roy K. Flannagan to Ferrell, February 26, 1921, ser. 1.2, box 112, folder 1523, ibid.

75. Covington to Ferrell, May 11, 24, June 3, 13, 17, 1921, ser. 1.2, box 107, folder 1468, ibid.

76. Covington to Ferrell, June 13, 1921, ibid. For an example of this pattern, in Beauregard Parish, see Covington to Ferrell, October 28, 1921, ser. 1.1, box 48, folder 726, ibid. For later problems in Louisiana, see H. Muench to Covington, February 23, 1922, ser.

1.1, box 57, folder 827, ibid.; Kelly Miller to Ferrell, April 12, 1924, ser. 2, box 180, folder 2336, ibid.

77. "Narrative Report of State Director [of Rural Sanitation] for Tennessee, January 1 to June 30, 1922," ser. 4, box 3, folder 20, TDPH; E. L. Bishop to Ferrell, April 22, 1922, ser. 1.2, box 133, folder 1774, IHB. See also Bishop to Ferrell, October 3, 1923, ser. 1.2, box 157, folder 2059, IHB.

78. P. E. Blackerby to Ferrell, January 17, 1922 (box 129, folder 1725), Covington to Ferrell, January 22, 1922 (box 57, folder 827), Blackerby to Ferrell, January 2, 1925 (box 212, folder 2709), and Blackerby to Ferrell, June 21, 1926 (box 244, folder 3122), ser 1.2, IHB.

CHAPTER TEN

1. Tennessee was the last state to ratify. On August 18, 1920, Florida refused even to consider ratification. Taylor, "The Woman Suffrage Movement in Florida"; Johnson, "The Woman Suffrage Movement in Florida." On the suffrage fight, see Woloch, *Women and the American Experience*, pp. 349–58; O'Neill, *Everyone Was Brave*; Flexner, *Century of Struggle*, pp. 319–37; Wheeler, "New Women of the New South."

2. Many prohibitionist newspapers condemned the WCTU. See "The W.C.T.U.," editorial, *Alabama Christian Advocate*, August 9, 1988. Meanwhile, the WCTU in the South distanced itself from the national organization's support of woman suffrage. See "The W.C.T.U. in Alabama," ibid., February 28, 1889.

3. W. A. McCarty, "Woman Suffrage," March 22, 1888, and "Woman's Place in American Civilization," editorial, August 23, 1888, ibid. "To make a woman legally the equal of man," declared another southerner, "might cost her much of the sweet courtesy that goes to the weaker and the dependent." John R. Deering, "Woman's Relation to Man," *Nashville Christian Advocate*, May 10, 1890. See also *Richmond Virginian*, October 24, 1910.

4. W. A. Smith to Westmoreland Davis, August 25, 1919, box 82, Westmoreland Davis Papers, UVA (hereafter cited as Davis Papers); broadside, n.d., ibid; Watterson, reprint of editorial on woman suffrage, n.d., box 82, ibid. For an account of the antisuffrage movement in one state, see Elna C. Green, "Those Opposed."

5. "Extracts from an Open Letter to U.S. Senator Ransdell [of Louisiana] Opposing the Federal Amendment for Woman Suffrage by Harry Gamble, New Orleans," January 26, 1918, box 49, folder 419, EJG; Henry St. George Tucker to Westmoreland Davis, August 23, 1919, box 82, Davis Papers. In a resolution, the Louisiana General Assembly declared the suffrage amendment as an "attack upon State control" of its own electorate. It would "pave the way for further Federal control of State electorates to the final destruction of the liberties of the people." Resolution of the Louisiana General Assembly, November 22, 1919, box 49, folder 420, EJG.

6. "Federal Suffrage: A Racial Question in the South," address by Harry Gamble before the New Orleans Press Club, March 11, 1918 (box 49, folder 419), and L. A. Moresi to Gay, November 26, 1918 (box 50, folder 432), EJG; editorial reprint, *Richmond Evening*

Journal, May 4, 1915, box 82, Davis Papers; Gay, typescript of a speech delivered at the U.S. Senate, February 10, 1919, box 49, folder 420, EJG.

7. Adele Clark was later convinced of Tucker's involvement. Alluding to his use of the pamphlet in the ratification debate, she said: "I don't think that he would have waved it in his hand and read from it if he hadn't been involved in it." Adele Clark Interview, Oral History Collection, UVA.

8. Mary Johnston, "The Woman Movement in the South," 1910, box 27, Mary Johnston Papers, UVA (hereafter cited as Johnston Papers).

9. Lillie Archbell to the Editor, "Woman's Problem," *Raleigh News and Observer*, March 9, 1902.

10. See, for example, Miles Dillard to Warren A. Candler, September 13, 1893 (box 3, folder 10), Candler to ———, April 11, 1895 (box 5, folder 3), Candler to J. E. Sibley, May 2, 1892 (box 3, folder 7), and J. E. Sibley to Candler, July 3, 1894 (box 3, folder 10), ser. 1, Warren Akin Candler Papers, EUL.

11. Kearney, *A Slaveholder's Daughter*, p. 120; Taylor, "The Woman Suffrage Movement in Texas," pp. 207–8; *Why Women Should Oppose Equal Suffrage*, undated pamphlet, VWSP; Mrs. C. H. King to Westmoreland Davis, July 26, 1919, box 82, Davis Papers.

12. Minutes of meeting of Columbia, S.C., Equal Suffrage League, March 23, 1915, Ida Salley Reamer Papers, SCL; Taylor, "The Woman Suffrage Movement in Texas," p. 199; Alabama Association Opposed to Woman Suffrage, broadside, ca. 1920, box 82, Davis Papers; "A Protest against Woman Suffrage in Alabama," n.d., AESA; Evelyn B. Dodd to Edward J. Gay, December 30, 1918, box 50, folder 433, EJG.

13. Richmond made the largest financial contribution. See "Pledges Made at State Convention, 1917," November 1917, VWSP. On the Lynchburg movement, see Elizabeth D. Lewis, annual report for Lynchburg Equal Suffrage League, 1913–14, November 7, 1914, VWSP.

14. Barbara Henderson to Clara Savage, February 15, 1915, Mary Octavaine T. Cowper Papers, DUL; Helen Moore to Lillian Sherey, February 25, 1916, pt. 2, box 17, file 2, JYM; Mrs. Preston B. Moses to Edith Cowles, January 29, 1917, VWSP; Jessie E. Townsend to Alice M. Tyler, n.d., Adele Clark Papers, Special Collections and Archives Department, Virginia Commonwealth University Library, Richmond (hereafter cited as Clark Papers), box 53A; Elizabeth Lewis Otey Interview, August 7, 1973, Oral History Collection, UVA.

15. Mary Elizabeth Pidgeon to Lila Meade Valentine, November 2, 1919, and Mrs. John H. Lewis, "Report of Congressional Chairman for Virginia," November 1917, VWSP.

16. Pidgeon to Lila Meade Valentine, October 14, December 9, 26, 1919, and Pidgeon to Ida M. Thompson, December 12, 1918, ibid.

17. H. P. Sugg to Alice M. Tyler, March 5, 1912, box 53A, Clark Papers; Katharine Marchant to Tyler, November 11, 1912, Eloise Johnston, report for Bath County Equal Suffrage League, 1914, and Elizabeth H. Lewis to Alice Overbey Taylor, April 28, 1915, VWSP.

18. Dow Husbands to Madeline McDowell Breckinridge, October 9, 1914, BFP; Eleonore Raoul to Miss ——— Patterson, n.d., enclosed in Eleonore Raoul to Rosine Raoul, July 4, 1916, ser. 1, subser. 12, box 30, folder 14, RFP; Elizabeth H. Lewis to Lila Meade Valentine, October 11, 1918, VWSP; Emily C. McDougald to Clara Savage,

January 28, 1915, Georgia Women's Suffrage College, box 1, folder 1, GDAH; Eleonore Raoul to Rosine Raoul, July 17, 1915, ser. 1, subser. 12, box 30, folder 13, RFP.

19. Mrs. Clyde E. Purcell to Breckinridge, January 10, 1910, and Anna V. Becker to Breckinridge, August 14, 1913, BFP; M. W. Blakey to Ida M. Thompson, December 4, 1936, and Lila Ware to Thompson, November 30, 1936, VWSP.

20. Constance Ashton Myers, notes on an interview with Elisabeth Perry Collins, April 6, 1974, Constance Ashton Myers Papers, SCL; Charlotte Tullis Potter to Annette Finnigan, May 13, 1914 (box 11, file 8), and Perle P. Penfield, "Report of Work, Summer of 1914" (box 10, file 8), pt. 2, JYM; Pearl L. Lockridge to Breckinridge, September 28, 1910, BFP; Eloise Lewis to Mary Johnston, March 23, 1911, box 8, Johnston Papers. The women of Danville, Va., were described in 1912 as "a bit shy of suffrage." In that town, there prevailed "rather apathy than hostility, with a little old time Southern prejudice, due to conservatism or ultra-conservatism." Arthur H. Taylor to Alice M. Tyler, July 16, 1912, box 53A, Clark Papers. During the ratification campaign of 1919–20, Mary Pidgeon characterized a western Virginia community, probably typical of many rural communities, as as "sleepy as ever." There was "practically no opposition" there, but "indifference and fear of signing" prevailed. Pidgeon to Valentine, September 25, 1919, VWSP.

21. J. E. Firth to Breckinridge, August 13, 1913, BFP; Kearney, "State Correspondence," *Woman's Journal*, April 13, 1907, box 2, Belle Kearney Papers, MDAH (hereafter cited as Kearney Papers); Lewis to Ida M. Thompson, October 3, 1918, VWSP. According to Lewis, when a group of suffragists later "eagerly took him to task," Flood *"brimmingly* asserted that if the women *wanted* the suffrage," "he was willing [that] they have it!"

22. Beard to Breckinridge, October 28, 1911, BFP.

23. Merrie P. Sugg to Lila Meade Valentine, January 18, 1912, box 53A, Clark Papers; James H. Pride to Bossie O'Brien Hundley, December 12, 1914, Hundley Scrapbook, Pidgeon to Valentine, October 26, 1919, and Pidgeon to Edith Clark Cowles, October 29, 1919, VWSP. "A majority of voters, and, indeed, a majority of women in my district" opposed woman suffrage, a legislator informed Valentine in 1913. Nonetheless, he promised his support because it was "the duty of every public man to be in advance of, rather than following, the sentiment of his constituents." John W. Chalkley to Valentine, November 11, 1913, VWSP.

24. Neal L. Anderson, "Child Labor Legislation," pp. 497, 500, 502–7.

25. McKelway, "Law without Enforcement," *Child Labor Bulletin* 3 (May 1914): 34–35; "Legislative Hints for Social Reformers," undated MS (ca. 1913), p. 23, Alexander Jeffrey McKelway Papers, LC (hereafter cited as McKelway Papers/LC); McKelway, speech in MS proceedings of the NCLC, Third Annual Convention, Cincinnati, December 13–15, 1906, NCLC.

26. Hine, "Alabama Investigation," November 1910, NCLC.

27. Hine, "Child Labor in the Cotton Mills of Mississippi," May 1911, and "Law Enforcement in Mississippi Canneries, February and March 1916," NCLC. Hine discovered the same false reporting of ages in Georgia. Hine, "Child Labor in Georgia," April 1913, NCLC.

28. Hine, "Some Information about the State Factory Inspector of Mississippi," March 1916, ibid. Gratuities to the inspector were also reported in Hine, "Law Enforcement in Mississippi Canneries."

29. McKelway, "Law without Enforcement," *Child Labor Bulletin*, p. 39; McKelway, "Child Labor in Mississippi," ca. 1911, McKelway Papers/LC; Edward F. Brown, "Neglected Human Resources of the Gulf Coast States," *Child Labor Bulletin* 2 (May 1913): 113–14,; Mrs. E. L. Bailey, "Mississippi," *Child Labor Bulletin* 2 (May 1913): 132; Herschel H. Jones, "Notes on the Need for Factory Inspection in Mississippi," December 1913–January 1914, and Jones, "Mississippi Reports and Interviews," December 1913–14, entry dated January 2, 1914, NCLC; Helen C. Dwight, "In Mississippi Canneries—A Continued Story," *Child Labor Bulletin* 5 (August 1916): 104–5.

30. Mrs. W. L. Murdoch, "Conditions of the Child Employing Industries in the South," *Child Labor Bulletin* 2 (May 1913): 125–26; McKelway, "Law without Enforcement," *Child Labor Bulletin*, pp. 38–40; Neal L. Anderson, "Child Labor Legislation," p. 499. As late as 1929, a reformer said that Georgia child labor legislation was "in need of additional means of its enforcement." Report of the Georgia Children's Code Commission to the Georgia General Assembly of 1929, ser. 2, box 10, folder 6, JMW.

31. John Porter Hollis to Charles Lee Coon, October 15, 1910, box 3, folder 29, Charles Lee Coon Papers, SHC (hereafter cited as Coon Papers); Lewis W. Hine, "Child Labor in South Carolina," May 1912, NCLC; McKelway, statement before North Carolina Legislation Committee, North Carolina House of Representatives, February 1905, and McKelway to the Editor, *Raleigh News and Observer*, typed copy, February 22, 1907, McKelway Papers/LC; McKelway, "Law without Enforcement," *Child Labor Bulletin*, pp. 35–36. The agent for the state NCLC committee witnessed "many" violations of the law in North Carolina. W. H. Swift, "The Campaign in North Carolina: The Mountain Whites—By One of Them," *Child Labor Bulletin* 2 (May 1913): 96.

32. Mrs. E. L. Bailey, "Mississippi," *Child Labor Bulletin* 2 (May 1913): 129–30. McKelway reported that in one southern state, the suggestion that the child labor campaign was financed by northerners was enough to doom passage of a law. The South, he wrote, was "suspicious of the disinterestedness of New England in matters of long-distance reform." McKelway, "Legislative Hints for Social Reformers," ca. 1913, McKelway Papers/LC.

33. *Charlotte Observer*, May 27, 1916, quoted in editorial, *Child Labor Bulletin* 5 (August 1916): 87; W. H. Swift, "The Campaign in North Carolina: The Mountain Whites—By One of Them," pp. 99–100; J. J. Hall to Coon, September 29, 1910 (folder 29), and Coon to B. V. Ferguson, March 19, 1912 (folder 38), box 3, Coon Papers.

34. E. N. Johnson to Mill Superintendent, May 12, 1913, and John Spargel to Mill Superintendent, May 5, 1913, FBCM; C. W. Jeffreys to Coon, March 13, 1912, box 3, folder 38, Coon Papers.

35. Neal L. Anderson, "Child Labor Legislation," p. 498; "Children in the Mills," editorial, *Columbia State*, April 21, 1909; Harvey P. Vaughn, "Child Labor in Georgia," April 1913, NCLC; Mrs. Alonzon Richardson, "Inhuman and Antiquated Children's Laws Need Revision," 1929, ser. 2, box 11, folder 7, JMW.

36. Oscar Elvas to Frank Walsh, March 29, 1915, entitled "Commission on Industrial Relations," box 2, FBCM.

37. Mrs. Alonzon Richardson, "Inhuman and Antiquated Children's Laws Need Revision."

38. McKelway, "Child Labor in North Carolina," undated address, McKelway Papers/

LC; Vaughn, "Child Labor in Georgia," April 1913, and Jones, "Mississippi Reports and Interviews," December 1913–January 1914, entry dated January 2, 1914, NCLC.

39. McKelway, "Child Wages in the Cotton Mills: Our Modern Feudalism," *Child Labor Bulletin* 2 (May 1913): 14; John Porter Hollis to Coon, February 11, 1911, box 3, folder 32, Coon Papers; Hine, "A Photographic Investigation of Child Labor Conditions in the Cotton Mills of Georgia," January 31, 1910, NCLC.

40. Townshend, "My Trip Abroad," September 10–December 24, 1924, VWSP.

41. *Richmond Virginian*, March 30, 1910; "The South and Liquor-Selling," p. 944.

42. Bailey concluded that the only effective means of control was local option. Bailey, "Political Treatment of the Drink Evil," pp. 113–16.

43. "Alarming Drouth in the Brushies," *Raleigh News and Observer*, December 15, 1906.

44. W. C. Gaither, affidavit, March 21, 1912, enclosed in J. M. Wysor, Mannering, W. Va., to the Editor, n.d., *Richmond Virginian*, April 4, 1912; ibid., April 4, 1912. For a fuller treatment of moonshining, see Wilbur R. Miller, "The Revenue."

45. A. M. King to John Hollis Bankhead, ca. 1912, Subject Files: Prohibition, box 40, folder 5, John Hollis Bankhead Papers, ADAH; Jefferson Davis to Governor F. H. Lubbock, July 20, 1887, Elijah L. Shettles Papers, TSL; Holmes, "Moonshining and Whitecaps," pp. 33–35.

46. Editorial, "Pitt County 'White Cappers,'" *Raleigh News and Observer*, December 16, 1906.

47. *Richmond Virginian*, March 15–16, May 28, 1912. For other accounts of the Allen case, see M. D. A. to the Editor, September 22, 1912, and P. H. Hubard to the Editor, ibid., September 24, 1912; ibid., September 26, 1912.

48. Ibid., March 13, 1911; Josiah William Bailey to R. L. Davis, January 16, 1917, and Bailey, press release, July 1, 1920, Josiah William Bailey Papers, DUL (hereafter cited as Bailey Papers). In Warren County, in northeastern North Carolina, IRS agents in 1910 destroyed a rural still but then were forced to flee to the woods on the return of the moonshiners. Although U.S. revenue agent W. H. Chapman and his two possemen escaped harm, according to one account, their movement attracted shotgun fire from the moonshiners. *Richmond Virginian*, October 3, 1910. Chapman also conducted raids in Chatham County. *Richmond Virginian*, March 13, 1911.

49. On dispensaries, see Christensen, "State Dispensaries of South Carolina"; Eubanks, *Ben Tillman's Baby*, pp. 66–83; Hendricks, "The South Carolina Dispensary System, Part I," pp. 188–89.

50. Dargan, "A Last Word."

51. Ibid. Eubanks, *Ben Tillman's Baby*, pp. 87–104, provides the most complete account of the Darlington Riot, but see also Hendricks, "The South Carolina Dispensary System, Part I," pp. 188–89, 193–97. For contrasting views of the riot, see Tillman, "History of the South Carolina Liquor Law"; Dargan, "A Last Word," pp. 52–60.

52. Whitener, *Prohibition in North Carolina*, pp. 61–80; Holmes, "Moonshining and Collective Violence" and "Moonshining and Whitecaps in Alabama"; Davis, "Attacking the 'Matchless Evil,'" pp. 157–69; Hendricks, "The South Carolina Dispensary System, Part II," pp. 320–35, 337–42. In 1915 South Carolina enacted statewide prohibition.

53. McClean, "Prohibition and Southern Local Problems," p. 154.

54. *Richmond Virginian*, March 5, 1910.

55. Ibid., January 6, 1912; John S. Henderson to Josiah William Bailey, January 24, 1912, Victor S. Bryant to Bailey, January 15, 1912, box 102, Bailey Papers. Despite a "strong and growing public sentiment" favoring enforcement, Tennessee continued to experience violations. Tom C. Rye to Westmoreland Davis, March 14, 1918, box 78, Davis Papers. Bristol, which was divided into dry and wet halves lying in Tennessee and Virginia, respectively, became a vivid illustration of the impotence of statewide prohibition, for in the Virginia side of town the "open saloon" prevailed. *Richmond Virginian*, March 16, 1913. In Georgia, the WCTU complained in 1914 about the "shameless defiance" that occurred in that state; "good men," it warned, were becoming "exasperated" over the situation. Editorial, "Law Enforcement Campaign," *Georgia Bulletin*, February 1914, ser. 5, box 2, Georgia WCTU Records, EUL. See also C. J. Barrows to James P. Bowman, November 19, 1915, folder 58, James P. Bowman Family Papers, LLMV; Jess Johnson to Daniel C. Roper, December 15, 1919, carbon copy, box 47, folder 405, EJG; "A Study of Prohibition in the South," *The New Voice in Mississippi*, February 6, 1902, clipping, box 2, Kearney Papers.

56. *Richmond Virginian*, February 28, 1910.

57. Ibid., February 11, 1910.

58. E. C. Payne to J. Sidney Peters, January 18, 21, 1917, and Payne to Peters, October 30, 1917, Correspondence, 1916–30, VPC. See also J. Toomer Garrow to Peters, June 12, 1919, ibid.

59. Peters, circular letter, April 6, 1917, ibid. See also Peters to the Director of the Valley Turnpike, December 14, 1916, Mrs. W. B. Allen to Peters, February 13, 1917, and James H. Fletcher to Peters, July 8, 1917, ibid.

60. Unsigned letter to Peters, May 7, 1917, C. H. Jennings to Peters, June 6, 1917, C. E. D. Burtis to Peters, February 19, 1917, and Peters to Burtis, February 21, 1917, ibid.

61. T. T. Arnold to Peters, October 21, 1917, and Peters to Arnold, October 24, 1917, ibid.

62. Miss J. W. Hardy to S. B. Woodfin, March 1, 3, 1919, petition to Smith, July 18, 1922, Miss Ruth Webster to Smith, July 29, 1922, Mrs. A. E. Kincannon to Smith, September 20, 1923, and John E. Grasty to Smith, October 16, 1923, ibid. During the 1920s liquor was available and widely consumed in Charlottesville. See Atcheson Laughlin Interview (OH#1), Oral History Collection, UVA. See also "One of the Ladies of Doswell [Hanover County], Va.," November 1922, VPC.

63. *Richmond Times-Dispatch*, November 13, 1924, box 74, Davis Papers; Payne to Peters, December 30, 1916, and Staley to Peters, October 23, 31, 1917, ibid.

64. Staley to Peters, July 19, 1917, and W. S. Shelton to Peters, September 1, 1917, ibid.

65. J. Sidney Peters to C. C. Gaver, July 3, 1919, and E. C. Payne to Peters, October 20, 1917, ibid.

66. "Home of Pocahantas Pastor Dynamited," ca. February 1921, unidentified clipping, H. D. Coffey to Thomas Whitehead, June 13, 1922, J. T. Finch to Smith, August 29, 1922, and H. B. Smith to B. D. White, May 6, 1922, quoting telegram from Princess Anne County, ibid.

67. "Police Seeking Booze, and Thefts Continue," *Richmond Times-Dispatch*, Septem-

ber 20, 1916, clipping, and R. A. Buckner to J. Sidney Peters, February 10, 1917, ibid.; Dr. R. B. Sapp to Westmoreland Davis, April 5, 1919, box 82, Davis Papers.

68. Peters to Mrs. R. A. Allison, January 3, 1917, and Peters to Thomas H. Lion, September 14, 1917, VPC; Peters to Westmoreland Davis, April 25, 1918, box 78, Davis Papers.

69. "Communities Too Friendly to 'Wet' Men," *Richmond News-Leader*, December 27, 1920, clipping, Peters, circular letter, April 6, 1917, and E. C. Payne to Peters, April 22, 1917, VPC. On the legislative history of the VPC, see Kirby, *Westmoreland Davis*, pp. 131–35.

70. C. D. Lam to Peters, August 21, 1916, E. H. Staley to Peters, August 28, 1917, J. O. Babcock to Thomas Whitehead, June 8, 1922, and William Lloyd to Harry B. Smith, December 18, 1922, VPC.

71. Charles T. Beall to Peters, March 11, 1919, and Peters to Beall, March 14, 1919, ibid.; Peters to Westmoreland Davis, May 10, 1918, box 78, Davis Papers.

72. "Consumer and Bootlegger," ca. 1921, unidentified clipping, VPC. For a similar opinion, see *Richmond Times-Dispatch*, November 12, 1924, box 74, Davis Papers.

EPILOGUE

1. Odum, *Public Welfare and Social Work*, pp. 115–16, 121.

2. Roosevelt quoted in Schulman, *From Cotton Belt to Sunbelt*, p. 50.

3. Hoke, "The Politics of Fertility."

4. Kirby, *Rural Worlds Lost*, describes this transformation, as does Daniel, *Breaking the Land*.

5. Schulman, *From Cotton Belt to Sunbelt*.

6. Southern Growth Policies Board, *Halfway Home*, pp. 5–6. The report was written by Doris Betts. It provided for a ten-point program, including nationally competitive education, the elimination of adult functional illiteracy, the development of a "flexible, globally competitive work force," the strengthening of at-risk families, promoting the economic development role of higher education, and the initiation of new economic development strategies.

7. Ibid.

BIBLIOGRAPHY

———— ◆ ————

This bibliography is organized as follows:
Manuscript and archival material
Government documents
Newspapers and periodicals
Books, articles, dissertations, and theses

MANUSCRIPT AND ARCHIVAL MATERIAL

Alabama
Birmingham
   Archives and Manuscripts Department, Birmingham Public Library
      Bossie O'Brien Hundley Scrapbook
      Pattie Ruffner Jacobs Papers
Montgomery
   Alabama Department of Archives and History
      Alabama Department of Public Health Records
      Alabama Equal Suffrage Association Records
      Alabama Governors' Papers
      Alabama Superintendent of Public Instruction Records
      John Hollis Bankhead Papers
      Birmingham Equal Suffrage Association Papers
      W. P. Browne Collection
      J. L. M. Curry Family Papers

Florida
Tallahassee
   Florida State Archives
      Florida Department of Education Records
      Florida State Board of Health Records

Georgia
Atlanta
   Atlanta University Library
      Commission on Interracial Cooperation Records (microfilm copy)
   Special Collections Department, Emory University Library
      Frances Sage Bradley Papers
      Warren Akin Candler Papers
      Georgia WCTU Records

Emily Stewart Harrison Papers
Eleonore Raoul Series, Raoul Family Papers
Josephine Matheson Wilkins Papers
Georgia Department of Archives and History
Georgia Department of Education Records (microfilm copy)
Georgia Department of Archives Records
Georgia Women's Suffrage Collection
Special Collections Department, Georgia Institute of Technology Library
Fulton Bag and Cotton Mills Company Records
Rabun Gap
Rabun Gap-Nacoochee School
Rabun Gap-Nacoochee School Records

Kentucky
Lexington
Special Collections and Archives, University of Kentucky Library
Laura Clay Papers
Linda Neville Papers
Cora Wilson Stewart Papers

Louisiana
Baton Rouge
Louisiana State Archives
Louisiana Department of Education Records
Louisiana and Lower Mississippi Valley Collections, Louisiana State
University Library
James P. Bowman Family Papers
Judith Hyams Douglas Papers
Edward J. Gay Family Papers
New Orleans
Manuscripts Department, Tulane University Library
Ethel Hutson Papers
New Orleans Public Library
Woman's Anti-Lottery League of New Orleans Papers
ERA Club of New Orleans Papers

Mississippi
Jackson
Mississippi Department of Archives and History
William Walton Hoskins Papers
Belle Kearney Papers
Mississippi Department of Education Records
Samuel Davies Wheatley Papers

New York

North Tarrytown
  Rockefeller Archive Center
    Child Health Demonstration Series, Commonwealth Fund Records
    General Education Board Records
    Hospital Series, Commonwealth Fund Records
    International Health Board Records, Rockefeller Foundation Archives
    Laura Spellman Rockefeller Memorial Records
    The Messrs. Rockefeller Records
    Rockefeller Sanitary Commission for the Eradication of Hookworm Disease in the
      Southern States Records
    Southern Highland Division, Russell Sage Foundation Records
    Benjamin Earle Washburn Papers

North Carolina

Chapel Hill
  Southern Historical Collection, University of North Carolina at Chapel Hill Library
    Jessie Daniel Ames Papers
    Ivan Proctor Battle Papers
    Launcelot Minor Blackford Diary
    Eugene Cunningham Branson Papers
    John C. and Olive Dame Campbell Papers
    Heriot M. Clarkson Papers
    Charles Lee Coon Papers
    Joseph Goldberger Papers
    Elvira Evelyna Moffitt Papers
    North Carolina Interracial Committee Papers
    Howard Washington Odum Papers
    Southern Education Board Papers
    Edwin Yates Webb Papers
Durham
  Manuscript Department, Duke University Library
    Josiah William Bailey Papers
    Clement Claiborne Clay Papers
    Mary Octavaine T. Cowper Papers
    Salisbury-Spencer Ministerial Association Minutebook
Greensboro
  University Archives, University of North Carolina at Greensboro
    Charles Duncan McIver Papers
    Woman's Association for the Betterment of Public School Houses Records
Montreat
  Presbyterian Church (U.S.A.), Department of History
    Robert Fishburne Campbell Papers
    Walter Lee Lingle Papers

Alexander J. McKelway Papers
Raleigh
  North Carolina Division of Archives and History
    North Carolina Department of Public Instruction Records, Division of
      Negro Education Series
    North Carolina Department of Public Instruction Records, General
      Correspondence
    North Carolina Department of Social Services Records
    North Carolina Division of Health Services Records
Winston-Salem
  North Carolina Baptist Collection, Wake Forest University Library
    John Alexander Oates Papers

South Carolina
Columbia
  South Carolina Department of Archives and History
    Bennettsville, S.C., Board of Health Minutes
    South Carolina Department of Education Records
    Manuscripts Department, South Caroliniana Library, University of South Carolina
    Jessie Stokely Burnett (b. 1882) Interview, April 6, 1974, Constance Ashton Myers
      Papers
    Ellen Evans Cathcart Papers
    Lysander Childs Papers
    Elisabeth Perry Collins (b. 1892) Interview, April 6, 1974, Constance Ashton Myers
      Papers
    Wil Lou Gray Papers
    Constance Ashton Myers Papers
    Ida Salley Reamer Papers
    Sons of Temperance No. 45 Records, Bennettsville Division
    South Carolina League of Women Voters Records

Tennessee
Nashville
  Special Collections Department, Fisk University Library
    Julius Rosenwald Fund Archives
  Archives Branch, Tennessee State Library and Archives
    Tennessee Commissioner of Education Records
    Tennessee Department of Health Records

Texas
Austin
  Eugene C. Barker Texas History Center, University of Texas
    Alexander Caswell Ellis Papers
    Prohibition Scrapbook
    Amanda Stoltzfus Papers

Austin History Center, Austin Public Library
  Jane Yelvington McCallum Papers
Archives Branch, Texas State Library
  Jessie Daniel Ames Papers
  Erminia T. Folsom Papers
  Elijah L. Shettles Papers

Virginia
Charlottesville
  Manuscripts Department, University of Virginia Library
    Oral History Collection
    Adele Clark Interview, August 18, 1973
    Atcheson Laughlin Interview, March 15, 1972
    Elizabeth Lewis Otey Interview, August 7, 1973
    Westmoreland Davis Papers
    Mary Johnston Papers
    Frederick William Neve Papers
    Robert Wellford Papers
    Richmond WCTU Records
Richmond
  Special Collections and Archives Department, Virginia Commonwealth University
    Library
    Adele Clark Papers
  Virginia Historical Society
    Lila Meade Valentine Papers
  Archives Branch, Virginia State Library and Archives
    Virginia Prohibition Commission Records
    Virginia Woman Suffrage Papers

Washington, D.C.
  Manuscripts Division, Library of Congress
    Madeline McDowell Breckinridge Series, Breckinridge Family Papers
    Alexander J. McKelway Papers
    National Child Labor Committee Papers

GOVERNMENT DOCUMENTS

Annual Report of the Health Commissioner to the Governor of Virginia for the Year Ending September 30, 1915. Richmond: Davis Bottom, Superintendent of Public Printing, 1916.

Cook, William A. *Schoolhouse Sanitation: A Study of the Laws and Regulations Governing the Hygiene and Sanitation of Schoolhouses.* U.S. Bureau Of Education, Bulletin no. 21. Washington, D.C., 1915.

Dresslar, Fletcher B. "The Duty of the State in the Medical Inspection of Schools." *Jour-*

nal of Proceedings of the Fiftieth Annual Meeting Held at Chicago, Illinois, July 6–12, 1912, National Education Association. Ann Arbor, Mich., 1912.

———. Rural Schoolhouses and Grounds. U.S. Bureau of Education, Bulletin no. 12. Washington, D.C., 1914.

Ferrell, John A. The Rural School And Hookworm Disease. U.S. Bureau of Education, Bulletin no. 20. Washington, D.C., 1914.

Florida State Board of Health. Eleventh Annual Report of the State Board of Health of Florida. Jacksonville: East Florida Printing Co., 1900.

———. Twenty-first Annual Report of the State Board of Health of Florida, 1909. Jacksonville: N.p., 1910.

———. Twenty-fourth Annual Report of the State Board of Health of Florida, 1912. Jacksonville: E. O. Painter Co., 1913.

———. Twenty-seventh Annual Report of the State Board of Health of Florida, 1915. Jacksonville: Palatka News Co., 1916.

———. Thirtieth Annual Report of the State Board of Health of Florida, 1918. Jacksonville: N.p., 1919.

Florida Superintendent of Public Instruction. Biennial Report, 1912–1914. De Land, Fla.: N.p., 1914.

Georgia Department of Education. Annual Report, 1911. Athens: Georgia Department of Education, 1911.

International Health Board, Report of the General Director. The Rockefeller Foundation, Annual Report, 1916. New York: Rockefeller Foundation, 1916.

———. The Rockefeller Foundation, Annual Report, 1917. New York: Rockefeller Foundation, 1917.

———. The Rockefeller Foundation, Annual Report, 1920. New York: Rockefeller Foundation, 1920.

———. The Rockefeller Foundation, Annual Report, 1921. New York: Rockefeller Foundation, 1921.

———. The Rockefeller Foundation, Annual Report, 1922. New York: Rockefeller Foundation, 1922.

———. The Rockefeller Foundation, Annual Report, 1923. New York: Rockefeller Foundation, 1923.

———. The Rockefeller Foundation, Annual Report, 1924. New York: Rockefeller Foundation, 1924.

International Health Commission, Report of the General Director. The Rockefeller Foundation, Annual Report, 1913–1914. 2d ed. New York: Rockefeller Foundation, 1914.

———. The Rockefeller Foundation, Annual Report, 1915. New York: Rockefeller Foundation, 1915.

Kentucky Superintendent of Public Instruction. Biennial Report of the Superintendent of Public Instruction of Kentucky for the Two Years Ending June 30, 1911. Frankfort: State Journal Co., 1911.

———. Biennial Report of the Superintendent of Public Instruction of Kentucky for the Two Years Ending June 30, 1913. Frankfort: State Journal Co., 1913.

———. Biennial Report of the Superintendent of Public Instruction of Kentucky for the Two Years Ending December 31, 1917. Frankfort: State Journal Co., 1918.

————. *Biennial Report of the Superintendent of Public Instruction of Kentucky for the Two Years Ending December 31, 1919.* Frankfort: State Journal Co., 1919.

Louisiana State Board of Health. *Biennial Report of the Louisiana State Board of Health to the General Assembly of the State of Louisiana, 1910–1911.* New Orleans, Brandao Printing Co., 1911.

————. *Biennial Report of the Louisiana State Board of Health to the General Assembly of the State of Louisiana, 1914–1915.* New Orleans: Hauser Printing Co., 1915.

————. *Biennial Report of the Louisiana State Board of Health to the General Assembly of the State of Louisiana, 1916–1917.* New Orleans, Brandao Printing Co., n.d.

————. *Biennial Report of the Louisiana State Board of Health to the General Assembly of the State of Louisiana, 1918–1919.* New Orleans: Hauser Printing Co., 1919.

————. *Biennial Report of the Louisiana State Board of Health to the General Assembly of the State of Louisiana, 1920–1921.* New Orleans: Hauser Printing Co., 1921.

————. *Biennial Report of the Louisiana State Board of Health to the General Assembly of the State of Louisiana, 1924–1925.* N.p.: N.p., 1925.

Medical Association of Alabama. *The Report of the Board of Health of the State of Alabama for the Years 1883 and 1884.* Montgomery: Barrett and Co., 1885.

————. *Report of the Board of Health of the State of Alabama for the Year 1887.* Montgomery: W. D. Brown and Co., 1888.

Mississippi State Board of Health. *Biennial Report of the Mississippi State Board of Health, 1880–1881.* Jackson: J. L. Power, 1881.

————. *Biennial Report of the Mississippi State Board of Health, 1884–1885.* Jackson: J. L. Power, 1885.

————. *Biennial Report of the Mississippi State Board of Health, 1890–1891.* Jackson: Power and McNeily, 1892.

————. *Report of the Board of Health of Mississippi from September 30, 1909, to June 30, 1911.* Nashville, Tenn.: Press of the Brandon Printing Co., 1911.

————. *Report of the Board of Health of Mississippi from June 1, 1913, to June 30, 1915.* Memphis, Tenn.: Paul and Douglass Co., Printers, 1915.

North Carolina Superintendent of Public Instruction. *Biennial Report of the Superintendent of Public Instruction, North Carolina, for the Scholastic Years 1912–1913 and 1913–1914.* Raleigh, 1914.

Rockefeller Sanitary Commission. *Annual Reports, 1911–15.*

South Carolina Superintendent of Education. *Forty-first Annual Report of the State Superintendent of the State of South Carolina, 1909.* Columbia, 1910.

————. *Forty-second Annual Report of the State Superintendent of the State of South Carolina, 1910.* Columbia, 1911.

————. *Forty-third Annual Report of the State Superintendent of Education of the State of South Carolina.* Columbia, 1912.

Swearingen, R. M. *Annual Report on [Texas] Quarantine for the Year 1882.* Austin: F. W. Swindells, 1882.

————. *Report on [Texas] Quarantine for 1883–4.* Austin: D. and D. Asylum, 1884.

Tennessee Department of Public Health. *Biennial Report of the Department of Public Health, State of Tennessee for the Fiscal Years 1926–1927.* Nashville: State Department of Public Health, 1927.

————. *Biennial Report of the Department of Public Health, State of Tennessee, for the Fiscal Years, 1927–1929.* Nashville: State Department of Public Health, 1929.

————. *Hookworm Disease: Its Cure and Prevention.* Nashville: State Board of Health, n.d.

Texas State Board of Health. *Report of the State Health Officer of the State of Texas for the Years 1891 and 1892.* Austin: Ben C. Jones and Co., 1892.

NEWSPAPERS AND PERIODICALS

Alabama Baptist

Alabama Christian Advocate

Atlanta Constitution

Baltimore and Richmond Christian Advocate

The Baptist (Memphis)

Baptist Courier (Greenville, S.C.)

Baptist Record (Jackson, Miss.)

Bulletin of the North Carolina Board of Health

Bulletin of the State Board of Health of Kentucky

Charlotte Presbyterian Standard

Child Labor Bulletin

Clinton (Miss.) *Argus*

Clinton Sword and Shield

Columbia (S.C.) *State*

Florida Baptist Witness

Florida Health Notes

Greensboro (N.C.) *Battle Ground*

Nashville Baptist and Reflector

Nashville Christian Advocate

North Carolina Baptist

North Carolina Presbyterian

North Carolina Prohibitionist

Raleigh Friend of Temperance

Raleigh News and Observer

Raleigh Spirit of the Age

Richmond Religious Herald

Richmond Virginian

Social Service Quarterly (Raleigh, N.C.)

Southern Baptist Witness

Southern Medical Journal

The Southern Witness

Tennessee Baptist

Tennessee Baptist and Reflector

Virginia Health Bulletin

"Actual Results of the System [N.C. Dispensary Law]." *Outlook* 61 (April 8, 1899): 822–23.

Akenson, James E., and Harvey G. Neufeldt. "Alabama's Illiteracy Campaign for Black Adults, 1915–1930: An Analysis." *Journal of Negro Education* 54 (1985): 189–95.

Alderman, Edwin A. "The Southwestern Field." *Annals of the American Academy of Political and Social Science* 22 (June–December 1903): 287–92.

———. "The Achievement of a Generation." *South Atlantic Quarterly* 5 (July 1906): 236–53.

Allen, Lee Norcross. "The Woman Suffrage Movement in Alabama." M.S. thesis, Alabama Polytechnic Institute, 1949.

———. "The Woman Suffrage Movement in Alabama, 1910–1920." *Alabama Review* 11 (April 1958): 83–99.

Anderson, James D. "Northern Foundations and the Shaping of Southern Black Rural Education, 1902–1935." *History of Education Quarterly* 18 (Winter 1978): 371–96.

———. *The Education of Blacks in the South, 1860–1935*. Chapel Hill: University of North Carolina Press, 1988.

Anderson, Neal L. "Child Labor Legislation in the South." *Annals of the American Academy of Political and Social Science* 25 (May 1905): 491–507.

Angus, David L., and Jeffrey E. Mirel. "From Spellers to Spindles: Work-Force Entry by Children of Textile Workers, 1888–1890." *Social Science History* 9 (1985): 127–43.

Appleby, Joyce. "Value and Society." In *Colonial British America: Essays in the New History of the Early Modern Era*, edited by Jack P. Greene and J. R. Pole, pp. 290–316. Baltimore: Johns Hopkins University Press, 1984.

Appleton, Thomas Howard, Jr. "'Like Banquo's Ghost': The Emergence of the Prohibition Issue in Kentucky Politics." Ph.D. dissertation, University of Kentucky, 1981.

"Arisen South." *World's Work* 14 (July 1907): 9040–42.

Armor, Mary Harris. "Local Option and Its Results in Georgia." *Annals of the American Academy of Political and Social Science* 32 (1908): 480–81.

Ashby, Irene M. "Child-Labor in Southern Cotton Mills." *World's Work* 2 (October 1901): 1290–95.

Atkins, Emily Howard. "The 1913 Campaign for Child Labor in Florida." *Florida Historical Quarterly* 35 (January 1957): 233–40.

Ayers, Edward L. *Vengeance and Justice: Crime and Punishment in the Nineteenth-Century American South*. New York: Oxford University Press, 1983.

Bacote, Clarence A. "Some Aspects of Negro Life in Georgia, 1880–1908." *Journal of Negro History* 43 (July 1959): 186–213.

———. "Negro Proscriptions, Protests, and Proposed Solutions in Georgia, 1880–1908." *Journal of Southern History* 25 (November 1959): 471–98.

Bailey, Hugh C. "Edgar Gardner Murphy and the Child Labor Movement." *Alabama Review* 18 (January 1965): 47–59.

———. *Edgar Gardner Murphy: Gentle Progressive*. Coral Gables, Fla.: University of Miami Press, 1968.

————. *Liberalism in the New South: Southern Social Reformers and the Progressive Movement.* Coral Cables, Fla.: University of Miami Press, 1969.

Bailey, Josiah William. "Case for the South." *Forum* 31 (April 1901): 225–30.

————. "The Political Treatment of the Drink Evil." *South Atlantic Quarterly* 6 (1907): 109–24.

Bailey, Kenneth K. "Southern White Protestantism at the Turn of the Century." *American Historical Review* 68 (April 1963): 618–35.

Bailey, Richard Ray. "Morris Sheppard of Texas: Southern Progressive and Prohibitionist." Ph.D. dissertation, Texas Christian University, 1980.

Baker, Paula. *The Moral Frameworks of Public Life: Gender, Politics, and the State in Rural New York, 1870–1930.* New York: Oxford University Press, 1991.

Ball, S. Mays. "Alabama's Fierce Struggle over Prohibition." *Leslie's Weekly* 109 (1909): 652.

————. "Prohibition in Georgia; Its Failure to Prevent Drinking in Atlanta and Other Cities." *Putnam's* 5 (March 1909): 694–701.

Barron, Hal S. "Rural Social Surveys." *Agricultural History* (April 1984): 113–17.

————. *Those Who Stayed Behind: Rural Society in Nineteenth-Century New England.* New York: Cambridge University Press, 1984.

Bassett, John Spencer. "Stirring Up the Fires of Race Antipathy." *South Atlantic Quarterly* 2 (October 1903): 297–305.

Baxley, Thomas L. "Prison Reformers during the Donaghey Administration." *Arkansas Historical Quarterly* 22 (Spring 1963): 76–84.

Bailey, Kenneth K. *Southern White Protestantism in the Twentieth Century.* New York: Harper and Row, 1964.

Barbour, Philip F. "The Importance of Medical Inspection of Schools." *Southern Medical Journal* 7 (1914): 184–190.

Beardsley, Edward H. *A History of Neglect: Health Care for Blacks and Mill Workers in the Twentieth-Century South.* Knoxville: University of Tennessee Press, 1987.

Beattie, Donald Weldon. "Sons of Temperance: Pioneers in Total Abstinence and 'Constitutional' Prohibition." Ph.D. dissertation, Boston University, 1966.

Beatty, Bess. "Textile Labor in the North Carolina Piedmont: Mill Owner Images and Mill Worker Response, 1830–1900." *Labor History* 25 (Fall 1984): 485–503.

Berkeley, Kathleen Christine. "Elizabeth Avery Meriwether [1824–1917]: 'An Advocate for Her Sex': Feminism and Conservatism in the Post–Civil War South." *Tennessee Historical Quarterly* 43 (Winter 1984): 390–407.

————. "The Ladies Want to Bring About Reform in the Public Schools: Public Education and Women's Rights in the Post–Civil War South." *History of Education Quarterly* 24 (Spring 1984): 45–58.

"Billups' Booze Bill." *Outlook* 89 (June 13, 1908): 311–12.

Blake, Nelson M. *Water for the Cities: A History of the Urban Water Supply Problem in the United States.* Syracuse, N.Y.: Syracuse University Press, 1956.

Blanton, Wyndham B. *Medicine in Virginia in the Seventeenth Century.* 1930. Reprint. Spartanburg, S.C.: Reprint Co., 1973.

Blocker, Jack S. *Retreat from Reform: The Prohibition Movement in the United States, 1890–1913.* Westport, Conn.: Greenwood Press, 1976.

Bordin, Ruth. *Women and Temperance: The Quest for Power and Liberty, 1873–1900.* Philadelphia: Temple University Press, 1981.

Boyer, Paul S. *Urban Masses and Moral Order in America, 1820–1920.* Cambridge: Harvard University Press, 1978.

Brandon, Betty Jane. "Alexander Jeffrey McKelway: Statesman of the New Order." Ph.D. dissertation, University of North Carolina at Chapel Hill, 1969.

————. "Wilsonian Progressive—Alexander Jeffrey McKelway." *Journal of Presbyterian History* 48 (Spring 1970): 2–17.

Brandt, Allen M. *No Magic Bullet: A Social History of Venereal Disease in the United States since 1880.* New York: Oxford University Press, 1985.

Branson, Eugene C. "The Real Southern Question." *World's Work* 3 (March 1902): 1888–91.

————. "The Real Southern Question." *World's Work* 3 (May 1902): 2066–72.

Breckinridge, Sophonisba Preston. *Madeline McDowell Breckinridge: A Leader in the New South.* Chicago: University of Chicago Press, 1921.

Brenaman, J. N. *A History of Virginia Conventions.* Richmond: J. L. Hill Printing Co., 1902.

Brough, Charles Hillman. "Work of the Commission of Southern Universities on the Race Question." *Annals of the American Academy of Political and Social Science* 49 (September 1913): 47–57.

Brown, E. Richard. *Rockefeller Medicine Men: Medicine and Capitalism in America.* Berkeley: University of California Press, 1979.

Brown, Roy M. *Public Poor Relief in North Carolina.* Chapel Hill: University of North Carolina Press, 1928.

Brown, William Garrott. "Of the North's Part in Southern Betterment." *Outlook* 78 (October 15, 1904): 415–18.

————. "The South and the Saloon." *Century Magazine* 76 (July 1908): 462–66.

————. *The New Politics, and Other Papers.* Boston: Houghton Mifflin Co., 1914.

Brownell, Blaine A. "Birmingham, Alabama: New South City in the 1920s." *Journal of Southern History* 38 (1972): 21–48.

Bryant, Keith L. "Kate Barnard, Organized Labor, and Social Justice in Oklahoma during the Progressive Era." *Journal of Southern History* 35 (May 1969): 145–64.

Burrow, James G. *Organized Medicine in the Progressive Era: The Move toward Monopoly.* Baltimore: Johns Hopkins University Press, 1977.

Burrows, Edward Flud. "The Commission on Interracial Cooperation, 1919–1944: A Case Study of the Interracial Movement in the South." Ph.D. dissertation, University of Wisconsin, 1954.

Caldwell, B. C. "Work of the Jeanes and Slater Funds." *Annals of the American Academy of Political and Social Science* 49 (September 1913): 173–76.

Campbell, John C. *The Southern Highlander and His Homeland.* New York: Russell Sage Foundation, 1921.

Campbell, Robert Fishburne. *Classification of Mountain Whites.* Hampton, Va.: Hampton Institute Press, 1901.

"Can Georgia Do It?" *Outlook* 107 (August 15, 1914): 888.

Carlton, David L. "'Builders of a New State': The Town Classes and Early Industrialization of South Carolina, 1880–1907." In *From the Old South to the New: Essays on the Transitional South*, edited by Walter J. Fraser, Jr., and Winifred B. Moore, pp. 43–62. Westport, Conn.: Greenwood Press, 1981.

───── . *Mill and Town in South Carolina, 1880–1920.* Baton Rouge: Louisiana State University Press, 1982.

───── . "The Revolution from Above: The National Market and the Beginnings of Industrialization in North Carolina." *Journal of American History* 77 (September 1990): 445–75.

Carlton, Mark T. *Politics and Punishment: A History of the Louisiana State Penal System.* Baton Rouge: Louisiana State University Press, 1971.

Chapin, Charles V. *A Report on State Public Health Work Based on a Survey of State Boards of Health.* 1916. Reprint. New York: Arno Press, 1977.

Christensen, Niels, Jr. "The State Dispensaries of South Carolina." *Annals of the American Academy of Political and Social Science* 32 (November 1908): 75–85.

───── . "Fifty Years of Freedom: Conditions in the Sea Coast Regions." *Annals of the American Academy of Political and Social Science* 49 (September 1913): 58–66.

Clark, Norman. *Deliver Us from Evil: An Interpretation of American Prohibition.* New York: Norton, 1976.

Claxton, Philander Priestley. "A Model School." *Annals of the American Academy of Political and Social Science* 22 (1903): 245–48.

───── . "A Substitute for Child Labor." *Child Labor Bulletin* 1 (June 1912): 73.

Clayton, Bruce L. "The Racial Thought of a Southern Intellectual at the Beginning of the Century: William Garrott Brown." *South Atlantic Quarterly* 63 (Winter 1964): 93–103.

───── . "An Intellectual on Politics: William Garrott Brown and the Ideal of a Two-Party South." *North Carolina Historical Review* 62 (Summer 1965): 319–34.

───── . *The Savage Ideal: Intolerance and Intellectual Leadership in the South, 1890–1914.* Baltimore: Johns Hopkins University Press, 1972.

Clemmons, William. "Volunteer Missions among Twentieth-Century Southern Baptists." *Baptist History and Heritage* 14 (January 1979): 37–49.

Cochran, Thomas E. *History of the Public-School Education in Florida.* Lancaster, Pa.: Press of the New Era Printing Co., 1922.

Cohen, William. "Negro Involuntary Servitude in the South, 1865–1940: A Preliminary Analysis." *Journal of Southern History* 42 (1976): 31–60.

Compton, Stephen C. "Edgar Gardner Murphy and the Child Labor Movement." *Historical Magazine of the Protestant Episcopal Church* (June 1983): 181–94.

───── . "Reform and Persecution in North Carolina Methodism." *Methodist History* (April 1984): 189–99.

Connor, Robert D. W. "The Peabody Education Fund." *South Atlantic Quarterly* 4 (April 1905): 169–81.

Coon, Charles L. "Where Negroes May Not Go." *Harper's Weekly* 48 (January 16, 1904): 102.

Cooper, George M. "Local Health Work under State Board Supervision with Special Reference to School Inspection and Typhoid Fever." *Southern Medical Journal* 10, no. 7 (1917): 554–59.

————. "Medical Inspection of Schools in North Carolina." *Southern Medical Journal* 11 (1918): 112–15.

Corrigan, John. "The Prohibition Wave in the South." *American Review of Reviews* 36 (September 1907): 328–34.

Coulter, E. Merton. "The Athens Dispensary." *Georgia Historical Quarterly* 50 (March 1966): 14–36.

Crunden, Robert M. *Ministers of Reform: The Progressives' Achievement in American Civilization, 1889–1920*. New York: Basic Books, 1982.

Dabney, Charles William. *Universal Education in the South*. 2 vols. Chapel Hill: University of North Carolina Press, 1936.

Dabney, Virginius. *Dry Messiah: The Life of Bishop Cannon*. New York: Alfred A. Knopf, 1949.

Daniel, Pete. *The Shadow of Slavery: Peonage in the South, 1901–1969*. Urbana: University of Illinois Press, 1972.

————. *Breaking the Land: The Transformation of Cotton, Tobacco, and Rice Cultures since 1880*. Urbana: University of Illinois Press, 1985.

Daniels, Richard S. "'Blind Tigers and Blind Justice': The Arkansas Raid on Island 37, Tennessee." *Arkansas Historical Quarterly* 38 (Autumn 1979): 259–70.

Dargan, W. F. "A Last Word in the South Carolina Liquor Law." *North American Review* 159 (1894): 52–60.

Davidson, Elizabeth Huey. "The Child-Labor Problem in North Carolina." *North Carolina Historical Review* 13 (April 1936): 105–21.

————. *Child Labor Legislation in the Southern Textile States*. Chapel Hill: University of North Carolina Press, 1939.

Davis, William Graham. "Attacking 'The Matchless Evil': Temperance and Prohibition in Mississippi, 1817–1908." Ph.D. dissertation, Mississippi State University, 1975.

D'Emilio, John, and Estelle B. Freedman. *Intimate Matters: A History of Sexuality in America*. New York: Harper and Row, 1988.

DeNatale, Douglas Paul. "Bynum: The Coming of Mill Village Life to a North Carolina County." Ph.D. dissertation, University of Pennsylvania, 1985.

Denson, D. "First Child-Labor Law Enacted in North Carolina." *Charities* 10 (April 25, 1903): 411–12.

Dillard, James Hardy. "County Machinery for Colored Schools in the South." *School and Society* 6 (September 8, 1917): 293–95.

Dodd, Ruth A. "Opportunities of the Rural Public Health Nurse to Develop Child Hygiene." *Southern Medical Journal* 13 (1920): 658–62.

Doherty, Herbert J. "Alexander J. McKelway: Preacher to Progressive." *Journal of Southern History* 24 (May 1958): 177–90.

Dowling, Harry F. *Fighting Infection: Conquests of the Twentieth Century*. Cambridge: Harvard University Press, 1977.

Duis, Perry R. *The Saloon: Public Drinking in Chicago and Boston, 1880–1920*. Urbana: University of Illinois Press, 1983.

Dunn, Durwood. *Cades Cove: The Life and Death of a Southern Appalachian Community, 1818–1937*. Knoxville: University of Tennessee Press, 1988.

Durrill, Wayne K. "Producing Poverty: Local Government and Economic Development in a New South County, 1874–1884." *Journal of American History* 71 (1985): 764–81.

———. *War of Another Kind: A Southern Community in the Great Rebellion*. New York: Oxford University Press, 1990.

Dykeman, Wilma, and James Stokely. *Seeds of Southern Change: The Life of Will Alexander*. Chicago: University of Chicago Press, 1962.

Eakin, Sue Lyles. "The Black Struggle for Education in Louisiana, 1877–1930." Ph.D. dissertation, Southwestern Louisiana University, 1980.

Eaton, Clement. "Edwin A. Alderman—Liberal of the New South." *North Carolina Historical Review* 23 (April 1946): 206–21.

———. "Breaking a Path for the Liberation of Women in the South." *Georgia Historical Review* 28 (September 1974): 187–99.

Eggleston, Joseph D., and Robert W. Bruère. *Work of the Rural School*. New York: Harper and Brothers, 1913.

Eighmy, John Lee. "Religious Liberalism in the South during the Progressive Era." *Church History* 38 (September 1969): 359–72.

———. *Churches in Cultural Captivity: A History of the Social Attitudes of Southern Baptists*. Knoxville, Tenn.: Abingdon Press, 1972.

Ellis, Ann Wells. "The Commission on Interracial Cooperation, 1919–1944: Its Activities and Results." Ph.D. dissertation, Georgia State University, 1975.

Ellis, Leonora Beck. "New Class of Labor in the South." *Forum* 31 (May 1901): 306–10.

———. "Industrial Awakening of the South." *Gunton's Magazine* 20 (June 1901): 527–36.

———. "Child Labor Legislation in the South." *Gunton's Magazine* 21 (July 1901): 45–53.

———. "Child Operatives in Southern Mills." *Independent* 53 (November 7, 1901): 2637–47.

———. "A Study of Southern Cotton-Mill Communities." *American Journal of Sociology* 8 (March 1903): 623–30.

———. "Educating Southern Factory Children." *Gunton's Magazine* 24 (May 1903): 459–70.

———. "Factory Children of Georgia." *Era* 12 (July 1903): 49–57.

Enck, Henry S. "Tuskegee Institute and Northern White Philanthropy: A Case Study in Fund Raising, 1900–1915." *Journal of Negro History* 65 (Fall 1980): 336–48.

Engelman, Larry. *Intemperance: The Lost War against Liquor*. New York: Free Press, 1979.

English, Peter C. *Shock, Physiological Surgery, and George Washington Crile: Medical Innovation in the Progressive Era*. Westport, Conn.: Greenwood Press, 1980.

Epstein, Barbara Leslie. *The Politics of Domesticity: Women, Evangelicalism, and Temperance in Nineteenth-Century America*. Middleton, Conn.: Wesleyan University Press, 1981.

Erickson, J. E., and James H. McCrocklin. "From Religion to Commerce: The Evolution and Enforcement of Blue Laws in Texas." *Southwestern Social Science Quarterly* 45 (1964): 50–58.

Eslinger, Ellen. "Antebellum Liquor Reform in Lexington, Virginia." *Virginia Magazine of History and Biography* 99 (April 1991): 163–86.

Estes, Florence S. "Cora Wilson Stewart and the Moonlight Schools of Kentucky, 1911–1920: A Case Study in the Rhetorical Uses of Illiteracy." Ph.D. dissertation, University of Kentucky, 1988.

Etheridge, Elizabeth W. *The Butterfly Caste: A Social History of Pellagra in the South.* Westport, Conn.: Greenwood Press, 1972.

Ettling, John. *The Germ of Laziness: Rockefeller Philanthropy and Public Health in the New South.* Cambridge: Harvard University Press, 1981.

Eubanks, John Evans. *Ben Tillman's Baby: The Dispensary System of South Carolina, 1892–1915.* Augusta, Ga.: The author, 1950.

Ewing, Quincy. "The Heart of the Race Problem." *Atlantic Monthly* 103 (March 1909): 389–97.

Farish, Hunter Dickinson. *The Circuit Rider Dismounts: A Social History of Southern Methodists, 1865–1900.* 1938. Reprint. New York: Da Capo Press, 1969.

Farmer, Harry Frank, Jr. "The Hookworm Eradication Program in the South, 1909–1925." Ph.D. dissertation, University of Georgia, 1970.

Ferrell, Henry C., Jr. "Prohibition, Reform, and Politics in Virginia, 1895–1916." In *Studies in the History of the South, 1875–1922,* pp. 175–242. Vol. 3 of East Carolina College Publications in History. Greenville, N.C., 1966.

Ferrell, John A. "The North Carolina Campaign against Hookworm Disease." *South Atlantic Quarterly* 11 (1912): 128–35.

Few, William P. "The Constructive Philanthropy of a Southern Cotton Mill." *South Atlantic Quarterly* 8 (January 1909): 82–90.

Flannagan, Roy K. "Medical Inspection of Rural Schools—Methods, Results, Possibilities." *Southern Medical Journal* 8 (1915): 123–28.

———. "Rural School Inspection and How It May Be Secured." *Virginia Journal of Education* 10 (1915–16): 112–15.

Flexner, Eleanor. *Century of Struggle: The Woman's Rights Movement in the United States.* Rev. ed. Cambridge: Harvard University Press, 1975.

Floyd, Josephine Bone. "Rebecca Latimer Felton: Champion of Women's Rights." *Georgia Historical Quarterly* 30 (1946): 81–104.

Flynt, Wayne. "Dissent in Zion: Alabama Baptists and Social Issues, 1900–1914." *Journal of Southern History* 35 (November 1969): 523–42.

———. "Alabama White Protestantism and Labor, 1900–1914." *Alabama Review* 25 (July 1972): 192–217.

———. "Southern Baptists and Reform, 1890–1920." *Baptist History and Heritage* 7 (October 1972): 211–24.

———. "Religion in the Urban South: The Divided Religious Mind of Birmingham, 1900–1930." *Alabama Review* 30 (April 1977): 108–34.

Ford, Lacy K. "Rednecks and Merchants: Economic Development and Social Tensions in the South Carolina Upcountry, 1865–1900." *Journal of American History* 71 (September 1984): 294–318.

———. *The Origins of Southern Radicalism: The South Carolina Upcountry, 1800–1860.* New York: Oxford University Press, 1988.

Forderhase, Nancy K. "The Clear Call of Thoroughbred Women: The Kentucky Federation of Women's Clubs and the Crusade for Educational Reform, 1903–1909."

Register of the Kentucky Historical Society 83 (1985): 19–85.

————. "Limited Only by Earth and Sky: The Louisville Woman's Club and Progressive Reform, 1900–1910." Filson Club Historical Quarterly 59 (1985): 327–43.

Fosdick, Raymond Blaine. The Story of the Rockefeller Foundation. New York: Harper Brothers, 1952.

————. Adventure in Giving: The Story of the General Education Board. New York: Harper and Row, 1962.

Foster, Gaines M. Ghosts of the Confederacy: Defeat, the Last Cause, and the Emergence of the New South, 1865 to 1913. New York: Oxford University Press, 1987.

Foxcroft, Frank. "Prohibition in the South." Atlantic Monthly 101 (May 1908): 627–34.

Fraser, Walter J., R. Frank Saunders, Jr., and Jon Wakelyn, eds. The Web of Southern Social Relations: Women, Family, and Education. Athens: University of Georgia Press, 1985.

"Freedom of Opinion in the South." Nation 82 (January 4, 1906): 6.

Freeman, Allen W. "Rural Sanitation." Southern Medical Journal 4, no. 12 (1911–12): 869–74.

Friedman, Jean F. The Enclosed Garden: Women and Community in the Evangelical South. Chapel Hill: University of North Carolina Press, 1985.

Galishoff, Stuart. Safeguarding the Public Health: Newark, 1895–1918. Westport, Conn.: Greenwood Press, 1975.

Gardner, Sarah Elizabeth. "Medical Men versus Granny Women: The Professional Obstetricians' Campaign against Midwives in the Rural South." M.A. thesis, Miami University, 1990.

"Georgia's Example to the Nation." Independent 64 (January 16, 1908): 162–63.

Gifford, Carolyn DeSwarte. "Sisterhoods of Service and Reform: Organized Methodist Women in the Late Nineteenth Century: An Essay on the State of the Research." Methodist History 24 (January 1985): 15–30.

Glasson, William H. "The Rockefeller Commission's Campaign against the Hookworm." South Atlantic Quarterly 10 (April 1911): 142–48.

Going, Allen J. "The Reverend Edgar Gardner Murphy: His Ideas and Influence." Historical Journal of the Protestant Episcopal Church 25 (December 1956): 391–402.

Goodman, Clavia. Bitter Harvest: Laura Clay's Suffrage Work. Lexington: University Press of Kentucky, 1946.

Goodrich, Gillian. "Romance and Reality: The Birmingham Suffragists, 1892–1920." Journal of the Birmingham Historical Society 5 (January 1978): 5–21.

Gould, Lewis L. Progressives and Prohibitionists: Texas Democrats in the Wilson Era. Austin: University of Texas Press, 1973.

Graham, Joseph B. "Current Problems in Alabama." Annals of the American Academy of Political and Social Science 22 (June–December 1903): 280–83.

Grantham, Dewey W., Jr. "The Regional Imagination: Social Scientists and the American South." Journal of Southern History 34 (1968): 3–32.

————. Southern Progressivism: The Reconciliation of Progress and Tradition. Knoxville: University of Tennessee Press, 1983.

Graves, John Temple. "Georgia Pioneers the Prohibition." Cosmopolitan 45 (June 1908): 83–90.

Green, Elna C. "Those Opposed: The Antisuffragists in North Carolina, 1900–1920." *North Carolina Historical Review* 67 (July 1990): 315–33.

Green, Fletcher M. "Some Aspects of the Convict Lease System in the Southern States." In *Essays in Southern History Presented to Joseph Gregoire De Roulhac Hamilton*, edited by Fletcher M. Green, pp. 112–23. Chapel Hill: University of North Carolina Press, 1949.

Gusfield, Joseph R. *Symbolic Crusade: Status Politics and the American Temperance Movement.* Urbana: University of Illinois Press, 1963.

Hahn, Steven. *The Roots of Southern Populism: The Transformation of the Georgia Upcountry, 1850–1890.* New York: Oxford University Press, 1982.

Hall, Jacquelyn Dowd. *Revolt against Chivalry: Jessie Daniel Ames and the Women's Campaign against Lynching.* New York: Columbia University Press, 1979.

———. Hall, Jacquelyn Dowd, James LeLoudis, Robert Korstad, Mary Murphy, and Christopher B. Daly. *Like a Family: The Making of a Southern Cotton Mill World.* Chapel Hill: University of North Carolina Press, 1987.

Hamm, Richard. "Origins of the Eighteenth Amendment: Prohibition in the Federal System, 1880–1920." Ph.D. dissertation, University of Virginia, 1987.

Hammond, L. H. "The White Man's Debt to the Negro." *Annals of the American Academy of Political and Social Science* 49 (September 1913): 67–73.

Hanchett, Thomas W. "The Rosenwald Schools and Black Education in North Carolina." *North Carolina Historical Review* 65 (October 1988): 387–427.

Harlan, Louis R. "The Southern Education Board and the Race Issue in Public Education." *Journal of Southern History* 23 (May 1957): 189–202.

———. *Separate and Unequal: Public School Campaigns and Racism in the Southern Seaboard States, 1901–1915.* Chapel Hill: University of North Carolina Press, 1958.

———. *Booker T. Washington: The Making of a Black Leader, 1856–1901.* New York: Oxford University Press, 1972.

———. *Booker T. Washington: The Wizard of Tuskegee, 1901–1915.* New York: Oxford University Press, 1983.

Harris, Carl V. *Political Power in Birmingham, 1871–1921.* Knoxville: University of Tennessee Press, 1977.

———. "Stability and Change in Discrimination against Black Public Schools." *Journal of Southern History* 61 (August 1985): 375–416.

Hart, Albert Bushnell. "Conditions of the Southern Problem." *Independent* 58 (March 23, 1905): 644–49.

———. *The Southern South.* New York: D. Appleton and Co:, 1910.

Hay, Melba Porter. "Madeline McDowell Breckinridge: Kentucky Suffragist and Progressive Reformer." Ph.D. dissertation, University of Kentucky, 1980.

Hendricks, Ellen Alexander. "The South Carolina Dispensary System, Part I." *North Carolina Historical Review* 22 (April 1945): 176–97.

———. "The South Carolina Dispensary System, Part II." *North Carolina Historical Review* 22 (July 1945): 320–49.

Hill, Walter B. "Negro Education in the South." *Annals of the American Academy of Political and Social Science* 22 (June–December 1903): 320–28.

Hine, Lewis W. "Child Labor in Gulf Coast Canneries: Photographic Investigation

Made February 1911." *Annals of the American Academy of Political and Social Science* (Supplement) 38 (July 1911): 118–22.

Hogan, David John. *Class and Reform: School and Society in Chicago, 1880–1930.* Philadelphia: University of Pennsylvania Press, 1985.

Hoge, Sara H. "Organization and Accomplishments of the W.C.T.U. in Virginia." *Annals of the American Academy of Political and Social Science* 32 (1908): 527–30.

Hohner, Robert Arthur. "Prohibition and Virginia Politics, 1901–1916." Ph.D. dissertation, Duke University, 1965.

——— . "Prohibition and Virginia Politics: William Hodges Mann versus Henry St. George Tucker." *Virginia Magazine of History and Biography* 74 (January 1966): 88–107.

——— . "Prohibition Comes to Virginia: The Referendum of 1914." *Virginia Magazine of History and Biography* 75 (1967): 473–88.

——— . "Bishop Cannon's Apprenticeship in Temperance Politics, 1901–1918." *Journal of Southern History* 34 (February 1968): 33–49.

——— . "The Prohibitionists: Who Were They?" *South Atlantic Quarterly* 68 (Autumn 1969): 494–505.

Hoke, Kathleen E. "The Politics of Fertility: Coercive Sterilization and Public Health Birth Control in North Carolina, 1929–1960." M.A. thesis, University of North Carolina at Greensboro, 1991.

Hollis, John Porter. "Child Labor Legislation in the Carolinas." *Annals of the American Academy of Political and Social Science* 38 (Supplement) (July 1911): 114–17.

Holmes, William F. "Whitecapping: Agrarian Violence in Mississippi, 1902–1906." *Journal of Southern History* 35 (May 1969): 165–85.

——— . "Moonshining and Collective Violence, 1890–1895." *Journal of American History* 67 (1980): 589–611.

——— . "Moonshining and Whitecaps in Alabama, 1893." *Alabama Review* 34 (1981): 31–49.

Hunt, Robert Eno. "Organizing a New South: Education Reformers in Antebellum Alabama, 1840–1860." Ph.D. dissertation, University of Missouri-Columbia, 1988.

Ireland, Robert E. *Entering the Auto Age: The Early Automobile in North Carolina, 1900–1930.* Raleigh: North Carolina Division of Archives and History, 1990.

Isaac, Paul E. *Prohibition and Politics: Turbulent Decades in Tennessee, 1885–1920.* Knoxville: University of Tennessee Press, 1965.

Jackson, Harvey H. "The Middle-Class Democracy Victorious: The Mitcham War of Clarke County, Alabama, 1893." *Journal of Southern History* 57 (August 1991): 453–78.

Jackson, J. C. "The Work of the Anti–Saloon League." *Annals of the American Academy of Political and Social Science* 32 (1908): 482–96.

James, Arthur Wilson. *Virginia's Social Awakening: The Contribution of Dr. Mastin and the Board of Charities and Corrections.* Richmond: Garret and Massie, 1939.

Johnson, Kenneth R. "The Woman Suffrage Movement in Florida." Ph.D. dissertation, Florida State University, 1966.

——— . "Kate Gordon and the Woman Suffrage Movement in the South." *Journal of Southern History* 38 (August 1972): 365–92.

Jones, James H. *Bad Blood: The Tuskegee Syphilis Experiment*. New York: Free Press, 1981.

Jones, M. Ashby. "The Approach to the South's Race Question." *Journal of Social Forces* 1 (November 1922): 40–41.

Jones, William M. "Medical Inspection of Children in Rural Schools." *Southern Medical Journal* 7 (1914): 198–200.

Kearney, Belle. *A Slaveholder's Daughter*. New York: Abbey Press, 1900.

Kemp, Kathryn W. "Jean and Kate Gordon: New Orleans Social Reformers, 1898–1933." *Louisiana History* 24 (Fall 1983): 389–401.

Kerr, K. Austin. *Organized for Prohibition: A New History of the Anti-Saloon League*. New Haven: Yale University Press, 1985.

Kett, Joseph F. *The Formation of the American Medical Profession: The Role of Institutions, 1780–1860*. New Haven: Yale University Press, 1968.

Kilgo, John Carlisle. "An Inquiry regarding Lynching." *South Atlantic Quarterly* 1 (January 1902): 4–13.

———. "Our Duty to the Negro." *South Atlantic Quarterly* 2 (October 1903): 369–85.

Kipp, Samuel M. "Urban Growth and Social Change in the South, 1870–1920: Greensboro, North Carolina, as a Case Study." Ph.D. dissertation, Princeton University, 1974.

———. "Old Notables and Newcomers: The Economic and Political Elite of Greensboro, North Carolina, 1880–1920." *Journal of Southern History* 43 (1977): 373–410.

Kirby, Jack Temple. *Westmoreland Davis: Planter-Politician, 1859–1942*. Charlottesville: University Press of Virginia, 1968.

———. *Darkness at the Dawning: Race and Reform in the Progressive South*. Philadelphia: J. B. Lippincott, 1972.

———. "Black and White in the Rural South." *Agricultural History* 58 (July 1984): 411–22.

———. *Rural Worlds Lost: The American South, 1920–1960*. Baton Rouge: Louisiana State University Press, 1987.

Klotter, James. "The Black South and White Appalachia." *Journal of American History* 66 (March 1980): 832–49.

———. *The Breckinridges of Kentucky, 1760–1981*. Lexington: University Press of Kentucky, 1986.

Kneebone, John T. *Southern Liberal Journalists and the Issue of Race, 1920–1944*. Chapel Hill: University of North Carolina Press, 1985.

Kousser, J. Morgan. "Progressivism—For Middle-Class Whites Only: North Carolina Education, 1880–1910." *Journal of Southern History* 46 (May 1980): 169–94.

Kramer, Howard D. "The Beginnings of the Public Health Movement in the United States." *Bulletin of the History of Medicine* 21 (May–June 1947): 352–76.

———. "Early Municipal and State Boards of Health." *Bulletin of the History of Medicine* 24 (November–December 1950): 503–29.

Kyvig, David. *Repealing National Prohibition*. Chicago: University of Chicago Press, 1979.

Lacy, Eric Russell. "Tennessee Teetotalism: Social Forces and the Politics of Progressivism." *Tennessee Historical Quarterly* 24 (Fall 1965).

Leab, Grace. "Tennessee Temperance Activities, 1870–1899." *East Tennessee Historical Society Publications* 21 (1949): 52–68.

Lefever, Harry G. "The Involvement of the Men and Religion Forward Movement in the Cause of Labor Justice, Atlanta, Georgia, 1912–1916." *Labor History* 14 (Fall 1973): 521–35.

Legan, Marshall Scott. "The Evolution of Public Health Services in Mississippi, 1865–1910." Ph.D. dissertation, University of Mississippi, 1968.

Leloudis, James L. "School Reform in the New South: The Woman's Association for the Betterment of Public School Houses in North Carolina, 1902–1919." *Journal of American History* 69 (March 1983): 886–909.

————. "'A More Certain Means of Grace': Pedagogy, Self, and Society in North Carolina, 1880–1920." Ph.D. dissertation, University of North Carolina at Chapel Hill, 1989.

Lerner, Gerda. "Early Community Work of Black Club Women." *Journal of Negro History* 59 (April 1974): 158–67.

Letsinger, Norman H. "The Status of Women in the Southern Baptist Convention in Historical Perspective." *Baptist History and Heritage* 12 (January 1977): 37–44.

Levine, Daniel. "Edgar Gardner Murphy: Conservative Reformer." *Alabama Review* 15 (April 1962): 100–16.

Link, Arthur S. "The Progressive Movement in the South, 1870–1914." *North Carolina Historical Review* 23 (April 1946): 172–95.

Link, William A. *A Hard Country and a Lonely Place: Schooling, Society, and Reform in Rural Virginia, 1870–1920.* Chapel Hill: University of North Carolina Press, 1986.

————. "Privies, Progressivism, and Public Schools: Health Reform and Education in the Rural South, 1909–1920." *Journal of Southern History* 54 (November 1988): 623–42.

————. "'The Harvest Is Ripe, but the Laborers Are Few': The Hookworm Crusade in North Carolina, 1909–1915." *North Carolina Historical Review* 67 (January 1990): 1–27.

————. "The Social Context of Southern Progressivism, 1880–1930." In *The Wilson Era: Essays in Honor of Arthur S. Link,* edited by John Milton Cooper, Jr., and Charles Neu, pp. 55–82. Arlington Heights, Ill.: Harlan Davidson, Inc., 1991.

Lissner, E. "Dry Days in the South." *Harper's Weekly* 51 (July 1907): 1057.

Locke, James H., Jr. "The Struggle for the Mind: The Child Labor Movement in North Carolina, 1900–1916." M.A. thesis, University of North Carolina at Greensboro, 1988.

Logan, Rayford W. *The Negro in American Life and Thought: The Nadir, 1877–1901.* New York: Dial Press, Inc., 1954.

Louis, James P. "Sue Shelton White and the Woman Suffrage Movement in Tennessee, 1913–1920." *Tennessee Historical Quarterly* 22 (June 1963): 172–77.

Luker, Ralph E. *The Social Gospel in Black and White: American Racial Reform, 1885–1912.* Chapel Hill: University of North Carolina Press, 1991.

McBeth, Henry Leon. "The Role of Women in Southern Baptist History." *Baptist History and Heritage* 12 (January 1977): 3–25.

McCormick, Richard L. "The Party Period and Public Policy." *Journal of American History* 66 (1979): 279–98.

———. "The Discovery That Business Corrupts Politics: A Reappraisal of the Origins of Progressivism." *American Historical Review* 86 (April 1981): 247–74.

McDowell, John Patrick. *The Social Gospel in the South: The Woman's Home Mission Movement in the Methodist Episcopal Church, South, 1886–1939.* Baton Rouge: Louisiana State University Press, 1982.

MacFayden, Irene Ashby. "Child Labor in the South." *Current Literature* 33 (July 1902): 77–79.

McGovern, James R. "'Sporting Life on the Line': Prostitution in Progressive Era Pensacola." *Florida Historical Quarterly* 14 (1975): 131–44.

McIver, Charles Duncan. "Current Problems in North Carolina." *Annals of the American Academy of Political and Social Science* 22 (June–December 1903): 293–302.

McKelvey, Blake. "A Half Century of Southern Penal Exploitation." *Social Forces* 13 (October 1934): 112–23.

McKelway, Alexander J. "The Dispensary in North Carolina." *Outlook* 61 (April 8, 1899): 820–22.

———. "Child Labor in Southern Industry." *Annals of the American Academy of Political and Social Science* 35 (January–June 1905): 430–36.

———. "The Child Labor Problem—A Study in Degeneracy." *Annals of the American Academy of Political and Social Science* 27 (January–June 1906): 312–26.

———. "Child Labor in the Southern Cotton Mills." *Annals of the American Academy of Political and Social Science* 27 (January–June 1906): 259–69.

———. "The Atlanta Riots: A Southern White Point of View." *Outlook* 84 (November 3, 1906): 557–62.

———. "The Awakening of the South against Child Labor." *Annals of the American Academy of Political and Social Science* 29 (January 1907): 9–18.

———. "Child Labor in the South." *Outlook* 85 (April 27, 1907): 917–19, 999–1000.

———. "State Prohibition in Georgia and the South." *Outlook* 86 (August 31, 1907): 947–49.

———. "Local Option and State Prohibition in the South." *Charities* 19 (January 25, 1908): 1452–53.

———. "Child Labor and Its Attendant Evils." *Sewanee Review* 16 (April 1908): 214–27.

———. "State Prohibition in North Carolina." *Outlook* 89 (June 6, 1908): 271–72.

———. "Fight for Child Labor Reform in the Carolinas." *Charities* 21 (March 10, 1909): 1224–26.

———. "Child Labor in the South." *Annals of the American Academy of Political and Social Science* 35 (January 1910): 156–64.

———. "The Cotton Mill: The Herod among Industries." *Annals of the American Academy of Political and Social Science* 38 (Supplement) (July 1911): 49–50.

———. "Child Labor Campaign in the South." *Survey* 27 (October 21, 1911): 1023–26.

———. "Fighting Child Labor in Three States." *Survey* 28 (April 20, 1912): 121–22.

———. "Child Labor and Poverty." *Survey* 30 (April 12, 1913): 60–62.

———. "The Florida Child Labor Campaign." *Survey* 30 (July 12, 1913): 497–98.

————. "Arkansas Child Labor Law Secured by the Initiative." *Survey* 33 (October 10, 1914): 44.

McLean, Francis H. "Prohibition and Southern Local Problems." *Charities* 20 (May 2, 1908): 154.

Mann, Harold W. *Atticus Greene Haygood: Methodist Bishop, Editor, and Educator.* Athens: University of Georgia Press, 1965.

Margo, Robert A. "Teacher Salaries in Black and White: The South in 1910." *Explorations in Economic History* 21 (July 1984): 306–26.

————. *Disenfranchisement, School Finance, and the Economics of Segregated Schools in the United States South.* New York: Garland, 1985.

Mathews, John H. "Black Newspapermen and the Black Community in Georgia, 1890–1930." *Georgia Historical Quarterly* 68 (Fall 1984): 356–81.

Miller, E. E. "When Prohibition Fails and Why." *Outlook* 101 (July 20, 1912): 639–43.

Miller, Wilbur R. "The Revenue: Federal Law Enforcement in the Mountain South, 1870–1900." *Journal of Southern History* 55 (May 1989): 195–216.

Mitchell, Samuel Chiles. "The Nationalization of Southern Sentiment." *South Atlantic Quarterly* 7 (1908): 107–13.

Mitchell, Theodore R. "From Black to White: The Transformation of Educational Reform in the New South, 1890–1910." *Educational Theory* 39 (Fall 1989): 144–50.

Mixon, Wayne. *Southern Writers and the New South Movement, 1865–1913.* Chapel Hill: University of North Carolina Press, 1980.

Modey, Yao Foli. "The Struggle over Prohibition in Memphis, 1880–1930." Ph.D. dissertation, Memphis State University, 1983.

Moore, John Hammond. "The Negro and Prohibition in Atlanta, 1885–1887." *South Atlantic Quarterly* 69 (1970): 38–57.

Moos, Malcolm C. *State Penal Administration in Alabama.* University, Ala.: University of Alabama Press, 1942.

"Moral Dignity of Prohibition in the South." *American Review of Reviews* 37 (April 1908): 479–80.

Morrow, Honoré (McCue) Willsie. *Tiger! Tiger! The Life Story of John B. Gough.* New York: W. Morrow and Co., 1930.

Murphy, Edgar Gardner. "Progress in the South." *Outlook* 67 (June 29, 1901): 475–76.

————. *Child Labor in Alabama: An Appeal to the People and Press of New England with a Resulting Correspondence.* Montgomery: Alabama Child Labor Committee, 1902.

————. *Pictures from Life: Mill Children in Alabama.* Montgomery: Alabama Child Labor Committee, 1903.

————. "Child Labor in Alabama." *Annals of the American Academy of Political and Social Science* 21 (March 1903): 331–32.

————. *Problems of the Present South: A Discussion of Certain of the Educational, Industrial, and Political Issues in the Southern States.* New York: Macmillan Co., 1904.

————. "The National Child-Labor Committee." *Charities* 12 (June 4, 1904): 574–76.

————. "The Task of the Leader." *Sewanee Review* 15 (January 1907): 1–30.

————. "Backward or Forward?" *South Atlantic Quarterly* 8 (January 1909): 19–38.

————. *The Basis of Ascendancy: A Discussion of Certain Principles of Public Policy Involved in the Development of the Southern States*. New York: Longmans, Green, and Co., 1910.

Nelms, Willie E. "Cora Wilson Stewart and the Crusade against Illiteracy in Kentucky, 1916–1920." *Register of the Kentucky Historical Society* (Spring 1984): 151–69.

Newby, Idus A. *Jim Crow's Defense: Anti-Negro Thought in America, 1900–1930*. Baton Rouge: Louisiana State University Press, 1965.

————. *Plain Folk in the New South: Social Change and Cultural Persistence, 1880–1915*. Baton Rouge: Louisiana State University Press, 1989.

Nolen, Claude H. *The Negro's Image in the South: The Anatomy of White Supremacy*. Lexington: University Press of Kentucky, 1967.

Odum, Howard Washington. *An Approach to Public Welfare and Social Work*. Chapel Hill: University of North Carolina Press, 1926.

Ogden, Robert C. "The Conference for Education in the South." *Annals of the American Academy of Political and Social Science* 22 (July–December 1903): 271–79.

O'Neill, William L. *Everyone Was Brave: A History of Feminism in America*. Chicago: University of Chicago Press, 1971.

Orery, David H. "When the Wicked Beareth Rule: A Southern Critique of Industrial America." *Journal of Presbyterian History* 98 (Summer 1970): 130–42.

Orr, Dorothy. *History of Education in Georgia*. Chapel Hill: University of North Carolina Press, 1950.

Ownby, Ted. *Subduing Satan: Religion, Recreation, and Manhood in the Rural South, 1865–1920*. Chapel Hill: University of North Carolina Press, 1990.

Page, Walter Hines. *The Rebuilding of Old Commonwealths*. New York: Doubleday, Page, 1902.

Pannell, Anne Gary, and Dorothea E. Wyatt. *Julia S. Tutwiler and Social Progress in Alabama*. University, Ala.: University of Alabama Press, 1961.

Parker, Lewis W. "Conditions of Labor in Southern Cotton Mills." *Annals of the American Academy of Political and Social Science* 33 (January–June 1909): 278–86.

Parker, Thomas F. "The South Carolina Cotton Mill—A Manufacturer's View." *South Atlantic Quarterly* 8 (October 1909): 328–37.

Pearson, Charles Chilton, and J. Edwin Hendricks. *Liquor and Anti-Liquor in Virginia, 1619–1919*. Durham, N.C.: Duke University Press, 1967.

Pilkington, Charles Kirk. "The Trials of Brotherhood: The Founding of the Commission on Interracial Cooperation." *Georgia Historical Quarterly* 69 (1985): 55–80.

Plank, David N., and Rick Ginsberg. *Southern Cities, Southern Schools: Public Education in the Urban South*. New York: Greenwood Press, 1990.

Plank, David N., and Paul E. Peterson. "Does Urban Reform Imply Class Conflict? The Case of Atlanta's Schools." *History of Education Quarterly* 24 (Summer 1983): 151–73.

"Plantation as a Civilizing Factor." *Review of Reviews* 30 (September 1904): 357–58.

Pocock, J. G. A. *The Machiavellian Moment: Florentine Political Thought and the Atlantic Republican Tradition*. Princeton: Princeton University Press, 1975.

Pope, Paul G. "Factors Involved in Medical Inspection of School Children." *Southern Medical Journal* 14 (1921): 205–16.

Porter, Melba Dean. "Madeline McDowell Breckinridge: Her Role in the Kentucky Woman Suffrage Movement, 1908–1920." *Register of the Kentucky Historical Society* 72 (October 1974): 342–63.

Prather, A. Leon, Sr. *Resurgent Politics and Educational Progressivism in the New South: North Carolina, 1890–1913.* Rutherford, N.J.: Fairleigh Dickinson Press, 1979.

Prescott, Grace Elizabeth. "The Woman Suffrage Movement in Memphis: Its Place in the State, Sectional, and National Movements." *West Tennessee Historical Society Papers* 18 (1964): 87–94.

Pritchard, R. E. "The Failure of Prohibition in the South." *Harper's Weekly* 55 (March 18, 1911): 12.

"Prohibition in Alabama." *Outlook* 87 (November 30, 1907): 707.

"Prohibition in Georgia." *Outlook* 86 (August 10, 1907): 757–78.

"The Prohibition Wave over the South." *World's Work* 14 (September 1907): 9278.

Pudup, Mary Beth. "The Limits of Subsistence: Agriculture and Industry in Central Appalachia." *Agricultural History* 64 (Winter 1990): 61–89.

Rabinowitz, Howard N. *The First New South, 1865–1920.* Arlington Heights, Ill.: Harlan Davidson, Inc., 1992.

Richardson, Joe M. *Christian Reconstruction: The American Missionary Association and Southern Blacks, 1861–1890.* Athens: University of Georgia Press, 1986.

Ritchie, John Woodside. *Primer of Sanitation: Being a Simple Textbook on Disease Germs and How to Fight Them.* Yonkers-on-Hudson, N.Y.: World Book Company, 1910.

Roblyer, Leslie F. "The Fight for Local Prohibition in Knoxville, Tennessee, 1917." *East Tennessee Historical Society Publications* 26 (1954): 27–37.

Rodgers, Daniel T. "In Search of Progressivism." *Reviews in American History* 10 (December 1982): 113–32.

Rorabaugh, William J. *The Alcoholic Republic: An American Tradition.* New York: Oxford University Press, 1979.

———. "The Sons of Temperance in Antebellum Jasper County." *Georgia Historical Quarterly* 64 (Fall 1980): 263–79.

Rosen, George. "Political Order and Human Health in Jeffersonian Thought." *Bulletin of the History of Medicine* 26 (January–February 1952): 32–44.

———. "Problems in the Application of Statistical Analysis to Questions of Health: 1700–1880." *Bulletin of the History of Medicine* 29 (1955): 27–45.

———. "The Fate of the Concept of Medical Police, 1780–1890." *Centaurus* 5 (1957): 97–113.

———. *A History of Public Health.* New York: MD Publications, 1958.

Rosen, Ruth. *The Lost Sisterhood: Prostitution in America, 1908–1918.* Baltimore: Johns Hopkins University Press, 1982.

Rosenberg, Charles. "The Cause of Cholera: Aspects of Etiological Thought in Nineteenth-Century America." *Bulletin of the History of Medicine* 34 (July–August 1960): 331–54.

———. *The Cholera Years: The United States in 1832, 1849, and 1866.* Chicago: University of Chicago Press, 1962.

———. "The Practice of Medicine in New York a Century Ago." *Bulletin of the History of Medicine* 41 (1967): 223–53.

————. "The Female Animal: Medical and Biological Views of Woman and Her Role in Nineteenth-Century America." *Journal of American History* 60 (1973): 332–56.

————. "Social Class and Medical Care in Nineteenth-Century America: The Rise and Fall of the Dispensary." *Journal of the History of Medicine* 29 (1974): 32–54.

————. "And Heal the Sick: Hospital and Patient in Nineteenth-Century America." *Journal of Southern History* 10 (1977): 428–47.

————. "The Therapeutic Revolution: Medicine, Meaning, and Social Change in Nineteenth-Century America." *Perspectives in Biology and Medicine* 20 (1977): 485–506.

————. "Inward Vision and Outward Glance: The Shaping of the American Hospital, 1880–1914." *Bulletin of the History of Medicine* 53 (1979): 346–91.

————. "The Origins of the American Hospital System." *Bulletin of the New York Academy of Medicine* 55 (1979): 17.

Rosencrantz, Barbara Gutmann. *Public Health and the State: Changing Views in Massachusetts, 1842–1936.* Cambridge: Harvard University Press, 1972.

Rouse, Jacqueline Anne. *Lugenia Burns Hope: Black Southern Reformer.* Athens: University of Georgia Press, 1989.

"The Saloon in the South." *Outlook* 88 (March 14, 1908): 581–82.

Savitt, Todd L. *Medicine and Slavery: The Diseases and Health Care of Blacks in Antebellum Virginia.* Urbana: University of Illinois Press, 1978.

Schulman, Bruce J. *From Cotton Belt to Sunbelt: Federal Policy, Economic Development, and the Transformation of the South, 1938–1980.* New York: Oxford University Press, 1991.

Schultz, Stanley K. "Temperance Reform in the Antebellum South: Social Control and Urban Order." *South Atlantic Quarterly* (Summer 1984): 323–39.

Scott, Anne Firor. "The 'New Woman' in the New South." *South Atlantic Quarterly* 61 (Autumn 1962): 473–83.

————. "A Progressive Wind from the South, 1906–1913." *Journal of Southern History* 29 (February 1963): 53–70.

————. *The Southern Lady from Pedestal to Politics, 1880–1930.* Chicago: University of Chicago Press, 1970.

————. "Women, Religion, and Social Change in the South, 1830–1930." In *Religion and the Solid South,* edited by Samuel S. Hill, Jr., pp. 92–121. Nashville, 1972.

————. "On Seeing and Not Seeing: A Case of Historical Invisibility." *Journal of American History* 71 (June 1984): 7–21.

Scott, Emmett J. "Brightening up the Rural South." *Outlook* 119 (July 10, 1918): 412–14.

Sellers, Charles Grier, Jr. "Walter Hines Page and the Spirit of the New South." *North Carolina Historical Review* 29 (October 1952): 481–99.

Sellers, James Benson. *The Prohibition Movement in Alabama, 1702 to 1943.* Edited by Albert Ray Newsome, William Whatley Pierson, Mitchell B. Garrett, Fletcher M. Green, and Keener C. Frazer. James Sprunt Series in History and Political Science, vol. 26. Chapel Hill: University of North Carolina Press, 1943.

Shapiro, Henry D. *Appalachia on Our Mind: The Southern Mountains and Mountaineers in the American Consciousness, 1870–1920.* Chapel Hill: University of North Carolina Press, 1978.

Shelby, Annette. "The Southern Lady Becomes an Advocate." In *Oratory in the New South*, edited by Waldo W. Braden, pp. 204–36. Baton Rouge: Louisiana University Press, 1979.

Sheldon, Richard N. "Richmond Pearson Hobson as a Progressive Reformer." *Alabama Review* 25 (October 1972): 243–61.

Simpson, R. W. "Near-Prohibition in the South." *Harper's Weekly* 53 (July 10, 1909): 15.

Sims, Anastatia. "'The Sword of the Spirit': The WCTU and Moral Reform in North Carolina, 1883–1933." *North Carolina Historical Review* 64 (October 1987): 394–415.

Skates, John R. "Fred Sullens and Prohibition." *Journal of Mississippi History* 29 (May 1967): 83–94.

Smith, Hilrie Shelton. *In His Image, but . . . Racism in Southern Religion, 1780–1910.* Durham, N.C.: Duke University Press, 1972.

"Some Thoughts on Lynching." *South Atlantic Quarterly* 5 (October 1906): 349–54.

Southern Growth Policies Board. *Halfway Home and a Long Way to Go.* Research Triangle Park, N.C.: Southern Growth Policies Board, 1988.

"Southern Question." *Outlook* 76 (January 16, 1904): 189–90.

"Southern Race Feeling." *Independent* 56 (March 17, 1904): 594–99.

"The South and Liquor-Selling." *Outlook* 86 (August 31, 1907): 943–44.

Spain, Rufus B. *At Ease in Zion: A Social History of Southern Baptists, 1865–1900.* Nashville, Tenn.: Vanderbilt University Press, 1967.

Spears, R. "Beating Prohibition on the Mississippi." *Harper's Weekly* 53 (May 29 1909): 27.

Speer, James Brooks. "Contagion and the Constitution: Public Health in the Texas Coastal Region, 1836–1909." Ph.D. dissertation, Rice University, 1974.

Spiers, Patricia Loraine. "The Woman Suffrage Movement in New Orleans." M.A. thesis, Southeastern Louisiana College, 1962.

Spivey, Donald. *Schooling for the New Slavery: Black Industrial Education, 1868–1915.* Westport, Conn.: Greenwood Press, 1978.

Stanfield, John H. *Philanthropy and Jim Crow in American Social Science.* Westport, Conn.: Greenwood Press, 1985.

Steiner, Jesse F., and Roy M. Brown. *The North Carolina Chain Gang: A Study of County Convict Road Work.* Chapel Hill: University of North Carolina Press, 1927.

Stephenson, Wendell H. "John Spencer Bassett as a Historian of the South." *North Carolina Historical Review* 25 (July 1948): 289–317.

Talmadge, John Erwin. *Rebecca Latimer Felton: Nine Stormy Decades.* Athens: University of Georgia Press, 1960.

———. *Corra Harris: Lady of Purpose.* Athens: University of Georgia Press, 1968.

Tatum, Noreen Dunn. *A Crown of Service: A Story of Woman's Work in the Methodist Episcopal Church, South, from 1878 to 1940.* Nashville: Parthenon Press, 1960.

Taylor, Antoinette Elizabeth. "The Convict Lease System in Georgia, 1866–1908." M.A. thesis, University of North Carolina, 1940.

———. "The Abolition of the Convict Lease System in Georgia." *Georgia Historical Quarterly* 26 (December 1942): 273–87.

———. "The Origin of the Woman Suffrage Movement in Georgia." *Georgia Historical Quarterly* 28 (June 1944): 63–79.

———. "The Woman Suffrage Movement in Texas." *Journal of Southern History* 17 (May 1951): 194–209.

———. "The Woman Suffrage Movement in Arkansas." *Arkansas Historical Quarterly* 15 (Spring 1956): 17–52.

———. *The Woman Suffrage Movement in Tennessee*. New York: Bookman Associates, 1957.

———. "The Woman Suffrage Movement in Florida." *Florida Historical Quarterly* 36 (July 1957): 42–60.

———. "Revival and Development of the Woman Suffrage Movement in Georgia." *Georgia Historical Quarterly* 42 (December 1958): 338–54.

———. "The Last Phase of the Woman Suffrage Movement in Georgia." *Georgia Historical Quarterly* 43 (March 1959): 16–21.

———. "The Woman Suffrage Movement in Mississippi, 1890–1920." *Journal of Mississippi History* 30 (February 1968): 1–21.

———. "South Carolina and the Enfranchisement of Women: The Later Years." *South Carolina Historical Magazine* 80 (October 1979): 298–310.

Thelen, David P. "Where Did Progressivism Go? A Search around the South." *Georgia Historical Quarterly* 68 (Spring 1984): 60–70.

———. *Paths of Resistance: Tradition and Dignity in Industrializing Missouri*. New York: Oxford University Press, 1986.

Thompson, Holland. "Some Effects of Industrialism in an Agricultural State." *South Atlantic Quarterly* 4 (January 1905): 71–77.

———. "Effects of Industrialism upon Political and Social Ideas." *Annals of the American Academy of Political and Social Science* 35 (January 1910): 134–42.

Tillinghast, Joseph Alexander. "Race Heterogeneity in a Democratic Society." *South Atlantic Quarterly* 2 (1903): 152–56.

Tillman, Benjamin. "History of the South Carolina Liquor Law." *North American Review* 158 (1892): 140–49.

———. "Our Whiskey Rebellion." *North American Review* 158 (1892): 513–19.

Tindall, George B. *The Emergence of the New South, 1913–1945*. Baton Rouge: Louisiana State University Press, 1967.

Trattner, Walter I. *Crusade for the Children: A History of the National Child Labor Committee and Child Labor Reform in America*. Chicago: Quadrangle Books, 1970.

Tyrrell, Ian R. *Sobering Up: From Temperance to Prohibition in Antebellum America, 1800–1860*. Westport, Conn.: Greenwood Press, 1979.

———. "Drink and Temperance in the Old South: An Overview and Interpretation." *Journal of Southern History* 48 (1982): 485–510.

Vogel, Morris J., and Charles Rosenberg, eds. *The Therapeutic Revolution: Essays in the Social History of American Medicine*. Philadelphia: Temple University Press, 1979.

Wade, Grace Adelaide Van Duyn Wade, and Joel Taylor Wade. *Our Life Story*. Chattanooga, Tenn.: George C. Hudson Company, 1954.

Wallenstein, Peter. *From Slave South to New South: Public Policy in Nineteenth-Century Georgia*. Chapel Hill: University of North Carolina Press, 1987.

Waller, Altina L. *Feud: Hatfields, McCoys, and Social Change in Appalachia, 1860–1900*. Chapel Hill: University of North Carolina Press, 1988.

Walton, Hanes, Jr. "Another Force for Disfranchisement: Blacks and the Prohibitionists in Tennessee." *Journal of Human Relations* 18 (1st Quarter 1970): 728–38.

———. "The Negro and the Prohibition Movement: Georgia and Alabama." *Negro History Bulletin* (March 1971): 247–59.

Walton, Hanes, Jr., and James E. Taylor. "Blacks and the Southern Prohibition Movement." *Phylon* 32 (Fall 1971): 247–59.

Ware, Louise. *George Foster Peabody: Banker, Philanthropist, Publicist*. Athens: University of Georgia Press, 1951.

Warner, Margaret. "Local Control versus National Interest: The Debate over Southern Public Health, 1878–1884." *Journal of Southern History* 50 (1984): 407–28.

Washburn, Benjamin Earle. *The Hookworm Campaign in Alamance County, North Carolina*. Raleigh: E. M. Uzzell and Co., 1914.

———. *As I Recall: The Hookworm Campaigns Initiated by the Rockefeller Sanitary Commission and the Rockefeller Foundation in the Southern United States and Tropical America*. New York: Rockefeller Foundation, 1960.

———. *History of the North Carolina State Board of Health, 1877–1925*. Raleigh: North Carolina State Board of Health, 1966.

Washington, Booker T. "Prohibition and the Negro." *Outlook* 88 (March 14, 1908): 587–89.

———. "Relation of Industrial Education to National Progress." *Annals of the American Academy of Political and Social Science* 33 (January–June 1909): 1–12.

———. "The Negro's Part in System Development." *Annals of the American Academy of Political and Social Science* 35 (January–June 1910): 124–33.

Weatherford, Willis Duke. *Interracial Cooperation: A Study of the Various Agencies Working in the Field of Social Welfare*. New York: Interracial Committee of the YMCA, 1920.

———. "Race Relationships in the South." *Annals of the American Academy of Political and Social Science* 49 (September 1913): 164–71.

Wheeler, Marjorie Spruill. "New Women of the New South: The Leaders of the Woman Suffrage Movement in the Southern States." Ph.D. dissertation, University of Virginia, 1990.

Whisnant, David E. *All That Is Native and Fine: The Politics of Culture in an American Region*. Chapel Hill: University of North Carolina Press, 1983.

White, Arthur O. "State Leadership and Black Education in Florida." *Phylon* 43 (March 1982): 15–28.

White, John E. "Prohibition: The New Task and Opportunity of the South." *South Atlantic Quarterly* 7 (April 1908): 130–42.

White, Ronald C., Jr. *Liberty and Justice for All: Racial Reform and the Social Gospel (1877–1925)*. New York: Harper and Row, 1990.

Whitener, Daniel Jay. *Prohibition in North Carolina, 1715–1945*. Edited by Albert Ray Newsome, William Whatley Pierson, Mitchell B. Garrett, Fletcher M. Green, and Keener C. Frazer. James Sprunt Series in History and Political Science, vol. 27. Chapel Hill: University of North Carolina Press, 1946.

Whites, LeeAnn. "The DeGraffenreid Controversy: Class, Race, and Gender in the New South." *Journal of Southern History* 54 (August 1988): 449–78.

Wiebe, Robert H. *The Search for Order, 1877–1920*. New York: Hill and Wang, 1967.

Wilson, Charles Reagan. *Baptized in Blood: The Religion of the Lost Cause, 1865–1920*. Athens: University of Georgia Press, 1980.

Wisner, Elizabeth. *Public Welfare Administration in Louisiana*. Chicago: University of Chicago Press, 1930.

———. *Social Welfare in the South: From Colonial Times to World War I*. Baton Rouge: Louisiana State University Press, 1970.

Woloch, Nancy. *Women and the American Experience*. New York: Alfred A. Knopf, 1984.

Wood, Stephen B. *Constitutional Politics in the Progressive Era: Child Labor and the Law*. Chicago: University of Chicago Press, 1968.

Woodward, C. Vann. *Origins of the New South, 1877–1913*. Baton Rouge: Louisiana State University Press, 1951.

Woofter, Thomas Jackson. *Teaching in Rural Schools*. Boston: Houghton Mifflin Co., 1917.

Wyatt-Brown, Bertram. *Southern Honor: Ethics and Behavior in the Old South*. New York: Oxford University Press, 1982.

Zimmerman, Hilda Jane. "Penal Systems and Penal Reform in the South since the Civil War." Ph.D. dissertation, University of North Carolina, 1947.

INDEX

———————— ◆ ————————

modernization, 274–75; moonshining in, 312

Georgia State Department of Education, 205

Georgia State Department of Labor, 307

Georgia State Normal School, 59

Giles County, Tenn., 232

Glade Springs, Va., 86

Glasgow, Ellen, 184, 196

Goldsboro, N.C., 120

Gompers, Samuel, 175

Good-government reform, 31

Good Templars, Independent Order of, 35, 41

Gordon, Kate, 72, 189, 196

Grady, Henry: statue of (Atlanta), 72

Grant County, Ky., 236

Grantham, Dewey W., 95

Gray, Wil Lou, 140, 233

Great Migration: of southern blacks to north, 248–49, 262

Great Society, 324

Greene County, Ga., 274

Greensboro, N.C., 105, 123, 138, 256

Greenville, N.C., 154

Gretna, Va., 319

Guerrant, Edward O., 79, 84

Guilford County, N.C., 123, 138, 218

Guilford County Medical Society, 287

Gulf Coast canneries: child labor in, 163, 176, 179, 306

Habersham County, Ga., 17

Hagerstown, Md., 318

Halifax County, N.C., 150, 233

Harlan, Louis R., 241

Harrison, Emily Stewart, 134, 175

Hart, Albert Bushnell, 8, 9, 63

Haskin, Sara Estelle, 254

Hayesville, N.C., 133

Haynes, Elizabeth Ross, 262–63

Haywood County, N.C., 81

Health Train: in Louisiana and Tennessee, 146–47

Heart disease, 27

Hempstead County, Ark., 244

Henderson County, N.C., 277

High schools: and reformers, 212–13, 232, 237; for blacks, 245–46; and school consolidation, 275

Hill, Walter B., 65–66, 75–76

Hindman, Ky., 83, 127

Hindman Settlement School, 83–84, 127

Hine, Lewis W., 179, 181, 305–7, 310–11

Hobdy, J. B., 213

Hoey, Clyde R., 110

Hollister, Mo., 253

Holmes, William F., 312

Hoodoo doctors, 89–90

Hookworm Field Research, 289

Hookworms, 84; crusade against, 142–59, 206, 216–20; and child labor reform, 171; opposition to crusade, 288–89

Hope, John, 251, 266–67

Hope, Lugenia Burns, 254

Houston, Tex., 183

Hundley, Bossie O'Brien, 187, 197

Illiteracy: efforts against, 139–41

Infant hygiene. See Child welfare

Infant welfare, 84

Intensive community work, 216–17, 292

International Health Board, 214–22, 226–27, 284–85, 289, 291–94

International Health Commission, 214, 216–17, 292

International Social Hygiene Board, 228–29

Interracialism: and black education, 243; and CIC, 248–67

Interracial marriage: whites' fear of, 67–68

Intestinal tract infections, 207

Iredell County, N.C., 276

Ivy, Va., 80

Jackson, Thomas "Stonewall," 128

Jackson County, Ala., 22, 28

Jackson County, N.C., 240, 279

Jacksonville, Fla., 223

Jacobs, Pattie Ruffner, 183–84, 197

Jacocks, W. P., 156

Jeanes Fund, 241–44

Jefferson County, Fla., 288

Jefferson County, Ky., 151

Jeffress, Va., 318

Jews: and Protestant-led reform, 121, 122, 181; and woman suffrage, 195; and opposition to public health, 287

Johns Hopkins University, 144

Johnson, Carrie Parks, 254–56, 263

Johnson, Charles Spurgeon, 230

Johnston, Mary, 119, 188, 191–96, 299

Johnston County, N.C., 161

Jonas Ridge, N.C., 275

Jones, Herschel, 310

Jones, Meredith Ashby, 251, 265

Jones, Robert Elijah, 251

Jones, Thomas Jesse, 249

Journal of Social Forces, 265

Joyner, James Yadkin, 127, 131, 142, 233

Julius Rosenwald Fund, 215, 229–31, 243, 246–47, 252

Kansas City, Mo., 254

Kearney, Belle, 4, 64, 73, 299, 303

Keller, Alvin E., 287

Kelley, Florence, 193

Kentucky: mountain missions in, 79, 83, 87, 127; Bluegrass region of, 79, 83, 280; prohibition in, 101; school crusade in, 127, 133, 137, 139–41; and anti-hookworm campaign, 147, 151, 152; woman suffrage movement in, 189–90, 196; and public health, 206–7, 230, 293–94, 297–98, 302–3; school inspection in, 232–35; black schools in, 242; CIC in, 256–57; agricultural economy of, 271–72; opposition to school modernization in, 275, 280; and resistance to child labor reform, 307; and resistance to prohibition, 315

Kentucky Equal Rights Association, 196, 302

Kentucky State Board of Health, 285

Kentucky State Federation of Women's Clubs, 83, 127, 191

Key West, Fla., 158

King, Richard Hayne, 251

Kingdom of God: and mountain missions, 84; and prohibition, 111; and child labor reform, 161–62

King's Daughters, 176

Kittrell, Tenn., 237

Knott County, Ky., 83

Knotts Island, N.C., 216

Knowlton, Millard, 228

Kosciusko, Miss., 181

Ku Klux Klan: and public health, 287

Lakeland, Fla., 220

Latin America: and yellow fever, 24

Lauderdale County, Ala., 132

Laughinghouse, Charles, 154

Laura Spellman Rockefeller Memorial, 252, 270, 272

Laurens County, S.C., 233

Lebanon, Va., 317

Lee, Robert E., 65, 128, 138

Lee County, Ala., 132

Leesburg, Va., 320

Leloudis, James, 134

Lewis, Elizabeth H., 303

Lexington, Ky., 119

Licensing of alcohol, 48–49, 111

Life Extension Program (N.C.), 223–24

Little Brasstown Creek, N.C., 277

Little Rock, Ark., 213

Local option, 42, 45–47, 100–101, 315–16

London, 311

Longfellow, Henry W., 138

Louisa County, Va., 319

Louisiana: and public health, 6, 205–6, 210, 217, 219, 230, 288, 293–94; schools in, 17, 18; moral reform in,